Garry O'Connor is married an[...] five children in Oxford. Forn[...] Shakespeare Company and a the[...] writer. He edited *Olivier: In Cer[...] His other biographies are *The Pursuit of [...]* of *Maggie Teyte*, *Darlings of the Gods: One Y[...] Li[...] of Laurence Olivier and Vivien Leigh* and *Ralph Richardson: An Actor's Life*.

GARRY O'CONNOR

Sean O'Casey

A Life

Mrs Henderson: Them words is true, Mr Gallicker,
and they aren't. For to be wise is to be a fool,
an' to be a fool is to be wise.

Mr Gallogher (*with deprecating tolerance*): Oh,
Mrs Henderson, that's a parrotox.

The Shadow of a Gunman

PALADIN
GRAFTON BOOKS
A Division of the Collins Publishing Group

LONDON GLASGOW
TORONTO SYDNEY AUCKLAND

Paladin
Grafton Books
A Division of the Collins Publishing Group
8 Grafton Street, London W1X 3LA

Published in Paladin Books 1989

First published in Great Britain by
Hodder & Stoughton Ltd 1988

Printed and bound in Great Britain by
Collins, Glasgow

Set in Bembo

Permission to quote from the following works of Sean O'Casey is gratefully
acknowledged:

First edition of *Juno and the Paycock*, *The Shadow of a Gunman*, 1925; first edition
of *The Plough and the Stars*, 1926: first issued in St Martin's Library 1957 as
Three Plays by Sean O'Casey. Reprinted by permission of St Martin's Press.

Purple Dust (copyright 1940 by Sean O'Casey, renewed 1968 by Eileen
O'Casey); *Red Roses For Me* (copyright 1943, 1944 by Sean O'Casey, renewed
1971, 1972 by Eileen O'Casey, Breon O'Casey and Shivaun Kenig); *The
Bishop's Bonfire* (copyright 1955 by Sean O'Casey, renewed 1983 by Eileen
O'Casey and Breon O'Casey); *Autobiography*, vol. 1 (copyright 1939 by
Macmillan Publishing Company, renewed 1967 by Eileen O'Casey, Breon
O'Casey and Shivaun Kenig); *Autobiography*, vol. 2 (copyright 1942 by Sean
O'Casey, renewed 1970 by Eileen O'Casey, Breon O'Casey and Shivaun
O'Casey); *Autobiography*, vol. 3 (copyright 1945, 1946 by Sean O'Casey,
renewed 1973, 1974 by Eileen O'Casey, Breon O'Casey and Shivaun
O'Casey); *Autobiography*, vol. 4 (copyright 1949 by Sean O'Casey, renewed
1977 by Eileen O'Casey, Breon O'Casey and Shivaun O'Casey); *Autobiography*,
vol. 5 (copyright 1952 by Sean O'Casey, renewed 1980 by Eileen O'Casey);
Autobiography, vol. 6 (copyright 1954 by Sean O'Casey, renewed 1982 by
Eileen O'Casey). Reprinted with permission of Macmillan Publishing
Company.

Letters, ed. David Krause, vols. 1 and 2 (Macmillan, New York); vol. 3
(Catholic University of America Press). Reprinted by permission of Catholic
University of America Press.

To Catharine Carver

CONTENTS

Prologue   3

ACT ONE   *SWORDS OF LIGHT*
1880–1921
1   Two Eternities   11
2   The First Sword   25
3   Fiery Blossoms   39
4   The Third Eye   61
5   They Dreamed and Are Dead   86
6   Lethe's Wharf   104

ACT TWO   *ON THE RUN*
1921–1927
7   The Shaft Which Flies in Darkness   123
8   Hearts of Flesh and Stone   143
9   Green, White, Orange – or Yellow   163
10   Divine Afflatus   187
11   Free Wheeling   205
12   A Part in Life   220

ACT THREE   *THE SHAPE OF A NEW WORLD*
1927–1964
13   Slouching Towards Bethlehem   241
14   A New Character   260
15   The Phantoms of Hyde Park   279
16   Pink Wilderness   303
17   A Detrimental Temper   324
18   Divorce, Irish-Style   349
19   Th' Gentle Ripple of a Rose   359

Epilogue – Saint or Gunman?   375

Notes   385
Acknowledgments   431
Index   435

LIST OF ILLUSTRATIONS

Susan Casey with one of her grandchildren[1]
Mick Casey as a young man[1]
Brother Tom[1]
Bella[1]
Nicholas Beaver[1]
Mick during World War I[1]
St Barnabas Church[2]
St Laurence O'Toole Church[2]
18 Abercorn Road[2]
Sean O'Casey aged thirty
The room at 422[3]
Sean O'Casey in his forties
W. B. Yeats[4]
Lady Gregory[4]
Eileen Carey Reynolds[3]
F. J. McCormick as Joxer
The 1927 production of *The Shadow of a Gunman*[3]
Sara Allgood as Juno
The O'Caseys on their wedding day[3]
Number 19 Woronzow Road[3]
Gaby Fallon
Cartoon by O'Casey[3]
O'Casey in Chalfont St Giles[3]
Breon O'Casey and Sean[5]
Tingrith, Totnes[3]
Family group in Totnes[6]
O'Casey with Eileen[7]
With Gauguin and Joseph Stalin[6]
"We cannot always suffer ecstasy"[8]

ACKNOWLEDGMENTS

1 By courtesy of Martin B. Margulies
2 Photograph by Martin B. Margulies
3 By courtesy of Eileen O'Casey
4 By courtesy of BBC Hulton Picture Library
5 Photograph by Alfred Eris
6 Photograph by Gjon Mili © *Time & Life* Inc.
7 Photograph by Wolf Suschitzky
8 Photograph by Robert Emmett Ginna

Pages 8 and 9
Map of Dublin by Martin Lubikowski

pages 7, 88 and 239
Cartoons by Sean O'Casey, courtesy of Eileen O'Casey

page 121
Pen drawing of M. J. Dolan in
The Shadow of a Gunman by Grace Plunkett

SEAN O'CASEY

PROLOGUE

Imagine Falstaff as a paragon of virtue, a sainted character akin to Jesus; as a representative of a decaying aristocracy; as a dietician's example of the wrong kind of eating and drinking; as a slapstick comedian – or as a figure of pure wish-fulfilment. No single label provides a satisfactory description. The complete Falstaff is the sum of his parts: remove one element, one strength or weakness, and you diminish his glory.

Sean O'Casey, the great dramatist born in Dublin in 1880 and who died in Devon, England, in 1964, was another such type. He created many rich characters, but none richer or more many-sided than himself. A good number of the weak and self-indulgent figures in his plays were based on himself, or on brothers and friends who resented his depiction of them. He was never much interested in foreign travel or in expanding his mental horizons. The inner animus he fed on excluded everything that was not connected with it: cultivating grievances, he was always spoiling for a fight. Yet he had an intense and eloquent vision of humanity which aligns him with some of the Christian prophets. And, paradoxically, for all his bitterness, he became a great comedian, developing a generous capacity for laughter, and turning the ferocity, the dark inequalities and passions of his times into a cleansing and liberating release of high spirits.

Lady Gregory, a director of the Abbey Theatre, Dublin, where O'Casey's first five plays, among them the "Dublin Trilogy": *The Shadow of a Gunman, Juno and the Paycock* and *The Plough and the Stars*, were produced, once defined as the Irish frailty "our incorrigible genius for myth-making". The author of those plays, christened John Casey and known as Jack, before he orchestrated his name into Sean O'Cathasaigh, Johnny Casside or Cassidy, and eventually Sean O'Casey, gave the idea (seized on by others as fact) that he was born one of thirteen. Hugh Kenner, the American literary critic, has recently called the vagaries of exaggeration, hearsay, and personal vanity one is likely to encounter in writing the biography of an Irish writer, "Irish fact". The size of the Casey brood is perhaps the first Irish fact we encounter in the O'Casey story.

Significantly, twelve of its components occurred before Sean's birth, he being the youngest in the family. But the birth of only eight Casey children was actually recorded or spoken about. Three of them died in infancy and five reached maturity. One of thirteen would mean that eight were stillborn or died as infants – a "fact" reiterated by those who have perpetuated the myth of O'Casey the underdog. Yet, judging by other records, the rate of stillbirths and early infant mortality in areas of Dublin other than slums in the late nineteenth century was not especially high. Moreover, the Casey family lived in a relatively spacious and well-aired part of the city. The Rotunda Hospital, only a short distance away, had been one of the great centres of obstetrical knowledge in Europe, and the rate of mortality among the thousands of children born there was lower than in much of Europe; in 1840, for example (unless this is also Irish fact), 0.53 per cent for 10,785 deliveries. Susan Casey, O'Casey's mother, may have given birth to thirteen children, but some of them should perhaps be put down to that incorrigible genius for myth-making.

So was O'Casey unreliable in what he said about himself? In the worst slums of nineteenth-century Dublin the figures for death and disease were, to be sure, as bad as in Calcutta: O'Casey was certainly not brought up in such a slum. Yet he later assessed his background: "It had often been recorded in the Press, by those who could guess shrewdly, that Sean was a slum dramatist, a guttersnipe who could jingle a few words together out of what he had seen and heard. The terms were suitable and accurate."

They were suitable, but accurate only perhaps in a sense very different from what O'Casey meant, or was understood to mean. In accounts of himself that he gave to others he frequently misrepresented his age – those who defend his doing this say he did not properly know how old he was, but this is just not supported by the evidence – while in his *Autobiographies*, 1939–54 (collected in two volumes of three books each, over half a million words in all), he even wrongly located the street of his birth.

More gravely – or defiantly – from the point of view of truth, he rearranged the sequence of events to suit himself and showed a mocking contempt for dates. Evidence of certain kinds did not impress him, unless it supported what he wanted to say. His process of recall was imaginative and emotional: suffering from poor eyesight throughout his life, he based his vision of the past on his scrupulous ear for the rhythms of speech heard round him, but his sweet tooth for rhetoric sometimes made him as self-indulgent as someone who can never refuse another cream cake. The truths in his autobiography belong more to the ear and heart than to history.

"Lying for its own sake", wrote a fellow Dubliner, Oscar Wilde, still remembered in O'Casey's day by old ladies who had known him as a young man, is not only "absolutely beyond reproach" but "the proper aim of art". George Bernard Shaw, known at the same period in some Dublin circles as Georgie, and who in O'Casey's middle age became his friend and mentor, shared his contempt for factual truth: "No man is real", Shaw said, "until he has been turned into a work of art." GBS applauded vigorously the strong rhetorical element in O'Casey: praise from such a quarter boosted his ego and encouraged him to fabricate more.

In the following pages I attempt to show how Sean O'Casey, slum dramatist and guttersnipe, hobnail-booted labourer and communist freethinker, who disdained a tie and thumbed his nose at conventional bourgeois behaviour, painstakingly created himself out of the real-life John Casey. For the character O'Casey designed for himself became real and inhabitable – much greater, perhaps, in scope, dimension, humour and sadness, than any of the great stage characters he carved out of his Dublin upbringing.

But there were some highly disagreeable elements in this character. O'Casey was far from being a Class I Soviet working-class hero; his powers were much more subtle and more complicated than his "socialist realist" admirers (i.e. from the Communist bloc), or his more sentimental Irish-American adulators, with their rags-to-riches mythology, like to imagine. The portrait O'Casey held up for the world to see, wearing it and thrusting it where it would cause the greatest guilt and outrage, was skilfully tattered and cunningly stained with, in his own phrase, "the diseased sweat of the tenements".

Of course O'Casey had bad eyes; he had been humiliated by deprivation and deeply hurt, in his early life, by loss. But his assumption of poverty was, like a saint's, ultimately an act of will. He fashioned out of actual materials the image, part fact, part fiction, by which he came to be recognised. He saw the opportunity to become the poetic symbol of the Dublin slums: he seized it. Such an assumption was very middle-class – and with O'Casey, also the result of a strongly Protestant outlook.

"Where we are dealing with a man of such tremendous spirit as Sean O'Casey one must be honest," wrote Sean O'Faolain. O'Casey

was fastidious, touchy, a prey to both colourful and irritating contradictions and obsessions, capable, almost at the same instant, of biting
the hand that fed him, and cutting off his own nose to spite his face.
As much lazy as hard-working, as much fragmented as a man of
integrity, he was in many ways perhaps the ultimate affront to
his own background – as much English as Irish. Narrow-minded,
sometimes to the point of bigotry, he was a man of many creeds
jostling at different times for self-expression.

But above all he was a man of his times – times that were, for all
their cruelty and inhumanity, of great intellectual generosity and
artistic scope. When he wrote his best work man was still (at least in
Ireland) the measure of all things, and O'Casey was able to employ
successfully a truly Elizabethan breadth of language and emotion. It
is, above all, his humanity which everyone can recognise and love.
If we discover that there is as much weakness in it as strength, as
much self-deception as truth, this still does not weaken its appeal,
but should help to build or restore our faith in ourselves as indivisible,
and united in one "tremendous and glorious bond".

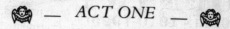 — *ACT ONE* —

Swords of Light

1880 – 1921

It is said God never ceases
working out His way,
so why the hell should I?

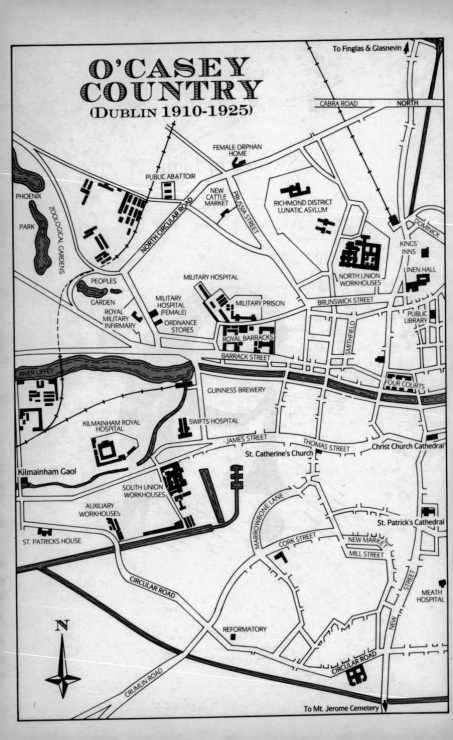

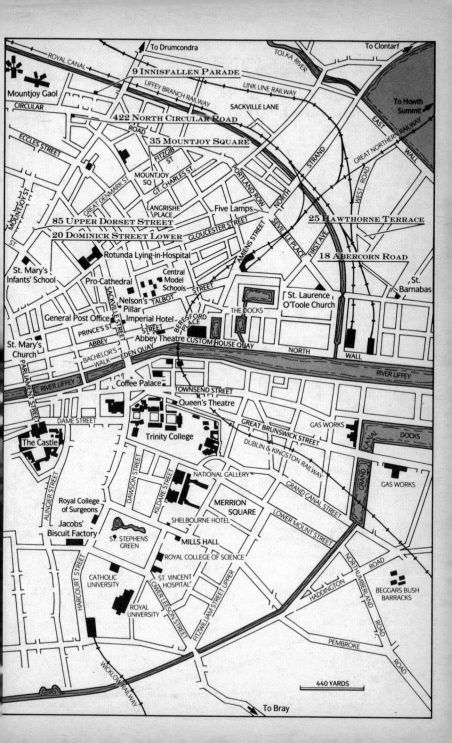

TWO ETERNITIES

Archer was the maiden name of O'Casey's mother Susan: when he was sixty-five years old, he wrote to Nan Archer, no relation, of Rush, County Dublin, about his family tree: "That's curious about the Archers of Galway or Wicklow. My mother's mother came from Wicklow, and, I think, my own mother was born in Delgany. And I have heard when I was a kid that she spent some years when she was young in Galway – possibly with some relatives." O'Casey understood from an alderman, Tom Kelly, that the Archers had come to Ireland with the Normans; there had been Archers in Dublin for 800 years.

O'Casey's father was "of the Limerick branch of the O'Caseys", and would claim, when in expansively Gaelic mood, that the original form of his name, O'Cathasaigh, came from a very old sept of an old clan. The only property the family ever possessed, as O'Casey once tartly observed, was the family plot in Mount Jerome graveyard, plot A 35–247–7166, for which they paid five shillings a year. Michael Casey, of farming stock, settled when young on the south side of Dublin, near St Patrick's Cathedral, and there met and married Susan Archer, who lived in the same street. Michael, unlike the rest of his family, was a Protestant: Susan, whose father, Abraham, was a prosperous auctioneer, echoed his faith through her own Anglo-Protestant origins. They were married in 1863 in the Protestant church of St Catherine where, sixty years before, Robert Emmet had been hanged, drawn and quartered for his part in an abortive rising against England.

– Is it a roman catholic church? asked Johnny.
– No, no, said Uncle Tom; it's a protestant one.
– You'd think they'd hang a roman catholic rebel outside a roman catholic church, said Johnny.
– But poor Emmet was a protestant, Johnny.

To have so strong a Protestant background stamped Sean O'Casey from the start. Although by no means a passport to wealth or social superiority, it did mean that he had, like his brothers and his sister, at least initially the chance of entering a profession denied to someone of the Catholic faith. That he chose for the most part not to take the proffered opportunities, working for many years with little to distinguish him from an ordinary Catholic labourer, did not mean that he abandoned for one moment his deeply ingrained Protestant attitude to life, and especially to the Catholic Church. As a Catholic contemporary observed the difference, a Dublin child was at once aware of two separate and immiscible kinds of citizen, his own kind and the Protestants, a hostile element, "vaguely menacing us with horrors as Mrs Smylie's houses for orphans where children might be brought and turned into Protestants". Protestants were proselytisers, a trait O'Casey kept all his life, never losing the habit, even while professing atheism, of trying to convert someone to something or other.

For the first twenty or so years of their married life the Caseys, while never prosperous or part of the ruling Protestant garrison, were comfortably off, moving house several times, usually to larger premises within the same area of Dublin, a cheerless but clean and tidy district to the north of the city centre and halfway to Drumcondra, a suburb in which the clerical and skilled working class, generally with nationalist leanings, predominated. The Caseys' own area was much more volatile terrain, reflecting rapid upward or downward social mobility in that city of amazing contrasts. This mobility was evident in the volatile emotions of the family into which O'Casey was born.

As a Protestant clerk earning five pounds, fifteen shillings and eight pence a month, roughly twice the average wage of a manual labourer – and moonlighting as a teacher for an extra fifteen shillings – Michael Casey belonged to Class 3 in a social structure of five strata. Above him were the professional men such as lawyers and doctors, the employers and senior clerks: below were the semi-skilled, the transport workers, and, last of all in the pecking order, the vast mass of unskilled labour. This last numbered a fifth of the working population, and included a large contingent of street beggars, hawkers and vagabonds. The poverty among this lowest class was appalling, the great majority of them lodging in unheated tenement dwellings where they slept and ate, inadequately, among their own filth, with families of six commonly housed in one room; but there were also, in this city of stark contradictions, numerous charitable agencies for the alleviation of the destitute, many of which were also proselytising bodies. The largest were orphanages catering for every religion and social class. It was for one of these bodies, the Society for Church Missions, that Michael Casey may• have worked for as long as twenty-two years, before he retired – whether forced to through ill health or because his contract had expired is unclear.

Michael and Susan's first child, Isabella Charlotte (known as Bella), was born in 1865. She and O'Casey's three older brothers – Michael, born in 1866, Thomas (1869), and Isaac (1873) – came far more under their father's influence than Sean. Their development gives little indication of decisive and firm fatherly control, although Bella appeared the most hard-working member of the family. Michael Casey may have been more of a Limerick Catholic than he liked to admit. According to her burial document Susan Archer Casey was eighty-five when she died in 1918 and therefore four years older than her husband: this and the more prosperous background she came from may have had something to do with her being clearly the dominant partner in the marriage.

Michael Casey did not send his children into the national school system, which would have been free, but to the fee-charging Central Model Schools where they could grow up among their middle-class peers. Isaac was the most proficient at his lessons, which included music, drawing, bookkeeping, handicrafts and algebra, and he gained in the family the reputation of being a mathematical wizard. Later he was to fancy himself as an actor. From their school reports Michael and Tom appear to have failed to reach the required standard some of the time, although in the general view they were considered bright. Their father, who had ambitions for them and hoped that Michael, who could draw well, might become an architect, paid for additional tutoring by the headmaster.

Both the older boys were set to become teachers; however, upon their father's death their propensity for taking the easy way out – and poor application to learning – again asserted itself and they began to drift downwards socially. This is what turned them, particularly Mick, into characters O'Casey could later draw on in his plays; working all their lives at jobs far below their training or ability, they generated in their brother a terrible sense of waste. Only Isaac, though his schooling suffered as a result of his father's death, was to keep the status of a clerk.

Sean had two tragic predecessors: two other John Caseys were born, the first in August 1871 and the second in May 1876, both of whom lived long enough to be christened by the Revd John Black, who officiated at most of the Casey baptisms. Neither of these boys was buried in the family plot at Mount Jerome; and there is no record of the birth of a sister whom O'Casey mentions in his autobiography, where no reason is given for her death. The first John's death O'Casey attributes to croup, while the second, living a year and contracting a bad cough, is depicted as a victim of poor medical attention: waiting in hospital to be seen by a doctor, he choked to death, and his distraught mother, sooner than leave him behind, carried his little body home to his father. O'Casey, ironically referring to himself as the "third Johnny" and, in an Elizabethan phrase, the "shake of the bag", believed his parents did not rate his own chances of survival as high. But Michael and Susan's defiant naming of him, their determined care of him in infancy, gave him that extra push in life which was lacking not only for the two earlier Johns, but for his older brothers who lived.

O'Casey's birth in 1880 he describes in terms similar to animal parturition, which shocked people in 1939 when he published the first volume of his autobiography. His mother, he wrote, clenched her teeth, "dug her knees home into the bed, became a tense living mass of agony and effort, sweated and panted, pressed and groaned, and pressed and pressed till a man-child dropped from her womb down into the world". This suggests that O'Casey had an extremely hazy notion of obstetrics, and had not witnessed a child's birth, even that of one of his own. His wife, Eileen, later verified this. The notion that a woman in labour could find the anatomical resources to dig her knees "home" in a bed suggests that he had, for all his vaunted working-class earthiness, a middle-class fastidiousness towards matters of the flesh. That he was born with a caul, the womb membrane that sometimes covers a child's head, seems incontestable, although he does not mention it in his first volume. His mother sold the caul, considered a charm that could ward off drowning, to a sea captain to keep in his cabin.

———◆◆◆◆———

The year of O'Casey's birth, 1880, was marked by unprecedented labour unrest in Dublin, reflecting the scarcity of employment: demonstrations were as yet unorganised, although one particular grievance, the award of a Dublin Corporation sewer contract to a Scottish company, pointed ominously to the diminished standing of the Dublin worker in the face of competitors both from the north and overseas.

The neighbourhood into which O'Casey was born was comfortable and secure, however. His father, according to how one interprets the evidence, was either the rate-payer or principal tenant, even sub-landlord, of the large house at 85 Upper Dorset Street. Michael Casey may well have made up part of the rent from subletting rooms in the house. In any event, he and his family occupied considerably more than the single room which was the usual accommodation for a poorer family. They were respectable people, with a parlour kept swept and ready to impress visitors, with refreshments to serve them. The house itself was of brick, consisting of four storeys and a basement, and had been built in the mid-eighteenth century. Not far away was the birthplace of Richard Brinsley Sheridan, while round the corner, in Eccles Street, James Joyce later set up a fictitious house for Leopold and Molly Bloom.

Contrary to popular belief, ownership of real estate was very common among shopkeepers and publicans, the class that formed the Catholic backbone of Dublin at this time. Some tenements were said to have five levels of ownership, thus ensuring a wide, but highly primitive, distribution of wealth from property. Tenement ownership (or occupancy) was by no means considered disreputable. The grievances of those at the lowest level, reduced to living little better than pigs, showed on the other hand how stagnant Dublin's commercial life had grown, for as a manufacturing town it had been overtaken by Belfast. It had all but stopped producing wealth and its people had, instead, become obsessed with the declining value of their property.

The landlords had their own grumbles. In the tenement houses piping and gutters were stripped off and sold as scrap metal, banisters were used for firewood, corridors and privies soiled with human excrement; for average tenement dwellers, it was said, "to beat the landlords is the first great object of their lives". In 1914 the Lord Mayor of Dublin claimed that 30,000 eviction notices were served annually on tenants – roughly one for every ten of the population, although only a small proportion were followed by notices to quit. At the same time it was estimated that in a single year nearly three million pawn tickets were issued, most of them to members of the working classes, and the loans worked out at an average of two pounds, four shillings per head of the population. (Joyce later, in a typical Dublin aside complaining of his supporters and hagiographers in the United States, said they "would bring out a collection of my selected pawn tickets".)

Tenements in Dublin were large houses under multi-family occupancy, on which the rates were paid by the landlord. The house at 85 Upper Dorset Street was not a tenement, nor was the smaller terraced house of two storeys a short walk away from it at 9 Innisfallen

Parade, "below St Ignatius Road, beside Father Gaffney's School", to which the Caseys moved two years after Sean's birth. There, in what would now be called "unfurnished accommodation", the Caseys had their own furniture, including, at one stage, a piano; Susan loved flowers and kept potted plants, in particular a most mysterious one, which apparently had no tuber, root or bulb: "in the spring it thrust up a rosy tip of life, and in the summer turned into a wealth of variegated leaves, garnished by thick velvety blossoms of a rich red, with a saucy blob of tasselled gold in its centre. She called it the Resurrection Plant."

It was in Innisfallen Parade that the Casey children had scarlet fever, and were nursed by Susan; she put Tom, who did not contract the illness, in the same bed with Mick, who had the worst case, but Tom remained mysteriously immune in spite of his mother's efforts. Here, too, the young Sean faced the greatest torment of his life, and its greatest challenge. One day when he was five (according to him), "small, hard, shiny, pearly specks appeared on the balls of his eyes. He began to dread the light; to keep his eyes closed; to sit and moan restlessly in the darkest places he could find." His brothers, on the advice of a friend, plunged his head under cold water in a bucket to cure the weakness, and when he struggled,

> they pushed him further down till the water flowing through his nostrils gurgled down his throat, almost choking him, leaving him panting for breath, shivering and wet, in the centre of reproaches and abuse because he had kept his eyes fiercely closed underneath the water.

The complaint was later diagnosed as chronic conjunctivitis, or trachoma, brought on by reduced circumstances; but the Caseys were in such circumstances only later, after Michael Casey died in 1886.

O'Casey knew little of his father, who died when he was six. The cause of Michael Casey's death, as recorded on the death certificate, was "disease of the spine" believed to be the result of a fall. In recollection his son could offer only general notions of him, such as that he knew his Bible well, "most of it in the letter and all of it in the spirit", showing that a man "could always go straight to God without passing round saints and angels". Michael Casey knew he wanted to give his five surviving children the best education, and had worked hard to provide it. He had a fine love of learning, had studied Latin, and among his books, tucked away in a recess at the side of the fire, O'Casey listed d'Aubigné's *History of the Reformation*, Milner's *End of Controversy*, Foxe's *Book of Martyrs*, as well as the English Bible, the Latin Vulgate, and even the opposition's version from Douai. There were Gibbon, Shakespeare, Dickens, Scott; the poets noted by his son included Pope, Milton and Keats. Locke's *Essay on Human Understanding* was clearly a favourite with the elder Casey, while Bishop Berkeley's more dangerous teachings, which supported God through human perception and cast doubts on the existence of the real world, were locked away in a drawer, it being understood such books were only for those minds "big enough to understand that they were rubbish". The neighbourhood respected Michael as a scholar; to help him spend his life among his books he smoked Cavendish cut plug.

O'Casey's description of his father as having a "sometime gentle, sometime fierce habit of criticism" and as being "famed by all as one who spat out his thoughts into the middle of a body's face" sounds very much as if the son were describing himself. And the retrospective scene he makes of Michael Casey reclining crippled in a horsehair armchair with a spine injury, the result of a fall from a ladder which slipped from under him, while the young Sean, sent by his mother, runs out to buy him tobacco, gripping the money in his little fist, is rather stereotyped, although it may be true. Unlike O'Casey's best autobiographical writing it does not seem to be based on his own memory, and was probably concocted from something his mother told him. It is also echoed in his own play, *The Silver Tassie*, in which the crippled soldier and ex-football hero, Heegan, confined to a wheelchair, jerks his way round spying on his old girlfriend making love to his best friend.

But while O'Casey was able to give Heegan a ferocious, bitter vitality, poor Michael Casey, in his son's portrait of him, has none, or little, of that life. Sean attends his funeral, eavesdropping on the cab-drivers who arrive to pick up the mourners, and who boast of their drinking the night before. O'Casey's acoustical sensitivity is beautifully registered in the way he almost scores their dialogue, receiving, as if in compensation for his damaged eyes, an enlarged delight in speech rhythms. Sean does not want to kiss his father: "– I couldn't, I couldn't, he sobbed. Don't ask me, mother, don't ask me to kiss him, I'm frightened to kiss a dead man." No other views or reports of his father exist.

Although O'Casey says his eye trouble had already begun when he was five, as he continually underestimated his age by three or four years until he was well on in life, its onset should probably be placed at around 1888 or 1889. In his account in the autobiography his father is already dead when Susan Casey takes Sean to St Mark's Ophthalmic Hospital for treatment with a Mr Story. The painful symptoms – watering of the eye, sticky lids, and acute sensitivity to light – today respond to antibiotics, and trachoma caused by poor living conditions, especially inadequate water, is now more a social problem than a medical one. But in O'Casey's childhood the treatment was laborious, bathing the eyes in hot water, frequent applications of lotions and ointments, and the wearing of bandages; rest and the tonic, Parrish's Food, were also prescribed. But the boy's eyes did not deteriorate as feared, while in the long term the pain he endured was more than compensated for by a fierce desire to possess books, the only thing in life towards which he ever showed acquisitive passion.

In the early parts of his autobiography O'Casey is intent on showing how he grew up defiantly individual in the face of conditions which would have stifled a lesser man: he blames an unjust and inhumane God, whom he does his best to mock and vilify, and a corrupt and occupying foreign power, the British. But there was another side to the Imperial presence; when nearly seventy, he recalled having visited Stonybatter, a North Dublin working-class area, as a child, and watched the redcoats going in and out of a soldier's home there, and wished he was one of them.

It is hard not to believe that the older Casey boys at least continued to pass a comfortable if unchallenging time for some years after the death of their father. Christopher (Kit) Casey, Sean's nephew, who was a stevedore, spoke out unequivocally against the picture O'Casey paints of his family circumstances: "They weren't as poverty-stricken as the books say. He wasn't a poor boy as depicted by some writers. While he was with the Caseys he never knew what want was."

Other evidence bears out this testimony. The daughter of O'Casey's sister Bella was photographed with her grandmother in the early 1890s: in the picture Susan Casey appears plump and well dressed. The photograph itself is the work of a professional photographer, whose services no slum dwellers of the time could have afforded. Another of the Casey grandchildren, Tom's son, John Joseph Casey, described how when he visited his grandmother, which was often, he found her pleasant-mannered, and dressed in a spotless white apron. At mealtimes they always had meat. There is also a photograph of O'Casey himself, taken during the same period, which shows him elegantly dressed, in a suit of good material whose buttonhole displays a splendid flower. The crowning sartorial touch is a new soft flannel hat with turned-up brim and a cord going round under the chin. Also photographed were Mick and Tom, Bella and her husband Nicholas. Mick appears as a proud, broad little peacock of a man, an instantly recognisable O'Casey character.

As the oldest Casey child, Bella's advantages were considerable, and it was she who emerged from childhood with a coherent career structure: at seventeen she entered a teacher training college, passing the final examination in 1885, just before her father died. She then left home to take up a teaching post. For the next five years, critical to the Casey family fortunes, she taught and lived at St Mary's Infants' School, Mountjoy Street. There confidential reports from inspectors describe her as "attentive", with "a very attractive manner". "Discipline is well maintained," runs another evaluation, "teacher's manner is gentle, and seems to suit young children well."

From Dublin records it can be established that during Bella's tenure of her teaching post at St Mary's, Sean began attending school there. Even he, in an unguarded moment in his early seventies, admitted his presence there, and recalled in a genuine rather than fabricated memory being promoted from wearing a red and black plaid petticoat, to trousers. The records show that his attendance became more regular with the years, and that his standard of reading, arithmetic and spelling was satisfactory.

In 1887, the year after his father's death, he received the prize of *Alone in Zulu Land* for "proficiency in Holy Scripture and Church Formularies", which he explained away later as having been achieved by his capacity to repeat from memory passages he had not been able to read. This seems unlikely, and it too contradicts his contention that he had no learning until much older; at another time he recalls, "in a bible Sean had had when a kid . . . a marginal note telling the world that Adam meant red earth".

O'Casey was to tell Lady Gregory, when he was in his early forties and beginning to make headway with his plays, that he had not been to school until he was sixteen and up till then had not learned to read and write. What he presumably meant was "read seriously" – at another time he mentioned classics he had not read by that age; this was similar to the report that "O'Casey never drank" – what people meant by this was, "never drank heavily". The aristocratic Lady Gregory, who had wealth and intellectual acumen but no great worldliness, was deeply impressed by his admission:

Casey told me he is a labourer, and as we talked of masons said he had "carried the hod". He said "I was among books as a child, but I was sixteen before I learned to read or write. My father loved books, he had a big library, I remember the look of the books high up on shelves." I asked why his father had not taught him and he said "He died when I was three years old, through those same books. There was a little ladder in the room to get to the shelves, and one day when he was standing on it, it broke and he fell and was killed."

In 1887 both Mick and Tom Casey left their jobs in the Post Office and enlisted in the army, Tom in the Royal Dublin Fusiliers, and Mick as a telegraphist in the sappers. This represented a decline in their status, for serving men were mostly working-class Catholics while the Post Office was a Protestant-staffed establishment. The wound to their mother's sense of social position was deepened when in 1889 Bella, up to that time the ascendant star in the fortunes of the Casey family, married an acquaintance of her brothers, Nicholas Beaver, a Protestant serving in the 1st Company of the King's Liverpools. Two years older than he, she had clearly been drawn to his striking good looks and dark hair. O'Casey unfairly demotes Beaver from the rank of lance-corporal which he held:

an' I'm here waitin' for tomorrow's darkness when a girl that never lifted her clothes an inch above her ankles'll have to take them all off an' give everything she holds dear to the man of her choice in spite of me mother for ever pickin' at me because poor Nicholas isn't anything higher than a drummer, as if rank mattered in any way to a true-hearted an' pure girl who truly loved a man.

This impulsive marriage confirms that the Casey children, for all their puritanism, basically pleased themselves, suggesting that Michael Casey, had he been alive, might have encouraged his daughter's self-indulgence, or that Bella reacted strongly against her mother's stricter and more typically Protestant attitudes. But the children were not especially ambitious; rather the reverse, even the beautiful and hard-working Bella.

When she and Beaver married, Beaver had five years still to serve; stationed in England, he was in Dublin only on leave. Bella was living in a top-floor flat provided by St Mary's School, and her mother, although she refused to attend the marriage ceremony, now moved in with her, together with Sean and his brother Isaac. The latter had left school at the age of fourteen and was working as an office boy for the Dublin *Daily Express*. The flat was in a building that is now a Dominican home for boys; its magnificent entrance hall had been decorated by Robert West, a famous Irish stuccoist, and the interior included a "Venus room". It was not at all the cheerless dwelling O'Casey describes, in which Bella takes her bath – "she brought from the little yard a galvanised bath . . . Then she stripped herself naked, stepped into the bath, and washed her body all over."

One day, against his wishes, Sean was taken by the newly-weds to the sea at Bray: he felt deeply alienated as they kissed, held hands, and looked at each other. Sent off to play on the beach, he cautiously watches the sea "glide in over the brown sand", and while dwelling on his misery fails to spot a wave washing up his ankles. He is then afraid his mother will punish him if she discovers that he has got wet – she believed sea-water "would decay you" – so he removes his boots to dry them, using one to beat a crab to death. Everything about the sea makes him sick, and he longs to be taken home to his nice dark house. When Bella forces him to say "goodbye" aloud to the sea, he adds under his breath "blast you sea and all that in you is, and each flame of sun that smites be damned forever". Later O'Casey omitted from his autobiography this painful account of what may well have been his first trip to the seaside.

Although the family was not as well off as during Michael Casey's lifetime, they were still comfortable. But in 1890 Bella became pregnant, left her job and they had to vacate the school premises. Their new address was in a different area, over to the east and near the East Wall, and Sean who was nearly ten changed schools, from the one at which his sister taught to St Barnabas' National School.

He and Bella would quarrel, even after her baby was born: according to an unpublished sketch of his, he is reciting from a poetry book when Bella snatches the book and sits on it; when he tries to tip her off the chair, she threatens to tear up the book. The chair hits the floor and Sean pushes Bella's legs up over her head – "If your drummer boy was here now, he'd see something worth while." The argument makes the new baby scream, so if it happened Sean could not have been much more than eleven.

No. 25 Hawthorne Terrace was a cheerful one-storey cottage of two rooms and a kitchen; rates and rent were both lower than the last address at which the family had lived when Michael Casey was alive. But there was a small garden plot in front and a yard to the rear, with a water tap and a dry privy of which the family had sole use. Sparsely populated and with wide tracts of open ground, the new neighbourhood, Susan Casey's choice, was less central, and there were fewer professional people among the residents; it was a sober locality of ship's officers, bottle-blowers and artisans employed in local factories. Its character has changed little in a hundred years; now, as then, it houses the lower middle class.

For the eleven- or twelve-year-old Sean the neighbourhood buzzed with sounds: "Women standing at their doors this side of the street were talking to women standing at their doors on the other side of the street, and murmuring against the confusion that had come upon them." Relating more often to the world through voices and smells than through what he sees, Sean hears the drying clothes "flutterin' on the lines", dislikes the smell of beer, but rejoices in the "spice of Ireland", the hawthorn tree, whose "scented message of summer's arrival came pouring out in her blossoms, and went streaming down the little narrow street".

The Protestant vicar of St Barnabas' parish, the Revd J. S. Fletcher, was an unkind man to whom O'Casey, in his autobiography, gives the name Hunter, because the vicar's son, the Revd Harry Arthur Fletcher, later became a friend of his; thirteen years O'Casey's senior, this man showed him great kindness. The senior Fletcher, if O'Casey is to be believed, persecuted him on account of his poor attendance at school, and insisted on his being punished when the boy one day turned on the schoolmaster Slogan (actually John Hogan, a hard-drinking Galway man). Goaded into a rage by being unfairly treated in class, Sean dealt the schoolmaster a savage blow on the head with a large and heavy ruler, following this up with a kick in the shins before fleeing home to the protection of his mother.

It is impossible to determine whether this vividly created incident really took place. Only one contemporary of O'Casey's at St Barnabas' school has been traced, and this man, George Rocliffe, testified to Hogan's barbarity but knew nothing of the episode. Rocliffe did, however, although two years O'Casey's junior, remember that Sean missed many classes, and that when he was present, his eyes were frequently bandaged. "This led his classmates to tease him, but O'Casey won their respect by his eagerness to participate in their games in spite of his handicap. A determined youngster, he was not an aggressive one", never to Rocliffe's knowledge getting into a fight. All the pupils at St Barnabas' appeared to Rocliffe well fed and comfortably clad. His bandaged eyes apart, O'Casey did not stand out from the others.

The way "Hunter" is described by O'Casey reveals that by this time the boy Sean not only missed having a father, but that his sense of loss had developed, perhaps exaggeratedly, into a deep resentment towards any man who wanted to exercise over him any paternal authority.

– There is to be no putting-off of the punishment, Mrs Casside [Casey], the hard mouth said; remember that. The caning must be given while the blaguardly act is fresh in the mind of the boy.

The soft quivering mouth of the woman sitting on the butter-box covered with the old red cloth hardened to the hardness round the mouth of the minister.

– Tomorrow morning, the soft mouth that had hardened said, the boy will be where God, through the doctors, may give ease to his eyes. The harsh hand that fell on him today shall not fall on him tomorrow, or the next day, and its dark shadow shall he never see again. Tell that to Slogan from the boy's mother.

His mother's protection was possibly not wholly beneficial. While Hunter clearly deserved the contempt O'Casey shows him, O'Casey was increasingly to adopt, and develop for the sake of his image, a violently anti-authoritarian stand. Where witnesses at the time, like Rocliffe, saw a gentle, pacific boy, O'Casey when he recalled his early days portrays himself as a lawless upstart, especially ill-disposed towards those men who did not give him unqualified praise or attention. But he worshipped women: the whole sex, practically, became in his eyes hallowed by the uncritical love and devotion his mother gave him. She even supported him when he "fecked" or stole a lump of bacon and an egg from Liptons: after admonishing him severely, "Take no thought for your life, what ye shall eat; nor yet for your body, what ye shall put on", she dons bonnet and cape and leaves the house with sixpence to buy a "couple o' nice heads of cabbage" to go with the bacon.

For all his mother's exclusive care, however, Sean was not to have the good fortune granted his three oldest siblings – although not to Isaac – of being educated to the age of seventeen or eighteen. In 1894, the year after Nicholas Beaver was discharged from the army and signed on as a porter on the Great Northern Railway, and after Bella and her baby daughter had moved out of Hawthorne Terrace into a cottage of their own, Sean, not quite fourteen years old, was sent out to work. Although his attendance record at St Barnabas' School had been poor, he had benefited enormously from his qualified sister's constant presence at Hawthorne Terrace. She tutored him at home and he could read, even on his own admission, the stories in *The Boys of London and New York*.

He was now thin and lanky, with masses of hair which his mother was at pains to brush back from his forehead. His first job interview was with the wholesale chandlers, Hampton and Leedon, on the same side of Henry Street as the General Post Office from which the defeated Republicans were to break out in 1916. And so he set out one warm spring day in 1894, dressed in an Eton collar and blue Melton coat, carrying a reference from "Isabella Beaver", as his sister signed herself, to meet Mr Anthony Deverell, one of two brothers who owned the firm. Upon learning that O'Casey was a Protestant, Deverell engaged him to start at eight the following morning at a salary of three shillings and sixpence a week.

2

THE FIRST SWORD

In November 1890 when O'Casey was a little over ten years old, Charles Stewart Parnell was overtaken by a sexual scandal, which, in the words of James Joyce, befouled and smeared "the exalted name". Parnell, the first of O'Casey's heroes, had been for some time an important figure in Casey family lore: a Protestant aristocrat who led the Irish Home Rule Party in the House of Commons – it held eighty-five seats there, including seventeen of the thirty-three Ulster seats – he had over ten years raised Irish expectations of self-government to their highest point since January 1801, when the Irish Parliament was formally abolished and Ireland made part of Great Britain. Parnell was a solitary individual, admired across the political spectrum, by rich and poor, by Joyce as much as by W. B. Yeats; the latter put him alongside his earlier Protestant champions, Grattan, Swift, and Bishop Berkeley, although an antithetical tone later entered Yeats's attitude:

> Parnell came down the road, he said to a cheering man:
> "Ireland shall get her freedom and you still break stone."

Just when his party's alliance with Gladstone's Liberals seemed about to achieve power both for the Liberals and himself, when he was being lionised in English Liberal society and had been given the freedom of Edinburgh, Parnell was cited as co-respondent in the divorce action of a fellow MP, Captain O'Shea, with whose wife he had been having an affair for ten years. With the Catholic clergy mobilised against him, the party was irredeemably split, and although he tried to exonerate himself (at least with the clergy) by quickly marrying Mrs O'Shea, he made little headway against the clergy. He died, aged only forty-five, less than a year after the verdict in the divorce case was handed down. The whole scandal was a grave blow to the Irish nationalist cause.

Parnell makes his first appearance in the later mythicising of

O'Casey's own life at a particularly significant juncture – just before Sean's birth, when the body of the "second Johnny" is being carried home by his mother from the hospital where she has waited in vain for medical attention. A festive crowd halts the cab, "bringing Charlie Stewart Parnell to the Rotunda with bands and banners, where he's to speak on the furtherance of Home Rule for Ireland". "Ireland's greatest son," declares the cab-driver. "I'd sell me hat, I'd sell me horse an' cab, I'd sell meself for him, be Jasus."

Parnell, a father figure for the whole of Ireland, is at once related to, even identified with, Sean's own father, soon to die, and becomes the first of O'Casey's father-substitutes, a strong but misty presence at first who is gradually defined more clearly and worshipped more deeply as the young Sean's vision of life widens. So, when Parnell dies, in England at his wife's home in Brighton, as a result of overstretching himself in a by-election tour of North Kilkenny in October 1891, the event forms the basis of a moving and dirge-like section entitled "A Coffin Comes to Ireland", describing the impact of the death on the Casey household.

The impact of Parnell's death on O'Casey did not lessen, as did that of earlier Protestant Irish leaders such as Robert Emmet and Wolfe Tone, with the passage of years. Here was the essential difference between the years when O'Casey was entering his teens and earlier periods of Irish history: the pace of Irish nationalism now began to accelerate. Not only in O'Casey's own retrospective vision, but in the work of Lady Gregory, George Moore, Synge and others, Parnell was a decisive figure; he inspired Joyce's famous lines:

> This lovely land that always sent
> Her writers and artists to banishment
> And in a spirit of Irish fun
> Betrayed her own leaders, one by one.
> 'Twas Irish humour, wet and dry
> Flung quicklime into Parnell's eye

The quicklime referred to was cement thrown in his eyes by Irish workers in Kilkenny – which, as O'Casey pointed out some fifty-six years later in a letter to a friend, showed he got damned little gratitude for his efforts "to serve the Irish peasant".

Not only Parnell's fall, but the founding of the Gaelic League, by Douglas Hyde, to restore Irish as the national language, and the anti-Jubilee demonstration of 1897, in which Yeats took part with Maud Gonne and James Connolly, the ex-British Army socialist who later commanded the Republican garrison during the Easter Rising – these were important elements in the nationalist ferment. O'Casey was at an impressionable age, and these events helped to form his vision of the Ireland of his time. It was as if the scene designers and lighting men were for twenty or more years hammering and sawing and moving material and equipment into position, and then – with the actors given only a few skimpy rehearsals – had suddenly to switch everything on for the Easter Rising of 1916. The whole of Ireland became a stage ringed with footlights, blazing with drama. O'Casey, as the witness on the spot, not only observed the preparations, he grew into and out of each act in the tragedy, as his country gave birth to a national identity. He was able, in the end, to record the process as much from within as by means of his observant but often cynical eye.

As stock boy at Hampton and Leedon, the wholesale chandlers to whom he later gave the mocking names of Hymdim and Leadem, to express his disgust at the Protestant mercantile superiority in his native city, his powers of observation were sharpened too, as for the first time he became interested in the processes of life. The hundreds of Hampton and Leedon employees were part of the lower-middle-class world of Dublin in the '90s, a world whose vanities, aspirations and sad deficiencies, compared with those of the outside world, were delineated with scrupulous tenderness by Joyce in *Dubliners*, published in 1914. There was a significant difference between Joyce's observation and O'Casey's, however. Joyce's characters yearn for the great outside, rebelling against the shabbiness of the Dublin streets. The atmosphere he paints is a claustrophobic one: everyone knows everyone else, gossip and details of personal scandal pass quickly from ear to ear, nothing remains in darkness and mystery. O'Casey's view of the same world is intolerant and extreme – and more self-centred. He depicts the Hampton management as a conspiratorial hierarchy which calculatedly robs the poor and exploits the weak and helpless. The Deverell brothers embody evil:

A cloudy sneer rippled over the tight thin lips of Anthony, and his bony fingers twisted round each other, like the snakes on the head of Medusa. From a side squint, Johnny saw his pallid face redden, and his frosty eyes glitter with a cold glare.

O'Casey too, like a character in a Jonsonian comedy, adopted a humour: his was impudence and he begins pilfering on a large scale, giving the impression that he stole anything that could be hidden under his coat. When his mother discovers this she proposes deeper and wider pockets so that he can filch more, and with greater ease. But was O'Casey's picture of this activity true? He never referred to it later, in letters to friends, although he did mention, when he was over seventy, that he was sent to collect a monthly cheque on behalf of his employers from the Guinness office in St James's Street; this hardly suggests that Hamptons considered him unreliable.

Compared with Joyce's careful revelations of sexual awakening in *Dubliners* and *A Portrait of the Artist as a Young Man*, O'Casey's awareness borders on impersonality. In Hamptons he apparently fancied a Presbyterian girl who sorted dusty china in an out-of-the-way attic, on a step-ladder which gave him a liberal view up to the "lacy halo" of her drawers. But when a more serious sexual passion threatens to engulf the two young Protestants, their innate puritanism slams on the brakes: "He was clawing at her skirt when her eyes opened again, with a start; she tore his hands away, panting and pressing herself out of his grasp, till she stood, breathless and flushed, beside the little dusty window." He becomes more involved in the girl's response than in his own violence of feeling. Even as an adolescent O'Casey's view of sex was highly stagey: not experienced individually, but presented as if someone else was looking on. At no time, in no room or location, it seemed, could the door be locked, and some privacy of thought or feeling be established.

The unlocked door – a genuine symbol of Irish poverty – was to play a greater part in his life in the next few years. His brothers were becoming hardened drinkers, and while all three of them lived at home with their mother and Sean in Hawthorne Terrace, Tom and Mick, as serving soldiers, were absent except when on leave. Isaac exerted the greatest personal influence over Sean, with a result that neither of the brothers could have prophesied in 1894. Now in his early twenties and still working on the *Express*, Isaac had constructed a stage in the sitting room, and here the brothers, together with neighbourhood friends, began to act out plays; as Bella's eldest daughter said later, there were parts for everyone including the family mongrel.

But this was only the beginning: Isaac began to take part in charity performances, for example one at the Coffee Palace, Townsend Street, which included scenes from Boucicault's *The Shaughraun*, as well as a minstrel show and part of Shakespeare's *Henry VI Part 3*. Isaac had been assigned the role of Richard of Gloucester in the last, and wanted his younger brother to impersonate the victim-to-be,

Lancastrian King Henry. His mother was against Sean taking part, saying he was too young. But Isaac was her main financial support and so he had his way: he had also given Sean, until he began working, tuppence a week pocket money.

In 1895 Sean had the chance to act in what had already become his favourite work, *The Shaughraun*; he later confirmed in a letter that this was the first play he ever saw, performed at the Queen's Theatre, in Pearse Street, at that time a music hall. "It was a wonderful revelation. Then, it seemed the world was lit by footlights." Although Sean, like Mick, had shown ability at sketching and lettering and had hopes of becoming a painter and designer, from the time he saw his first Boucicault, the theatre began to rival his love of painting. His father had always held that Shakespeare was the greatest writer of all time, but Sean, despite Bella's sniffing at mention of the name, seemed inclined to champion Boucicault. In this he was emulating Isaac's friend, Charles D'Alton, the comedian and actor-manager, who said, "Shakespeare's good in bits; but for colour and stir, give me Boucicault."

Dion Boucicault had been born Dionysus Lardner Boursiquot in 1820, in Gardiner Street, Dublin, just round the corner from Hawthorne Terrace. Boucicault grew up unsure whether his father was the elderly wine merchant whose surname he bore, or the prolific Lardner, originator of the 134-volume *Cabinet Encyclopaedia*, from whom he took his two forenames. The son wrote hundreds of plays, most of them indescribably shoddy and derivative, but in *The Shaughraun* (1874), his best play, he displayed a comic inventiveness which had a profound effect on later playwrights, among them Lady Gregory, Synge, O'Casey, Behan and even Beckett. What was daring as well as seminal in *The Shaughraun* was that Boucicault moved its stock Irish comic rogue from being a peripheral figure right into the centre of the play.

"Shaughraun" means literally "wandering" or "straying". There had always been an Irish vagabond or slave figure on the English stage, cunning, clownlike or simple. There had also been stock Irish characters of the more pompous kind, such as the braggart Captain Macmorris in Shakespeare's *Henry V*. Boucicault, however, saw that if you put the two types together you might make something more than a stage stereotype. The perception was based on himself and his own superb skill as a comic actor: what if he could embody both the vain and insufferably ridiculous pretension and the parasite's subversive wit in a single character? Would this not be something of a revolution?

The characters of Myles-na-Coppaleen (in *The Colleen Bawn*, 1860), Shaun the Post (in *Arrah-na-Pogue*, 1864) and Conn the Shaughraun won universal popularity for the Irish rogue-hero. His heroic mockery also accorded with the new mood of Irish nationalism in the ten years after Boucicault's death in 1890: here were the traditional weapons, trickery and irreverence, with which the Irish had always fought their masters, but suddenly infused with new combative possibilities as Irish nationhood became more than a fantasy.

It is not difficult to see why O'Casey responded so positively to *The Shaughraun*, for he was himself becoming something of a Shaughraun in life. The Fenian Brotherhood during the late 1860s had made unsuccessful attacks on the British, and Boucicault's farcical plot involves not only a Fenian rebel on the run, but a police spy colluding with the 41st Regiment of Foot, along with other fantastic ingredients. But the play is held together by its hero, Conn the Shaughraun, whose lies are forgivable because they are so monstrously comic. His whole end in life is uninterrupted leisure, in parody of the idle rich who had long been Ireland's landlords; yet when it comes to the various comic crunches in the plot, Conn shows himself resourceful to the point of glorious absurdity. After simulating death from a British bullet, he acts the corpse at his own sham wake, and, unobserved, helps himself to whiskey provided for the sustenance of the keening mourners. As his sweetheart points out after his resurrection, when his mother falls on his neck, then whacks him for his deceit, "If he hadn't been murdered, he couldn't have saved us." It was not only by the speech rhythms of Boucicault's play that the teenage O'Casey became intoxicated, learning some of the lines by heart, but also by the triumphantly irreverent attitudes behind those rhythms; he could not have failed to note that the best comedy often emerged from the most marked contradictions.

Isaac Casey, too, under whose influence Sean lived at this time, was a bit of a Boucicault character: he fancied himself as an actor but, according to some contemporaries, quarrelled with the director, wouldn't learn his lines properly, and was generally short on stage discipline, sometimes making his entrance from the wrong side of the stage and dubbing in his own lines. He had a reputation for being moody and snappish, a bit pompous: O'Casey shows him as unpredictable and liable to dash expectations. But Isaac's passion for the theatre was constant; first a member of the Townsend Dramatic Society, which performed in disused stables, he later joined the Liberty Hall Players who, with proper sets and costumes, played to audiences of forty or fifty, in scenes from Shakespeare or Boucicault in which Sean sometimes took part.

When extolling the virtues of Boucicault Isaac's friend D'Alton had quoted a passage from *The Shaughraun*:

FATHER DOLAN: I'd rather see her tumble down in death an' hear the sods fallin' on her coffin, than speak the holy words that would make her your wife; for now I know, Corry Kinchella, that it was by your means and to serve this end that my darling boy, her lover, was denounced and convicted.

C. KINCHELLA: 'Tis false!

FATHER DOLAN: 'Tis thrue. But the thruth is locked in my soul (*he points finger at heaven*), an' heaven keeps the key!

declaring, "How could anyone beat this." Isaac for a while acted in D'Alton's company, the Mechanics' Theatre, in Abbey Street, giving his brother a free pass to watch from the bench placed at the front. D'Alton's brother-in-law Charlie Sullivan often played the leading Boucicault roles, with Isaac in small parts. One day when they were performing *The Shaughraun* they needed a last-minute replacement for an actor who had fallen ill. The part was that of Father Dolan, and Sean, being tall and ascetic-looking, as well as already knowing much of the script by heart, was quickly rehearsed, costumed, and had the make-up of a Roman priest hurriedly smeared over his face: thin streaks of brown across the forehead, wrinkles under his eyes, and flour over his hair to make it grey. Clutching a breviary in his left hand, and gesturing with his right, he appears to have acquitted himself well.

O'Casey had now left the wholesale chandlers where he had worked for over a year, whether of his own free will, or following a row with his employers over a fine imposed unfairly, cannot be verified. His own later account too easily slips into gratifying what was by that time his image of himself as a downtrodden but impudent and defiant member of the working class. His account of his next job, at Eason and Son the newsagent, where he worked as a van boy, starting at four in the morning, and which lasted only a week, shows him refusing to remove his cap to show suitable respect to his employers when collecting his wages. He narrates the incident proudly, feeling the "hero-heat that surged through Cuchullain in the core of a fight", displaying a mock-heroic bravery which O'Casey intends to be ironic. No recriminations from his tolerant mother appear to have followed his dismissal, so clearly the family could afford, if only barely, for Sean to adopt this stance towards the world of business and employment. He was now sixteen and it may have been at this point that his health deteriorated sharply: he was later to claim that he suffered so badly from beri-beri, caused by hunger, that everyone thought he would die or never walk again.

O'Casey said he obtained his position at Eason's through the Revd Harry Fletcher, son of the hated J. S. Fletcher, a Trinity College graduate who was standing in as curate at St Barnabas' during an illness of his father. Under the influence of the new curate – tall, kind and handsome, and roughly the same age as Sean's brother Tom – Sean developed into a more deeply committed Anglican. His father's books were what one would expect to find in the collection of a man all his life associated with Protestant principles: it was these principles which the most intellectually gifted of Michael Casey's four sons was to explore over the next year or two.

Reflecting perhaps the religious ambivalence of his father's Limerick family, Sean responded enthusiastically to the High Church ritual which Harry Fletcher introduced into St Barnabas' services. He was receiving instruction from Fletcher himself, who encouraged his wider reading and supplied him with books (out of church funds Fletcher bought books for poor children in the East Wall area); O'Casey also began at about this time to study Irish and to think of changing his name from John to Sean, "his right name", although he had always been known in his family circle as Jack and this never changed.

With Tom convalescing from a serious illness after leaving the Dublin Fusiliers, and Sean disinclined to pursue anything – other than reading – more than half-heartedly, the Casey family resources were dwindling, and in 1897 Susan and her four boys moved again, this time to 18 Abercorn Road. The nondescript grey pebbledash terraced house, lying in the formidable shadow of St Barnabas' itself, looked out from its upper-storey window on to the Great Northern railroad and the Royal Canal alongside. Over both of these a narrow bridge carried the pedestrian to the courtyard of the other giant house of worship of the area, the Catholic St Laurence O'Toole church, "with its ugly bloated spire", to which O'Casey was later to transfer his allegiance, at least socially. As in Hawthorne Terrace the family had a dry privy and water tap in the yard, but this time, significantly, they shared the house and its amenities with another family, the Sheelds, who lived downstairs. Again O'Casey makes an important distortion of circumstances in his autobiography, for by placing the

Sheelds family upstairs and the Caseys downstairs, he exaggerates the noise and disturbance caused, as he claims, by eight children always running up and down the stairs and shouting above his head; he also says that the Sheelds children were half-fed, dressed in shreds and patches, and forever quarrelling. The house, too, according to him, was alive with bugs.

The area was indeed a shabbier one than that of Hawthorne Terrace, with the docks of the North Wall several blocks away, beyond the cattle yards; but – and there are still neighbours who remember the Caseys living in Abercorn Road – it was not a slum. In what was to be her last home, Susan Casey strove with her customary Protestant zeal to keep up appearances. Bella's and Isaac's children later testified to the spotless state of the rooms, the cloth on the kitchen table and the plentiful supply of meat, as well as tea, bread, butter and jam. Susan Beaver recalled her granny's piercing eyes. One main cause of family friction, a nephew remembered, was studious Sean's refusal to find work.

In March 1898, on a lovely sunny spring day just before his eighteenth birthday, his head having been touched by the hand of a bishop of the Church of Ireland, O'Casey was confirmed a Protestant in Clontarf parish church. Here he publicly renewed his baptismal vows; sang "*Veni Creator Spiritus*"; and received , as he says, "a fuller grace from the Holy Ghost". As he passed with his companion, Nicholas Stitt, into the church, he met Jenny Clitheroe, an early sweetheart, whom he had once encountered in a field of poppies and daisies and defiantly kissed, although even then, with her studies of Euclid and her shy grey eyes fixed on the future, she had been too grand for him: now as they walked by each other "she closed her eyes, and gave a little disdainful toss to her head". Jenny worked as a cashier in Sir John Arnott's select drapery house.

But the richness of High Church ritual made up to O'Casey to some degree for his feeling of poverty. Future wealth of spirit was the promise:

From the big east window ahead of him, there were the twelve apostles, baked in brightly-coloured glass, looking down on them, carnivalled in bellalluring robes of blue, yellow, red, green, black, brown, purple, orange, Hebrew umber, Chinese white, and Hindoo crimson, glowing like titan tulips in a Persian garden. The sunlight, now, came strolling through them, their eager faces shone with a thousand tints, their coloured cloaks rippled as if blown by a gentle breeze from heaven, their limbs quivered as if they were about to step forward in a sparkling procession over the heads of the congregation.

The splendour of this Anglican ritual had an uncomfortable sequel: the popular Harry Fletcher fell foul of the Loyal Orange Order: at first the loyalists began a hissing campaign when they saw his black cassock, defiantly spoke the creed while the choir sang and shouted "Popery!" But as Fletcher went on bravely challenging them with his fine vestments and ritual, which appealed to the poorer members of the church, they withdrew funds from him, flung stones at the church windows and generally made life so unpleasant that he had to contemplate leaving the parish.

He called one night on Sean to say goodbye and found him deep in conversation with his Catholic friend Ayamonn O'Farrel, a tram conductor, who had given him O'Growney's *Simple Lessons in Irish* and had first called him "Sean". After praising the young man for his industry at his books, Fletcher tells them the reason for his visit is that he is being driven out by his congregation's "deep-set emotions of an ignorant evangelism". After Fletcher has gone, Sean argues with O'Farrel that he belongs to the one Catholic and Apostolic Church, to which his friend replies, "I always thought yous were protestants." Ah, ripostes Sean, "St Patrick founded our Church as he founded yours." To be Irish transcended both Catholicism and Protestantism.

O'Casey was now keenly learning Irish, although ashamed to say too much about it in public. And while he stalwartly maintained his position as a communicant Anglican, giving classes at Sunday School, his mother, her true-blue heart fortified by his continuing adherence to her faith and standards, suffered a set-back with Isaac, who one day announced he was going to marry a frail girl, Johanna, or "Josie", Fairtlough. As he was the first of her sons to marry, one might have assumed Susan Casey would be glad; as Isaac was betrothing himself, moreover, to the daughter of a thriving family of grocers and trades-people whose name went back to the Norman Conquest – genealogy being always an important consideration in Ireland – Susan might look for an alleviation of the family circumstances. Josie's brother, William, was clearly set to become an influential man and later held office in the Transport and General Workers' Union. He also owned a fleet of lorries which, in the preparations for the Easter Rising, he used for gun-running from Howth.

But Susan Casey was a Protestant and Josie a Catholic. The marriage took place in the Catholic Pro-Cathedral of Dublin and she refused to attend. She could be very severe and disapproving. O'Casey himself appears not to have liked Josie, calling her "stumpy", a "perky-faced lass" with an air proclaiming she was a born lady. Isaac, however, seemed only too pleased to flee into Catholic security, adopting the superior tone of his in-laws and insisting his brothers dress properly when visiting them, which enraged Sean, who by now, having awarded himself the status of "poor scholar", was abandoning his earlier habits of clerical attire. "O'Casey and Mick were commanded to wear collars and ties. . . . O'Casey, the more bashful of the two, would redden and leave, but Mick would storm in unbidden, snarling he was 'as good a man with a muffler'. And Isaac himself would greet Bella's children with a broad, conspiratorial wink and caution them – in tones imitative of Josie's carefully cultivated accent – 'Now, boys and girls, we have to be precise'."

Demonstrating the Casey family's almost Russian volatility of nomenclature, Isaac had with marriage become Joseph – he had loathed being called Isaac – and himself converted to Catholicism. But while he pursued greater middle-class respectability, the marriage did not transform his predilection for the easy life, and he still drank heavily, pulling his hat down over his eyes when he'd taken a drop too much. He drank not only evenings but afternoons, using the takings from his inlaws' grocery shop, and paying for Mick and Tom to join him. Fortunately O'Casey had already formed a strong aversion to drink – had squashed in himself that active ingredient of his brothers' subsequent decline.

With the loss of Isaac's earnings, with the recall of both Tom and Mick to the colours for the duration of the Boer War in 1899–1900, and with Bella no longer working, the Casey household was finally on the downward slide. At first it was on a gentle and comfortable incline, making Sean skimp a bit on food and clothing but not disturbing his dedicated study of Irish, of German – he claims he learnt some German at this time – nor the leisured life he led arguing with his friends, attending nationalist or religious meetings, or participating in noisy demonstrations such as the anti-Boer War riot in 1899. There he spotted James Connolly, Arthur Griffith, and the lovely Maud Gonne, before the hoof of a charging police horse grazed his leg and split his trousers from knee to ankle. In this episode, as he reports it, he is then taken home by a glamorous fellow demonstrator who feeds him an egg and tea and retires, complaining that her skirt and petticoat have been "creased an' twisted with the crush of the crowd". She emerges from her bedroom a little later dressed in a dark-green shawl, which is fastened with a large brooch decorated with the picture of a naked girl. This signals the loss of his virginity. After leaving the girl half dead from his amorous exertions, he never mentions her again.

Catching .
Recruits. .

John Kelly, aged 10, arrested for having "kicked up his feet" and thrown a piece of bread at a woman in the streets of Limerick. He was let out on condition he became a drummer boy in the English Army.

An anti-recruitment cartoon from *An Poblacht*

Close to his mighty mother's side, O'Casey's Shaughraun-like leisure in shabby declining Dublin was little interrupted between 1900 and 1903 by work, although he always had an enormous number of self-appointed tasks on hand: Susan Casey connived in his self-improvement, cooking and caring for him as ever. While he repeated passages from Shakespeare or Goldsmith, Susan did the washing for his sister's family as well as for her own and was presumably paid for it by Bella; she also washed for another woman, her remuneration for this being sixpence and a glass of porter. His mother did more than feed Sean's body, she fed his idealism during the first years of his full manhood. His Protestant nationalism was given a boost too, when the Revd Harry Fletcher was replaced, not by a regalia-sporting Orangeman, but by Edward Morgan Griffin, gentle son of a Methodist and ex-secretary of the Hibernian Bible Society. O'Casey got on well with him, joined his Bible classes and became secretary to the church's Foreign Missions work. Griffin now took over from Harry Fletcher the role of mentor priest in the Casey family.

O'Casey's brighter conception of the Christian faith persisted. Mentally, he was broadening his horizons, but he was to remain a non-conformist Protestant in outlook even upon abandoning the Church some years later. He was gradually becoming more of a non-conformist in Shaw's definition of a Protestant as "theoretically an anarchist as far as anarchism is practicable in human society: that is, he is an individualist, a freethinker, a self-helper, a Whig, a Liberal, a mistruster and vilifier of the State, a rebel". But in the period from 1900 to 1903 when he was embarking on manhood without work, dreaming for a while first of a career as a painter, only later of becoming a writer, O'Casey's Protestant outlook was mingled with an ardent nationalism. Sometimes the two commitments were movingly fused: "A holy city's our city of Dublin . . . more ancient than Athens; more sacred than Rome; as holy as Zion." Yet he would never fight for her, for all too often she was also "Rotten Dublin; lousy Dublin, what had it for anyone? What had it for him? Poverty and pain and penance. They were its three castles." He knew even at this time, long before the drums of revolution and then civil war beat under his windows, that he would never be a soldier, he had neither the character nor the constitution. Even in the crowd, defying the mounted police in Parliament Street in the anti-Boer War demonstration, he knew at heart he was scared and it was no use pretending otherwise.

His favourite brother, Tom, returning to Post Office employment after his discharge from the Royal Dublin Fusiliers at the end of 1900 (he had taken part in the Relief of Ladysmith), regaining by this time his former status and a decent wage, followed Isaac into marriage in February 1903. The girl he chose, Mary Kelly, to Susan Casey's horror was another Catholic, a plumber's daughter, far lower down the social scale than Josie and even unable to read. At least she and Tom were not married in a papist church, but even so Susan refused once again to be present at the event, in a Register Office. Now, in Abercorn Road, only Mick and Sean were left with Susan.

O'Casey was still teaching himself Irish and was soon to embrace the emblem of the Gaelic League, *An Claidheamh Soluis*, or the Sword of Light, first in half-farcical circumstances over a bookshop in Tyler

Street, later at a branch of the League he attended regularly for some years before becoming himself an official in the organisation. It was paradoxical that he, with his weak eyes, became increasingly an organiser, and inevitably figured sooner or later as secretary to any organisation he joined. He was also developing a taste for the sport of hurling, although here too, poor eyesight was unlikely to help him.

So where should he turn? He was at the crossing of many paths: each, in Gaelic imagery, with its own sword to grasp. Which one should he follow? "The Sword of Light! An Claidheamh Soluis, the Christian Faith; the sword of the spirit; the freedom of Ireland; the good of the common people; the flaming sword which turned every way, to keep the way of the tree of life – which was it? Where would he find it?"

Over the next twenty years he was to follow each of these paths in turn, until he found that none led where he wanted to go. The pattern was the same: his involvement with a particular cause would reach a pitch of intensity before he began to see the flaws in it. By this means he would re-enact the expansion of the hopes of his early years and their dramatic foreshortening caused by his father's death.

Eventually he perceived that what he held in his hand was no longer a sword but a pen, a more subtle and provocative instrument, that could be turned many ways at once and at the same time, and could produce unexpected effects, not least laughter at the causes he had formerly embraced.

3

FIERY BLOSSOMS

O'Casey, aged twenty-three, was by now extremely well read, and could, had he so chosen, have found employment in a clerical job, or tried to qualify for something higher. Instead, shunning the advantages his reading and his contacts might have commanded, he adopted the more positive persona, for an intellectual, of a common labourer. On the suggestion of his old school friend George Middleton, a member of a Loyal Orange lodge, he started work for the Great Northern Railway of Ireland. Once again O'Casey owed employment to a privileged social position, and had himself taken no action to find it.

How solidly did he work on the railways? His autobiography devotes fewer pages to his nine years on the railways than to his week's work at Eason's. His other rapidly expanding interests, among them now that of writing, suggest the work was casual, even seasonal. Probably he found, while working on the GNR, not the exploitation he depicted to make socialist propaganda much later in life, but the laziness and even comically incompetent corruption which he satirised in a series of articles for the Larkinite *Irish Worker* in 1912 and 1913, the years immediately after he left the railways.

But it was only the persona of a working man he adopted – and that mainly in relation to his middle-class friends. He made little effort to communicate with other members of his railway gang, while he defied his loyalist superiors by making a show of studying Irish during meal breaks. With something of the reputation of a "scholar", he would sometimes be entrusted with collecting the weekly wages from the cashier and distributing them to the gang. Mick, now a well-paid postal worker, was still the main support of the Casey household, and was, by all accounts, the more attentive of the two sons to their mother, helping her by cleaning and running errands. Had O'Casey left the GNR in 1904 or 1905 he could have borne witness to Shaw's philosophy of the true artist by letting his mother "drudge for his living at seventy [Susan Casey was seventy in 1905], sooner than work at anything but his art". But he must have found the work experience valuable, and the hours were perhaps flexible enough to allow him to remain on the job, while the outdoor labouring improved his physical health.

For some years at any rate O'Casey felt proud of his work, claiming that his body caught up to, and fell into alignment with, his developing mind. His first job was as a bricklayer's assistant; he worked six days a week, twelve hours a day, for a total of eighteen shillings a week. He would carry bricks in a hod, help erect scaffolding, dig earth or concrete with a pick. At another time he carried sleepers, "slippy, hot and pungent with the soak of creosote". For this work he was paid on the basis of how many "quarters" – periods of three hours – he put in per day; he might work twelve days in a fourteen-day period, and for the next fourteen days might not necessarily work at all.

The proof that he did not work full-time lay in the number of other activities in which he immersed himself between 1903 and 1911, when his allegiance next shifted significantly. Judging by the scant reference made to this period in the autobiography, and the way in which he transferred into it tragic events, like the death of his brother Tom, which happened much later, one can only assume that these years were, as Tolstoy observed of happy families, all alike, and had no history.

When O'Casey laboured alongside navvies who were laying a monster drain he still knew his own identity as separate from theirs: "Not one of these brawny boys had ever heard of Griffith or of Yeats. . . . What to them were the three Gaelic candles that light up every darkness: truth, nature, and knowledge? Three pints of porter, one after the other, would light up the world for them." He was, as his fellow workers observed, "odd", and not much of a mixer; not that he was truculent or aggressive in his defiance of authority, but he seemed eccentric. They recalled that often he did not turn up for work. His superiors found him "a cranky devil", one of them saying he was often to be seen leaning on his shovel, staring into space and day-dreaming, and that, as at school, he was often absent. Although he was cautioned frequently by his superiors, in particular on his laziness, they tolerated him, presumably because while being cussed he was not an actively disruptive force in the work gangs.

He was also remembered for his refusal to join in the various little rackets that went on, such as paying the foreman a commission to obtain building materials for use at home; on the occasion of Edward

VII's Coronation in 1902, he refused a day's pay given to workers for the holiday and boycotted St Barnabas' church when he found it covered with flags.

Tom Casey quickly started a family, ultimately having two boys and a girl, while Bella now had a family nearly as large as her mother's. She lost a son, Nicholas, who died in 1904, aged two, of a stomach ailment, and Josie and Joseph (*né* Isaac) in the same year lost a daughter, Eileen, who was only a month old. But Tom's position in the Post Office improved over the next few years – he became head sorter on the Belfast mail – and he remained part of the Casey family circle, leaving his wife at home and out of it. On Sundays they would gather for afternoon dinner, usually at the Beavers'. As Martin Margulies, the first chronicler of O'Casey's early life, records:

> Tom and Mick would drift over several hours early, so that they could stroll through the country with Beaver while Beaver – a bird fancier who kept a large parrot at home – flew his pigeons. When O'Casey arrived later with his mother, he would settle himself in the best armchair, take a book from the shelf, and read placidly through the evening as the conversation swirled around him. Sometimes he would pause to sip at his cup of cocoa, which he prepared himself from a packet of chocolate which he carried in his pocket.

At other times O'Casey participated in prayer meetings, "voluntering long fervent prayers" which were dreaded because of their length. "We heard his voice ringing out loud and clear, in that drawling, lilting way he had of speaking . . .", Edward Griffin's daughter said later, and added, "He would have made a great preacher." After Sunday services he would escort the rector's two oldest daughters home to the Rectory in Charles Street, often accompanied by his sister's children, whom he dropped off at Rutland Street. While walking he would playfully mock the essays the children were preparing for school.

O'Casey's first direct contact with the Gaelic League was in 1905 or 1906, at the Mulachy branch which assembled over a boot shop in Talbot Street, round the corner from where he had acted at the old Mechanics' Theatre in Abbey Street. The meetings there were irregular and ill attended, and soon were abandoned: he and a fellow railway worker, Peadar O'Nuallain, watched the benches being taken away after the last meeting, and Peadar was in tears. Next they assembled more regularly in Drumcondra, in Carlingford Road, very near Richmond Road where Tom lived, and the Botanic Gardens. Their use of these premises did not last long either, although O'Casey, somewhat inconsistently with his supposed six-day week on the railway, would spend Saturday half-holidays coating the walls with paint; another member, Paddy Callan, used to drop by to see how he was getting on. The meeting place was unconventional, a ground-floor shop front with an unfinished room above it, the result of a neighbour's complaint over lack of light. They were driven from Carlingford Road by another neighbour who claimed they were lowering the "caste" of the road.

The Drumcondra branch, called Lámhdearg (Red Hand), finally came to rest in more modest quarters, what O'Casey called a tumble-down shack in Seery's or Boylan's Lane, a squalid charnel house, at one time used as a place to deposit the dead, near North Strand. The air here was foul, but the learning of Irish gathered pace and soon O'Casey himself was an instructor, although conscious that he did not belong to the class that ran the League – "the Civil Servants, Customs Officers, Teachers, and others of the budding Irish Gentry". These would not attend such a poor branch – although some of them put their noses round the door once or twice a year, and O'Casey recalled visitors such as Seamus Deakin, a chemist, and Sinéad Ni Fhlannagáin, the future Mrs Eamon de Valera, who challenged the opinion that a woman's place was in the kitchen. Sinéad Ni Fhlannagáin, who was very pretty, once acted the part of the Fairy in Douglas Hyde's *The Fairy and the Tinker*: when she asked George Moore about taking up a stage career he replied, "Height five feet four; hair, red; name, Flanagan; no, my dear."

O'Casey arrived early before each meeting, in the bad weather ploughing through frost and snow, and then used to open up, sweep the floor, light the fire, and get the room ready: he admitted that he worked a lot harder at night time than during the day. There was a workers' club next to the League premises, and here they ate supper and brewed tea. Sometimes, perhaps two evenings a week, they would hold an all-night *ceilidh* with dancing, and he also contributed articles and ideas to a "Manuscript Journal".

O'Casey, as was his wont, assumed the position of secretary, and it was at this time also that he began to take a serious interest in hurling. He flung himself into the sport with more gusto than finesse – he was said to have killed a sparrow in flight, mistaking it for the ball. He would regale club members with humorous tales of a mythical brother named Adolphus O'Casey, a character based on Joseph: Adolphus, a social climber, scorned common girls, affected a posh accent, pronouncing his name "O'Caysay". Adolphus opposed the activities of the Gaelic League. In reality, so too did Mick, who displayed the average Irish mentality, growling at O'Casey, "Irish, what good's Irish in a British country?"

Later, probably because the game was better organised there, O'Casey hurled in the Ard Chraobh, or Central Branch, with two Aran men, and with his former companion, Peadar O'Nuallain, who ticked him off for wearing a muffler instead of a collar. Another team-mate, Ernest Blythe, who also suffered from poor eyesight, remembered being taken home to meet Susan Casey and being given tea, butter, bread and jam in O'Casey's "ordinary working-class home"; he and O'Casey, with others, campaigned for church services in Irish, wrote letters soliciting money. One night O'Casey spoke to Blythe about the Fenians, at first in a roundabout way, then, having sounded him out, asked him directly if he would join the organisation known as the Irish Republican Brotherhood, to the Teeling Circle of which O'Casey now belonged. "I don't believe in assassination," Blythe told him, to which O'Casey replied, "Nor do we, we're organising for open warfare."

Blythe, who found O'Casey confident, without self-pity, a man who could take as well as administer a joke, was induced to join the much more sinister Brotherhood, although its activities were as yet extremely low-keyed and, according to Blythe, monotonous. But Mick Casey, when he heard of his younger brother's participation in the organisation, was fiercely critical: "Join that crowd," he told Sean, "and you're finished. You've lost your freedom." O'Casey all during this time favoured a separate republic for Ireland, while others espoused the moderate policies of Arthur Griffith, with his "dual monarchy" idea.

The Casey family received its next major blow in 1905, when Bella's husband, Nicholas Beaver, fell seriously ill – "quietly going mad", as O'Casey put it, with GPI, or general paralysis of the insane. Beaver, who by then had attained a good position as head of the GNR parcels office, was taken to the Richmond District Lunatic Asylum, off the North Circular Road, at the other end of which O'Casey himself was later to live. He describes how his brother-in-law was driven to "the house of strident shadows, to dress in the rough grey tweed of the loony pauper, to wear the red woollen handkerchief so tied that when one became restless, a keeper could seize it, pull, and choke all movement . . ." He took him in himself, he claims, noticing his fellow inmates:

> Dotted here and there in the grounds were the dismal brothers of disorders grey, their red mufflers making them look as if their tormented heads had been cut off, and pushed crookedly back on to their necks again.

Bella, selling off her possessions all the while, had to move with her five children from Rutland Street, where they had lived in modest comfort, to a shabby tenement in Fitzgibbon Street, where they survived for a while on Beaver's savings, although unable to disguise that they had crossed the significant line dividing those who could still cling to respectability from those who had become downright pathetic:

> She had married a man who had destroyed every struggling gift she had had when her heart was young and her careless mind was blooming. He had given her, with God's help, a child for every year, or less, that they had been together. Five living, and one, born unsound, had gone the way of the young and good, after being kept alive for three years . . . Ah! faded into the forgotten past were the recitation of bits from Racine's *Andromaque* and *Iphigénie*, or from Scott's *Lady of the Lake*, the confident playing of waltz, schottische, polka, and gavotte on a piano in a friend's house . . . Now she went about everything like a near-drowned fly in a jar full of water.

Even Susan Casey could not startle her daughter into resistance to this decline.

Here at last, through his sister, was O'Casey's first direct and painful experience of poverty, genuine cause for the "poor mouth" he puts on when describing his early life. It was no longer, however, early life; O'Casey was now twenty-five: his sensitivity to Bella's tragedy shows how much of the quality and richness of life he had perceived by that time, how deeply and broadly he still, with regard to his own future, registered potentiality. But he still thought of it as early life because he still lived exactly as he had when a child, cared for entirely by his mother, now a toothless old lady of seventy, over whose five feet he towered but to whose cantankerous virtues he remained entirely obedient. Susan Casey had slaved for twenty-five years to keep him well fed and comfortable, but it was his sister who, from an early age, had nourished him intellectually, and in the devoted care Bella had shown him before she married, and in the early years of her marriage when Beaver had been absent, she had been an extension of his mother. The degree to which his feelings had been protected and cocooned by his family and his religion showed in one of the first poems he wrote. "The Soul of Man", dated November 1905, ends with the lines:

> When Life's bright dawn the world was gilding,
> Man's infant mind went Babel building.
> But want of knowledge man defeated,
> And left the work but half-completed:
> For broadening powers of mind alone
> Can climb upon God's highest throne.
>
> And man, unshaken, still shall seek –
> Ignoring all the gods' derision –
> To make eternal silence speak
> To look behind life's hidden vision,
> Till Thought may weigh and sift and scatter,
> And mould again the life of matter.

The by now absurd genteel pretensions of the Casey family were seen again when Bella's eldest daughter, Susan, who had, like Bella, been sent to the fee-paying Central Model Schools, was not allowed to work at anything which might demean her position as a lady. Bella herself was reduced to scrubbing floors three or four times a week at a shilling a time.

O'Casey had been putting down his political ideas in school exercise books since he was about twenty: one of these early scribblings, in the form of a "Petition", approved Protestant opposition to the idea of Home Rule, claiming it would reduce Ireland to "a state of chaos equal to that which troubled Nature before the World was Born". In May 1907, in the midst of the family trials, O'Casey had his first article published, in the *Peasant and Irish Ireland*; this was "a satiric fantasy throwing a mockery of glory" over the chief secretary for Ireland, Augustus Birrell's, policy speech on Irish education. O'Casey savagely denounced Birrell's views as alien to the interests of the new spirit in Ireland: "After all, what is Irish Education to a fresh battalion, a new gunboat, or the comfort of the police force? To gain a huge lump of the world as Empire would evoke the admiration of the gods; what doth Séaghan Buidhe [John Bull: literally 'Yellow John'] profit if Ireland should save her national soul?" Appropriately entitled "Sound the Loud Trumpet", the article appeared under an early pseudonym, *An Gall Fada*, the "Tall Foreigner" or Protestant. O'Casey read out the piece at Gaelic League meetings, convincing himself, because it had convinced others, that he could write.

One of O'Casey's earliest manuscripts

But the heartening effect of such publication must have palled, later in the same year, when Nicholas Beaver died and was placed in a coffin, to be subjected to his brothers–in–law's scrutiny. Mick said you could see from "the marks around his head where . . . the skull had been lifted, and the brain removed: 'Practising on him they were'." So died a man who, in the words of his former C.O., Captain Campbell of the King's Liverpool Regiment, had "always borne a good character".

Bella had to move, but where? The list of his sister's possessions which Sean brought back early one morning in November 1907 to his mother's home in Abercorn Road was wonderfully precise: as if the wool of false poverty had suddenly been pulled from his eyes on confronting the real thing. He felt a quite desperate fear that he might be seen herding these possessions by a Gaelic League friend or Republican brother. The inevitable scavengers – omnipresent witnesses to Irish misery – gathered:

> A group of them were even now standing to stare at the unhappy little heap of scrap in the kennel, then over at Sean leaning against the railings of the rotting houses; for this sort of thing was to them a song . . . Someone in trouble, someone in sorrow, a fight between neighbours, a coffin carried from a house, were things that coloured their lives and shook down fiery blossoms where they walked.

For the time being Bella and her family created a hellish state in Abercorn Road that fitted O'Casey's worst nightmare: nine of them were squashed into the two small bedrooms. Their living conditions were now nearly like those prevailing in the true slum Georgian tenements with their hosts of ragged poor, sometimes as many as a hundred to one house. Even so, O'Casey himself, as he makes clear, never went hungry; the GNR had become absolutely crucial both to his survival and his self-respect. He says bluntly that if he gave his sister sixpence a week, it meant doing without a book, or part of a book. It was his ambition to write, his middle-class aspiration not his very life, that Bella's decline threatened:

> It wasn't a pleasant job for him to be eating a dinner with a little army of hungry eyes watching him, so, working near or far, he took his dinner with him. Taking his breakfast wasn't so bad, for they were all still asleep, though it wasn't easy always to arrange table and chair so that the legs didn't pinch their prostrate bodies; and the smell of the room from the breaths of the sleeping bodies made the air of the room thick and sluggish, even though he kept the window open, especially to him, in from a first quarter's work in the fresh and frosty air. At times, a surge of hatred swept through him against those scarecrow figures asleep at his feet, for they were in his way, and hampered all he strove to do, and a venomous dislike of Ella [Bella] charged his heart . . .

In the meantime Dublin had become drama-mad. While O'Casey's energies were being asserted in the humbler areas of national revival, the high flyers, Yeats and Maud Gonne, had resigned from the Irish Republican Brotherhood. Maud Gonne had formed the Inghínídhe na hÉireann, the Daughters of Erin revolutionary society, whose first success, she claimed, was virtually to stop Dubliners from enlisting in the British Army. She had joined forces early in 1901 with W. G. Fay's National Dramatic Company, an enterprising group run by the brothers Willie and Frank Fay, who were as deeply committed to an Irish dramatic revival as Maud Gonne was to Republicanism. "We thought it was time," wrote Frank Fay, "to make the Irish accent and idiom in the speaking of English a vehicle for expression of Irish character on the stage and not for the sole purpose of providing laughter." After several years of indifferent success, during which the new movement achieved renown with productions such as that of Yeats's *Cathleen Ni Houlihan*, in which Maud Gonne played the lead, *In the Shadow of the Glen* proclaimed the arrival of the astonishing talent of J. M. Synge.

A permanent home was found in the building where nine years before O'Casey had trod the boards as Father Dolan: the Mechanics' Hall was rebuilt and transformed into the Abbey Theatre at an estimated cost of £13,000, under the supervision of Annie M. Horniman. This English heiress to a tea fortune did more than anyone else to make sure the theatre was built. She later made Manchester a centre of serious theatre, and inspired Lilian Baylis to turn the Royal Victoria Coffee Music Hall in London into the Old Vic Theatre. Although Miss Horniman had been Yeats's close associate for five years, she soon fell out with the nationalist aspirations of the Fays' company: later she wrote that "love of wicked politics, which teach you to hate each other so intensely, has spoiled my efforts at the Abbey Theatre". It was perhaps as well she was out of the way by the time O'Casey came along.

The Abbey Theatre opened its first season on 27 December 1904, a Tuesday, with Yeats's *On Baile's Strand*; Lady Gregory's *Spreading the News* was the curtain-raiser. Yeats made a speech on the opening night. Two years later, in 1906, the theatre rejected Shaw's *John Bull's Other Island*, provoking its author to declare to a reporter, "Here's a play by an Irishman on Ireland as original as anything could be, as sympathetic with the genius of the people and in every way racy of the soil. Why don't the National Theatre people give it?" One reason, Shaw said, was that certain speeches in it "would so enrage all Nationalist auditors that they'd rise as one man and burn the house down".

There was no truth in this; the Abbey rejected *John Bull's Other Island* on the grounds of casting: no actor in the company was considered good enough to play Broadbent. Also Yeats did not much like the play, although he later changed his mind. Otherwise, apart from a flock of internal troubles, all predictable, the Abbey's modest reputation continued to increase until 1907, the crucial year in its history. In January of that year the curtain rose on Flaherty's public house, on a dark autumn evening on a wild coast of Mayo, with Pegeen Mike mulling over her shopping list. In J. M. Synge's *The Playboy of the Western World* the Abbey management had at last found a play that not only provoked riots but was itself a symptom of the rising national temperature. Trouble was anticipated from some quarters over the daring inclusion in the text of such words as "God" and "bloody" – hardly an innovation as far as Irish speech was concerned – but no one considered the devastating effect the use of a five-letter word, the feminine of "shirt", denoting a long-obsolete garment lying close to a woman's skin, would have.

"AUDIENCE BROKE UP IN DISORDER AT THE WORD SHIFT," Lady Gregory informed Yeats, away in Scotland, by telegram. The row over this word, which has seemed extraordinarily infantile to later generations, was nevertheless what sparked off the *Playboy* riots. There were deeper causes, however, as was claimed by both sides in the dispute: there was the religious objection to playwriting itself, and the position that "art for art's sake" was against the national interest. Many people, not all of them stupid, genuinely believed that Synge's play constituted a slander on the fair name of Ireland. O'Casey observed the effects of the *Playboy* in his local branch of the Gaelic League, where everyone was tense and aflame with indignation. Ayamonn O'Farrel was the worst: "Some blasted little theatre or other has put on a play by a fellow named Singe or Sinje or something . . . a woeful, wanton play; bittherin', bitherin', th'n, th'n th' bittherest thing th' bittherest enemy of Ireland could say agin' her!"

Even more upsetting than a garment's proximity to woman's naked flesh, was the Shaughraun element in the *Playboy*. The challenging irreverence of Boucicault's prototypical comic Irish hero, shaped into Christy Mahon by the hand of a literary genius, threatened the established order. What hurt in the play – and still does – was its truthfulness to life. Maxim Gorky later wrote, "In it the comical side passes quite naturally into the terrible, while the terrible becomes comical just as easily." For J. M. Synge, a truly wise artist, did not inject his own point of view; he just exhibited the people. "They are half gods and half beasts, and are possessed of the childish desire to find a 'hero' among themselves."

Thanks only to the tenacity of the directors of the Abbey, the *Playboy* continued to be performed, the reactionary audiences kept in order by rows of policemen standing in the aisles. Railway worker O'Casey was not yet part of this Dublin, where, as Mary Colum wrote, "Between Abbey Street and College Green, a five minutes walk, one could meet everyone of importance in the life of the city at a certain time in the afternoon." But the Dublin literary tradition of supplying great playwrights to the English-speaking stage had again been demonstrated.

Although an outsider on the Dublin literary scene, O'Casey had not abandoned, even in the reduced family circumstances after Beaver's death, his search for a meaning to his life; nor did he lose that margin of energy which he had begun to commit to the Irish revival. Like many of his countrymen, even the dullest and most frustrated of tenement dwellers, he had a passion for freedom. One of the first restraints he threw off, in the year following the *Playboy* riots and the death of his brother-in-law, was that of Anglicanism. How this came about is not clear, for he later recorded very little about his early religious feelings, but it may have had something to do with the reaction of Edward Griffin, to whom he sent his satirical article, "Sound the Loud Trumpet". Being deeply fond of Griffin, he expected encouragement, but the response from the rector was a profound silence. Some weeks later O'Casey ventured to ask him what he had thought of the piece. Griffin placed a hand gently on his shoulder: "The man who wrote that article, John, is a traitor and ought to be in jail."

According to George Rocliffe, the parishioner of St Barnabas' who had been his contemporary at school, O'Casey left St Barnabas' in 1908 because the new church organ had been built in England. However, he stayed in touch with Griffin, and never ceased to be favourably disposed towards him. A further reason for lapsing from Protestantism was the strain, now intolerable, imposed on his belief in a just and fair God by the suffering in his own family.

After living for several months in Abercorn Road, Bella moved with her five children into new lodgings, a small cottage round the corner in Brady's Lane, where George Middleton had been O'Casey's champion in his school days against the local bully boys. Having defaulted on the rent, Bella was evicted from this place, humiliation which O'Casey, again with Middleton, helped her overcome by moving her furniture into a vacant one-room cottage in near-by Church Place; there she lived rent-free for six months until she was able to move to a larger place next door. By now O'Casey's attitude to his sister was rather grudging: he saw little of the family, he says, and never enough to give him a worrying thought. But he did complain that she had lifted a jug from his dresser, and that some of his mother's blankets were gone from the sofa where she dossed down.

Another irritating aspect of Bella's family which helped to keep O'Casey away from church was their begging: he says that his sister used to solicit a few pence from him after the morning service in order to feed her children, and that he would stay behind in church to avoid meeting them. If O'Casey had as yet produced none of the work of an artist, he was certainly displaying the egotism of one, at least the struggle, as Shaw defined it, "between the artist man and the mother woman". His treatment of his sister's family was at odds with the selfless charity of actions he later performed – and records himself as performing – towards other people's poor children. But by then he had an audience and saw himself as working in the cause of his fellow men.

Other considerations were in 1908 turning him away from the Established Church. Although the Gaelic League was led by Douglas Hyde, the Trinity College-educated son of a Protestant rector, the Catholic outlook had soon come to dominate the organisation, in turn influencing O'Casey. He had seen attempts to have the Irish language introduced into Anglican services, both in his own parish and at St Patrick's Cathedral, if not fail outright, be only tepidly embraced. Now a new Catholic and nationalist friend, Frank Cahill, a teacher in the Christian Brothers' School at St Laurence O'Toole's, the church whose dirty, squat spire O'Casey could see from the window of his room, invited him to join the Laurence O'Toole Club of which he, Cahill, was a founder.

Cahill, two years younger than O'Casey, became a great influence on him. O'Casey never mentions him in the autobiography – they later fell out – even though Cahill was the model for the central figure in O'Casey's first play. A great story-teller and mimic, the younger man had a habit of visiting the Four Courts of Dublin's judicial system to find material for his ready wit and observation. According to Margulies:

. . . on weekends, he and O'Casey would stroll together along the Royal Canal, bringing their lunches with them, while Cahill spun stories of what he had seen. These walks lasted the better part of the day. Often, after they had returned, the two would stand outside Cahill's house and talk until two or three in the morning. If Cahill was a remarkable yarn-spinner, O'Casey was a patient listener, and . . . was blessed with an unusually retentive memory besides. He took no notes of their many conversations, but he paid close attention to what was said, interrupting occasionally to ejaculate, "Ah, there's a good one, Frank!"

O'Casey, too, was developing his gift for mimicry and his insatiable curiosity about his fellow beings. He was still with the GNR, and we have the clearest picture of his activities at this time late in 1908, when he was working at the Dynamo Room in Sutton, from which the trams were driven up to Howth Summit and pulled down again. From the roof, where he was adding parapet coping to the gables and doing repairs, he saw fields of corn and ploughs in action for the first time. He remembered one winter in Howth,

> when all telegraph-poles were down with a weight of snow, & coming down, in the tram, [they] had to dig a way along through the snow-drifts. At the Station, making for the train, every second wave came tumbling over the wall, sending itself right over train & station buildings. A dash for the train as soon as a wave went over, or we would have been swallowed up be the salt sea.

Later, after he had left the GNR, he listed his grievances against it in lively style in a series of articles for the *Irish Worker*, inveighing against the "Pomps and Charities" of the foreman, Reid, as well as another overseer, Hayden, at the Dublin running shed. Reid, he alleged, was ever anxious for the comfort of his gang, "selling them off bad clothes – a pair of blankets like tissue paper . . .", while Hayden, "a genteel cultured 'boy', had a habit of receiving money from the cleaners to get his own selection". He also cast withering scorn upon one Turkington, the superintendent of goods, who was trying to found a temperance union among the men; it reminded O'Casey of Conn the Shaughraun: "Sure Conn's father was a real good man when he was sober." But he never was sober . . .

To judge by the cutting sharpness of the detail, O'Casey also participated in chaotically wasteful schemes like the innovation of a special "motor service" to Howth, the carriages to be housed in a huge, incompetently designed shed, the brainchild of "Birmingham and Yorkshire and London importations". He tried later to incorporate in his autobiography a mocking account of this battery- or dynamo-driven "new-fangled" train on its first experimental run, but abandoned it after a few pages.

There was also the construction of cattle "banks", to simplify the dispatch of cattle by rail, a "long-drawn-out comedy". This task was confided to "a so-called carpenter, general pimp and spy, and particular confidential servant named Higgins. This creature – huge of stomach, huge of limb and huge of head, in which was said to be a microscopical brain, of which I have my doubts – was a genius for doing everything wrong." A day came when the bank was smooth and level beneath the complacent gaze of "the doughty Milling", an engineer at the Dublin end, and his henchman. "They wouldn't let a crow alight on the bank till it was 'dry and settled'." But a few months after, the pitching had forced its way through the sand and clay, and "very soon that bank was as bad as a rocky and flinty ravine in the heart of the Rocky Mountains". The savage tone audible here is as much that of Jonathan Swift as of the authentic O'Casey, who had yet to emerge.

But O'Casey's personality and appearance were by now distinctive, while his impetuous and high-handed Republican behaviour often created bad feeling, especially among socialists. An observer at a Drumcondra Gaelic League meeting found him one night sitting at the back of the hall during a lecture, "a dour and fiery figure swathed in labourer's garb . . . His neck and throat are bound in the coils of a thick white muffler," and he looks like "a Jacobin of Jacobins" as his red-rimmed eyes "stab all the beauty and sorrow of the world".

He speaks first, and very fluently and eloquently in Irish, then launches out into a violent Republican oration in English, stark and forceful, biblical in diction with gorgeous tints of rhetoric and bursts of anti-English Nationalism of the most uncompromising style . . . Yes, he reminds them, when roused by his sharp words they murmur interruptions taunting him with the poverty and degradation of the Dublin workers, there is all that in life. Half to himself he speaks, lowering his voice to an intense whisper, but there is something else: joy.

Walter Carpenter, a leading socialist propagandist, rises and would argue with O'Casey. "O'Casey rises in a fury and growls in Irish like a thunderstorm that he wishes no Englishman to teach him." He strides through the door "with flames in his eye and his fists clenched", as Carpenter protests, "'Tell him for Gawd's sike that I am not an Englishman but a Scotchman and that I 'ad the honour to drop a tear in the grive of Charles Stuart Parnell.'"

His behaviour was not always aggressive: Paddy McDonnell, another Gaelic enthusiast of the period, recalled how determined and tenacious O'Casey was, especially strong and able as an organiser, but also a lover of argument. He liked to draw people out by playing devil's advocate: if a student expressed interest in learning Irish he would test his seriousness by declaring, "It's a damn language – dead as a dodo." He had a hearty laugh, despite often looking ill, and was a fine impromptu speaker. He loved to appear before Protestant debating societies to defend the capacity of the Irish to rule themselves, and knew how to draw laughter from a hostile audience. If a book he had not read came up for discussion he would go off and read it, coming back later to give his opinion. Stephen Synott, who worked in Webb's Bookstore, on the South Quay, remembered the tall, shabbily dressed O'Casey, in hobnailed boots and a muffler and wearing spectacles, calling twice a week to browse through the stock and buy cheap or second-hand books. Synott grew to know his tastes and set aside favourites, "Dostoevsky, Chekhov, Ibsen, or a Chambers Dictionary or occasional English grammar".

A less sympathetic view was expressed by Bulmer Hobson, a prominent Republican who was writing manuals on guerrilla warfare and who often dined with O'Casey on Saturday nights in 1909 and 1910 at the house of Seamus Deakin. Deakin, another leading Sinn Feiner and member of the Supreme Council of the IRB, used to invite O'Casey, said Hobson,

> partly because he was an entertaining talker, and partly because we thought he needed a meal. He was an unskilled labourer, frequently unemployed . . . He suffered from a very distressing complaint; he had in-growing eyelashes and they had to be plucked out at frequent intervals – this was extremely painful and his eyelids were also red and sore . . . He was guided by his emotions and never listened to reason. He poured violent abuse on everybody who did not agree with him.

Hobson's character assessment may owe something to the unconvivial treatment his former dinner companion later meted out to him:

> Bulmer Hobson . . . editor of *Irish Freedom* and head bottle-washer of all National activities, with his moony face, bulbous nose, long hair half-covered by a mutton-pie hat, a wrapped [rapt?] look on his face, moving about mysterious, surrounded by the ghostly guns of Dungannon:

> Ireland awoke when Hobson spoke – with fear was England shaken.

As if this was not enough, O'Casey heaps scorn on Hobson's writings in *Irish Freedom* as "nothing more than hundreds of dead thoughts on thousands of cold, leaden slabs of words".

Tom Clarke, the old Fenian who had spent half a lifetime in British prisons, was another prominent member of the Teeling Circle, in which it seemed at times O'Casey functioned as court jester, delivering himself of a wry song like Feste or spitting his venom at the audience with the bitterness of Thersites. Clarke owned a number of tobacconist's shops, two in Amiens Street near the landmark of the Five Lamps, and later one in Parnell Square. O'Casey found Clarke impatient with the timidity and caution of many of the younger members of the Brotherhood. This he applauded, and became a staunch helper to Clarke. Clarke's wife remembered O'Casey calling by for her husband, speaking little to her, "giving her only a curt nod as she stood behind the counter, and leaving with a shrug of the shoulders when Clarke was not in". O'Casey, in his dogsbody role, discharged without pay or publicity such tasks as the loading and unloading of copies of *Irish Freedom*, sold in Clarke's shop, but subjected the older man to much chivvying about Hobson, provoking Clarke till he would awake from his doze, spring to his feet and, "fire flashing from his remarkable, eagle-like eyes", order O'Casey to desist or leave the shop. Clarke was to be closely involved in 1916 in planning the Easter Rising, of which he was one of the leaders; he was subsequently court-martialled, sentenced to death, and executed in Kilmainham Gaol.

Having transferred much of his allegiance from his own parish church to the St Laurence O'Toole Club, O'Casey now helped Cahill organise a pipers' band. Among his first published letters, written in 1910, was a fund-raising circular dispatched to various local worthies who might be counted on to support the "strictly non-sectarian and non-party" revival of the Irish War Pipes whose music "led the Irishmen to victory on many a hard fought field". This was a canny way to foster the nationalist spirit, ostensibly harmless, but essential to the morale of any future freedom fighters. O'Casey, to whom the idea of a band had an instantaneous appeal, became the Hon. Sec., signing himself with an official flourish "S. O'Cathasaigh". In the following year he sent the same circular, with a covering letter in Irish, to Lord Castletown of Upper Ossory, a well-known supporter of the Gaelic-language revival, enclosing also a highly competent drawing in red, green and black ink, of an Irish piper. "It's surprising how the picture enticed people to send us a subscription," he said later. Tom Clarke became the band's nominal head.

The band itself, initially rehearsed by a flute-player as no expert piper could be found, was first seen in the streets of Dublin in 1910, making it the oldest pipers' band on record – it still exists today. Marching in kilts knitted by Cahill's sister, and displaying a banner presented by Douglas Hyde and Padraic Pearse, the pipers led the procession from Seville Place to Wolfe Tone's grave at Bodenstown. O'Casey accompanied them but did not play. On one occasion he was brought before a judge by a policeman who alleged that the pipers were playing within the limits of St Mary's church during a service. By the church gates they had been playing "The Peeler and the Goat", the ballad of a goat arrested for high treason, to taunt their police escort. O'Casey addressed the court in Irish, meekly pointing out that the band had only been marching, not playing, and saying that as he himself had been baptised in St Mary's no offence could possibly have been meant. The case was dismissed. One night Sean borrowed some pipes and practised them at home; the noise was so terrible that, according to Kit Casey, Tom's younger boy, Mick got hold of a gimlet and bored a hole through the pipes.

The O'Toole clubroom was "as big a slum hovel as the [Gaelic League] one in Seery's Lane, a back shanty off of Strandville Avenue, North Strand". Some of the pipers were also hurlers, and had a flag with the O'Toole emblem of a silver lion embroidered on it. Later O'Casey recalled many of his old friends, bewailing the "great scatter since I walked beneath the glimpses of the moon in the street of the parish of O'Toole":

> Tommy Lynch and his brother of the dour face – Feardorcha [the dark man]; M. Lawless, Mackey, called Lar, Colgan – a very devoted labour man now [in 1947], and a baiter of the poor communists; Carroll, the well-dressed, who married Miss Wisely – Molly to her friends; Fitzharris, gone the way of all flesh; Seumas Moore of whom I've heard nothing for a long time . . . Sean, Michael and Tom, the clarinetist; and last, but by no means least, the bould Kevin O'Lochlain.

O'Casey omitted from this list another piper, Thomas Ashe, whose death at the hands of the British in 1917 was to inspire his moving lament for a wasted life.

O'Lochlain, a civil servant with a thin sunken chest and the odd capacity of flicking a book from the top of his head by exerting strong scalp muscles, dreaded smutty stories, as did O'Casey, but had the history of the Gaelic Athletic Association on the tip of his tongue. The great passion he communicated to O'Casey was for the writings of Bernard Shaw, whom O'Lochlain called "the cleverest Irishman the world knows, Sean. A wit of wonder. A godsend to men who try to think, who's creating a new world out of new thought. Read *John Bull's Other Island* and the Ireland you think you know and love will vanish before your eyes." O'Casey did not much want it to, and later, in his seventies, admitted to his relative good fortune: "On the whole, they weren't bad days . . . and I would neither be unwilling nor ashamed to live them all over again." At the time his truthful response to the poverty round him was tolerance: "We were then, apparently, unconscious of the way in which we lived, and stayed so till Jim Larkin came to show us all how shocking were the conditions that surrounded us."

In 1909 the circumstances of the Casey household improved sharply, for the British Government began paying old age pensions and from January Susan Casey received the maximum allowance, five shillings a week. "That's a feather in your cap," chortled Mick, who was still bringing home his respectable Post Office wage, or that part of it which he did not drink away: one day someone upset a bowl of stout and he was on all fours, lapping it up from the floor with his tongue. Susan Casey's grandchildren now had strict instructions not to make a noise when they visited Abercorn Road, and had to tiptoe through the parlour in order not to disturb their Uncle Jack, when he was busy reading or writing. Kit Casey recalled being in the room one day with a friend who was fingering some of O'Casey's books, when they heard "Uncle Jack's footsteps coming up the stairs. Well he caught my friend with the book, *The Imitations* (sic) *of Christ* it was, and took it off him, looked at it and then he blamed me for it. Then he threw another book at me and told me to read it but when I looked at it I wasn't interested in it and I told him so. 'You know as much about Charlie Chaplin and Tom Mix as Peter and Paul,' he said." Later O'Casey inserted this phrase, slightly altered, into the mouth of Captain Boyle in *Juno and the Paycock*. Kit found his uncle a disagreeable fellow, who "never worked. Only fifteen months with the Great Northern Railway and a few months with a builder that he knew, but if his mother hadn't some hot scones ready for him when he came in in the evening she'd get a scolding from that terrible tongue of his."

O'Casey had hero-worshipped Parnell with the imagination of a child. His next great father figure had heroic dimensions, but was man-sized and real. In a passage deliberately echoing that on Parnell's return, in "A Coffin Comes to Ireland", Jim Larkin, the great Irish labour leader, lands in Dublin one day to address the Irish masses. As on that other day of bitter cold and black sky, Larkin's epiphany was marked by harsh weather:

> Through the streets he strode, shouting into every dark and evil-smelling hallway, The great day of a change has come; Circe's swine had a better time than you have; come from your vomit; out into the sun. Larkin is calling you all!

But the time of O'Casey's mind had never been quite the same as the time of the clock, and he had first seen and met Larkin at least two years before the "Prometheus Hibernica" arrived in Dublin to rouse his union to confront the wicked employers before the great Dublin lock-out of 1913. The Liverpool-born Larkin had come from Belfast, in 1908, to organise the Irish Transport and General Workers' Union, then called the Irish Workers' Union, and during that year had successfully called strikes by the carters, canalmen and maltmen, despite the hostility of traditional trade unionists, threats of black-legging, and the high unemployment. O'Casey had already persuaded the IRB to select a committee to see how it could be brought into closer touch with Larkin's militant labour movement. O'Casey and a friend were chosen to visit Larkin, by now running the *Irish Worker*, to publicise the committee's activity, and the enthusiastic Larkin promised he would do all he could to help. O'Casey's other IRB colleagues ignored the contact made, and let the whole idea slip, leaving O'Casey nursing a potential grievance.

His new sword of light had, however, been located, and in 1911 he himself joined the Irish Transport and General Workers' Union. A fellow worker in the GNR later claimed that O'Casey never belonged to that union, only to the National Union of Railwaymen, but whatever the truth, O'Casey was fast heading towards a show-down with his railway employers. Earlier in that year he had refused, out of sheer cussedness, to join a compulsory pension scheme. How his dismissal at the end of 1911 actually came about is once again, and typically, obscured by contradictory explanations and "Irish fact". George Wisdom, a GNR workman, said O'Casey was working one day on the building site for a staff dining hall in Amiens Street, opposite Mullett's pub, when the foreman, Reid, seeing him leaning on his shovel, reprimanded him, whereupon O'Casey snapped back. He was suspended for insubordination. Others say that as a casual worker he left by default, simply not turning up for work.

O'Casey had his own angle; the reason for his dismissal, he said, was that he had been overheard attacking working conditions in the GNR, and praising Jim Larkin. He wrote two letters, on 7 and 18 December, to try to find out the exact cause of his dismissal, but received no satisfaction; he then sent off his letters and the replies he had received to the *Irish Worker*, to create a stir and some pro-labour, anti-British propaganda. He rounded off what was printed with a biting appeal for justice: "In the department in which I worked (the engineering) the unfortunate men were at the feet of a sleeven English engineer named Whilden. Well, God made him, so we'll call him a man; and a cold, wolfish-hearted foreman named Reid, in whom is neither truth, honour, nor candidness." He claimed, moreover, that in his ten years' service on the GNR he had missed only about eighteen hours' work; that he was a total abstainer from alcohol, and had been ill for only a fortnight – yet, he concluded, he had been "dismissed because he refused to be a slave to an Irish cur or an English importation".

Whilden's own memorandum on O'Casey's dismissal acknowledged that the cause was his refusal to join the pension fund: "In addition his eyesight is defective and it is doubtful if the Company's doctor would pass him – further he is inclined to be idle and has been warned on several occasions." O'Casey omitted these considerations in putting his case in the *Worker*; it is possible that he did not see them. He later gave a further reason for his dismissal: his refusal to sign a form circulated by the Employers' Federation, forswearing allegiance to Larkin's union – though in fact the form was not in use until some two years later, *after* the 1913 lock-out.

Perhaps the most valid reason of all for O'Casey's discharge lay in four words that he had added to his account in the *Worker*, after his description of the foreman, Reid. The words were "Of these more anon". For by now Larkin had offered O'Casey the opportunity to expand on his views of the GNR in a series of articles for the *Irish Worker*, or else O'Casey had gone to Larkin with an idea for these articles. They represented O'Casey's first big opportunity to express in print a succession of views, and he was not going to miss it in order to lift or turn another sleeper, or repair another rail – especially as he had now established his credentials as a working man.

The twentieth century, said Ibsen in a speech to a workers' procession in Trondheim in 1885, would belong to the workers, and to women. O'Casey had fulfilled his aspiration and won his new identity in the fertile breeding ground of Dublin's highly mobile society. His own obstinate character, combined with his mother's devotion to him and her resourcefulness on his behalf, had maintained his freedom to develop. He would continue for some years to sacrifice at twin altars, of idealism and discontent, without knowing whether the fire that consumed his offerings was a purification or a waste, leading ultimately to victory or defeat.

4

THE THIRD EYE

"He could put a loaf on a plate and a vase on the table," O'Casey said of Larkin. The two men had much in common, but with significant differences. When he came to Dublin in 1908 Larkin was thirty-two years of age, four years older than O'Casey; he had proved his power in Belfast with masterly organisation of the new weapons against employers: the paralysing dock strike, his campaign to stop people buying "tainted" goods – made by black-leg labour – and his volcanic oratory. He had managed to smash through sectarian divisions, persuading Orangemen and Catholic nationalists to march together in unprecedented unity. He achieved little immediately, though with the shooting of Catholics in the Falls Road by troops, and the mutiny in the Royal Irish Constabulary, the myth of Larkin's power began to grow. He was condemned as a socialist, an anarchist, a papist, or, by the Dublin press, an Orangeman. He wore a dark, wide-brimmed hat – obliged to do so, according to some, to hide the third eye set in his forehead, proving beyond all doubt that he was the Antichrist.

Larkin's background was more truly urban working class than O'Casey's, although a grandfather had farmed in County Armagh and wielded a shillelagh to emphasise his Fenian opinions. As with O'Casey, there was always a touch of the countryside in his speech, a "glow of poetry and idealism", according to one biographer. His father had emigrated to Liverpool where he worked in a factory for twenty years, while Jim himself began in the same factory as an apprentice. At seventeen he threw up the job and stowed away in a ship of the Harrison Line bound for New York. He was discovered, and showed his defiance of authority by refusing to work for the rest of the voyage unless paid the proper crewman's rate. The captain was not impressed: Larkin spent the rest of the crossing in irons while rats ate through his leather toe-caps.

On reaching New York he was sent to gaol, and here began avidly reading literature and social theory. Even these hagiographical details were not enough to satisfy the Irish predilection for mythology: in one version of the stowaway story Larkin reached the River Plate with eleven other rebels who went on strike for better conditions, finally securing as wages a square-faced bottle of gin each day.

Repeated humiliation at the hands of employers formed the basis of Larkin's rise. He accepted every set-back or harsh word not as an individual, but on behalf of the lowest-paid workers, transforming the slights into a wider persecution of "Labour"; he took all his fellow workers' sufferings personally. The blows to pride and dignity fuelled his sense of inferiority to such an extent that it erupted in a glow of superiority, and his rhetoric became flavoured with phrases such as that his enemies ought to "bow down before the labourer's son". But if in argument he could be savage, intolerant and completely disregarding of facts, paradoxically, he could also show unexpected generosity and kindness towards his foes. Infinitely more conciliatory than O'Casey, in no way did he cultivate, or sink into, a disgruntled or downtrodden appearance. He wore a collar and tie always, a waistcoat and well-polished shoes: in his lapel he sported the union insignia of the red hand. Yet he took, as O'Casey would in future take, his authority from poverty, and while in Dublin from its slums: "Hell has no terrors for me," he answered a churchman once:

> I've lived there. Thirty-six years of hunger and poverty have been my portion. The mother who bore me had to starve and work, and the father I loved had to fight for a living. I knew what it was to work when I was nine years old. They can't terrify me with hell.

Like O'Casey Larkin did not drink, and campaigned vigorously against alcohol, and the practice of paying dock labourers their wages in public houses, with its consequent abuses.

When he set out to organise the Irish Transport and General Workers' Union in Dublin, the mounting unrest was particularly ripe for Larkin's brand of preaching: "the divine mission", he called it, "of discontent". He did not have to look far to find the social attitudes he wished to change; one such was expressed in a Chamber of Commerce paper, on the deterioration of slum-dwellers:

> Once drawn into the abyss they speedily lose, not merely their sense of self-respect, but their capacity for sustained exertion. At

the same time the thought of all that is implied in this vicious housing system . . . should make us chary of playing the role of critic to employers who have to use this damaged material.

Larkin's own weekly paper, the *Irish Worker*, began publication on 27 May 1911 and except for a few weeks when he was either in gaol or travelling abroad he edited all of its 189 issues before he left for America in the autumn of 1914. The stamp of his personality is evident in the colourful mix of satire, opinion, reportage, poetry and songs that filled its four pages. The *Worker* tried to combine Irish nationalism with Larkin's avowed aim to free the worker from industrial oppression, but it was opposed by the Parnellite Irish Parliamentary Party, and Larkin would not tolerate spurious nationalist sentiment: he was condemned heartily by Arthur Griffith, who listed the consequences of his policies as "workless fathers, mourning mothers, hungry children and broken homes. Not the capitalist but the policy of Larkin has raised the price of food until the poorest in Dublin are in a state of semi-famine – the curses of women are being poured on this man's head." The arguments have a familiar, circular ring.

O'Casey resisted all-out commitment to the Larkinite position for some time, still thinking of himself first and foremost as an Irishman, and only second as a worker, in spite of his spirited attacks on corruption in the GNR. But, largely on Larkin's side, the paradoxical spirit of Bernard Shaw – of whom O'Casey's fellow O'Tooler, Kevin O'Lochlain, was such a passionate advocate – had seized his imagination.

The figure of St Laurence O'Toole towering over the top of the Pro-Cathedral had changed the head of the holy man for the head of the smiling sage. Sometimes, when Sean was swinging his pick, the red beard came close to his ear and the musical voice said – Take it easy, man; don't kill yourself for any employing exploiter . . . England cannot do without its Irish and its Scots today, because it cannot do without at least a little sanity.

He grasped at once the drunken side of Shaw's teetotalism – saw how ideas for him had become an alternative to drink – and in this observation there was perhaps more than a sidelong glance at his brother Mick: "Then the musical voice went into a laugh, and added, Idolatrous Englishman and fact-facing Irishman are proved today, for though I shock you, you are fearlessly facing me, aren't you? Of course you are;

and a lot the better for it." O'Casey had read the paper-covered edition of *John Bull's Other Island*, while in the 10 February 1912 issue of the *Worker* Larkin published the shortened Preface; these more than coloured O'Casey's thinking, they upset him. "– A man without a soul, said the Gaelic Leaguers; nothing is sacred to him – not even the slums!" Two ideas fought one another in this new view of Ireland learned from Shaw: the Irish dream without efficiency, and the English efficiency without a dream. Efficiency, O'Casey concluded, could come from a dream, but not vice versa.

At the end of 1912 it was clear that O'Casey, in spite of having become a more frequent contributor to the *Worker* – sometimes he now signed himself *Craobh na nDealg* (the Thorny Branch, in deliberate contrast to Douglas Hyde's pseudonym, the Pleasant Little Branch) – was still protecting himself with a shield of reluctance and doubt, although in an article, "Leather Away the Wattle, O", he reported sympathetically on a Larkin meeting. When you attend a meeting at Liberty Hall, the headquarters of the ITGWU on Custom House Quay – later the nerve centre of all workers' unrest in Dublin – he said, "You leave on the doorstep your Religion, your Nationality, and your Respectability." Of Big Jim in action, he noted:

> The lecture was brimful of force, argument, statistics, and humour. Jim's himself! The Lecturer also used the wattle on some husbands who devoutly believe that from the day their sweethearts become their wives they bid goodbye to the world for ever and all the innocent joys thereof.

O'Casey chastised the Gaelic League for offering only a "hesitating and an insecure hand to the General Worker and the Docker", and concluded, "Although we cannot agree with all Jim's opinions, National, Social and Biological, we are constrained to say what Schumann said to his friend Chopin, 'Hats off, gentlemen; a genius!'" O'Casey made an attempt at this time to write a play on the subject of Liberty Hall, but abandoned it.

Larkin received a weekly wage of two pounds, ten shillings as General Secretary of the Union; he was living in a rented flat in Auburn Street with his wife and three sons. It is not clear whether O'Casey received any payment for his contributions to the *Irish Worker*. He never mentioned his penniless state to his Gaelic League friends such as Clarke or Cahill, although he readily accepted hospitality; it may be that he was paid minimal expenses for some of the numerous secretarial functions he performed – in 1913 he was to add to these another secretaryship, that of the Wolfe Tone Memorial Committee – but if so these could hardly have constituted a living wage. He continued to read avidly at night, his back room in Abercorn Road lit by a single candle.

As late as February 1913 he was defending Irish nationalism against "Euchan", a columnist in the *Worker*, who argued that they were living in a purely commercial world and that the battle of the future in Ireland would be between Capital and Labour. O'Casey now wielded a quite distinctive sardonic tone: "So, Euchan, you sneer at the pike. It's not the first sneer that winked at the Gael from the face of *The Worker*. The weapon only bruises the hand that flings it." He challenged "Euchan" – the actor-journalist who in Ireland called himself A. Patrick Wilson, in Scotland, Andrew P. Wilson – to a public debate in "an old spot by the river". Euchan refused with a scathing rebuke to O'Casey's two columns of "aimless futility, tinged here and there with obvious spite", condemning him as a "poor old Rip Van Winkle . . . [with a] motley collection of prehistoric red-herrings". O'Casey, bloodied but unbowed, clearly loved the fight, released a new flow of invective, prompting Euchan's rejoinder, "What a complicated piece of decayed mechanism this writer's brain must be."

O'Casey, still taking the part of nationalism against labour, was finding his allegiance more and more strained, especially in a controversial case which surfaced during 1913. The Revd Michael P. O'Hickey, Professor of Irish at St Patrick's College, Maynooth, and a former President of the Gaelic League, wanted to introduce compulsory Irish at the National University, a notion which had O'Casey's full support. He campaigned vigorously, "while cheers", as he put it, "went rippling from one end of Ireland to the other". But the official Catholic clergy, identified for the first time as an object of O'Casey's hatred – a strong leftover trace of Protestantism here – turned on O'Hickey, calling on him to resign or be dismissed from his Maynooth post. He resigned, and a furious campaign was initiated to reinstate him. O'Casey thought all Sinn Fein Republicans ought to support O'Hickey vigorously, and although some did, among them Douglas Hyde and Eoin MacNeill, the Professor of Early Irish History at University College, their efforts were not militant enough or sufficiently backed up by other Republicans. O'Casey outlined the reasons sardonically:

– We can't afford to have the bishops against us, said the Sinn Fein Republican, and, besides, Dr O'Hickey himself would never give permission for such an action.

– Oh, no-one suggests he should be asked, retorted Sean impatiently; and as for the bishops – shall we, who have nothing to lose, run away from them, while O'Hickey, who has everything to lose, be left to face them alone?

– We're with him in spirit, said the Republican unctuously. Now I have work to do for the Sinn Fein Bank, and I must be off, so *slán leat*, he said, speaking the only Irish words he knew.

O'Hickey took his case to Rome, O'Casey contributing towards his expenses the money he was saving to buy a new coat; however, scurrilous reports were circulated about O'Hickey's incompetence and insubordination in Ireland, and the case dragged on in the Vatican for years, while various evidence was considered. O'Casey portrays even Hyde as turning on O'Hickey.

Finally the appeal made by the Pope himself to the Rota, the ecclesiastical court, was withdrawn; and O'Hickey died in 1916, by then a broken and neglected figure.

It was just the kind of *cause célèbre* to become part of O'Casey's mental furniture, and he carried it around with him for years, championing both O'Hickey's dead cause, as something with which to whip the Catholic Church, and O'Hickey's friend and supporter, Dr Walter McDonald. O'Casey believed that five years after O'Hickey died betrayed by his Gaelic friends, although they bought him a costly coffin and gave him a splendid funeral, with "me Lord Archbishop taking Hyde and his friends out to dinner, and back to the Cathedral again, where a rousing sermon was given eulogising the quiet-minded, harmless dead man for compiling five wee books of cuckoo Irish for beginners". Another of O'Casey's swords of light was beginning to tarnish.

———◆◆◆———

But there were so many shifts in belief and cross-currents of disillusionment in the years 1912 and 1913 that no one in Ireland quite knew to what they were committed. Padraic Pearse in 1912 supported a big Home Rule meeting, yet even then, according to O'Casey, was in his heart an IRB man, although "there was an IRB doubt about him". Later O'Casey was to call Pearse "a great humanist, stretching out his deep affection for all men", but in singing his praises he had to ignore the fact that Pearse took the side of the employers against the strikers in 1913 and often rode the Dublin trams, a flagrant act of strike-breaking.

As a member of the Teeling Circle in 1912-13, O'Casey made a further attempt to unite his nationalism with his growing labour convictions by helping Pearse, then a teacher at the Irish language school, St Enda's College, with his Irish pageant of *The Cattle Raid of Cooley*. O'Casey did the publicity, exhorting the *Worker*'s readers to attend, "The Boy Corps of Ulster hurling on the field. The news of Cuchulain's wounding; the march of the boys to defend the frontiers, till the Hero recovers; the scene of the men of Ireland around their Camp Fires." But two months after Pearse's pageant, the men around the camp fires became a reality, as the clouds of uncertainty rolled back to reveal two opposing armies, the workers and the employers.

In August 1913 a form (the one O'Casey claimed he had signed two years earlier) was issued by the newly formed Federation of Employers, containing a disclaimer which ran, "I agree to immediately resign my membership of the Irish Transport and General Workers' Union (if a member) and I further undertake that I will not join or in any other way support that union."

Ever since Larkin had established himself in Liberty Hall labour relations had been deteriorating – and accelerating towards crisis since the beginning of 1913. Strikes and lock-outs swiftly followed one after another, while, ignoring libel writs, the *Irish Worker* rapidly expanded its circulation through its non-stop lampooning of employers and criticism of social conditions; the libellous pieces appeared under such sobriquets as "Mother of Seven", "Liberty Boy", "Caliban", "Locked Out", and "One of the Oppressed". The leaders of the respective sides were well matched: Liverpool's Larkin against William Martin Murphy, owner of Clery's department store, the Imperial Hotel, the *Irish Independent* and, most significantly of all, the Dublin United Tramways Company.

On 19 August Murphy paid off the distributors of his newspaper because they refused to sever connections with Larkin's union; next day employees at Eason's, where O'Casey had worked, walked out because they too refused to handle the *Independent*. On 21 August Larkin was struck violently in the face by one Peter Sheridan, a clerk, who wielded a stick and drew blood. Sheridan was sentenced to six weeks in prison, but Larkin interceded on his behalf to have him freed. Such impulsive generosity won Larkin great support, and when the next move in the fight, the calling out of the tramwaymen, came on 26 August, the stoppage assumed threatening proportions:

The Dublin United Tramways Company (1896), Ltd.

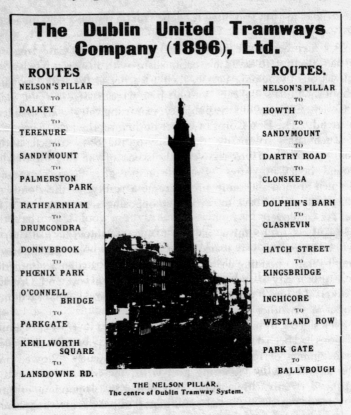

ROUTES	ROUTES.
NELSON'S PILLAR	NELSON'S PILLAR
TO	TO
DALKEY	HOWTH
TO	TO
TERENURE	SANDYMOUNT
TO	TO
SANDYMOUNT	DARTRY ROAD
TO	TO
PALMERSTON PARK	CLONSKEA
RATHFARNHAM	DOLPHIN'S BARN
TO	TO
DRUMCONDRA	GLASNEVIN
DONNYBROOK	HATCH STREET
TO	TO
PHŒNIX PARK	KINGSBRIDGE
O'CONNELL BRIDGE	INCHICORE
TO	TO
PARKGATE	WESTLAND ROW
KENILWORTH SQUARE	PARK GATE
TO	TO
LANSDOWNE RD.	BALLYBOUGH

THE NELSON PILLAR.
The centre of Dublin Tramway System.

SCENE: A TRAM STOP ON THE DALKEY LINE

1ST GENTLEMAN: Conductor – does this car go to Ballsbridge?

CONDUCTOR: I'm no longer on duty, sir. I'm on strike. (*Shouting*) Hey, Puddiner! It's ten o'clock!

DRIVER: Wha . . .?

CONDUCTOR: It's ten o'clock.

DRIVER: Right – me hearty. We stop where we are! I'll take off the trolley.

1ST GENTLEMAN (*unbelievingly*): On strike . . .? In Horse Show Week –!

The troops were put on alert, police reinforcements were drafted in from the countryside, pensioners were sworn in as gaolers: on the streets horse and foot patrols appeared everywhere.

On the evening of the 26th Larkin seized the initiative: speaking to strikers outside Liberty Hall he said, "This is not a strike, it is a lock-out of the men who have been tyrannically treated by a most unscrupulous scoundrel . . . We will demonstrate in O'Connell Street. It is our street as well as William Martin Murphy's. We are fighting for bread and butter. We will hold our meetings in the street and if any one of our men fall, there must be justice. By the living God, if they want war, they can have it!"

In the next few days there were scuffles and fights between strikers and "scabs", and with police; Larkin and four others were arrested for libel and conspiracy on Thursday the 28th, but released the next day on bail. On the Friday the police banned the mass rally Larkin had called for Sunday, but Larkin burned the order paper at a meeting. Everyone eagerly awaited the big Sunday demonstration: would Larkin have the courage to turn up, as promised, at the Imperial Hotel? The gladiatorial combat between Larkin and Murphy caught the whole city as it moved to its climax: "Larkin will meet his Waterloo," gloated the *Independent*; "Murphy will reach St Helena," the *Worker* snarled back. With money and the forces of the Crown on his side, Murphy was convinced he had beaten his antagonist: "I have broken the malign influence of Mr Larkin and set him on the run. It is now up to the employers to keep him going . . . this convicted and mean thief had nearly become the labour dictator of the city."

On Saturday the police tried again to arrest Larkin, but failed, taking off two of his lieutenants instead: one, James Connolly, a slow-spoken Edinburgh-born Irishman who rarely smiled, told the court that he did not recognise the proclamation banning the Sunday meeting in O'Connell Street, "because he did not recognise the English Government in this country". Connolly refused to give surety for bail: he was sentenced to three months in Mountjoy Gaol where, going on hunger strike, he was released after one week.

On the Saturday afternoon there was more trouble in the docks, with pitched battles between strikers and police. During a baton charge at Eden Quay, two union men, James Nolan and James Byrne, were beaten to death. O'Casey was later among the crowd on the pavement in O'Connell Street as their funerals passed: "Here it came, the *Dead March in Saul*, flooding the street, and flowing into the windows of the street's rich buildings, followed by the bannered Labour Unions, the colours sobered by cordons of crêpe, a host of hodden grey following a murdered comrade."

These casualties and others, not fatal but equally bloody, did not prevent the courts and police proceeding with ruthless vigour to stamp out the unrest. But Larkin eluded them: he had powerful protectors, in particular Countess Constance Markiewicz, eldest child of the Anglo-Irish landowner Sir Henry Gore-Booth: born in Buckingham Gate, London, she was married to the Polish Count Casimir Markiewicz. She now hid Larkin in Surrey House, her residence on the fashionable outskirts of Dublin.

"Sitting there, listening to Larkin, I realised that I was in the presence of something that I had never come across before, some great primeval force, rather than a man. A tornado, a storm-driven wave, the rush into life of spring and the blasting breath of autumn, all seemed to emanate from the power that spoke" – so wrote the forty-seven-year-old Con Markiewicz, not yet over her first flush of left-wing idealism. She and her husband, however, had to disguise their protégé as something other than a primeval force if they were to get him past the hundreds of police clustering in O'Connell Street – at that time still called Sackville Street – to prevent him addressing the rally on Sunday the 31st. The working-class leader was encased in the Count's frock coat, bent himself double to assume crabbed age, and with the straggly growth of beard of an old and enfeebled clergyman glued to his face and chin by the Abbey Theatre actress, Helena Moloney, dispatched with his "niece' in a taxi to the Imperial Hotel.

According to Miss Moloney, Larkin's physical courage failed him at the last moment and he did not want to appear: she and the Countess insisted.

O'Connell Street was jammed with thousands of people, most of whom were there to see if Larkin would keep his promise. Mick Casey was there, as a spectator: unlike his younger brother, he began as a cynic and ended so. The gladiatorial combat had reached its killing time: even at this climax there was never the sense of a clash of impersonal forces which, as Marx believed, shaped human destiny; nothing, either, of the deliberately cold alienation effect that Bertolt Brecht tried to impose on his political characters. Politics had not yet become dehumanised or humourless. At one thirty p.m., on the Imperial's balcony, in full sight of those in the street below, Larkin, wearing his beard and frock coat, addressed the crowd with his familiar roar. His first words, delivered with a bow, were that he was there as promised to address a public meeting. The police reacted violently, a score of them rushing to the hotel, where they entered and seized Larkin: he now, according to Miss Moloney, cringed with fear, saying, "Don't strike me now, don't strike me now, I'll go quietly."

Downstairs the cheering grew, but not many people understood that Larkin's appearance was also the signal for the massed forces of police to charge the crowd, possibly out of panic – 200 of them were hurt in the ensuing fray – driving the demonstrators towards O'Connell Bridge and also into Prince's Street where they were met, and trapped, by a large body of reserves. The police had no compunction about ferociously batoning the heads of the fleeing crowd.

Larkin, hustled away under arrest, had won the day, for by goading the police into over-reacting he had turned public sympathy in his favour. But the bosses' attitude further hardened: three days later 400 employers met – the largest gathering of its kind ever held in Ireland – under the chairmanship of Murphy himself, and resolved "not to employ any persons who continue to be members of the Irish Transport and General Workers' Union". The lock-out was a reality: Larkin had achieved unification not only of the workers, but of the bosses.

O'Casey was one of those who, in his own account, fled from the police onslaught. This was the day when the "big-headed, dark, big-mouthed man, with a weighty moustache that gave a bend to his shoulders and curtained off the big mouth completely" became the symbol of living Ireland, of the only Ireland worth belonging to. The Irish worker had at last turned against his oppressors. But O'Casey also perceived that while his passions were aroused by "Bloody Sunday", he was not himself a hero, and, shivering with fear and shame, wished he had not come. He measured his own courage against Larkin, his "Prometheus Hibernica", admitting he cut a poor figure. He describes the apparition of his hero at the window of the Imperial Hotel, mistakenly claiming that Larkin swept the beard from his chin (photographs of his arrest show the copious disguise still in place). In the charge O'Casey desperately sought to escape, the crowd suffocating him with its breath which, steamy and thick, was like that of a herd of "frightened cattle in a cattle-boat tossed about in a storm". He could not get away, and expected at any moment a baton to crunch down sickeningly on his skull.

The crowd bore him in its surge down the narrow lane leading to the Pro-Cathedral, where he nearly fainted, but reached safety – and fell at once into a fictional reverie, both celestial and farcical, involving the Dublin statues of St Patrick and St Laurence O'Toole. The two saints are furious with Larkin the rabble-rouser. They blame Bishop Eblananus; when the feeble, gasping bishop is summoned to the top of Nelson's Pillar, he tries to excuse himself to Patrick, who accuses him of not doing his duty to the people. "Control yourselves, gentlemen," Nelson cautions them, and Patrick can't take any more, discharging all his pent-up fury on the Admiral: "Control yourself!" he shouts. "If you could, you wouldn't send your murdherous polis out to maim an' desthroy poor men lookin' for no more than a decent livin'. Gah! If me crozier could only reach up to you, I'd knock your other eye out!" The reverie ends as O'Casey is brutally brought down to earth:

> Along a wide lane of littered bodies, amid the tinkling of busy ambulances picking them up, one by one, pushed, shoved, and kicked by constables, the man with the cleft jaw trudged to jail, the wide stitches in his wounded face showing raw against his livid skin, the torn bandages flapping round his neck; shouting, he trudged on, Up Jim Larkin! Nor baton, bayonet, nor bishop can ever down us now – the Irish workers are loose at last!

In a grotesque parallel, the events of the Horse Show, Ladies' Day and the usual parties had proceeded, unscathed by Larkin's hundred-headed Hydra; that year it was reckoned to have been the best ever held. But in the socially dead season that followed Dublin for ever lost its late-nineteenth-century imperial innocence. The lock-out forced everyone to take sides: the police raided the poor in their tenement dwellings, smashing their ragged belongings and decorations, assaulting women and children in a reprisal which roused Larkin's uncouth followers to attack ordinary citizens who still tried to work. Dublin was not a city in which, numerically, the working class predominated, and middle-class opinion, while disparaging the severity of the police response, deplored the disruption and violence. The dialogue of two ordinary law-abiding workers trying to make their way home renders the unhappy atmosphere:

> "Looks like rain, Mick."
> "Aye," – (*pause*) – "I wish the bloody strike was over, that a man didn't have to thramp the sthreets into Dublin, and could ride the bloody tram, ordinary."
> "Aye, indeed. A lousy road, into the city, on a wet night especial." (*pause*) "There's a meeting at Inchicore Cross just after knock-off time."
> "Oh! Should be good . . ."
> "They say Jem Larkin'll be out here himself, speakin' tonight."
> "Uh-huh. *That'll* be broke up of course" – (*pause*) "There's no

way of gettin' past the bloody polis at Inchicore Cross. That means the long way round for anyone who wants to miss the meetin'."

"Uh-huh. An' I hate that bloody road, on a wet night."

"Me, too." (*pause*) "To hell with them. I'm going by Inchicore Cross."

"Sure, sure." (*more briskly*) "You'll be shoeing a shaft, then?"

"Aye."

"Make it two."

A shaft was a sledge-hammer handle which was "shod" with a piece of red-hot iron piping. The men were ensuring that no one would mess them about, not even the police, armed with shorter and lighter batons.

But the violence being used by the police had a new ally, starvation, which Murphy thought would quickly force the workers into submission. He did not reckon on the stiffening resistance and the widespread support the workers and their families were gaining, especially abroad – in England and, not surprisingly, in Russia. A pamphlet by V. I. Lenin applauded "the Irish Proletariat . . . awakening to class-consciousness", and Larkin, a "man of seething Irish energy performing miracles among the unskilled".

The literati of Dublin, hitherto aloof, declared their feelings in a letter to the press from George Russell, who signed himself "AE", addressed to the "Four hundred masters of Dublin". "You may succeed," he told them, but "the men whose manhood you have broken will loathe you, and will always be brooding and scheming to strike a fresh blow . . . It is not they – it is you who are blind Samsons pulling down the pillars of the social order." At Liberty Hall O'Casey was introduced to Russell: "O'Casey – another rebel," said Larkin.

O'Casey, the ubiquitous secretary, now offered his skills to the Women's and Children's Relief Fund, and he was party, along with Con Markiewicz and Larkin, to the planning of measures such as the temporary evacuation of workers' children to Catholic families in the north of England – an impractical scheme impulsively supported by Larkin for its daring, but scuppered, amidst general approval, by the Catholic Archbishop of Dublin. The Fund also set up a food depot in Liberty Hall, with stocks augmented by the arrival of two supply-laden ships from the Cooperative Society in England. O'Casey himself was concerned more with clothing than with food, but, seriously undernourished himself, and with gnawing pains in his legs, he says he hobbled down on a stick to be from ten in the morning until twelve at night in and out of Liberty Hall. But his faith was now strong:

What life would remain in the human body if the heart were plucked out and cast away?

We know that the Transport Union is the heart of all our strength and all our hope.

A drawing of a food kitchen in Liberty Hall by William Orpen

The conflict witnessed by O'Casey in 1913 fed an imagination already disposed to view life in strong dramatic colours, but the spawning in the wake of the strike of a unique militant organisation did more than anything else prior to 1916 to spark off his talent. Again, it was Larkin who was midwife to a new idea, in the British Isles, at least: an army to support the workers.

The idea came from a wayward ex-British serving officer, Captain Jack White, DSO, an Ulster Protestant nationalist. Son of Field Marshal White, Governor of Gibraltar and a friend of Kitchener, White was something of a soldier of fortune. He had gallantly fought with a Scottish regiment in the Boer War, although he later resigned his commission and became a believer in free love, a Tolstoyan, then an international socialist. Why not, he suggested, form a citizen army along the lines of the Ulster Volunteer Force which Edward Carson had begun in Belfast the previous year to defend the Protestant loyalists against the eventuality of Home Rule? The justification for such a force – namely, unchecked police brutality and violation of the rights of working men – was to hand: it needed only the will.

The providing of political will was Larkin's speciality, and in October he held a meeting in Beresford Place to launch the Irish Citizen Army, in the course of which he declared: "Labour in its own defence must begin to train itself to act with disciplined courage." If Carson had permission to train his braves of the North to fight against the aspirations of the Irish people, he said, then it was "legitimate and fair for labour to organise in the same militant way".

But, as the Army's first chronicler, "P. Ó Cathasaigh" – O'Casey himself – remarked, the response was not nearly as great as was hoped for, and nowhere near that received in the North by Carson. The launching itself was greeted with enthusiasm; O'Casey's own discontent gave way to hope, so that when he writes of Dublin as "surging with a passion full, daring, and fiercely expectant; a passion strange, enjoyable, which it had never felt before with such intensity and emotion," the passion he was describing was perhaps as much his own as the city's. Yet even among the ranks of the first recruits, numbering clerks, artisans, labourers, United Irish Leaguers, Republicans, Sinn Feiners and students of Gaelic, O'Casey sensed impending disillusionment. He could see the people of Ireland were "not ripe enough to be shaken from the green tree of Nationalism into the wide basket of an Irish Labour Army". Here was one reason, surely, that it inspired him: he knew it was bound to fail, and that, quixotically, he was destined to become its champion.

It certainly supplied him, on the non-stop carousel of Dublin politics, with the excuse he was now seeking to leave the Irish Republican Brotherhood, to which he had previously looked to defend with force the workers against the implacable unity of law-enforcement bodies. He had grown too much aware of the shortcomings of other members of the Brotherhood and would not stop voicing his criticisms of Bulmer Hobson to Tom Clarke. Intellectually, with the exception of Pearse and Seamus Deakin, his chemist friend, and Clarke, he found the movement lacking, making the point that *Sinn Fein* or *Irish Freedom* never mentioned art, science, or music: all of them "feared the singing of Yeats".

It might not have mattered if he had kept these opinions to himself, but what irked Deakin and Clarke – whose dedication, the intense flame of whose hatred for England, had burnt away all enjoyment, so that Clarke's fifteen years of distorted life in jail seemed to O'Casey a waste – was that he argued perpetually with them, exposing their shortcomings, picking holes in their commitment, especially to the working class. O'Casey himself championed "union between the separatist and the railway labourer, the factory hand and the transport worker". One day Deakin asked him in his shop if he was prepared to obey the leaders and cease his criticisms; O'Casey replied no.

So he left the Brotherhood, pulling out of it three others, Kevin O'Lochlain, Jimmy Moore and Frank O'Growney, who shared his feelings. The "purer flame" of the Citizen Army now enjoyed his exclusive patronage, and he transferred for a while much of his former religious feeling – he could now be outspokenly atheistic – into its symbols and rituals, which he supported with evangelical fervour.

The struggle was hard. The Citizen Army enjoyed some initial success, but soon struck leaner times, for the bosses stepped up the pressure to return to work and men began to dribble back in their hundreds. Worse, only a month after the founding of the Citizen Army, a rival force, the Irish Volunteers, with the aim of uniting all shades of nationalist opinion, was launched by the Brotherhood. It had much more middle-class appeal than the Army and was eagerly supported by young men who were impatient of waiting for Home Rule and had grown weary of the older politicians, such as John Redmond of the Parliamentary Party. Recruits came from the very groups of which O'Casey had once been part, in particular the Gaelic Athletic Association, and the Gaelic League itself, which supplied leaders like Padraic Pearse and Eoin MacNeill.

O'Casey went along with some worker comrades to the Volunteers' enlistment meeting at the Rotunda Rink on 25 November, where, as Bulmer Hobson wrote: "The audience was unanimous in its support of the Irish Volunteers, but an unpleasant scene was created by an organised crowd from Liberty Hall, . . . who refused L. J. Kettle a hearing . . . Kettle read the Manifesto, but the din created by the Liberty Hall men made his voice inaudible."

Hobson became secretary of the Volunteers, while Sir Roger Casement, a former British diplomat, was made treasurer. A predominantly moderate organisation at first, the Volunteer Army was seen by a more militant wing of the IRB, which planned to seize control of it, as a potential force of insurrection. Above all it was not proscribed by the authorities, so while the lock-out lasted, which it did until January 1914, support for the Citizen Army dwindled.

O'Casey grumbled at their rivals' superior facilities: they had halls to drill in, and when the Citizen Army Council asked the Volunteers for the use of these rooms on certain nights of the week they were emphatically refused; the Volunteer leaders had more energy and time to devote to their force than the labour leaders, whose responsibilities were wider and greater. Drills of the Citizen Army became irregular, numbers were further reduced, until the down-hearted Captain White found himself with only one company of faithful stalwarts.

The end of the lock-out in early 1914 was a godsend to the Army. Food and money had run out. On 30 January Larkin declared in public, "We are beaten. We make no bones about it; but we are not too badly beaten still to fight." Two days later 3,000 builders signed the employers' form promising not to join the ITGWU: this began the drift back to work on Murphy's terms. James Connolly provided the bitter lament: "And so we Irish workers must go down into Hell, bow our backs to the lash of the slave driver . . . eat the dust of defeat and betrayal." He and Larkin turned their fury on their British counterparts for failing to support them with a sympathy strike. But they could claim victory of a kind, for, in their own terms, they had raised the level of class-consciousness and, as believers in the class war, had produced for those ready to applaud it a magnificent curtain-raiser, the only one of its kind in Europe, to the Bolshevik Revolution of 1917; they had also awakened the public conscience to the appalling conditions of the Dublin poor.

It may be that Thomas Casey, Sean's favourite brother, would not have become seriously ill and died on 6 February 1914, at the age of forty-four, if he had not gone out drinking so often with his two brothers, Joseph and Mick, and weakened his constitution. The soldierly boy of the three, Tom had kindness of heart. His son Kit later said he was a steadying influence at home and was quiet and easy-going; Kit and his brother were made to attend the Roman services, the religion of their mother, Tom's wife, Mary. O'Casey's charity reaches its nadir in his account of Mary, whom he rechristens Agatha, calling her toweringly ignorant, badly built in body, slovenly, unrefined: above all her superstition seared his imagination. She would sit and sip her beer answering a flat "yes" or even flatter "no" to every question, till one crept away: "She had got Tom, and there she sat, thick and stout, like a queen cactus on a kitchen chair of state."

Sean's feelings about Tom were as possessive and Protestant as those of his mother: Tom was too good for Mary, and when he was dying, of peritonitis, it was O'Casey who demonstrated his great love for his brother by bringing him home and carrying him up to his room, where he laid him down gently in the easy armchair, watched by Mary: "Tom's yellow-skinned wife glared at them sleepily from the half-lidded eye, and balefully from the wide-open one, like a lassie direct in descent from the one-eyed coon – no, like a woman Balor of the Blows." O'Casey's invective turns more sour, even repellent:

> Ah, Tom, if it had only been a comely face, a rustling petticoat, and a slender leg that had betrayed your poor life to a woman, enhanced by a shimmer of a little silk. But no! It was pendulous breasts, a ponderous belly, a clumsy foot, and a vacant yellow face that brought you close to this.

He could hardly have considered Tom's own feelings, for Tom had been living in apparent harmony with his wife since they married eleven years before. O'Casey's anti-Catholicism, too, reaches morbid proportions in his recreation of Tom's death: having already sent for his mother and Bella, he calls in the Protestant rector of St Barnabas', the Revd Edward Griffin, to offer prayers for the dying man. Griffin will, he assures his mother, read the service at the graveside. When they arrive at the house Catholic Mary curses the Caseys – "I don't want his home to be a clusther of the ragged Casside [Casey] army, for the one that's just gone was the only decent specimen among yous, so he was, an' all who knew him, knows that. Me husband, me poor husband, you come of a dirty lot."

After a row about the expense of the funeral O'Casey leaves the destitute widow, who soon after has to begin scrubbing floors to support her children: "He gripped her angrily by the shoulder, putting his face close to hers to say venomously, Go in a carriage with you, is it? Why, you yellow-skinned Jezebel, if I could I'd put a wide sea between us both, and never bathe in it if I thought you were anyway near its margin!"

Such intemperate treatment was possibly more a reflection of O'Casey's condition of self-pity when he came to write this, than of any feeling that could truly be called love for Tom. Its pathology is almost Swiftian, especially as, according to Tom's children, Sean was not even present at Tom's death: if this is indeed true, his depiction of himself as a dark avenging angel is pure fiction. To O'Casey's claim that he paid for the funeral himself, Tom's son Kit answered later that his own family paid and that he still had the bill – from "Kerrigan in the North Strand who traded under the name of O'Neill". Moreover, Kit Casey said Sean borrowed twenty sovereigns from his mother after Tom's death and never paid them back.

If O'Casey was fictionalising events yet again, misrepresenting his family, this time displaying an exaggerated hostility which the mild-mannered, very quiet "Uncle Jack" would have been unlikely to show even had he been there, a more significant distortion of the truth is in the matter of time. To achieve a cumulative effect of misery, and make a procession of family corpses, he places Tom's death *before* that of his brother-in-law, Beaver, who in fact died seven years earlier. He then has Tom's death follow that of Bella, who still had another four years to live. Great fiction it may be, but as autobiography it shows a curious lack of respect, as if brothers and sister were little more than models to be placed in whatever arrangements may satisfy the artist. That O'Casey loved Tom is never in doubt, and he pays a heartfelt tribute to him: but he has no compunction about sacrificing his brother to that inner Protestant animus against the Catholic Church, making his wife Mary a symbol of its petrifying influence. How did it come about that a writer who could so vividly evoke sympathy for the sufferings of characters he invented, could so coldly withhold it from the living? Hatred can be as vitalising a force as love: Yeats might have had O'Casey in mind when he later wrote:

> Out of Ireland have we come,
> Great hatred, little room.

------◆◆◆◆------

In the meantime, in early 1914, O'Casey had been sniping at the growing army of Volunteers from the columns of the *Worker*: quoting John Mitchel's demand for an "Ireland for the Irish, not for the gentry alone", he accused the Volunteers of being a crowd of "chattering well-fed aristocrats and commercial bugs", basing their movement on Henry Grattan's "Tinsel Volunteers" of the 1780s, and he tried to woo away from them the Irish peasants and workers who were joining in such large numbers. A former Citizen Army man, James MacGowan, who had sat with O'Casey at the recruiting table, repudiated his attack as the "croaking of a self-constituted prophet", and claimed that the identification with the movement of such men as Padraic Pearse, P. Macken and Tom Kelly was a guarantee of workers' interests. Ah, O'Casey replied, Pearse went on using the trams in 1913 "while the workers of Dublin were waging a life and death struggle". He was indefatigable at seizing on points with which to wound, although MacGowan scorned his arguments as vague, evasive, and as misrepresenting his own. While O'Casey showed agility in being able to jump over "troublesome points", MacGowan wrote, "the whole tone of his letters is evidence of the spite which frustrated ambition engenders. In them is reflected the narrow-mindedness, the shallowness and the pessimism which are the chief characteristics of the cynic and sceptic."

In March 1914 O'Casey was asked if he would assume the post of secretary of the Citizen Army, and he accepted. He then escalated the minor but significant war of his own devising, fomenting Larkinite discontent against the Irish Volunteers. The Citizen Army was re-organised, given its own constitution and plan of action, which included recruitment, the proper supply of uniforms, regular drilling, and camping out during the summer months. The provision of uniforms had its comical side, not that O'Casey was yet in a mood to see it: Captain White ordered from the tailors, Messrs Arnott, fifty uniforms of dark green serge, with broad slouch hats in the same colour, "jauntily turned up at one side", but the Council decided that no man could bring his uniform home until he had paid for it. The result of this, says O'Casey, was that when there was a parade in Croydon Park the confusion of undressing and redressing "rivalled some of the tragic episodes depicted in Dante's *Inferno*".

The boots issued created a different kind of problem in the early days of this workers' army, while O'Casey quickly saw the Commandant's limits:

Captain White was indeed the son of a general, but that makes him no better than if he had been the son of a gun. I know more about the boots given to those whose broken boots "prevented them from marching" . . . Most of those who got these boots pawned them – some for food, some for drink – a few days later. Captain White had a bad habit of distributing largesse to those who flattered him, and when advised against this practice, resented it. On one occasion, he promised a fine topcoat he was wearing to three different men. No one could depend on his enthusiasm for more than a day. He ordered the uniforms from Arnott's, guaranteeing fifty pounds for them, without a by your leave from the Army Committee; and the collection of this money meant work night and day to promote a festival in Croydon Park that the Captain shouldn't be short. The fact is that Captain White was a noble fellow, but a nuisance.

The recruiting drive in the countryside was an uphill struggle, too: O'Casey relates how he, Captain White, Countess Markiewicz and P. T. Daly journeyed to Lucan in the Captain's car. On arrival they found "ominous quietude" and O'Casey felt it would be a long time before the locals grew "sufficiently class-conscious to understand the elementary principles of Labour thought". The same indifference was shown in Clondalkin, with the residents "gazing fixedly towards the Captain's motor car as if it were some dangerous machine calculated, if approached too closely, to upset for ever the quiet rhythm of the pastoral life".

O'Casey was celibate in this period, without even a steady girl-friend, although he found some girls attractive, among them Frank Cahill's sister Josie. A passing girl or woman often evoked a casual sexual response: he was never averse to noticing a shapely calf, or a sudden flash of white thigh, as the wind whipped up a skirt, but in these months of involvement with the Citizen Army it was the flag which held his attention most, provoking in him bursts of intense lyrical feeling, perhaps a sublimation of sexual desire:

> Then the flag came – the Plough and the Stars. A blanket was spread over a wall, and the flag spread over the blanket so that it couldn't be defiled by the grimy evil of the wall. All pressed back to have a good look at it, and a murmur of reverent approval gave the flag a grave salute . . . There it was; the most beautiful flag among the flags of the world's nations: a rich, deep poplin field of blue; across its whole length and breadth stretched the formalised shape of a plough, a golden-brown colour, seamed with a rusty red, while through all glittered the gorgeous group of stars enriching and ennobling the northern skies.

O'Casey mentions the fabric advisedly, for he had earlier had the imported satin of Republican badges changed for Irish-made poplin. His reverent, even jealous, feelings for that flag were never to leave him; nor the emotive force with which he was able to wave it, or trail it before audiences in his plays, sometimes thrusting it at them like a goad, sometimes tantalising them and seducing them with its magic.

One reason that, while devoting himself completely to the Army's cause, O'Casey gradually uncovered a further bone of contention – even while fulfilling his heart's desire, for the mock-heroic antics of the Citizen Army had completely captured his imagination – was his growing instinct for drama. Having now read so deeply, not only Shakespeare and Boucicault but more recently, thanks to a generous gift of books from Deakin, a wide range of other authors including Butler, Landor, Washington Irving and Jack London, he viewed the rivalry between the Citizen Army and the Volunteers not only in ruthless Darwinian terms, but also as having the pomp and ceremony of a Shakespearean Roman or history play.

He *wanted* the armies to be rivals, and as secretary agitated towards that end, fighting for his version of the truth with divisive fury. He was sensitive to the Volunteers' great charm and appeal to all sections of the public. Bulmer Hobson's persistent attitude towards labour he called "the attitude of the witches towards the intrusion of Faust and Mephistopheles: – 'Who are ye? What would ye here? Who hath come slinking in? The plague of fire into your bones!'" He challenged the Volunteers' President Eoin MacNeill to debate with the Citizen Army's executive council "the ambiguous principles of the Volunteers' Constitution, and the class basis of the Provisional Executive . . . consistently antagonistic to Labour". MacNeill curtly replied that he was ignorant of the distinction. O'Casey's former friend, Tom Clarke, turned against him and declared, in a letter in May 1914 to a friend: "Larkin's people for some time have been making war on the Irish Volunteers. I think this is largely inspired by a disgruntled fellow named O'Casey."

The Citizen Army was now a thousand strong. O'Casey recruited actively, creating confidence in timid youngsters who were not quite sure of their suitability, participating with Larkin in a festive pilgrimage to Wolfe Tone's grave in June. The summer of 1914 saw, as well as the drilling with broomsticks and hurling clubs, concerts held in Croydon Park, when Jim Larkin would sometimes get up and sing "in a hoarse, tremulous voice", a shy side of him which O'Casey noted, "The Red Flag" or "The Risin' of the Moon". They organised a marathon, and a "Citizen Army's attack on a Cowboy

Stockade"; during warm nights they camped under the stars, which led O'Casey to reflect, in contemplating the beauties of nature, "to what a small compass shrinks even the Constitution of the Irish Citizen Army! How horrible is the glistening, oily rifle to one of the tiny daisies, that cowers in a rosy sleep at my very feet."

But the glistening, oily instruments were in short supply, although the Citizen Army managed to pick up some of those smuggled into Howth in July 1914 for the Volunteers. Joseph Casey, himself an ICA man, brought some of these in with his brother-in-law, who owned a fleet of trucks and took part in the gun-running. This event, described by O'Casey as a "fraternal mingling" of the Volunteers and the Citizen Army, led to casualties when the Castle authorities made a half-hearted attempt to seize the arms but failed. Confronted by a jeering, stone-throwing mob on the march home the Scottish Borderers opened fire in Bachelor's Walk and killed three civilians. Public opinion rallied to the side of the Volunteers, and even O'Casey noted the glow of fellow-feeling engendered between the rival armies as the guards of honour "around the funeral cortèges were composed of alternate units of members of the Citizen Army and Volunteers".

Although he quoted, as epigraph to a three-page chapter in *The Story of the Irish Citizen Army* (1919) devoted to his break with the Army, Cassius's comment, "In such times as these it is not meet that every nice offence should bear its comment", O'Casey's actions over the next few weeks *were* comments on a "nice offence". Countess Markiewicz, a member of the Citizen Army Council, also belonged to the women's auxiliary, Cumann na mBan, of the Volunteers. O'Casey wanted her expelled. He took exception anyway to certain elements in her character. First, she was a member of the upper class, and O'Casey had at this time – he was later to relax this attitude towards members of that class who favoured him – a hatred on principle of such people, saying even of the Countess, who was noted for her wide espousal of causes, that she was a "spluttering Catherine-wheel of irresponsibility". She had wounded him with a disparaging remark about his Plough and Stars flag – before returning to oiling her automatic. At another time she held a rehearsal in the Citizen Army room in Liberty Hall and left a piano behind for O'Casey to move: he took this as a slight. To the actress Helena Moloney, who called the Countess a fine woman, he once said, "Nyah – all that type ever wants is to get what it can out of the workers."

When Captain White resigned from the Army – "trying too hard," said O'Casey, and disappointed at results; White said he was accused of being an "uncontrolled military dictator" and that O'Casey drove him out – and when in his place Larkin was appointed Commandant, O'Casey introduced a motion that it should not be expected that "Madame could retain the confidence of the Council", and that she should be asked to sever her connection either with the Volunteers or the Citizen Army. In forcing her to choose, O'Casey was supported by Larkin's sister, Delia, an active union organiser. But Larkin himself, together with four other members of the council, opposed O'Casey's motion, which was defeated by seven votes to six – the Countess voting for herself – and then moved that an apology should be tendered to the Countess, who now thought she deserved one. Secretary O'Casey, stung to the quick, said he could not apologise for what he "believed to be the truth", and wrote out his resignation.

At a meeting called a few days later expressly to paper over the differences, Larkin explained the attack made on the Countess, appealing to O'Casey to withdraw his accusations and cooperate with everyone. Those present were told by Larkin, according to his greatest admirer, that some people "lacked the broadmindedness one would expect from them". But his speech was mainly conciliatory and noncommittal. O'Casey then clashed heatedly with Larkin, counter-attacking with a new resolution that the Countess be expelled "for bourgeois tendencies and fraternisation with the enemy", i.e. the Volunteers. When he finished he stood sideways to the platform, with arms spread, saying, "I fear no man, physically or morally, not even the great Jim Larkin." Larkin tried to speak, but O'Casey went on and on, and when Larkin finally broke in O'Casey, together with several friends, walked out of the meeting. This time it was pain, not disillusionment, which struck O'Casey.

Soon after that clash, still in October 1914, Larkin left Ireland for America, to raise funds there to rebuild the union, and with his allegiance to class before nationality, remained in America through the First World War; in his absence the Citizen Army passed into the hands of his deputy, James Connolly. Although Larkin had taken the side of his patron and protector, Countess Markiewicz, in the dispute, O'Casey at once forgave his great hero: his love for him was total and unqualified, and he never spoke or wrote a word against him. But his defiance of Larkin over the Countess revealed a curious streak, almost a deliberate blindness, to Larkin's clear liking for a woman towards whom, in her old age, O'Casey was gratuitously insulting. The defiant little "chiseleur" inside O'Casey still balked at authority and refused to obey.

Larkin's sudden, impulsive departure established the distance necessary for the continuation of hero-worship. The most effulgent of O'Casey's father-figures, Larkin was the hero O'Casey would like to have been but wasn't, and his place in the pantheon was ensured by his sudden departure for the USA. Like O'Casey's own father, Larkin had gone before O'Casey had a chance to know him better, and before his propensity for fault-seeking inevitably came into play.

O'Casey also remained true to Larkinism, his hero's political philosophy, which he later and mistakenly saw as embodied in the Bolshevik Revolution of 1917. The communism or socialism of "Red Jim", as he was later depicted in O'Casey's play *The Star Turns Red*, was in essence a gentlemanly and British affair, with courtesy and fair-mindedness displayed towards enemies, an idealistic belief in justice, and a tolerance of cultural values even if they differed from his own. He always allowed his workers to hold dissenting views. O'Casey was right that he was a giant, but he was a giant who could only have existed on the stage of Irish history in 1913 and 1914. He fixed the scale of O'Casey's political imagination, gave it breadth, colour and humanity. O'Casey owed him a great debt, which throughout his life he continuously and generously repaid.

5

THEY DREAMED AND ARE DEAD

"He could relax now in a kind of way," writes O'Casey of his autobiographical hero, upon the severance of his connection with the Citizen Army. But in what kind of a way? He had no regular job, and not much paying work of any kind – he still wrote for the *Worker* until it ceased publication at the end of 1914 – and looked for support from his mother and his brother Mick. He had made one attempt to write a play, but had given it up, so that even at thirty-five, as he became at the end of March 1915, he was having to content himself with O'Toole Club meetings where he could sing songs and declaim satirical poems. His life at this time revolved round his reading, his family, and the friendships he had formed at the Club in Seville Place.

The 1914 War, at first expected to last only a short time, postponed the promised Home Rule for Ireland; but as it went on, it stimulated the ailing Irish economy. In the summer of 1915 Mick Casey, now aged forty-six, volunteered and was accepted for re-enlistment in the Inland Water Corps of the Royal Engineers; apparently he saved men from drowning on two different occasions. But with him gone, and O'Casey himself not working, Sean and his mother had scant resources. He received occasional gifts from friends and did from time to time, according to his nephew, borrow money; but he was intensely proud about asking for help: Tom Clarke's wife, in later years, was astonished that the former frequent caller at her husband's shop had never mentioned his straitened circumstances. Sean and his mother paid their weekly bills at Murphy's shop in Church Street. O'Casey did once mention to his O'Toole friend, Paddy McDonnell, that he had not eaten meat for five years, but this is at odds with his glowing account of summer weekends at Croydon Park, when he breakfasted with the Army on a substantial bowl of porridge and milk, followed by bacon, eggs, bread, butter and tea.

Ill-health was a recurrent problem: this time it was tubercular swellings in his neck. He had suffered these when younger, and his mother, on a neighbour's advice, had painted them with iodine three times a day. O'Casey recalled that Jim Larkin, noticing the lumps, sent him to a clinic where he was rudely handled but advised to have surgery. Eventually he was allotted a Union bed in the Laurence O'Toole ward of St Vincent de Paul Hospital, although not until 15 August 1915, after Larkin's departure from Dublin.

By then O'Casey was something of an outsider to the ITGWU, although he still frequented Liberty Hall. The impulsive, flamboyant leadership of Larkin had been succeeded by the more accommodating manner of James Connolly, who had started out on the Marxist left, but was now stepping into what O'Casey called "the broad and crowded highway of Irish Nationalism". ("We all regarded Jim Connolly as Red," Frank Daly reported. "But after he met Pearse no one ever heard a word of Communism out of him again.") O'Casey and his fellow malcontents were now impelled to find their platform outside the Hall: ranging themselves on the steps outside, they harangued those who entered and left, earning themselves the derisive title of "the Steps Committee".

O'Casey's operation was performed successfully by an almost deaf surgeon called Mr Tobin, who had lost his only son in Flanders and who identified with the numbers of British Army wounded shipped from France that he had to treat. In his free moments he would ask soldiers, "Where did you get your blighty, son?" and when he heard the name of the place, murmur, "Ah! my son spent his last moment a long way off: but yours was near enough, son; near enough." He seemed to think that when he was close to these men he was closer to his son.

O'Casey's growing insight into a mother's emotions declares itself when he writes of Tobin attempting to conjure up his son by joining in the singing of war songs: "You wouldn't get a mother doing it . . . She'd feel it too deep . . . Neither in noise of song nor murmur of story would she bring back the sad, sunny dust of his shape again, but in the deep and bitter loneliness of remembrance." Although nursing a painful and hacked-about neck, he was forming a deeper emotional identification with the mother losing her son, which one day he would forcefully express through Bessie Burgess:

There's a storm of anger tossin' in me heart, thinkin' of all th' poor Tommies . . . dhrenched in water an' soaked in blood, gropin' their way to a shattherin' death, in a shower o' shells! Young men with th' sunny lust o' life beamin' in them, layin' down their white bodies, shredded into torn an' bloody pieces, on th' altar that God Himself has built for th' sacrifice of heroes!

O'Casey set the first act of *The Plough and the Stars*, which he did not write until 1924-25, in November 1915, just a few months after he left hospital and was recuperating at home. That date was highly significant: not only was the first performance of *The Plough*, in February 1926, followed shortly after by his actual exile from Ireland later that year, but the earlier moment of November 1915, when the play begins its account of the Easter Rising of 1916, signalled O'Casey's own inward exile from events and the intellectual ferment around him. Through a mixture of his own physical frailty and his mother's intense protectiveness, his pain and frustration was deepening into the negative capability of a writer.

During this period, too, he was notably silent in the letter columns of the press. He had abandoned the "romantic cult of Nationalism", as he said sixty years later, "and saw the real Ireland when I read the cheap edition of Shaw's *John Bull's Other Island*; hating only poverty, hunger and disease". The involvement with the Citizen Army had been his last sustained attempt to act purely within the dictates of his ideals, and even here he had been bitterly frustrated: "Labour", he commented, "had laid its precious gift of independence on the Altar of Irish Nationalism."

O'Casey sent this drawing of himself to his friend, Leo Rush

So he withdrew into the shadows, growing a beard to cover the scars of the operation, and becoming more and more of an autodidact. He now saw the rising strength of the Irish Volunteers with the eyes of a cynic, and particularly he viewed its romantic thirst for blood in the cause of Irish independence as irrelevant to the struggle of the working class. Although he was never directly to dramatise the events of 1913 with success – his comic gift, when it came to writing a play with a message, always remained subservient to abstract ideas and propaganda – it was to this defeated hope of the workers coming to power that he remained loyal. But in the shadows where he lay, and was to remain for years – subsisting, it is said, on only the barest of necessities – he could not but respond emotionally to the way ordinary Dublin people were affected by the events of the next few months. There was an added dimension to his experience of those events: although he was no longer a member of the Republican leadership, he had known most of the leaders well. So he participated and yet did not participate; part of him remained an insider, in his own imagination close to former friends like Pearse, Clarke and even Bulmer Hobson. Another part of him remained the commentator and outsider: the mocking chorus to the national catastrophe about to unfold.

There were, in the Volunteers, two active groups with opposing intentions: one was headed by MacNeill, the Volunteers' chief of staff, and Hobson, who now repudiated IRB strategy and envisaged a cautious defensive policy until the end of the war; the other was led by Arthur Griffith, Tom Clarke, who now took an anti-Hobson line, and Padraic Pearse, who openly advocated bloodshed – "The old earth of the battlefields is thirsty for the wine of our blood."

The first of these factions was still, on paper, in charge of the Volunteers, but the second, bent on securing martyrdom – or more than martyrdom, crucifixion – wrested control away from the moderates. James Connolly, commandant of the 300-strong Citizen Army, was also a prime mover in the idea of an insurrection: Pearse had managed to win him over to a plan for concerted action of the two forces. Pearse and his staff planned their rebellion to take place on Easter Day 1916, but without telling MacNeill. The authorities could see Irish Volunteers and Citizen Army units parading openly, but took the chances of a rising lightly, failing to understand the idea of deliberate self-sacrifice which, together with hope of aid from Germany, now motivated Pearse and his fellow conspirators.

On the Tuesday before Easter, a rumour of the mooted rebellion reached Hobson, who at once went to MacNeill; in the early hours of Good Friday morning he and MacNeill visited Pearse, who admitted the rumour was true. In the ensuing confusion MacNeill countermanded the order for "manœuvres" on Sunday, which had been Pearse's signal for the Rising to begin. A further blow to Pearse's plan was the scuttling of a German ship, the *Aud*, which had arrived off the coast of Kerry with a cargo of arms: no one was there to meet her. Roger Casement, the Republican who had been negotiating with the German High Command, landed on the west coast off the submarine which had escorted the *Aud*, and fell into the hands of the authorities. Unlike the others, he was widely regarded as a German spy. Father Breen, O'Casey's friend in the St Laurence O'Toole church, persisted in this view until "the British rope was around the indomitable man's neck".

Indeed, as O'Casey said, there was in the whole affair "too much of an Irish heaven . . . and too little of the Irish earth", or, as a character remarks in the novel *The Red and the Green*, by the Dublin-born Iris Murdoch, "Why could the Irish get nothing right? Such dunces deserved their slavery." O'Casey relished the farcical side to the claims of the Republicans, as when, years earlier, Seamus Deakin, who like himself did not take part in the Rising, had outlined the means by which the British Empire could be brought to dust:

In a room, back of the shop, he showed me pictures and diagrams of Airplane stations & Zeppelin sheds in the Rhineland facing Britain. They were in, if I remember right, Stead's Review of Reviews. He, Deakin, was quivering with excitement. The airplane was going to win the freedom of all little subject nations, & make them secure forever – including our own homeland, of course. "An airoplane" says he "will cost only £50, & so, from a military point of view, every little nation will be as mighty as the biggest." Then he paused for breath. "England," says he, when he got it again, "is going to go up in dust." When I demurred, saying I dunno about that, & that, like everything else, aeroplanes were bound to go up in price, he said "Nonsense; you'll see, Sean." By now, I've seen pretty clearly, though all the way home I couldn't help thinking how easy it was for a man to believe what he wished to believe.

The reality was not so farcical; when the Rising did take place, on the Monday instead of Easter Sunday, far fewer supported it than the leaders had hoped. It was a force of less than 2,000, including one hundred women, which seized virtually the whole of the centre of Dublin and held out for nearly a week until the British were reinforced. But the appeal of the Volunteers to the country as a whole fell flat, for, as Captain White, now commandant of the Derry Volunteers, said, "The Irish National Volunteer Movement had no definite ideals and no definite objective. I was a blind leader of the blind."

Public opinion as a whole was hostile to the Republicans: most of middle-class Dublin favoured the status quo, and Bulmer Hobson, a leader whose opinions were typical of the "silent majority", was kidnapped by Republicans just before the Rising so that he should have no influence over events. Those who fought did so with extraordinary bravery and tenacity, although fewer than one in twenty died in the fighting. Two O'Toole friends of O'Casey, Jimmy Shiels and Johnny McDonnell, were combatants, although Johnny's brother, Paddy, just twenty-one years of age and O'Casey's close friend, stayed at home, on the principle that two sons of one family should not both be put at risk. Another O'Tooler, Mick Smith, was holed up in Jacobs' Biscuit Factory: he told O'Casey that he could see through the window of a flat opposite, the tiny coffin of a child which stayed there unburied because the family dared not venture out. Later, in *The Plough and the Stars*, O'Casey developed this emotive detail in a subplot.

O'Casey watched the Citizen Army parade in front of Liberty Hall before taking up its rebel positions; he himself, he said, was "a little loose on his legs, and nursing a septic neck-wound". He resented Connolly's not raising over Liberty Hall the Citizen Army flag of the Plough and the Stars, which he had so lovingly sponsored, but a plain green Republican ensign instead. He had advocated the underground guerrilla tactics of the Boers, not the formal insurrectionary methods the Republicans actually used. Take off your uniforms, he had said, and keep them for the wedding. But no one heeded his advice, and the *Volunteer* refused his article on the subject.

On Thursday of Easter Week O'Casey, as a former nationalist activist, was arrested, and herded with others into St Barnabas' church where he was locked up for the night. He had a copy of Keats in his pocket and he remarked, as he grew in grace and wisdom, his status as a hero rapidly diminished. The British gunboat, *Helga*, firing from the mouth of the Liffey, had reduced Liberty Hall to a shell and toppled Connolly's green flag; O'Casey was worried about his mother because the *Helga*'s shells were hitting the East Wall. On the same morning field artillery opened fire on the Republican stronghold in the GPO and while incendiary mortars were lobbed on to the roof, surrounding buildings blazed.

Next day, while fighting still raged in O'Connell Street, giving it the look of a town in war-ravaged Belgium, O'Casey was allowed home, only to be re-arrested with a hundred other men on the Friday night and marched by a detachment of Welsh soldiers to a grain store, where he was again locked up for the night. The following morning they were released a second time. "Will we have to come back tonight?" asked a detainee. "If we want you, we'll fetch you," answered the Tommy. O'Casey returned home accompanied by a kind-hearted soldier who commandeered some grub for him and his mother from Murphy's.

At six on the Friday, in the GPO, Clarke, Sean MacDermott, Joseph Plunkett and a founder member of the Volunteers known as The O'Rahilly, who the week before had been Eoin MacNeill's chief courier for cancelling the Rising, gathered round Connolly. Unable to walk from two wounds, and scorning advice that he should be removed to hospital, Connolly stationed himself under the portico where the fiercest assault from the enemy was expected. They held a council, as a result of which the sixteen wounded and twelve women were smuggled out to Jervis Street Hospital under the care of a captured British MO who had been tending wounded Republicans. Then, from floors now smouldering with cinders, The O'Rahilly led a diversionary attack of thirty men on a barricade placed to cut off their retreat.

> What remains to sing about
> But of the death he met
> Stretched under a doorway
> Somewhere off Henry Street;
> They that found him found upon
> The door above his head
> "Here died the O'Rahilly
> R.I.P." writ in blood.
> How goes the weather?

He fell at the doorway of Kelly's fish shop at the corner of Sackville Lane, where he scrawled a note to his American wife.

Next morning after breaking out of the Post Office and burrowing and hacking their way through the walls of Moore Street shops and basements to Number 16, a poultry shop, Pearse and the rest capitulated. Fourteen leading Republicans were finally executed, out of the ninety-seven condemned to death by General Sir John Maxwell's courts martial; they included Clarke, Pearse, Joseph Plunkett, who married Grace Gifford in Kilmainham Gaol on the eve of his execution, and the badly wounded Connolly, who had to be propped up on a chair in the prison yard. Countess Markiewicz, as a woman, was spared. So was Eamon de Valera, who carried an American passport. Pearse, the man who had contrived the whole sacrifice, spent his last moments writing about the beauty of this world:

> Sometimes my heart hath shaken with great joy
> To see a leaping squirrel in a tree,
> Or a red ladybird upon a stalk.

As for the Citizen Army flag, "Some say it was burned in Liberty Hall," when it was shelled by the *Helga*; "some that it fell from the top of a building held by the ICA when the building went up in flames; some that a British Officer took it away with him after the surrender of the IRA."

It was the failure of the rebellion which became its final glory: had the English, to turn Shaw's clever-sounding but ultimately foolish phrase on its head, not been so stupid in their wisdom and not begun executing the leaders, until popular outcry forced them to halt, then the Christ-like sanctity of those leaders would never have been established, and the rebellion would never have been seen as a holy event in Irish history. It was Padraic Pearse, a devout Catholic, who carried the identification with Christ to its ultimate limit: as Jesus had died for the ungodly so he, in dying for Holy Ireland, gave his life for the disbelievers in independence and won a moral victory over his oppressors. And as in the case of Jesus, it was his own people – the likes of Murphy, but even some of the Volunteers themselves – who betrayed him.

O'Casey's account, twenty-nine years later, in his autobiography, of Pearse appearing steady before his captors was contradicted by the Ulster Protestant playwright and critic St John Ervine: Pearse, Ervine said, according to a Castle official had reeled like a drunken man, "His great head, made hideous by a squinting eye, lolling from side to side as if it were about to fall out." O'Casey replied that although Pearse did have a very slight cast in one eye, he feared death no more than the legendary hero, Cuchulain. The exchange shows two Protestants of a fundamentally nineteenth-century cast of mind making the mistake of seeing Pearse's death, like Christ's, as an act of moral exemplism, not of fidelity. Both forgot, possibly, that Christ at one point felt forsaken by the Lord, while Peter thrice denied his Master. Bernard Shaw questioned the value of the entire Rising: the event which it followed, he said, the "mutiny of the British officers against the Home Rule Act", was far more important, and "shattered the whole cause for parliamentary government throughout the world".

But the potent image had been created. When O'Casey came to treat the Rising in his irreverent Boucicault manner, in 1926 in *The Plough and the Stars*, the image had hardened into orthodoxy. O'Casey's emotions in 1916 were volatile, he was both moved by and excluded emotionally from the rebellion: how could he not feel his own cowardice – with a deep, self-consuming bitterness that the revolt had not followed the path he wanted – in the face of so much heroism? Even his hated "Madame" had behaved with impeccable courage: after surrendering at the College of Surgeons, Countess Markiewicz refused a chivalrous British officer's proffered transport and marched her detachment away. She, too, had been tried and sentenced to death – a sentence later commuted to life imprisonment. Worse and worse, from O'Casey's point of view, she became, on her release in the general amnesty of June 1917, a convert to Catholicism.

O'Casey's fluctuating emotions, which could also be construed as excuses for not doing more, later became fixed when he fiercely dismissed the Rising as a "fiery-tale, a die-dream showing a false dream that no soul saw", or more simply as "naked foolishness a child's patthern of war". Nearer the event, although with a touch of cussedness even then, he identified its true hero as the peripheral but much loved figure of the pacifist, Francis Sheehy-Skeffington. He was "like all really sincere pacifists," Captain White said, "the most pugnacious of men . . . there was no one in Dublin who had not at one time or another broken an umbrella over his head." Out in the streets, at imminent risk of his life from stray bullets, Sheehy-Skeffington was trying to stop people looting, and had already, in front of Dublin Castle, pulled a bleeding British officer to safety, when he was arrested. He fell into the hands of a sadistic British officer, Captain Bowen-Colthurst, who had been stimulating his own ferocity with Old Testament texts, and this man had Sheehy-Skeffington shot in cold blood. The atrocity was hushed up until another officer, Major Sir Francis Vane, persistently called attention to the case. Later Colthurst was "detained during the King's pleasure" at Broadmoor asylum for the criminally insane.

O'Casey, in a calculated insult to Connolly, referred to Sheehy-Skeffington in *The Story of the Irish Citizen Army* as "the first martyr to Irish Socialism". Sheehy-Skeffington's spirit of peace was the "living antithesis of the Easter Insurrection", he was "the purified soul of revolt against not only one nation's injustice to another, but he was also the soul of revolt against man's inhumanity to man".

Here O'Casey lapsed into writing propaganda, which so often cancelled itself out, as when later he fiercely, and with equal cussedness, defended those looters whom Sheehy-Skeffington was trying to dissuade from their unholy actions. Sometimes – perhaps increasingly, as he grew older – chaos appealed more than order to O'Casey: "Now the looters gambled before they went looting, and to go looting was a brave thing to do, for the streets sang songs of menace from bullets flying about everywhere."

Sean watched their wonderful activity, and couldn't desecrate their disorder with dishonour. All these are they who go to Mass every Sunday and holy day of obligation; whose noses are ground down by the clergy on the grindstone of eternal destiny; who go in mortal fear of the threat of a priest, he thought; but now he was glad to see they hadn't lost their taste for things material.

As a supporter of Labour he could find comfort in the decision taken at the Irish Trades Union Congress in August 1916 to opt out of the national struggle; as an atheist, he despised the moral victory over oppression. But the conflict in him over not taking part – as much to do with his mother as with himself – simmered in him for years, and was only finally exorcised by writing *The Plough and the Stars*.

But he did pay tribute to the insurrectionists: "The bonfires of Sinn Fein began to blaze on every Irish hillside, and thousands of the Irish people danced around the blaze of Sinn Fein, as if they warmed themselves at the fire of life. Parliamentarism was a sinking fire." He could have been thinking when he wrote this that he spent much of the summer of 1916 with about ten of the rebels whom Frank Cahill had smuggled out of the city centre to County Meath. Sean pitched down with them in a large meadow owned by Cahill's cousin, while Cahill, who had a bad leg and limped, slept in his cousin's house.

Others of his friends had not been so lucky: Shiels and Johnny

McDonnell had given themselves up and suffered the jeering of crowds lining the route to the dockside from which they were deported to Frongoch detention camp in Wales. O'Casey wrote to Shiels with a witty cartoon of a female aid worker and Frank Cahill with his arm around her, each holding a large can inscribed "Volunteer Fund", which he captioned "Frank kicks two birds with the wan stone"; he also referred to McDonnell's brother, Paddy, who "felt ashamed" – at not having been allowed to go out and fight.

In the same letter he described the horrible time they had had in his district: "Death was facing us back and front for days, but there must have been more righteous men amongst us than were found in Sodom and Gomorrah, for most of us came out safely, and could now listen to the 'ping' of bullets as serenely as to the chirrup of 'the little dickie birds sitting in the tree'."

He sent further cartoons: of looting in the slums, of himself dodging bullets, of himself and Cahill as hobos round a campfire. He was in excellent spirits: "I try to laugh at the world – nay, I do not laugh *at* the world, but with the world, for a cheerful spirit will serve a man in Heaven or in Hell."

———◆◆◆———

"When I danced, & I danced often and I danced long, I always had on a pair of hobnailed boots," O'Casey said later; but if the boots were the proof of a working man's identity, there was little work, apparently, to go with them. Scant reference to manual work of any kind is to be found in his letters, articles, or the memories of his friends or family. There are plenty of glimpses of O'Casey enjoying himself at the Club in the company of friends who were many years his junior. Some marvelled at his boisterous humour, at his booming laugh, at how little hostility or self-pity he showed in the face of poverty and illness. He would sing comic and sentimental songs, tell stories, and was the life and soul of *ceilidhs*, although to one young woman he could be "a puzzling figure, given to sitting and staring at some distant object, especially after someone had contradicted him". To the same woman he would pay old-fashioned compliments: "Ah, you have lovely hair, Josie." Another found him a clumsy dancing partner, unattached to any girl in particular.

One night the O'Tooles piped Douglas Hyde to the Mansion House on his return from a triumphant tour of America: afterwards they held a *ceilidh*, and then the pipers left, each with a girl on his arm. "O'Casey staggered home alone, on his shoulders the band's huge drum." At thirty-six he was still gaunt and lean of figure and although he slouched along the street in a shuffling, ungraceful manner, he looked tall and aloof. A friend arranged work for him at the *Irish Independent*: "I don't need any work," O'Casey snapped at him. Others said he resembled a scarecrow; when, just to provoke him, street urchins would ask the time, he answered them in Irish.

In 1917 a new lay teacher joined Cahill on the staff of the Christian Brothers' School. Good-looking, with a strong face and soft hazel eyes, Mary, or Maire, Keating looked like the traditional maid of many a poignant air. She lived in a two-storey house near the East Wall with two sisters, her mother and father. They were Catholics. Cahill introduced her in the Club. To O'Casey, who met her when she was twenty-two, he thirty-seven, she was much more than a decent and attractive girl:

> How quickly "Maire" may be written, how rapidly it can be uttered! . . . What a beautiful and adorable vision the little word conjures up before *me*. The vision of gentle grey-blue eyes, of lightbrown golden hair, of soft cheeks, whose colour is the most delicate blend of the pale white lily and the blushing rose, the full white throat, but before all these, beautiful as they are – the gracious, gentle, loving, winning manner of my dear little loved one.

After the passion of lock-outs, street violence, rebellion and martyrdom, O'Casey's new sword of light gave to his eye a distinctly different glint. Even grim-visaged poverty was courting an amorous looking-glass – without any of Gloucester's cynicism. The gallant ex-labourer was smitten with "a love so ardent and so deep that it resembles the fabled tree of which it is said that its roots penetrated to the earth's centre while its branches blossomed in the higher heavens".

He began to write poems to Maire, and to post them to her, sometimes with a covering excuse such as "Forgive me for my execrable attempts at poetry", sometimes without even a date. He would lend her books – not his usual serious reading, but more frivolous offerings, such as *Chevalier de la Maison Rouge* or *The Forty-Five Guardsmen*. Once he told her he had written a ballad which could become a national anthem, and had shown it to his friends at Liberty Hall, who told him it was good but later handed it back to him without doing anything about it. Entitled "The Call of the Tribe", its rejection had been a great disappointment:

Like vultures from dark clouded skies they come swooping
To feast themselves full on inanimate prey,
The legends of England to Ireland come trooping
To bear the best sons of our mothers away.

REFRAIN: But the children of Ireland with hearts fixed and true
Shall ever be faithful dear Eire to you!

He had better luck with a more irreverent ballad, "The Grand Oul'
Dame Britannia", which had first been printed in June 1916 under
his pseudonym, *An Gall Fada*, and subsequently much reprinted as
a "Broadsheet Ballad".

In early October 1917, for the second time that year, Maire fell ill
– this time much more seriously. Sean was extremely upset; unable
to visit her, he kept a diary, which, later, he posted to her: "Unhappy
Sean!" he wrote on Saturday, 6 October, "An untrammelled spirit
may make a universe of a tiny cell, but today illimitable space
has become a prison surrounded by the dark walls of bitter disappointment." The following Monday morning he expected a
letter, but none came, and by the next day the uncertainty made
him "almost frantic". Between three and four-thirty p.m. of that
day he waited in East Road to see "Birdie", Maire's sister, walk
home from school, but she did not pass. He returned home sick at
heart.

Wednesday saw him "hovering about Seville Place", where he saw
Maire's mother going home from the Force Depot – Mr Keating was
a policeman; here he "was sorely tempted to implore her to have pity
upon me and tell me how my sweet Maire was". The thirty-seven-
year-old ex-labourer fell prey to love-sickness deeper that afternoon
than on the previous one:

Waited in East Road again from three to five in the hope of seeing
Birdie, but she came not. Drank a cup of cocoa, and took the tram
to the Park, waited outside the Shell Factory from 5.45 to 7 in the
hope of seeing Maire's Aunt Katie; did not see her. Filled with
heart-breaking visions of Maire's illness and its ultimate termin-
ation. Oh! Should Maire die, may God send death to me as well!
Stood at the corner of 1st Avenue 10.30 p.m. tried to pierce the
gloom and perceive with spiritual vision the face of my beloved
Darling, I love you, I love you, I love you, I love you! Oh! Why
should I be ashamed?

Next afternoon he again waited in vain for Birdie, until he concluded she, too, must be ill. On Friday O'Casey wrote some lines of verse, but gave up in despair; on Saturday, he went along with three friends, Kevin O'Lochlain, Frank O'Growney and Matt Carroll, to a diversionary funeral, keeping up, as he wrote, "a lively conversation which made them laugh frequently, while I'm near to tears myself and my heart was bursting with grief". In the evening, when at William Kelly's shop discussing events with Charlie Russel, he was at last put out of his misery, for Mrs Keating came in, carrying parcels, and he overheard her say to Kelly – clearly he could not ask her himself – "Oh she is better now."

This was the week when on the other side of Europe, Lenin returned from hiding in Finland to St Petersburg, and when the momentous news of the October Revolution began to break in Dublin, yet O'Casey remained completely unaffected, slave as he was to a very different passion. Maire's improvement was all that mattered in life, and when he heard of it, he talked so vehemently and quickly that Kelly and Russell thought he had been drinking. "May Christ be thanked!" he wrote. "Oh, God be praised!"

All the summer of 1917 O'Casey had kept up his delicate and repetitive attentions. Recently Douglas Hyde had published translations of *The Love Songs of Connacht*, written in Irish by an anonymous woman who died romantically when very young: there was in O'Casey's lyrical outpourings to Maire Keating something of the same direct and vulnerable feeling, although its expression was technically not as adept. When she left for a short holiday he wrote,

The gentle flowers, the gentle flowers – Their softening charm
  is fled,
For now they seem like blossoms strewn about the silent dead;
They're symbols now of sorrow deep and Joy's swift sad decay –
For my heart is filled with woe, with woe, since Mary went away.

More than their difference in age, their difference in religion made difficulties for the pair from the start. Although O'Casey in the autobiography describes Maire's house as if he had been there – "the bedrooms were so small that a dim glance from one eye enfolded all that might be there. If you stretched out of the bed from the far side, you could put your head out of the window" – he was never once invited in, and, if he had gone there, would have been very unwelcome. Her parents could never have tolerated a Protestant for a son-in-law; her father was the more lenient of the two, but her mother was adamant. The relationship was doomed from the start; sometimes and suddenly Maire would disappoint his hopes of seeing her; he would plead:

> Let me crave your forgiveness for expecting you to risk additional pain by acceding to my selfish appeal to meet me when the weather emphatically forbids it . . . It is my love which makes me selfish . . . It may be rash but it is passionate and strong. My only joy . . . is when I am with you, intensified when I hold you in my arms, and when I press ardent kisses on your sweet little mouth.

But – ardent kisses apart – it was, strictly in accordance with the prevailing *mœurs*, an unconsummated passion. They attended dances, took part in the activities of the O'Toole drama club, rode on trams to view the cliffs at Howth or pace the beach at Dun Laoghaire. A favourite walk was in Finglas, west County Dublin, where they trod the lane, Stella's Walk, where Stella and Swift had enjoyed each other's company. Maire, too, was excellent company for Sean and the warmth of her character, and the fun they had together relieved his former attachment to "mere complexity". Although he now contributed an occasional article to *Irish Opinion* and seemed to accept that Ireland's political aims had to be achieved before the class war could be begun (the Dublin *Saturday Post* in September 1917 published a letter of his on the issue of Labour and Sinn Fein), he had developed a wider view of himself which Maire, with her gentle manner, "wistfully patient in listening to his talk", fed.

In late September the death of an Easter Rebellion hero who had been sentenced to death, reprieved, then released in the general amnesty, gave new impetus to his ambition to write. Thomas Ashe, a handsome golden-haired Kerryman, over six foot with a leonine head, had been an O'Toole piper and as such known to O'Casey. In August 1917 Ashe had made a seditious speech at Ballinalee in County Longford, "sowing the seed of Human Liberty in the hearts of the people". A few days later, walking in O'Connell Street, he was arrested by two members of the RIC and subsequently sentenced to two years in prison. He began a hunger strike in Mountjoy Gaol in September. Six days later, from a combination of pneumonia, forced feeding and ill treatment, he was dead.

O'Casey first claimed Ashe as a supporter of the Great Strike of 1913, as much a labour hero as a Republican one. In a letter to the

Saturday Post, he wrote: "It never made him less Irish to love and to fix his hope on the ultimate Emancipation of the Masses." There was just then a great revival in Republican hopes; the survivors of 1916 were now in key positions. "Was he out in Easter Week?" became the touchstone of Irish life. Eamon de Valera, the last commandant of Easter Week to surrender, and the ablest tactician of them all, was elected President of Sinn Fein in October, and of the Volunteers in November: "It was a curious choice to Sean, for to him de Valera seemed to be no Gael either in substance or in face, though he was probably one in theory." O'Casey could never envisage an excited de Valera on the hurling field, and, pulling a bit of rank, remarked he had never known him in his own Central Branch team. Worst of all, as far as O'Casey was concerned, de Valera knew nothing about the common people.

An enterprising Dublin publisher, Fergus O'Connor, who had printed Republican pamphlets and been interned in Frongoch along with Shiels and McDonnell, undertook to print the lament for Ashe which O'Casey was now writing. It was a hurried piece of work, composed in the heat of the moment, melodramatic and overstated, but it had a strong, continuous emotion beating through it, with the whole account of Ashe's end set out in the brooding, forceful tone of a soliloquy. Saturated with his reading of many books, O'Casey had found a power of utterance, if not yet a voice of his own, markedly different from anything he had shown till then.

Thomas Ashe, Thomas Ashe, take a last look at the Irish sky, for when these grim gates open to let you forth, your strong body will be limp and helpless, your brave heart will faintly beat in a final effort to live for the people, and your eyes will be too dim to see clearly the kindly Irish skies that have watched your life-long efforts to free your Country and to uplift Her People. The gate closes: Thomas Ashe is separated forever from his relatives, his friends, and the Irish People – when once more they look upon him they find him dead!

As O'Connor prepared *The Story of Thomas Ashe* for publication in 1918, together with some booklets of songs by "Sean Ó Cathasaigh", the tempo of O'Casey's life began to quicken. In November 1917 he was rehearsing, with Maire helping behind the scenes, a charity show in aid of Meals for Necessitous Schoolchildren. To keep himself from idleness, as he put it, he arranged a concert, to include the performance of a one-act play, *The Nabocklish* (a rough approximation in Irish of "never mind"), in which he himself had a part. The whole occasion, which took place at the Empire Theatre on Sunday, 25 November, proved a great success. The house was packed, and hundreds of people were turned away.

O'Casey commented that the one failure was himself. The *Saturday Post* was not quite so harsh, saying that O'Casey, as a dim-witted English tourist who wants to meet Irish rebels, "strove valiantly in a part that was altogether unsuited for him". An English accent was never O'Casey's strong point, either then or later, even on the printed page. But he also sang, with a friend, a "topical song" – a euphemism for a ballad – satirising John Redmond's Irish Parliamentary Party, called "The Constitutional Movement Must Go On", which he and Fergus O'Connor had written together, and another, "I Don't Believe It, Do You?" – items which won the "applause of the night". Paddy McDonnell also took part in *The Nabocklish*, playing Jeremiah Cullinam, displaying nervousness as well as talent. Later they did *The Nabocklish* at 41 Parnell Square and "at the back of the houses in Leinster Avenue".

When Tom Clarke was executed in Kilmainham Gaol he left £3,100 for his wife to distribute to the distressed; one of his tobacconist's shops, at 77 Amiens Street, where in 1916 the Republican Nurse O'Farrell had met General Lowe prior to Pearse's surrender and discussed terms, passed to the charge of William Kelly, who had now become a close friend of O'Casey. In mid-December Kelly and his wife took O'Casey to the Abbey Theatre to see *Blight: The Tragedy of Dublin* by "Alpha and Omega" (Oliver St John Gogarty and Joseph O'Connor), one of the first plays O'Casey claims to have seen there.

They may have been accompanied by Frank Cahill, for at about this time Cahill, by now with a permanent limp, accompanied O'Casey home after they had seen a play at the Abbey; neither of them had much liked the play, and at the Five Lamps, near the O'Toole Club, where O'Casey had to turn off to the right, Frank told him, "You know, Sean, you could write a better play than the one we saw tonight!" O'Casey stopped and thought this over: "D'ye know Frank, I believe I could. I think I will."

There may have been some irony in his reply, because the first play he sketched out, *The Frost in the Flower*, about which little is known before it was rejected by the Abbey Theatre two years later, has Frank Cahill as a central character. But, on the night he parted company from Frank, it is more likely his thoughts switched immediately, as he began walking home to Abercorn Road, to Maire, who lived at 14 First Avenue, just across from the Five Lamps. Little did he know then, with the auspicious moves his new literary friends such as the Kellys and Fergus O'Connor were making on his behalf, that in the following and fateful year, 1918, the two women to whom he had been closest all his life would die, while in the year following that Maire herself would fall seriously ill.

6

LETHE'S WHARF

When he was seventy-four O'Casey wrote to the American critic, John Gassner, with whom he was discussing the idea of a one-volume abridgement of his autobiography, "Your suggestion that I should travel through the old territory again, & put up sign-posts of dates on the way, is a good and terrible idea! Recollection of dates is the one thing under God's heaven & in man's earth I can't remember."

Bella died on New Year's Day, 1918. She had risen early to wake and give her son Valentine breakfast; he left for work and she crept back into bed, never to awaken again. She probably died from influenza, for there was a lot of it about even before the Spanish flu epidemic of the 1918-19 winter; O'Casey says the only symptoms she showed were the red and inflamed skin of erysipelas, and headaches which had gradually grown worse till she ceased working and donned a shawl.

In the autobiography he placed her death some ten or more years earlier than it actually took place, adding it to the chronicle of earlier Casey family misfortunes. By doing so he obviated the need to describe in detail the long years his sister had spent in shabby, declining gentility, scraping to keep up appearances in her widow-hood, with her five children to support – scrubbing floors in a pair of spotless white gloves, cutting an incongruous figure so that she was known locally as "the Duchess".

Of her five children, three were soon working, although her eldest daughter, Susan, was still prevented from exerting herself beneath her station, kept in a state of ladylike luxury to which her broken-down mother still aspired. The other daughter was a box-maker, however, while Valentine – the name itself conjures up the plush world of the department store – wielded a coal-yard shovel; his brother, "Sonny", beat the usual Casey trail: apprenticed first to a printer, he became a timberman and then a quay foreman. The youngest son, O'Casey's namesake John, at first got on well with his uncle, with whom he shared a taste for books; when Bella was still alive O'Casey allowed him the run of his library, until one day he found a book was missing and accused John of stealing it. "My mother was so angry", said John, "she refused to set foot in 18 Abercorn Road till the book was found. When it did finally turn up Uncle Jack hastened round to apologise. Having sunk a foot in my estimation by calling me a thief, he rose two feet by admitting his error."

On Bella's death it was found that the insurance policy to pay for the funeral had not been allowed to lapse, in spite of O'Casey's inveighing against the evil insurance companies, which he called "asps on the breasts of the poor". The funeral, however, rubbed home the emotional dereliction – that gap between former hopes and actual achievements – the Caseys now felt. Bella had been the main thrust of their father's efforts to give his children a good education and therefore a better position in life. But at her funeral there wasn't even the postmen's band playing, as there had been at Tom's. Her hearse was drawn by a "scraggy mare bare of a plume" to Mount Jerome where her coffin joined that of her father, her husband, and younger brother.

Why did O'Casey not want Bella's death, in his own subsequent re-arrangement of events, to happen when it did? There are two likely explanations. The year 1918 began a busy time for him, more full of hope than any previous year of his life. His Fenian friend, Fergus O'Connor, whose costly cap and well-cut Irish tweeds contrasted strangely with his own shabby attire, was actively promoting his pamphlets in the flurry of pro-Fenian activity of 1918. Sinn Fein clubs were sprouting up all over Dublin and O'Casey's reputation as a pamphleteer and a "quare fellow" grew and grew, in the hothouse atmosphere of the city, through advertisements and readings. Three seven- or eight-page booklets of his songs – *Songs of the Wren, Humorous and Sentimental*, so called because of an old Irish song, "The Wren", attributed to earlier rebels known as the Wren Boys – were in various stages of preparation. In January and February O'Casey wrote to O'Connor full of plans for future publications, telling him of friends of his, William Kelly and a Mr King, who also wanted to commission "reading matter", as he called it.

By now he was earning modest, certainly not negligible, amounts from his writing, in one letter mentioning having had at least five pounds from work published – one pound was a labourer's average weekly wage, while his mother's pension was ten shillings. O'Connor printed 10,000 copies of the first booklet of songs, selling them at one penny, and it was likely O'Casey received more than five pounds of the proceeds of £400 from this sale. With a Sinn Fein ballad he sent O'Connor he excused himself for his handwriting – he was using a new fountain pen, his first and one of the very latest kind, a Waterman, which Maire had given him. Later Maire Keating pointed out that O'Casey's claim that he couldn't afford a pen was exaggerated. "I know that wasn't true," she said.

The year 1918 was a happy one for this courting couple; while they were never formally engaged, it was believed that they would eventually marry, in spite of the disapproval of Maire's father, and also of a new clerical friend O'Casey made at this time, Canon Brady. This priest strove for a time to convert him, "only to make him recite from the Koran in reply".

But the second, possibly the main, reason O'Casey shifted poor Bella's death to an earlier epoch of sorrow was that 1918 held for him the greatest personal loss of all: this he foreshadowed in writing to O'Connor on 13 February that he could not call round as much as usual because of the "continued feebleness of my mother who has nobody to look after her but myself". Bella's death had hit him badly in this respect, for Bella, living just round the corner in Church Place, had cared for him also in a very practical way: as he told O'Connor a week later, "I could call up now and again, but should you not be in I cannot wait as I formerly used to do, for since my sister died, I have to do all the washing, cooking & scrubbing in the house, unless I am prepared to reign in dirt, which I am not prepared to do."

His relationship with O'Connor soon soured, in spite of the extra work he was also doing for him producing "Homely Greetings" – personal, sincere and Irish – when the latter objected to his producing a similar line in greeting cards for a rival press. O'Connor then declined to publish some songs O'Casey submitted to him, affronting him so much that he wrote, "I cannot humiliate myself so as to allow you to become the arbiter as to whom I shall, or shall not, sell the poor effusions of my mind."

O'Casey used as epigraph to the preface of *The Story of the Irish Citizen Army*, which he had begun writing for another publisher, Maunsel & Co., the lines from *Julius Caesar*:

SEC. CIT: Answer every man directly.
FIRST CIT: Ay, and briefly.
FOURTH CIT: Ay, and wisely.
THIRD CIT: Ay, and truly, you were best.

The work drew deeply on Shakespeare's depiction of civil disturbance as well as of rival armies. With agony piled on to its completion in September, when the British Censor returned it to him for amendment with his longhand underscored on every page in red, green and blue pencil, it was finally revised in October, after which the Censor passed it at proof stage.

———◆◆◆———

His mother's feebleness began to assert itself over her will to live. She was now over eighty years of age, and had taken her daughter's death deeply to heart. Mick Casey was back in Abercorn Road. He had been discharged from the army because of a partial but worsening disability – arthritis in his right hand – on the basis of which he eventually qualified for a full pension, granted him in 1920, of twelve shillings a week. His discharge papers commended him on his sobriety, which when he strutted and boasted of this testimonial in the neighbourhood, must have raised an eyebrow or two. Mick's presence at home again aroused murderous feeling in O'Casey, especially when Mick would get his ailing mother up to help him settle down to sleep.

Maunsel & Co. paid O'Casey fifteen pounds advance for *The Story of the Citizen Army* – enough, he reckoned, with his mother's pension, to keep the pair of them for seven months. But Susan Casey's life was ebbing away quickly. O'Casey begins the justly celebrated and moving chapter of his autobiography called "Mrs Casside Takes a Holiday" with an account of his frantic need to cash the fifteen-pound cheque in time to buy her food to revive her strength – a hot-water bottle to keep her feet cosy, oranges to cool her hot tongue, beef tea. But when he had been fund-raiser, recruiting officer, treasurer, secretary of this and that, a functionary in a score or more of different organisations and a well-known local figure, perhaps it was stretching credulity to show himself, at the age of thirty-eight, ignorant of cashing a fifteen-pound cheque. Still, it is a glorious passage, as with great comi-tragic effect he projects his guilty feelings about his dying mother on to a gallimaufry of the hard-hearted commercial classes. The effect he wanted to give was that he, his mother, his sister and his brothers had been hard done by.

The rest of the chapter makes a fitting elegy, powerfully expressing the depth of his gratitude towards his mother and her selfless support of him. For thirty-eight years he had lived with her under the same roof, the only one of her children to have been with her all the time. He imbues his sense of loss with enormous depth of feeling and emotional truth, all the better for including in it some self-mocking awareness:

> His beginning of bravery wasn't too good . . . Self-pity had ambushed his hardy designs, and before he knew it, tears had welled from his eyes, and had splashed down on to the pale face so full of settled peace. The black eyes of her suddenly opened and, startled, stared up at his anxious face . . .
> – Ah! Jack, she murmured pitifully.

But facts, again, took a holiday. In his grief he excluded the rights of all others, including his two brothers who were still living, as well as Susan's grandchildren, to feel anything for themselves. He showed, like a jealous lover, almost inhuman possessiveness; "Life," he wrote, "had wasted all her fine possessions." And, "None, save he, could recognise her for what she was. . . . Who was there to weep for her going? The poor had precious little time or chance to weep."

This superior, even patronising attitude of his was resisted and resented by the rest of his family. It was as if he were saying, on the one hand, the Casey family were the victims of social forces over which they had no control: all they could do was to struggle, uselessly, against their fate. Yet on the other hand he contradicted this view in his bitter personal assessment of his three brothers and his sister – writing that they "were all four failures: no one was there to point a way further on from where they found themselves when they entered into personal and responsible life".

Of course he could not blame Susan's own narrowness of mental outlook for the failure of her children – and of himself up to that point – because, as he viewed it, it was only her courage which had enabled him to survive. It was a courage, moreover – and O'Casey never quite had honesty or perception enough to grasp or admit this – that was based upon prejudice, even bigotry, a Protestant conviction that deep down inside, somewhere, in spite of the conditions she had to struggle under, she was one of God's elect. It was this quality, carried on in her son, which brought out the best, but also the worst, in him.

From independent accounts it appears that O'Casey's control, both emotional and practical, over his mother's death and burial was far from total. He was not alone with her when she died. He did not bury her without assistance – the name "M. Casey" appears on the funeral records – while a former Volunteer, Joe Adams, sat up with him the night after Susan's death for the wake. He spent most of the night crying; according to his niece, he rose at one point, "draped a red cloth over a little table, set flowers on it, and placed the table next to the coffin". The publican's wife, Mrs Brady, who lived at the back of Abercorn Road, in Church Street, provided the sheets and the candlestick for Susan's wake: Mrs Brady who was "fond of the sup" was great friends with Susan because, according to a letter O'Casey wrote much later, "my mother took her part when Mrs Brady's childer abused their mother for making 'a show of them'. The children were, in a sense, right; but they didn't mind because the drink injured Mrs Brady, and hastened her end, but because when she was tight, it offended their growing bourgeois sense of respectability."

If the two versions of Susan Casey's death are set alongside one another, the picture of O'Casey that emerges is more fascinating and complex than he was perhaps himself ever able to show, for it can be seen how his emotions manipulated reality: sometimes the effect hit its target square and fair, sometimes went lamentably wide of the mark. "Target" is the operative word here – the by this time sixty-eight-year-old autobiographer was, in the contemplation of his thirty-eight-year-old former self, often keen to notch up points, pay off old scores, and redress the balance of former feelings of inadequacy or inequality.

The younger man turned to more immediate consolations after his mother's funeral, at which, incidentally, Isaac (Joseph) failed to arrive from Liverpool – he had not had time before the funeral to make the necessary travel arrangements – and from which the Revd Edward Griffin was another notable absentee. Griffin had retired from his rectorship the year before, and fallen seriously ill, becoming an invalid. But friends still saw O'Casey out walking often with Maire, who for the sake of propriety would sometimes take him to see a friend of hers, Susie O'Brien, who enabled them to be together on their own. Maire did not mind his careless manner of dressing, saying he was never unkempt or dirty. When his eyes were tired, she noted, he would crinkle them up, and sometimes would not recognise someone he knew on the other side of the street; yet he did notice, one day when they were out walking and Maire's sister and her boyfriend approached them, that Maire turned and hurried away from them, with him following. This humiliated him for days. Another time, when they were on the Glasnevin tram, the conductor, who knew Maire, came round for the fare and didn't ask for money but handed O'Casey two tickets – in return for a kindness Maire had shown one of his children at school. O'Casey was up in arms: "Does he not think I can pay my own fare and yours too? Do I look in need of charity?"

Maire called this the "sour pride he often talked about". It could be both a weakness and an embarrassment, she found. She criticised him later for misrepresenting his home: "In this way he was a bit two-faced. He had a thing about poverty. He liked to put on the Irishman's poor mouth." But she liked his continual talk and humour, with its often sarcastic turn. Outwardly abrasive, he was still driven by an inner passion. The loss of his mother had sharpened his need for another person, a need that sometimes, in the period immediately after her death, became obsessive. The pure sentiment of the songs was giving way, in a world less structured without his mother, to a dangerous restlessness of feeling.

In spite of the publication in April 1919 of *The Story of the Citizen Army*, and reviews in the *Irish Independent* and the *Irish Statesman*, his restlessness deepened as the year went on. From a letter he wrote to Maire in July, in a hand that had grown markedly less elaborate – the result of the Waterman – about a Sunday walk with his friend Joe Adams, it is clear that his political allegiances were being increasingly subjected to the alchemical action of his imagination. In Glasnevin village, he related, they visited a Protestant church

> reported to be the original site of a cell of Msoni Mopti – the patron of the district, and it is also the spot to which a loud-tongued tradition assigns the burial place of Robert Emmet . . . the church-yard was very interesting, evidently very ancient, but in a splendid state of preservation. Fanciful as ever, I seemed to see in the silent church an enlarged tomb in which every Sunday the dead had a meeting, and that we have been just in time to witness their exit, and their quiet and chill return to the surrounding graves that they had temporarily abandoned. Joe intercepted a little boy that wore on his breast a white medal . . . whom he asked to point out the place where Robert Emmett [sic] was buried. He shook his head and passed on. My God, said Joe, I suppose he never heard of Robert Emmett – I rebuffed Joe by murmuring "De mortuis nil nisi bonum [honour] . . ." so we bade farewell to the dead.

This Sunday communion with ghosts was followed, not by a Monday of hard work, to begin a new week, but a day, so he told Maire in the same letter, in which he wandered aimlessly about thinking of her, until heavy rain forced him to take shelter. His bitterness was such that he told her it would have been better had they never met, for now the "serpent of separation" was coiled round their hearts. He exhorted her to see other men: "Be kind to them . . . allow them to enjoy the pleasure of your personality." If she cannot give that joy to him, why should she deny it to others? And, he concluded, in a burst of overmastering self-pity: "Go, dear love, and danse, and let all who will admire you, for Sean will not be jealous, but proud of his dear love's charms" – almost hastening to add, "But I indeed am very lonely".

If he was still suffering from adolescent passion at the advanced age of thirty-nine, one part of him was mature enough to be working, goaded not only by Maire's keeping him at arm's length, but perhaps also affected by feelings of insecurity at his mother's absence. He made a radical new departure. He had begun in a dark blue notebook the year before a dialogue, called *The Crimson Cornkrakes*, on the subject of Bernard Shaw. The characters are identified only by initials:

R. There is nothing solid in his writings. He treats of things that nobody is interested in.
J. He treats of things in which everybody ought to be interested.

In the same exercise book he had written an outline for a play, *The Harvest Festival*, which he was now engaged in turning into a first draft. But this was by no means his only effort at playwriting. He was determined to put to use the meagre sum he had earned from Maunsel & Co. – a fortune to him, as he had observed – to "create things out of his own life". He was beginning to do things for himself: "pictures . . . that would be worth hanging in the Hallway for other people to see".

———◆———

But even the most modest of hallways, where he had won local recognition with his acting, ballad-mongering and political haranguing, would not take his first picture, *The Frost in the Flower*. The O'Toole Club was still the focus of much of his social energy, and he and his friends, notably Cahill, had their own clique. But they were an older generation now, and O'Casey was visibly intolerant of the younger men, especially of their cold nationalist aspirations, stripped of all the cultural embellishments he loved. They were potential gunmen of another breed: "What are they fighting for Ireland for," he snarled at them once, "when they can't even speak their own language?"

The tactful Catholic schoolteacher tried to get him to moderate his temper, but often took the side of the younger members. Cahill also attempted to persuade O'Casey to change his opinion of Mick, pointing out how often in the past his brother had supported him; he also found himself at odds with O'Casey's impatience with his old friend Griffin, who had faithfully helped the Caseys in a variety of ways over many years. O'Casey would not listen to Cahill and went his own obstinate way. Worse, he found in the teacher's modesty and his shortcomings, together with the raconteur's wit and richness of character he displayed, a subject for satire; this portrait he swiftly set down, with little skill as yet in plotting or development of theme. He called his play *The Frost in the Flower*, the hurtful implications for his friend being clear even in its title: it was understandable that Cahill should have been wounded by this onslaught on his "indecision and failure to make anything of himself".

Later O'Casey described the main character in the play as "full of confidence on gigantic questions he was never called upon to touch", but "timid as a new-born mouse over simple questions concerning himself". Betraying professional insensitivity even in very amateur circumstances, O'Casey submitted the play to the O'Toole Club. His old friend Paddy McDonnell reacted: "We wouldn't touch it at all, it was too personal." This first, handwritten version of *The Frost in the Flower* O'Casey also sent to the Abbey Theatre, where it was rejected sometime in 1919 – returned, he says, with a note saying "not far from being a good play", but that one of the main characters had the tiresome habit of being too critical. Neither it nor a second version, which he re-submitted after re-drafting it, survives from these years.

But he had made a beginning. He continued until late summer writing *The Harvest Festival*, willingly swopping the torments of "splashing his thoughts over what he had seen and heard", for his earlier frustrated attempts "to form Ireland's life". It was a significant advance and, like previous stages, one reached slowly and with pain. But in the formal attempt at playwriting on which he was now engaged, his choice of subject matter lagged far behind actual experience: he had returned to the strike and lock-out of 1913.

Possibly it brought him a sense of security, to go back five or six years. The world of the past was simpler than the one he had to contend with in the present, and, as he demonstrated later on an epic scale in his autobiography, the past could be arranged to fulfil his deepest wishes. Although he had thought about beginning the play before Susan Casey's death, one of *The Harvest Festival*'s main successes is the life it brings to the character of the hero's widowed mother, Mrs Rocliffe. Through her, O'Casey brought his own mother back to life, although he did not yet have the gift of rounding out a character as he later did in reincarnating Susan Casey, conferring upon her immortality. But, as the first of the line, an often wooden prototype, Mrs Rocliffe has an authenticity in some of her speeches which shows the care O'Casey took to base his characters on real relationships, in this case his own relationship with his mother:

I wish to God this strike was over, I'm never easy in me mind, the way Jack does be talkin' about things. He has such a terrible temper, though he was always very gentle with me; an' if he got into any trouble, I suppose they'd take the old-age pension off me; not that it'ud be much loss, though we'd miss it now, with nothing else comin' into the house. I hope he'll be in soon; he knows I want to go to the Harvest Festival tonight, an' he promised he'd be in time to get his dinner & tea so that I could go. [*She begins to sweep the floor.*] I don't think it'll be long till Higgins turns Turk on us, it's the long, sour face he had on him this mornin' when I went in for a loaf an' some tea an' sugar, because he knew there was no money comin' into the house, an' maybe, wouldn't be for a long time. An' the winter comin' on us too, as well. It would be better for me to be dead than to be sufferin' like this at the end of me days.

He also vividly depicts through Jack Rocliffe his own estrangement from the Church, putting forward, with a tolerance he learned from Larkin, the Church's own conviction, through the mouthpiece of the Rector, the Revd T. Jennings, whom he based closely on Griffin. Indeed O'Casey's defence of Jennings's philosophy – against Rocliffe's choice of Labour over God's law – clearly re-enacts arguments they had at the time. The Rector is able to put forward his argument with greater human conviction than Jack:

Oh, John, you wrong us, you wrong us. You know we sympathize with the poor, with God's own poor. But we cannot escape from the existence of poverty. "The poor we shall always have with us" – the Master says so, and we must, we must believe it. It is our duty to preach patience and submission to God's will to those that sit in the darkness of poverty, for we are told that these light afflictions will work an exceeding weight of glory. And you know, John, that the arms of the Church are ever around the poor; praying with and for them always, advising them constantly, and helping them whenever we can . . . But our ways are not your ways, John –

But Jack is not convinced by the Rector that violence will accomplish nothing, and that the real obstacle to a good social life is sin or selfishness. He throws himself into the workers' struggle, when, as happened on "Bloody Sunday", they clash with the police. Choosing between attending his local Harvest Festival and the street affray, he disappoints his mother, and the Rector, by asserting his new-found class-consciousness and leaving them. It is "the readin' that has ruined him, the readin', the readin'," says Mrs Rocliffe: "after a while when he began readin' I noticed a change in him." Attacking lorries loaded with flour and driven by scabs, Jack is shot at and meets a hero's death.

The play then moves, in a third act, to vindicate his life of sacrifice, as his mother and the Rector – Jennings now becomes the earlier ritual-loving Revd Fletcher in disguise, with his local quarrels at St Barnabas' brought to the fore in the drama – consort together to have Jack's body properly buried: "I cannot turn a man away because he may be a Fenian, a Trades' Unionist or an Orangeman." However the Rector, finally intimidated by the powerful interests ranged against him, has to back down, and turn away Rocliffe's cortège. Later O'Casey recognised the Rector as being the only worthwhile character in the play.

The Harvest Festival showed O'Casey's competent stage craft emerging; the use of off-stage violence, with its repercussions for those on stage, was something he had clearly studied both in Synge's *Playboy of the Western World* and Ibsen's *An Enemy of the People*; the settings were imaginatively changed, the climaxes neatly, if predictably, handled. But the play had overriding weaknesses. There were far too many two-handed scenes, a flaw common to beginners, while O'Casey's susceptibility to propaganda and abstract ideas ruined the central character of Rocliffe, his *alter ego*, or a projection of what he himself would like to have been (and yet could not, while remaining alive). Rocliffe has completely swallowed Larkin's gospel of discontent, and regurgitates it in swollen, humourless chunks:

TOM: And this is the glorious Brotherhood about which you are always preachin'.

JACK: No Brotherhood can exist between you and me. You are a link in the chain that fetters me, & the sooner you are smashed to pieces the sooner I shall be free.

TOM: And you call the employers beasts, an' what in the name of God are you?

JACK: A claw in the foot and a fang in the mouth of the great Beast of Labour. But such as you are a muzzle on Labour's mouth, and a sheathe on its claw, so that we are rent and cannot rend again; are torn asunder and cannot injure the power that destroys us.

The Harvest Festival contains no mention of the Gaelic League, or Irish nationalism: no gods or holy myths are yet in evidence to tempt O'Casey's profanity. The social chaos, or "chassis", he predicates, caused by rival systems, is a very dull state compared to that he was later to depict as caused by complicated and paradoxical individuals, whose desires or ideals expose them to ridicule. To this extent the cartoons which he sent in 1916 to his Republican friends in Frongoch – Cahill touching up a female Volunteer fund-raiser, himself performing antic somersaults to avoid bullets during the revolt – more truly anticipated his comic genius than the valuable exercise of writing *The Harvest Festival*. Still, he was learning the hard way, and one of the first lessons he learned – a lesson which much later, unfortunately, he forgot, or wilfully ignored – was that he would not succeed with a play which had socialism as its central theme.

The Harvest Festival is also revealing in a way O'Casey did not intend, for in spite of his trying to make it vindicate Jack Rocliffe – and possibly to justify himself for not taking a more active role both in the lock-out and the Easter Revolt of 1916 – the play is really more a vindication of his mother's protectiveness: finally it seems to have been Susan Casey's voice which had swayed him from taking part. The universality of the views which O'Casey puts into Mrs Rocliffe's mouth, and which he later developed so movingly, was surely his own mother's. When Rocliffe's "butty", Bill, tries to cheer Mrs Rocliffe up by saying they have disposed of the scab who shot her son and flung his body in the river, she answers, "I don't know, Bill, I don't know; maybe he, too, was the only son of some poor, old, heartbroken mother."

O'Casey owed his life to his mother in a much wider sense than the many years he existed under her practical love and care: he owed it to her because her broader humanity protected him from his own idealism. This is why he had a weakness for disillusionment, a weakness which now had a further motivating force, beyond the basic one that disillusionment helps you to survive. He hoped some-where to find, behind all the tempting illusions of this world, his solid old mother again.

After sending off the closely handwritten sheets of *The Harvest Festival*, fifty-six in all, with "S. Ó Cathasaigh" on the title-page, to the Abbey Theatre, O'Casey's love for Maire began to take on a new dimension of suffering. Without resources or professional confidence to back him up, he knew of no other way to make her capitulate than to inflict his own pain on her, intimidate her through guilt – while protesting that the very last thing he desired was to harm her in any way. Emotional exhaustion – perhaps from the effort of finishing *The Harvest Festival* – made him write more of his naïvely felt songs which, when they were later collected and published in *Windfalls*, were described by Samuel Beckett as "the model palace of a dyna-miter's leisure moments".

He had no one, now, to talk to at home, for he avoided Mick whenever possible, while his nephew John, who had lived for a while at Abercorn Road after Susan's death, had moved on to stay with his married sister Susan. Mick was now fifty-two and his mother's death had had no reforming effect on his drinking. He still believed in reincarnation: during John Beaver's stay he told him that one day he would return as a goat and butt him. O'Casey and Mick quarrelled frequently over Mick's dog, a lively, sturdily built Irish terrier which became friendly with O'Casey, but which Mick would force to crouch before him to show how superior man was to the lower animals.

In May 1919 O'Casey had written to Maire, in spite of his atheistic convictions, "I hope you did not forget to pray for me last night; remember me always in your prayers, I beseech you, my gentle Maire. May God lift upon you the Light of His countenance now and forever." Later when he wrote about her in his autobiography he spent several pages justifying the stance he took against her religion, attacking the clerical advice she was given. Yet Maire later claimed that the local priest was extremely sympathetic to the problem:

My mother did speak to Father Flood about my relationship with Sean and told him that she considered it wrong for a Catholic girl to be going around with a man of little or no religious persuasion. But the priest did not advise her to stop me seeing Sean, nor did he ever advise me to stop seeing him. He said to my mother, "there's good in the worst of us and bad in the best of us". He told me to try and bring Sean to Benediction if I ever got the chance. He felt this would help to convert him.

In spite of their differences in faith they had been happy that summer, meeting far out in the country, so they might, as he put it, escape from prying eyes, and walk the hedge-lined roads: "She listened – how well she listened to all he said, to all he quoted." Enchanted by her presence he had written a poem of three stanzas which began:

> The summer sun is tightly folding
> Dear nature in a warm embrace
> With joy his ardent love beholding
> All mirrored in her flushing face;
> So, Mary, when I'm fondly gazing
> Upon your face so richly fair,
> Your tender glance sweet hope is raising,
> For me deep love seems pictured there.
> The seasons shall forget to come,
> The summer skies shall ne'er be blue,
> And voiceful birds in Spring be dumb
> When my heart shall lose its love for you.

and to which he added the note, "Maire – Dear, Gentle, Beloved – I offer this little effort to you, not because of any merit therein, but as an expression from a heart pressed full with ardent love for you. Maire, I love you. SEAN."

In late September, either of her own volition or through her family putting pressure on her, Maire broke off with Sean. At first he did not take it too seriously. It had happened before that, expecting to meet her, he had received an agonised little note saying she could never see him again. Several weeks had passed, he had withdrawn into his own company, then she had written again asking him to see her and they had resumed their meetings.

This time, however, there was no recantation. September passed into October, October into November. Waiting to hear about his scripts at the Abbey, O'Casey prepared for possible publication a little collection of his published articles on nationalism, the Gaelic language and Irish labour which he called *Three Shouts on a Hill*. He sent the collection to Adelphi Terrace, London, where Bernard Shaw was living at the time, to ask the great man to contribute an introduction, but no answering cry was received, only an ungracious grumble. He liked, Shaw said, "the forword and afterword much better than the shouts, which are prodigiously overwritten". Shaw was impatient, too, with O'Casey's Gaelic leanings. To the request for a preface he flatly said no: "get published for your own sake, not for mine." (He received one such letter a fortnight.) And he threw in some parting advice: "You ought to work out your position positively & definitely. This objecting to everyone else is Irish, but useless."

At the O'Toole Club, where he still went, although less frequently, they saw how short-fused O'Casey's temper was growing in Maire's absence. Group feeling, being sensitive to a man when he was down, focused unhappily on him when they had one of the mock battles they held to keep in training for the eventual war to win Irish independence. Actual clashes between Republican forces and the police and military were becoming more frequent towards the end of 1919, and sums of money were pouring in from the United States to boost the Republican cause. Lloyd George's postwar coalition came under great pressure to resolve the crisis without resorting again to the open warfare of 1916.

One Sunday night the O'Tooles started a mock attack at Seville Place, barring the doors and windows and making O'Casey the "enemy" who had to try and break his way in. Finding the resistance strong, O'Casey grew furious and tried even harder. When he thrust his way in through a window they beat him back with sticks and brushes, but he wouldn't give up and finally broke through. By then he was seething with rage, which he turned on all of them: "He cursed us all and the language was terrible," said Paddy McDonnell. Later O'Casey was "brought up" before the O'Toole disciplinary committee for using bad language, but not expelled from the Club.

Some degree of persecution may have been essential to him, but how much could he stand? Almost daily he was writing tortured letters to Maire, appealing to her to see him again. A few days before Christmas it was clear to him that everything was finished between them – she had written yet again beseeching him to accept her announcement that she had given him up. He decided then that he had better finally sever the relationship on his own part, and on Monday 22 December he wrote to her:

My Dearly treasured Deeply loved Darling Maire:
    I'm afraid that you will assume from the letters that I have written before this that I am primarily selfish. But love is always

selfish. I cling to you because it is life and joy to me. I write to you because this action gives me joy too. I'm sure for your sake I should do neither one nor the other.

You have said that my letters upset you terribly, and yet does it not seem that I have been, and am, indifferent to your – anguish? But I am not wholly indifferent, and if you still wish it, I shall write to you no more, and will from now seek to forget you. If ceasing to love should make you happy; if forgetfulness of me should make you happy – then try to cease from loving – and forget.

I know you will not think too harshly of me for manifesting my love for you in such a passionate and persistent manner. It was impossible that I should have loved in any other way my truly beautiful and sensitively cultured darling –

Underlining, unusually for O'Casey, his sexual deprivation, he then went on to praise her physical attractions in Solomonic terms: her temples like pomegranates, her breasts like two fawns that were twins of a roe . . . But self-justification, for him, always lurked in the shadow of self-hatred: he felt horror and detestation at forcing his love on her, yet if he measured his stature against that of his rivals he could not "help thinking that I am worthy of offering you the full". In some ways his view of love was similar to his view of class – feelings of inferiority rapidly transformed themselves into feelings of superiority.

After more assertions of love he acceded to her wish for them to cease seeing each other, concluding, "I can only do this because I love you dearly . . . it is not Fate neither is it the will of God that thus separates us, but the tyranny of old-fashioned thought that has come between. My love forever and forever shall be yours."

To alleviate his misery, he had but one hope left, his plays. The one in particular about the lay teacher in a Christian Brothers' School, which ended in a big party given for him which then turned out to be his crowning humiliation: O'Casey had a high opinion of this work, *The Frost in the Flower*, and high hopes of a production. It was based so closely on the life and people he knew.

He passed an exceptionally lonely Christmas – even then his least favourite time of year: it was the second after his mother's death. Dominating him still was his feeling for her: "I thought the world vanished when my mother left me." Now the shock was being transformed into a permanent sense of loss.

But there was hope, as there always is, in the New Year, in the new decade, although it could not be far from his mind that, a few months after the decade began, his fortieth birthday would fall.

He was little prepared for the return by the Abbey Theatre of both his scripts at the end of January: "We are sorry to have to return these plays for the author's work interests us, but we don't think either would succeed on the stage."

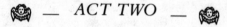 — *ACT TWO* —

On the Run

1921 – 1927

I had to live on, live on, and fight and like
Yeats's red cock, even lifted the head, clapped
the wings and crew.

7

THE SHAFT WHICH FLIES IN DARKNESS

No letters either from or to O'Casey have been preserved from the period February 1920 to June 1921. In the wake of his mother's death he abandoned his occasional journalism and withdrew into greater anonymity than before; nursing and moulding the emotions which remained locked inside him, he was practising a desperate patience. The loyal Protestant had gone; vanished, too, was the devoted son, the nationalist, the labour agitator and polemicist; the gentleman wooer, dallying and versifying, had been crushed. What was to take the place of these personae?

The letter of rejection he had received from the Abbey Theatre contained encouragement, especially for *The Frost in the Flower*: the reader had found its characters more lifelike than those in *The Harvest Festival*. Its faults were that it was "set too much in the one key throughout, and the endless bickerings of the family end by becoming wearisome. The decision of the hero to throw up his job is too well prepared for and does not come as a surprise." O'Casey had sent them an earlier version of the same play, and this on the whole they had preferred, "except for the character of Shawn who was stilted and who is in this [second] version quite natural, though the author seems to have gone to the other extreme and made him almost common-place". The implication was plain, and depressing: he was not even improving.

The report on *The Harvest Festival*, on whose text O'Casey was to draw many years later for *Red Roses for Me* and for *The Drums of Father Ned*, contained sound advice which, in his determination to continue writing plays, he took deeply to heart:

This play is interestingly conceived but not well executed. It is seldom dramatic and many of the characters suffer from being too typical of their class or profession (Williamson, Sir J. Vane, for instance). They are conventional conceptions, as unreal as the

"Stage Irishman" of 20 years ago. If the author has got these typical figures firmly planted in his imagination we should advise him to try to replace them by figures drawn as accurately as possible from his own experience.

The failure of his writing projects accelerated the deterioration of relations between O'Casey and his brother Mick. The ex-sapper Mick had begun to receive his partial disability pension of twelve shillings per week, and now only needed work of an irregular kind to top up his income, which meant he could fuel his contentiousness by heavy drinking. The brothers had never got on well and the years brought no growth of tolerance in either. Mick would try to force drinks on Sean, and once, as John Casey alleged, when stopped by the police for disorderly behaviour, gave Sean's name instead of his own, with the consequence that O'Casey later spent a night in a cell.

Both resented, in differing ways, the degree to which Sean had been supported by Mick over the past twenty years; and their mother was no longer there to act as buffer between them. There were various quarrels over Mick's Irish terrier, and the dog left Abercorn Road. Sean lived there for over a year after his mother's death. In what must have been the winter months of late 1920 Mick, according to his brother, had dwindled into a wreck:

> His glittering gate had always been the door of a public-house, and drunkenness was to him an inward sign of outward majesty and strength . . . Paint him as he was twenty golden years ago, and paint him as he is now, and one would have a horrifying picture of a worker Dorian Gray.

Had it not been for his mother, Sean claimed, he would have choked Mick to death long before; but now it was different: "no mother to wail, to plead, to sigh her heart half away from herself". The brothers were clashing almost nightly, and Mrs Cunningham, downstairs in Abercorn Road, where the children had once kept O'Casey awake, complained she could not sleep.

One night, according to O'Casey, when he had just received payment for an article and for once had some money, Mick returned home late. Stumbling up the stairs, with the "raucous beery voice forcing itself to shape a song", he deliberately knocked the ink bottle off the table where Sean was working. He launched into a vituperative assault: "– Writin', be God, again! murmured the blurred voice of his brother; some fellas are able to give themselves airs! Scholar, is it? Scholar, me arse!"

Twenty-three years they had lived together in Abercorn Road, and Mick – apart from his absences in the army – had been a main source of the family income. But O'Casey was in no mood, later, to spare him. Prince Hal was rejecting Falstaff – prior to refashioning him as some of his greatest characters: "– Who d'ye think y'are, eh? were sodden words borne to his ear by a gust of rotting breath . . . while the wobbling mouth slobbered out a black rosary of curses, many of the soiled words slimy with self-pity." Sean barged into Mick's chest with his shoulder, and sent him crashing to the floor, where he stayed in a drunken stupor. In his fortieth year O'Casey was leaving home for the very first time.

O'Casey's depiction of his brother as in the last stages of alcoholic decay has been much contested. Tom Casey's son, Kit, indignantly repudiated it, pointing out that O'Casey only had the courage to publish such an account after Mick's death – he died in 1947, aged eighty-one, while the relevant volume of O'Casey's autobiography, *Inishfallen Fare Thee Well*, was not published until 1949 – and never said anything derogatory about him in his lifetime. Moreover, Kit Casey claimed, Mick "was responsible for all the wit in the first three plays".

Other relations attested to the fact that Mick was "never stupidly drunk", as some of them put it, and that he could always hold his liquor. His neighbours and friends saw no malice in him, and several insisted he never became obnoxious. Perhaps a truer picture of him would be as a pint-size Falstaff than as the drunken Caliban O'Casey depicted. In any event, O'Casey moved out. Just before Christmas 1920, he went to live at 35 Mountjoy Square, where he shared a room with Michael Mullen, an old friend from the Jim Larkin days. Like O'Casey, Mullen had written for the *Irish Worker* – twenty-seven articles in all, mostly about the illegal stuffing of ballot boxes. Far from being a Dubliner, Mullen had been born in the Aran Islands; his mother, a school teacher, was, so O'Casey wrote, "a hearty and insistent lass for the drink". Mullen at thirty was near-sighted – "as bad as I am now", recalled O'Casey at the age of eighty – and of an "odd slouching appearance . . . among the girls of Liberty Hall he was known as Pig's Cheek Face, and the nick-name was very suitable, for he had the curious wide-spreading cheeks of the animal though it was well-relieved by the most lovely, large, limpid dark eyes I've ever seen in a man's head". He spoke Gaelic fluently and was a prodigious worker; he had helped organise the Citizen Army.

O'Casey had now, as he reckoned, moved into the Dublin slums: he had become a true tenement-dweller, living in a decayed Georgian house in the same conditions as the 20,000 families he observed "wriggling together like worms in a putrid mass in horror-filled one-room tenements". "A long, lurching row of discontented incurables", he called the houses of Mountjoy Square,

> smirched with the age-long marks of ague, fevers, cancers, and consumption, the soured tears of little children, and the sighs of disappointed newly-married girls . . . the pillars were shaky, their stuccoed bloom long since peeled away, and they looked like crutches keeping the trembling doors standing on their palsied feet.

Yet, again, there were witnesses to the effect that the houses in Mountjoy Square, while shabby and let in multiple tenancies, were far from being in the condition O'Casey described.

Mullen's own account of 35 Mountjoy Square is not so bleak. He and O'Casey shared a small "return" room at the back on the ground floor; the two other large rooms on that floor housed "Fred" (his real name was Schweppe), a quiet, entirely reliable fellow deeply involved in the Republican cause. In the back room lived Fred's family, while the front room was used for putting up gunmen on the run from the authorities. This Sinn Fein "safe house" was raided eight times, by police, British soldiers or Black and Tans, while Mullen lived there. At one time, he said, the neighbours had the idea that O'Casey was on the run, and tried to be particularly nice to him.

The room-mates got on well. Although Mullen was a devout Catholic, went to daily Mass, and was "desperately superstitious and afraid of hell", he and O'Casey never quarrelled. They would discuss literature, the Irish language and politics for hours on end; Mullen said that O'Casey knew Burns, Shaw and Shakespeare backwards, but had never read a word by Swift (which was untrue). O'Casey read him his own plays, although Mullen preferred "fireside homespun folk stories to theatrical fireworks".

The two men would go to bed at eleven every night and talk for an hour before going to sleep. O'Casey slept in the middle of the room in a collapsible bed – their quarters were quite cramped, but with no wasted space. In the morning O'Casey woke first, singing a song by Burns. He had a "sweet soft voice", like that of a robin – "as a redbreast has a sweetness of its own, so did O'Casey".

Through Mullen, O'Casey became involved in the Larkin cause

again. Jim Larkin's sister, Delia, lived in a flat in Mountjoy Square. A forceful woman, she had helped educate her brother on feminist issues, had organised relief for women and children during the great lock-out, and had remained active as a trade-union organiser. Larkin was still in America raising funds to rebuild the union, although his wife and children had stayed behind in Dublin. Another resident of Charles Street, on the south side of Mountjoy Square, was the Revd Edward Griffin, now an invalid and nearing the end of his life. Dorset Street and Innisfallen Parade were only a stone's throw away; O'Casey had thus moved from the securely working-class area of his mother's life, near the Tolka and the East Wall, back into the grander but socially more volatile area where they had lived in his early childhood when his father was still alive.

During this time, in the aftermath of the First World War, the Republican leaders were strengthening their hand, and demonstrating that strength in the general election of December 1918, when seventy-three Sinn Fein candidates were returned, as against twenty-six Unionists; the Irish Parliamentary Party won only six seats. One of the new MPs, returned for St Patrick's Division, Dublin, was Constance Markiewicz, the first woman ever elected to the House of Commons. Always still, in O'Casey's eyes, "in hysterical terror", she had been converted to Roman Catholicism in 1917; later she served a term in Holloway Prison in London for her alleged part in a "German plot" and was still in prison when elected.

The Sinn Fein MPs did not take their seats at Westminster, and in January 1919 proclaimed themselves as the Dáil Éireann – Assembly of Ireland. De Valera, arrested the previous year, escaped from Lincoln Prison in February, and was elected President in April. Sinn Fein was declared illegal in August, and the Dáil in September, but the Irish hoped American pressure might still influence Britain to yield peacefully to their demands; the British themselves, hesitating between repression and conciliation, avoided a military solution.

In early 1920, however, the Irish Republican Army, as the reconstituted Irish Volunteers and Citizen Army now called themselves, began insurgency operations. Not with the foolhardy heroism of 1916, but in flying columns of fifteen to thirty strong, they planned to deliver disruptive blows on selected targets. By these they hoped to render Ireland ungovernable. In London a weak coalition government headed by Lloyd George, constantly under attack in Parliament and in the press, responded by forming two special forces outside the regular army, and a demoralised Royal Irish Constabulary: these were the Black and Tans, recruited mainly from among ex-soldiers in England and so named because their mixed dress of khaki coats, black trousers and caps brought to mind a well-known pack of Tipperary foxhounds; and a constabulary unit called the Auxiliaries, comprised of young ex-officers. As these special forces were largely undisciplined, and their enemy more or less unidentifiable, they became as much terrorists in their efforts to break the IRA and its sympathisers as the IRA were against them. A series of savage reprisals followed, described by O'Casey as "the Dublin slums at war with the British Empire", although the common people were generally more spectators than combatants – caught, as P. S. O'Hegarty wrote in 1924, between "the devil of the Auxiliary's pistol and incendiary bombs and the deep sea of the Irish Volunteer's home-made bomb".

On 20 February 1920, after the shooting of a policeman, a curfew was imposed on Dublin: it was on a night during this curfew that O'Casey set the drama of his departure from Abercorn Road, portraying himself as constantly in fear of being stopped and arrested in the street. However, the celebrated raid on 35 Mountjoy Square, which O'Casey depicted twice – first in *The Shadow of a Gunman* and later in his autobiography – happened on Maundy Thursday and Good Friday of 1921, and as O'Casey lived only six months or so in Mountjoy Square, he could not have gone there from Abercorn Road before late 1920.

In Mullen's own account of the 1921 raid, written in Irish and published thirty-four years later, the Black and Tans struck at about two thirty a.m. on 24 March. They broke the plate glass of the front door but were unable to smash down the door itself, bolted with iron at top and bottom. In the front room of the house two wanted IRA men were sleeping, one in bed with a child of the household; woken by the noise and the flashing armoured-car headlights, they crept to the back, where Fred was waiting to let them out into the yard. Then the Tans noticed something – a shadow, perhaps, of one of the fleeing men.

Mullen remarks that O'Casey grew absolutely terrified – "terror in the shape of a man" (admitting that he himself was not the hero Cuchulain at the gap either) – and begged him to unlock the door so the Tans wouldn't think he and Mullen were hiding. Mullen disagreed; it would be more suspicious, he thought, if the door were unlocked, as it might give them the idea the two men had stolen in there from somewhere else. O'Casey, petrified with fear, rushed in the wrong direction to find the door and fell over Mullen's bed, scratching and clawing at the wall above it.

In O'Casey's version of the raid, he is living alone on the ground floor at the front of the house; he sees, from his darkened room, the searchlight gliding up and down the street, he hears the party break down the front door and rush up the stairs and down. A large shed at the back of the house is broken into – a carpenter's shop used, he believes, for the manufacture of explosives. His door, left unlocked so as not to be battered down by the intruders, is opened and Mrs Ballynoy, the wife of another tenant, lets herself into the room, where he sees that "A shoulder-band of the overall had slipped down, and she had saucily drawn an arm out of it altogether so that near half of her body to the waist was bare, and he saw a breast, rather lovely in the light of a candle, looking like a golden cup with a misty ruby in its centre." O'Casey then comments, adding absurdity to likely improbability, "In the midst of death we are in life".

The lady's husband, it later turns out, is himself the arsenalist, wounded when he tries to stop the raiders entering his shed. A timid, insignificant man, Ballynoy stands up in the lorry as he is driven away, "clouts" of blood dripping from his hands as he shouts, "Up th' Republic". In the pattern of other sexual adventures in his autobiography, O'Casey's lust is thwarted as Mrs Ballynoy flees naked, clutching her flowered overall, up the stairs. While this is how he later – and fancifully – elaborates the incident, at the time what engaged him more was the plot of what became his first play to be staged, *The Shadow of a Gunman*, set (as he has it) in May 1920.

Mullen's testimony is closer to the play: the Tans came to their room, he says, where one shone a torch in, asking who was there. Mullen replied, the two of them asleep. Finally they took away Fred and one of the young men whom they had caught, alleging he was making bombs. Mullen went to make tea, while the other man on the run returned from outside, with cuts from climbing over the walls. Returning to O'Casey, Mullen found him still bothered: "I've got the minute book of the Citizen Army here," he told Mullen. "*She* asked me to look after it." (The book could have been lent by Delia Larkin; in *The Shadow of a Gunman* the hero hunts feverishly for a possibly dangerous piece of evidence.) O'Casey went out and hid the incriminating book, possibly under a floorboard in the hall, before the owner of the house, furious at the broken door and windows, arrived.

While he was in Mountjoy Square, when his money ran out, O'Casey was employed by Delia Larkin as a janitor in the old Forester's Hall, 10 Langrishe Place. He worked at cleaning and organising the hall for concerts and plays; and gathering funds "for Jim Larkin when he returned", knowing the "opposition Jim would meet when he came home from the self-centred, conventional, 'hero-frightened' leaders of the Irish Labour Movement". O'Casey was paid thirty shillings a week for this work, meanwhile acting the part of a cockney burglar in a production of *Special Pleading*, by Bernard Duffy. Daily he contemplated from the hall, which had been both a church and a Methodist chapel, the terrace from which Bella had been evicted with her five children after Beaver's death.

In America, Larkin had in 1919 been sentenced, in the wave of anti-Bolshevik feeling which swept the States, to ten years' penal servitude for what the court described as "criminal syndicalism". A committee was formed in Dublin to agitate for his release from Sing Sing; O'Casey later served for a time as its secretary. The activity hardly interrupted his efforts to replace with his own experience the stage stereotypes in the plays he was writing.

During 1920 and in early 1921 he completed his third full-length play, *The Crimson in the Tricolour*, on the struggle between Sinn Fein and labour. He described it as

a "play of ideas" moulded on Shaw's style. It had in it a character posed on A. Griffith, a Labour Leader, mean & despicable, posed on whomsoever you can guess & the "noble proletarian" in it was later "The Covey" in the *Plough & the Stars* [The Covey quotes from *John Bull's Other Island*], as was a carpenter who developed into "Fluther" [Fluther Good in *The Plough and the Stars*].

The "Labour Leader" was William O'Brien, who had usurped Larkin's post as General Secretary of the ITGWU, and whom O'Casey elsewhere described as "the big sharp shit".

O'Casey moved away from Mountjoy Square two or three weeks after the raid, which had left him going round in circles. "I wasn't lonely for him," Mullen commented on his departure. By the end of June 1921 he had changed his address to 422 North Circular Road, where a letter from Seamus O'Concubhair (James O'Connor), an old Republican friend and former Red Hand hurler, reached him. "Drifting", O'Casey called this period of his life. He had written to O'Concubhair on the question of a faulty will, a problem affecting another lodger at 422, John Moore, who lived with his family in the flat above O'Casey's new room. "The writing of the Will" engrossed O'Casey's imagination until, several years later, he made use of it in the plot of *Juno and the Paycock*.

In the North Circular Road he now lived on his own.

The handwritten script of *The Crimson in the Tricolour*, which Mullen took along to the Abbey for O'Casey, was kept by the theatre for longer than the two previous scripts. Lennox Robinson, the director and playwright, who was responsible for the day-to-day management of the Abbey, wrote to O'Casey to say that they had lost it, and O'Casey, who had no copy, prepared himself to write out another version. Robinson then found the script, which relieved O'Casey and raised his hopes of the play's being performed. These were further sustained by a detailed critique from Lady Gregory – at seventy still co-director, with Yeats, of the Abbey – which Robinson copied out for O'Casey:

"The Crimson in the Tricolour" (a very good name). This is a puzzling play – extremely interesting. Mrs Budrose is a jewel and her husband a good setting for her. I don't see any plot in it, unless the Labour unrest culminating in the turning off of the lights at the meeting may be called one. It is the expression of ideas that makes it interesting (besides feeling that the writer has something in him). But we could not put it on while the Revolution is still unaccomplished – it might hasten the Labour attack on Sinn Fein, which ought to be kept back till the fight with England is over and the new Government has had time to show what it can do. I think Eileen's rather disagreeable flirtation with O'Regan should be cut – their first entrance – or rather exit – or both, it seems to be leading to something that doesn't come. In Act II a good deal of O'Regan and Nora should be cut. In Act III almost all of the O'Malley and Eileen part should be cut. The end is, I think, good, the entry of the workmen, and Fagan and Tim Tracy. I feel that there is no personal interest worth developing – but that with as much as possible of those barren parts cut, we might find a possible play of ideas in it. I suggest that (with the author's leave) it would be worth typing the play at the Theatre's expense with or without those parts. For it is impossible to go through it again – or show it, or have a reading of it while in handwriting.

The following Friday at eight thirty p.m. O'Casey met Robinson for the first time. This had few immediate consequences, except for the typing of the manuscript. But O'Casey's enthusiasm must have been kindled, and he began to see more plays. Joseph Holloway, who kept a daily record of what went on at the Abbey, later recorded that O'Casey told him he had liked Daniel Corkery's *The Labour*

Leader, which dealt with Larkin and the 1913 lock-out. He had also seen James Stephens's *The Wooing of Julia Elizabeth*, set in a tenement, which was first performed in August 1920.

The Abbey Theatre in the 1920s

While *The Crimson in the Tricolour* awaited a final verdict, O'Casey wrote *The Seamless Coat of Kathleen*; this allegorical tale was printed in the Republican weekly *Poblacht na h'Éireann* on 29 March 1922. ★ O'Casey also sent a one-act dramatic version of it to Robinson, who swiftly rejected it. The "coat" of the title referred to the nominal unity of the new but highly controversial Irish Free State, product of the treaty negotiated by Lloyd George with the provisional Republican government headed by Griffith, Collins and a reluctant de Valera which had put an end to the Anglo-Irish war. To call the coat "seamless" was ironic, because the leaders of the rival Irish factions – Free State supporters on the one side, Irregulars or Diehards on the other – were organising for open conflict, and it must have come as little surprise to O'Casey to have his play declined by the Abbey directors at such a sensitive moment as "too definite a piece of propaganda for us to do". They asked if there was any chance of O'Casey's getting it done at Liberty Hall.

Patience was a necessary attribute for the playwright: in June 1922 Yeats reported on *The Crimson in the Tricolour*:

★ Later he mistakenly gave the name of the play as *The Robe of Rosheen*, stating it was published in *The Plain People*; but this was another early piece, which O'Casey had apparently forgotten.

I find this discursive play very hard to judge for it is a type of play I do not understand. The drama of it is loose & vague. At the end of Act I Kevin O'Regan is making very demonstrative love to Eileen Budrose, & the curtain falls on what (in all usual stage manners) should have been her early seduction. In Act II without a word of explanation one finds him making equally successful love to Nora. In Act III one learns for the first time that Eileen has married Shemus O'Malley. We have not even been told that they were courting. We have only seen her refuse his escort to supper. Regan talks constantly of his contempt for organised opinion & suddenly at the end we discover him as some kind of labour leader – one organised opinion exchanged for another. It is a story without meaning – a story where nothing happens except that a wife runs away from a husband to whom we had not the least idea that she was married, & the Mansion House lights are turned out because of some wrong to a man who never appears in the play.

On the other hand it is so constructed that in every scene there is something for pit & stalls to cheer or boo. In fact it is the old Irish idea of a good play – Queens Melodrama brought up to date would no doubt make a sensation – especially as everybody is as ill mannered as possible, & all truth considered as inseperable [sic] from spite and hatred.

If Robinson wants to produce it let him do so by all means & be damned to him. My fashion has gone out.

Yet it was not until the end of September, more than three months later, that Robinson finally said no to O'Casey, sending on Yeats's comments without identifying him, and without the first sentence, or the second and third paragraphs of his report. Robinson mentioned the possibility that he and O'Casey might work over the play once more together, or discuss any future scenario O'Casey had in mind, so he could avoid getting the shape wrong.

Six years later, by 1928, O'Casey would have taken mortal offence at such an idea, but the forty-two-year-old ex-labourer – fallen at first, he said, like Lucifer, "never to hope again" – still had to have a play produced. Even so, in his reply to Robinson he foreshadowed future differences with Yeats – without as yet knowing he had been the reader – by proudly reaffirming his faith in the play. "I have re-read the work and find it as interesting as ever, in no way deserving the contemptuous dismissal it has received." Bristling with contrariness, he went on to challenge various judgments Yeats had made – such as that the play was "loose & vague" – "what could be more loose and vague than life itself?" He even cited "Yeates", as he spelt the name, as an example of a man who behaved untypically and implausibly, which "the reader" had criticised O'Regan in the play for doing!

His crowning riposte was to Yeats's stricture that an important action should not be performed in a play by a man who never appears on stage: O'Casey intended, he said, to write a play about Jim Larkin, to be called *The Red Star*, in which Larkin would never appear and would be responsible for all the action! (He did this eighteen years later and the result, *The Star Turns Red*, is perhaps the crudest and certainly one of the least successful of his plays.) His reply read as empty expostulation on the part of an unknown playwright in response to the views of the newly created Senator Yeats – in the following year he was to be given the Nobel Prize – and Robinson must have smiled when he read it. But he had judged O'Casey well, for resentment spurred him on to do his best and – in spite of his grumbles – to adhere painstakingly to all the advice he had received from the Abbey. He had already begun, that summer, a new full-length play based on the Black and Tan raid in Mountjoy Square, and was incorporating as threads of sub-plot various other incidents in which he had been involved in 1921 and 1922.

"I've been among children all my life," O'Casey commented when seventy, to a friend, but he had never suffered such a concentration of them before moving to 422 North Circular Road, where he claimed there were twenty. He had the front downstairs room which looked on a small scraggy sycamore tree and a crossroads: Innisfallen Parade was scarcely a hundred yards away. As sole occupant of the room, his rent was five shillings a week.

He now possessed a typewriter, on which he had himself typed out *The Seamless Coat of Kathleen*. When the house was quiet he would begin work, continuing until two a.m. In the basement lived the Kavanagh family, whose floorboards were rotted away with damp. Sometimes, if he went on working after two, one of the Kavanagh sons, Jim, would hammer on the ceiling with a broom for him to give over. In the room directly above O'Casey lived the Moore family, later models for characters in *Juno and the Paycock*.

About this time, back in Mountjoy Square in Delia Larkin's flat, O'Casey met R. M. Fox, then an Oxford undergraduate, who later wrote a biography of Larkin and a history of the Citizen Army. O'Casey scorned both books, but at first he and Fox were friends. Fox had written an article calling for Larkin's release from Sing Sing, which O'Casey got *The Gael* to publish, expanding it with passages of his own of which Fox knew nothing, but still crediting the younger man with the authorship. Fox was shown by O'Casey round the Dublin of mixed rule and jostling factions, and he found O'Casey generous with his time and his help: though O'Casey was by now in his early forties, Fox's first impression was of "a man in his thirties, of slight build, straight, with quick nervous movements, sensitive features and peering eyes. Very soon I noted his gift for incisive comment."

O'Casey took Fox first to Fowler Hall, formerly an Orange Lodge but now housing Catholic refugees driven out of Belfast in the Protestant pogroms of summer 1920 and after. Men, women and children lived there, under Republican guard, in rough, makeshift conditions. "Round the walls were heavily framed, massive portraits of Queen Victoria, Lord Carson and other Orange workers, gazing down in glassy-eyed disapproval of the scene." The refugees told the two visitors of Northern Catholics who had had to jump from ships into Belfast Lough, swimming to safety while red-hot rivets, "orange confetti" thrown by the Belfast shipyard workers, fell round them. They heard too that the present position of all these refugees was perilous, because they were "cover" for a Diehard ammunition dump hidden in the basement.

Fox and O'Casey also visited the Four Courts, which Republican Diehards had occupied in defiance of the Free State Army. These Diehards, or Irregulars, were using law books to block up the windows in preparation for civil war, while Republican justice was being dispensed in the courts. They then mounted a tram; "as it swirled round College Green," wrote Fox, "a motor car in the street backfired loudly. Suddenly I saw that all my fellow passengers ducked their heads. They knew Dublin and didn't trust bangs. O'Casey smiled his sardonic smile."

The new play O'Casey was writing had the provisional title *On the Run*: he took for his setting the room he had lived in in Mountjoy Square, adapting the name to 'Hilljoy Square' – near-by Hill Street was where he had first acted with his brother Isaac's Townsend Players. He told Joseph Holloway that he had begun writing *On the Run* in Mountjoy Square, and the setting he described was later corroborated by Mullen as fitting Number 35:

A Return Room in a tenement house in Hilljoy Square. At the back two large windows looking out into the yard . . . Running parallel with the

*windows is a stretcher bed; another runs at right angles along the wall at
right . . . The aspect of the place is one of absolute untidiness, engendered
on the one hand by the congenital slovenliness of* SEUMAS SHIELDS *and on
the other by the temperament of* DONAL DAVOREN.

The time could be documented precisely: 19 May 1920, at the bitterest
period of the Anglo-Irish conflict. The two main characters who
share the bed-sitting room – the play required only a single set, by
no means an innovation at the Abbey – were modelled on Mullen and
himself; the former did not take kindly to seeing himself portrayed as
a pedlar of second-rate cutlery and a cynical commentator on the new
nationalism. O'Casey may have taken the shell of the character of
Shields from Mullen, but he filled it with much of himself – his bitter
disillusionment with earlier causes he had embraced, reinforced by
the authority of Shaw in *John Bull's Other Island* and its Preface.

> There's a fellow that thinks that the four cardinal virtues are not
> to be found outside an Irish Republic. I don't want to boast about
> myself – I don't want to boast about myself, and I suppose I could
> call meself as good a Gael as some of those that are knocking about
> now – knocking about now, – as good a Gael as some that are
> knocking about now – but I remember the time when I taught
> Irish six nights a week, when in the Irish Republican Brotherhood
> I paid me rifle levy like a man . . . Now, after all me work
> for Dark Rosaleen, the only answer you can get from a roarin'
> Republican to a simple question is "good-by . . . ee".

He also celebrated comically in Shields his own anti-heroic behaviour
during Easter Week and after, his withdrawal from political commitment – but deepened with the raw emotional directness of the Dublin
street-dweller:

> But this is the way I look at it – I look at it this way: You're not
> goin' – you're not goin' to beat the British Empire – the British
> Empire, by shootin' an occasional Tommy at the corner of an
> occasional street. Besides, when the Tommies have the wind up –
> when the Tommies have the wind up they let bang at everything
> they see – they don't give a God's curse who they plug.

Davoren, the aspiring poet, O'Casey based fully on himself: into
the character he put, with dispassionate, comic sharpness, sides of
himself even more unsympathetic than he put into Seumas. He had

a strong belief that Byron's humour – which in *Don Juan* he admired – diminished him as a poet while Shelley, who had no humour, was always taken more seriously. Therefore Shelley could more easily be "sent up", and so he depicted Davoren – whose presence in Hilljoy Square is mysterious to the other tenement dwellers – as moulding himself on Shelley, repeating lines from *Prometheus Unbound*, "Ah me, alas! Pain, pain, pain ever, for ever!" which in their deadly seriousness are intended to have an hilarious, and at the same time sad, effect. For, unlike Shelley, Davoren is a bad poet, a bit of a poseur – "poet and poltroon" – as well as a coward, prepared to exploit a pretty girl's mistaken view of him as a gunman on the run. Brutally O'Casey carries the pretence to its logical conclusion, having the pretty girl, Minnie Powell, die at the end to save her hero. He never redeems Davoren, as Synge redeems Christy Mahon in *The Playboy of the Western World*, or as a Conn the Shaughraun survives death and is revealed as the saviour of his friends.

Particularly truthful, in both a comic and painful sense, in *On the Run*, is the extent to which O'Casey heaps ridicule on himself in his most intense phase of loving Maire, at the time when he wrote and dedicated so many heartfelt lyrics to her. It seems as if, putting into Shields's mouth the cynical assessment of Minnie – a much more ignorant girl than Maire – he is purging himself of self-pity: "Surely a man that has read Shelley couldn't be interested in an ignorant little bitch that thinks of nothin' but jazz dances, fox-trots, picture theatres an' dress."

He may have won a kind of subtle, imaginary victory or revenge over Maire by having Minnie die for her imaginary gunman in the form of the worthless Davoren, while Maire had failed to show, as far as O'Casey was concerned, enough courage even to defy her own family and stand by him. Minnie Powell, the first woman character O'Casey shows suffering heroically as a result of the weakness and folly of men, gains authority from the contradictoriness of feeling O'Casey shows over her commitment: she never becomes a cardboard heroine, nor do those who follow her. As Seumas says:

> A Helen of Troy come to live in a tenement! You think a lot about her simply because she thinks a lot about you, an' she thinks a lot about you because she looks upon you as a hero – a kind o' Paris . . . she'd give the world an' all to be gaddin' about with a gunman. An' what ecstasy it 'ud give her if after a bit you were shot or hanged.

The misogyny was but one side of O'Casey's thought: Minnie, although in too accelerated a way to be wholly credible, takes on a tragic dimension.

But it is the attitude towards failure which transforms O'Casey's writing in *On the Run*. When he had seriously presented his lame friend, the alderman Frank Cahill's weakness, in *The Frost and the Flower*, he had wanted to make a point about it, project a personal judgment. But now he was writing of the one thing about which he, of all people, might have been expected to be touchy, namely his own failure as a writer: "Oh, Donal Og O'Davoren, your way's a thorny way [a reminder that O'Casey's early Gaelic pen-name had been "the Thorny Branch"?]. Your last state is worse than your first." He has the generosity of spirit to present the process of life itself, and, in doing so, to send himself up. The surroundings that so frustrated his ambition, namely the slums, are what make that ambition ridiculous. As Davoren says, "The poet ever strives to save the people; the people ever strive to destroy the poet." Here is another form of comic defiance to add to that of Shields's resilient pacifism.

O'Casey calls the unseen gunman friend of Shields Maguire; departing for an errand outside Dublin, he leaves a bag behind with Shields. Only later do Davoren and Seumas look inside, to find it full of Mills bombs: in taking the bag Minnie hopes to protect Davoren. The defiance shown by the self-sacrificing Minnie when she is hauled off is very similar to that of Ballynoy in O'Casey's autobiography, but not to the real-life Fred of Mullen's account, arrested during the raid. The gunman himself was based on James MacGowan, with whom O'Casey had shared recruiting during his Citizen Army days, and who later commanded the detachment of Volunteers left behind at Liberty Hall when the main body went to occupy the GPO. MacGowan definitely did not, at Knocksedan, catch something besides butterflies – in the play "two of them he got, one through each lung" – but lived on, carrying a bomb splinter in his head for some years, before it worked itself out. (He then carried the splinter around with him in a little tin box.) But in numerous other details *On the Run* was very close to life.

When writing this play O'Casey had all the Abbey criticism, particularly that of Lady Gregory, in the front of his mind; later he told Holloway how much *On the Run* owed to Lady Gregory, especially to her advice, "to cut out all expression of self and develop his peculiar aptness for character drawing". A handwritten draft he kept of the first scene shows only minor changes and three words crossed out. He had the play ready by mid-November, writing to

Lennox Robinson on the 17th to tell him he intended to bring it over to the theatre the following week: "The play is typed – not faultlessly, I'm afraid – but the result is obviously immeasurably above my fiendish handwriting. I have to thank you and Lady Gregory for the self-sacrifice displayed by the reading of such a manuscript as *The Crimson in the Tricolour*."

He heard from Robinson in February 1923 that *On the Run* had been accepted, although he was asked to change the title – another play had the same one – which he did, to *The Shadow of a Gunman*, an infinitely better and more subtle title which reflects the irony at the centre of the play. For "shadow" has a deeply Platonic implication – Plato's ideal substances were reflected as shadows dancing on the wall of his cave – and yet Plato would have excluded the poet from the Republic. That the weak-minded poet in the play should represent the essence of the patriotic gunman is the ultimate mockery. But it seemed that O'Casey, who had an instinctive gift for incorporating powerful images into his work, was not conscious of the Platonism he mocked – except that he chose Shelley, the most Platonic of all poets, to be Davoren's literary mentor.

The first performance of *The Shadow of a Gunman* took place just after O'Casey's forty-third birthday: it was the last play of the Abbey season, tacked on for three performances after *She Stoops to Conquer*. On the same bill – the Abbey management must have felt it was too slight without a curtain-raiser – was T. C. Murray's popular *Sovereign Love*. Two important funerals had taken place on the morning of that day of 12 April 1923: in London Sarah Bernhardt's, in Cork that of Liam Lynch, a Diehard leader who had earlier, during the Irish war of independence, led the party that captured the only British military installation to fall, Mallow Barracks. Lynch was shot dead by Free Staters. There was now a Free State detachment on duty at the Abbey, as the theatres were threatened by the Diehards if they remained open.

Lennox Robinson directed O'Casey's play, Arthur Shields played Davoren, F. J. McCormick played Shields, and Gertrude Murphy took the role of Minnie. O'Casey had tried, Robinson wrote later, "to write plays in which he pursued a moral idea; he only completely found himself when he was content to act as a reporter". But with *The Shadow of a Gunman* his plays became "reporting of the highest kind, almost of genius". The theatre on that Thursday night was less than half full, but the play immediately touched a chord: the audience, quick to pick up the political references, laughed and cheered frequently, and O'Casey, who watched from the wings, came forward at the end to take his bow.

Next day O'Casey pasted cuttings of some of the glowing notices over jottings in a dark red notebook. The critic of the *Irish Independent* wrote that there were few plays in the Abbey repertoire that rivalled it, and "in satire" it was "in a class by itself". All the character studies by the actors were praised. The *Irish Times* recommended that if O'Casey would remove "the small element of real tragedy from the end of his play . . . and [if he will] . . . call it a satire instead of a tragedy, there is no reason why it should not live for a very long time". "What it lacked in dramatic construction," recorded Joseph Holloway in his diary, "it certainly pulled up in telling dialogue of the most topical and biting kind . . . Out of the crudeness . . . truth and human nature leaped."

By the second night, thanks to "word of mouth", the Abbey was three-quarters full. Audiences were tired of war and of politics; here was someone at last getting back at both in a gutsy and irreverent manner, blowing both away in a gale of laughter. "A man should always be drunk," as Davoren says to Minnie, "when he talks politics – it's the only way in which to make them important"; uncovering a deeper passion of disillusionment with Shields's cry,

> I'm a Nationalist meself, right enough – a Nationalist right enough, but all the same – I'm a Nationalist right enough; I believe in the freedom of Ireland, an' that England has no right to be here, but I draw the line when I hear the gunmen blowin' about dyin' for the people, when it's the people that are dyin' for the gunmen!

The play's faults were its strengths, the gallery of weak men so funny, like a string of vaudeville turns – the vainglorious, self-interested types of Tommy Owens, Grigson and Gallogher, presented à la Boucicault, were instantly recognisable – that it had become caricature as much as character-drawing; it seemed O'Casey had now learnt to sketch dramatically with the same boldness and simplicity he used in his cartoons. To Dublin audiences self-mockery was always endearing: in a city so small and intimate it created a cabaret atmosphere. Everyone could identify with Mrs Grigson's query, "Do the insurance companies pay if a man is shot after curfew?" as with Davoren's vanity:

MINNIE: I know what you are.

DAVOREN: What am I?

MINNIE (*in a whisper*): A gunman on the run!

DAVOREN (*too pleased to deny it*): Maybe I am, and maybe I'm not.

MINNIE: Oh, I know, I know, I know. Do you never be afraid?

DAVOREN: Afraid! Afraid of what?

MINNIE: Why, the ambushes of course; *I'm* all of a tremble when I hear a shot go off, an' what must it be to be in the middle of the firin'?

DAVOREN (*delighted at* MINNIE's *obvious admiration; leaning back in his chair, and lighting a cigarette with placid affectation*): I'll admit one does be a little nervous at first.

By Saturday night Lady Gregory herself was thrilled, for the attendance was so huge – the largest, she said, since the first night of Shaw's *Blanco Posnet* in 1909 – that many were turned away. Before the start of the performance she brought O'Casey round to the foyer, "to share my joy in seeing the crowd surging in". O'Casey was now, by that third night, a celebrity, and Lady Gregory gave him her own reserved seat, next to Yeats, and herself sat in the stalls. O'Casey did not invite Mullen, who, not a bitter man, later remarked that "he forgot that my kind was alive". Holloway was watching too: "The author is a thin-faced, sharp-profiled man, with streaky hair, and wore a trench coat and a soft felt hat. He followed his play closely and laughed often, and I was told he was quiet-mannered almost to shyness." "The characters seemed strangers to me, but I enjoyed them," O'Casey told Holloway afterwards. He didn't know that his neighbour, Senator Yeats, had been the hypercritical reader of *The Crimson in the Tricolour*.

Later, the elderly O'Casey cast a veil of cynicism over his playwriting début: a run of only three nights, he wrote, was the first cause of vexation, the second the low box-office receipts – only thirteen pounds on opening night. Although Saturday's full house brought in over fifty pounds, his share of the total takings amounted to less than four pounds, for which, because of the Abbey's shaky finances and because he felt too proud to ask for it in cash, he would have to wait: "Less than four pounds! And he had bargained in his mind for twenty, at the least."

But there was a much stronger side to the younger O'Casey who now bathed in a glow of success, a side that linked him with the shadow gunman Davoren, poet and poltroon, and it was to this side of O'Casey that Lady Gregory responded most markedly when they talked together:

> I forget how I came to mention the Bible, and he asked "Do you like it?" I said, "Yes. I read it constantly, even for the beauty of the language." He said he admires that beauty, he was brought up as a Protestant but has lost belief in religious forms. Then, in talking of our war here, we came to Plato's *Republic*, his dream city, whether on earth or in heaven not far away from the city of God.

He had found a new church – the Abbey Theatre – and for the present the iconoclast in him gazed in wonder at the range of images on offer.

8

HEARTS OF FLESH AND STONE

As O'Casey grumbled about his four pounds, there was no reason that he should have known – or cared – that the Abbey building, formerly the Dublin City morgue, had recently been mortgaged to pay off a debt of £1,153. Although the authorities had just acknowledged the theatre's importance to the new Irish Free State by conferring on it an annual grant of £850, it could only employ six fully professional actors, each paid four pounds a week. Gabriel Fallon – Gallogher in *The Shadow of a Gunman* – was a civil servant by day; so, too, was Barry Fitzgerald, who, as Captain Boyle in *Juno and the Paycock*, was soon to be recognised as the great leading actor of the Abbey. The part-timers would dash from their offices at lunchtime, rehearse for half an hour, snatch a sandwich and coffee, and be back at their desks by two p.m. They would manage an hour and a half's rehearsal after work, the main meal of the day at six thirty, and then start making up for the evening performance. They each received thirty shillings a week.

Fallon worked in Transport Statistics in Dublin Castle, and Barry Fitzgerald (the stage name of William Shields, brother of Arthur Shields, the Abbey actor and stage manager) in an office two blocks away in the Department of Industry and Commerce. But F. J. McCormick (stage name of Peter Judge), who played Seamas in *Gunman*, the Abbey's leading depicter of Dublin character, was a full professional, who began work at eleven.

At first, O'Casey was in awe of the actors. Fallon recalled seeing "F. J." usher him into the wings during the first performance. "Certainly, why not? You'll be all right there." While the little pit orchestra under Dr John Larchet ("Larky") played Mendelssohn's "Son and Stranger" overture, O'Casey anxiously asked Fallon, "Are you sure I won't be in the way here?" Fallon gruffly replied, "Dammit, you've written the play, you've every right to be here." But

O'Casey told him in a soft, persuasive voice, "The stage is really the actor's place. Only *he* has the right to be here."

When the Abbey, angling for Horse Show Week custom, reopened in August, *Gunman* was the natural choice with which to begin the new season. But now F. J. – as subtle an actor as the Abbey had ever known – became a target for O'Casey's revived critical spirit. After one performance he mounted the fourteen wooden steps which led from the stage to the flimsily timbered dressing rooms, to inform F. J.:

"You're after making a hames of my play, Mr Mac." "How did I make a hames of your play?" asked F. J. "You made a hames of it at that particular line when Donal says 'I remember the time when you yourself believed in nothing but the gun,' and Shields says, 'Aye, when there wasn't a bloody gun in the country.'" Anyway F. J. asked him, "How would you say the line?" and O'Casey replied, "Oh, but I'm not an actor."

Particular lines apart, O'Casey felt McCormick made Shields too sympathetic a figure.

Gunman was now a sell-out and later became one of the most often revived plays in the Abbey's repertoire. O'Casey worked less and less often as a casual labourer, although he did not own up to his new-found independence of means until the following year. He had completed two more one-act plays, *The Cooing of Doves* – full, as he said, "of wild discussions and rows in a public-house" – and *Cathleen Listens In*, "a jovial sardonic sketch on the various parties in conflict over Irish politics – Sinn Fein, Free State, and Labour". He preferred the first work, and received a shock when it was turned down in favour of the second. And although he later used *The Cooing of Doves* as the basis for the second act of *The Plough and the Stars*, he never admitted that the Abbey had done him a good turn by rejecting it when it did.

Concentrating on playwriting to the exclusion of almost everything else, O'Casey had by now withdrawn socially from the St Laurence O'Toole Club (but he still hurled), from his earlier friendships such as that with Cahill, and from family life. He still saw himself as a martyr, more now perhaps in the sense of the Greek, i.e. witness – and depended wholly upon himself. Applause from the public had to some extent become a substitute for personal love. Defending F. J. against O'Casey in an amiable discussion about F. J.'s acting in Terence MacSwiney's *The Revolutionist*, M. J. Dolan, another actor-director at the Abbey, said, "Mac made one fatal mistake in the part; he occasionally played for applause, and thus became self-conscious."

O'Casey told him, "Sure, we all play for applause in life, from Jim Larkin down."

Larkin was released from Sing Sing in 1923, on the order of Governor Al Smith of New York: fêted at the dockside when he left America, his progress through Southampton was no less triumphant, and in Dublin people stood shoulder to shoulder from Westland Row Station to Liberty Hall. But he soon found he could not take up just where he had left off after the great lock-out: O'Brien was firmly established in the ITGWU, and the executive refused to reinstate Larkin. Larkin distrusted the outlook of Arthur Griffith's successors, who controlled the Free State: "Nobody in Ireland did anything but Sinn Fein," he wrote; "Connolly and the other boys all recanted Socialism and labour and were good Sinn Feiners. My God, it is sickening." His view was roughly now that of O'Casey, who in 1919 had written in his Citizen Army history that Labour would "probably have to fight Sinn Fein".

As he fought to re-establish himself in Dublin politics, later forming a rival union to the ITGWU, Larkin found other things had changed, in particular his marriage. Later, in a rare personal judgment passed on one of his greatest heroes, O'Casey said, "Of course, Jim was always religious – in the good sense of the word. I don't think he acted quite justly to Mrs L. After all, it must have been a tough job to have been tied to Jim. He had very little time for any home-life. I think he made a mistake in not living with her when he came back. But I never said so to him – that sort of thing's too private to be discussed with anyone."

If O'Casey had little time for Larkin in 1923, he had also severed connections with his former friends, the priests of both Catholic and Protestant denomination, such as Griffin's successor, or Canon Brady, to whom O'Casey used to quote the Koran. He was in a virulently anti-Catholic mood, having mocked, in *Gunman*, the Church's holy rituals:

> Instead of counting their beads now they're countin' bullets; their Hail Marys and paternosters are burstin' bombs – burstin' bombs, an' the rattle of machine-guns; petrol is their holy water; their Mass is a burnin' buildin'; their De Profundis is "The Soldiers' Song" . . .

and now he turned on the stones of St Laurence O'Toole, with its "brawny and vulgar" façade, abusing it for refusing to shelter the body of a dead Fenian for a night.

In May he began sketching out a new play which he called *Juno and the Peacock*: on the inside cover of a seventy-two-page pink Grattan school exercise book he pinned an *Irish Times* cutting dated 8 May describing King George V, in "naval undress" and Queen Mary, wearing a heliotrope dress trimmed with Parma violets, visiting Raphael's tomb in Rome. It was his custom to embellish work in progress with news snippets and reviews. Opposite he wrote out a scenario of the first two acts:

Act I –
   Annie on strike; mother going out to work. Joxer outside enters when Juno leaves: enters singing. His talk with Andy. Interrupted by entrance of Juno. The dispute between the two of them. The lover of Annie's.
   The entrance of the Schoolteacher
   The writing of the Will,
      End I

Second act details included "The cultivation of the teacher's society, his love affair with Annie . . . The will to be proved. The borrowing of the money."

The rest of the Grattan exercise book, except for eight blank pages, he filled, at different times, working from both ends of the book, with drafts of the first two acts (to be expanded in the finished script) and brief sections of Act III. He also used some pages for lists of characters and for experimenting with snatches of dialogue, e.g. "When are we going to get our – Quatta? – Quota"; "Thine to the point of Emancipation"; "Procrastinator & Prognosticator", and the impressionistic, possibly overheard, "Andy Murphy . . . he lives in – where's this he lived . . . it wasn't in – no not in in in, it doesn't matter. He was the son of oh you know him well . . . of one o' oh what this his name was . . ."

During the summer of 1923 O'Casey also rewrote *The Crimson in the Tricolour*, and forwarded it to Robinson, who again said no. He tried to interest Dolan in producing it, and Dolan had given him suggestions, such as transforming the setting from outside a convent, where characters were "spouting socialism", to inside a pub. But the play lacked characterisation or a solid enough plot for Dolan. "Always keep the interest on the move," was his advice to O'Casey, giving him the example of Lennox Robinson's popular *The Whiteheaded Boy*, which had been the last play produced by the Abbey before the Easter Rising of 1916, and which was now being revived late in 1923.

Robinson was rehearsing *Cathleen Listens In* in September but the production, presented at the end of the month in a triple bill with Shaw's *The Man of Destiny* and Lady Gregory's *The Rising of the Moon*, was a dismal failure. Holloway noted:

> Somehow or other, despite . . . being a good skit, it missed the mark I think and fizzled out somewhat. It was full of subtle touches, most of which didn't fit into dramatic effectiveness . . . It was types and not characters that made up the cast; therefore, none of the players made their parts live . . . There was a fine audience present, and excitement ran high to see how O'Casey would succeed in his second dramatic effort. The audience was eager to laugh with him, but couldn't, only by fits and starts.

O'Casey himself was mortified by the audience rising in silence at the end, as he saw it, and filing out of the auditorium. He was the only Abbey playwright, he said, ever to be deprived of even a single timid handclap: it looked as if his talent "would have to perish in silence".

But, in this most fertile period of his life, failure was a better tonic than success, for out of *The Crimson in the Tricolour*'s rejection had come *Gunman*: now, seething with disappointment, cap well down and hands in pockets, he walked home uphill to Number 422. "Once inside he swore an oath that he would write a play which would be such that the Abbey would not be big enough to hold the audience that would want to see it."

This meant intensifying the hasty and almost illegible efforts he had begun to make in the pink Grattan notebook.

<hr />

Ulster, as was expected, having voted itself out of the Free State at the end of 1922, Ireland as a whole, under the separate governments of North and South, had gradually been settling down, although fighting continued in 1923 between the Free State Army and the Irregulars. Griffith had died, Michael Collins been killed in an ambush, but their successors, W. T. Cosgrave and Kevin O'Higgins, sternly implemented measures which led their main opponent, de Valera, to seek a cease-fire at the end of May 1923. But they were in no mood to respond. One of the main factors in undermining the power of the Irregulars had been the Catholic hierarchy, whose weight was thrown in on the side of the Free State (hence O'Casey's increasing derision of it).

Living as he did in Diehard country, O'Casey's sympathies were with the new breed of martyrs, the Irregulars, hunted down in the final revenge of the Irish Free State against its potential usurpers. In the week of 3 September 1923, even though de Valera had declared a unilateral truce, the killing went on. One of the victims was the sweetheart of Mary Moore, daughter of the family who lived in "the two pair back" above O'Casey in Number 422.

The CID had raided 422 several times; on one occasion, hauling the sheets off O'Casey, and pulling him roughly out of bed, they had pointed their revolvers at him till he could establish his identity. Both sons, and then the daughter, of Mrs Moore were dragged off to jail; but the girl's sweetheart's end was particularly savage. Captain Hogan – such was his name – had shot a Free-Stater, and had no benefit from the armistice terms. He was caught at the Dorset Street end of the North Circular Road. O'Casey had a picture of this man given to him later by Mary Moore, which he kept for many years.

Hogan was taken, as O'Casey told Holloway at the Abbey, "in the middle of the night . . . and brought out towards Finglas and brutally beaten with the butt end of their revolvers, and then told to run for his life while they fired revolver shots after him, taking bits off his ears, etc., and catching up on him again renewed their beating." Next day O'Casey had seen him dead – "more than just dead, for his belly had been kicked in, his right eye was a purple pulp, an ear had been partly shot off, and now, jagged and red-edged, stood out like a tiny fin from the side of his head." Finglas was where O'Casey had particularly enjoyed Maire's company when they had strolled together down Stella's Walk.

The image of the crippled Diehard victim was from the start central to the conception of *Juno*. From the first draft it would appear that the duplicated form of this image – Robbie Tancred first, and then his former comrade, Johnny Boyle, who "shopped" him – emerged only later, for Johnny hardly appears in the draft of Act I; another character called Jim, who later becomes Mary Boyle's sweetheart, Jerry, fills his place. The notion of Johnny as an off-stage presence – a theatrical ploy which O'Casey always found attractive – he dispensed with as the urgency and immediacy of the theme, and of the real circumstances to which it related, dictated its own conditions. So in Act II:

JOHNNY (*passionately*): I won't go! Haven't I done enough for Ireland! I've lost me arm, an' me hip's desthroyed so that I'll never be able to walk right agen! Good God, haven't I done enough for Ireland?

THE YOUNG MAN: Boyle, no man can do enough for Ireland!

The Hogan atrocity supplied O'Casey with the first line of his play: Mary Boyle's noticing a news item in the paper: "On a little bye-road, out beyant Finglas, he was found." So he could have written that line before *Cathleen Listens In*, but only just. The response of the Moore mother to this death and to the wholesale arrest of her children stirred him profoundly:

> the kindly soul of the old woman found rest only in restlessness. One night, while her old husband slept, she had wandered out into a windy, sleety night, to be found the morning after, stretched calmly out, indifferent to the stinging rain and the bustling wind, on the streaming pavement of a windy turning, in a last, long sleep.

Mrs Moore's death and her funeral, which he attended – to help, as he said, "hedge the old man's sorrow in" – aroused deep feelings, which had been but sleeping, about the death of his own mother, and about motherhood in general. He had dramatised these feelings once before, but unsuccessfully, in *The Harvest Festival*.

The comic plot of *Juno* also came, miraculously, from the Moore family. O'Casey remembered that this same family had been a different kind of victim more than two years before, when Mr Moore had been made the beneficiary of a faulty will. O'Casey had sent him for advice to his lawyer friend, James O'Connor, who tried – unsuccessfully, or so it appeared from O'Casey's subsequent treatment of the subject – to have the will established in Mr Moore's favour. O'Connor wrote to O'Casey to try and get the witnesses he required, "otherwise I fear that the first and second cousins would come in and with the investigations etc. necessary, would stretch out the final distribution of the estate to a very far distant date". O'Casey's master stroke is to combine the two narrative elements – one potentially comic, the other potentially tragic – in the same play.

This mingling of elements was there in the first draft. Joxer, the typical Dublin wastrel – deceitful, lazy, hypocritical – and Boyle, the public-house lounger with the title "Captain" from being "only wanst on the wather" on a Liverpool–Dublin coal boat, were there, much of their dialogue untouched in the final version from this first scribbling – or if changed expanded from an impressionistic shorthand:

B. I often of a . . . cold & wathery night looked up at the stars & I assed meself the question – What is the stars, and it blowed & blowed & blowed, blew is the right word, Joxer, but we sailors always cry blowed.

JOXER: A darlin' word, a darlin' word.

So was Juno, some of her great emotional outbursts intact and almost complete even then, including the one that became in its final version at the end of Act III:

> I forgot, Mary, I forgot; your poor oul' selfish mother was only thinkin' of herself. No, no, you musn't come – it wouldn't be good for you. You go on to me sisther's an' I'll face th' ordeal meself. Maybe I didn't feel sorry enough for Mrs Tancred when her poor son was found as Johnny's been found now – because he was a Diehard! Ah, why didn't I remember that then he wasn't a Diehard or a Stater, but only a poor dead son! It's well I remember all that she said – an' it's my turn to say it now: What was the pain I suffered, Johnny, bringin' you into the world to carry you to your cradle, to the pains I'll suffer carryin' you out o' the world to bring you to your grave! Mother o'God, Mother o'God, have pity on us all! Blessed Virgin, where were you when me darlin' son was riddled with bullets, when me darlin' son was riddled with bullets? Sacred Heart o' Jesus, take away our hearts o' stone, and give us hearts o' flesh! Take away this murdherin' hate, an' give us Thine own eternal love!

It is, from the start, these three great characters who provide the play's dynamism: its subtleties, its skilfully complex organisation of the rise and fall of the Boyle legacy, news of which the theosophist and schoolteacher Charles Bentham brings into the Boyle household, and Mary's pregnancy, her rejection by her overspent and shattered father – all apparently came later. The poetic repetitions, such as Boyle's

> I'm telling you . . . Joxer . . . th' whole worl's . . . in a terr . . . ible state o' . . . . chassis!

rode through successive drafts. But some of Boyle's Shakespearean expansiveness was cut down, for example when Mrs Madigan challenges him about his rank at sea:

> MRS. I gather from what you say Mr that you were in your young days a sailor.
> B. (*expansively*) Mrs I trod the decks o' the finest ships that ever put into the port of (Glenrose?) Ah thems, thems was days, thems was days!

JX. A life on the rollin' wave, a life on the boundin' sea . . .

MRS. What were you Mr . . . Mate first or second (rank) class.

B. (*solemnly*) This is a democratic age Mrs . . . we wont discover
about rank . . . "Rank is but a name" . . .

In place of this O'Casey wrote:

BOYLE: Another dhrop o' whisky, Mrs Madigan?

thus concentrating the feeling Boyle's call of the sea has awakened in
Mrs Madigan.

The less strong characters, such as Mary and Jerry, grew more
slowly. In the final version the pair have become more condensed,
more rounded in what they say, while the semi-farcical interruptions
– Johnny objecting offstage to Boyle putting on his moleskin trousers
– have doubled in richness. In places the earlier script has some
of the fussy, music-hall abruptness of *Gunman*: but unnecessary
characters and extraneous business were later cut.

O'Casey included few songs and snatches of verse in his first draft:
these, and most of the stage directions, were added later. To begin with
Boyle's walk is a "slow, semi-pompous strut"; later, a "slow, consequen-
tial strut". His stomach, "perceptibly protruding", becomes "slightly
thrust forward". O'Casey sketched Boyle's head in the pink exercise
book, and once or twice totted up his own rent and other costs of living.

Like *Gunman*, although more rich and complex in plot, *Juno* depends
ultimately upon its characters' foibles for its humour. Mr Moore, of
Number 422, bereaved husband and thwarted father, who had stood
at his wife's funeral, his few white tufts of hair saturated with rain,
embodied the opposite of vanity, but O'Casey had portrayed that
failing so well in *Gunman*, with Davoren, that he saw even greater
comic and tragic possibilities in it now. So, in place of Moore he
has Captain Boyle, who combines Davoren's vanity with Seumas
Shields's illusionism. O'Casey took the name of Boyle from a well-
known Dublin character whom he used to visit at his flat in Gloucester
Street, often finding there a quick-tempered down-and-out called
Jack Daly who would call in regularly for a cup of tea. The pair
would gossip for hours, while O'Casey sat near the fire listening,
occasionally jotting down snatches of their talk on bits of paper
(neither suspected him of doing this). Boyle also wrote verses, and
those in Act II of *Juno* may originally have been his.

But like many rich creations, Boyle stemmed from more than one source: the character shared with O'Casey's own brother Mick, and with Shakespeare's Falstaff, his terrible thirst and his phobia towards work. Lennox Robinson gave O'Casey a volume of Chekhov's plays at about the time he was working on *Juno*: it is perhaps, then, no mere coincidence that Boyle is deemed "Captain" for nautical exploits that are boastful lies, like those of the hired "General" in Chekhov's farcical *The Wedding Party*, "You sail the seas without a care in the world." Above all Boyle is a victim of the illusion that he will become free of debt and poverty – and, like the new Ireland, deliriously drunk and happy with its independence, he is to be cruelly disillusioned. Perhaps O'Casey – this time anticipating his habit of becoming disillusioned – was also issuing a warning to himself not to be too much affected by the slowly but significantly increasing royalty payments he received from the Abbey. (In the May 1923 exercise book an item of thirty-seven pounds is recorded, although this cannot be dated.)

As in *The Shadow of a Gunman*, the setting of *Juno and the Paycock* never changes. But while *Gunman* is more about a people at war, *Juno*, for all its deeply emotional pacifism – in which O'Casey, through Juno and Mrs Tancred, rejustifies and re-affirms his own non-combatant stance on taking up arms for a cause (or expiates, and apologises for, his own cowardice) – takes place in a poor tenement and addresses itself to the subject of poverty and human aspiration. Susan Casey, both materially and emotionally, had protected her Johnny, whose intellectuality had in any case made him superior to the issues at stake. But Juno – so named, with typical O'Casey irony and comic deviousness, not, he said, after the Roman goddess of the hearth, but because the significant events of her life happened in June – has no such luck or ability to protect her Johnny. In Johnny Boyle O'Casey was depicting a "might-have-been" version of himself (as he did with Jack Rocliffe) although, fortunately for *Juno*, he did not allow the character to become much more than a sketch.

Much more powerfully and confidently than in *Gunman*, O'Casey shows without comment the processes of life. There had been plays before at the Abbey about the Dublin poor: A. Patrick Wilson's *The Slough*; the harsh satire called *Blight*, which O'Casey had seen; Daniel Corkery's *The Labour Leader* – but none of these made the audiences laugh, and each had emptied the theatre. O'Casey's slice of life showed no one being exemplary, while the wonderful influence the Abbey triumvirate exerted over O'Casey squashed all ideology. We see the best and worst of everyone involved, and retain sympathy even for the obnoxious Boyle, whose escape from his sordid confinement into drink and dreams is lovingly felt, and for Joxer, whose wheedling acceptance of his Plautine lord's dominance conceals the malice of the born arse-licker.

At forty-three O'Casey, not yet married, demonstrated through Boyle and Joxer how he, like countless other unmarried Irishmen, could conduct a non-sexual relationship with a "butty" based on overlooking the other's faults in pursuit of a common aim such as drinking – to most intents and purposes a marriage. The great Irish gift for celibacy was possessed by O'Casey himself, who existed more or less happily in this condition for upwards of half his life. *Juno* shows, although only incidentally, how O'Casey coped with the state of non-marriage. The playwright embodies in Juno's and Boyle's loveless marriage what V. S. Pritchett once called "the ambition of every Dublin husband . . . never to go home", and the basic Irish male fear of women and of sex. The Irish man never grows up: he keeps not only the little boy alive in him, and the anarchic spirit, but the basic fear. Comically engaging in his infantilism, he is tragically inadequate when facing reality. And the basic fear – in marriage the fear of pregnancy – keeps the sexes polarised more effectively than anything else.

But woman has the courage: Juno, exalting the mother above the useless, segregated male, is a triumphant assertion of woman's superiority over man: when Mary, rejected by her father and sweet-heart, complains, "My poor little child that'll have no father!" Juno replies, "It'll have what's far betther – it'll have two mothers."

Would O'Casey always portray men disparagingly, as if trying to get back at his own father for dying on him so young? Nowhere else in his later plays is his distrust of men displayed so effectively as in *Juno*: it seems that he can only see men as betraying each other, failing in their ideals – as in the case of Johnny Boyle and Mrs Tancred's son – or "gratifying" themselves in an essentially false, comic double act on the Laurel and Hardy principle (an example publicists later took up by trying to pair him with, for example, Barry Fitzgerald). He savagely parodies the whole masculine state of life, not only its ideals and its organisation but its petty and pathetic aches and pains. Perhaps he felt emotionally secure only in the mother–son relationship: what makes *Juno and the Paycock* cumulatively moving, in spite of its volatility of feeling and its sudden, unexpected and comic changes of pace, is the way it asserts the primacy of a mother's emotions in counterpoint to the decline of the Boyle family's hopes and aspirations.

After a cruel build-up of the family from poverty to a range of middle-class hopes and acquisitions – and O'Casey is here in his best vein of self-mockery, because he was himself filling up his room at Number 422 with books and new furniture bought with the royalties of *Gunman*, yet wary that his affluence wouldn't last – he telescopes beautifully the deterioration of the Boyle household, intensifying its decline against a civil war background of savage reprisals. To do this he draws instinctively – and in the urgency of what he wants to show – on his own past experience, purging his family ghosts and at the same time bringing Susan Casey back to life as Juno. As Paul Claudel wrote to Jacques Rivière in 1912, "Do you believe for a moment that Shakespeare or Dostoevsky or Rubens or Titian or Wagner did their work for art's sake? No! They did it to free themselves of a great incubus of living matter, *opus non factum*." The same motive underlay the making of O'Casey's supreme masterpiece.

Apart from the overriding unity which *Juno*, in its diversity, possesses, there were many other biographically revealing touches. The play shows, to begin with, how little difference there was in Dublin at that time between a working-class man and his lower-middle-class counterpart. Boyle lives not in the fixed world of the poorest slums, but in the mobile world of middle-class aspiration, of hire-purchase and legal disputes, though, like O'Casey, for all his high opinion of himself he is quite happy to do casual part-time labouring – and even more happy to shirk it, mocking the once acute pains in his legs:

BOYLE: Won't it be a climbin' job? How d'ye expect me to be able to go up a ladder with these legs? An', if I get up aself, how am I goin' to get down agen?

MRS BOYLE (*viciously*): Get wan o' the labourers to carry you down in a hod! You can't climb a laddher, but you can skip like a goat into a snug!

There is Mick there, too, scorning Sean's ambitions, when Boyle attacks his daughter: "What did th' likes of her, born in a tenement house, want with readin'? Her readin's afther bringin' her to a nice pass." And there are echoes of his treatment by Maire Keating, although O'Casey reverses the roles, with Bentham throwing over Mary Boyle:

MARY: I imagine . . . he thought . . . we weren't . . . good enough for him.

MRS BOYLE: An' what was he himself, only a school teacher?

In *Juno* O'Casey also goes on mocking all the causes he had previously believed in, but he sticks with his image of Ireland as the stoical mother. What could be nearer the tone of Susan Casey, when she rebuked Mick or Tom before he married, as O'Casey has Juno rebuking the fear-tormented Johnny:

> . . . it's yourself that has yourself the way y'are; sleepin' wan night in me sisther's, an' the nex' in your father's brother's – you'll get no rest goin' on that way.

O'Casey never directly based a character in *Juno* on himself, but his unseen presence can be felt all through, pulling the strings, splashing on colour that came to him unsolicited through his unlocked door at 422. The momentum of a Boucicault play drives *Juno* forward, characters appearing and disappearing with all the unexpectedness of vaudeville turns, uttering the comic lies and deceits of knockers and desecrators who abhor holiness and hypocrisy of all kinds, but with one significant difference: the surroundings are scorchingly real.

O'Casey's genius is that he has substituted the contradictions of changeable personality for the twists and turns of a Boucicault plot. He succeeded triumphantly in refining his model, deepening it emotionally, giving his own characters both lasting power and universal significance. Ireland in its history from 1916 to 1923 played out in miniature, and ahead of any other country, the dramas of nationalism and revolution that have absorbed the rest of the world for most of this century (and that still absorb Ireland); O'Casey, in depicting that Ireland, projected a lasting image of the vulnerable yet defiant human family caught in the tragic conflict between, on the one hand, its own failure and hopeful delusions, on the other the bitter, inhuman circumstances of war.

O'Casey completed *Juno* in the last weeks of 1923 and gave it to Lennox Robinson to read: perhaps he had in mind its future when he wrote to Robinson on 29 December, that he envied him "every word of the White-headed Boy": he had certainly read Robinson's play, *The Whiteheaded Boy*, before writing *Juno* and had implemented Dolan's advice to "always keep the interest on the move". He told Holloway he had also been reading and enjoying Chekhov who "seems to let his characters speak as they please and get them into his play's scheme".

The keepers of O'Casey's new temple were Yeats and Lady Gregory, but he still stood reverently on the steps, "the timid drama postulant," as he said, "ready to wear any habit offered to him and take any vow required": they had yet to embrace him socially, to grant him the status of novice or even son. Although his loyalty to Larkin's ideals remained firm, Larkin himself was by now a discarded father figure: Yeats, who received the Nobel Prize in November 1923, became the new object of O'Casey's hero-worship.

It was a measure of O'Casey's innocence, continuing well into middle age, that while cynicism had affected so many sides of his personality, for his new mentors he had nothing but trust and admiration, although he had balked at Yeats's criticism of *The Crimson in the Tricolour*. Here were demi-gods. He could not have known that an earlier hero of his, Padraic Pearse, had judged them both: "Lady G. enjoying her own pieces and laughing at her own jokes. Yeats does the same. Truly they were both like little children in their ways," and complained in 1912 that the Abbey was "run too much on Ascendancy principles".

O'Casey's first perception of Yeats, as recorded in his autobiography, was as a powerful and mysterious figure. He had spotted him (or says he had) at the Abbey during the *Playboy* riots in 1907, "a stately-looking man with long black hair, a lock of it half covering an eye, who had come to the entrance, and, in the light of a street lamp, stood looking dreamily at the agitated crowd". But sixteen years passed before O'Casey was invited by Yeats to dinner, Robinson providing the link, at a well-known Dublin restaurant "bearing a sturdy poetical name". O'Casey's sense of humour did not desert him when he found himself at a table for three, with Robinson and Arthur Shields, in a far corner of the room (he was acutely sensitive of such placings):

Away in the dim distance, a far larger table served a number of persons whom Sean did not know yet, though, through a murmur of submissive conversation, he heard the booming voice of Yeats chatting in a lordly lilt about Utumara, Brahmin Mohini, birds born out of the fire, the two inflows to man's nature.

O'Casey was awakened out of the booming by Robinson asking him if he'd enjoyed the dinner: he answered, the rhubarb and custard, yes, but the rest was badly cooked. His bluntness shocked Robinson, in turn embarrassing Sean. He remembered how good a cook his mother had been, especially with anything worthwhile, on the plain open coal fire. "A ceremonial meal to Megarithma, or any other deity", wasn't going to make him tell polite lies to his hosts.

On 12 February 1924, O'Casey told Holloway that *Juno*, now accepted, had not yet been put into rehearsal, although down to open on 25 February: clearly the Abbey management could respond with alacrity when they smelled the possibility of success. But Robinson had bowed out of directing the new O'Casey, his place being taken by Dolan whom, Holloway reported, O'Casey liked "best of all the actors in the company". It was Robinson, however, who first told O'Casey they had F. J. McCormick in mind to play Boyle. O'Casey had fallen slightly foul of McCormick over his criticism of him as Seumas Shields; and since seeing Barry Fitzgerald appear in St John Ervine's *Mary, Mary, Quite Contrary*, he had thought him a born clown, ideal for the Captain with his arrogant, boozy humour.

O'Casey seemingly had little trouble in persuading Robinson that his was the better choice, although his tactless stating of his preference ruffled a few feathers, among them those of McCormick himself, who enjoyed a much higher status in the company than the part-timer Fitzgerald. Fitzgerald needed a great deal of persuasion: O'Casey and Gaby Fallon, newly become O'Casey's close friend within the Abbey, spent much time trying to convince him, and he finally said yes.

The new company assembled on a February afternoon at five p.m., to give the part-timers a chance to be present, to read *Juno* for the first time. Wrote Fallon:

It seemed to be a strange baffling mixture of comedy and tragedy; and none of us could say, with any certainty, whether or not it would stand up on the stage. Sara Allgood [cast as Juno, she was Lady Gregory's favourite actress, and tragic queen of the Abbey] had some difficulty in reading her script – several times she referred to "Joxer Daly" as "*Boxer* Daly" and had to be corrected . . . Barry Fitzgerald mumbled his way through the part of Captain Boyle and gave not the slightest indication that it was likely to be funny. F. J. McCormick applied his well-known Dublin technique to the part of Joxer yet nothing much worthwhile seemed to be emerging from it. All were agreed that the title of the play was not a good one and that the dialogue written for the part of Jerry

Devine . . . was possibly the most stilted ever written in the history of the Abbey Theatre. There was a general feeling that the play lacked form, that it was much too "bitty", that the mixture of tragedy and comedy "would not go" and that the author of *The Gunman* might well have overshot his mark.

Even the eavesdropping and ever-present Holloway could not report much about *Juno* in rehearsal, and to most of the cast it was a routine production of another new play. Robinson said O'Casey disturbed him at one point by saying that all the characters were literally taken from life. "Would they," wondered Robinson, "come to the back pit, recognise themselves and wreck the theatre?" But O'Casey told him no, they never visited theatres – and he named the pubs they frequented.

In the week preceding the dress rehearsal, fixed for Sunday 2 March, Lady Gregory, who spent most of her time in her family home at Coole, County Galway, came to Dublin, but she, also a painstaking recorder of her theatre's history, could find nothing to note. An end-of-run party for the previous play held up commencement of the dress rehearsal until five p.m. on Sunday. Abbey revelry was famed, and at this time the parties were held under armed guard – as in O'Casey's play, Diehard retribution still took a grisly toll of those who had deserted its banner – so the cast, in particular Sara Allgood, an unquenchably festive spirit, arrived both tired and late.

O'Casey sat waiting in the stalls from four thirty, looking glum, and wondered if the dress rehearsal would actually take place – he couldn't find a soul. He had an additional problem: his eyes had been playing him up badly, an ulcerated cornea not being helped by the extra pressure he had put on them by his feverish efforts at composition by poor light in the early hours of the morning, and by his constant retyping of *Juno*. He was now under the care of Dr Joe Cummins, Senior Surgeon at the Royal Ear and Eye Hospital, whom he visited at 38 Merrion Square East (Yeats lived at Number 82) and who kept him chatting till past midnight: they were "great friends", O'Casey said later, although Cummins was "a strange man, one I could never quite fathom".

At last there was some action at the Abbey. As Fallon wrote:

Gradually the players filed in and quietly went to their dressing rooms . . . Lady Gregory and Robinson took seats in the stalls . . . The curtain rose about 5.36 p.m. So far as I could see and hear while waiting for my cue in the wings the rehearsal seemed to be proceeding smoothly. As soon as I had finished my part of Bentham at the end of the second act I went down into the stalls and sat two seats behind the author . . . I was stunned by the tragic quality of the third act which the magnificent playing of Sara Allgood made almost unbearable. But it was the blistering irony of the final scene which convinced me that this man sitting two seats in front of me was a dramatist of genius.

In spite of the apparently casual attitude of the players to rehearsal, the opening, on Monday night, proved a total triumph. O'Casey this time sat in the second row of the stalls with a friend, and "with his cap on all the while" while underneath his trench coat – it's "a fella in a Thrench coat" who calls on Johnny Boyle, when Joxer refuses to stick his head out of the window "an' mebbe get a bullet in the kisser" – he wore a collar and tie. Rough serge trousers and the heavy Dublin boots known as "bluchers" completed his first-night garb. "A strange, odd fish," commented Holloway.

In Act III, the audience began to laugh as tragedy entered the Boyle family but soon became gripped by the awful actuality – there was always a safe margin in O'Casey for laughing in the wrong places, although not for crying. Afterwards they called for the author.

Juno and the Paycock: pen drawing by Grace Plunkett of Sara Allgood as Juno, F. J. McCormick as Joxer and Barry Fitzgerald as Captain Boyle

The critics were not wholly favourable: the mixture of tragedy and comedy was hard on traditional penpushers, and one called it outrageous, while "Jacques" (J. J. Rice) in the *Irish Independent* objected to the author's verbal padding, attributing it to a thirst for "dialogue with a dig in it". Jacques was otherwise approving. W. J. Lawrence in the *Irish Statesman* was the warmest and most accurate: O'Casey, he wrote,

> is at once an iconoclast and a neo–Elizabethan . . . He lures us into the theatre under the pretext of affording us hearty laughter, and he sends us away with tears in our eyes and with the impression of direst tragedy heavy on our hearts. None but a neo–Elizabethan could accomplish this, since the secret of juxtaposing and harmonising the comic with the tragic, and thereby throwing the elements of terror and pathos into greater relief, have been lost to the English-speaking stage for over a couple of centuries.

Yet O'Casey, whose admirers often provided him with the biggest glass to be shattered, would probably have insisted that Boucicault and old melodramas such as *The Harbour Lights*, *Saved from the Sea*, *The Unknown*, *Peep o'day Boys*, were more crucial antecedents.

The Abbey rapidly became booked out for the rest of the week, ensuring that O'Casey would earn at least twenty-five pounds. While he had been dubious, even hurt, about the cutting of a scene during rehearsal – the main cut Dolan asked for, of a heavy-handed Act III scene taking place at night by the road and showing the actual shooting of Johnny Boyle – O'Casey also seems to have been uncertain of the quality of some of *Juno*'s finer touches, such as the drunken coda of Joxer and Boyle. To him the play still revolved around the figure of Johnny Boyle, who had been expanded from the first version.

Lady Gregory returned to see *Juno* a second time on Friday, bringing Yeats, who hadn't seen it before. He thought it "very fine", and it reminded him of Tolstoy: he told Lady Gregory, when they talked of *The Crimson in the Tricolour*, of which he had been critical, "Casey was bad in writing of the vices of the rich which he knows nothing about, but he thoroughly understands the vices of the poor." Lady Gregory rejoiced in the packed house, the play itself, and what she termed "the call of the Mother for the putting away of hatred". She told Yeats, "This is one of the evenings at the Abbey which makes me glad to have been born."

She had a little talk afterwards with O'Casey in the Green Room.

I asked him to come to tea after the next day, the matinee, as I had brought up a barmbrack [Gort cake] for the players, but he said, "No. I can't come. I'll be at work till the afternoon and I'm working with cement, and that takes such a long time to get off."

"But after that?"

"Then I have to cook my dinner. I have but one room and cook for myself since my mother died."

O'Casey's excuse presumably did not stretch Lady Gregory's credibility on this occasion, though she might have reflected that the tea party was to be late on a Saturday; anyway, as he confessed afterwards in a letter, he used at this time to "buy cooked pork in Yorkstetters"; he might have been hurling, however, with Jim Kavanagh from the basement at Number 422.

There was now a new crowd at the club – "Paddy Callan & his brother Phil; O'Reilly, Michael O'Murchadhu, Leo Rush, Brown, Bennett, the Dunshaughlin lad who broke a leg & thrust a spike through his hand, trying to reclaim a ball beyond the chevaux-de-frise of the Magazine Fort." O'Casey could not afford to compromise his image at the Abbey. If the patrician Yeats kept his mask firmly on by haughtily talking down to "Casey", O'Casey certainly could not for a moment allow his "poor mouth" pose to drop. Anyway, he must have sensed it wise to keep his distance – as well as not to be drawn into risking an opinion on the monstrous barmbrack. He eluded such small patronising gestures, perhaps holding out for higher invitations. Later he admitted he had told a white lie – "Fact I wasn't working when Lady Gregory put the question to me," he said – because he did not want her to find him a more suitable job than labouring.

But he did genuinely thank Lady Gregory for his success, saying (as she recalled):

"I owe a great deal to you and Mr Yeats and Mr Robinson, but to you above all. You gave me encouragement. And it was you who said to me upstairs in the office – I could show you the very spot where you stood – 'Mr O'Casey, your gift is characterisation'. And so I threw over my theories and worked at characters, and this is the result."

Soon after *Juno* opened Jack Daly visited the Abbey, with the real-life Boyle himself in tow. Daly wore a pair of boots given to him for church-going by a lady – he had thanked her profusely, saying, "Now I can kick anyone who annoys me into a blooming pulp". He was furious at the play and brought a lawyer along with a view to suing O'Casey for defamation, but Boyle would not agree, saying the cap did not fit.

Juno did so well in its first week that it was kept on for a second, guaranteeing O'Casey further royalties. Yeats's brother, Jack, the painter, came on the first Saturday night; so did James Stephens: they could find no seats so Dolan and Lady Gregory, after the overture was over, brought them chairs. Augusta Gregory had "Casey" with her, and they sat together: she was taking him under her maternal wing.

When the mother whose son had been killed – "Leader of an ambush where my neighbour's Free State soldier son was killed," cries out, "Mother of Jesus put away from us this murderous hatred and give us thine own eternal love" I whispered to Casey, "that is the prayer we must all use, it is the only thing that will save us, the teaching of Christ". He said "Of humanity".

9

GREEN, WHITE, ORANGE – OR YELLOW

Friendship with William Butler Yeats eluded O'Casey, although he tried hard, in 1924, to get behind the great man's mask; but shyness, in the acute form manifested by Yeats, was inconceivable to O'Casey, more gregarious and used to people, and he took the haughtiness at its face value. Yet he could see that the poet, fifteen years his senior, was in many ways a prisoner of the exalted position he held, surrounded by his hangers-on, whom O'Casey called his "Gaeligorian guards"; without them, O'Casey felt, another side of Yeats might have been seen: gossipy, innocent, ready to laugh.

This may have been a naïve view, but behind, on the one hand, the elaborate artifices of the esoteric dreamer for whom complete knowledge of the higher mysteries of life was the goal, and on the other hand the legerdemain of the highly successful literary operator who had, like his swan with Leda, the instinctive knowledge of when to apply the "brute blood" of power, there could in Yeats be detected something he had in common with O'Casey. Both were Protestant to the core. "I am proud", Yeats was to say in the Irish Senate in 1925, in a speech defending divorce, "to consider myself a typical man of that minority." Although O'Casey would not have gone as far as to declare arrogantly, with Yeats, that "We are one of the great stocks of Europe. We are the people of Burke; we are the people of Grattan; we are the people of Swift, the people of Emmet, the people of Parnell. We have created the most of the modern literature of this country. We have created the best of its political intelligence," he did feel that he possessed the same independent spirit.

Both men also believed in the value of literature, particularly of poetry, and in the poet as hero, seeing his consciousness of liberty as the implacable enemy of religion. Yeats followed in the footsteps of his father who had written:

Religion is the denial of liberty. An enforced peace is set up among the warring feelings. By the help of something quite external, as for instance the fear of hell, some feelings are chained up and thrust into dungeons that some other feelings may hold sway, and all the ethical systems yet invented are a similar denial of liberty, that is why the true poet is neither moral nor religious.

And, in contrast to George Moore, he had been even more directly outspoken against censorship: "I believe that literature is the principal voice of the conscience, and that it is its duty age after age to affirm its morality against the special moralities of clergymen and churches, and of kings and parliaments *and peoples.*" Both Yeats and O'Casey also found in Ireland their area for action, a battleground for their inner convictions as well as a potent symbol that could totally suffice their needs and preoccupations.

Underlying Yeats's early dramatic theory as exemplified in *The Countess Cathleen*, first performed at the Abbey in 1899, had been the notion that spiritual reality was of paramount importance, and that plays should manifest "in one way or other the existence of an invisible world": "My own theory of poetical or legendary drama," he said, "is that it should have no realistic, or elaborate, but only a symbolic and decorative setting." However, in the twenty-odd years that separate *The Countess Cathleen* from the production of *The Shadow of a Gunman*, Yeats's original notion had undergone considerable modification, reflecting his typical flexibility and his subtle and intricate attempts to balance and integrate the opposites within himself. Synge had brought into the movement a fantasy of realism based on traditional Irish parricidal feelings. Lady Gregory brought a lively sense of comedy, and a natural ear for local dialect – Yeats, echoing Wordsworth, wrote approvingly of this to a friend in 1905, "I believe more strongly that the element of strength in poetic language is common idiom, just as the element of strength in poetic construction is common passion." Later, during the First World War, the younger American poet, Ezra Pound, persuaded him to turn *The Player Queen*, the tragedy with which Yeats had been wrestling for many years, trying to sort out his characters' problems of secret daemons and antithetical selves, into something lighter, so that he could escape from allegory: he did this at last, "when I had mocked in a comedy my own thought". At that point Yeats would clearly have been able to recognise the irreverent appeal of such a writer as O'Casey when he came along.

But the pendulum swung the other way, for Pound also tempted

Yeats back into esoteric drama, through his advocacy of the Noh play, so that the Faustian spirit of the much older man was again stirred to experiment with what Pound called "an art for the few, for the nobles; for those trained to catch the allusion . . . it is a symbolic stage, a drama of masks – at least they have masks for spirits and gods and young women". Yeats then began writing *At the Hawk's Well*, another of his plays dramatising the myth of Cuchulain, returning to his earlier ideal of theatre as an unpopular, mysterious art, directed towards an "audience like a secret society where admission is by favour and never to many".

A few weeks after the opening of *Juno* and its wide public acclaim Yeats invited O'Casey to join that society: "Will you come in on Monday March 31 at 8.15? My play the 'Hawk's Well' is being done that evening with masks, costumes and music by Edmund Dulac." He told O'Casey that it would be a quite informal gathering, attended only by those connected with the arts. And, "No day passes without my hearing praise of your play."

O'Casey may have left behind his bluchers on this occasion but later he was still projecting his sense of incongruity in the poet's Merrion Square drawing room, finding it full of the Gaeligorian guard, the men "immaculate in shiny sober black, the women gay and glittering in silk sonorous, and brilliant brocade". No one spoke to O'Casey and he felt they were ill at ease with a tenement-dweller among them. "Yeats suddenly caught sight of him, came quick to him, and guided Sean to the front, where he wheeled over a deep and downy armchair. – You'll be able to see well here, he said."

Conversation between the pair did not progress further: Yeats would probably not have known what else to say. O'Casey, for his part, found the evening ridiculous; he was oblivious to such concerns as Yeats's "terse, vivid diction" which recommended *At the Hawk's Well* to T. S. Eliot as "modern" when he saw it in Islington. But Mick Dolan holding a spear and spouting "I am named Cuchullain; I am Sualtam's sin" didn't exactly translate the Noh convention into Irish with any degree of success for O'Casey, and he was impelled to retreat into riotous imaginings:

he wondered how they would feel, what would happen, if Fluther, furiously drunk, came tumbling into the room, looking for someone to fight him.

– Any two o' yous, any three o' yous; your own selection; anywhere yous like – here or in th' sthreet!

Fluther Good, the "well-oiled" carpenter of *The Plough and the Stars*, had hardly been conceived, let alone written, when O'Casey visited Merrion Square on the day after his forty-fourth birthday. He had made a few jottings about the play, however. When Holloway met him at Webbs, on 20 May, he "happened to mention something about stars and he said that is strange. I am thinking of writing a play called *The Plough and the Stars* about Liberty Hall and Easter Week 1916."

———————

As might be expected, the wooing was the other way in Augusta Gregory's case, even though she was now in her seventy-third year. O'Casey found it much easier to respond unequivocally to her, both in her image as Protestant aristocrat landowner and the warmer reality of her as endearing Mother Superior to the Abbey players and writers, whom, from Yeats and Lennox Robinson on down, she fussed over and cared for as if they were her own children. O'Casey became a particular favourite, at any rate at first, as he accepted her patronage gratefully, and submitted willingly to her advice – she always rather fancied herself, with justification, as a play doctor.

Lady Gregory and O'Casey had much in common, including a stern streak of Protestant moralising, and a commitment to the working class and to pacifism. Her mother had been a proselytiser of peasant Catholics, while O'Casey's father, Michael Casey, had worked for a proselytising mission. Above all O'Casey fulfilled an ambition of Lady Gregory's: to see a genuine working-class playwright rise from the slums (or almost), embodying the new nationalism – pulling himself up, as it were by his own bootstraps – repaid the tremendous efforts she had made on behalf of Irish theatre. Yet sometimes, perhaps, she hankered more than a little after the role of the English patroness and lady of letters for which she had neither quite the stature nor the financial resources.

She too was a commercially successful playwright – a success which had eluded Yeats, so that by now his ambition no longer seriously operated in this sphere – and she and O'Casey shared the ability to entertain an audience. In 1924, she earned royalties of £467, no mean income in those days, and an indication, perhaps, of what O'Casey's plays would earn in the next year or two. But she was never very rich and on principle travelled third class in trains, practising stringent economies in her household which must have reminded O'Casey of his own mother. In a restaurant, she would empty the sugar basin and take its contents home in a used envelope.

O'Casey, who was responsive to external gestures, admired her composure and common touch in the third-class compartment when she met him for the last stage of his journey to her country house at Coole, to which he was invited in June 1924. Touchy as he was towards those with any power or authority, in her case these were authentic externals, and he never turned on her later. As he wrote, reviewing her *Journals* twenty years later, "Living her own life with insistent intensity, Lady Gregory lived, at the same time, ardently, a life among the plain people. She knew Curley the Piper as well as she knew Yeats, and Ardrahan Church better than Westminster Abbey . . . Though far from being well-off, she gave of what she had and added a large part of herself to the gift."

Others, however, have remarked on Lady Gregory's aloofness and condescension, finding her possessed of an annoying and insincere vein of flattery and "a mouth that was inflexible". And O'Casey, oddly in one of his political leanings, overlooked the fact that her long-deceased husband's fortune, with which he had acquired Coole Park, had been made mostly out of India. Perhaps he found it a little too easy to waive his class hatred in the case of certain individuals who took him warmly to their hearts. Perhaps Lady Gregory, too, was playing her part in the game by accepting without question his statements about his early illiteracy and his refusal to take tea with her in the Green Room because he had to attend to the setting of some concrete. There may have been an element of willing self-deception on both sides.

"June is coming & the sun is gaining strength . . . There are the woods to wander in, & there is quiet for writing," Lady Gregory had written, to which he had answered, tongue in cheek, "Isn't it a pity that there are no amusements there? How splended it would be if the Woods of Coole were vibrating with throngs of Joywheels and Charoplanes."

He stayed a week, instead of the two he had been invited for, and was her sole guest. A "trim, stout, sturdy figure", with a bit of a lisp – Lennox Robinson complained later of the way O'Casey caricatured her speech defect in print – she made him very comfortable in the Georgian house, which swarmed with servants who could be summoned with the snap of a finger against a tiny Burmese gong, "that gave a soft, pensive, penetrating note". She told him her sorrows, the loss in the war of her beloved son Robert, leading his air squadron in Italy, the drowning of her nephew, Hugh Lane, when the *Lusitania* was sunk off the Cork coast – leaving, like Boyle's deceased cousin in *Juno*, a disputed will which enabled the British authorities to carry out their "despicable robbery" of his fine picture collection. But she also told him of her joys – her grandchildren, the house at Coole, and, of course, the Abbey.

In the evenings she indulged with O'Casey her love of literature, which he later affectionately recalled, especially her reading to him from Thomas Hardy's *The Dynasts*, that huge sprawling epic drama of the Napoleonic Wars, which she pegged away at night after night, while he battled away to keep himself awake and "be polite to the Spirit of the Years, the Spirit of Pity, the Spirit of Rumour, the Spirits Ironic and Sinister . . . [till] she could murmur, half-exhausted, Dat's de end!"

Did he really enjoy the splendid scenery at Coole? In his thank-you letter – what could be a greater sign of middle-class civility than an eloquent encomium? – he wrote, "I have long pondered over whether the beautiful pictures & statuary, the glorious books, or the wonderful woods, river & Lake of Coole deserve the apple of praise – for they are like the three competitors that stood before & showed their charms to Paris – but I think I must choose the woods, the Lake and the river." But much later he said he "never cottoned on to the woods", because they were gloomy – perhaps reflecting a weak-sighted man's understandable dislike of an ill-lit place – although he acknowledged that Yeats loved them. Any individual response to the river and the lovely lake seemed anyway to have been pre-empted by Yeats (not to mention Shakespeare, in Mercutio's "Queen Mab" speech), and O'Casey sank in artificial, gooey reverence. This wasn't O'Casey country.

He could manage only one original image on this well-beaten literary track: a heath covered with butterflies, a "host of blue evanescent divinity", and fancifully placed Lady Gregory among them: "How delightful the sturdy black figure of her ladyship would look doing a slow, graceful, if a little stiff, minuet among the brilliant-blue fluttering things." But even here he was still looking over his shoulder at Yeats: "Sean wondered if Yeats had ever set eyes on these." There were decided disadvantages in arriving at the tail-end of a literary movement, especially when it came to visiting Coole Park.

———◆◆◆———

In July O'Casey began the play, the consequences of whose production led more directly than anything else to his self-imposed departure from Ireland. He was thinking of calling it *The Plough and the Stars*, "after the name of the flag of the Citizen Army", wrote Fallon, the design for which had been suggested by the poet George Russell. He didn't like work. (Who did?) He had to drive himself to it. In fact he had to write on a piece of paste-board which he displayed on his mantel-piece: GET ON WITH THE BLOODY PLAY! He *was* getting on with it. Would I like to hear some which he had written that day? . . . So far as I remember, it was a very funny scene and mainly concerned the Covey.

The character called the Covey was by this stage more developed than the others, for O'Casey lifted him from *The Crimson in the Tricolour*, displaying his wisdom in not, now that he was established, allowing other theatres to consider those earlier plays rejected by the Abbey, but to keep them as a source of dialogue for later plays.

But he was also writing a new one-act play, which quickly overtook the longer project, and he submitted the shorter piece, after cutting it down heavily, towards the end of the month of July. A comic vignette of North Dublin life, taking place in a provision store O'Casey knew in Dorset Street, *Nannie's Night Out* centred on a meths-drinking nannie who is wooed by an assortment of suitors, and displays a reckless penchant for chaos in her drinking bouts.

In the same month, as a gesture of reconciliation, the Free State Government released Eamon de Valera, who had been in Arbour Hill Prison for almost a year. De Valera's name was again on everybody's lips, and O'Casey wrote to Lady Gregory, "I am glad that de Valera is out again, & read that he says we must go back to 1917. I wish he would read *Back to Methuselah*, and long a little less earnestly for the salvation of his countrymen. A great many of us are really too anxious about the souls of other men." The release prompted him to reminisce, and Holloway noted, "Of all whom he met with in the old Sinn Fein Days, he liked Mrs de Valera the best. She was a very bright, unassuming, intelligent woman; he knew her as Miss O'Flanagan, and heard her lecture very agreeably in Sinn Fein halls. 'It is such as she should represent Ireland in Parliament.'" But much later, when de Valera was President of the Republic, O'Casey told another friend that Mrs de Valera had fallen by the wayside, for "all she does now, seemingly, is to write little plays in Gaelic for production by convent childer".

In late August O'Casey received news that *Juno* and *The Gunman* were to be published together early in the following year, by Macmillans of London. Daniel Macmillan, elder grandson of the founder of the firm, handled some of the most significant figures of the Irish literary revival, including Yeats; he now sought a puff for

O'Casey from James Stephens, who had introduced him to the plays, and who had apparently said that O'Casey was "the greatest dramatic find of modern times". With packed houses continuing at the Abbey, O'Casey was now accounted something of a miracle-worker, one newspaper correspondent noting how audiences had become psychologically transformed. From their usual dour receptivity, "the habit of laughter" had seized them, so that "even in the most poignant moments of Mr O'Casey's plays, a meaningless titter will set your nerves on edge".

Outwardly O'Casey remained much the same, making the Abbey the centre of his social activities – his "club" – watching the audience thronging the vestibule before and after performances, "proud of the fact, but in no way swell-headed, his cloth cap cocked over his left eye, as his right looked short-sightedly at the audience's eager rush". Still a lonely figure, he "foraged for himself", knowing, and calling on, a range of friends and acquaintances, from the very high to the very low. One day an old friend, now married to a Free State general, and affecting a "cockney [i.e. smart and English] accent", stopped to give him a lift and invited him home to tea. "Now?" he said by way of interrogation, but she interpreted this as "no". For godsake, he told her, stop affecting the cockney and speak as you used to in the old days.

The new rich were in the saddle – "beggars on horseback riding to the Devil" – and money flashed in their eyes and pockets. O'Casey's antithetical self could still make a point of his poverty: as when he asked Holloway if he'd ever been to the Labour Exchange:

> He had been there lately and tried to get to the hutch his docket was made out for, but the great crush of men in the queue almost made him faintish, and after about an hour and a half of it (and he still hours away from the hutch) he had to try and push his way out of the crowd. It is a terrible sight to see so many men out of work . . . He should like to show Yeats or Robinson such sights. Then they would be less ready to advocate the use of the lash.

But he had difficulty in keeping his critical spirit on a leash, even with the sympathetic Holloway acting as safety valve, and, after only a short while as the successful author O'Casey began to show dangerous symptoms of the cantankerous fellow who had turned (if he did) on his manager at Hampton and Leedon, insulted his railway employers, and quarrelled with Madame Markiewicz and his idol Larkin.

He thinks Robinson has too many irons in the fire – his *Never the Time and the Place* is but poor stuff . . . I said, "He'd never be forgiven if he dispraised a piece of Robby's." "And why not, if one has an opinion, be allowed to express it?" he queried, and I replied: "I don't know but such is the case when the Abbey is concerned. They never forgive those who criticize their work adversely . . ."

How long would it take for him to turn on his new masters at the Abbey?

Although he was to "put on a poor mouth" to describe the Georgian house at 422 North Circular Road, for the Act III setting of *The Plough and the Stars*, as

> a long, gaunt, five-story tenement; its brick front is chipped and scarred with age and neglect. The wide and heavy hall door, flanked by two pillars, has a look of having been charred by a fire in the distant past. The door lurches a little to one side, disjointed by the continual and reckless banging when it is being closed by most of the residents. The diamond-paned fan-light is destitute of a single pane . . .

Gabriel Fallon found it a "*respectable* tenement", its hall door closed, on "Landlord's orders", O'Casey said, when Fallon called one warm evening in September – his first visit to the playwright's room:

> Its most remarkable feature was its fireplace and the fire it held. I felt the heat of it as soon as I entered. There was a stretcher-bed to the left of the door, its head towards the near window; a washstand beside the bed-head. Rough book-shelves lined with second-hand books stood between the windows. There was a small table under the far window and on it the well-worn typewriter; beside it a plain chair. Each side of the fireplace there were shelved cupboards. On the right-hand wall going in, more book-shelves. In the centre of the room stood a round mahogany table; on it stood an oil lamp, books and papers. To the right of the fireplace there was an easy chair; and, facing the fireplace, a small settee.
>
> "Did you have your tea, Gaby?" Again one is conscious of the quietly insistent, almost regal, note of hospitality. A throwback to the high halls and the groaning tables of royal Kincora . . . He offers me a choice of the easy chair or the settee. I take the easy chair . . . He asks me about rehearsals of *Nannie's Night Out* now in progress.

The one-acter opened towards the end of the month; but although exciting a great deal of attention it flopped (being a tail-ender to the main bill, a revival of Shaw's *Arms and the Man*, it did not, however, turn away the crowds, and the houses were, on the whole, good). "But no sign of life came from the audience," remarked the actress Beatrice Coogan, then still in her teens. "Not a laugh. Not a clap. An actor came off-stage shrugging ruefully." But just as the failure of *Cathleen Listens In* had spurred on O'Casey to carry his talent to new heights with *Juno*, so the tepid response to his one-act absurdity, which, he later wrote to Lady Gregory, he did not like very much, seems to have goaded him into assembling all the power he could muster to continue work on *The Plough and the Stars*.

This took much more protracted labour than *Juno*, and was a broader and more diverse subject than any he had so far attempted. He did not have in mind a simple theme like the one so helpful to the construction of *Juno*, of the crippled IRA man whose stony and appalling fate underpins the comic self-deceptions of the Boyle family. The huge canvas to which he now addressed himself depicted a whole class – the tenement class he knew so well, and with which he had now proved his gift for characterisation – caught up in an epic historical event, the Easter Rebellion of 1916, itself a central part of the dramatic action.

The scale of events was exactly right for representation. The dramatist's instinctive choice of a subject the scope of which was suited both to his writing and to the resources of the Abbey stage and company, was completely justified. Unlike Shakespeare in *Henry V*, where the Chorus constantly apologises for a lack of material means to bring the colourful action fully alive, O'Casey had no sense of shortcomings. To begin with, he did not see the Rebellion of 1916 as at all heroic. His ragged tenement army was in the business of debunking.

For the emotion driving O'Casey to write *The Plough and the Stars* was hatred of the Irish Free State as it had emerged from the strife-torn years of 1916–23, "a discordant symphony in green". He hated the leaders, jockeying for position, seeing their actions as entirely guided by self-interest or revenge – "the stag dead, the hounds hunted the hounds" – and their betrayal of the hopes he and his fellow labour supporters had cherished prior to 1916. De Valera knew nothing of the common people, he was worse than Cosgrave – whom he devoured, like a "Cronus swallowing Zeus". At least Cosgrave had joviality, a streak of erring humanity, but the "pietistic Spaniard" de

Valera was dull and lacked magnetism. O'Casey could not understand the hold that he gained over the Irish people.

He despised, too, the new bourgeoisification of Ireland, the growth of the power of money, the new social stratification and snobbery that became rife. He revived, in his hatred, the old causes which even though he had become disillusioned with them, once evoked his loyalty and affection: the Irish language, for one, with the "cruiskeen lawn" rejected for the cocktail glass, while the teachers of the "adventists" and new Irish aristocracy were "working day and night educating the vulgar hilarity of jig and reel" from their joints. Having cast off British rule, the Irish were feverishly aping its refinements: even – an untypical posture of condemnation for O'Casey – its growing sexual licence. Women were employing experts to make "blue-prints to see how far their bodices could be lowered and still be consonant with diocesan doctrine and Dublin's desperate need of attraction".

The growth of the Church's power – or rather its failure to decline – in the new State excited his irascibility to its highest pitch. Greater humiliation was there none, he believed, than de Valera kneeling before a visiting Cardinal from the Vatican. He ardently embraced the cause of Dr Walter McDonald, whose *Reminiscences of a Maynooth Professor* were posthumously published in 1925, and whose progressive theories he saw as threatening the power and secrecy of Rome. The new Ireland was "a theocracy, fashioned by the Vatican, and decked in the brightest sacerdotal array by the bishops of Maynooth".

Much though he might have liked to, O'Casey did not set out in *The Plough and the Stars* to show how the cause of the Easter Rising was betrayed by the Irish middle classes. Fortunately he was still influenced by the rejection of his early didactic plays, and he had the Robinson–Lady Gregory – even the Yeats – aesthetic firmly lodged in his mind while at work in 1924-5. So he managed, and with genius, to incorporate into the play's conception the opinion of his old Citizen Army commandant, Captain White, that "the Irish question was the sexual problem writ large". Showing the battle between a married pair, the Clitheroes – between Nora with her possessive ideal of motherhood, and Jack with his commitment to the Republican cause, which required sacrifice and which led ultimately to his death – he presented a fundamental conflict in any society facing violent change.

Eight years after the event, he could also, through the Clitheroes, relive the doubts and torn emotions he had experienced during the months prior to Easter 1916 and during Easter Week itself. The Rising had come at a critical time for him, when, long cherished by his mother, long unconsciously rejecting any obstacle in the path of his future development as a writer, he had begun to overcome the active sides of his personality and to develop a negative capability – of watching, observing, recording, feeling. It is ridiculous to assert that O'Casey could not have played an active role in the Rising because of his deficient eyesight: an extremely vigorous hurler, and hard-working secretary, he could have performed a dozen crucial jobs, from courier to staff officer, and an army always needs more noncombatants than combatants. But his sense of his own worth, his preciousness, as cocooned by his mother's care and feelings for him, had outgrown his recognition of the validity of any brave, self-sacrificing gesture.

In real life his mother's side had won, and the two of them lived through the Rising, as he said, dodging bullets with Frank Cahill. With good cause he later dedicated *The Plough and the Stars*, in its published form, "To the gay laugh of my mother at the gate of the grave", for in it her spirit is triumphantly resurrected. His capacity for feeling had been preserved over the need for action – and with it his sympathy for the rogue, the looter, the coward, the wastrel. This was the unholy "Oisin spirit" as opposed to the "St Patrick purity and commitment" exemplified by Pearse and the other heroes of 1916. No wonder O'Casey hated de Valera, who had taken part in the Rebellion and survived, his masculine ethic finally emerging as all-powerful – while O'Casey had avoided action, elevating cowardice into a virtue while feeling a deeper conflict, if not shame, over doing so.

But it was O'Casey who wrote *The Plough and the Stars*, and not de Valera. In the play O'Casey reverses what actually happened to him and shows the destructive, heroic principle winning – with Clitheroe being killed as a result, Nora losing her baby and retreating into madness, Bessie Burgess being shot by a stray bullet intended for a sniper, while the consumptive girl Mollser – neglected victim as much of poverty as of war – ends up sharing a coffin with Nora's premature child. Even the Tommies who swarm over the tenements are, as O'Casey sketched them in, not such bad chaps; they don't murder and rape on sight, but brew up tea and have a mocking compassion for those they hunt down. Cumulatively, then, in O'Casey's dark vision of the events of 1916, his irreverence becomes far more than comic: it becomes a deliberate kind of profanity, a calculated act of desecration of what was now considered the most holy event in the emergence of the new Ireland, combining a nativity with a paschal sacrifice.

All through 1924, more under the tutelage of Lady Gregory than of anyone else, O'Casey was broadening his technical knowledge of playwriting and the range of his general reading. He borrowed Mark Twain's *Personal Recollections of Joan of Arc*, finding it a "worthy supplement" to Shaw's play, which he had read and was to see the following year at the Abbey; Upton Sinclair's *The Singing Jailbirds*, on which he commented, "Honestly, I don't think much of it as Drama, & very little of it as an expression of life. The Play is, I think, hysterical."

He had regularly been attending productions of the Dublin Drama League, founded in 1918, which performed at the Abbey on Sunday and Monday nights, and which introduced him to the work of other contemporary playwrights, among them Eugene O'Neill and Ernst Toller. So he was able further to dismiss *The Singing Jailbirds* as "not comparable" to either O'Neill's *Hairy Ape* or Toller's *Masses and Men*. Cautiously he was experimenting with one or two innovatory notions culled from these two authors in particular (as well as from Strindberg), and he also drew on the experience gained from *Nannie's Night Out*, in which he had used expressionist methods in presenting deliberate stereotypes such as the Free-Stater, Farmer, Republican, and Labourer. The shortcomings of such effects having been powerfully, although not indelibly, recorded, he toned down similar stylistic devices in *The Plough and the Stars*, till they chimed perfectly with the overriding, sometimes almost photographic, realism.

The intermittent use in Act II of the offstage speech of the Republican leader – clearly based on Padraic Pearse – is one such expressionist device and helps to make that act, set in a "commodious publichouse", a theatrical image as universal as Shakespeare's Boar's Head in Eastcheap in *Henry IV*. The "voices in a lilting chant", in Act IV, crying their "Red Cr . . . oss, Red Cr . . . oss! Ambu . . . lance, Ambu . . . lance!" in a much more frenetic and German manner, add to the confusion and hysteria O'Casey shows in the tenement as the British forces mount their final counter-attack on the Post Office, and the "*glare in the sky seen through the window flares into a fuller and a deeper red*".

Lady Gregory's tutelage of her latest and greatest find was at its most inspired when she read to O'Casey from *The Dynasts*, for, tedious and long-winded as much of it is, Hardy's work conveys a strong and brooding atmosphere of inevitable fate – as if the powerful protagonists were but puppets being manipulated by some amoral destiny. It is this sense of historical inevitability which, imported into O'Casey's own chronicle, gives it unity and a confidence in its tragic progression, for *The Plough and the Stars* has no plot, as *Juno* had, no inexhaustible and grabbing music-hall mentality as in *Gunman*. The later play, in its multiplicity and subtlety of vision, could dispense with conventional plot, and could trace events with the flexibility and spontaneity of a camera recording actuality as it followed, in the jargon of later decades, the first "National Liberation Movement" of the twentieth century.

While O'Casey repeatedly claimed that he took his inspiration from the Citizen Army's Plough and Stars flag – "a sacrament to the Citizen Army members" – he also took, as he had in *Gunman* and *Juno*, much from other people's lives. Clitheroe (whose forename, Jack, links him not only to his author but to Rocliffe in *The Harvest Festival* – another martyr, but to a different cause) was based largely on Sean Connolly, the Abbey actor and Citizen Army captain who commanded the City Hall garrison (which included three of his brothers and his sister); Connolly died on Easter Monday, which prevented the opening of a double bill at the Abbey on Thursday 25 April.

Fluther Good, the main comic protagonist, who bickers with his companions Peter Flynn and the Young Covey – the three together provide a mocking chorus to the Rising as well as other aspects of Dublin life – had, like Captain Boyle, a real-life counterpart, John Good, dubbed "Fluther" when he once hit an itinerant flautist on the head with his own instrument. Similarity went no further than the name.

Much of O'Casey's brother, Mick, went into Fluther: according to their nephew, Kit Casey, the playwright reproduced verbatim what Mick used to say, especially his comically pompous tricks of repeating words like "derogatory" and his drunken but always courteous pride: "What d'ye take Fluther for? You must think Fluther's a right gom. D'ye think Fluther's like yourself, destitute of a titther of undherstandin'?" Mick's absurd self-protectiveness – the self-indulgence of a middle-aged man cosseted and pampered by his mother, as both Mick and Sean apparently had been – is revealed in his response to Mrs Gogan describing the onset of the killer consumption: "It's only a little cold I have; there's nothing derogatory wrong with me" and, later, "A man in th' pink o' health should have a holy horror of allowin' thoughts o' death to be festherin' in his mind, for (*with a frightened cough*) be God, I think I'm afther gettin' a little catch in me chest that time – it's a creepy thing to be thinkin' about." When Mrs Gogan leaves, having punctured his weak vanity, which needs alcohol to sustain it, he collapses on a chair: "You can't sneeze but that oul' one wants to know th' why an' th' wherefore . . . I feel as dizzy as bedamned! I hope I didn't give up th' beer too suddenly."

O'Casey presented his brother affectionately in Fluther, showing him as he was, but underlining his capacity for courage in his vanity and weakness. It is Fluther who bravely rushes out to look for Nora when she madly follows her husband through the barricades; it is Fluther, alone, who defiantly, in the face of the Tommies rounding up the men, puts in a word for the rebels: "Fight fair! A few hundhred scrawls o' chaps with a couple o' guns an' Rosary beads, again' a hundhred thousand thrained men with horse, fut an' artillery . . . an' he wants us to fight fair!"

A failed Irish marriage, similar to that of Boyle and Joxer, is shown in the profane squabbles of the Covey and Peter. This, with Fluther's anti-heroic tirades, Rosie Redmond, the prostitute's, fleshy baiting of political theorists, Bessie Burgess's Protestant defence of the British war effort on the side of Belgium – "call themselves Catholics", she sneers at the Irish nationalists, "when they won't lift a finger to help poor little Catholic Belgium" – make *The Plough* a savage indictment of Ireland's independence. Above all, this is crowned with Pearse's cry for the redemptive blood sacrifice of heroes: "Bloodshed is a cleansing and sanctifying thing, and the nation that regards it as the final horror has lost its manhood."

But O'Casey never departs from capturing life accurately: as with Fluther, there was a real-life Covey, but the force of Covey's character comes from O'Casey's ironic depiction, in this narrow-minded left-wing idealist, of an earlier self: the basic inequality of his feeling is scornfully unmasked by Rosie, whose opinions he dismisses as a "prostitute's" – a taboo, inflammatory word: "You louse, you louse, you! . . . You're no man . . . You're no man . . . I'm a woman, anyhow, an' if I'm a prostitute aself, I have me feelin's . . . Thryin' to put his arm around me a minute ago, an givin' me th' glad eye, th' little wrigglin' lump of desolation turns on me now, because he saw there was nothin' doin'." According to Maire Keating, with whom O'Casey was "walking out" again – after the first flush of his success he had renewed their on-and-off relationship – he made a big effort to authenticate Rosie:

One evening he left off his collar and tie and put on a scarf instead – he said it made him look disreputable – and he went down to Burgh Quay. He hoped to meet the right sort of girl there. He didn't have long to wait before one came up to him. He asked her a lot of questions and when he had got most of his information he put on the poor mouth and pretended he had no money. She took pity on the poor starving writer and took him to a café and bought him a cup of coffee.

Others found the seed of Rosie in "Honour Bright" a well-known tart, later a murder victim.

As for other characters, O'Casey drew on the rooms above and below in 422, and elsewhere in his locality; "Mrs Gogan" and "Bessie Burgess" were tenement-dwellers he introduced to May Craig, now F. J. McCormick's wife, when she came to play Mrs Gogan. Mollser was based on an ailing Kavanagh child in the basement; for the dead Clitheroe baby he drew on the memory (or his mother's) of his buried siblings. Captain Brennan, the Diehard of the Citizen Army who stiffens Clitheroe's loyalty, wavering in the face of Nora's onslaughts, was based on "Padjo" (Patrick Joseph) Flannagan, a Moore Street chicken butcher killed in Church Street, which explains Bessie's lines, "th' professor of chicken-butcherin' there, finds he's up against somethin' a little tougher even than his own chickens, an' that's sayin' a lot! . . . Choke th' chicken, choke th' chicken, choke th' chicken!" Reversing reality, and making Brennan humiliatingly seek in civilian clothes to save his own skin – while having urged Clitheroe to his death – O'Casey again soils the heroic image.

But the manner in which little details remained sharp in his memory from real events which time and imagination transmuted into art is best shown by the oak coffin of Mollser which stands on stage on two kitchen chairs, lit by two candles, while Peter, the Covey, and Fluther play cards, waiting for the undertaker's men to carry it away and while the street outside is "hot shop", the air "shakin' with the firin' o'rifles, an' machine-guns". This recalled the experience of the O'Toole Club member, Mick Smith, fighting from inside Jacobs' Biscuit Factory, who could see on the other side of the street, through the window of a flat, a tiny coffin waiting for burial: all during Easter Week the family had been too terrified to move it out to the cemetery.

The creation of *The Plough* was a painstaking act of willing a form to emerge "of its own birth", as Coleridge described the poet's imaginative procedure, which could express, to distort Wordsworth's phrase, volatile emotions reactivated in tranquillity. There was none of the white heat of *Juno* about it, and O'Casey confessed early in 1925 that his work was often interrupted. As Holloway reported, "I . . . heard one workman say to another in D'Olier Street, 'You're a bloody fool to work for anyone if you can help it,' and when I told O'Casey what

I overheard, he replied, 'Work was made for mugs.' He hasn't been working at the new play of late. He is lazy." He told Fallon he was worried about the Voice of the Man in Act II. "'You see, Gaby,' he said, 'that speech is made up of extracts from speeches delivered by Padraic Pearse and there are people who knew Pearse who might object.'"

For a man who sucked power and inspiration from failure, O'Casey now had to contend with growing success. Part of this was highly enjoyable even if, as he informed Lady Gregory, "I am very busy laying down linoleum in my room; having the floor sides stained & waxed & the window frames painted, and all the bother makes me feel far from friendly towards civilisation." To R. M. Fox, busy in London writing an article and seeking information, he replied with cantankerous certainty, an echo of the tone in which Shaw had paid him off when he sought help from him:

> I'm afraid you'll have to write your article without any help from me. Desire for quietude is stronger in me than desire for publicity – the spirit is stronger than the flesh. It's not due to modesty; I'd love to blow my own trumpet, but the work's too hard. And even if others supply the trumpet, they expect you to provide the wind. This refusal isn't singular; I have just declined to allow an artist to sketch my face, simply because I was too lazy.

In February 1925 Macmillan published *Juno* and *The Gunman* as *Two Plays*. They were widely and enthusiastically noticed; 1,500 copies were printed originally, priced at seven shillings and sixpence, and the book was reprinted before the end of the year, and three times in 1927; in New York, where *Two Plays* was published by J. J. Little and Ives Company, the print run was 15,000. Dedicated "To Maura and to the Abbey Theatre", the copy O'Casey gave to Maire was further inscribed, "To the lovely and loveable Maura in whom the author found his first inspiration".

A London management made plans to produce *Juno*, while a New York theatre also began negotiations to put it on. But, while he bathed everywhere in this glow of success – the usual backbiting comments of a few Dublin critics on the published plays in no way denting his well-being – O'Casey's enthusiasm for the Abbey, the sword of light which he had carried for now well over three years, began to flicker. Perhaps success threatened the anger that kept the flame lustrous – or perhaps, as a commentator observed, he could only ever keep one enthusiasm alive at a time. For whatever reason, during the middle and towards the end of 1925 his relationship with the Abbey Theatre – although not yet with Yeats and Lady Gregory – began to deteriorate.

The Abbey Theatre had, by today's London standards for either commercial or subsidised theatre, small means to meet enormous demands: it responded to these at its own modest level, and had developed extraordinary resourcefulness and flexibility. On the barest of lifelines provided by the backers, notably Annie Horniman, Lady Gregory, and latterly the Irish Free State, its company existed barely above subsistence level, most of its members subsidising their acting by working outside: for instance, F. J. Dolan, who as the director of *Juno* had been instrumental in O'Casey's success, still worked in a Guinness brewery.

Yeats's plays had, as Micheál MacLiammóir wrote, "thinned down the stalls to a few ecstatic readers of poetry", but by the early 1920s his hopes for a poetic theatre were fading. The perfect diction and artificial style of acting instilled by Frank Fay and his brother W. G. (Willie), which had brought out the peculiar inflections of the Irish voice, were also on the wane, although clarity of meaning and careful attention to the sounds of words were still a powerful legacy. But Yeats had restored words to their sovereignty. The words now spoken were in the rich dialect of the Dublin tenements, with an urban directness and accessibility – some would say coarseness – of which Yeats had not dreamed.

Yeats did not want his actors to have physicality, but to be as nearly as possible abstract mouthpieces. As O'Casey amusingly reported later, Yeats once even thought of "putting actors into barrels and, armed with a long pole, pushing them into any new position he wanted them to take" (the barrels were to be mounted on castors). But he and Lady Gregory managed to get the actors to stay still, and in so doing "sent into the world a number of the finest actors the world ever saw".

The Fay style had another side to it – a side which looked towards the naturalism of Antoine, and the more robust genius of Coquelin – which was wonderfully adapted to O'Casey's heightened naturalism. But Yeats was not entirely happy with the way the naturalistic vein of playwriting had emerged conqueror over the poetic vein. He complained afterwards, "We were to find ourselves in a quarrel with public opinion that compelled us against our own will and the will of our players to become always more realistic, substituting dialect for verse, common speech for dialect", disciplining that same thought in his lines:

> But actors lacking music
> Do most excite my spleen
> They say it is more human
> To shuffle grunt and moan
> Not knowing what unearthly stuff
> Rounds a mighty scene.

O'Casey's shuffles, grunts and moans had cemented a new style of acting which gave to his work as much as it took from it: both were based on direct observation of the life and theatricality of the Dublin people.

Of the Abbey players, although Barry Fitzgerald impressed O'Casey more, F. J. McCormick was probably the greater actor. He embodied the essence of impersonal dedication, even mediumship, that Yeats advocated as a necessary adjunct to art. F. J. was a self-effacing man, avoiding publicity, passing

from juvenile leads to middle-aged character parts. He was unknown to the English stage and in fact unknown to all but Abbey Theatre goers . . . Even to his fellow players, McCormick remained little known except professionally. He came from his home to his dressing-room and then to the wings to wait to go on. As he stood there McCormick ceased to be and the character he was playing took over. If any of the other actors spoke to him he seemed not to hear.

Fallon compared McCormick as Joxer with Fitzgerald as Boyle, finding in the former a deeper intensity of character, while Fitzgerald, in the manner of Laurence Olivier, seemed to have assumed the character he was playing as he put on each feature of the disguise:

As he stepped back to survey in his dressing-room mirror the effect of his application of grease paint one noticed his right shoulder beginning to droop. As he completed his make-up this effect began to harden. By the time he was satisfied with his appearance as Boyle, his walk – in heavy boots – had become a slither and the drooped right shoulder had become a permanent feature of his characterisation. This I attribute to the inward conviction of his characterisation.

There was no doubt in the actress Siobhan McKenna's mind that McCormick, who descended visibly to Joxer's level – even cracking coarsely profane jokes in his dressing-room as Joxer – was "incomparably the greater". Siobhan McKenna, too, had a very high opinion of Lennox Robinson as a director: "Very underestimated," she called him, "very inconspicuous, but he had a wonderful way of bringing out the best in any part, and didn't mind where you moved or sat." Robinson adhered to the policy of overriding trust the Abbey management had for its actors, allowing them to be largely self-directing.

The small group of actors who made up the company were to all intents and purposes a family, bound together not only in some cases by blood ties or by marriage, but united, as a family is, by shared tensions, loyalties and feuds. The company did not always display harmonious family affection, as Cyril Cusack, who joined it later for a revival of *The Plough and the Stars* at the Embassy Theatre in London, noted:

> The Allgood sisters not on speaking terms; O'Rorke (according to Agate, "a magnificent Fluther") and myself (the young Covey) at purse-lipped loggerheads; then, finally, and to crown all "togetherness", Miss Allgood – Sara – in the wings suddenly, belligerently addressing me:
> "Do you think I'm fat?"
> "Well . . ." I began, a little defensively, "no-o . . ."
> "What, then?"
> "Well, I'd say . . ." – I thought I had hit on the right word – "I'd say . . . plump!"
> Just then, by the grace of God, Bessie Burgess had to make an entrance on-stage. But Miss Allgood never spoke to me again.

The Abbey's genuine tradition, Cusack believed, was founded on the actors' summoning of "stage presence", which he defined as a quality distinct from personality – "which, as often as not, is just a page torn from the gossip-column"; and distinct also from "a real character – usually no more than a public-house adornment".

O'Casey should have had the good sense not to start finding fault with these "presences", and have understood that the relationship between playwright and actors is a most delicate one, and likely to be upset by a single ill-judged word of criticism on the playwright's part. Actors may pitch in and fight among themselves but they quickly kiss and make up; the playwright has a different status altogether, and many actors like to keep him at arm's length: he can be an inhibiting presence – as well as hurtful.

O'Casey may well have understood this, but his greater need was to express himself with a blunt honesty, and he tended always to see his own opinions as causes to be fought for. He had already incurred some ill-will for criticising F. J. (as Seumas Shields) for getting laughs in the wrong places – a story given wide currency in the numerous versions in which it has been circulated. He had insisted on his own choice of Fitzgerald to play Boyle, overriding Robinson's choice of F. J.: not a bad thing in itself except that O'Casey subsequently took credit for it, and went out of his way to refer to the Abbey's misjudgment in as wounding a way as possible. More recently, Holloway had warned him to be tactful in voicing his opinion of Robinson's play, *The White Blackbird*. But towards the end of the summer of 1925 O'Casey became involved in a bitter wrangle – totally unnecessary – with the whole Abbey company.

The summer of 1925 passed well for O'Casey, as he continued to lead the life of a celebrity, while working on his new play. Though steadily, and apparently without hope, continuing his now much more sedate wooing of Maire, more desperate methods of courtship manifested themselves in his dealings with the Abbey actress, Beatrice Coogan, with whom, she recalled, he walked the streets reminiscing about the past. On one of these walks he was talking about his play in progress, when "the Church of the Three Patrons, Rathgar, loomed up, its door still open". "I'm going in here," said Beatrice:

> A few yards round the corner was my home in Kenilworth Square. Every few moments my father would be out on the steps scanning all approaches. The church offered a strategic moment for parting from Sean. "Are you coming in to say a prayer?" I quipped, thinking that he wouldn't, but wanting to soften my abruptness.
>
> His answer surprised me. "I'm not a Catholic" – I had assumed with a name like his that he was sure to be. "I am an agnostic," he continued. "I believe in Christ and I consider that St Augustine was the only Christian after Christ." Then after that rather sententious remark his voice and even his face seemed to alter as he added, "But if *you* want me to, I'll go inside and kneel with you while you pray."

She found his words strangely humbling; much later when he had walked her back to Kenilworth Square, disparagingly dismissing it as a "bloomin' rich man's square", he refused to go away, but remained in front of the hedge that enclosed the park, a sinister presence in his trench coat. Next day while walking her dogs she came across him again: he had been out there all night and fallen asleep exhausted.

Beatrice Coogan might just have been exercising a proclivity for "Irish fact"; but she continues with an account of the books he showered upon her as presents, among them G. K. Chesterton's *Life of St Francis*, where she hits upon the truth: "I had the impression that there was a basic spirituality always striving within him." She repulsed his attempts to kiss her. There was another girl she knew he had fallen for (presumably Maire), who "had found his preoccupation with the severities of life and its inequalities, and this business of retaining the aura of poverty and shabbiness, rather offsetting. So, I thought, was this business of breaking off from some grave discourse to administer a kiss like a wallop."

O'Casey's own view of his gallivanting was more spirited, although just as inconclusive: he wrote to Fallon, "Had Joyce Chancellor [another Abbey actress], [Raymond] Brugère [École Normale professor spending a year at Trinity] and Will [Shields, i.e. Barry Fitzgerald] with me on Thursday evening. The Brugère Butterfly was comically fluttherin' around the chancellorian Rose all the evening. Poor little Joyce! a wistful little body, full of quaint charm." But the tension of his own unrelieved sexual appetite, though it found an outlet in the almost orgasmic as well as tragic ending of *The Plough and the Stars*, may well have contributed to the big bust-up with the Abbey actors in mid-August. It exactly coincided with his letter to Lady Gregory telling her he had finished the new play. He now had merely to give it a final look – "type the Caste" – and he would be ready to avail himself of her "brimming kindness" and pay another visit to her, to "plunge enthusiastically into the wonderful woods of Coole".

On 10 August Shaw's *Man and Superman* opened at the Abbey. For O'Casey the play was the equivalent, possibly, of brother Mick's indulgence in drink: it gave him psychic and emotional relief, an escape, from the huge effort he had put into *The Plough and the Stars*. Shaw's verbal assault intoxicated him. Drink and quarrelling alike assuage the sexual urge; as Captain White, given to epigrams, observed, "in the words of the Gaelic proverb, fighting is better than loneliness".

O'Casey went backstage after the Shaw play. F. J. was acting Tanner, in a performance O'Casey hated, and the director was Michael Dolan. O'Casey, wielding a sword for Bernard Shaw, at once launched an onslaught on the company, an attack he later defended with mock innocence and hardly convincing bewilderment: he said it was a patchy production which had little merit or consistency and deserved general ridicule. Shocked, the actors tried to hush him up, while F. J. (in O'Casey's version) warned, "'I hear you've been criticising our rendering of Shaw's play. You've got a bit of a name now, and you must not say these things about an Abbey production. If you do, we'll have to report it to the Directors.'"

Not content to leave it at that – and rubbing salt into the effect of the bad notices next day – O'Casey wrote to Dolan that his first impressions were "confirmed and intensified" upon reflection, and restated them, directing a strong personal attack at Dolan over his loyalty to F. J.'s performance. "Extravagant vehemence. . . marred the whole pattern of the play, and the thing that astonishes me is that you seem to fail to see it." He went on to exempt from his indictment his favourite in the company, Barry Fitzgerald, playing Roebuck Ramsden, who "admits he was bad", and Ria Mooney (Violet Robinson). But Ann (played by Eileen Crowe, later F. J.'s wife) was "the weakest manifestation of the surging life force one could imagine".

O'Casey's old demons – the Deverell brothers of Leedon's, the foreman Reid and the engineers on the GNR, the bosses and bourgeois nationalists such as Bulmer Hobson, or his brother Mick – had assumed a new and unlikely form: that of a pathetically touching and gifted family of actors. As he had done with every other organisation with which he became involved, he now split up the Abbey into phantom goodies and baddies, pinning his own dark inner hostilities on to good and well-meaning people.

There was also something of the holy fool about the way O'Casey voiced the self-defeating vanity of his opinions:

I have written this primarily to show that no savage attack upon me by you or by Mr F. J. McCormack [sic] will prevent me from venturing to give an answer for the hope that is in me, and to point out that while the Abbey Players have often turned water into wine, they may occasionally, (as in this instance, in my opinion) turn wine back again into water . . .

– especially as he then, with these words, handed over the first typed copy of *The Plough and the Stars* to the Abbey for its consideration.

Perhaps he was also saying, "I dare you not to perform it . . ."

Dolan, a hard uncompromising man, cast in the role of O'Casey's scourge, responded by pinning his wine-and-water letter up on the theatre notice board. A few nights later Seághan Barlow, the stage carpenter and painter, stopped O'Casey on his way to the Green Room:

> BARLOW: May I ask what you're doin' on th' stage?
> SEAN: I'm on my way to the Green Room.
> BARLOW: There's none but the actors and officials allowed on the stage, and we'd be glad if you came this way no more.

Success must have been a terrible strain. It brought no comfort, only more exposure, while failure had always its own compensations for one of the unlucky Caseys.

10

DIVINE AFFLATUS

But O'Casey had written his masterpiece, so – for perhaps the only time in his life – his cantankerousness was borne, while the inflamed feelings of those he had attacked were waved aside but not forgotten. McCormick seemed to be a saint of another kind, however, one who bore no grudge at all. Riding high, O'Casey set out for Coole on 19 August 1925 for a fortnight's holiday, with its agreeable prospect of meeting Jack Yeats, W. B.'s painter brother, and his wife, Mary, who were also guests.

The night he arrived, Lady Gregory received the copy of his *The Plough and the Stars* from Lennox Robinson, who had previously sent it to Yeats. Both men had found it "probably the best thing O'Casey has done". Lady Gregory read the play aloud to her house guests – the first act on Sunday, the other three on Monday evening. Her opinion bore out those of Robinson and Yeats. "It was rather embarrassing to me," O'Casey wrote to Fallon, "to hear her reading the saucy song sung by Rosie & Fluther in the second act, but she is an extraordinarily broadminded woman & objects only to the line 'put your leg over mine, Nora'; not because it is objectionable, but because she's afraid it may provoke a laugh from the wrong people." The play was then sent off to George O'Brien, Professor of Economics at University College, who had been appointed government watchdog of the theatre that summer when the Abbey received its first annual subsidy from the Free State.

O'Casey had designed his new play like a projectile aimed at stirring up the wasps' nest of the new Ireland. He had worried over what friends and supporters of the Easter Rising might think, but not Abbey Theatre employees. M. J. Dolan, slow to forgive O'Casey after their row, made the first sabotage attempt, writing to Lady Gregory on 2 September, "I would think twice before having anything to do with it. The language in it is – to use an Abbey phrase –

beyond the beyonds. The song at the end of the second act, sung by the 'girl-in-the-streets', is unpardonable.''

Dolan successfully lobbied George O'Brien, who had now read the script. He declared that the introduction in Act II of Rosie Redmond, one of O'Casey's master strokes, was quite unnecessary to the action. Prostitutes *per se*, O'Brien thought, were not in themselves objectionable, but "The lady's professional side is unduly emphasised in her actions and conversation and I think that the greater part of this scene should be re-written." He also found fault with O'Casey's numerous profanities and "vituperative vocabulary" – words such as "bitch", "lowsers" and "lice" – and with the Clitheroes' Act I love scene, which did not "read true". He thought, with Lady Gregory, that Jack's "put your leg over mine" should be cut, and in addition, "Little rogue of th' white breast".

Fortunately – for he would probably have publicised them – O'Casey did not know of these comments; Yeats and Robinson tactfully disposed of O'Brien, agreeing about Clitheroe in Act I, but putting the economist, now self-appointed censor, firmly in his place:

> O'Casey is contrasting the ideal dream with the normal grossness of life and of that she [the prostitute] is an essential part. It is no use putting her in if she does not express herself vividly and in character, if her "professional" side is not emphasised. Almost certainly a phrase here and there must be altered in rehearsal but the scene as a whole is admirable, one of the finest O'Casey has written. To eliminate any part of it on grounds that have nothing to do with dramatic literature would be to deny all our traditions.

O'Brien, prophetically as it turned out, stuck to his point, replying to Yeats and Robinson on 13 September: "I feel however that there are certain other considerations affecting the production to which it is, in a peculiar way, my duty to have regard. One of these is the possibility that the play *might offend any section of public opinion so seriously as to provoke an attack on the theatre* [my italics] of a kind that would endanger the continuance of the subsidy. Rightly or wrongly, I look upon myself as the watchdog of the subsidy. Now, I think that the play, just as it stands, might easily provoke such an attack . . ."

Returning to Dublin, O'Casey found he had developed a taste for the countryside, especially the cock that sat on his windowsill every morning: "They are mending the road just outside my window, & a lumbering road-engine, with its monstrous, monotonous rumble has taken the place of the cock. He had a rare three-course meal the last day I was with him – bread & butter, barm-brack and ginger-cake." Yeats had rung O'Casey at the Abbey and invited him round to Merrion Square to discuss alterations to the text of *The Plough and the Stars* – Yeats felt in particular that the first act love scene needed altering. The full force of Yeats's approval turned on O'Casey warmed him so much that he exclaimed excitedly to Lady Gregory, "Speaking to me across the telephone, Mr Yeats said he thought *The Plough & the Stars* a wonderful play, and I am very pleased to rank with you, and Yeats, Robinson & Synge in the great glory of the Abbey Theatre." He babbled on to Lady Gregory like an excited schoolboy, enclosed cuttings about the Abbey, and revealed that he was now the hero of his former hero's followers:

Jim Larkin had a great meeting here on Wednesday night. His men were jubilant, for five boats laden with coal, purchased by the Union, had berthed in the Liffey, and some food ships are expected too.

He spoke again of "the little Theatre, over the river", at the meeting, and I know that many coal-heavers, dockers, Carters & labourers have been in the Abbey, & good is sure to come from their visits. Many grumbling to me because they couldn't get in wanted to know "why the hell we didn't take the Tivoli [a music hall theatre]!"

Calling on Yeats in his Merrion Square study, O'Casey was almost overcome, first, by the "onslaught of venomous warmth", and, second, by the ear-splitting scream of fifty canaries in a gold-barred cage – "Dose derrible birds," Lady Gregory called them, in O'Casey's mocking rendering of her slight speech impediment. He found the great man ready to address him.

"O'Casey," Yeats boomed, "you have written a great play; this play is the finest thing you have done. In an Irish way, you have depicted the brutality, the tenderness, the kindling humanity of the Russian writer, Dostoevsky." At Coole, prodding the logs with a brass poker, Lady Gregory had smilingly and ingenuously told O'Casey how shocked she had been to find Yeats had read nothing by Dostoevsky; she had immediately lent him two of the novels. So now, when Yeats announced "O'Casey, you are the Irish Dostoev-sky!" O'Casey's comment was, "And Yeats only after reading the man's book for the first time the night before."

Back at the more modest North Circular Road O'Casey sat down to alter his love scene, and to read *The Idiot* himself with "reverent avidity", commenting to its generous lender Lady Gregory in words that she must have wanted to hear from her all too often defiantly atheistic protégé, "It is a great story . . . The central figure is a Christ that was born in Russia. Not Revolutions, but men must bring about the Brotherhood of Man."

<hr>

The Plough and the Stars had other faults, although they were not in any way obstacles to production; rather, they were flaws endemic in O'Casey's nature, which his judgment could or should have modified rather than developed with time. Minnie in *Gunman* was not an altogether successful character, and the same might be said of Mary Boyle: Nora Clitheroe, a much more important and central character than the other two, also fails to be wholly convincing. Respectable, straightforward heroines are not susceptible to the accretions of character or presence that O'Casey is so adept at applying: Rosie Redmond, the more dangerous and provocative female, stirred his imagination at a deeper level. Here, perhaps, is the answer to why he did not marry Maire: it was not, ultimately, as he presented it, that she thought she was too good for him, but that her virtue and goodness palled on him.

Other faults in *The Plough and the Stars* were potentially more serious. The Abbey guardians had curbed his proselytising tendency, made him concern himself wholly with character and with reproducing the processes of Dublin life. But in the character of the Covey and especially in the verbal duels he has with Fluther and Peter, O'Casey was beginning to revert to his old practice, before the acceptance of his first play, of using his characters as spokesmen for ideological points of view.

> THE COVEY (*loudly*): There's no use o'arguin' with you; it's education you want, comrade.
> FLUTHER: The Covey an' God made the world, I suppose, wha'?
> THE COVEY: When I hear some men talkin' I'm inclined to disbelieve that th' world's eight-hundhred million years old, for it's not long since th' fathers o' some o' them crawled out o' th' sheltherin' slime o' the sea.

These exchanges reveal the start of the considerable negative influence Shaw had on O'Casey, which increased when the two men later became friends. All Shaw's debaters have brilliant minds, but

O'Casey's verbal brawlers are not in the same league; they scatter shrapnel instead of forging sharp points.

Also, in *The Plough and the Stars*, O'Casey began to display an ominous if still only slight capacity for self-parody, a long-windedness which shows with what care the dividing line needs to be drawn between self-mockery and pomposity:

> FLUTHER (*scornfully*): Then Fluther has a vice versa opinion of them that put ivy leaves into their prayer-books, scabbin' it on th' clergy, an' thryin' to out-do th' haloes o' th' saints be lookin' as if he was wearin' around his head a glittherin' aroree boree allis!

or

> PETER: . . . isn't it a poor thing for a man who wouldn't say a word against his greatest enemy to have to listen to that Covey's twartin' animosities, shovin' poor, patient people into a lashin' out of curses that darken his soul with th' shadow of th' wrath of th' last day!

The stage directions, too, tend to become overdetailed and elaborate. Significantly, the Act I setting of the Clitheroes' flat – used for only a quarter of the play – is described at twice the length of the Boyles' living room in *Juno*, from which the action never moves.

O'Casey was determined that Lennox Robinson should direct *The Plough and the Stars*, and his wish was granted. The casting proved fraught with difficulties. Fallon charged Robinson with choosing players to weaken the production, for the reason that he was now jealous of O'Casey's reputation, but this seems unlikely. Robinson, not very strong himself and increasingly given to drink, assembled a cast every bit as strong as Dolan had for *Juno*. O'Casey had his way with Fluther (Barry Fitzgerald), while F. J., the Jack Tanner he had despised, seemed no bad choice for Clitheroe. The part of Nora was given to a relative newcomer, Shelah Richards, but she went on to establish herself as an Abbey stalwart. O'Casey chose for "The Voice" (of Pearse) John Stephenson, while the tough and dour M. J. Dolan agreed to be the Covey: an ironic choice in view of his and O'Casey's feud, for the Covey is the most autobiographical, as well as the most spiteful, character in the play. Eileen Crowe, who was to marry F. J. at the end of 1925, was cast first as Rosie, but – perhaps with her own marriage in mind, and a sense of shyness at being cast in a role so opposite – shied away from the part, and elected to do Mrs Gogan. Ria Mooney, hotly championed by O'Casey in *Man and Superman*, replaced her as Rosie.

The greatest setback to the casting spelled good fortune in another guise. Sara Allgood, triumphant as Juno, had been the natural choice for Bessie Burgess, and the part had been written for her. But she had been released from the Abbey for the first London production of *Juno*, directed by J. B. Fagan at the Royalty Theatre. O'Casey considered their second choice, Maureen Delaney, "too merry" even for Mrs Gogan, for whom May Craig was originally suggested. (O'Casey had dismissed her as "impossible".) In the event Maureen Delaney was chosen. O'Casey also felt Fallon ought to play Peter Flynn, persuading his friend, against his better judgment, to take the role.

Juno opened in London in mid-November. O'Casey at one stage considered attending – it would have been his first journey outside Ireland. But he elected to remain quietly in Dublin, resting his eyes and chatting to Joe Cummins, enjoying the painting, "The Tops of the Mountains", he had just purchased from Jack Yeats, and helping to breathe life into his new play, instead of going with *Juno* "to live among the shades", as he told Lady Gregory. But whether he knew it or not, those shades were soon to assume an enticing shape, ready to rescue him from his "apotheosis" of the following year.

The London critics were highly enthusiastic about *Juno*, especially James Agate, who called it "as much a tragedy as *Macbeth*, but a tragedy taking place in the porter's family". But O'Casey took a lofty view of the whole matter, exhorting his leading lady not to get a swelled head:

A dramatic success is as big a nuisance as a dramatic failure. I have been flooded with letters, till I feel, like Job, I could curse God & die!

All the same, Sally, I'm delighted "Juno" is going so well, & sincerely hope she may have a long and useful life.

I hope you are pleased with the grand notices you are getting; while they make your heart flutter, I hope they won't fill your head with contempt for your poorer brothers and sisters.

The best way is to take them quietly & murmur – Well, what the hell else could they say. I cannot offer you congratulations, for you have done nothing that I did not know was in you to do.

Could the stern moral warning he issued really be for Sara? More likely for himself.

When *The Plough and the Stars* went into rehearsal, in early January of 1926, there was already a pro-O'Casey and an anti-O'Casey faction in the cast, and while rumours of the inflammatory content of the play spread, these divisions also took hold of the public. "Dublin was too close to everyone." Fallon, on O'Casey's side, claimed that Robinson "consciously or unconsciously . . . was out to damage O'Casey's play", but Robinson gave O'Casey a very different impression, for he wrote to Sara Allgood in London with hopes that while she was missing the Dublin premiere, she might one day play Bessie Burgess: "I see where Robbie [L. R.] read the last act of the play at a lecture he gave in the Liverpool University. He thinks the last act splendid, & Bessie has a fine part in it. I'm looking forward to seeing you enthrall audiences in the interpretation."

The actors, antipathetic to the abrasive language, now rebelled at some of the coarser expressions and gestures. The newly wed Eileen Crowe objected to her line, as Mrs Gogan, "any kid, livin' or dead, that Jinnie Gogan's had . . . was got between th' bordhers of the Ten Commandments"; her husband, cast as Clitheroe, disliked saying the word "snotty"; he and others balked at "bum", "bastard", and "lousy". Even the brave Ria Mooney, risking her reputation by playing Rosie Redmond, complained to Robinson about "the horror of her part".

O'Casey rejected their views. "Were corrections of this kind to be suffered," he said, "the work would be one of fear, for everyone would start a canonical pruning", and threatened to withdraw the play. Yeats backed up O'Casey, and Eileen Crowe was replaced as Mrs Gogan by May Craig; O'Casey had in the first instance refused to countenance her in the part, although he later described her playing of it as "perfection".

The pressure put on the pro-O'Casey actors, in particular Ria Mooney and Fitzgerald, made the atmosphere uneasy. Fallon begged to be released from playing Peter Flynn, and wanted to do Captain Brennan instead: this was allowed. Ria Mooney responded to the hostility with typical O'Casey defiance, putting more fire into the part of Rosie because of the opposition, but Fitzgerald grew "more nervous than ever, for he had none of the arrogant courage, and none of the jovial determination, which, under different conditions, might have made a great man of Fluther". For Robinson, too, the rehearsals became a strain, for one day when Sean ventured to suggest the kind of instrument needed for some offstage effect, he burst out, "Oh, shut up, for Christ's sake, man! I've got enough to do to deal with the cast!"

The tension did not escape O'Casey, whose eyes worsened before the first night; this time ingrowing eyelashes "pricked like red-hot needles". Dr Cummins, his strangely fastidious and sensitive eye doctor – an odd companion, as he thought, for his rough-and-ready proletarian self – ameliorated his condition.

The indefatigable diarist, Holloway, was now shifting fast to the anti-O'Casey camp: a queer fish, O'Casey had called him once, to his face: "You are hard to understand." He commented on the dress rehearsal of *The Plough and the Stars*, held on Sunday, 7 February 1926, and which lasted over four hours:

> The last act will save the play; the second . . . is quite unnecessary. On the whole, I imagine, as far as I can judge from such a performance, [it] is not nearly as interesting and gripping a piece as *Juno and the Paycock*. Will Shields [Barry Fitzgerald, i.e. Fluther] was most indistinct in his utterance. May Craig was consistently good, and Shelah Richards promises to be a big success . . . Ria Mooney's part, a prostitute, in Act II, is quite unnecessary; and the incident in Act I about the naked female on the calendar [Giorgione's Venus] is lugged in for nastiness' sake alone . . .
>
> Robinson mostly reviewed the rehearsal from the pit, going up on stage every now and then to tell the players what he wanted them to do with this or that situation, and always giving them effective advice. . . . O'Casey was about on the stage between acts and seated alone in the front row of the stalls, and later on with some of the players in the stalls. He seemed anxious, but not excited. He wore his cloth cap and trench coat.

In the meantime, Yeats, shrewdly, had created a great deal of advance publicity: he had spotted another possibility of making his cockpit, Ireland, and its microcosm, the Abbey, the centre of world attention: the achievement of national independence had been succeeded by dullness. Like O'Casey, Yeats had himself known these leaders of the Easter Rebellion, and found them little more than ordinary – especially MacBride, "the drunken, vainglorious lout", his rival who had won Maud Gonne (although not for long, for they separated). He was long past his moment of fervid eulogy –

> I write it out in a verse –
> MacDonagh and MacBride
> And Connolly and Pearse
> Now and in time to be,

> Wherever green is worn,
> Are changed, changed utterly:
> A terrible beauty is born

– and was now more responsive to shock, bitterness, caricature of those same heroes. He hired men to carry sandwich boards and splashed out on posters and newspaper advertising, hoping to make as big a stir as possible.

By the opening night the word had certainly got around: Holloway reported on Monday, 8 February:

There was electricity in the air before and behind the curtain at The Abbey tonight when Sean O'Casey's play *The Plough and the Stars* was first produced. The theatre was thronged with distinguished people, and before the doors opened the queues to the pit entrance extended past old Abbey Street – not a quarter of them got in. The play was followed with feverish interest, and the players being called and recalled at the end of the piece. Loud calls for "Author!" brought O'Casey on the stage, and he received an ovation. Monty [James Montgomery, the Irish film censor] said after Act II, "I'm glad I'm off duty."

ABBEY THEATRE
— DUBLIN. —

Proprietors — THE NATIONAL THEATRE SOCIETY, Ltd
Directors — W. B. YEATS, LADY GREGORY.
GEORGE O'BRIEN, LENNOX ROBINSON
Manager — MICHAEL J. DOLAN

Producer — LENNOX ROBINSON
Assistant Producer — ARTHUR SHIELDS
Stage Manager — F. J. McCORMICK

All seats in Theatre with exception of Back Pit may be Booked. Seats Reserved by Telephone and not paid for, will not be kept later than 7.45 p.m.   Telephone 3988

Monday, Feb. 8th, 1926, and following nights at 8
Matinee, Saturday, at 2.30

FIRST PRODUCTION OF
THE PLOUGH AND THE STARS
A Tragedy in Four Acts, by SEAN O'CASEY

Characters :

COMMANDANT JACK CLITHEROE (of the Irish Citizen Army)	F. J. McCormick
NORA CLITHEROE (his wife)	Shelah Richards
PETER FLYNN (Nora's uncle)	Eric Gorman
THE YOUNG COVEY (Clitheroe's cousin)	Michael J. Dolan
FLUTHER GOOD	Barry Fitzgerald
BESSIE BURGESS	Maureen Delany
MRS. GOGAN (a charwoman)	May Craig
MOLLSER (her consumptive daughter)	Kitty Curling
CAPTAIN BRENNAN (of the I.C.A.)	Gabriel J. Fallon
LIEUT. LANGON (of the Irish Volunteers)	Arthur Shields
ROSIE REDMOND	Ria Mooney
A BARMAN	P. J. Carolan
A WOMAN	Eileen Crowe
THE VOICE	J. Stephenson
CORPORAL STODDARD (of the Wiltshires)	P. J. Carolan
SERGEANT TINLEY (of the Wiltshires)	J. Stephenson

NOTICE—Owing to numerous Complaints, the Management must insist that ladies Sitting in the Stalls shall remove their hats

ACT I. Scene—The living-room of the Clitheroe's three-room flat in a tenement house in Dublin

ACT II. Scene—A corner public-house in the street where a meeting is being held

ACT III. Scene—The outside of the tenement house in which Clitheroes live

ACT IV. Scene—Bessie Burgess's room in the same tenement

A few hours elapse between Acts I. and II., Some months between Acts II. and III. and a few days between Acts III. and IV.

Period of Play—Acts I. and II. November 1915 ; Acts III. and IV. Easter Week 1916

The Orchestra, under the Direction of Dr. J. F. LARCHET, will perform the following selections :

Overture	"Mireila"	Gounod (1818-1893)
Fantasy	"La Bohème"	Puccini (1858-1924)
Slow Movement	"The New World" Symphony	Dvorak (1841-1904)
Irish Reel	"Molly on the Shore"	Grainger (b. 1882)

ANNOUNCEMENT

Tuesday, February 16th, 1926, and following nights at 8
Matinee Saturday, at 2.30.

DOCTOR KNOCK
By JULES ROMAIN

TEA ROOMS IN VESTIBULE
CHOCOLATES, ETC.

REFRESHMENTS WILL BE SERVED IN
THEATRE IF DESIRED

Holloway changed his tune about Act II – although it "carries realism to extremes" – when Rosie and the two women were long applauded.

O'Casey, before the performance, showed animation (if not anxiety), with his eyes all screwed up, and once it was under way, because of his painful lashes, found it hard to keep his eyes focused on the "bright zone" of the stage, although he was delighted with the way the actors gave of their best: indeed, given the ill omens, the evening passed very well. The applause was sustained and tumultuous. And while O'Casey found F. J. McCormick as the tragic hero a bit on the reluctant side – he mumbled the word "snotty", although Shelah Richards as Nora, when she had to repeat it after him, made a point of making it heard – he singled out Ria Mooney for particular praise.

"Afterwards I met him," she said later. "I was going home and you had to cross over the stage . . . Well the stage was empty and Sean was coming over from the other side and . . . his face was white, expressionless . . . He stopped me and thanked me for the way I played Rosie. He said I saved his play. If the people had disliked Rosie the other two acts would have failed." This episode shows the depth of commitment O'Casey felt for the character of Rosie: as the woman taken in adultery, about to be stoned by the Pharisees, had excited Christ's compassion and drawn from him his most profound judgment, so had O'Casey, with his deep and early absorption of biblical stories, provided an image with which to confront the Irish people. As word of the play spread, most Dubliners were outraged, and could find little self-identification, for as one Cumann na mBan woman later told him, "I'd like you to know that there isn't a prostitute in Ireland from one end of it to th' other."

There was not much in the next day's notices that the over-sensitive O'Casey could object to. The *Irish Times* found the play's meaning to reside in Mollser's line "Is there anybody goin' with a titther o' sense?", while "Great events are outlined only in so far as they have had reactions on the lives of the men and women O'Casey recreates." But he did make his audience feel the Rising was not worth it; "that one drop of human kindness is worth more than the deepest draughts of the red wine of idealism." The *Irish Independent* believed that he had not taken sides: "What the play brings home is the strength of the common ties that bind humanity." It predicted, rightly as it was to turn out, that this would become O'Casey's most popular play. The *Irish Statesman*'s reviewer, Dr Walter Starkie, soon to become a director of the Abbey and as such to have a crucial influence on O'Casey's future, wrote that although O'Casey pardons all,

"He never fails to expose hypocrites and evil to the gaze of humanity . . . we have rarely seen an audience more moved than in the last act."

From the reviews it began to look as if O'Casey's deliberate act of desecration, his flagrant irreverence, would fail to make the impact both he and Yeats had hoped, and his insult would have the halo of "artistic masterpiece" conferred on it, to float above and give it protection. As Holloway forcefully told George O'Brien during the show, Abbey audiences would suffer the devils in hell to exhibit their worst pranks sooner than by their disapproval give another objectionable play like *The Playboy of the Western World* the advantage of notoriety.

But Irish womanhood was made of sterner stuff. On Tuesday half a dozen young women – one of them the sister of a noted volunteer captured by the Tans in 1920, tortured (the details of this taken down in a sworn statement before a JP) and finally hanged in Mountjoy Gaol – began hissing in the pit when the Plough and Stars flag was brought into the pub in Act II. They were ignored, although more hissing and moaning from the pit followed on Wednesday night at the same moment, and Arthur Shields, playing Langon, made a point of unfolding his tricolour in a defiant way – "He's usually out for cheap notoriety," said Holloway.

On Tuesday O'Casey was blithely signing autographs for female admirers, but turning down young men, saying, "I only do so for young and pretty girls." But on Thursday night the protesters gathered in force, and began interrupting during the first act; mostly they were members of Cumann na mBan – the Society of Women, or "Women Squealers" as O'Casey called them. Prominent among them were the widows of his former heroes, Padraic Pearse and Tom Clarke, while, paradoxically, their leader was the fifty-year-old Mrs Hanna Sheehy-Skeffington, widow of the gentle pacifist who had been sadistically tortured and then executed in 1916. Francis Sheehy-Skeffington had been strongly opposed to the Rising, and so earned a moving eulogy in O'Casey's *Irish Citizen Army* as "the ripest ear of corn that fell in Easter Week". It could be said that *The Plough and the Stars* was conceived and written as fruit from Sheehy-Skeffington's "sown body". No wonder O'Casey contemplated his widow's participation in the outcry against his play with rising incomprehension.

Before the beginning of Act II a student went up to Dr Larchet, conductor of the orchestra, and said, "I suppose that some of those instruments are valuable," adding, "if I were you, I'd have them moved." "Larky" locked the piano and other musicians took away their instruments. As soon as Rosie came on a voice called out loudly from the front, "O'Casey out", while others shouted "Honour Bright!" Fallon wrote, "I can still hear the Joxer-Daly-like accents of that fruity Dublin voice that wanted 'that wumman taken offa th' stay-age'." The uproar intensified throughout the whole of Act II, which went on in dumb show, with Mrs Sheehy-Skeffington screeching down from the balcony, she being abused by one man as a disgrace to her sex, and others calling out, "O'Casey the coward!" – he had not, incidentally, arrived. Other snatches of protest heard were: "We fought in 1916 and did not frequent pubs nor associate with prostitutes", "The Government is subsidising the Abbey to malign Pearse and Connolly."

When the curtain rose for Act III a section of the audience, about a dozen women and one or two men, invaded the stage, causing some of the cast to behave "with uncommon roughness", or "heroically", depending which side you were on. One young invader was pinned to the floor by two actors who sat on her chest while another was attacked by Barry Fitzgerald, who now became, according to O'Casey, "a genuine Fluther Good", sending his enemy flying into the stalls with a "flutherian punch on the jaw". In fact Fitzgerald fell on the piano and hurt his side. McCormick led the more moderate actors, making a plea – hardly very loyal to O'Casey – that the actors should be treated as distinct from the play in which they were appearing.

Vividly though O'Casey described the "two plays" now under way, with the stink bombs, the violence, the constables flooding into the theatre to restore order, he did not take the stage and defend his play, but remained in the foyer surrounded by a crowd of questioning women to whom his attitude – according to Holloway's now hostile view of him – was "I want to make money."

But Yeats was seen to be calling for silence from the stage; earlier he had slipped out to visit the offices of the *Irish Times* to deliver the text of a speech he had prepared and was intending to deliver at the appropriate moment. Nothing illustrates better Yeats's control of the apparatus of public relations than his behaviour on this night: master of the media, he shaped the event entirely to suit his own aims. He had risen and was attempting to get a hearing above all the hullaballoo on stage and in the auditorium: of course he couldn't,

Susan Casey with one of her grandchildren

Mick Casey as a young man

Brother Tom, on the left, in the Boer War period

Sean O'Casey's sister, Bella

Nicholas Beaver with daughter, Susan Archer

Mick, seated left, during World War I

Left: St Barnabas Church (now demolished)

Below left: St Laurence O'Toole Church as seen from Abercorn Road

Below right: Number 18 (formerly 4) Abercorn Road: O'Casey's home

Sean O'Casey aged thirty

Above: The room at 422
North Circular Road

Right: Sean O'Casey in his
forties

Above: W. B. Yeats

Right: Lady Gregory

Eileen Carey Reynolds

Above: F.J. McCormick as Joxer

Right: The 1927 production of *The Shadow of a Gunman* at the Royal Court Theatre, London, with Eileen Carey as Minnie and Harry Hutchinson as Davoren

and loud though he roared, not a word he spoke could be heard by anyone. As the angry Nurse Maguire wrote in the Republican weekly *An Poblacht*, "Mr Yeats struck an attitude – legs wide apart – hand well raised and bent over the head – result pandemonium!" This was exactly why he had absented himself earlier: he had known his words would be drowned.

Finally the demonstrators were driven out, with Mrs Sheehy-Skeffington declaiming, "We are now leaving the hall under police protection. (Cheers and jeers.) I am one of the widows of Easter Week. It is no wonder that you do not remember the men of Easter Week, because none of you fought on either side. The play is going to London soon to be advertised there because it belies Ireland. We have no quarrel with the players – we realise that they at least have to earn their bread. But I say that if they were men they would refuse to play in some of the parts. All you need do now is sing 'God Save the King'." The performance continued quietly to the end: no serious damage was done: some sheets of music were torn, two footlights broken, while the double bass player lost the cover of his instrument.

Next morning in its description of the riot, the *Irish Times* "reported" what Senator Yeats had said: that he had not been heard above the storm did nothing to lessen the news impact of the event as arranged by him, or of his "stiff, pompous and furious" style, as another commentator called it:

You have disgraced yourselves again. Is this to be an ever-recurring celebration of the arrival of Irish genius? Synge first, and then O'Casey! The news of the happenings of the past few minutes will go from country to country. Dublin has once more rocked the cradle of genius. From such a scene in this theatre went forth the fame of Synge. Equally the fame of O'Casey is born here tonight. This is his apotheosis.

The Catholic press disgustedly claimed that the whole commotion was over-inflated by the "Ascendancy organ" (the *Irish Times*) and its "Mutual Boosters" – a magnificent opportunity for them to "throw dirt on the Catholic City of Dublin". A "shoneen" (contemptuous term for a lower-class person who puts on airs) clique in the Abbey was led by Yeats who "dictates, Mussolini-like" to a Dublin audience, complained one correspondent. Another, "For the life of me I could see no British or Free State propaganda, only much washing of our dirty linen in public (about which I rather agree with the lady – Mrs Sheehy-Skeffington). I take it O'Casey is a rather disillusioned fellow about heroes and the like.''

Subsequent performances were not only packed, but took place under police protection: times had changed since the captive Republicans, after the Rising, had been jeered at by crowds on the way to the deportation ships. Ria Mooney recounted the terror she lived in, and that the nationalists tried to kidnap her, Barry Fitzgerald, and Shelah Richards. "Someone came knocking at our door but I wouldn't let me father open the door and let them in." Barry Fitzgerald's mother bawled out the raiders and they lost their nerve and ran away. "We had to go to the Theatre every other night by car. During my act the lights would be put on in the auditorium and the walls were lined with detectives. They threw pieces of coal, pennies, anything they had."

Yeats quarrelled with the noted gunman Dan Breen, and O'Casey with many of his former Republican friends, especially his close companion and fellow hurler, the Marxist Frank Ryan, who was twenty years his junior: he fell out as well not only with Holloway, but with some of his new literary friends, in particular Liam O'Flaherty and the poets Austin Clarke and Fred O'Higgins, and with R. M. Fox.

The dispute rumbled on for several weeks. In two long letters to the *Irish Independent*, Mrs Sheehy-Skeffington passionately argued her case against *The Plough*; in the first she decried O'Casey's realism: "It is the realism that would paint not only the wart on Cromwell's nose, but that would add carbuncles and running sores in a reaction against idealisation. In no country save in Ireland could a State-subsidised theatre presume on popular patience to the extent of making a mockery and a byword of a revolutionary movement on which the present structure claims to stand." In the second she repeated this point with even greater force: "Shakespeare pandered to the prejudices of his time and country by representing Joan of Arc (in *Henry IV*) as a ribald, degraded camp-follower. Could one imagine his play being received with enthusiasm in the French theatre of the time, subsidised by the State?"

Her attack went on to become more personal in the second letter: "Since receiving Mr Yeats' police-protected 'apotheosis' Mr O'Casey appears to take himself over-seriously, not sparing those of us who decline to bow the knee before his godhead." She attacked again the police enforcement of the production, saying Yeats had struck a blow at the freedom of the theatre in Ireland, as he had over *Playboy* in 1907, when Arthur Griffith wrote savagely against the police presence, "'If squalidness, coarseness, and crime are to be found in Ireland, so are cancer, smallpox, and policemen.'"

She also responded to O'Casey's widening of the debate in his first reply, when he defended Nora Clitheroe's womanhood ("The safety of her brood is the true mark of every woman"). Nonsense, thundered Mrs Sheehy-Skeffington: "Nora Clitheroe is no more 'typical of Irish womanhood' than her futile snivelling husband is of Irish manhood. The women of Easter Week, as we know them, are typified rather in the mother of Padraic Pearse, that valiant woman who gave both her sons for freedom. Such breathe the spirit of Volumnia, of the Mother of the Gracchi."

O'Casey defended himself in print against these attacks with memorable verve and humour, making the point over and over again that he was showing life as it was: men were mixed in qualities, he said: "The Staff of Stonewall Jackson [once] complained bitterly to him of the impiety of one of their number. 'A blasphemous scoundrel,' said the General, 'but a damned fine artillery officer.' Some of the men of Easter Week liked a bottle of stout, and I can see nothing derogatory in that."

All men, too, showed fear, he wrote, quoting Job in his defence: "Upon the earth there is not his like, who is made without fear," and giving illustrious examples, such as Hector (chased round the walls of Troy), and the Red Branch champions, Laoghaire and Conall, who fled leaving Cuchulain alone to face death "'in the heaviness of dark sorrow'". His parrying of Mrs Sheehy-Skeffington's attack on his so-called "obscenities and indecencies" had a Miltonic splendour: "We know as well as Mrs Sheehy-Skeffington that obscene and indecent expressions do not make great literature, but we know, too, that great literature may make use of obscene and indecent expressions, without altogether destroying its beauty and its richness." But, as might be expected, his most eloquent defence concerned his introduction of the Citizen Army flag.

They objected to the display of the Tricolour, saying that that flag was never in a public-house. I myself have seen it there. I have seen the Green, White and Gold in strange places. I have seen it painted on a lavatory in "The Gloucester Diamond"; it has been flown from some of the worst slums in Dublin; I've seen it thrust from the window of a shebeen in "The Digs"; but perhaps the funniest use it was put to was when it was made to function as a State robe for a Southern Mayor of Waterford.

With such powerfully uttered truths set down O'Casey perhaps did not need to go further in his own defence, but he had an unfortunate weakness for polemics. And although, as he wrote to Sara Allgood in London, both his eyes were bad and painful, he seemed to be enjoying the "something of a whirlwind" the play had raised. He therefore agreed to take part in a public debate with Mrs Sheehy-Skeffington, organised by Ryan, on 1 March 1926, at Mills Hall; perhaps having, in an earlier phase of his controversy-mongering, challenged so many of his adversaries to verbal tournament he could hardly back down (as they all, without fail, had done) and keep his colours flying.

The hall was packed: actors, playwrights, journalists, politicians and Republican personalities turned out in force. O'Casey was applauded as he took his seat; the chairman was Arthur Clery, Professor of Law at UCD and member of the Supreme Court. Mrs Sheehy-Skeffington spoke first; as a leading light of the Cumann na mBan she was a skilful public speaker and commanded attention easily. She repeated the charges she had made in the *Independent*, tellingly, adding a question: would O'Casey put on a travesty of Ulster Volunteers in Belfast before Sir James Craig and Lord Carson and not expect to have his theatre wrecked? She seemed to have much of the audience's support, as in her low and soft, but carrying, tones she went on, "With regard to Mr O'Casey my own impression of him is that he has 'a grouch'. He likes to see rather the meanness, the littleness, the squalor, the slum squabbles, the women barging each other, and the little vanities and jealousies of the Irish Citizen Army. He has rather the art of the photographer rather than the art of the dramatist."

In the meantime, listening to her address, O'Casey was feeling something similar to what he had felt on visiting Yeats in Merrion Square to discuss cuts in the play: the effects of an "airless room", this time crowded, which "always made him sick". "Neuralgic pain" was also "pressing on his eyeballs" – while his eyes were riveted with disgust on Maud Gonne MacBride, sitting next to Mrs Sheehy-Skeffington. She had, he believed, never understood Yeats, and was now a querulous old woman who uttered bitter words – "the colonel's daughter still". When he stood up to answer Mrs Sheehy-Skeffington, the implosive force of the atmosphere and its hostile presences overcame him, and he had to sit down again.

Some people alleged that he collapsed from a pitiable lack of guts, but Mrs Sheehy-Skeffington, as her son Owen later said, saw that "he was clearly unwell, his sight was apparently not good, he had difficulty in reading his notes, and he was under great emotional stress before an unfriendly audience. When he was unable to go on and had to stop dead, my mother's reaction was one of genuine sympathy. She . . . was well aware that *she* had started with the initial sympathy of the audience."

O'Casey's back-up man, Lyle Donaghy, a Trinity College student, stepped into the breach, but he, too, apparently, after a spirited defence, felt suffocated, and sat down. Rallying, O'Casey rose a second time, determined not to be beaten, and then, if we can believe Holloway, drifted into "a sort of Salvationist address at a street corner":

I am anxious [he said] to bring everyone into the public houses to make them proper places of amusement and refreshment. The play, in my opinion, is the best of the three produced. It has been said I have been writing for England. I am not writing for England. I am writing for England as well as for Ireland, and I don't see why I should not.

Afterwards, weary and scornful, he went home to 422, thankful for a lift "in the little car of Frank Hugh O'Donnell", author of the play *Anti-Christ*. Thrust under the room door – or so he wrote – he found a telegram from J. B. Fagan, in London, "telling him that his play was coming off at one theatre, but another had been engaged, and the play [*Juno*] would go on there; but there wasn't much chance of a new success, unless Sean came over for the first night, and so created a little publicity for the newer effort".

England!

The "apotheosis" had become the crowning disillusionment: like his feelings towards the once lovely Maud Gonne, he now felt a surge of hatred towards Cathleen ni Houlihan: "He saw now that the one who had the walk of a queen could be a bitch at times. She galled the hearts of her children who dared to be above the ordinary, and she often slew her best ones." But, in the curious selective way his antagonisms worked, he exempted Mrs Sheehy-Skeffington from all ill-feeling, even his scornful humour, and later spoke of her with affection.

It may be that Mrs Sheehy-Skeffington's approach to him after the debate had mollified him: she shook hands with him with tears in her eyes, saying she had just read for the first time his tribute to her dead husband in his *Story of the Citizen Army*. Of Frank Ryan, who had led the attack on *The Plough*, and who later commanded the "Communist Irish" in the Spanish Civil War, O'Casey not only spoke proudly, but stated, "I was never an enemy of his."

11

FREE WHEELING

A few days after the fiasco of the debate, O'Casey, now approaching his forty-sixth birthday, made his first visit abroad, crossing from Ireland to Scotland – "tramped the quarter-deck like a man head-on to the wind & felt at home on the billows". Arriving in London at the weekend of 6 March, he was excited to be in the capital of Ireland's ancient enemy, especially as he felt something of a conqueror there. Escorted everywhere by J. B. Fagan, who was organising *Juno*'s transfer from the Royalty to the tiny Fortune Theatre, he was "pulled here, pulled there; brought, bowing, before young men and women, before elderly men, before anyone who could write about him in the daily papers and in the weekly journals . . . Coriolanus O'Casside hurried here and there by Menenius Fagan."

The journalists identified him as a man in his forties, Irish of feature, silver-grey hair over his temples, eyes heavy-lidded but brown and twinkling, voice soft and mysterious, with the speech of a writer and the accent of a workman. "I live in the slums of Dublin . . . At sunset you stand on the quays and look around at the blue mountains." He regaled them with tales of collecting a daily dole of two shillings and sixpence, of pawning his trousers for five shillings before *Juno* was produced; he told them about his childhood, how his father died when he was six, how his brothers were better fed and better educated than he was. The journalists laid on thick the homespun charm: "There is material for a first-class film drama in O'Casey," noted one. A truer O'Casey was revealed when he was asked, at a photocall, to pin a bunch of shamrock to Sara Allgood's breast: "You can have it if you want it but it's pinning it on her arse I'll be and not on her breast at all."

When he broadcast on London 2LO, he became much oversimplified; the *Daily Sketch* had him saying to its reporter, "Sometimes Oi wish Oi was a labourer again – it's a grand loife for a man – a grand loife. It gives me almost a homesickness to pass men now knocking down houses and building roads."

The journalist Beverley Nichols interviewed him in a noisy tea-shop; even here, above the roar of traffic, clattering tea-cups, and the low moan of other customers, O'Casey wove a spell, as he described the experience of standing in Hyde Park. But Nichols and he soon crossed swords over Noël Coward's *The Vortex*, which O'Casey had just read:

"Didn't you think it a fine play?"

"No." Rather fiercely he put five lumps of sugar into his tea-cup. "The people in it are absolutely artificial."

"But they're meant to be artificial. If he'd drawn them in any other way, he'd have been telling lies."

"Nobody's artificial." O'Casey looked at me kindly, rather as though I were a child who could not quite understand why $a \times a = a^2$. "Nobody's artificial," he said. "Even insects aren't artificial. Shakespeare drew artificial characters, but he gave them humanity. My point about these people is that they haven't got humanity."

His character – or rather a caricature of his character – was becoming defined: in making him out to be a "rough diamond", a Jack London type – the original, hobnail booted, working-class man, the equivalent of Rousseau's noble savage of an earlier time – the journalists were representing him as the very opposite of what he was. O'Casey may have been a natural aristocrat, but his aristocracy was by no means that of an untutored peasant; it was more the refinement, indeed the essence, of Protestantism, allied to a belief that the successful practice of an art made one into a *superior* being. But being cast as an Irish working man gave him an immense psychological advantage in the drawing rooms of aristocratic ladies. He could clown, tweak noses, say all kinds of outrageous things, and his generous-minded but essentially timid British hosts would not blame him directly: they would put it down to the injustice their own fellow countrymen had inflicted on the poor, backward Irish.

All this must have produced a sense of inner distortion, which was finally to emerge as contempt. Not only did O'Casey display a certain kind of refinement, but, within the compass of his resources, he had always, like his mother, been a tremendous snob. This snobbery was now to be turned upon the English as selectively as it had, up till then, been focused on the Irish. Nichols, who had been so generous about him, was later dismissed with a wave of the hand: "Never saw a hobnailed boot in his life, not even in a shop window. Mignonette among the nettles." O'Casey had set his sights on higher contacts: "friends in spirit" like Lady Londonderry, who "quietly and cleverly placed a mantle of courtesy and kindness" round his shoulders when he came "lumbering into Londonderry House with Mary Grey and J. B. Fagan". The alacrity with which the intellectual aristocracy, the Londonderrys, the Astors, the Macmillans, put him on their invitation lists showed not only how responsive they were to the newest hero of the hour, but how available he was as a celebrity: within only a few days of being in London he had been taken by Lady Londonderry to see Rutland Boughton's *The Immortal Hour*, had lunched with Lady Gregory, who had come over to help advance her protégé, while a portrait of him by the doyen of portrait painters, Augustus John, had been commissioned and was soon to be begun. Rejected as he felt by Dublin's literary élite, he became, almost at once, the new theatrical sensation of London.

Part of O'Casey behaved as a new immigrant, "a guttersnipe", and he identified with the many Irishmen and women before him who had first been confronted with the impressive sights of London. Yet, unlike most of them – and whisked as he was from place to place by taxi – he was hardly a poor newcomer. He found the bright young things, the flappers and "gem-like lads" encountered in the big houses, desperately sad, "already of life's down and out". And where was the England of his imagination? Shakespeare was "unmentioned; Shelley apparently forgotten; Milton ignored". Stepping up wide and deeply carpeted staircases, "in the twilight of the goods", and bumping into men with orders dangling from their coats, Sean feels little else but defiance, belonging, as he sees it, to a greater and better aristocracy: that of thought.

The momentum of *Juno*'s success did not slacken with its transfer to the Fortune Theatre, where it went on finally to chalk up over 200 performances before Arthur Sinclair, who played Boyle, took it on a no less triumphant tour of the Midlands. Not many plays have the wit and power to captivate both a Dublin and a London audience. Probably owing to a poor cast, *Juno* was not able to repeat this success in its first New York production, in 1926 at the Mayfair: it had to wait for Abbey Company tours in the 1930s, and a 1940 production at the Ambassador with Allgood and Fitzgerald in their original roles, to deliver its full impact. The English critic, James Agate, had defined, in his *Sunday Times* review of the original London production, the essential lesson O'Casey had learned in *Juno*, which made the play so acceptable, namely that the English didn't like their tragedy undiluted: "Mr O'Casey's extraordinary knowledge of English taste . . . is shown by the fact that the tragic element in [*Juno*] occupies at the most some twenty minutes, and that for the remaining two hours and a half the piece is given up to gorgeous and incredible fooling."

The Committee of Selection for the coveted Hawthornden Literary Prize, which included Laurence Binyon and Edward Marsh, had already chosen O'Casey to receive the 1926 award. Lady Gregory later recalled that when O'Casey asked her if he should accept, she said, "Certainly. It is a compliment and the £100 will buy a good many new trousers." At the end of March, in a ceremony at the Aeolian Hall, O'Casey was presented with the £100 cheque by the Earl of Oxford and Asquith, who had been Liberal Prime Minister during the eight years up to the Rising and had approved the execution of the leaders in 1916. At the ceremony, Asquith called *Juno* the "most moving and impressive drama that we have seen for ten, fifteen or twenty years". O'Casey, wearing a grey lounge suit, varicoloured cardigan, and the black and yellow tie of the St Laurence O'Toole Club, responded to Asquith with several "sentences fervently spoken in Gaelic", as the *Irish Times* reported; he continued in English, saying that the prize "would be a happy memento of his visit to England, and, to use his own words, 'a very darling example' of his visit". He accepted the award, he said, as a tribute to the Abbey and the wonderful acting of its players.

At the ceremony Lady Gregory proudly gave a thumbnail sketch of her protégé's poor background, as outlined to her by O'Casey: but no one knew, least of all O'Casey (if we are to believe his uncritical admirers), that strictly speaking he did not qualify for the prize. Asquith described the Committee of Selection's "relief and . . . revelation in the discovery of a still young man, who satisfied the conditions . . . in that he was *under forty years of age* [my italics]". For some time now O'Casey had been saying he was three to four years younger than he was; but even by this sliding scale he was well past forty when *Juno* was first performed at the Abbey in 1924. He was trading on English ignorance of Irish efficiency. There is in Ireland, as Kenner notes, a "xenophobic delight in misinforming the stranger". Yet even English journalists who had interviewed him in Dublin the year before, notably J. L. Hodson in *The Observer*, had his age correct to within a year. But he must have thought he could get away with it – and did. And there is no doubt he deserved a prize such as the Hawthornden.

The heady circulating kept up: "great buttie now of Sybil Thorndike," he wrote to Fallon, "very natural kind, & lovable woman"; lunch with Maurice Macmillan, the chairman of his publishers – "made him wait a fortnight". He played golf in Hyde Park, was elected an honorary member of the Garrick Club, and attended the Irish Club banquet on St Patrick's Day night at which the Prince of Wales was also present.

Bernard Shaw, the object of O'Casey's adulation ever since he had opened the green paper-covered edition of *John Bull's Other Island*, became a new acquaintance, although not, at least to begin with, a close one. Indeed after a month in London O'Casey grew homesick, complaining to Fallon, "This is a lonely City after all: I wish sometimes I was singing 'Goodbye Piccadilly, Farewell Leicester Square', for they're so damned busy here, they haven't time to make friends." He sent a pound to his carpenter friend Jim Kavanagh at 422 North Circular Road, asking him to pay his rent there up to 8 May.

His greatest need – and sense of greatest deprivation, all the more keenly felt for the success showered on him from all sides – was now for a woman. He still had a strong sentimental attachment to Maire Keating, to whom in February he had inscribed a newly published copy of *The Plough and the Stars* with "Dear Maire: There is none like unto thee in gentle loveliness, in kindness and in truth. Sean." But there was another, darker side to the relationship with Maire, which he revealed years later, from the relative security of marriage to someone else, expressing in violent wish-fulfilment what had been a tormenting absence of sex:

She went too far altogether without going far enough. It was a bit thick to applaud desire till it was a passion ready to overthrow everything, and then to expect a sudden thought of shyness or fear to trim it down to a cool-centred flame of torturing self-control. Pandering to passion; playing with passion, and then asking passion to behave itself.

He even went so far as to imagine that if Maire gave in, even fainted, he would not stop: "In fact a faintness would make the job easier. When she weakened with emotion, that was the time to hammer a job on her."

Besides Maire, there remained other, less powerful attachments in Ireland. The actress Beatrice Coogan reported that, on a stroll along the Liffey, O'Casey had asked her to marry him, promising if she did he wouldn't leave Ireland. The sudden proposal, she wrote, sprang from his "angry hurt, his need for sympathy. He had spoken to me often about his first love and I suspected that even during my phase, and afterwards up to the time when he left Ireland and met the love that was to crown his life, he was still in love with the Maire to whom he had dedicated his first success." He had also, for a spell before leaving Dublin, and later in London, pursued Shelah Richards.

But now, at the end of April 1926, as a result of Fagan's decision to replace *Juno and the Paycock* with *The Plough and the Stars* (and still keep most of the cast of *Juno*), O'Casey met in the management office at the Fortune Theatre a young Dublin-born actress called Eileen Carey, who by far outrivalled all his previous girlfriends not only in exquisiteness of looks and charm of manner, but in another and no less important ingredient, for a man whose name was now on everyone's lips – worldliness.

Eileen Carey Reynolds, who took her mother's maiden name, when she went on the stage, was exactly half O'Casey's age when they met: but in her twenty-three years she had experienced much pain and disaster – as much, perhaps, as O'Casey in his forty-six – over a much shorter period and in more concentrated form. Her father, Edward Reynolds, had been an accountant; from Athlone farming stock, he had qualified in Dublin and emigrated to South Africa where he worked for a mining firm. Her mother, Kathleen Carey, who had trained as a nurse, joined Reynolds in Africa, where they married and settled down, and where two sons were born. The elder died; when the Boer War began Reynolds returned with his family to Dublin, where he began to gamble and failed to find work. At this point Eileen was born. Later, living in furnished rooms in London, the family suffered a further deterioration in its fortunes: Kathleen fell ill with rheumatic fever, while Eileen's remaining brother, not properly cared for, got bronchitis and died. The shock to Kathleen Reynolds was dreadful, and she found in Eileen no compensation for the loss of her two sons.

After the Boer War Edward Reynolds set out to recoup his fortunes in South Africa, leaving wife and daughter behind; but he succeeded no better out there the second time than he had the first, and suffered a nervous breakdown. About 1910 he returned to England where, although never a serious mental case, he became a more or less permanent inmate of the Bethlehem Royal Hospital in London. He was not only ill but demoralised: his wife nagged him continually;

and while his Catholic faith had lapsed, Kathleen had become a rigid and obsessive practitioner. Eileen visited him in hospital: "an enormous place . . . where people were sitting about in groups and my parents and myself were together." When he died, of pneumonia in 1913, she had a "dazed notion" that she was "playing a part and had to keep looking sad for days".

Kathleen Reynolds struggled valiantly to provide for her daughter and send her to school – sorrowfully reminding her how good-looking and like her father she was. As their circumstances grew shabbier, she insisted more passionately on her standards. Her family at home in Mayo had kept servants, and in South Africa they had had coloured houseboys, but now she herself sank into domestic service, becoming nurse-companion to an elderly lady. Eileen had to be dispatched to a convent. When Eileen reached adolescence her mother had become an even more doctrinaire Catholic: if you failed in any part of your faith you were "bad", and that was that. Kathleen loathed sex, condemning it as "disgusting" without explaining why. The idea of escape through drink began to attract her.

At the Ursuline Convent in Brentwood, Eileen had her own problems, which reached a climax during her last term when she started to sleepwalk and have mild fits in her sleep:

> The doctor said we must consult a nerve specialist, and he told us why I had broken down: a perfectly normal cause, the stoppage of my periods. I had not mentioned it to the nuns because in our code it was . . . secret and personal . . . My mother was sure I had inherited something from my father and must be going slightly mad.

But even at that time Eileen had a resilient personality – and a forgiving spirit, and she quickly resolved to escape her depressing background through her ambition to sing and to act. She soon found sponsors, and when she was ready for auditions she landed a job in the D'Oyly Carte Opera Company, graduating from this into the exciting yet dangerous life of a London chorus girl.

To Kathleen Reynolds such a way of life was deeply shocking. Life with her grew progressively trying:

> instead of seeing she was ill – for compulsive drinking is an illness – looked upon it sternly as a disgrace to us both. On recovering . . . she would . . . go to bed and send for the doctor, and if I were going out she would cry and say how dreadful it was for a child

to leave her mother. I hated it, but convent training can make one submissive – a mixture of submission and revolt. At last I had to rebel in earnest. When she pawned one of my dresses I threatened to leave her.

Leave her Eileen did in time, and although her mood fluctuated between hopelessness and extreme assurance, she began in general to have a good time as part of "café society", modelling clothes and hats as well as keeping herself in work. She played a chiffon-draped harem girl in Pablo Luna's *The First Kiss*, and a Cornish lass in a Napoleonic musical, Reginald Hargreaves's *Love's Prisoner*; then, in early 1925, she landed a job in the chorus of Rudolf Friml's "Canadian Rockies Romance", *Rose Marie* – one of sixty girls drilled to perfection by an American production team.

When *Rose Marie* entered on a long run at Drury Lane, Eileen had two steady boyfriends: one, a naval sub-lieutenant, would take her out after the performance. With the other, scion of a banking family, she frequented the Gargoyle in Dean Street and once went to a hunt ball. Soon Lee Ephraim, the American impresario of *Rose Marie*, began asking her to lunch and supper dances. Jewish, married, in his early forties, Ephraim was "unassertive, kind and husky-voiced", said Eileen; he attracted her more strongly than the younger men she had been seeing. Having been virtually fatherless herself, she had deep need of an older man.

So Ephraim became her lover, although instinct warned her to keep their relationship a secret, not only for Ephraim's sake but especially from her mother. She felt some pangs of conscience, for Kathleen's religion still strongly affected her. But with Ephraim, and with the long and lucrative run of *Rose Marie*, at least she could now afford the clothes she felt were right for her: smart pleated skirts, polo-necked sweaters, tempting lacy underwear.

In the autumn of 1925 Eileen sailed for New York, where she had arranged to meet Ephraim, and hoped to join the American cast of *Rose Marie*. After some unpleasant adventures avoiding the casting couch, she joined instead a touring company in George M. Cohan's *American Born*. The tour ended in failure, she was being bombarded with hysterical telegrams from her mother, and on Ephraim's advice, and after a painful bout of sciatica, she decided to return to London. But before she left, a friend, Joan MacLean, who had just been given a part in the New York production of *Juno and the Paycock*, asked Eileen for her help with the brogue.

When she read the script Eileen's imagination at once took fire:

she felt a powerful affinity with the deeply disturbing and volatile emotions of the play. She left on the *Mauretania* determined on arrival to see *Juno* at the Fortune Theatre: she also set her heart on meeting the author, and if possible joining the touring company of *Juno*. The faithful Ephraim arranged an appointment for her with J. B. Fagan, not of course knowing that in so doing he was conniving in his own downfall.

Meanwhile there had been a last-minute hitch in the casting of *The Plough and the Stars*, which was to replace *Juno* at the Fortune. Kathleen O'Regan, cast as Nora Clitheroe, fell ill two weeks before the opening night and a substitute was needed. So Eileen found herself being interviewed as a possible understudy by O'Casey and Fagan at the end of April. "Sean," wrote Eileen in her memoir of O'Casey, "then aged forty-six, was a lean man with hazel eyes that were weak but strangely penetrating: he looked directly at you when he spoke. Now he stepped forward, took both my hands in his, and said in his rich and lovely Irish voice, 'There is no need to be nervous.'" They chatted warmly and she at once lost her anxiety: she hardly noticed Fagan's presence in the office.

She was invited to play the part of Nora at a second meeting. But, having had little experience as a straight actress, she was full of misgivings: when she started rehearsals she found that some of the cast, sensing perhaps she had been preferred over other, better-qualified applicants because of her appeal to O'Casey, gave her little help. In particular Sara Allgood (Bessie) and Fagan's wife, Mary Grey, cold-shouldered her. Still troubled with sciatica, she was taking strong pain-killers which left her dazed: Sean, she said, was "infatuated and did not hide it". On 12 May, the sixth day of the 1926 General Strike, *The Plough* opened: desperately unsure of herself, Eileen had almost to hypnotise herself in order to get through the performance.

Next day, when O'Casey wrote to Fallon, he made no mention of how Eileen had affected him: he even complained, after describing how well *The Plough* had gone on its first night, that he was weary of "many things", and that no woman had anything to do with it, adding "Nine weeks here now, & haven't yet clicked with a woman." But, along with the success of *The Plough*, he could boast of a new triumph: the next day he was to sit for his portrait by Augustus John, adding, self-mockingly, "& the end thereof shall be honour and great glory". His comments on John do not show great perception of character: "He's a splendid fellow, & utterly unspoiled. Says I'm a great Dramatist & slaps me on the back for breaking every damned rule of the Stage."

O'Casey had met John through another great new "buttie", William (Billy) McElroy, a tall, picaresque Belfaster with white hair who dealt in coal slag, making the trains, as O'Casey once joked, run half as fast as they should. McElroy, with his strong accent and spontaneous manner, had a number of Dublin literary friends, among them Oliver St John Gogarty, and had even been seen in the company of the great Trinity College classicist, the Provost, J. P. Mahaffy, who, as John pointed out, "could hardly be expected to greet a tradesman with enthusiasm". McElroy and O'Casey had taken to each other at once, O'Casey warming to the other's humour, his volubility and his dubious air of prosperity. As well as owning racehorses, McElroy backed plays, and had money in both *Juno* and *The Plough*: to some extent he played Mephistopheles to O'Casey's Faust, instructing the innocent Dubliner in the wicked ways of the world. John called McElroy "a kind of minor Horatio Bottomley".

John, commanding and bearded, was at the peak of his fame and influence, and his adoption of O'Casey was extremely flattering to the playwright. O'Casey also liked the portrait, completed in one all-day sitting, from eleven a.m. to four thirty, telling Fallon that it was: "uncanny, powerful, embarrassingly vivid: an alert concentration wearing a look of (to me) shuddering agony". John, said O'Casey, liked it and thought it the finest work he'd done.

John, O'Casey and McElroy would dine together in the Queen's, an Italian restaurant off Sloane Square, O'Casey finding nothing incongruous in the fact that McElroy and he could not, ideologically, be further apart. Having spent what he had made out of *Juno* and, according to O'Casey, no longer rich, McElroy had to find a new field for speculation. Because of the miners' strike which continued after the collapse of the short-lived General Strike, coal was hard to come by; but a friend of McElroy's had discovered a huge slag dump in the north, over which grass was growing. Unlikely as it may seem, when McElroy asked O'Casey to join him in the scheme to exploit this find, he consented and placed all he had at his disposal, signing a guarantee with his banker, Tom Berry of the Hendon Branch of Lloyd's Bank. "It was terrible stuff, but it sold, for then, business firms would take anything, and it gave out some heat. It was bought cheap and sold dear. Fortunately for him (and for Me), it was a success, and he was able to give back the guarantee after a few months . . . Actually, he made more out of me than I made out of him."

Glorious companionship overrode ideology: in this carefree period

O'Casey had cast himself in a very English role: Prince Hal among the "base, contagious clouds". He became something of a dandy and, like John, smoked cigarettes of a special blend of tobacco bought at Morlands. O'Casey and John, noted Eileen, had two traits in common: both were intolerant in company unless themselves talking, and both unnerved those who intruded on their company by completely ignoring them. It was fortunate for Eileen that John found her attractive, for O'Casey was extremely sensitive to the opinion of his new friends. John, showing a heavy-handedness of which O'Casey might not have believed him capable, later commented on the playwright's behaviour at a theatrical gathering:

> There was nothing to drink but champagne; even the austere Sean had to have a glass. *His* intemperance is purely literary, and I used to think if he only drank more he'd blabber less. Pathos should be administered in drops, like medicine, never in a bucket; a subtle flavour rather than a thirst-quencher, to be guessed rather than gulped . . .
> However that may be, I could swallow any quantity of O'Casey's superb fun, and ask for more.

Unlike Shaw, with whom he lunched in John's company a short while after the portrait was completed (on 3 June), O'Casey never came to understand the English dislike of what John called, in his description of him, "stupid and even indecent" displays of sincerity.

But he did, almost at once, understand Eileen, and she found herself increasingly touched by the concern and tact of his attentions. He invited her to Trafalgar Square, Chelsea, where he was now living. The landlady, Mrs Sparrow, had laid the tea, but every time O'Casey made an approach to Eileen, Mrs Sparrow appeared with "Do you want any more milk?", "What about some sugar?" or "Shall I clear?" They gave up and went for a walk in Hyde Park.

O'Casey then wrote to her, somewhat in the persona of a Protestant pastor, ostensibly about the role of Nora, but with deeper implications:

> Be brave and be confident in the power and possibilities that are in you . . . If you should want any help in any way, any advice about a particular phrase or incident, ask me & all the fullness of sympathetic help that is in me will be freely given to you.

In contrast with her other admirers, he bought her no expensive gifts: her first present from him was a box of six macaroons. He did offer her money, which she refused: "Receiving his royalties, he had no idea what money meant; through life he never cared for it."

After she played Nora for three weeks, all the time gaining confidence, Kathleen O'Regan asked for the part back; so Eileen found herself out of a job. Ephraim arranged for her to play the soubrette on tour in Frederick Lonsdale's *The Street Singer*. O'Casey wrote to her with bracing words: "Remember the advice of Saint Teresa – 'Pray as if everything depended upon God; work as if everything depended upon yourself'." But she was soon afflicted again with sciatica, the pain of which the other girls in the show tried to alleviate by ironing her leg with a hot iron and brown paper. One night she swallowed so many aspirins that she passed out just after coming off stage. O'Casey wrote and telephoned often, exhorting her to sleep and rest: but the tenderness he offered did not quite win out over the late supper dances which she still enjoyed with Ephraim.

She found herself increasingly divided over the two men. They could not have been more opposite in type, but there was one key card O'Casey held: he was single, while the married Ephraim still showed every sign of being a devoted husband. Moreover O'Casey's affection continued to grow: if he were to leave Ireland, a thought increasingly in his mind, what would better keep his dear motherland alive for him than a wife with whom he shared his Irish origins? Not only had he "rarely seen a lovelier face or figure anywhere in this world"; Eileen was "as Irish as the heather on Howth Hill". He even grew chauvinist in his description: "nothing in her of Harry Lauder's Scotch Bluebell . . . Sean did not believe there was such a lass in Scotland either, down in the Lowlands or up in the Highlands." Yet when he pinpointed her crowning quality as her gloriously human sense of humour – "There's nothing lovelier in life than a lively laugh" – memory again played him false. He did not at first like her laugh: "That sharp, sinister, cynical laugh saturated with bitterness of sound that always made me shiver." It was only *after* she had known him for two years that her laugh became "bright & free & joyous to hear".

To some extent, then, Eileen was a study for an O'Casey stage character. Having suffered in her early life, she could emerge comically defiant, with her loveliness and appealing qualities intact. Young though she was, she already embodied many of the qualities he worshipped in a woman, while others, such as a strong mothering power, were there *in potentia*. He viewed her as a great gift to him from life itself. He perceived, too, with acuteness, that she was much more tolerant and truly kind than he could be himself: she could get on with all sorts of people.

Over the next weeks he grew determined to win her, "quietly, patiently, and persistently". But he knew little of the pain in her background, and she did not know him well enough to tell of it. Once, in a taxi on the way to the Fortune, he placed his hand on her knee, watching "her unmoved face". He hated "Ephraim & his cool-blooded maddening manifestation of ownership. 'God had created you for him, or he had created you for himself.'"

There was a danger, too, in finding his dreams fulfilled in such a complete woman as Eileen. Would she not rob him of that generative emotion which had driven him throughout the writing of the Dublin trilogy: his sense of loss of the woman he had held most precious, and wanted to have living there with him again – his mother, and his cumulative shame and resentment at those years of poverty and thwarted ideals? Would she not, in fulfilling his sexual and domestic needs, rob him of that genuine comic pathos of isolation that could move people and make them laugh? Of the burning sense of identification he felt with his country's fate? Wasn't the greatest danger of all that she would make him a happy and richly fulfilled husband and father?

Whatever his fears, those practical fighting qualities which had, through successive disillusionments with causes, been transformed into the negative capability of a poet and dramatist – and had found expression in great work – were now roused again. The first positive step he took, in the months after meeting Eileen – and perhaps this was the boldest step of all, for a future with Eileen was by no means a certainty, merely a challenging possibility – was to turn his visit to England into a permanent stay. Increasing success and the stimulus of new friends and contacts – to which was now added the luck of finding "a very lovely lass" – clinched it.

❖❖❖❖❖

In mid-May O'Casey cancelled plans for a temporary return to Dublin. He found himself increasingly drawn into the organisational side of the London runs of his plays, helping to find the New Theatre for the transfer of *The Plough* from the Fortune. Near the end of June he wrote to Fallon, in contrast to what he had said before, "I must say I feel at home in London now. It feels funny to read the Irish correspondents writing about Ireland in the London papers. The Free State – what the hell, & where the hell is it anyhow! I am going to a

Dance on Thursday given by The English-Speaking Union: imagine a Gael going to an event like that." By July he had signed a three-year lease for a small flat in Clareville Street, South Kensington, and he crossed over briefly to Dublin to arrange the dispatch of some of his personal effects, leaving the rest behind to be auctioned off. Before leaving London, he wrote a letter to Maire asking her to see him: "many have I tried to love, but none have I loved". But they did not meet then, or ever again.

He now announced his intention, in an interview in the *Daily Sketch* under the headline "FORSAKING IRELAND – SEAN O'CASEY MAKES PERMANENT HOME IN LONDON". He had taken a flat in Chelsea as his "permanent home and workshop", and intended, he said, to write a play about London people: "Human nature is just the same in a Chelsea environment as in Dublin, but in so many plays about London people one sees only artificial puppets moving." He knew it would be a challenge, and probably his first London play would be a failure, but "I'm determined to make them see themselves as they are, sooner or later." Besides, people did not seem to like him in Ireland any more: "I should not care to write a play about Ireland just now, with a possible bitterness in my heart." There was one telling detail: it is significant that he should have claimed his address was in Chelsea, not Kensington. To the *Irish Independent*'s London correspondent he spoke on a more personal note, saying he lacked the patience to remain in Ireland: "The Irish have no time for those that don't agree with their ideas and I have no time for those that don't agree with mine."

It can have been no surprise to him that such a view increased Dublin hostility towards him, although performances of *The Plough and the Stars* at the Abbey were as thronged as ever: but the backbiting in the press grew more pronounced, best shown in a *Catholic Bulletin* editorial:

British Drama knows its own. It was not for nothing that the Asquith, whose hands drip with the best blood of Ireland, ever since the week after Easter Week, 1916, should have been selected, when *The Plough and the Stars* was being put forward in Dublin, to present the writer of *Juno and the Paycock* with a special prize for excellence in British Drama. Here is the illuminating commentary on the central theme of the travesty of Easter Week and the men and ideals of Easter Week, the doctrine of *The Plough and the Stars*, the doctrine that "There's no such thing as an Irishman".

To Joseph Holloway, his ear ever cocked for Abbey gossip, the writer, Brinsley MacNamara, commented that whereas in Dublin O'Casey had avoided all photos, interviews and so on, he now courted publicity at every turn. "Snobbery", MacNamara called his stage-Irishman stunt in London, and continued that O'Casey's plays lowered the tone of the Abbey. "Now that Ireland is getting re-Anglicised, O'Casey's plays just suit the new class of audience who come to see them."

Ingratitude, insincerity, arrogance, inverted snobbery – the charges against him, past and present, piled up, retailed with malice by Holloway, indicative of the bad feeling he now engendered in the wake of his departure. Mrs Frank Fay thought that when, long before, she asked him to dinner on a Sunday he displayed "the snobbery of humility", for he told her he always stayed in bed on a Sunday and even though his brother was ill wouldn't get up to enquire for him. "Monty [James Montgomery] thought this rather callous on his part," wrote Holloway, "and said to him, 'I am sure if your mother were ill you'd get up to see *her*?' And he replied, 'Not damn likely; why should I?' Mrs Fay lost all interest in him after that."

Neither M. J. Dolan nor F. J. McCormick now had any place for O'Casey as a friend, and Holloway himself even withdrew his early praise of the plays, calling O'Casey "as a depicter of the Irish . . . a false prophet with an insincere and distorted view of persons and things". But another friend of Holloway's, John Burke, had the final word – a typical Irish word: "'Last year it was all Sean O'Casey; now it is all shun O'Casey.'"

12

A PART IN LIFE

If O'Casey had made the right pro-Irish noises when in London, it would have been a very different story: but his deliberately callous comments were those of a husband wanting to justify separation from a wife with whom he had long had close emotional ties, but knowing he must now finally make the break. To provoke anger in the injured party was a help in making a clean separation: it also lifted some of the responsibility from the husband's shoulders.

O'Casey's final departure from Ireland, then, was not so much the exile he and most commentators called it, but the breakup of a long and stormy marriage, which had begun when, as a young man, he embraced the Gaelic language and nationalist causes, and which had lasted until his final expression of disillusionment in *The Plough and the Stars* – a span of twenty-five years. No one could truthfully say that he had not tried to make a go of it, or that he had been unfaithful: even his deep attachment to Maire, taxing though that had been, had not come near to rivalling it. It also could not be compared, in more than a superficial way, to the exiles of Shaw and Joyce: Shaw left at twenty for London and assimilation into English literary society: of his more than fifty plays only one, or with *O'Flaherty, V.C.* one and a half, had a wholly Irish theme. And Joyce's flight – also at twenty, but to Paris – was that of the conscious artist determined to seek the liberty and mobility of wider perspectives: "When the soul of a man is born in this country," he wrote in 1916, "there are nets flung at it to hold it back from flight. You talk to me of nationality, language, religion. I shall try to fly by those nets."

Caught in those same nets, O'Casey's resilience and humour had flourished and turned the nets into trapeze wires and trampolines, on which he had bounded into dizzying eminence. Who could blame him, now, for seeking the greater scope and security England had to offer, especially as he had the prospect of a *real* wife, with a real family life to follow? He was wise enough even then to see his status as a celebrity as being only a temporary condition.

But graceful parting was not O'Casey's style: what had been a progressive disillusionment (but with signs that idealism still lived) now hardened into retrospective bitterness. Unfortunately for his future, he had to have right on his side. Just as he had denounced the officials of the GNR before throwing up his job on the railway, or accused Countess Markiewicz before resigning from the Citizen Army, he had to prove himself justified in his rejection of Ireland. So he drew up a long recriminatory list: some of the items on it were grievances he had already voiced in one way or another, but others were new, or almost new; every one related to himself and his position in Ireland, from his early days to the time of his leaving. These grievances, elaborated with infinite diversity, became a further but much more diffused and fragmented cause for which he would fight during the remainder of his life. But it could not, unfortunately, be called a fresh sword of light, nor was it an incubus of living matter that had to be discharged. Most of it was already dead matter – the past.

High on the list of immediate *casi belli* was the way he had been treated over *The Plough and the Stars*. "People just don't seem to like me in Ireland any more," he had told the *Irish Independent*. Later he listed criticisms with which his work had been "stoned": "His plays are phases of Dublin life as abnormal as they are transient . . . Is O'Casey a dramatist, or is he but a combination of the cinema and the dictaphone?" (Andrew E. Malone); "A bad play" (Liam O'Flaherty on *The Plough and the Stars*); "O'Casey in his new play entirely lacks the sincerity of the artist" (Fred O'Higgins); "Mr O'Casey's work was a crude exploitation of our poorer people in the Anglo-Irish tradition that is now moribund" (Austin Clarke); "The Drama of the Dregs . . . The peasant plays have been followed by slum plays, but their reign will not be long, though as entertainment these slum dramas are permissible. But truth is wanted as well as entertainment" (R. M. Fox).

There were not many such adverse criticisms, compared with the chorus of praise – and had he studied the past he would have found that every great work had its detractors. But his new recruitment drive was *for* detractors, just as the new factions he was beginning to define consisted of one that was pro-O'Casey and one that was anti.

His tolerance, too, of his literary peers in Dublin appeared to have evaporated as he contemplated the possibility of greater freedom and comfort available in London. His amazement knew no bounds when, on a visit to Yeats in the poet's Lancaster Gate pied-à-terre, he discovered crime novels and Wild West stories on the shelves, and was informed by the poet, "I turn for shelter and rest to Zane Grey and Dorothy Sayers. One can read them while the mind sleeps." Oliver Gogarty too, O'Casey discovered, read Edgar Wallace, while Lady Gregory was not above dipping into *Peg o' My Heart*, though snapping it shut quickly when he came into view; "Dope", pronounced O'Casey. He himself had tried one or two detective stories, but they tired his mind quicker than Locke's *Essay on Human Understanding*.

But the figure who best symbolised for O'Casey the narrow, parochial literary scene from which he was departing – and on which he wished to cast his dazzling scorn – was George Russell (AE). Yet those who knew him well portray a Russell who would have been the last person to try to make O'Casey feel socially inferior. Mary Colum, one of the best chroniclers of this period, describes the difference between a gathering at his house and one at Yeats's: "AE liked to have every sort of person and had no awareness of class differences or the difference between the mind of a man and the mind of a woman. W. B.'s guests were selected . . . in AE's one talked on draughts of tea or coffee, but in W. B.'s one's tongue was loosed on sherry." Moreover, Mrs Colum continues, Russell was "magnanimous . . . unenvious, courageous, he had no prejudices, he was a free being". A strong supporter of Larkin during the lock-out of 1913, he had even courageously declared, "All the real manhood of this city is to be found amongst those who earn less than a pound a week." Workers looked to him as one of their spokesmen and counsellors.

The terms in which Russell and Yeats are described, in twenty densely written pages of his autobiography in which O'Casey and two friends discuss the pair, are completely the obverse (though the two are still counterposed) of those used by Mrs Colum. "There's a genuine humility in Yeats's arrogance, but there's a deeper arrogance in AE's humility", and "AE thinks he's God's own crooner" are just opening shots to pinpoint the target, which is then raked with salvo upon salvo of bitter invective; the whole chapter, which O'Casey calls "Dublin's Glittering Guy", might serve as a model, if one were needed, of how to control, diversify and infinitely extend, gratuitous insult. Russell became the literary butt, the scapegoat for departure, embodying all the falsity of the Celtic revival ("Celtic twalette", Joyce called it) which lingered on, and from which O'Casey was prepared to single out only Yeats as a major figure.

Russell's counterpart in the religious sphere, for O'Casey, was a man in almost every respect his opposite: a humble Dublin workman called Matt Talbot, who on Trinity Sunday, 7 June 1925, some nine months before O'Casey's departure for London, collapsed from heart failure in Cranby Street, just round the corner from where O'Casey had lived briefly as a child, with his sister Bella. It was soon discovered, as stories emerged about him, that Talbot's life had been a saga of religious devotion and self-imposed poverty. He attended Mass many times a day and observed spiritual disciplines that rivalled those of the most pious saints: for forty-one years, as one witness at his beatification said, "He had trod the rugged paths of penance." Working men respected him: when they used bad language he would take a large crucifix from his pocket, hold it up and say, "Look, boys, see who you are insulting."

When Talbot died they found a chain, "about the size of a horse's trace, the links half an inch long, wound round the body; on one arm a lighter chain, on the other a cord. There was also a chain below one knee, immediately below the kneecap . . . so placed that it must have caused pain when kneeling." Although he himself had often said that wages were too low and that "No one can starve the poor into submission," it was Talbot's lack of militancy, his simple and austere support of the Catholic Church in Ireland that inflamed O'Casey's anger.

Talbot worshipped at the altar of St Laurence O'Toole church, on O'Casey's own former territory. He refused strike pay in 1913, preferring to borrow money and pay it back afterwards. Talbot would, wrote O'Casey sneeringly, stretch himself flat on the pavement to say his preliminary prayers, crawl up the steps on his belly to the big door closed against him, and lie on the stones till first Mass, after which he would go to work.

Ecce hobo sapiens. Blow, crumpeter, blow! So workers of Dublin, and the world, you know now what you have to do. Follow Matt Talbot up to heaven. You've nothing to lose but the world, and you've the holy chains to gain. Read this Glynn's *Life of Matt Talbot*, then read Stalin's *Life of Lenin*; and take your choice.

Communism was the one positive article of faith O'Casey declared in England, but his interviewers, protecting him, did not make an issue of it. New friends, such as Bernard Shaw, cautioned him not to be so combative when, less intemperately and with a truly Shavian sense of paradox, O'Casey took the side of another Catholic hero, this time a dissident. Dr Walter McDonald, whose influential and controversial book, *Reminiscences of a Maynooth Professor*, was published posthumously in 1925, had been Professor of Theology at Maynooth, a colleague of the Irish-language enthusiast, Dr Michael O'Hickey, for whom O'Casey had campaigned vigorously in his early days. During the lock-out of 1913 McDonald showed himself, in articles and sermons, sympathetic to the workers' cause. He was a supporter, too, of total abstinence, the only possible way, he claimed, "to wrest industrial supremacy in this land from the Saxon and prove that we are able to do our own business".

McDonald addressed himself to large questions which few Irish Catholics allowed themselves to be troubled by at that time; his reasoning, viewed in the light of the Church's own development, was very near present-day "liberation theology". For example, in *Some Ethical Aspects of the Social Question*, published in 1920, the year of his death, McDonald had gone straight to the heart of the dispute between socialists and Catholics: "I cannot see that the concept of history on which their [Marx and the leading socialists] economic theories are based is of necessity materialistic." He developed this view defiantly, against middle-class Catholic theology:

> Property in capital . . . is the consequence of inordinate appetites, not a necessity of human nature as such. Socialists look forward to a time when in the course of evolution the race will have attained to what will be practically a state of innocence, when there will be no inordinate lusts.

McDonald was not popular at all, which recommended him to O'Casey, who later devoted a whole chapter of the valedictory volume of his autobiography – as well as dedicating that volume to him – to his silencing by the bishops ("ecclesiastical electrocution"). O'Casey put his finger on a central weakness in the Church which McDonald was one of the first to identify, and which became the reason that "so many Catholic countries are in revolt today – clerical domination in lay activities has gone too far to be put up with any longer".

Many years later, in a long polemical letter to the *Daily Worker*, O'Casey quoted the Catholic McDonald on press freedom: "A debating society or journal that is kept in leading-strings will do little good to its members or readers. If the Catholic Church has in her service hardly one strong, well-conducted newspaper or periodical, that is the price she pays for *keeping all her journalists in bondage* [italics

O'Casey's]." The communist *Worker* was hardly likely to endorse such sentiments. They did not publish the letter.

────◆◆◆◆────

Another reason, and a far more harmful one to his future as a playwright, for O'Casey's leaving Ireland was the deterioration of his relationship with the Abbey Theatre personnel. He had already responded badly to F. J. McCormick's public dissociation of the actors from the text of *The Plough and the Stars*, when it would have been wise of him to treat their embarrassment in a more conciliatory way – it was they, after all, who suffered the audience's abuse on his behalf. McCormick had, whatever his views, served the plays faithfully, but O'Casey had not tempered his criticism; moreover, he had come increasingly to believe that the Abbey depended more on him than he on the Abbey. Resentment had been simmering on both sides, especially over the acting in *Man and Superman* and the incident when the brusque little carpenter, Seághan Barlow, had denied O'Casey access to the stage. This, O'Casey later wrote, was the decisive moment which convinced him that he should leave for England. But as the playwright Denis Johnston observed much later, "There are many of us who have been spoken to roughly by one of the two oldest inhabitants of the Abbey Theatre, but we don't suffer deeply on that account. Still less do we publicise so minor an incident as a reason for never setting foot in the place again."

O'Casey was never again to form so close a relationship with a theatre, or to involve himself so intimately in the production of his plays as he had at the Abbey. There probably could not have been a Dublin trilogy without the Abbey Theatre, but, said Lennox Robinson, "You mustn't tell him, for he thinks there could be no Abbey Theatre without him."

But the Abbey had been more than a matrix for his talent: it was also a natural habitat for the species O'Casey, as described by bird-watcher Holloway: earnestly standing, cloth cap on head, demolishing an interlocutor's argument, gaunt, often dominating physically, a finger poking and stabbing his opponent's chest as he made his points. Perhaps guilt over the success which came only after his mother's death activated in him something which it would be an exaggeration to call a death-wish, yet was a deliberate placing at risk of his talent.

But all these reasons (or excuses) for separation from Ireland stemmed from a deep-rooted emotional need: they were not rational, or the result of conscious judgment. To be surrounded by the results of his former nationalism was humiliating; to see on every side no change in the stifling morality which suppressed, as he saw it, the needs of the individual, was demoralising to him – it would have been a remarkable and brave decision to stay on, given that he had the resources to move away. Success is a notorious destroyer of first marriages. Later, when inveighing against Ireland with all the psychological conviction he could muster, O'Casey forgot how many friends he had also made.

———— ❧ ————

The delights and freedoms of England blew away dark thoughts of Ireland. A well-heeled patronage created for him a rich and variegated tapestry on which his imagination could feast. The centrepiece of his new life was the fascinating Eileen on whose pretty face and figure his ambitions became day by day more unshakeably fastened. He was, in middle age, escaping from a narrow self-consuming world to begin a different life: who could blame him for his new-found sense of celebration, his impulsive response to the call of a healthy young woman to experience life to the full?

What emerged in his next play, *The Silver Tassie*, which he began in 1926 and took until early 1928 to finish, was a stronger, more callous attitude than that of the more complex Dublin plays, which had observed ironically the discrepancy between the actual world and the ideal. In the protagonist of the piece, Harry Heegan, a former Dublin football hero mutilated by the war in the trenches, O'Casey buried once and for all the victim inside himself; and the play, despite his intention of making a powerful protest against the horror and pity of war, seemed more to justify a selfish, hedonistic approach to life – to espouse the philosophy of a winner. As Susie says at the end of the play,

> We can't give sight to the blind or make the lame walk. We would if we could. It is the misfortune of war . . . But we, who have come through the fire unharmed, must go on living. (*Pulling Jessie from the chair*) Come along, and take your part in life! (*To Barney*) Come along, Barney, and take your partner into the dance!

This was exactly what O'Casey was himself attempting to do with Eileen, and it meant numerous and fundamental readjustments. He seemed slightly, perhaps, to be gaining the upper hand in Eileen's affections: in the four months in which she played Violette, the soubrette, in *The Street Singer*, O'Casey took over from Ephraim more of the role of protector, inviting her frequently out to "a simple dinner" in the Queen's. One day he was seen, by the biographer Peter Quennell, sitting on the "rather shabby red-plush banquettes . . . grim and silent", while Eileen "gave way to a desperate flood of weeping".

Ephraim had been telling her that "it was my name englamoured you!", as O'Casey complained, but as he looked into her "big, soft, humorous blue-grey eyes" it was more his quiet and tender persistence. He reflected in a letter to Fallon, in October, with a wonderful (no doubt unintentionally) phallic drawing of himself holding a pen, crouched down behind a bottle of ink, on the proximity he still felt to Ireland: "Isn't it strange that the biggest bastard I've met over here is an Irishman, and a Catholic (or was) as well. However the most adorable woman I ever met was Irish, and a good Catholic too, so the whole thing remains a mystery." Eileen was still suffering from sciatica, and one afternoon in Bond Street she met O'Casey by chance: "My dear child," he said, "you look ill. Come and talk." His role in her life as father, lover and tutor grew larger as the autumn passed.

In December the scales tipped in O'Casey's favour: Eileen, on holiday on the Riviera, went one evening with friends to dine in Monte Carlo, and met Ephraim's wife: "an attractive woman," she wrote, "to whom he was most attentive". "Somehow I saw that my position was false," she remembered, and told Ephraim "that we should end our relationship". But they were both "exceedingly upset . . . and agreed to do nothing more until we had got back". O'Casey wrote to her curtly after her return: "I hope you had a good time in Monaco."

O'Casey had begun thinking about *The Silver Tassie* in London a few months after he arrived: he claimed he got the idea from the man he affectionately labelled "the biggest bastard" he'd met in London, Billy McElroy. One day during the miners' strike, McElroy had been sitting idly in his office when he started humming a tune which O'Casey had never heard before. He began to sing the words:

> Gae fetch to me a pint o' wine,
> An' full it in a sulver tossie;
> That I may drink before I gae
> A service tae my bonnie lossie.

> But it's no' the roar of sea or shore
> Wad mak' me langer wish tae tarry;
> Nor shout o' war that's heard afar –
> It's leavin' thee, my bonnie lossie.

O'Casey found the tune humming in his mind long afterwards: he would, he decided, give his next play the title of the song.

However, if Burns's romantic lyric – and McElroy's raucous and defiant rendering of it when the coal market had caved in and there wasn't so much as "a bean in th' locker" – helped build in O'Casey some central emotion he wanted to express through the play, Wilfred Owen's bleak and scorching poem, "Disabled", first published in his *Poems* of 1920, provided the more compelling and realistic image of the crippled soldier which became the framework of the play:

> He sat in a wheeled chair, waiting for dark,
> And shivered in his ghastly suit of grey,
> Legless, sewn short at elbow. Through the park
> Voices of boys rang saddening like a hymn,
> Voices of play and pleasure after day,
> Till gathering sleep had mothered them from him . . .
>
> One time he liked a bloodsmear down his leg,
> After the matches carried shoulder-high.
> It was after football, when he'd drunk a peg,
> He thought he'd better join. He wonders why . . .
> Someone had said he'd look a god in kilts,
>
> That's why; and maybe, too, to please his Meg,
> Aye, that was it, to please the giddy jilts,
> He asked to join. He didn't have to beg . . .
>
> Now, he will spend a few sick years in Institutes,
> And do what things the rules consider wise,
> And take whatever pity they may dole.
> To-night he noticed how the women's eyes
> Passed from him to the strong men that were whole . . .

Owen's poem even, if we include the brief flashback in a stanza not quoted, up to the line in which the disabled man had poured his "colour . . . down shell-holes till the veins ran dry", gave O'Casey his four-act structure for *The Silver Tassie*. Act I shows the hero, on leave in Dublin during the war, as the full-blooded football idol and courtier of his girlfriend Jessie; Act II, the shell-holes and trenches; Acts III and IV, the pitiable condition of the hero revealed after the war – although in O'Casey's treatment considerably, and dramatically, inflamed.

Although it is impossible to determine the exact chronology, O'Casey had never worked so slowly on a play as he worked on *Tassie*. Act I, set in Harry Heegan's Dublin home overlooking the dockside – familiar O'Casey territory – was probably completed during 1926: it depicts Harry's father arguing politics and religion with his friend Simon in the expected O'Casey manner. The name Heegan is reminiscent of the mutilated Captain Logan found "beyant Finglas", his ear shot in pieces – but between them there are significant differences. The family is better off than any previous O'Casey family, and, by contrast with the previous plays, no character displays passionate, volatile feelings about the war. Less distinct, too, is Susie's religious orientation: she is depicted as a fanatic but whether she is a Catholic or Protestant fanatic is not made clear.

Heegan's mother, too – perhaps a sign that O'Casey was outgrowing a dependence on such feelings, or growing to depend on someone besides his mother – is shallowly, almost sterilely drawn, scared as she is that Harry may miss his boat back to the front (via England), and she lose her weekly allowance. But vitality and humour remain evident in the character, which bears the signature of O'Casey's distinctly individual naturalism.

By the end of 1926, he had this act finished. Eileen's absence in France made his thoughts revolve fondly towards Lady Gregory, and he dispatched a warm Christmas Eve missive:

I suppose you think (forgive me for not writing to you) I have allowed former memories to be submerged by Glamour of London. I haven't, & feelings for & remembrance of you are as deeply affectionate as ever. I am living here as quietly as I have lived in Dublin; abiding alone even throughout the Christmas Festival. I am now – very tranquilly – working on a new play.

In the next month he sent off a request for eardrops to Jim Kavanagh in the North Circular Road, enclosing a prescription which proved to be the wrong one: the lonely winter had sent his thoughts back to Dublin.

There appeared to be little pressure on him to complete the new play and so he took his time, while his designs, especially as to how to develop it in the second act, grew more ambitious. His reputation as an international playwright also grew rapidly: far-flung managements perceived universal relevance in his tin-pot Dublin; foreign audiences identified their own social predicaments with those of his characters. Production of the three Dublin plays was mooted in Russia, Germany and Sweden, while others were to follow all over the world. The effect of all this "colour and stir" was to make him determined not to repeat himself in his fourth major play, just as he had not repeated himself in any of his previous three.

He now took his courage in both hands and made a dangerous leap, with Act II, into a form of dramatic vision he had up to then only mildly touched on – a vision explored in the so-called "expressionist" plays of Ernst Toller, Gerhart Hauptmann, Frank Wedekind, and Strindberg in his *Dream Play*. In *The Plough and the Stars* he had pitched his second act in a very different key – illustrating poetically, rather than directly developing the action – and had included in that act one or two expressionist devices. This had been wholly successful, although many people had found the act unnecessary: but Yeats, who understood its motivation and poetic force, had been its most appreciative supporter.

If the motivation of Act II of *The Tassie* was the same as that of *The Plough*, its poetic force was to be very different. O'Casey had absorbed dramatic theory directly from plays such as *Masses and Men* and *Hinkemann*, but also from powerful advocates of expressionism such as Huntly Carter, whose books on Russian cinema and theatre and on European drama he read in 1926. Carter in many of his challenging statements gave a tempting lead to O'Casey: "Certain plays of Ernst Toller", he wrote, citing *Masse-Mensch*, "contain a succession of scenes that pass from actuality to dreamland and back again." He called such writers as Toller "dramatists of the Chaos" (remember O'Casey's famous phrase in *Juno*, "The world's in a state of chassis"), showing how they created the form of their drama out of the despair and neurosis of the defeated German people – showing "a strange enthusiasm for destruction for the purpose of exalting a humanistic ideal":

> This sort of destructive drama brought a demand for an equally destructive treatment. Something was required to give fullest expression to the attack, something that would knock the play-goer senseless and leave him to recover fully converted to the "message" of the play. Hence came an aggressive kind of representation called Expressionism.

O'Casey, too, wanted to see the old world order destroyed. A poor Bolshy who was "shaking the devil's paw", the light for him glowed beyond Germany, in the East. He put his name on a "virulent Red pamphlet" issued during the Leith by-election in March 1927. He had, as he wrote to Lady Londonderry, a "fierce, jagged Communistic outlook"; a desire to put over a message, which had, from the point of view of the Abbey's directors, severely blemished earlier plays such as *The Harvest Festival*, seized hold of him once more.

His bold conception for Act II starkly contrasted, in an Irish and paradoxical fashion, with the delightful outcome, from O'Casey's point of view, of his rivalry with Ephraim for Eileen's hand. While he brooded theoretically and Miltonically on the horrors of the Great War – and his infernal landscape has as much of Satan's Stygian gulf and gloomy plain in it as of Flanders – another, lighter, part of his sensibility was engaged in a marital comedy nearer to the work of playwrights such as Lonsdale and Coward, for whom he expressed a mocking contempt. Eileen, now out of work in London, was contemplating auditioning for Ephraim's new musical, *The Desert Song*, with Rudolf Friml's score, due to open at Drury Lane in April. O'Casey made it a test of her feelings towards him: if she auditioned it meant she would lose him.

She now found O'Casey the dominating force, explaining that it was his power of words, in his letters and in what he said to her, which had won her. While as for him, she was now "within me darling as it is said that the Kingdom of Heaven is within a man". There had been a time when he could do without her – but no longer. He did not think it was within him to love her as he did: they were "captives of each other".

So she did not try for the Drury Lane part. Unfortunately, once when she had fixed to meet O'Casey at her flat in St Andrew's Mansions, Ephraim turned up, and there followed a nasty confrontation. She described O'Casey as frail, "but almost ready to knock Lee down", while Ephraim was "stockily built and resolute". They disappeared together around the block to talk things out. O'Casey reappeared to tell her that he wanted them to marry and that he had made this clear to Ephraim.

After this, life settled down for both of them. They went about together, visited theatres and art galleries and enjoyed a rich companionship. Eileen's mother hovered over them threateningly, pointing out that O'Casey was a Protestant, considerably older than Eileen, and came from a poor family: moreover, that he was embarked on a perilously insecure career and would never be able to provide for her properly. But neither of them found it difficult to evade Mrs Reynolds's clumsy tactics, although in 1927 she moved in with Eileen for a time. Eileen tended very carefully to her appearance – Sean, she said, always noticed dress and colour, liked "good legs, and skirts then were short and free". Some hefty dress bills arrived which she could not meet: "You mustn't send them to Ephraim," O'Casey told her, and promptly settled them from his royalties.

They were now lovers, he enjoying her "knee and thighs looking out from under the folds of your skirt . . . to fondle your legs, & caress your white thighs . . . press you panting to me". But a part of her still strongly missed Ephraim. She admitted frankly that her affair with him had been very physical and sexual – while O'Casey's notion of sex was very romantic, very ethereal. Not as strong and full-blooded, but with its own endearing force and purity, so that he was now finding his own love coming back "verified" in the "look of love in your beautiful eyes".

She, too, found her protective feelings awoken: "Take care of yourself," she wrote to him in her earliest preserved letter, headed Savoy Hotel, "and your work which is very precious, the very best is always worthy of care; therefore darling try and save all your nerve and energy for your work; get into the air in the day, eat what you can enjoy . . . My most ardent hopes are for your work dearest."

———◆◆◆———

After Easter O'Casey was working on the second act. Gaby Fallon asked him to come home, tempting him with the joyful sights of an Irish spring, but O'Casey replied, "I have no home – the foxes have holes & the birds of the air have nests, & I have just a place to rest my head." But his head during the night times when he wrote was full of the grim litany of destruction with which he was committed to tearing away the veil of the ordinary bourgeois appearances of Act I. He unleashed the Chaos of War, as he saw it, in the *"jagged and lacerated ruin of what was once a monastery"*. Religion, or the echo of its observance, is littered among the "blood dance of His self-slaying children". A howitzer broods over the broken remnants of men – a "Croucher" chorus figure made up like a death's head, a man tied to a wheel, a fatigue party who move ammunition boxes, a fussy observer, a staff-wallah issuing gas-mask instructions. Wounded men are carried on, tipped up on the stretcher to sing a song, then carried off.

This became O'Casey's descent into hell, his equivalent to Virgil's Avernus, or the Circe section in Joyce's *Ulysses*: he laboured hard at it, knowing that if this act were finally to work it would need several drafts to bring it to the right level of compressed power. He believed he was on to something infinitely more powerful than *Journey's End*, "that backboneless & ribless play" – failing to see that R. C. Sherriff's play in its own way encoded and registered the futility and heroism of the conflict for the officer class and their families, who suffered proportionately much higher casualties than the workers. Indeed O'Casey rejected *Journey's End* as he now rejected *Juno* – both plays being about people up against the *reality* of living through war. Above all he was escaping from "burlesque, photographic realism, or slices of life".

This did not mean he abandoned his ritualistic thrashing of *monstres sacrées*, among whom he placed William Archer with his *The Old Drama and the New* (1923) which he called "the worst book on the theatre ever opened under the nose of man". (It was possibly "dethrimental" to O'Casey that he never studied Archer's other, and better, book on the craft of playwriting.) Also included in his list of the damned were James Agate, Arthur Wing Pinero, and the members of the Garrick Club who kept their musty library under lock and key. He fell out with J. B. Fagan; he'd already referred disparagingly to him as a "little manager – born within view of Oxford University", and disliked his objections to O'Casey's rowdy friends McElroy and his son, who visited *The Plough* and shouted "It's a bloody great play, it tis thawt": "I gently tapped the little evening-clad pumpkin on his dainty shoulder" and said, "Next time they come, show them into a box". But he outraged Fagan most with his cavalier treatment of the manager's own script, *And So To Bed*, which Fagan gave him to read: first he forgot about it in "the excitement of his lady's loveliness and the roar of London", then, when pressed, told him not to waste his time by making him read such trivial things.

It was not Fagan, anyway, who was presenting the next O'Casey, but Billy McElroy himself; O'Casey had no more need of Fagan, for McElroy and a partner had subleased the Royal Court from Sir Barry Jackson, and put on *The Shadow of a Gunman* in May 1927 for a two-month run, with an outstanding cast which included Arthur Sinclair (who also directed) as Seumas Shields and the Allgood sisters as Mrs Grigson and Mrs Henderson. The behaviour of the audience on the first night was, according to *The Times*, "criminally unintelligent", and "saddening". Eileen played Minnie Powell, and during the run of this play O'Casey continued work on Act II of *The Silver Tassie*. It was now clear to both him and Eileen that they wished to begin a family. Eileen claimed that she was keener than Sean to marry: O'Casey, "one of the most truly moral men I had known", would have behaved the same had they merely decided to set up house together. However, on Billy McElroy's suggestion, O'Casey bought Eileen an engagement ring, of platinum with a sapphire surrounded by small diamonds. By the time they began seriously to think of marriage Eileen, who now spent more time in Clareville Street than she did in St Andrew's Mansions, was pregnant.

But there were still separations, provoking, on O'Casey's part, passionate outbursts with a Solomoniac ring:

Bright, fascinating things that often made me linger have lost their colour, & are pale gaunt shadows in the soft light of my love for you. When I lie down you are with me, & when I wake in the morning, behold you are there; your white hand is under my head, & I hear your voice like the distant singing of many birds.

My little Eileen, & she is fair, she is very fair; she is fair to look upon and very graceful, and the kisses of her mouth are desirable and lovely.

In June, when houses at *The Shadow of a Gunman* were tailing off – they had been poor compared to those for *Juno* – Yeats called unexpectedly on O'Casey at the Royal Court. Refusing a whisky, on doctor's orders, Yeats asked brusquely if O'Casey intended to give the script of his new play to the Abbey. There were rumours in Dublin, said Yeats, that he had decided to ignore the Abbey. O'Casey assured him that this was not so; yet he had – or so he later wrote – already promised to offer the script first to Sir Barry Jackson; in other words he did not necessarily intend to have the world première of his new play take place in Dublin.

In July O'Casey had finished half of his experimental second act when he decided to change the whole idea, so he went back to the beginning and started again. He had established a working routine in London: he would idle away the day, resting his eyes in the afternoon and bandaging them from the light until about four o'clock, then grow brisk and alert and start work. This he would continue until about eight, then break off for an evening meal. (Eileen, by her own admission, was at this time not much of a cook, although she later improved.) The pace of life was leisurely. "Myself, I've done no work," he wrote to her in early August. "I have spent the passing hours sitting, walking, rambling, idling voluptuously in Kensington Gardens: Sean and carelessness have met together: idleness and he have kissed each other. Hallelujah!"

But Mrs Reynolds returned to plague Eileen at St Andrew's Mansions, prying into her life, reading her mail, and doing her best to dissuade her daughter from marrying O'Casey, whom she placed in her own generation rather than Eileen's. Pressure on Eileen built up. *Gunman* had now closed and she left for a holiday in Bognor with friends. Both she and O'Casey were nervous at the prospect of marriage, although sure that they wanted each other: Eileen, in addition, had sunk into deep guilt on becoming pregnant. Although O'Casey was an atheist she still remained, as she termed it, "about the most bewildered Catholic ever", and wanted to be married in church.

"I love you," wrote Eileen from "The Bungie" in Bognor, where rain bucketed down and where her "esteemed" mother bombarded her with letters – four arrived in one day. She could picture him sitting in the front room, first in the chair,

> then getting up with that quick movement . . . as if some thought would urge you. Then sitting on the sofa: hands clasped & un-clasped as you think – then the careful settling of your cigarette in those ½ holders of white & gold. The smoke, all the while a movement, hand in pocket then out; over to the desk, an idle look through the papers; then perhaps a pause as one letter catches your eye. A long look along your book shelves, perhaps one taken down with a breath of contentment, then you will settle on to the sofa, almost patting the book before you open it, & read!

Her remarkable vision of him continued even to seeing how he used the fire: "I forgot the fire it should be on, to gaze into; some centre of colour to look at; to go away from & come back to." She exhorted him not to eat too many eggs, but to go to the Queen's, teasing him at the end of the letter, and echoing some gentle mockery of his, "Ah! What a strange girl you are!"

In spite of Mrs Reynolds's attempts to dissuade Eileen, they made their plans to marry at the Church of Our Most Holy Redeemer in Cheyne Row: but Eileen's declaration of love frightened him, he replied, "because of the possibility of pain and disappointment to you. Day by day a dread of giving pain to others flickers in me to a fuller strength, and how much to me are you above all the others!" But she was not to worry about his diet: "Very good," he called her pen-picture of himself and all his movements. "Very true indeed."

Meanwhile Eileen worried about the impending ceremony, and suffered increasing sickness in the early months of her pregnancy. On her return from Bognor she made her escape from the clutches of a grumbling mother to stay with a friend, Helen Elliott, who lived in Charles Street, near Berkeley Square, as O'Casey made a spurt forward with *The Silver Tassie*. He quickly sketched out Acts III and IV. In these, Harry Heegan, with little chance in the meantime to develop, had changed from the powerful and innocent football player into the broken-spirited *mutilé de guerre*.

Act III discovers him in a hospital bed, his blinded friend Teddy at his side and surrounded, like an uncomplaining Job, by feckless relations; here O'Casey was drawing on his three weeks in the ward of the St Vincent de Paul Hospital during 1915, when he himself had seen many badly wounded soldiers. In Act IV the football hero motif of Act I is reintroduced with ironic bitterness: Harry propels himself round the Avondale Club dance with ferocious resentment, forced to play the voyeur as his former sweetheart, Jessie, falls in love with his old pal Barney, who won the VC for rescuing him on the battlefield. Finally, he crushes the Silver Tassie, symbol of his glory, in despair and leaves for the twilight world of Wilfred Owen's disabled figure.

This last act, tragic in its intention, also owed a great deal to *Hinkemann*, although in Toller's play the eponymous hero, more explicitly impotent and unable to satisfy his wife sexually, undergoes a much more prolonged and Teutonic humiliation. O'Casey's tragedy is still relieved by farcical touches, with flashes of *Juno*esque wit, although the ratio is far from the one Agate admired, of twenty minutes' tragedy to two hours' sheer comedy. O'Casey, in *The Silver Tassie*, dismissed such approval with contempt.

As well as exploring powerful models such as *Hinkemann* in his own idiosyncratic way, in *The Silver Tassie* O'Casey was also dramatising his relationship with Eileen – although why he should have turned the successful outcome of his rivalry with Ephraim into its obverse in the play, and why he should have presented Heegan, the character based on himself – or the one with whom he most identified – as a nihilistic vision of a defeated nationalist spirit, cannot be explained in any way other than that he had not really adapted to the new reality of his life. He was himself no longer the victim of the poverty, nationalism, religious bigotry, loneliness and literary failure that he had in his earlier plays so cunningly and self-mockingly projected, without any desire to preach a message or indulge a feeling of self-pity. Then he had been content to show the processes of life through living characters presented with love and without being judged. The people he created were always greater than their models.

But now the situation was reversed. The overall expressionist aim of intensifying character and making it more abstract removed the flesh from much of the characterisation of *The Silver Tassie*. The process had become reductive. Jessie, based on Eileen, is an enticing but cheap flirt, while Susie Monican's abrupt transformation from religious hysteria to sexy nurse makes the accelerated development of Nora Clitheroe in *The Plough and the Stars* seem, by comparison, Ibsenesque in its preparation. Harry is a character whose emotions are overstated but who remains shallow and passionless: a cartoon character who betrays his creator's propagandist intentions. In his avowed aim of not repeating himself, O'Casey, alas, mutilated his own talent, reducing his great capacity for humour, sympathy, and warmth into a bold abstract attempt to make a shocking impact.

But it was a precedent to be much followed by politically motivated playwrights in the latter, more affluent, decades of the century: to this extent *The Silver Tassie* was a prophetic work. The curiosity of its composition is that it was written at a time when O'Casey felt the greatest personal happiness and financial security, and was full of hope for the future. Perhaps some darkness was hovering at the back of his mind – guilt that success had come too late to be of help to his mother who had so faithfully supported him; apprehension, too, that he was too old to change and develop. Perhaps, too, he did not see that success would pose a greater threat to his identity and a challenge to his courage than ever failure had.

For the moment he was greatly ambitious: *The Silver Tassie* had the strengths and the weaknesses of a play written purely out of ambition. Far from the impotent Hinkemann, or the wheelchair-confined Heegan, he was active, a father-to-be, a welcome guest in great salons commanding the attention of prime ministers, famous authors and distinguished hostesses, a figure courted by the newspapers. The very last thing he could claim himself to be was a victim. Quite the reverse: he was about to embark on the second half of a long life, as rich as the first had been, but in a very different way. It would have roughly the same measure of trials, setbacks, joys and heartaches, with the one great difference that he was no longer an obscure would-be playwright, a penniless stay-at-home shielding himself under his mother's skirts. He was out in the world.

Most of all he had found and succeeded in possessing a replacement for his mother, with a laugh to rival hers "at the gate of the grave", but a laugh which pointed forward to the future. He was submitting himself to a new process of life, the starting of a family, an act more courageous than writing a new play. His wife-to-be was feeling sick and needed reassurance. Her mother was trying to create every kind of trouble, even to waylaying the priest and stopping the ceremony, when, on 23 September 1927, the guests assembled at the Chelsea church. Fortunately the priest, Father Perceval Howell, did not mind mixed marriages, nor, it seems, self-confessed atheists darkening the doors of his church.

Eileen wore an expensive blue chiffon dress given to her by Helen Elliott, Sean his plum-coloured suit. Billy McElroy was the best man, while another friend, Captain Corby, gave Eileen away. She noticed Ephraim flitting about at the back of the church, and anxiously suppressed a surge of emotion towards him. O'Casey, at ease when talking to the priest, wryly set his mouth at the ceremony, but could not conceal a mocking smile: he never mentioned the wedding in his autobiography and later referred to the marriage certificate "of my own wife" – never "of myself". On that piece of paper he displayed his contempt for temporal certainty – and perhaps ceremony, too – by boldly inscribing his age as forty.

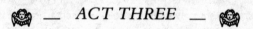

The Shape of a New World

1927 – 1964

Maybe he saw the shilling in th' shape
of a new world.

13

SLOUCHING TOWARDS BETHLEHEM

O'Casey took Eileen back to Ireland for their fortnight's honeymoon following the wedding. Ireland he had rejected – yet to Ireland he returned in the triumphant role of husband, introducing his new wife to his old friends such as Oliver Gogarty, Gabriel Fallon, Barry Fitzgerald, and his eye doctor Joe Cummins. Proud of everything, according to Eileen, he even had her guided round Trinity College by Dr Owen Sheehy-Skeffington, son of his former pacifist hero and of his un-pacific adversary over *The Plough and the Stars*. The whole visit, otherwise unaccountably strange, must have proved immensely flattering: the Lord Mayor of Dublin, Alfred Byrne, asked to meet O'Casey, who granted the request. They visited Leinster House, then Charlemont House, where they saw Augustus John's painting of his own son, and Epstein's Aeschylean but unlifelike bust of Lady Gregory: the gallery attendants showed as great excitement at O'Casey's presence as at visiting British royalty.

What O'Casey did not expose to Eileen was his own real background: 422 North Circular Road, the St Laurence O'Toole Club, the houses he had lived in as a child. Nor did he take her to see his brother Mick, or his nieces and nephews who lived in North and East Dublin. Probably he did not want anything to darken Eileen's view of the city he still held in deep affection: he declared to her that nothing in the world was lovelier than the Silver Strands outside Dublin. And she found him a marvellous companion: "humorous, watchful, and content to be with you, never wishing to stray; later I would be the restless one, needing at times to be on my own."

At first they stayed in Howth, then moved to the Hotel Russell, on St Stephen's Green, where it proved easier to run hot baths and visit the theatre, where *Juno* had been revived. Of Eileen's love of baths, not shared by him, O'Casey would exclaim, "God, Eileen! These baths again! However often do you have to take one?" But the baths did not alleviate the morning sickness and one night, having fully intended to have Sean's child, Eileen panicked and "took all and sundry to get rid of it".

What with the pregnancy, and with confused feelings about her Catholic faith, her health began to suffer. She tried to alleviate her guilt by attending Mass but discovered her attachment to the Church on the wane: "I knew that I had been cheating for a long time: a Catholic is not meant to have love affairs." O'Casey, with his proselytising, and reassuring, manner, helped her loosen the bond, so that finally she lapsed wholly, to her mother's horror. For the present he sought and found, through Cummins, a first-class gynae-cologist who was "wonderfully soothing", and informed her that to have O'Casey as the child's father would be perfect.

Apart from impending fatherhood O'Casey had plenty to occupy his mind, *Juno* having returned to the Abbey Theatre repertoire, and with an Abbey American tour planned for the late autumn (it was later called off). Back in London on 9 October he wrote to Fallon for the address of an actor to help in the casting of the first New York production, in November, of *The Plough and the Stars*. He was happy, he said, to be back among the "beeches, Larches, Willows, Oaks, & Chestnut trees of London". Four days later he confessed a new difficulty to his old friend – that he was trying to "solve an Einstein problem of how to buy a £4,000 house for 25/-". Now again hard at work on *The Tassie*, about which Lady Gregory wooed him encouragingly in November – "I hope all goes well with you – and your bride – and that you won't forsake us", he did not mention to the Abbey that he had already promised first sight of the script to Barry Jackson at the Court Theatre: Jackson's Birmingham Repertory Company, with two theatres in the West End, one in Birmingham, and a touring company, had something of the prestige of a National Theatre.

The house he and Eileen found was not the one they had originally sought: this one was smaller, cheaper, and on a shorter lease, only seven and a half years. A two-storey semi-detached in a Georgian terrace in Woronzow Road, St John's Wood, NW8, it had a basement kitchen equipped with a huge range – noticed more by O'Casey than by Eileen, who was not yet in the mood to settle down to domesticity. She still loved clothes, gaiety, but also the lilac, laburnum and apple trees in the front and back gardens. O'Casey hated the disruption of the move, in January 1928, and the extra spending it entailed at Heals and Harrods, the plumbing needed for a hot bath, and numerous other headaches (they hadn't money enough to carpet the rooms right up to the walls). But they were better set up than most, with a Bechstein piano, and John's *Head of a Gitana*, which O'Casey bought off the painter at a Chelsea gallery for twenty-five pounds. As a wedding present John gave the couple the first of his two paintings of Sean – "a princely gift", O'Casey called it. This was hung on the sitting-room wall over the mantelpiece; one visitor noticed how everything in the room was organised to match it in scale and taste.

O'Casey, who now wore spectacles, with large lenses and silver rims, soon noticed that he did not much like the neighbourhood. It was expensive to shop in and full of rich people. He discovered that ownership, even if only of a lease on a small house, caused all kinds of problems not hitherto met by the tenement, or bed-sit, dweller: "Jasus, it wasn't half as easy as it had looked!" The anti-property hackles began to rise, and he heard Proudhon's dictum, "*La propriété, c'est le vol*", beating in his head. Of course he and Eileen could have purchased outright a freehold further out, say in Hendon or in Edgware, but they would have had to forfeit their "gipsy-aristocrat" status and come down to earth.

Neither was prepared to do this. But O'Casey kept his tenement room intact, carrying it everywhere with him. From now on it became his study. Perhaps this single room, in which he always kept a made-up bed, remained the true home of his heart, in which he still lived with his mother, but now enclosed securely in a house of his own, with a wife and family. "Wherever it was, it would be full of his personality, even to the fact that he hung his hat and coat behind the door, never in the hall. He would change his boots when he came in, so his slippers stood ready by the fire." In Woronzow Road this space of his own reminded him of the return room in Mountjoy Square: small, furnished with shelves of books, it had a small desk, an armchair, and a narrow bed against one wall.

A more humble suburban life would not have suited a couple still courted by the very rich. They now employed as a daily Eileen's former dresser, Mrs Earle, who cooked and cleaned for them. From Woronzow Road they went to dine at Londonderry House in Park Lane, and met Ramsay MacDonald, the former socialist Prime Minister, Stanley Baldwin, the incumbent Conservative, Lord Carson, leader of the Ulster breakaway Protestants, as well as poets and musicians such as Rutland Boughton and James Stephens. One evening O'Casey asked his hostess, "I wonder if it would be a great deal of trouble if I had a little pot of tea?" She granted his wish, and soon others wanted tea as well: Edith Londonderry established "a pot in the small room at the back" – O'Casey, even in Park Lane, established his snug little Dublin corner.

Later, he issued his usual disclaimer for North American admirers:

> Lady Londonderry had to live through a decline and fall; a shock, for she, and all of her class, refused to believe that social evolution was bound to write Ichabod on the lintel of every grandee house in the land. Lady L. had formed a society of her personal friends; a society to which she gave the name of THE ARK. Each member received, or chose, the name of some animal. On being accepted by 'Circe', the animal received a badge, a bronze square piece, having the image of Noah's Ark on it, surmounted by a broad ribbon-bow of the Stewart tartan. I think Eileen still has hers . . . I didn't join in, refusing to get entangled in anything like a coalition of antagonistic forces.

But O'Casey did belong to the Order of the Rainbow, as it was called, whose other members included Churchill, Princess Helena Victoria and John Buchan:

> You will find there a Queen,
> A jockey, a Dean,
> With perfect affinities sorted;
> A sculptor, an actress,
> A world's benefactress,
> By crowned heads and clergymen courted

Members were called after a bird, insect, beast or reptile, or a magical or mythological creature whose first letter accorded with the first letter of his or her christian or surname. Winston Churchill was the Warlock, Sean O'Casey the Spider.

He found Edith Londonderry "charming", and was "content with her friendship without even seeming to agree with political affinities". Well he might not: her view of the Southern Irish was that they were not fit for democracy. "They are of a different race. They want firm, wise but powerful control, to prevent them from trying to eat each other up. Someday someone may arise who is powerful enough to be loyal to the Crown and great enough to be humble, and lead the people back into the United Kingdom." Yet at the time O'Casey was content to soak up her hospitality, preparing to explode his own bomb – his new play – which he hoped would help blow the social order apart.

In one sense, O'Casey felt more at home in London than in Dublin: England had, with its first Labour government, that of Ramsay MacDonald, passed a peak of socialism, while the country, still cherishing illusions of an Empire which had even then lost economic power, was beginning to embark on a series of leadership crises which were to continue on and off for forty years at least. Socialism had proved it was not a radical force in British society, while conservatives like Winston Churchill, who had warned of the new Soviet imperialist attitude ("The bear is padding on bloody paws across the snows to the Peace Conference"), were disheartened and isolated. Although O'Casey had little in common with the leaders of the Bloomsbury group, who he thought were out to devitalise literature – just as certain Church of England clerics such as William Temple, Bishop of Manchester, later Archbishop of York and Canterbury, were doing with religion, removing from Christian belief its specific spirituality in favour of more Marxist and materialist concerns – he did share the former group's pacifism, its atheism and its anti-imperialism. Its more languid addiction to "the higher sodomy" O'Casey later roundly denounced: "I know some of these 'Literateurs' – nancy boys in art."

He did, however, early in 1928, dine with Lady Ottoline Morrell in Bloomsbury Street, where he and Eileen met Julian Huxley and his wife, Juliette, formerly the Morrells' governess. The evening provided some authentic O'Casey comedy. Eileen, now heavily pregnant, wore a black lace dress pleated from the neck, and when they arrived realised she had forgotten to put on the heavy silk slip that went under it; her underclothes were all on show. Lady Ottoline, herself in startling white silk with white face powder and her dark red-purple hair, responded to the humour of the situation. O'Casey burst out laughing, so did Eileen, who wore her coat through dinner. O'Casey tucked into the fish, but failed to notice he had also helped himself to lemon, which he loathed, and reacted with a horrified squeak.

O'Casey never encountered Bertrand Russell, nor did he feel challenged in his continuing admiration for Soviet Russia by Russell's description of it as "a close tyrannical bureaucracy with a spy system more elaborate and terrible than the Tsar's, and an aristocracy as insolent and unfeeling". Russell had gone there himself to see. But for O'Casey, as for many English intellectuals, Russia had become Utopia on earth, an atheist's substitute for heaven. O'Casey never went to Russia – indeed never crossed the English Channel – but Julian Huxley, who journeyed over routes carefully arranged by the Soviet authorities during the great Russian famine of 1932, found "a level of physique and general health rather above that to be seen in

England", while Shaw, too, was an ardent admirer and later met Stalin during a brief visit.

But, O'Casey promised Lady Gregory in early 1928, there was no politics in his new play. By the end of February he had finished it hurriedly, and on 28 February wrote to her with the glad tidings, saying he would show it to no one else until he heard that they had received it in Dublin,

> so that I may be able to say that The Abbey Theatre was the first to get my new effort.
>
> I hope it may be suitable, & that you will like it. Personally, I think the play is the best work I have yet done.
>
> I have certainly put my best into it, & have written the work solely because of love & a deep feeling that what I have written should have been written.

But by his own admission, he had already passed a copy to Barry Jackson, who had not yet responded.

In mid-March O'Casey followed up the play's dispatch with an excited flow of letters anticipating acceptance and with suggestions, both rash and premature, as to how it should be cast, as well as blustering assertions of its imminent publication by Macmillan and of the large sum (£500) he was being offered for newspaper articles (he did not like writing journalism and did none at this time). Confident of returning again shortly to Ireland, he discussed sympathetically with Lady Gregory one of her own great causes, the return to the Dublin National Gallery, from the Tate, of her dead nephew, Sir Hugh Lane's, famous picture collection. With a touching personal affection – but perhaps rather cynically loaded, given the depth of his need and the response he was expecting – he wrote:

> I don't believe you'll ever really grow old, for there always was, & always will be, a lot of the child in your soul. Like my mother, who aged & aged, but kept her keen, bright eyes, her intelligent mind & her humourful laugh for ever.

----◆◆◆◆----

Robinson was the first of the Abbey triumvirate to read *The Silver Tassie*: he went through it three times and his initial feeling was one of satisfaction that O'Casey had made an attempt to do something new, for, as O'Casey himself believed, he could not go on writing slum plays for ever. But the word Robinson employed for this

Sara Allgood as Juno

Above: The O'Caseys on their wedding day

Right: Number 19 Woronzow Road

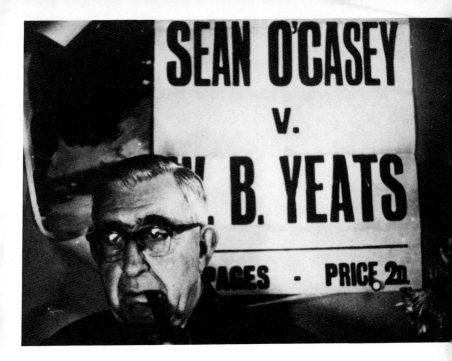

Above: Gaby Fallon with a poster of the celebrated quarrel

Right: Cartoon by O'Casey of himself preparing to fight

O'Casey in Chalfont St Giles

Right: Breon O'Casey and Sean

Below: Tingrith, Totnes

Family group, 1953, in Totnes: Shivaun, O'Casey, Eileen, Niall

Above: O'Casey with Eileen

Right: With Gauguin and
Joseph Stalin

"We cannot always suffer ecstasy": O'Casey at the sink

attempt was "groping" – he did not believe O'Casey had wholly succeeded. He liked the expressionist second act: "difficult to do and get right but not impossible . . . should be very effective." His reservations concerned the last two acts, which reminded him of the early O'Casey in *The Frost in the Flower*; his judgment here was astute, for O'Casey was slipping back, almost in reverse – with success the keynote instead of failure – into that earlier mode of writing.

Robinson, who apparently expected the theatre, as a matter of course, to produce *The Tassie*, passed it to Lady Gregory whose opinion, recorded as she said in her diary, was "I absolutely agree with LR's criticism, the beginning is fine, the two first acts – then such a falling off, especially in the last – the 'persons lost in rowdiness'." She then, to keep a copy by her, typed the first three acts and copied the fourth by hand. What greater sign of devotion could there be?

The script was forwarded to Yeats in Rapallo, but missed him there, for he had already left for Dublin; it arrived back on 16 April, whereupon Yeats, without consultation with Lady Gregory or Robinson, read it himself. He took three nights – feeling increasing disappointment: "You were interested in the Irish civil war," he wrote to O'Casey, "and at every moment of those plays wrote out of your own amusement with life or your sense of its tragedy; you were excited, and we all caught your excitement; you were exasperated almost beyond endurance by what you had seen or heard as a man is by what happens under his window, and you moved us as Swift moved his contemporaries."

But, he went on, O'Casey was not interested in the Great War, had never stood on its battlefields or walked its hospitals, and so had written

> out of your opinions. You illustrate those opinions by a series of almost unrelated scenes as you might in a leading article; there is no dominating character, no dominating action, neither psychological unity nor unity of action, and your great power of the past has been the creation of some unique character who dominated all about him and was himself a main impulse in some action that filled the play from beginning to end.

The size, the scale, of the World War, was wrong for O'Casey's dramatic imagination: "the whole history of the world must be reduced to wallpaper in front of which the characters must pose and speak." He then asked if Shakespeare educated Hamlet and King Lear by telling them what he thought and believed? No, he answered, Hamlet and Lear educated Shakespeare. "The control must be theirs."

Yeats only marginally softened this central damning criticism by saying, in his high-handed covering note to Lady Gregory, that his was only "an opinion" and did "not absolutely reject". But it was far from being a tactful and considerate exhortation by a sympathetic friend to the author to make some changes. And Yeats went on to recommend to Lady Gregory devious means by which O'Casey could save face by publicly declaring that he had himself withdrawn the script for revision – if he agreed with the criticism, that is; if he did not, he could offer it to a London management. And if no London management took it, he could "keep it by him revising or not revising as he pleases".

That Yeats's criticism of the play had validity cannot be denied: but it was tactlessly expressed and showed abysmal lack of understanding of any author's – never mind O'Casey's – susceptibilities. Yeats should have known by now what he was like. To suggest that O'Casey should withdraw his play could be construed as a calculated insult, especially as Yeats had gone on – in his letter to O'Casey – to upbraid him for the evidently huge effort he had put into writing *The Silver Tassie*. "I can imagine how you have toiled over this play," but "A good scenario writes itself. . . What business have we with anything but the unique?"

Why did Yeats take such an extreme view? He himself attributed it to splenetic age; in a few months he would come near to death with congestion of the lungs. Others ascribed his response to jealousy: O'Casey's plays had attained a popularity with audiences to which Yeats could never aspire. He might have felt that to let O'Casey experiment in his own literary domain would be to risk seeing him succeed, and become a great dramatic poet where he himself had failed. Yet, in the light of his judgments on earlier O'Casey scripts, Yeats's opinion did show consistency. He was a harsh critic: the standards he set himself were the standards he applied to others. He could never, as O'Casey himself well understood, descend to show ordinary human considerateness in matters of artistic judgment, which he put on a different plane. Part of the force of his reaction came from his genuine disappointment: a wiser, more worldly man might have seen that with all the personal upheavals O'Casey had been undergoing he might not produce – at least for the time being – another *Juno*.

Yeats's expectations were in any case excessive, when O'Casey had already given the Abbey three outstanding plays. Everybody had learned from those plays – including Yeats himself, some of whose grit and power as an elderly poet stemmed from the abandonment of his lyrical, pastoral voice and his adoption of a harder, more disillusioned and essentially *urban* tone. Where else could he have got this from but O'Casey? To say he owed part of his enduring greatness to O'Casey is not an exaggeration, for the popular acceptance of O'Casey's work forced Yeats to see that he himself had to make contact with the real world of his day. An increasing awareness that he had not many years to live made him appreciate the processes of life, especially love, as never before.

Perhaps, unbeknownst to him, O'Casey had become a mentor, a model for Yeats, and pointed the way to make him give up his poetic isolation and esotericism, and directly engage the heart. Hence Yeats's particular scorn of O'Casey's Act II "technical experiment", hence his sense of betrayal at O'Casey's attempting to tackle something outside his own direct experience. Yeats himself had never been deeply aroused by the World War, beyond the powerful lines in "The Second Coming":

> The blood–dimmed tide is loosed, and everywhere
> The ceremony of innocence is drowned.

As it brought only passive suffering it remained remote, peripheral to his central obsessions, one of which was that tragedy causes joy in the man who suffers.

In many of its particulars Yeats's opinion was right, although his sweeping dogmatic generalisations could be argued with (and were, of course, scorned by O'Casey). But what did weaken *The Silver Tassie* compared with the three previous plays was its absence of any emotionally unifying series of events in which all the characters participated, whether they liked it or not. The Great War was an intelligent but not an underlyingly cohesive substitute for the historical integrity of the other plays. A fatal deficiency – one that Yeats did not notice – was that it lacked their humanity and humour.

Bessie Burgess's stinging comment to the revolutionaries in *The Plough and the Stars*, "Call themselves Catholics, when they won't lift a finger to help poor little Catholic Belgium", was truer, and demonstrated greater perception about the involvement of Ireland in the Great War, than any comparable statement in *The Silver Tassie*. The nihilistic aims of expressionist drama ill suited O'Casey's instinct for warmth and cocky defiance in the face of authority and repression. The darkness, the seriousness, of *The Tassie* is manufactured. The ritual slaughter in Act II, intended to mock the ritual of the Church, makes the act ponderous. Yet somewhere within the play the laughter was trapped and waiting to be released. Perhaps, more in the Bouci- cault manner, O'Casey should have treated the whole field of slaugh- ter as a farcical wake. Had he been more miserable inside, he might have found release in laughter: personal happiness made him solemn.

Yet Yeats's judgment – and particularly the action of rejection undertaken on the basis of it – was profoundly unfair, and unwise. Every artist has a right to fail sometimes, and O'Casey had certainly earned himself the right to experiment with a play which was by no means wholly a failure, and which over the years, with changing styles of production, won many more admirers than Yeats's stilted verse dramas. *The Tassie* is a play which, as Robinson pointed out, challenges the theatrical imagination – a director's piece. The Abbey had shown itself all too willing to produce, not only honest failures, but works of drivelling and hopeless incompetence – as O'Casey and everyone else well knew. As the influential drama critic, St John Ervine, himself a playwright and a Northern Irishman, said later, in support of O'Casey:

> When "A. E." experimented with the dramatic form and wrote a play on Deirdre . . . the Directors did not tell him that his play was hopeless. They produced it. I remember "A. E." telling me that it ought to have been done behind a gauze net. This was not, as you may suppose, for the protection of the company, but for the purpose of making the play appear remote.

Yeats's bloody-minded judgment was one thing; but the subsequent behaviour of the Abbey directors was something else altogether. In the past, as Robinson reminded Lady Gregory, with his first plays like *The Crimson in the Tricolour*, O'Casey had been handled with sensitivity. Robinson had edited Yeats's harsher comments, only showing O'Casey the constructive or encouraging ones, while later he and others, such as Holloway, had acted as buffers, filtering criticism to (or from) O'Casey. It was the first important consequence of O'Casey's physical severance from the Abbey that his haunting, characteristic presence and soft, instinctive vocal charm, which had often contradicted the effect of harsh and bitter utterances, were not there to impose caution and tactful handling in the directors' dealings with him. Simply, they had forgotten what he was like.

Of course they should have sent for him, and Robinson, not Lady Gregory, should have edited Yeats's criticism. But they were older,

Robinson was more often drunk and Yeats more ill, Lady Gregory more dotty and idealistic. First impressions had lingered, or hardened with time, and they all somehow still expected O'Casey to be acting the poor supplicant, cap in hand, glad to serve and comply. Arrogant, Protestant, yet deeply spoilt and childish themselves, by virtue of the aristocratic, Ascendancy style of life they led, the directors forgot that "Casey" – as Yeats still called him – was also a Protestant, and now thought himself their equal, if not their superior (as a writer). He was finding a world-wide audience for his plays, which none of them had ever found.

Moreover the breakdown in communication was heightened by O'Casey's now publicly stated disdain towards Dublin and his departure from Ireland, leaving behind him a lot of ill-feeling. Yeats, while spending most of his time elsewhere, had cannily pretended to remain in Dublin, Robinson and Lady Gregory perhaps had no choice – but so many others from the Abbey stable had fled. Why should they be kind and treat with kid gloves a favourite son who had too often bitten the hand that fed him, and was forever causing minor but irritating trouble about rights and royalty payments? Now once again, over his new play, they could assert their authority, sure that while they were in what was only a backwater, it was one that should command respect.

Lady Gregory may not have had these motives consciously in mind when, on 27 April 1928, she sent O'Casey the whole of Yeats's two letters (the "opinion", along with the confidential note to her about how "Casey" should be treated), plus Robinson's, with a covering letter from her. She seems to have expected O'Casey to respond most untypically. Could there have been more than a touch of Job's comforter in her assertion of friendly honesty?

I think I ought to mail it [Yeats's letter] to you at once though I am afraid it might hurt you – or at least disappoint you – (as his criticism did me, on my first draft of "Sancho"). But it is right you should at once know what he – what we all – feel and think – I won't make any more comment – I know you will prefer this to any attempt to "soften" things and will believe that I, that we all – feel you would rather have the exact truth than evasions.

Expecting far too much from O'Casey, she was soon to become the victim of her own propaganda about artists. Some of her patronising words suggest that the unconscious contempt O'Casey had displayed towards her when lying about himself in the past might have been well founded. "My comfort is that you have such courage (far beyond mine!) and tenacity that I know you will, as of old, when the 'Banner' went back – set your teeth and 'turn a defeat to a victory' as you did then –." The reference to *The Crimson in the Tricolour* could not have been much comfort to O'Casey.

––◆◆◆◆◆––

In the meantime O'Casey and Eileen were preparing for the birth of their child. Rich in theatrical personality even when young, Eileen was also superstitious and in awe of fortune-tellers, and when one of them predicted some great disaster for her, she naturally assumed it concerned her baby. They still dined out, and attended a performance of the marathon *Back to Methuselah*, at which Eileen lost her shoes. But she was now huge – too huge, warned her specialist, threatening to induce labour a month before the promised date (unless this was another example of O'Casey chronology).

They hurriedly ordered a cot: on its arrival at Woronzow Road Mrs Earle remarked that it looked like a coffin. Eileen was nervy and sought full-time medical attention; her mother, sipping tea round at the house, warned her to prepare herself, what with Sean, an eccentric, and her own unbalanced father, for the birth of a mad child. Eileen broke down; Sean, cocooned in his study, rushed downstairs, shouting at his mother-in-law, "What the hell are you up to, woman?"

With the help of two doctors and an anaesthetist, Eileen gave birth during the night of 30 April to a healthy boy, whom they called Breon. It was a costly affair, O'Casey later remarked, "the doctor taking fifty pounds, plus the cost of a nurse who stayed with them for six weeks". Advised to spend the night of delivery elsewhere, he stayed with Billy McElroy, but when he arrived home next morning all joy in the wonderful event was crushed by the letter postmarked Dublin lying on the hall table. He tore it open, quickly absorbed its contents, then ran upstairs to Eileen, who was glowing with pride and happiness at the arrival of her son. O'Casey kept his bad news to himself.

In the weeks before the rejection of his play he had been keyed up with hope and excitement, even to the extent of picking F. J. McCormick to play Harry Heegan. But later, in retrospect, he sketched a scenario of gloom and expected disaster. He had anticipated the play's being turned down, he told Bernard Shaw: it was a predetermined plot. The style of the play could not in any case have been a surprise to Yeats, because he had been told about it – even told that it was about the Great War. Yeats had not objected.

The Abbey guardians had committed evasion after evasion, the first being Robinson's "'I will read it as soon as possible. Very busy now with a new Murray (play) & a Borkman production.' Though I knew he had read it, & could hardly read it quick enough," said O'Casey. The second was Yeats's statement "in his letter to me saying [he had dictated his letter before he opened the letters of the other directors], which is countered by a statement in a letter from L[ady] G[regory] 'that she couldn't remember writing this letter' (though she recorded in her diary that she agreed with L. R[obinson]'s opinion." There was

a third, a fourth, a fifth grievance listed in the intense paranoia the rejected author was still suffering two months later.

Yet even in his darkest moments, O'Casey, in the richness and many-sidedness of his character, never wholly became an obsessive case, and as he wrote out his numerous responses to this terrible disaster he relieved his feelings by drawing spirited caricatures, such as the one reproduced on p. 253. The dialogue under this drawing reads:

> YEATS: We decree that thou art a heretic.
> ROBBIE: Cast out from the unity of the Abbey.
> YEATS: Sundered from her body.
> ROBBIE: Segregated & abandoned for evermore.
> LADY GREGORY: Amen.

In another, the monocled Yeats leads a procession over a cliff (while gazing at the stars); Lady Gregory holds a banner reading "We're all as God made us", with Robinson's obscene shape supporting it:

A third caricature depicted the blighter and blaster O'Casey ready to defend his script.

He could also confirm that in spite of the Abbey's rejection Macmillan would still publish *The Silver Tassie*. The text was already in the press, and they had commissioned a charcoal sketch of O'Casey by Evan Walters, a young Welsh artist liked by both O'Casey and Augustus John, for the frontispiece. O'Casey sent the Abbey directors' letters, with his replies, to Daniel Macmillan, suggesting that they should be published as an introduction to the play. Macmillan promptly declined, but knowing that the book-buying public like nothing better than a good row between distinguished writers, brought the play's publication date forward. O'Casey was hurt that they would not publish the correspondence: "I have no intention of pressing for their publication in this way, for it would not be fair to bring Macmillans into the controversy against their wishes," he declared huffily, adding, "I am satisfied that I have acted in a square way with your Firm."

By now it must have been clear that O'Casey intended to milk the rejection for all its potential publicity. Feelings that had been confined to art, ironically reflecting and mocking one another, were now about to spill out hideously into life. Intrepidly, and yet foolhardily, for it is possible to view the action as demonstrating two elements of his character which existed side by side, he posted the exchange of letters, once Macmillan returned it, to the *Irish Statesman* and, in London, to *The Observer*, without consulting his Abbey correspondents or seeking their permission.

In his replies to the three directors O'Casey had not pulled his punches: he had scrawled over Yeats's letter, "Could anything equal the assumption of Zeusian infallibility." He told Robinson (on 2 May) that he had bet his wife ("curious word that for me to be using") that the play would not "be fondled by the Abbey". Of Yeats's wounding and confidential advice to Lady Gregory, which she had quite unnecessarily sent him, he wrote to Robinson:

I am too big for this sort of mean and petty shuffling, this lousy perversion of the truth. There is going to be no damned secrecy with me surrounding the Abbey's rejection of the play. Does he think that I would practise in my life the prevarication and wretchedness that I laugh at in my plays?

He did not stop, in further correspondence, from taking every point of Yeats's magisterial judgment and hotly arguing its opposite.

Yeats was stirred at first to reply soothingly, and (apparently for the first time) placed a conciliatory "O'" before Casey: "Had my admiration for your genius been less, my criticism had been less severe." This did little to calm O'Casey, who on 11 May produced his final word:

> You seem Mr Yeats, to be getting beautifully worse; you astonish me more and more. There seem to be shallows in you of which no one ever dreamed.
>
> What have packed houses, enthusiastic (cheering, says Mr Robinson) audiences for *The Plough* got to do with your contention that *The Silver Tassie* is a bad play?
>
> Perhaps this thought is due, as a journalist might say, to your delightful sense of Irish humour. – Farewell.

To Lady Gregory O'Casey was more kind, having already acknowledged to Robinson that she had written "in her kind way" and given him a "full, perfect and sufficient account" of the directors' action, he did allow himself, to her, a further swipe at Yeats's suggestion that he withdraw the play: "Does he take me to be such a dish of skimmed milk that I would do such a shuffling, lying thing as that?"

George Russell, as editor, at first balked at publishing the correspondence in the *Irish Statesman*, but O'Casey assured him, "You can take it from me that neither Mr Robinson nor Mr Yeats will mind the publication of the letters . . . what really concerned them was the fear that the rejection of the play would be a very great blow to me. The realization that the blow wasn't so great as they thought will be rather a relief to them, and they will welcome instead of objecting to the publication of the letters." But the appearance of the letters in *The Observer* on 3 June provoked Yeats's ire and proved the opposite was true: he asked the Society of Authors to take action against *The Observer*.

Walter Starkie, the literary critic, now an Abbey director, had not been in Dublin during the earlier exchanges with the other directors: he had now read *The Tassie*, and Yeats had his opinion inserted in the *Irish Statesman* when it published the other correspondence on 9 June. Accepting that the suppression of the letters was impossible, Yeats now wanted the record to be complete. Starkie's view at first echoed those of Yeats and Robinson:

In *The Silver Tassie* the characters seem to come from a shadow world . . . I feel that the author had a great idea at the back of his mind and fugitive symbols presented themselves to him . . . Many visions, many ideas crowd into his mind, but he is unable to make the synthesis and enclose them within the framework of drama. In spite of all this, I feel that the author is experimenting in a new world of drama; for this reason I feel strongly that the Abbey Theatre should produce the play.

Starkie's view, passionate and sensible, demonstrates ultimately how the Abbey bungled its decision and let down its audiences, as well as O'Casey: how frustrating that had a vote been taken, it would probably have been three to one for producing the play, with only Yeats dissenting. "A fight was the honest way out of it," O'Casey later claimed, also pointing out that on a man with a wife and tiny baby, loss of expected revenue was a grave financial imposition. He now paid English taxes and kept a tally of expenses on taxis, typewriter repairs, and entertaining foreign visitors: one night in June 1927 he and Eileen sat up in bed trying to sort out their accounts. His eyes were paining him and he cancelled visits to *The Dance of Death* and *The Way of the World*: with all the uncertainty he was "hopping about like a gold finch on the rim of a bowl".

But the dispute with the Abbey hoisted his name higher than ever before in the world's print, across America and Europe, and "tossed the names of Yeats and O'Casey into minds which had never bothered about them before". It was, as O'Casey had already shown in his unsent cartoons, a wonderful subject for caricature. The most celebrated appeared in the *Irish Statesman* on 9 June; Yeats, in spats and monocle, boots a hobnail-shod O'Casey out of the Abbey while telling him, "Of course, Mr O'Casey, you must on no account take this as being in the nature of a rejection. I would suggest that you simply tell the Press that my foot slipped." The *Catholic Bulletin* found it ideal summer reading:

Mr S. O'Casey, dramatic writer and military historian, deals for our delectation with Dr William Butler Pollexfen Yeats, and eke with Professor Dr Don Gualtero Fitzwilliam Starkie. This follows on what, not so long ago, the Proud Pollexfen proclaimed in the Abbey Theatre (subsidised; Government Director, Prof. Dr Don Gualtero himself) to be "the Apotheosis of O'Casey". The Apotheosis, like the German warships lifted at Scapa Flow, has been towed into harbour, keel upwards, to be broken up.

O'Casey did also partly exult in this colour and stir, even upbraiding the *Irish Times* for not making enough of it.

But Yeats continued to view the dispute with distaste: he told Lady Gregory, "So far as Dublin is concerned I think we will gain . . . and elsewhere when the play is published. The tragedy is that O'Casey is now out of our saga." If he was on the defensive, Lady Gregory showed pure bewilderment, confiding to her journal that she had sent O'Casey Yeats's letter to her, "that he might see there was nothing kept back and my own note of criticism in my diary. He had stayed here [at Coole] and I looked on him and treated him as a friend I could speak or write openly to. He had accepted our criticism in other cases . . ." She did not admit that those "other cases" were minor by comparison and she was so upset that she continued for months afterwards to write conciliatory letters to O'Casey: he would reply but he would not forgive.

Nor would he stop raging. The balanced and generous Starkie became "a toff" who "wears a stole of authority from the literary apostolate and epistolate of Dublin, so that everything he writes is stamped with a scholarly image and superscription". Yeats underwent further comic and hyperbolic transformations: "Born into the proletariat, [he] would have made a magnificent docker."

Sir Barry Jackson's rejection of *The Silver Tassie*, which came in June, did not make O'Casey more cautious: Jackson arrived in person at Woronzow Road to return the script, telling O'Casey that the play would be impossible for him to do and that an English audience could not stand it: it would "lacerate our feelings . . . be unbearable". He later added, "I am convinced that it is one of the greatest postwar plays and is certain to be widely read – and, although perhaps this is not the desired result of a work written for the public stage, it is at all events a very good stepping-stone."

O'Casey dispatched further lengthy letters to the *Manchester Guardian*, the *Irish Times*, and an even more discursive counterblast to the *Irish Statesman*, with his own and Starkie's arguments set out in the form of a dialogue. Russell refused to publish this last contribution; cutting it down, O'Casey then sent it to the *Irish Times*, which also declined it.

He rejected the good advice he received from all sides, in particular from St John Ervine, who agreed with his "justifiable anger" at the Abbey's "brilliant bungling" but appealed to O'Casey to stop being hurt. He was, Ervine said, first and foremost a distinguished Irish dramatist, and "the life of the Abbey is more important to Ireland than the life of you or me or Yeats or any other individual. It has kept what mind there is in Dublin – Heaven knows there is not much to boast about – and it must therefore, not be hurt."

O'Casey still took no heed. He had now resolved to wheel up the Big Berthas of literary controversy to escalate the bitterness, and even more than before to engulf in it his own pride and commitment. His atheism may have been in deep contradiction to his need for a father (and the constant need, stronger in him than in most, for an eternal father), but he now sought, in this controversy in particular, both an earthly father and an eternal arbiter.

There was one man alive in England whose literary authority was unquestioned and whose image had not been assaulted in O'Casey's passion for throwing down idols. To this man, and to submit to his fatherly judgment, O'Casey sent *The Silver Tassie* as soon as he had a finished copy in his hand.

14

A NEW CHARACTER

George Bernard Shaw, asked in June 1928 to deliver a verdict in the divorce action of O'Casey v. O'Casey (O'Casey versus Ireland, or the new O'Casey versus the old), quickly ruled in favour of the former, granting a decree nisi – with a glowing testimonial calculated to serve O'Casey's side in the controversy. From Passfield Corner in Hampshire, where he was staying with Beatrice and Sidney Webb, he wrote to O'Casey, "What a hell of a play! I wonder how it will hit the public." After overthrowing Starkie's and Robinson's opinion ("the hitting gets harder and harder right through to the end"), he commended *The Tassie*'s nihilism:

> You really are a ruthless ironfisted blaster and blighter of your species; and in this play there is none righteous – no, not one. Your moral is always that the Irish ought not to exist; and you are suspected of opining, like Shakespear, that the human race ought not to exist – unless, indeed, you like them like that, which you can hardly expect Lady Gregory, with her kindness for Kiltartan, to do. Yeats himself, with all his extraordinary cleverness and subtlety . . . is not a man of this world; and when you hurl an enormous smashing chunk of it at him he dodges it, small blame to him.

Shaw followed this with a rebuke sent off to Lady Gregory in which he boldly stated that she and Yeats had been treating O'Casey "as a baby", that Starkie was right, and that they should have done the play. Yeats, whatever he thought, should have submitted to it as to an act of God; on this occasion he had been "extraordinarily wrong", although typically himself: "Give him a job with which you feel sure he will play Bunthorne and he will astonish you with his unique cleverness and subtlety. Give him one that any second-rater could manage with credit and as likely as not he will make an appalling mess of it." To Lady Gregory Shaw repeated his description of *The Silver Tassie*: "It is literally a hell of a play."

There were, however, one or two personal considerations which lead one to question the impartiality of the judge. Over seventy, and twenty-four years older than O'Casey, Shaw was tired of a dangerously undiscriminating England in which his reforming wit, his radicalism, his gentle gradualistic Fabian socialism had been absorbed, and nothing changed for the better. He had, since the rise of Lenin and the propaganda success of the Russian Revolution, and in particular since Ramsay MacDonald had so spectacularly failed to implement Fabian socialism by means of the democratic process, shifted to more brutal beliefs, as exemplified by the Liberal MP, Cecil L'Estrange Malone, who at an Albert Hall meeting to commemorate the Russian Revolution popped the question, "What are a few Churchills or Curzons on lamp-posts compared to the massacre of thousands of human beings?"

Further considerations: Shaw hated Irish nationalism as much as O'Casey. He had, as an aspiring writer, gone through much the same kind of rejection O'Casey had experienced. Over *John Bull's Other Island* he had even received from the Abbey directors something of the same treatment. He and Yeats, although ostensibly friends, even allies – they were working together to set up an Irish literary academy – were temperamentally poles apart.

Early failure had affected Shaw even more deeply than it had O'Casey, but he hid his inner vulnerability more successfully. As long as he could command attention it provided the artificial self-esteem which he felt, as much from family and personal reasons as from his early lack of success, he needed to sustain him in the face of his ultimate belief that he was unlovable. What, sadly, he found himself so sympathetic to in *The Silver Tassie* was the nihilism: "You are suspected of opining . . . that the human race ought not to exist." The play had exercised his feelings about war. No wonder he signed himself off to O'Casey, "Cheerio, Titan". His approval of O'Casey's ruthlessly expressionist drive revealed a shocking truth: his disenchantment with the human race. The old man may be suspected of having grown callous – did a bit more slaughter really matter?

Shaw did not praise *The Silver Tassie* for being, as O'Casey intended, a great, warm-hearted attack on the horror of war; he lauded it for being "literally a hell of a play". It was not the first time, nor the last, that O'Casey's intentions had been misunderstood, but never was such a misunderstanding more crucial for his future. But O'Casey, too, put a false construction on Shaw's remark. There were, in any case, several possible meanings to "a hell of a play!" (but only one to "literally a hell of a play"). O'Casey did not understand that Shaw liked *The Tassie* for reasons which, had he perceived their full import, would have horrified him. Being two-edged, playing the divine fool, was by now second nature to Shaw, while he had perfected, as no one else could, the disarming wit which ultimately made his deepest convictions less than serious. Nobody needed to believe that he *meant* what he said. Thus he had often found himself the unwitting supporter of much that he wished to destroy (what greater affirmation of religious faith is there than *Saint Joan*?). Disillusionment with himself and his methods made Shaw speak up for O'Casey.

At a kindlier, and more mundane, level, he was also giving a leg up to a fellow Irishman in an alien land: he knew how difficult it was, so near and yet so far from Dublin, to settle down and become accepted. Possibly his sensitivity to O'Casey's vulnerability was not in the long run helpful: the earlier rebuke he dealt him over his early collection of articles, *Three Shouts on a Hill*, may have had a more salutary effect.

But the short-term effect of Shaw's championing him was immensely gratifying to O'Casey, to Eileen, to Macmillans – who included an extract from Shaw's rebuke of the Abbey in publicity for the published version of *The Tassie* – and to C. B. Cochran, who after lengthy consideration agreed to present the play in London. It refuelled the fires of O'Casey's self-justification: he had lost a mother and father but won a new father figure. Yeats and Lady Gregory could be ditched. Victor over his past, he could trumpet Shaw's approval in Ireland: a new confidence entered his polemical outbursts. He sent a copy of the published play to Lady Gregory, and she replied in an affectionate tone, trying to reweave the threads of friendship. He disposed of a review of the published *Tassie* by "Desmond", in the *Irish News*, by sending a copy of Shaw's approbation for the paper to print, ending, "And there I'll leave you Desmond, peeping at the world beneath the legs of Shaw".

It was a wasteful and unnecessary exercise: O'Casey did not recognise his true friends, nor see the limits he needed to place on his critics' influence over his highly volatile art. But he could not ignore them. He had, possibly, some sense that he had not come up to his own expectations, any more than to theirs, in writing *The Tassie*. All too evident in the play was a dislocation of his talent caused by his move from Ireland, while his own exaggerated response to rejection possibly betrayed the fact that his energies had not been wholly engaged during the writing of the play: had they been, he might have trusted more in its quality, as he had trusted in that of his previous plays.

But if the theme of *The Tassie* did not engage him at the deepest unconscious level, the effort he had put into the play had been stupendous. Yeats – "a bad scenario excites the most miserable toil" – knew much more about O'Casey's unconscious creative processes than Shaw (who never commented on them). Shaw ministered to the conscious ego, Yeats tried to apply drastic medicine to the artist's psyche: O'Casey, whether he was aware of it or not, chose between them. He chose Shaw.

Some delicate balance between his negative capability and a fierce Irish independence of mind was seriously harmed. The controversy, this time, came *before* the production, the cart before the horse, and with a play as experimental as *The Tassie* O'Casey desperately needed to sit among an audience and experience their reactions. A lot of abstract opinions were useless to him and he should not have bothered with them. But he had abandoned his former patience, while transplanting his gift on to English soil, and neither he nor anyone else yet knew whether it would thrive.

Eileen and Sean lunched with Shaw and his wife Charlotte on 21 June 1928 in the Shaws' second-floor flat in Whitehall Court. At the front door Shaw hurried forward to take both Eileen's hands in his – "the same gesture", she recalled, "the same warmth of feeling I remembered from my first meeting with Sean."

Over lunch Charlotte Shaw warned O'Casey not to be so angry with the press, but Eileen gently contradicted her, pointing out that if O'Casey felt resentful he must express his feelings. She had begun by supporting him in his individuality, his waywardness, and was never to stop. O'Casey recalled that GBS's support was being deflected from his own still combative anger with the Abbey "towards the silencing of Sean; and towards soft persuasion to be used on Yeats". During an animated talk O'Casey reminded Shaw of his having written to ask him for a preface to *Three Shouts on a Hill*. Shaw had refused, but he had carried the letter round in his wallet till it creased and frayed. Now "eight years later, he was equally moved by the salute to *The Silver Tassie*". Was he establishing, without saying so openly, that he had got his way at last with Shaw? To all intents Shaw's letter about *The Tassie* had become its preface. But neither writer appeared to notice the irony that in the case of the former letter it had been Shaw's rejection which had been the spur to success, not his approval.

The Shaws did put pressure on O'Casey to conform – for his own good: Shaw, for all his polemical impishness, was neither unkind nor irresponsible. Eileen, as far as can be judged, merely wanted Shaw to protect Sean: "Through the delicate fume of the conversation, Eileen's silvery voice suggested the compromise of Sean submitting any further letters to Shaw, who, if he disapproved of a paragraph or sentence, would edit it into a more suitable and tactful expression." This sensible advice was applauded by Charlotte Shaw and GBS, but O'Casey said nothing, and the pair left with a return lunch date suggested but not confirmed.

Shaw wrote on 3 July to O'Casey that he had heard from Lady Gregory that she had been on his side all through: he advised O'Casey not to run down Lennox Robinson or make conditions – it seemed in the curious slant of O'Casey's mind that he was gradually transferring from Yeats to Robinson the blame for *The Tassie*'s rejection. "Say that he is the rottenest producer on God's earth, and would kill a play even if St Luke and St Gabriel collaborated to write it. He won't mind that; and the conditions will follow spontaneously."

Shaw reminded O'Casey to be cautious: "Playwriting is a desperate trade. £300 a week for just long enough to get you living at that rate, and then nothing for two years. Your wife must support you (what is she for?), and when she is out of work you must go into debt, and borrow, and pawn and so on – the usual routine."

But the cancer of rejection was spreading: there was no second lunch between the Shaws and the O'Caseys. O'Casey drafted a reply to Shaw in which discontent boiled over into malevolence and paranoia. He knew the play had been rejected before he sent it in: he was the victim of a huge plot which pursued convoluted twists and turns of secrecy as the three evil guardians of the Abbey, aided and abetted by Russell, tried

> to prevent the publication of the letters shown by AE writing & wiring to me to show his fright over the possibility of an action for breach of [copyright] against him by Yeats, & the only way I could reply to the stirring of his fourth dimensional conscience was to write saying, No AE, "don't be trying to act the bloody Gaum!"

Dr Starkie's criticism, too, had been deliberately concealed from him ("the one criticism that was in any way favourable to me"). "How do I know these things! Ah! how did I know that Yeats was coming to London, & coming to see you before he stepped on the ship in Dublin Bay."

These outbursts would have been hilarious and vital in the mouth of an O'Casey character on stage, but O'Casey was playing them for real, in his own life. He had lost objectivity, the self-mockery he once possessed. His draft reply finished with a resounding condemnation of the Abbey ("a silly little temple, darkened with figures past vitality").

The Shaws now extricated themselves with alacrity from the complications looming – they must have received this letter in some form or other – Charlotte insisting that Yeats had not come to see Shaw about the play. She further told Eileen that she was all the more sorry they could not see the O'Caseys again for a while (the Shaws were just off abroad), as

I do feel "Sean" wants a lot of looking after just now. He is going to be very naughty & fierce & resentful – & he is a terribly hard hitter!

That idea of letting G.B.S. see his letters to his "friends" is a grand one. Do keep him up to it. Any letters addressed to 4 Whitehall Court, will be forwarded *at once*, and I will send you our address the moment we are settled, & he must write about all he is doing, & G.B.S. will answer *quickly*, & try to act as a lightning conductor!

O'Casey would have none of it. "He had refused the counsel of Uncle Yeats, and he had no intention of taking the counsel of Auntie Shaw." He would not submit to his own emasculation.

He also thought "Mrs Shaw, in her heart, resented Sean's independent critical outcry, and remembered it against him". When Russell reviewed the published *Tassie* in the *Irish Statesman*, O'Casey attacked him, rounding off his reply, "London with the sun out"; his attack on the "toff" Starkie's report, in the September issue of *Nineteenth Century*, was equally unnecessary and carping. Russell reproached him, "Try to be a little good natured about our imperfections. There was something else out besides the sun when you wrote those letters."

Russell in a further editorial comment in the *Statesman* put his finger exactly on what had been happening to O'Casey since he left Dublin. "DEAR SEAN, – You are creating a new character, and when you have finished annihilating your critics the portrait of the annihilator will be as vivid in the consciousness of your readers as Joxer or the Paycock." The birth of this new character had been painful: moulded in his new life in London as a married man, it had been taking shape, unseen, alongside the crippled hero Harry Heegan, who had a little but not much to do with O'Casey himself, and had soon sucked all the energy from Heegan.

The rejection of *The Silver Tassie* was this new character's baptismal fire, but O'Casey would not, like Harry Heegan, become the victim of himself (having, before, been the victim of others' blind hate). He would turn and fight: not for those causes which, expressed in his plays, had bound him to other men, but for himself, and for his work – especially if people attacked it, made it the object of their criticism. He no longer had need of motherly protection, or of idealised father-substitutes:

> He would fight alone; one alone and not a second. He would fence in his own sour way, thrust, parry, and cut with his own blade of argument . . . according to the measure of his own heart, the rhythm of his own mind, logical now, savage and sudden a moment after: in this fight, he would face any opponent, and thrust straight at the side where the heart lay.

While Maire Keating's rejection of O'Casey had provided the basis of a wonderfully and comically distorted vision of a relationship in *The Shadow of a Gunman*, O'Casey's fulfilled love for Eileen had led to a failure of representation in *The Tassie*: the portrait of Jessie Taite is tantalising, sexy and compelling, but unsatisfactory. Eileen, in reality, had embraced the self-mocking O'Casey and loved him, preferring him to his much richer and better-established rival Ephraim. As a result, the cynicism of Jessie Taite has a manufactured feel, the bitterness is too literary: it doesn't reveal the pressure of unexpected passion, or heartbreak. O'Casey did not have to mock himself: he could take himself seriously.

In August 1928 Eileen took Breon away with her, for a rest, to Amersham Common: O'Casey stayed behind in Woronzow Road. Alone for the first time for months, he felt curiously quiet, uneasy and restless. Nothing could remove this, he told Eileen, but the "clasping in my arms once again of my lovely little Eileen". He looked at the things "in your room & in my room, & they, too, seem to have gathered in them something of the patient resentment of your absence". He longed to see her once more, he said in a further letter, in the black dress she had worn at Ottoline Morrell's.

While O'Casey negotiated the sale of rights in *The Tassie* to Cochran – wanting to "get as far away from the Irish Players as possible", as he told Fallon, "& to break the tradition that no 'Irish' play can be played without the 'Irish' players" – Eileen went on from Amersham to Angmering-on-Sea in Sussex. Here, in fine weather, she bathed in the sea and read *Jude the Obscure*, not perhaps the most heartening of stories for a nursing mother. "Isn't Jude a tragic tale, all life is tragic to the imaginative type of person, to eat, drink and 'live within the law' is so difficult for them to do. I hope to get a letter soon." O'Casey replied, on 20 September, gloomily, that she had to keep herself fit to battle for Breon if anything happened to him. "Even if nothing should happen, I'm not going to be, apparently, of very much use to you or him."

He soon cheered up, inscribing the flyleaf of her copy of *The Tassie* – they had now been married one year – with tender and affectionate compliments, ending, "From Sean, with deep and intense love that has been wedded into a sweet and lovely companionship". And at last, just before the end of the month, Cochran signed the option to present *The Silver Tassie*, which he was intending to back wholly himself. Costs would run as high as £5,000 – a sum inconceivable and awesome to the Dublin dramatist whose Abbey productions cost less than a tenth of that. Cochran wanted to do the play first in America, and seems to have paid O'Casey as much as £500 for the acting rights – much more than he could have hoped for out of an Abbey production. So he had only lukewarm interest in an *Irish Times* report which had Lennox Robinson saying that the Abbey would do *The Tassie*, "if I were willing & the Cochran production fell through".

Cochran and he went off together to do battle with C. L. Gordon of the Lord Chamberlain's office, who asked for fifteen omissions or modifications in the text of the play, mostly of religious blasphemies of a fairly straightforward and, by later standards, mild kind ("Holy God", "Goddam", etc.); the office also objected, in Act I, to "arse" and "we'll rape her", in Act II to "pissing", "does he whore well?"; in Act III to "Hurt her breast pulling your hand quick out of her bodice did you?" and "peering pimp". The pair found the censor alert and friendly and, having ultimately to change only six words, they had an "interesting discussion of the drama". Cochran's presence was a great salve to O'Casey's hurt feelings: he had himself produced, in his latest revue, a musical number, "Dance, Little Lady, Dance", noted by O'Casey as "a marvel of Expressionism".

A mixture of dreamer and financier, Cochran was the ruling showman of the West End; he managed entertainments like stocks and shares, but with an eye to Higher Art. He proclaimed *The Silver*

Tassie a great play: it will, he said, be our "classical war play – revived in ten and twenty and fifty years' time. It is a perspective of war by a great mind. It breaks rules . . . just as Coward breaks them in *Bitter Sweet* – What is wrong with our English theatre is that rules are not broken often enough." O'Casey overlooked the bracketing of himself with Noël Coward. He preferred instead to admire Cochran's taste in art: he owned pictures by "Cezanne, Renoir, V. Gogh, Degas & John".

In October Cochran disappeared to New York, where he presented a new revue bringing him receipts of £7,000 a week, prompting O'Casey's comment to his faithful buttie Fallon, "so you see my boy GENIUS and ART sometimes have a reward greater than a cup of cold water". O'Casey passed the time with frequent visits to the Tate Gallery, and showed pride in his own picture collection, writing to Lady Gregory, "We have six originals now, & some beautiful prints by modern artists. We have declared war on the clumsy, gaudy, garish, picture-degrading cult of gilt framing, & enclose them all in simple oak, walnut or ebony frames."

Gaby Fallon kept him in touch with the Abbey and its main autumn production of *King Lear*, with F. J. McCormick in the title role: O'Casey still read the Irish papers avidly, and asked, "Did you see see pee see's [Constantine P. Curran] praise of King Lear? He says, says he that K.L.'s a Katabolic Kharacter." The new O'Casey, who instead of feeding directly on life and observation now devoured articles and gossip, made much sport of the news that Robinson had taken a temporary post as drama adviser at the University of Michigan: "that's the place for Robbie. What about holding a class in the open on the shores of the Lake? Such a fin de siècle idea! Everybody bring a cushion. Lecturer in extraordinary to Thespis. And draw me salary from The Abbey all the while." When Yeats's highly praised volume, *The Tower*, appeared in 1928, he did more than pour scorn on it – he wasted valuable time reactivating his hostility over *The Tassie*, writing to Oliver Gogarty:

> I've read Yeats's "The Tower" in fact – as [Lennox] Robinson would say – three times in all, and it doesn't satisfy me. He builds better in wattles than he builds in stone. And all the silver-throated bugles that blew about this bloody book! There isn't a good line about life from one end of the book to the other, though there are several bad ones about death . . . Age like a tin can tied to a dog's

tail? . . . And that loud-lauded passage "Hollow of cheek as though it drank the wind and took a mess of shadows for its meat." Thought of by a quattrocento mind & written by quinquagesima fingers . . . There is nothing natural here; it is all forced.

O'Casey not only hated Yeats's imagery of cock or hen on golden bough ("May I be one of the passing gents that listen"), but the birds singing in the Woronzow Road garden also got on his nerves. Gogarty tried to put him right in a buccaneering, witty reply which veered close to giving offence but just about kept on the right side of O'Casey and his "philosophysing with an hammer":

There is no greater artificiality than being natural in literature. If it were possible that naturalness were literature, you and the rest would be well superseded by a dictagraph. Where would the fashioning faculty be? All we can do with our life in Art is to form, to shape something. That is why my family is a better achievement than my verses.

O'Casey valued the medical side of Gogarty's skill and later consulted him about having his tonsils out. Perhaps bad teeth were adding to his troubles now. Extensive extractions were followed by the planting of new ones in his mouth ("I don't know [he wrote to Fallon] . . . whether to condemn progress that takes away teeth, or progress that gives one a new set . . . However, they're feeling more hopeful now, & in years to come, I will be able to hang on to an iron bar"). A hard winter made the pipes burst in Woronzow Road in early 1929 and O'Casey took time off to watch the skaters on Hampstead's Whitestone Pond: "on every house [he wrote to Augustus John] you can see plumbers crawling over the roofs and along the walls massaging the pipes. Cascades of cursing everywhere."

Eileen was still feeding her young son, Breon, who was "going along like a house on fire" and now well over double his birth-weight. She played a decisive part in the staging of *The Tassie* by suggesting early in 1929 that John design the set for the controversial Act II. Cochran concurred, whereupon Eileen approached John, visiting him in his Chelsea studio. O'Casey, possibly embarrassed, wrote to John about the question which "her good & impetuous nature has thrust between us" – sounding like an indulgent father. "A remarkable girl," he declared; "over the year that is gone she has raced to a perception & enjoyment of art that is very gratifying." Elaborately humble, he continued that it was the case of "an angel rushing in where a devil feared to tread" and "though the present day English stage is unworthy of the consideration of any serious artist, yet I have the encouraging reflection that the play isn't beneath the thoughts even of Augustus John". John agreed to design the second act.

Another man might have been anxious about his wife visiting this notorious womaniser, but not O'Casey. Conscious of himself as a much older man, he encouraged Eileen – or so it seemed to her – to be attractive to other men. David Astor, who encountered the O'Caseys at this time, when they visited his mother, Lady Astor, was struck by Eileen's audacity: "I was very young," he recalled, "and she took my hand and half-flirted with me as we walked around the garden. She was very forward with men and gave them confidence." When they rejoined O'Casey, Astor noticed that he was "amused and didn't seem to mind".

Cochran, too, encouraged Eileen's independence: one weekend when they were with him in Cookham, and had finished discussing *The Tassie*, he took her aside and asked when she meant to return to work. She would find it hard, he said, to settle and needed to go out in the evenings. Pointing out how much older O'Casey was, he insisted that she ought to pick up the threads of her career. He invited her, a few weeks later, to audition for Noël Coward's *Bitter Sweet*.

O'Casey was not doing much writing: a short story, called "The Star-Jazzer", later collected in *Windfalls* (1934); a few autobiographical sketches which were to form the basis for his future autobiography. He had developed some ideas for the London play he had mentioned to journalists three years before, but not much, if anything at all, had been committed to paper. It was a vain boast that he made to Fallon, in April 1929, that *The Tassie* was rarely in his thoughts. He sold the film rights of *Juno* to British International Pictures for £1,000 during this spring; he was offered the job of scripting Liam O'Flaherty's *The Informer*, the picture John Ford directed, which he turned down at once, inspired by the example of Shaw – possibly a mistake considering the ease with which he could write brilliant vernacular dialogue.

Eileen was offered the part of Jane, one of the bridesmaids, in *Bitter Sweet*; her protracted absence on tour, their first long time apart, put a strain on the marriage. On the date of the pre-London opening in Manchester, O'Casey wrote to her, self-pityingly, that he was "fighting bravely, if hopelessly, in an effort to disassociate myself from a sense of loneliness and pain". He could hear Breon's teething cries, or his "peevishly proclaiming his hunger". Nanny, and Mrs

Reynolds as well, were there, and Sean took the child off to his room: "We must be careful not to let him feed too much on attention from women," He did not like Eileen's mother mixing too much with Breon, "particularly when you aren't there". While the tone of emotional blackmail was strong, he ended that she must not lose heart because she was away. He had tried, he said, to send a telegram to Noël Coward but could not.

When they were back together again he wrote to her, in the second of two letters dated 9 July, "Breon must only take you away from me for a few moments," although earlier he conceded that he does, "in his own little way, need his daily association with his mother". The separation was agony: "We pay the penalty of love with pain . . . I have done what I said I would do: I have made you love me." But he regretted he had not known her whole past earlier in their relationship, "& I would have been kinder and gentler & more useful to you".

When, a little later, he wrote the prose poem "Gold and Silver Will Not Do" (also in *Windfalls*), he addressed it to her: although eventually substituting another name. "Eileen most fair; Eileen most desirable of women; Eileen whose personality tempers my thought, and whose loveliness brings pride to my pleasure . . ."

Bitter Sweet triumphed in Manchester, with ten curtain calls on opening night and wonderful notices next day. It began its enormously successful and long run at His Majesty's Theatre on 19 July 1929. Eileen remained in the show until it closed nearly two years later, fulfilling what she described to Sean as her "deep, burning longing to earn something myself to leave you freer to do what you will with your writing". Although it meant she had to forgo appearing as the first Jessie Taite in *The Silver Tassie*, she was again in her element. Cochran sent her carnations on the first night. She regretted that O'Casey could not bring himself to send Coward a note (she had told Coward he would): "Would it really be wrong to your conscience to wish him success?" she asked. "If it be good and from God, then shall it stand," was his final word, and he did not revise his opinion.

On the day of *Bitter Sweet*'s London opening O'Casey answered yet another conciliatory letter from Lady Gregory ("believe me affectionately your friend", she had ended) in the same spirit, although he complained of his health and bad eyes, things that had "entrenched themselves in me in Childhood". But he had, he told his old friend, "many reasons indeed for believing that the goodness of God hasn't altogether left me alone". He then went on to describe his simple life and how little money they had. But his life-style that same evening somewhat belied the profession of "a simple life". *Bitter Sweet*'s opening cost him thirty-four pounds, the price of the tickets Eileen bought and sent to many friends, anxious that the show should be well received. O'Casey attended with Eileen's gynaecologist, Harold Waller, who thought the music bad; he himself found the "wording" worse. He must have been aware that Cochran's success with the Coward play would help him produce *The Silver Tassie*.

Augustus John had made no progress with his ideas for the set of Act II when Raymond Massey, who was to direct the play, called on him in September. Massey found the painter distracted and nervous, with "not only an open mind but a blank one". It was obvious that O'Casey's meticulous delineation of the setting, more than a page of script, left John feeling hampered and frustrated. He showed Massey some large charcoal drawings he had made as a war artist with the Canadian forces at the front: one of a ruined chapel had a resemblance to O'Casey's detailed description, and they settled on it as a basis for the design. Two days later Massey managed to extract two more sketches, "frightening, grizzly and jagged, O'Casey's scene was there". Massey proceeded, with the aid of some outstanding scene painters and builders, to translate John's ideas into reality. They hoped John might himself paint the figure of the Virgin on the stained-glass window of the chapel.

O'Casey, at his first meeting with Massey, had informed him he could be of no help with the second act. Over lunch at The Ivy, Massey asked about the play's inconsistencies and inaccuracies about the war, and if they were intentional. The question aroused O'Casey's ire. Massey told him that this would be the fifth war play he had directed in the past few years.

It was, however, the first which was in a symbolic or expressionistic form; the others had demanded complete authenticity. Sean with obvious anger said that of course the flouting of authenticity was intentional. It was done for dramatic or satirical effect. The character switch in the role of Susie – a religious fanatic in the first act and in the final two acts a gay party girl – was justified by the play's development.

O'Casey, however, kept quiet about the Abbey's rejection. Massey learned nothing about the play at lunch, except that there was no room for balanced opinion. "It was all out and no holds barred . . . there could be no compromise with reason. The emotional range was supreme and the act was no interpolation but the core and substance of the play."

The "whirl & sweep" of rehearsals – short, according to Massey – soon excited O'Casey, as did the high-calibre cast: Beatrix Lehmann played Susie, Binnie Barnes Jessie; O'Casey's favourite, Barry Fitzgerald, came over from Dublin to play Sylvester Heegan, while the "genius" Charles Laughton, as Harry, rehearsed, wrote O'Casey to Fallon, "with amazing strength & pathos". Not only were the international film careers of Fitzgerald and Binnie Barnes launched in this production but a young Welshman, just down from Oxford, also made his West End début, as The Trumpeter in the second act.

Emlyn Williams showed at once a sharp and satirical eye: "every day after rehearsal we spent a tedious hour standing round a piano repeating over and over again the Catholic Gregorian chants, in Latin and Greek . . . which we were to intone offstage in the weird second act; a posse of professional waiters at a wake." The group soon called itself "Cochran's Choir". Laughton, as Heegan, was described by Williams as "massively crouched in an old wheel-chair, knuckles white round the arms of it, eyes protruding wildly in a pale pudge of a moon-face. He looked nearer fifty than thirty." One young walk-on cracked, "Footballer my eye, looks more like the football!"

Laughton became deeply obsessed by the difficulties of his part; especially his Irish accent which he felt was up against the real thing all around:

Christ these Irish parts, but it can happen the other way round – when I went to Dublin recently to get the feel of this, I saw a tremendously Oriental play which started with the Muezzin in the market place and weird Arab music – fine until one of the hooded figures on his knees turned to his neighbour and said, "Methinks the wind of Allah boiteth mighty cold in the bazaar tonoight".

This exploded him into helpless laughter which transformed the smouldering sufferer into a mischievous fat cherub. Just as swiftly there was a dissolve back to the sufferer: he sighed, slumped forward and started to glower, ready for his next entrance. Then a hoarse near-Irish mutter of despair, "Will Oi ever get it roight, damn an' blast . . .?"

"Too intense to move me," Williams described the play as a whole.

The star, even one as bright as Laughton, was a poor substitute for the Abbey's twenty-year-long ensemble tradition, whose human and instinctively comic underpinning *The Tassie* possibly needed. O'Casey remained touchy about Yeats and the Abbey, and in mid-August when a report appeared in the *Birmingham Gazette*, the *Sheffield Independent* and the *Nottingham Journal* that the play had already been produced at the Abbey, and that, at a Wicklow house party, Yeats had made disparaging references to it, he wrote to Yeats and to the papers in question, demanding denials and apologies. Yeats later explained to Lady Gregory:

> The journalist claimed to have met us on the stormy & rainy night when the "Silver Tassie" – which afterwards went to America – was produced in Dublin for the first time. I replied that I had of course given no interview to anybody on the subject in Wicklow or elsewhere. However I did not get Casey's letter until seven or eight days after he had posted it.

In London O'Casey, swept along on the glamour of the impending first night, granted an interview to George Bishop of *The Observer*, which Bishop introduced with "The story of Mr Sean O'Casey is a modern epic." *Juno* was "the poorest thing I have had produced", O'Casey told Bishop and, with equal silliness, said that "I would make it a penal offence for any man to write a play without being able to declaim two or three of Shakespeare's plays by heart." He refused, with a bold flourish, to be interviewed by Hannen Swaffer for the *Sunday Express* – making sure that Swaffer felt the snub.

As usual when he was under pressure, his eyes hurt and he felt unfit, this time with tonsillitis, so that he called in Gogarty to inspect his throat. Lady Gregory delighted him with a report that a portrait of her granddaughter by George Russell was not very good, but when she sent her best wishes for the first night and informed him of her intention to see *The Tassie*, and hoped she might be able to visit him and meet his wife and son, he retaliated: "The production has made my mind a-flood again with thoughts about the play's rejection by the Abbey Directorate, & bitterness would certainly enter into things I would say about W. B. Yeats, & L. Robinson if we were to meet; bitterness that would hurt you, and I am determined to avoid hurting you as much as possible." He ended vindictively, "So knowing how I feel, & guessing what I would say about the many Artistic & Literary Shams squatting in their high places in

Dublin, I feel it would be much better to set aside, for the present, the honour & pleasure of seeing you & talking with you."

Many years later he regretted this letter and his "grim mistake" in refusing to listen to Eileen, who begged him to let Lady Gregory visit. She had been eager to meet the woman "of whom he had so often spoken affectionately and well". Lady Gregory kept her word, saw *The Tassie*, and departed again for Dublin not only without a word from O'Casey, but without "a last affectionate handshake, for he never laid eyes on her again".

Massey little expected Augustus John to arrive, even at the last moment, to paint the Madonna on the Act II stained-glass window: he had made alternative arrangements with a scene painter. At midnight on set-up day, John turned up drunk, "his great black hat cocked over his forehead", and sauntered down the aisle, climbing unsteadily on to the stage, where he surveyed the scene in silence:

> In the harsh work lights it looked like a bone yard it was meant to. The artist slowly moved towards the window frame lying on the stage, took up Alick's [the scene painter's] stick of charcoal and made a firm stroke on the oiled silk. He worked as though possessed and for more than two hours he never looked up. Cochran, Sean, Alick and I and the crew watched in fascination. At last he was done. He moved to the side of the stage and stood waiting. Without a word, two stagehands lifted the window piece and braced it in position. The master electrician connected the cable and set the lights for act 2. And there shone the Madonna of *The Silver Tassie* . . . We cheered Augustus John. He did not hear us; he just stood there looking at his scene. He was pleased with it. He left, swaying slightly.

The first night also passed to everyone's satisfaction. On the whole the critics were favourable, although, as Emlyn Williams noted, the *Telegraph* described the play as "puzzling", *The Times* as "a great stumbling failure". The first week's receipts broke the record of the Apollo for the last three years. Shaw, there on the first night, still championed the play vigorously; he was joined by T. E. Lawrence, who told John (so John informed O'Casey) that he found it "the greatest thing of our time". Lady Gregory wrote to O'Casey that the second act was impressive, but that the Abbey would have done the other three acts better: she had written to Yeats saying they should have accepted the play in the first place. Well meant, this comfort was cold and misplaced at a moment when, as Williams noted sardonically, on the Monday night of week two, there were empty seats. "Cochran the infallible had been misled by *Journey's End*; this was a war play that was not going to succeed."

Yeats himself, worried and ill, a spectre at the feast, flitted in and out of London: he reported to Lady Gregory in early November a rumour that audiences were falling off: "I hear only of people who greatly dislike the play or greatly like it. I met Sally [Sara Allgood] at Lady Ottoline's, she said we ought to have done it, but when I asked her how the audiences would have taken it said 'there would have been a row of course' and went on to explain why – general bad behaviour of everybody." To Lennox Robinson Yeats wrote flatteringly – both men were on the defensive, cast as villains in the piece – "I had tea with Gerald Heard yesterday and praised *Ever the Twain* [Robinson's 1924 play, *Never the Time and the Place*] to the rich young man. I said it was the greatest success we had ever had because though *Juno and the Paycock* had drawn as well *Juno* had the help of extraneous events." He didn't see *The Tassie*: "Illness kept me from seeing it, though I had my seat taken."

Meanwhile, O'Casey concealed from everyone – most of all himself – his growing fear that *The Tassie*'s financial return would not be what he had hoped, namely a decent living allowance for one year. Bravely, on 3 December, he told Fallon that it was still playing to "fine houses". But it was now in its last week. The Wall Street stock market had crashed in the second week of the run and Cochran could not risk more capital in an already expensive production: "It's the proudest failure I ever had," he declared.

In the following year Fallon tried to arrange a production in Dublin at the Gaiety, but it fell through because of vituperative denunciation by the Church, in particular from Father Michael Gaffney, who wrote in the *Catholic Mind*, "I fancy that Dublin is a little too wise . . . to put its lips to a cup that may possibly have been filled from a sewer. The play has been published in London, and is in our hands for cold inspection. It defies analysis. It is a vigorous medley of lust and hatred and vulgarity."

True to his Flutherian code O'Casey fought his way out of failure. George Russell and his sundered psyches "AE" and "YO" ("one in three and three in one") offered himself as a convenient target, with remarks in the *Irish Statesman* on Japanese art, Corot, and the photographer's art. Fluther opened up, "Vox AEius non vox Dei – non by a long chalk", and bingo! they had a new literary scrap going. Russell pontificated on the contradictions of human nature, and, parodying himself, quoted Walt Whitman who relished contradictions: Allow, dear Sean, he said, "your many-sided and complicated nature intellectual nourishment for the various elements from which it is compounded . . . repeat every morning this sentence from Emerson: 'A foolish consistency is the hobgoblin of little minds.'" O'Casey, tasting blood, waded in:

> I advise you to say three times every morning before you get up, and three times every night before you go to bed (murmur it, and it'll do just the same), "If God hasn't given a man something to say out of himself, why should he be permitted to acquire merit by saying again what some other artist has already said?" Keep at this hard enough, now, and it may save you from the bad habit of one day filling yourself, like a fattened goose, with Spengler, to spout Spengler; or, on another day . . . with Eddington, to spout Eddington. It may deliver you, too, from having to say what has already been said by Laotze or Li Hung Chang; Waldo Emerson or Billy Sunday; Signor Eddington or Monsieur Buffon . . .

It was all fairly good-natured knockabout, with Russell then unrepentantly quoting Blake's "One law for the lion and the ox is oppression". You ought to take up reading something simpler, he advised O'Casey, write another *Juno* but not worry about articles which "cause a red haze to form before your mind".

What turned sour a comically belligerent exchange was that Russell did not publish O'Casey's next long-winded and repetitive letter. The rejection became a cause which O'Casey expanded, inflated, continued to fight for in other papers – *An Poblacht*, the *New York Times*, the Dublin *Star* – dragging in, of course, the Abbey Theatre directorate. "Any more strokes from the Titan would have pulverized you," he wrote in a further letter which Russell also refused to publish.

O'Casey had the best of this row because only a couple of months later, in April 1930, the *Irish Statesman* itself folded, or, as O'Casey gleefully expressed it, "AE has been unhorsed too, arsed & unhorsed". No longer would the *Statesman* "like a little cuckoo clock in a soda-fountain parlour [hop] out at stated times", sing its little song and bell its little chimes, then hop "back for rest and further meditation".

One major moon of the great Irish literary revival was sinking below the horizon, and O'Casey had had his fun at its expense. He now wore outwardly, like a coat of armour, his disillusionment. Like a polemical journalist he could separate the private from the public, and had learned to control the public persona. Life and work were diverging fast, and rather than try to fuse them once again he was content to take the happier way out; so the art – or as it became, increasingly, the art of controversy – grew more abstract, rhetorical, or simply combative, like a hurling match, as he enjoyed more directly than before the processes of life. He and Yeats were moving, in strange symbiosis, in opposite directions.

Russell had dubbed this new O'Casey "the annihilator". Their preposterous tragi-comic fight had taken place offstage; *The Silver Tassie*, as O'Casey told George Bishop, was different "because the tragedy dominates the characters". O'Casey's characters, full of contradictions, at one minute kind and generous, at the next barging each other like angry fishwives, had fled the boards, and now roamed the stage of life.

15

THE PHANTOMS OF HYDE PARK

Dislocation, sometimes provocative and productive, more often disruptive, even seriously destructive of both work and relationships, is the keynote of the next four years. Divorce from Ireland had now become permanent exile: the emotions informing O'Casey's life and work became those of the displaced person, its logic the logic of the uprooted. Appropriately enough, it was during this period that he made his first and only visit to America. It may have been an affinity with dislocation that helped, in time, to establish his popularity in that country.

From the moment he set foot in London, in 1926, O'Casey had expressed his determination "to write a play about London people"; more explicitly, he said to Beverley Nichols, "What are your dramatists doing to neglect Hyde Park?" The rough diamond would show them. He conceived the idea of *Within the Gates* first as a film, which would be "geometrical" and "emotional", the emotion of the living characters to be projected against their own patterns and the patterns of the Park. The action was to begin at dawn, with the opening of the gates, and end at midnight as they closed again to the twelve chimes of Big Ben striking softly in the distance. He wrote to Alfred Hitchcock to come and have dinner with him and Eileen, so that they could talk it over, and Hitchcock agreed.

Hitchcock had by now made his "all-talkie" version of *Juno*, having gone to Dublin in search of "local colour". The film, released at the beginning of 1930, was not successful: it managed to lack both realism and suspense, two qualities in which Hitchcock later excelled, while instead of a comedy with Agate's twenty-minute quota of tragedy the piece became more of a slow-paced, brooding melodrama with comic touches. There were endless scenes of eating and handing round cups of tea, while for the most part the playing was pedestrian. Sara Allgood, repeating her role of Juno, looked past her prime and showed little grasp of screen acting; Joxer was played by Sidney

Morgan, Boyle by Edward Chapman; Barry Fitzgerald was relegated to playing an unnecessary Prologue figure called "The Orator". Worst of all, Hitchcock insisted on changing the cunning little tailor, "Needle" Nugent, into a stage-Jew whom he called Kelly. Twenty years later two American Jews who saw a revival of the film wrote to O'Casey to complain of its anti-Semitism. "I never saw it," replied O'Casey, and went on to condemn Hitchcock for his cheap trick.

But talking films were in their infancy, and the results did not yet measure up to the enthusiasm shown for them: O'Casey stuck in one of his exercise books clippings on the new medium and its superiority to the theatre. When Hitchcock had dinner at Woronzow Road O'Casey's new idea excited him and he left after dinner having delivered a hearty return invitation to discuss the project further. No such invitation was forthcoming, however. O'Casey continued to enjoy the suggestiveness of his chosen setting: he described to Edith Londonderry his sense of life overpowering art as he sauntered through Hyde Park, "'taking upon me the mystery of things, & acting as if I were one o' God's spies'". He enjoyed the theatre of it:

> From the little cock'ey'd sparrow watching a crumb in the hand of a fellow full of pity for the bird, & destitute of pity for himself, to the red-coated, gorgeously braided Salvation Army officer thunder-voicing God's love . . . [the] circles of people tossing troubles away into the singing of "Danny Boy", or, "Oh God, our help in ages past", led by conductors tense as steel moving their slender white wands as if from their tips flowed the energy that gave majestic & immortable motion to the planets and the stars . . . And here and there a lonely, static-faced preacher appealing piteously for someone to come along & shake the hand of Jesus.

The image of O'Casey, the gaunt exile, savouring these delights, is possibly a stronger one than any in the play itself. So fixed was he on Hyde Park he even wrote a preface to a book by the well-known Park orator, Bonar Thompson, claiming, in what was hardly a strong recommendation, that Thompson had not vividly observed the scene, and advising him, in a lofty Yeatsian manner, "Had he found the gathering of thoughts together a hard thing to do, he would have written a far, far better biography of himself." The preface also reflected that O'Casey was, at this time, gathering thoughts for his own autobiography. He tells Thompson to think less of himself and more of others.

O'Casey was far from being absorbed into English ways. Hyde

Park was a poor substitute, a tourists' surrogate for the dark, sombre area of Abercorn Road, which occasionally surfaced again in news from Fallon in Ireland, as when he heard that his old friend, Father Brady, had been appointed Archdeacon of Dublin: "Sooner or later an Archdeaconship comes along to St Laurence O'Toole's. How strange it would feel to me to walk slowly & pensively through that district now."

Leslie Rees, an Australian visitor to Woronzow Road, confirmed how actively the past still fermented inside O'Casey, during a long chat held in his upstairs room; also that his claims about Shakespeare were a load of bluff: "he was all", Rees wrote, "for quoting long passages from *Hamlet* and *Julius Caesar* but usually dried up after a few pentameters and turned to me with the words 'What is it? What is it?', an appeal that to my chagrin I never seemed able to gratify."

O'Casey, now over fifty, had become thinner and balder than in his outdoor days: he peered with small brown eyes through his silver-rimmed glasses and spoke in a raw Dublin accent whose tone was thin and whining rather than rich: to his Antipodean visitor he looked frail and flat-chested. Eileen, still appearing in *Bitter Sweet*, struck the visitor as chic and dainty, "with her West End voice that was not quite West End". Afternoon tea was brought in by a "wordless old duck of a servant", Mrs Earle. It seemed that London and success had aged O'Casey quickly: he was starting to dread, as he later said, "its powers & its attractions". He was even tiring of the art galleries: after visiting the Titians in the National Gallery one day he remarked that galleries were "imposing prisons for pictures . . . I never leave one without a sense of gloom", and dismissing them further as "memorials to one fellow that has been made a baron".

Yet happiness with Eileen was at its height, for although *The Tassie*'s failure still rankled, the loss of earnings had been made good to some extent by money from the Hitchcock picture, from royalties on his books and foreign rights on the earlier plays. Eileen, too, had a regular weekly salary, which she supplemented by modelling hats and stockings. Most evenings Sean would catch a bus from St John's Wood to the Haymarket and meet her after her show; they would eat, and travel back by bus. He was extremely appreciative of her clothes, and of the colour of the hat she might be wearing – colour for him was always of paramount importance. Later, back at Woronzow Road, he would lead her to his room, "that I may talk in secret with you, & caress and fondle you in secret". Or they would stay in the big downstairs room, so that he could see her charms mingle with the browns, yellows, greens and blues of the room. "I'll see to it you will be as helpless before me there as you would be in my own room . . ." His intimate letters to Eileen show his sexual gratification at its height.

He had done what he said he would do, namely make her love him, but without being proprietorial. He rejoiced in her freedom, although there was little doubt, he told himself, he needed to be cautious in his joy. As he had teased her at an earlier time, when she had written while away on tour that she missed his companionship, his caresses, his gentleness and fierceness, "Do you miss anything else? Try to think & remember & then tell me, my little love. How many times have you fondled another hand & kissed another mouth since you went away from me? On your guard, Sean, fight & do not give too much liberty to the love for a beautiful face, desirable form and charming nature."

But the greatest danger to their happiness came from practical problems: difficulties with the house, or some previous flat, the meeting of bills. Neither of them, even having responsibility for a child they both loved, developed – or wanted to develop – less extravagant or aristocratic tastes. It was, O'Casey remarked, a "pity these things should shove themselves in between the sweet exchanges of our love".

Eileen deeply cherished his genius, and she sent, whenever absent from him, motherly exhortations to eat well, look after himself, take proper walks – in other words, to put his work before everything. The highest praise she could have from him was to be compared with his mother. But she herself remained giddy and impressionable.

The summer of 1930 was exceptionally hot; she had booked rooms in a boarding house in Margate, but could only go at weekends. O'Casey took Breon and his nanny there. During the day O'Casey enjoyed the crowded beach, which was like a Hyde Park by the sea. At night the landlady gave him a coal fire. Eileen, who remained behind in Woronzow Road with Mrs Earle, picked up the threads of social life, responding once more to invitations to go out to supper after the show. One night, to her amazement, Ephraim turned up at the stage door of His Majesty's: "something to do with casting . . . not especially to see me." But, she remembered, "his mere presence was fatal".

Without Sean's protective influence, she accepted his renewed invitations, and found old emotions reviving. Ephraim still felt resentment over the marriage and the way "his property" had been taken from him. O'Casey himself had no great respect for marriage, far from it; he often referred to it contemptuously as "a permissive chit from a cleric". "Wife" – "strange word for me to be using", he had written to Lennox Robinson. He approved of passion, people flinging themselves down on couches "without prim and purposeful preparation for the roistering–doistering deed of love". He approved of "Tristan and Iseult, Abelard and Heloise, Romeo and Juliet, Paolo and Francesca, Parnell and Kitty O'Shea, Jennifer and Dubedat. Let them rave: the musk of love will ever cling to the rose of life."

Alone with Ephraim after the performances of *Bitter Sweet* Eileen danced and kissed: it was like *The Silver Tassie*, but with the victim tied not to a wheelchair but to a nanny and small son. Was Eileen trying to test O'Casey's love by hurting him? Perhaps there was no deeper reason than mutual attraction – and the freedom to act on it. But it became inevitable that she and Ephraim would go further, make love, and spend some nights together.

She kept the secret for several weeks, but then discovered, to her horror, that she was pregnant and had no alternative but to own up. O'Casey had returned to Woronzow Road, while Ephraim had left for America. One afternoon before setting off for the performance of *Bitter Sweet*, she told O'Casey, "I'm going to have a child," then admitted it wasn't his. He turned white as a sheet, knowing at once who the father was. He asked her to leave him; and off she went to His Majesty's for the evening show.

Deeply hurt, he brooded all evening, but love and generosity towards Eileen in the end overcame bitterness. For the most part he blamed himself, believing he was not providing properly for her. Later he collected her from the theatre in a taxi: he had forgiven her. She sobbed in his arms; they had supper and she was ill all night.

Next day O'Casey obtained from Billy McElroy, his "fixer", the name of a Harley Street specialist. The following Saturday Eileen drove straight from His Majesty's to the nursing home and to "an operation at midnight: a horrible and saddening psychological upset". O'Casey never spoke to her further about it, but she later found that the incident appeared to have fortified their marriage.

O'Casey kept knitting away, trying to join up the wild and wandering themes of *Within the Gates*, but, in the early months of 1931, both he and Eileen realised they could not go on living at the same standard and survive. O'Casey was not the only writer to feel the dissipating influence of living in London, but his experience of the concentrated, gossipy Dublin made it impossible for his imagination and mind to grasp the complexity of the huge metropolis in whose bewildering tangle, coldness and materialistic heartlessness he was trying to make a living.

Billy McElroy advised that the O'Caseys should withdraw into the seductive loneliness of Buckinghamshire, a plan which Charlotte and Bernard Shaw enthusiastically endorsed, as a means of simplifying their lives and cutting down on expenses. Knowing now that Eileen recognised his full qualities both of persistence and love, O'Casey agreed to McElroy's plan: he may have hoped country life might slow her down and that she might adopt a calmer rhythm in which he figured more. The parties at which she stayed out, sometimes till four or five, the constant attentions of admirers, irritated him, and it was with relief he anticipated the closing of *Bitter Sweet* in May 1931, and their move to a cottage owned by McElroy's sister, Evelyn, in the village of Chalfont St Giles. Mrs Earle was now leaving them, so was Nanny Trim, and with a new girl, Tessa, they moved into 2 Misbourne Cottages, just outside the village, overlooking the Misbourne valley. They sold the remainder of their lease at Woronzow Road to release capital and pay off debts, and put their furniture in Harrods' repository.

A typical O'Casey Lord of Misrule presided over the financial arrangements. A sum of twenty pounds was demanded from them for the previous tenant's arrears; when they sorted this out Eileen, arriving at the cottage first, found the telephone disconnected, with seven pounds owing: anxious to contact O'Casey, she signed a form, and O'Casey duly paid up. He didn't blame McElroy, he said later, but admitted his friend's "glorious irresponsibility" could, at times, be irritating.

In 1665, with the help of his Quaker friend, Thomas Ellwood, John Milton had fled the Plague in London to live in Chalfont St Giles: but from poverty, as O'Casey sourly pointed out, no flight was possible. London was not far anyway: a bus ran from nearby Amersham and the distance was nineteen miles, an hour by Green Line bus.

No. 2, Misbourne was an ordinary workman's cottage, two up, two down, dark, without electricity, with a bathroom but no inside lavatory. O'Casey was horrified: an Abercorn Road dwelling, depressingly damp, isolated in deep countryside without the compensating noise and companionship of city life. When "serious, thoughtful, and intent", as Jonathan Swift described the process of being "at stool", O'Casey faced slugs and snails on the wall beside the lavatory.

"A mass of wriggling twisting slime . . . A Walpurgis night of vermin."

Charlotte Shaw chirped in from Ayot St Lawrence with, "I rejoice to think of you both in your own home with the garden and peace and quiet," but said that they would have to wait for a visit from her and GBS: "he hates these lanes after dark, and meeting cars with blazing lights in fogs round corners." They never visited. Sean reproved Mrs Shaw from Misbourne Cottages for a new friendly warning about his belligerence: "God be my judge that I hate fighting. If I be damned for anything, I shall be damned for keeping the two-edged sword of thought tight in its scabbard when it should be searching the bowels of knaves and fools."

In the autumn of 1931 O'Casey – perhaps stimulated by the oil lamp near his head where he worked stretched on his belly, and having contracted "housemaid's knee" in his elbow – began to recall his early life. He recounted episodes from it to Eileen while they rambled in the surrounding countryside or took tea on the lawn (which was mown by the gardener from nearby Misbourne House). He wrote some of these down, using the first person, though later abandoning this practice.

The time at Misbourne Cottages passed slowly: O'Casey wrote, in a later stage of the autobiography he tentatively began there, that "*after a year* [my italics], they moved into a bungalow, which, though of no great shakes, at least was cleaner than the horrible cottage". They had stayed in the workman's cottage (rent £1 per week) little more than a month.

The new place was unfurnished, so they sent for their furniture from Harrods. An imposing brick bungalow on the other side of the village near Milton's cottage, with a garden in front, an orchard behind, "Hillcrest" brought relief and good health, for as O'Casey told Fallon, "I have, at last, got a chance of again using the hack & shovel, & have worked hard here with these glorious tools every day in the garden . . . I worked today hacking out a path facing the setting sun, with a heavy frost falling . . ." The lease, with three months' notice on either side, promised not to strain their resources, so they could settle down once more. O'Casey took as his workroom a little room at the back; he was, said Eileen, "a stoic of stoics". But there was little secretive love-making now.

Having made the mistake of talking about his new work, *Within the Gates*, on the radio, and regretting it, he began again, in November, to "get back to the play or film – or whatever it may turn out to be – & to the semi-biography to be called, A Child is Born". "Ireland was created by the Almighty to entertain the world, and Irishmen to lighten our darkness," announced J. L. Hodson, who visited O'Casey at this time, alighting from a bus in Chalfont St Giles to find the playwright deeply contented, wearing a "wideawake hat, a brown guernsey to the throat like a fisherman, a Harris tweed suit, and strong boots". He said O'Casey remarked that "England is lovely beyond his belief, that he likes the quiet, sober people . . ." Hodson had first met a very different O'Casey smouldering in his room in the North Circular Road: "I found he has kept an Irish and boyish love for being contrary and says a good many things for devilment," and that he still works "very slowly, writing and re-writing – never pens even a letter without great care".

What emerged from Hodson's vivid piece was how adept O'Casey had become at playing his greatest character, himself, and how Eileen could chime in as the perfect back-up and foil for this character. O'Casey repeated an assertion that he was soon to abandon: that he had finished with Dublin as a subject for plays, adding that he couldn't be bothered to emend *The Silver Tassie*, which he admitted had its faults. With a final flourish he told Hodson his ambitions were "that the next may be a great play – and *not* to send the boy to Oxford".

But notwithstanding the confidence he radiated to outsiders, Chalfont St Giles was an unhappy period. Eileen was emotionally unsettled, still intent on working in London, but troubled by her conscience. In early 1932 she gained a small part in *The Immortal Hour*, Rutland Boughton's fey exploration of the Celtic twilight with its winsome theme song, "How beautiful they are, the lordly ones" – O'Casey impishly referred to Barry Jackson, who revived this opera, as a "lordly amateur" (never forgetting he had turned down *The Tassie*) – and she took herself off to a room in London, commuting at weekends to Chalfont St Giles. By the fourth week of the run she had fallen in love with the conductor, Ernest Irving: she found life in the country lonely, informing Sean that it was all right for him, he always had his thoughts. "My thoughts, Eileen, my thoughts!" he expostulated. "They are in themselves an everspringing fountain of loneliness . . . my thoughts have made many Rate me, and some have tried even to injure me . . . They often divide me from the few that I dearly love."

Her crisis now precipitated one in him, and he complained that when she had first hurried him down to the country – she had been eager to seize on McElroy's offer – he had said very little to hinder her, punishing himself with hard work to "fence out" the feeling of dislike of the change of scene. Now she had dashed back to London he still hadn't said anything. But didn't they now need a complete and fundamental change?

Both were confused and did not know what to do. Perhaps the desperate passion Eileen had conceived for Irving was a symptom of the insecurity of life with O'Casey: there was emotional security, yes, but compared with what she was used to, practical poverty and social dullness. On most evenings she supped with the conductor. At weekends she discussed the affair with Sean, who listened patiently, and responded, in quiet tones, "Eileen, dear, I don't think this man would be any good to you. It doesn't sound as though he has any steady money."

O'Casey was sure she would forget the man, and his prediction soon proved true. A second time, by steadiness of love, he had overcome a threat. By March he and Eileen were sleeping together again, and he rejoiced once more in her "dear and lovely" body, with its white breasts and rosy nipples, but added ruefully that such a special treat "doesn't happen very often". He was wise enough to perceive that she needed rest more than "caresses".

Guilt over money and over a sense that he was squashing her independence and curtailing her freedom weighed heavily on him, however – while she admitted that he, at fifty-two, looked much older than she, and a trifle grim sometimes. These factors may have made him more magnanimous in action than he felt inside.

Some unconscious resentment may have been expressed in *Within the Gates*. The Young Woman at the centre of the story turns to the elderly Atheist, whom she calls 'dad', and begs him to comfort her: "You crept into a father's place when you took me away from the nuns who were moulding my life round the sin of my mother . . . Save me, Dad, oh, save me!" The character, although not outwardly based on Eileen, expresses continual fear and insecurity, not knowing who her real father was, forced to earn her living as a streetwalker (meaning, perhaps, the theatre?), constant prey to the advances of men. She voices sexual disgust:

> The other night I had a man with me, an' when I was half stripped it came on me as he was coming over to paw me. In a mist I saw the fright in his eyes, saw him huddling his clothes on an' hurrying away . . . How often have I told you that the swine of a manager

brings good-looking girls, one at a time, to a silent storeroom to sort chemises, and then sends his slimy paw flickering around under their skirts . . .

although a mood of hope dominates by the end, as the forces of poetic idealism overcome those of everyday reality.

Everyday reality encroached with true O'Caseyan vigour on the real life of the playwright: with that wonderful sense of paradox which his whole life, sometimes consciously but mostly unconsciously, embraced, we find him writing one day to his neighbour Ramsay MacDonald, the Prime Minister, at Chequers, inviting him over so that an Irishman and a Scotsman could sit down and have a quiet chat together; the next day to the Inland Revenue trying to stave off their claim on him for £236, with the *cri de cœur* that he had only twenty pounds in the world. He offered the inspector "Five pounds to keep the wolf from the door, leaving myself with Fifteen to keep myself, wife and kid, and help to promulgate the Gospel in foreign parts". He added best wishes for the Exchequer's scheme to convert a five per cent war loan into a three and a half per cent loan – as if this would help to mollify the local taxman. Ramsay MacDonald wrote back an affectionate letter, promising to call, but never did.

O'Casey had earned almost nothing in the previous tax year; so the £236 owed was on the sale of film rights in *Juno* to British International Pictures. Still, in that period of low taxation, £236 was a great deal of money, representing income in excess of £1,000, or nearly ten times the average annual wage of a British industrial worker. (O'Casey later said that one year he paid more than £1,000 in tax.) Short of money, he still refused to write articles, and turned down Shaw's invitation later in 1932 to join the new Irish Academy of Letters, thus ranging himself alongside George Moore and James Joyce. Eileen, as always, respected his integrity: she could be unfaithful but she never opposed his will. Loyalty to his spirit and principles carried more weight than physical fidelity.

Disintegration of two kinds was at work in the pair of one-act plays O'Casey wrote in Chalfont St Giles. The first, *The End of the Beginning*, has a vain and obstinate Paycock type, Darry Berrill, switching roles with his wife Lizzie, and launching into the domestic chores with his "buttie" Barry Derrill, who is so short-sighted that they soon turn the household into a "state of chassis": a genuine escape from the domestic round that showed, albeit farcically, that O'Casey had not lost contact with the basic impulses of his dramatic talent. In the second play, *A Pound on Demand*, with another feckless pair, Sammy and Jerry, the disintegration is of the more familiar, intoxicated kind, as they go through farcical motions of withdrawing one pound from a suburban post office.

If the reversal of roles with Eileen was what gave spontaneous life to the first play, what perhaps makes *A Pound on Demand* so light and hilarious was its basis in the serious financial problems besetting the O'Casey household, especially income tax. Good comedy is deadly serious: "That's the last penny of our money the Government'll ever get from us!" shouts Jerry at the end. Instinctive comic energy had been kindled once more in O'Casey's writing – one outcome of the move to the country, possibly, as well as a new "victory in defeat" over life. Samuel Beckett, in his review of the sketches on their publication the following year in *Windfalls*, applauded the "triumph of the principle of knockabout in situation, in all its elements, and in all its planes, from the furniture to the higher centres". Knockabout was the energy of O'Casey's theatre, for he "discerns the principle of disintegration in even the most complacent solidities and activates it to their explosion". If *Juno* was, "as seems likely", his best play so far, it was because it communicated most fully "mind and world come asunder in irreparable dissociation".

Lady Gregory would no doubt have also loved the unforced hilarity, the absence of rhetoric and the delight in simple character of these two short plays. She was not to see them for, on 22 May 1932, she died at Coole from cancer of the breast: "she an aristocrat and I a proletarian communist . . . I loved her and I think she was fond of me – why God only knows," O'Casey said, as an atheist oblivious to his invocation of the Almighty.

Her last visit to London had been in April 1931; she wrote beforehand to inform O'Casey of this and again expressed a hope that she might make the acquaintance of his wife and son. O'Casey did not take up the suggestion. In her last letter to him she described how she had been crippled by a rheumatic attack, but she sounded cheerful, still showing her motherly possessiveness of Yeats, who had been with her most of the summer, and hopeful that O'Casey would one day bring Eileen to Coole. She died feeling she had so much still to give to O'Casey.

Her death was followed by a further reminder – or so Eileen and O'Casey felt – of the financial harm the Abbey's refusal of *The Silver Tassie* had inflicted on them. The "careless and incompetent" Curtis Brown agency, handling O'Casey's rights abroad, failed to let them know of more than £350 which Samuel French of New York had collected on his behalf, as fees for amateur productions (the agents did not know about it themselves). O'Casey was then offered £300 by Samuel French in London for a half-share in the amateur rights during the term of copyright, i.e. throughout his own lifetime and for fifty years after his death. An "absurdly bad bargain", Shaw called it; "My advice is to let wife and child perish, and lay bricks for your last crust, sooner than part with an iota of your rights." O'Casey, in spite of Shaw's sensible warning, which included the offer of a £100 loan, accepted French's money; the ignominy of it was increased by his having the chore of supplying, from memory, details of the Dublin productions for amateur prompt copies – work which kept him from finishing *Within the Gates*. Small payments, such as nineteen dollars for an article to the *American Spectator* ("Laurel Leaves and Silver Trumpets"), afforded some respite, but O'Casey always found the spiritual cost of journalism high. Yet he sent back fifteen guineas to *Time and Tide* for a short story, "I Wanna Woman", which the magazine had accepted for publication but· which its printers refused to set up on account of its immoral subject – it contained the old favourite, an encounter with a prostitute.

Eileen, after the closing of *The Immortal Hour*, had been recruited into Max Reinhardt's *The Miracle*, and then, later in 1932, into Cochran's *Mother of Pearl*, in which once again she had a small part and was understudying the role of the French maid, Fifi. The play opened in Manchester at the Christmas of 1932: again O'Casey was left on his own with Breon and the girl Tessa, whom he now believed to be unreliable. Breon became ill with bronchitis, and Eileen had to sack Tessa, because, as she said, "Once Sean had turned against anybody, he would never look back." Christmas passed – not a happy one – and O'Casey asked Eileen why she was feeling lonely in Manchester. Didn't she have a crowd there, or was it only in London that she felt lonely? "It can't be worse there than it is here, for it's worse here than it could be anywhere." The only relief he expressed was that Christmas was over, so "no more kids [were] howling out a Hail to the ever blessed morn".

The Chiltern nights were bitterly cold at the New Year of 1933: Eileen wrote to Breon from Manchester and O'Casey reported that his son made him read the letter over and over again while he "listened and hummed & hummed, till he was satisfied & then tucked it under his pillow". Eileen grew frightened that Breon might forget her: she arrived back at Chalfont St Giles at five one morning, having managed to obtain a lift from a violinist who lived locally. When *Mother of Pearl* moved to London, she took Breon to stay with her in her Baker

Street room. O'Casey, in the meantime, applied himself to organising an education for his son. A school run by some Carmelite friars did not attract him at all – suspicious of their teaching methods, he believed they only wanted to indoctrinate the children entrusted to them. "Anyhow what more can they teach him than we ourselves do?" he asked.

The return of spring brought new hope, both of the completion of *Within the Gates* and of improvement in the O'Casey finances. The play was, he now emphasised, the "hardest job that I have ever attempted, making me exclaim with Yeats, 'my curse on plays that have to be set up in fifty ways!'" But *Within the Gates* was as yet some months away from being ready for production. Eileen was still in *Mother of Pearl* when on 20 May O'Casey, who never remembered birthdays, sent her a few pounds to buy a hat and his favourite item of female wear – camiknickers. "I wish it were a hundred & one," he declared. "It's really a bitter thing to know you want so much & that I can give you so little." By this time, however, Eileen, having played Fifi several times when her principal, Eve Manning, was off, had found her work in the theatre pulling against her marriage, and saw that the struggle to fulfil her ambition was counterproductive and futile. Her career was a self-indulgence she could no longer afford: she realised she had married a man who needed her with him constantly, and she resigned herself to slipping back into the Chalfont domestic routine.

———◆———

By now the strain on O'Casey had become great. The completion of *Within the Gates* brought a whole new wave of preoccupations and tensions: there were songs to be put to music, there was the torture of submitting the script – much more trying for the successful playwright than for the successful novelist, for an option acquired by a management by no means guarantees a production. Indeed Cochran, to whom O'Casey first sent the new play, turned it down straightaway, though with a rejection letter which did not displease:

> You have written some grand stuff and I am intrigued by your manner of introducing the singing, although you have created another difficulty for the producing manager, who must find an actress who can sing. The non-singing actress is difficult enough to find – the combination is very rare. I wish I could see my way to risk the production, but frankly I can't . . .
>
> You can't go on writing fine things, Sean, unless they bring

some material reward. I suppose you are tired of people advising you to get back to the method of "Juno". I wish you would.

But *Within the Gates* was very different from what he was writing ten years before. The Gates are symbolic as much as real, the battlefield universal in this morality play on prudery and sexual freedom, while the Hyde Park setting often seems like a cross between a Boucicault village green and a mystic Garden of Love. Words are the weapons chosen for O'Casey's attempt to "release drama from the pillory of naturalism and send her dancing through the streets". Jannice, the young prostitute and heroine, wants to give up her profession but rejects the salvation offered by the pious pedlars of goodness such as the Salvationist and the Bishop: true to her Shavian mould, in spite of the way the world has let her down, she dies with reckless defiance: "I'll go the last few steps of the way rejoicing". O'Casey intends every character to symbolise a type Jannice meets on life's journey, while the young whore herself is meant to represent young women to whom life fails to respond but who want to maintain their truth and integrity. Often the dialogue, bearing the signs of immense diligence, sounds awkward, especially when O'Casey tries to reproduce Cockney: "It's not 'ims afryde to come; it's you're afryde to stye. Spice-time gives a noo meanin' to th' universe."

Rejection of *Within the Gates* on the grounds that it was too "highbrow" may have flattered O'Casey's vanity – it was a bit like Jackson's rejection of *The Tassie* as "too shocking". He wrote to Cochran in an uncharacteristically meek vein: "Your advice to go back to the genius of 'Juno' might be good for me, but bad for my conception of the drama." Clearly he accepted the refusal at its face value. The impatience and agony of waiting, the bitterness and disappointment of rejection found no outlet: Fluther's derogatory temper could not find a target. O'Casey now smoked sixty or seventy cigarettes a day and had done so ever since he could afford to buy them: "Instead of being a drunkard he was a cigarette person," said Eileen; "he would even chain-smoke before breakfast."

After the months of tension he looked pale and had become breathless, with a severe pain in the region of his heart. The local doctor ordered an X-ray, but no irregularity was found (O'Casey claimed that a scarred lung hid his heart). But Eileen and O'Casey had worked themselves up to such a pitch of intensity that in desperation they called Edith Londonderry, who sent a car to Chalfont St Giles to collect O'Casey and bring him to Harley Street for the examination by Dr Bertram Nissé. This specialist told him and Eileen that there was nothing wrong with him, except that he had to stop smoking. "You don't look pleased, either of you," said Nissé. "We were thinking of the main scene," said Eileen; "him about to die, and me with the small child!"

Norman MacDermott, the licensee of the Royalty Theatre, where J. B. Fagan had so successfully presented *Juno*, brought further relief when he said he would like to produce *Within the Gates*. Compared with the dilatoriness that had attended the setting up of *The Tassie*, the speed with which MacDermott propelled *Within the Gates* on to the stage should have been a tonic for O'Casey's intemperate heart. He cut down his smoking drastically, noting on the back of each day's packet the previous day's total. Finally he took up a pipe. The advance, too, paid by MacDermott, was a beneficial accessory.

A new American pen friend, the critic George Jean Nathan, added his voice to the chorus of praise O'Casey was beginning to conjure into being. If Shaw could not generate the same full-blooded enthusiasm for *Within the Gates* as he had for *The Tassie* – saying now:

Sean O'Casey is all right now that his shift from Dublin slums to Hyde Park has shewn that his genius is not limited by frontiers. His plays are wonderfully impressive and *reproachful* without being irritating like mine. People fall crying into one another's arms saying God forgive us all! instead of refusing to speak and going to their solicitors for a divorce

– there was Nathan's friend, Eugene O'Neill, to take his place:

It is a splendid piece of work. My enthusiastic congratulations to you! I was especially moved – and greenly envious, I confess! – by its rare and sensitive poetical beauty. I wish to God I could write like that!

Moreover T. E. Lawrence, writing to Lady Astor (and signing himself "Your Airman"), having by this period reached his apogee of anonymity and limpid ecstasy, declared, "How far he has gone since he was in Ireland, on paper! This play is London and human (and inhuman) nature: all of us, in fact; and about as helpless . . . When a rare Irishman does go on growing, you see, he surpasses most men. Alas that they are so rare."

But Augustus John, painting the elaborately "anonymous" Air-craftsman Shaw, was more quizzical and down to earth. He found himself puzzled by O'Casey's summary treatment of Cockney dialect, "which is really pretty subtle & complicated with its numerous sub-dialects". He didn't know enough about Bishops and their sisters to judge what O'Casey was doing, but "whores I do know something about, so much indeed that I am unable to generalize with confidence as you have done. In any case that good old word has lost its pristine kick except as an expletive, & like 'Sin' & 'Virtue' belongs to an obsolete & Theological vocabulary." John, for all his posturing, spoke his mind, and O'Casey did not take kindly to his comment: the two men hardly met again.

The rehearsals were as auspicious as the advance praise. As far as O'Casey was concerned, they were conducted from the vantage point of the Astors' London town house, 4 St James's Square, where, as O'Casey wrote to Lady Astor, he was as comfortable as he ever hoped to be – "or wish to be saeculo saeculorum". In fact so agreeable and "cosy" did he find the aristocratic residence that he stayed there at weekends, rather than take on himself the "fatigue of a visit to Chalfont".

He was pleased with the casting: Marjorie Mars as the Young Woman, Douglas Jefferies as The Bishop, Sir Basil Bartlett as The Dreamer, and even MacDermott, the producer, struck him as an "Artist" and a very clever fellow.

But only at first: soon he and MacDermott were at loggerheads, and O'Casey revised his opinion abruptly downwards. He issued a stream of notes and directives to MacDermott about the staging, the incorporation of the music, and was categorical about what would, and would not, work. MacDermott objected – it emerged that he was not greatly experienced as a director – whereupon O'Casey pulled his self-justification lever: hadn't MacDermott, he asked, told him to feel free to criticise, but when he did so he was publicly rebuked for his interruptions. Wielding his powerful rhetoric, O'Casey advanced on his floundering interpreter with repeated "You will remember", "You frequently quote your experience", mercilessly pointing out MacDermott's shortcomings and inconsistencies. MacDermott was reduced to pacing up and down his office, shouting his opinions at the playwright, and an alternative scenario was played out, with the interpreter's difficulties becoming the author's opportunity.

The first night at the Royalty didn't satisfy O'Casey either: he sat, chin cupped in hands, in a box with Bernard Shaw and, according to the sardonic observation of Gordon Beckles in the *Express*, "with a twisted smile, listening to his own ranting denunciations of the world's hypocrisy". But O'Casey's private thoughts were full of dissatisfaction for the "timid and agitated" production. Charles Morgan, in *The Times*, was more respectful; "Mr O'Casey's fierce play is that very rare thing – a modern morality play that is not a pamphlet but a work of art . . . He is opening up a new country of the imagination from which, by its rigid photography, the fashionable theatre has hitherto been shut out." But neither praise, nor awareness of the production's shortcomings, stopped O'Casey's now Swiftian habit of savage retaliation: when Beckles challenged him to say what the play really meant he wrote to the *Express*; "My mission in life is not to give to Gordon Beckles a higher mind than he has, for I am not a worker of miracles."

James Agate made some more heavyweight criticisms. Having called O'Casey "the greatest living dramatist but one", he picked apart the richly coloured strands of his careful literary weave, labelling it pretentious, the characters "both real and unreal, earthbound and fantastic", so that the play read "like 'Alice in Wonderland' interleaved with Euclid". He identified one cause of the weakness – divorce from Ireland:

> Mr O'Casey is essentially an Irishman who, while labelling his characters English and dropping the accent, still retains the Irish idiom. Take the Old Woman, for example. Any drunken old lady who is Irish has that poetry in her which befits her for Kathleen-Ni-Houlihan, whereas the capacity to soar is not in the English Mrs Gamp. If this play were translated back into the Irish in which it was conceived one might take a very different view of it.

Agate was also cruelly revealing of O'Casey's rose-tinted view of the basic little scrubber: "the young street-walker is the idealised harlot that intellectual Bloomsbury is always running after. She prates rather than prattles, uses words like 'oblate' and talks about 'composing hymns to intellectual beauty'." John might have agreed with his assessment: Toulouse-Lautrec, too.

"A big sneer and a little snarl here," O'Casey snapped back in a 2,000-word reply to the *Sunday Times*, which published two-thirds of it. Yet he had failed to grasp the central point Agate was making – he admired O'Casey for its opposite in the Dublin plays – namely that he had lost his knack of understanding an *English* audience. Agate tacked a short note on to the end of O'Casey's agitated refutation:

"The difficulty is that I write in English and Mr O'Casey thinks in Irish."

As if to prove Agate's point, *Within the Gates* came off after only twenty-eight performances. The result was to shutter off a little more of O'Casey's understanding, and increase his power to nurse a grievance. Why didn't they see that to experiment was far greater and more noble an aim? To a request in 1934 from the publishers, Collins, to include an excerpt from *Juno* in a manual of English literature for schools, O'Casey reflected with plaintive incomprehension, "Curious they can't see that *Within the Gates* is better literature than *Juno*."

Just as the British Foreign Secretary, George Canning, once claimed that he had brought the New World into existence "to redress the balance of the Old", O'Casey redressed his inner balance of self-esteem and fury with the heartening comments of George Jean Nathan and, later, Brooks Atkinson, the *New York Times* critic. Never again in his life did he take note of English critics, except to abuse and vilify them. Even sympathetic voices, like that of Charles Morgan, he later dismissed scornfully.

"It is a proud thing to me to fondle in my mind the high opinion you have of my play," he had written to Nathan after Nathan's extravagant praise of *Within the Gates*. After the mauling the play received in London, O'Casey's hopes revived when his American agent, Richard Madden, negotiated a New York production for later in 1934 (an earlier bid by Nathan to have it produced by the prestigious Theatre Guild had failed). He managed to persuade himself that it would be the play's first "true" production. In July it had become clear that both from a personal and an artistic view the New York production would be exciting. George Markle and John Tuerk, the play's backers, met O'Casey in London and arranged for him to travel to America to attend rehearsals and the first night.

Suddenly here was the prospect of escape from the darkness, failure and impoverishment of these years which had followed hard on the success of the Dublin trilogy. Optimism rose in his breast: he would leave in September. Nathan invited him to be his guest. "It will be good", O'Casey told him, "to walk on a new earth, & sleep under a new sky."

Eileen shared in these hopes. She had apparently given up her stage career for good, and, having moved beyond her excitement over the insecurity and wildness of the café society *demi-monde*, took the logical next step and became pregnant. Only in this pregnancy did she recover fully from the emotional scars left by the abortion. But she accepted without complaint the financial restraints imposed by having to exist entirely on O'Casey's income – a little boosted by continuing royalties from *The Plough and the Stars*, *Juno*, and now by the American advance for *Within the Gates*. Poverty – living at rock-bottom subsistence level – never worried O'Casey, he had done it all his life, with the few interruptions caused by windfalls which had been quickly used up. Far from being a handicap, poverty helped him maintain his aristocratic independence.

It was of course now no longer the poverty of an earlier time; it was the poverty of a famous man who had rich and powerful friends and a position in line with his own imaginings. And there was always some money coming in, however little. More important, there was always hope. The Dublin trilogy provided, not only then but for the rest of his life, an intermittent return of interest similar in many ways to that provided by a lump sum of capital investment. As in the years with his mother, he and his family would never *wholly* starve. Indeed he was more comfortable than he had ever been: his index of a high standard of living was the same as it had always been—a coal fire constantly burning in his room and a full cellar from which to supply it. Coal was cheap and plentiful.

Eileen showed unquestioning fortitude and acceptance: "Don't look on the dull side of finance," she told him; "it is a waste of energy in our case." If the going became hard they would need energy to face *that*: in other words, ignore money. She did not complain when he spent days penning a 2,000-word letter to a newspaper – he composed such letters as carefully as dialogue in a play, sometimes with greater difficulty – nor did she mind when he turned down film offers, believing it was "beneath" an author to write scripts.

Eileen, her baby due to be born around Christmas 1934, did not accompany O'Casey when he left Liverpool for New York in mid-September on the liner *Britannic*. But she had convinced Sean that they should move back to London, and had found a large flat in Overstrand Mansions, Prince of Wales Drive, overlooking Battersea Park: money advanced by Macmillan paid for the first quarter's rent. While Eileen, six months pregnant, managed the worry and work of moving, O'Casey went off to spend the week prior to his departure for the USA in Northern Ireland with the Londonderrys. It was his first break since moving to Chalfont St Giles three years before: he and Eileen had not been able to afford a seaside holiday for six years.

He had a $3,000 advance, a first-class ticket, supplied by Messrs. Tuerk and Markle, a new suit bought for him by Lady Astor, a sober, working-class cloth cap which replaced the exotic fedora of his sporting days with Augustus John, a new upbeat to his stride, and a guarantee with the bank of £200 from Edith Londonderry, to tide the family over till his return from New York – with, it was hoped, fistfuls of dollars. But actual cash was still in short supply: he and Eileen found they had £30 and split it between them. (Later, he wrote from on board the *Britannic* saying he wished he'd taken the lot: travelling first class, he complained, perhaps with traces of the old poor mouth, he could barely scrape together enough for the tips. It was clear he also had $100 with him. Still, it was hardly a fortune.)

The visit to Mount Pleasant, County Down, became in his autobiography the subject of a turgid and ungrateful sermon on the decline of the British aristocracy – with gleeful interventions on the rise of communism:

> The Commies are comin', oho, oho,
> The Commies are comin', oho, oho.

and with sidelights on the Ulster spirit ("the god-confident protestant David is always going forth to fight boastful catholic Goliath"), as well as the shameful neglect of St Patrick's burial place in Saul Abbey, Downpatrick, and the sacred spot in Saul where St Patrick celebrated his first Mass in Ireland.

The actual visit was filled with lonely thoughts of Eileen and Breon, and a sinking feeling at the months ahead. Awe at the splendour of the Londonderrys' establishment, with its sea views, semi-tropical vegetation of orange, olive trees and hydrangeas growing like weeds, did not wholly remove his choked-up feeling of missing Eileen. He penned a benediction to his patrons: "Brigid and Columcille with all the Irish Saints beside them, be with you both, and with your charming household, now and forever." He had crossed over to Northern Ireland in a three-quarter gale: Edith Londonderry, promising to "keep an eye on Eileen", put him on another steamer at Kingston back to Liverpool to board the *Britannic*.

Soon he was passing Galway and having struck up a friendship with the ship's surgeon, a Dublin man, O'Casey became more settled on board the huge ship. He justified his departure on the grounds that he was collecting funds ("England couldn't afford to keep him"); he enjoyed life-belt drill, during which he was commended by the officer in charge as the most efficient member of the squad. Eileen sent him a wireless message and he responded with three or four passionate love letters, in which he noted that the English and American passengers, trying to amuse themselves, were "a melancholy sight"; elsewhere they were described as "a decrepit lot", and when attired for a ship's ball their fancy dress "looked like coloured shrouds".

George Jean Nathan later was accorded the stature that O'Casey gave his other heroes like Larkin and Shaw, but his overblown praise of the American critic has the ring of a reward: it was never an admiration conceived in the knowledge that the idol was indifferent to, or ignorant of, his devotee's existence. Whatever the merit of his critical opinions, Nathan's main claim to a place in the O'Casey pantheon was as an honest and passionate champion of the plays, in particular the unpopular ones: he called *Within the Gates* "one of the true masterpieces of the modern theatre". In the flesh, although something of a dilettante and a snob, Nathan at once showed himself a considerate and generous host. O'Casey was lodged in the hotel where he himself lived – the Royalton on West 44th Street – and O'Casey told Eileen, "I've rarely seen such a man who has such a beautiful smile. It lights up his whole face and makes one love him. The Irish smile is a mile or more behind his smile."

The pace of New York upset O'Casey at first, but one thing he observed with great admiration was the absence of the institutionalised conception of Divinity – all New York's cathedrals were "huge buildings of commerce and trade". He later compared favourably with Moscow's (when had he been to Moscow?) these steel and stone monuments which coldly ordered churches out of sight and which decreed "Come unto me all you who labour, and we will give you work. Work! Labour the *aspergas me* of life, the one great sacrament of humanity from which all other things flow – security, leisure, joy, art, literature, even divinity itself."

Rehearsals of *Within the Gates* began well and continued that way. A week after his arrival O'Casey moved to the Devon Hotel to stay with his managers Markle and Tuerk. As usual he found himself getting the slim end of the stick in the negotiation of subsidiary rights; he discovered that he would have to pay $250 for Herbert Hughes's score – elaborate orchestrations of tunes he mostly supplied himself – while he worried that the costumes might be a "bit too gorgeous". As the first night at the National Theatre approached, the full New York publicity network sprang into action: Nathan and Eugene O'Neill proclaimed the virtues of the play and its author;

there was a big spread in the Sunday *New York Times* on 21 October. After a run-through of the play the same night, O'Casey told Eileen that Lillian Gish, who headed the cast of seventy, was "good though she is a little frail, & may not have the great vitality needed to keep the part always in a high key, but on the whole she is fine". His apprehension, he was glad to find out, was completely mistaken.

The opening night audience mystified him; he was not sure if it was dumbfounded or spellbound – he suspected the first. But the lively and generally favourable reviews created a *succès d'estime* and his suspicions cleared. Audiences filled the large theatre for well over a month, and soon O'Casey found himself appreciably in pocket; having earned back his $3,000 advance, he began sending cheques for his share of the takings back to Eileen – £380 by the end of November, always hoping for more. But then the houses began to drop off, prompting some fears. "Don't say anything to anyone about the bad business," he instructed; "one thing's certain – if I hadn't come here the play wouldn't have run a week . . . When I leave they'll take it off."

He was probably right: O'Casey the character was equal to any of those in the new play and he had quickly become a New York celebrity. Eugene O'Neill liked him ("You haven't got a bad fellow for a husband and a sweetheart!" he told Eileen). Markle invited him to Pennsylvania for a weekend; he excited the disapproval of the coloured maid of Brooks Atkinson when he came to dinner at Atkinson's apartment wearing a turtle-neck sweater instead of a shirt and tie; he was sketched for the *Herald Tribune*. He could spin, as he did in the *New York Times* on 14 October, all the old myths of his Irish background, although he mysteriously omitted from them the one of his true age: "He was born in 1880, said he, 'so anyone can compute how old I am now'." He even found himself blessed by Catholic priests: one in Pennsylvania praised his play and sent his blessing – O'Casey took the blessing, he told Eileen, and thanked him seriously; another, a Jesuit, told him it was a great play. Better than approbatory priests, the Abbey Players from Dublin, visiting New York on tour, were spitting venom when they heard of his success – or so he was told by Barry Fitzgerald. Delight at this was only equalled by the emotion he felt when one reviewer, after seeing *Within the Gates*, said that beside it Noël Coward's *Conversation Piece*, which had also just opened in New York, looked "like a monkey on a stick".

But being a celebrity could also be tiring. He refused invitations to a dozen parties after the first night, so exhausted that he just slipped away from the first and hurled himself into bed; at another time, in a synagogue, having addressed his audience on the curious resemblance between the Jews and the Irish, he stood and shook hands with a hundred people – "and not a pretty girl among the whole of them"; he spoke in Boston, at Harvard, on "The Old Drama and the New", complaining that out of the seventy-five dollar fee he had to pay his hotel, his rail fare, and made the equivalent of four pounds. He met other, more faded celebrities, including Vera Brittain, a "tattered, worn & fragile figure – though she wore an elaborate orchid in her breast" who, at a Macmillan party, was listening to endless flattery from other guests and sucking it all in. When he wasn't thinking of the need to make "a little store of money" to keep them going for a year or two, he thought of Eileen, back in London with the new life inside her. He declared, in a yearning moment, "After we have nursed the baby we shall have a joyous time together renewing our courting." He had seen, he said, a good many pretty girls in New York, but not one came up to her. In imagination she was always in his arms, and – as he constantly reminded her – imagination was a "powerful thing" in him.

O'Casey left America on the *Britannic* on 14 December, before the New York run of *Within the Gates* finished, and prior to an American tour of the play, due to begin in Boston in January. He formed a higher opinion of the American character than of the English, and would, Eileen said later, have stayed on in comfortable America if he could – he always liked to stay on where he was comfortable. The American streak of generosity touched him most. The reverse was true of London, which he found cold and ungiving, its critics in particular unsociable and conceited.

One thing that did terrify him about America was the patriotic fervour expressed by its women's clubs, at one of which he spoke: prior to the speeches a full-voiced soprano sang "The Star-Spangled Banner", while he watched the flag itself unfurled in floodlights. Moved at first by terror and apprehension, he still found more than a measure of justification in the emotional tension which, he honestly reminded himself, he had once enjoyed at the sight of the Irish Republican tricolour – and then at the International's red flag. "Nationality was something even deeper than life in a man's nature . . . Good it must be, and it will persevere." Even the Roman Catholic Church frowned somewhat on it in the fear it might lead to the deification of the state – an added attraction.

The United States had flattered him above all as an Irishman. O'Neill's friendship, Nathan's sincere adoration, Atkinson's more

perceptive praise, these had made him proud to be Irish: and, paradoxically, this had all happened out of his attempt to write a wholly
English play. For the rest of his life, with one exception, he was
never again to seek a subject outside of Ireland.

Before addressing "America's mothers, sisters, daughters, sweet-
hearts, and wives", he had listened to Irving Stone describe the life
he had written of Van Gogh, and perceived the value of biography
as being that of "the making of a great man to live again". Another
speaker put forward a claim which touched the austere, patronising
disdain with which O'Casey had surveyed the reading habits of Yeats
and Russell, namely that, as he mockingly reported, "the nickname
of whodunnit given to detective fiction was conceived by star-crossed
envy engendered in those who couldn't achieve success in the creation
of convulsive consternation". But fortunately the speaker noted that
communist Russia didn't give this "art" much status!

O'Casey's own address came as an anti-climax – he lectured the
good women on the need to be cautious of success, and never afraid
of failure: how could one be sure that failure was not "success in a
shroud"? It left his bewildered audience pondering just exactly what
the phrase could mean: perhaps only the completely unknown Samuel
Beckett knew fully, having credited O'Casey with dramatising "the
slump in the human solid".

Had the American women understood that O'Casey himself deeply
and instinctively preferred failure ("chassis") to success, he might
have provoked a riot. But there was little evidence in their social or
cultural history that Americans loved failures, or extended to them
their glowing hospitality – it was O'Casey's success that attracted
them, they wanted to buy it and share in it because it reflected on
them. His story, that of the poor Irish boy who made good, was one
of those self-perpetuating myths that sustained the heart of America.
O'Casey, the character, and the struggle of his life interested the
patriotic women's clubs more than anything he actually wrote.

As the atheist set sail he sent his blessing to Eileen: "God be with
you, sweetheart."

16

PINK WILDERNESS

Once a proselytiser always a proselytiser: early 1935 brought O'Casey pricks of persecution sufficient to goad him into new zeal. The Irish Censorship of Publications Board banned his new volume, *Windfalls*, and the Mayor of Boston, Frederick W. Mansfield, refused to allow *Within the Gates* to open at the Shubert Theatre in Boston on 21 January, because it was "anti-religious and obscene". The first refusal did not hurt O'Casey's pocket, for there was no great sale for his "thing of shreds & patches", as he dismissively referred to the collection in a letter to Nancy Astor; but the second was a more serious blow to his harmless, Giraudoux-esque fantasy, and led to the cancellation of a tour of thirteen cities, and thus to the loss of some thousands of dollars of expected royalties. The churches – this time Methodist as well as Catholic – trotted out their now-familiar clichés about an O'Casey play. One may wonder whether it was by now not the song but the singer, to which the authorities in both countries were objecting. So powerful had been the publicity machine, so strong the projection of O'Casey as a working-class, atheistic rebel, that it was as though at a rival preacher that these touchy, backward-looking organisations were lashing out. As O'Casey kept plaintively pointing out, to friends and foes alike, worse language could be found in the Bible, as well as in many other unbanned plays and books.

But two souls, of preacher and poet, fought uneasily within O'Casey's breast over the next few years, and neither left the other entirely alone. Curiously though, on his return from New York the preacher grew strangely, perhaps dangerously, silent. While Harvard students collected signatures for a petition in support of their "master playwright and crusader in the drama", O'Casey sat in the Battersea flat with Eileen, heavily pregnant, waiting for their second child to be born. By now its delivery was a fortnight overdue: financial deprivation and the stress of waiting wore down his nerves. His temper was bad, and often, sitting at Eileen's bedside when she was moved to a nursing home, he would fume at the disgusting conditions he found in the place for which they were paying twelve guineas a week – the "wobbling walk of the housemaids, the dirty tray of slopped-over tea, the dirty window, the whole aspect of continual carelessness". Eileen tried gently to quieten him, pointing out that his temper would make "bad things worse". Although he had been with Eileen less than a month he wrote later that he would like to see a "celibate cleric stay with a pregnant woman day after day, hour after hour, during the last three months of her trial".

The trip to America finally severed O'Casey's remaining ties with Ireland, nourished and maintained for more than eight years through his correspondence with Gabriel Fallon. Nathan now took over as the "buttie" O'Casey was never to find in England, and to Nathan rather than to Fallon O'Casey described the "chassis" of Niall O'Casey's birth on 15 January. Eileen had complained of pains, and the matron wanted to keep the contractions on the move:

> the missus protesting & half afraid to stir, & I arguing with [the matron], seeing with a layman's eye that the moment wasn't far off, & telling the Matron her business. But the Lady-Matron kept on "Just a little walk," & we were fully cloaked & on the steps to go out, when the missus rushed back, tore off her clothes, & the kid was born inside of twenty minutes! And after four weeks in which to prepare, when the time came nothing was ready, & the poor kid actually had the baby herself while the nurse was telephoning for the doctor, & the Matron was washing her hands & looking for the chloroform.

Niall had a bruised head and a bruised eye, Eileen had to have stitches and later O'Casey complained that the doctor charged fifty guineas.

Unfortunately none of the fluency, unexpected comedy and realism of this account found its way into dramatic form; O'Casey as a playwright was now beginning the longest fallow period of his life, which lasted until 1940, when his pro-Soviet play, *The Star Turns Red*, was published.

However, at the beginning of 1935 money had to be found. 1935 turned out to be one of their best years: O'Casey received substantial royalties from a diversity of sources and on 28 June banked a cheque for $10,752.71 from the sale of the film rights in *The Plough and the Stars* to RKO, Hollywood. On 9 February he had made an unexpected guest appearance as a *New Statesman* reviewer, with a savage on-slaught on the published text of the long-running play, *Love on the Dole*, a powerful but sentimental treatment of the theme of unemployment. Perhaps stung with envy at the success of Ronald Gow and Walter Greenwood in his own area of experience – and still (as he wrote) filled with fears that his long-overdue second child might be stillborn (or Eileen need a Caesarean) – he claimed that *Love on the Dole*, "delivered" out of a novel of the same name, was "either dead before it was taken from the belly of the novel, or the two drama surgeons killed it as they were taking it out. There isn't a character in it worth a curse, and there isn't a thought in it worth remembering." He then, surprisingly, asserted the artist's superiority over the temporal powers of the world: "He is above the kings and princes of this world, and he is above the Labour Leaders and Proletariat, too."

This messianic utterance provoked a flaming row – of course. Disappointment over *Within the Gates*, displacement caused by having to move back to London into a mansion flat in what he thought of as a snob-ridden road in Battersea, conflict over the direction his writing was taking – all this inner pain needed alleviation.

But the row led, indirectly, to a touching reconciliation with Yeats. In the last years of her life Augusta Gregory had been so upset at not patching up the quarrel with O'Casey that she had instructed Yeats, as one of her last wishes, to win O'Casey's forgiveness. The attack by O'Casey on *Love on the Dole* gave the old and increasingly ill Machiavellian the opportunity he needed – especially when, soon after the review, he received a genial note from O'Casey – the "first sign of amity since our quarrel". This change in O'Casey, and his proclamation of the artist's superiority, pleased Yeats. "He has attacked propaganda plays in the *New Statesman* and that may have made him friendly to me," he told an intimate friend. Now, as in 1926, Yeats came to O'Casey's defence. Writing to Ethel Mannin, who had praised *Love on the Dole* for its cogent statement on behalf of Revolution, and abused O'Casey for being jealous because *Love on the Dole* had been compared to *Juno*, Yeats warned her:

He is very emotional, and your attack, perhaps, made him lonely. Since we quarrelled with him years ago he has refused to speak to anybody belonging to the Abbey Theatre. Only two years ago he refused an invitation to lunch because he heard I was to be there. Though your defence of propaganda has had this admirable result do not let it come too much into your life. I have lived in the midst of it, I have been always a propagandist though I have kept it out of my poems and it will embitter your soul with hatred as it has mine.

His comment showed perhaps how by always speaking his mind O'Casey avoided the same polluting bitterness. – "You are doubly a woman", Yeats continued to Mannin – and his remarks may have been as relevant to O'Casey's creative process as to his own – "first because of yourself and secondly because of the muses, whereas I am but once a woman. Bitterness is more fatal to us than it is to lawyers and journalists who have nothing to do with the feminine muses."

Yeats thus displayed his need to make amends; the practical outcome of this was that in May 1935, having been in London for six weeks, and having for the second time recovered from an attack of congestion of the lungs, he invited O'Casey to dine alone with him in his Lancaster Gate flat. O'Casey's later account of the occasion begins with an awful travesty: Mrs Yeats watching over her famous husband, "pushing death away" from him, as she set the dinner on the table for the two men to eat alone. (Yeats had stated quite baldly in his letter of invitation that his wife wasn't at present staying at Lancaster Gate – there wasn't room for her.)

Yet – still – the whole scene as depicted by O'Casey is imbued with sympathy and love of the younger man for the pain-racked poet, culminating in his longing to lay a warm and sympathetic hand on his heaving shoulders: "to say silently so that Yeats could hear, God knows, if power were mine, you would be for ever young; no cough would ever come to warn you that the body withers."

It was a symbolic enactment of reconciliation, then, between O'Casey and his spiritual father Yeats, with its sonorous overtones of the son being forgiven by the father for his prodigality of beliefs and his headstrong temperament. It also fulfilled a need in O'Casey to believe again in Yeats, to believe in that side of himself Yeats had so potently activated in him as a young man: the integrity of the poet, which remained, O'Casey found, beneath the mask, under the "cabbalistic cloak". He might be vain and childlike, fearful of humiliation, an actor "posing about in trismegistic mask on a painted stage", but Yeats was a true rebel, a "truer rebel than truest politician; and eager, like the upsprung husband of Malfi's duchess, to fashion the world right". No braver man was there "among the men of Eireann than W. B. Yeats". In Lancaster Gate, O'Casey effected also some shadowy form of *rapprochement* with Lady Gregory, whose spirit he perceived to be always with Yeats.

But O'Casey, reconstructing their last talk somewhat along the lines of Landor's *Conversations*, still had to have the final word. He showed Yeats challenging him about his communism: what is it, the poet asked: "What is its divinity?"

Harold Macmillan, grandson of the founder of the publishing firm, had taken over from his brother Daniel as O'Casey's publisher in late 1933, during the negotiations over the publication of *Within the Gates*. He was a first-rate publisher, sensitive towards authors, with a great grasp of detail and an indifference to profit which made him warmly liked. "Publishers exist to satisfy their authors", was his motto. He had handled, at various times, the work of Yeats, Kipling, Hugh Walpole, Oliver Gogarty, James Stephens and Charles Morgan. Of Yeats he said, "He used to come in unannounced to my room in St Martin's Street: I can recall his splendid figure, his tie flowing through a fine ring, his somewhat dramatised appearance of the poet and dreamer. But he was a practical man and by no means despised the mundane problems of publishing." Unlike Yeats, Macmillan had read Dostoevsky at an early age.

Perhaps the seeming unworldliness of Macmillans as a firm appealed to the Irish literary imagination. They had turned down Shaw's early novels, and so did not publish him later, but none of the other Irish authors they published ever left them. H. G. Wells, by contrast, found them unadventurous, out of touch with the present day and not prepared to advertise (they sold 180 copies of *Kipps* in one year, but when Wells transferred the book to Nelsons, 43,000 copies of a cheaper edition were sold in a few months). Most of Macmillans' Irish writers belonged to the Protestant Ascendancy, and the Macmillan family – in particular Harold, who was High Church and connected with the aristocracy through marriage and political ambition – consoled themselves with literary connections for what their list failed to realise in hard cash.

Harold Macmillan particularly liked Irish writers. They amused him: of Gogarty, for instance, like him a member of the Beefsteak Club, he said, "rather lightweight. You'd ask him about another friend, someone it would be a privilege to know, and he'd say 'Oh yes, I know old so-and-so'. 'When did you last see him,' you'd then ask. 'Not for some time, perhaps a year ago, or was it five – it's a kind of absentee friendship.' That's the kind of Irishman he was."

But there were similarities in background, as well as the strong mutual attraction of dissimilarity in wealth, between him and

O'Casey which made the friendship deepen. While O'Casey was an Irish Celt (at least partly, on his father's side), Macmillan's family came from the Scottish Celtic Isle of Arran, and had shared with O'Casey the instinct for emigration to England. The reason, according to Harold Macmillan, that O'Casey settled in England "was the reason all Irishmen settle – they're comfortable here – all that Lake Isle of Innisfree stuff is just imagination". Both, too, had strong mothers, in Macmillan's case one of American birth, a widow before she married Macmillan's father, a sculptor in her own right and an amateur singer. Like O'Casey's mother, she was loving, strongly protective, a tower of strength and a pillar to the developing youth.

Although, of course, their circumstances were poles apart, the wounds Macmillan received in the Great War as an officer in France, his solitary convalescence, his natural shyness and intellectual reserve, gave him an awareness of social problems unusual in a man of his class: as his three early political books and his later *The Middle Way* showed, he was a Tory very much on the left of his party. As O'Casey told Nathan: "Harold Macmillan is one of the young Conservatives [he was then forty-one] – full of resolution to bring about a better state of things." "The dynamic of social change", Macmillan himself warned, "resides in our discontent with things as they are. If that discontent is shared by the comfortable as well as the uncomfortable then these changes can be accomplished by a process of peaceful evolution through which we shall continue to preserve the heritage of our liberty." Discontent was, of course, the essence of O'Casey's spirit.

O'Casey was fourteen years older than Macmillan, who remembered him as a "fine character, who wore a polo neck sweater at all times of the day and night. He was very popular but he would never change – even for dinner." (Unlike New York maids, the British aristocracy found such solecisms amusing.) "He was often with Lady Londonderry. He was a great favourite of hers, either at Londonderry House or the Berkeley, a big hotel where they used to entertain. Outwardly he was rather a severe man, but he wasn't like other writers, not conceited: he had a very modest [sic] view of himself. He was a very simple man."

Macmillan always felt comfortable with him and found him a much more attractive character than Shaw, whom he didn't like, and thought a great show-off. For him, O'Casey had "something of the greatness of Hardy, something of the strength of Hardy, which is to say that while both of them wrote a lot – some of it not very good – what they wrote came from a deep sincerity. That's why they live, that's why Hardy lives. O'Casey talked with sincerity, too, I would call him a saintly kind of man. In spite of the characters he created he was a sensible man *au fond*."

The older, famous author, and the younger, rising publisher and politician, who represented, as a radical Tory, the stricken North-East constituency of Stockton, shared an idealism, although Macmillan differed with O'Casey over his belief that the outcome would be communism. Macmillan told O'Casey on the telephone that he thought *Within the Gates* was the finest thing he had written. O'Casey sent on to him Nathan's praise of the play. In 1934, when Macmillan published *Reconstruction: A Plea for a National Policy*, O'Casey wrote to Ramsay MacDonald, giving his younger MP friend a glowing report, combining this with an invitation to see *Within the Gates*. MacDonald replied: "My dear Sean . . . I have almost had to forget that there is such a thing as a theatre in existence . . ." But he had read Macmillan's book, and with masterly condescension declared that he found in it "many echoes of what I myself have been saying and writing for years". He rather wrote off Macmillan as an ineffectual dreamer, pointing out the wide gap that existed between an idea and the working out of it in detail: this was where all the difficult problems were to be located, "as I am sure you know when you first get hold of an idea for a play and then sit down and work it out in its stage situations".

By the end of 1933 O'Casey and Macmillan had formed a close and friendly relationship, so that O'Casey could even secure his reading matter at discount prices through "Mr Harold", at one point ordering George Russell's *The Avatars* and Lennox Robinson's *Is Life Worth Living* – pabulum for his literary hatred. O'Casey heard Macmillan give a radio talk on the trades unions and wrote approvingly, only cavilling at the name of Tolpuddle for the famous martyrs: how could such a name "juggle inspiration" into the hearts of the workers? Anyway, did they need to go back so far, when they had the much better example of a battle for collective bargaining in Ireland in 1913? – the strike and lock-out in which he himself had been involved. It was in this letter to Macmillan, of 28 June 1934, that he made his first mention of the subject of *The Star Turns Red*: it was indeed a paradox that the seed of O'Casey's most committedly communist play should emerge from his contact with a future Tory Prime Minister.

But political idealism was the heroin of the 1930s: it established a hold on the young of rich and privileged families even more dangerous than on those predisposed towards addiction of another kind.

Intellectuals under the spell of G. E. Moore found it the very best kind of spiritual painkiller, destroying as it did all thoughts of God. Moore's *Principia Ethica* attacked religious and patriotic absolutes, substituting the pleasure principle based on human relationships, and refined the political aspect of idealism until it became a delicious flavour attendant upon what Lytton Strachey called "the best feelings", namely those that were "sodomitical". "It had become evident that the structure of Capitalist society in its old form had broken down," wrote Macmillan; ". . . the whole system had to be reassessed. Perhaps it could not survive at all . . . Something like a revolutionary situation had developed, not only at home but overseas." The Marxist writer, John Strachey, had maintained in *The Menace of Fascism*, published at the end of 1932, that "there is no force on earth which can long prevent the workers of the world from building a new and stable civilization for themselves on the basis of the common ownership of the means of production". With the prevalence of a general disillusionment, and not only with the old class and colonial structure, there was little to be surprised at in the build-up of a climate of national treachery, if not treason, which Rebecca West and Andrew Boyle were later to describe. Malcolm Muggeridge, who believed that the Russian Revolution quite surpassed in importance the Crucifixion of Christ, when he went to Moscow in 1932 as the *Manchester Guardian*'s correspondent found particular delight, on the eve of departure, in burning his marriage licence, along with his "ridiculous BA hood and certificate". O'Casey believed exactly as did Muggeridge, Strachey – and Shaw: that the old bourgeois order and certainties had broken down.

Still, a great gulf separated those who had been to Russia from those who had not. Macmillan, who believed in the abolition of privilege in education, although himself a product of Summerfields, Eton and Balliol (he had left Eton under circumstances unconvincingly explained as ill-health and for a long period was tutored privately), visited Russia late in 1932, at a time when Stalin was tightening his grip on the country. He met Maxim Litvinoff, the then Foreign Minister; he travelled in the country, and was impressed by much that he saw; but his response displayed that ambiguity of which he became increasingly the master, afterwards declaring that when he left Russia he was "stepping back from a kind of nightmare world into the world of reality". Muggeridge was less equivocal: he returned to London in 1933, disillusioned by the "harshness and incompetence of the regime", by the "cutting or softening" of the dispatches he sent to the *Guardian*, and by "the succession of western luminaries who came to Moscow to be gulled". Shaw, however, was a most steadfast believer in Stalin, and nothing could shake his faith: he visited Russia in 1931 and met his hero. He had declared himself already a "born Communist and Iconoclast", himself adopting as rigid a position as those he spent a lifetime in mocking.

O'Casey's communism, like Shaw's, was impervious to reality. Like Shaw he was at ease in the drawing rooms of the aristocracy; unlike Shaw he was, although highly selective, never above accepting loans and gifts (the herringbone tweed suit from Lady Astor, for example). When Karl Marx was told by a lady in Karlsbad, where he had gone to take the waters, that she could not imagine him in a classless society because of his aristocratic "preferences and habits", Marx replied: "I cannot either. Those times will come, but we must be gone by then." Lady Astor told O'Casey roughly the same thing: "I would like to take you to Russia – I don't know anybody who would be less fitted to live under an autocracy than you, unless it is myself!"

* * *

O'Casey was forever aware of being older than Eileen and unable to provide the style of life to which she had been accustomed before their marriage. He had even once heard Shaw at a party asking the Irish High Commissioner, John Dulanty, how it was "lovely Eileen Carey had come to marry such an ugly fellow as Sean". He stood at these parties often, like Harry Heegan in *The Silver Tassie*, watching Eileen talking excitedly with a young male guest, but unlike Heegan, with no bitterness in his heart.

When O'Casey travelled to America in 1934 Eileen began seeing Harold Macmillan on her own. In an advanced stage of pregnancy, she was taken out to lunch by the tall, reserved publisher and MP who had a keen eye for a good-looking woman. O'Casey applauded. He was glad she was seeing "Mr Harold" as he always addressed him, and when she reported a week later how much she liked Macmillan, he echoed her: "He is, as you say, a fine fellow, indeed." Eileen and Macmillan began then a close friendship which was to last more than fifty years. Both of them loved and respected O'Casey, and Eileen always put Sean and her children first. As Macmillan, who spoke about her with great depth of feeling, said, "O'Casey lived very much in himself, didn't need people, he had very poor eyesight, and then he had Eileen. She was his kind of ambassador . . . he was a kind of medieval saint."

Eileen, not wanting to hurt O'Casey, by now kept quiet about relationships she pursued outside their marriage. She would, she admitted, not have told him about her renewed affair with Ephraim, but for the resulting pregnancy. By remaining silent now she was merely saving both of them pain and heartache.

O'Casey received more gratification from his communism than from a straying eye; also from his continuing controversies with critics and the editors of journals. The massively prolonged row over *Love on the Dole* yielded him the distinction of being called an "Irish guttersnipe" by Kingsley Martin in *Time and Tide*. "Capitalism", he proclaimed in a later issue of the same journal, "is the regimentation of life towards death, but Communism is the regimentation of life towards life." He praised a book, W. H. Chamberlain's *The Russian Revolution*, published by Macmillan, in which one would find, he said, that "soldiers of rotten cardboard under the Czar became soldiers of steel under Communism", that "out of ruin, famine, bewildering disorder, and pitiful impotence, Communism has created one of the strongest, if not the greatest nation in the world." To Harold Macmillan himself he wrote, at the start of the Spanish Civil War, and with his typical ambiguity – a trait both men shared and enjoyed in one another – "I am praying to God that the Spanish Communists may win. I wish I could be with them. However, if I haven't manned a tank, or fired a rifle for the cause of Communism, I have, at least, in my day, fired stones at the police."

Macmillan did not take O'Casey's communism too seriously: he said, "He wasn't much of a thinker and he didn't have an idea about what life was like in the Soviet Union, but then nor were the saints great thinkers. He thought that everyone ought to be equal out of kindness."

By now, with the death of his father, Macmillan had inherited the family house, Birch Grove, Chelwood Gate, in Sussex: the O'Caseys were invited to stay for weekends. Macmillan, prompted by Eileen, became positive on O'Casey's behalf. He issued a collection of *Five Irish Plays* (the Dublin trilogy plus *End of the Beginning* and *A Pound on Demand*), which sold well. Noting that O'Casey did not talk a great deal, he listened to him reading after dinner "bits of his autobiography", proud, later, that it was he who had first encouraged him to write it. He suggested that a two shillings and sixpenny edition of *The Plough and the Stars* should be issued when the Hollywood film – every bit as bad as, if not worse than, Hitchcock's *Juno* – directed by John Ford for RKO was ready to be screened. But he balked somewhat at publishing the volume O'Casey handed him in August of 1936: a collection of his various articles and letters, published and rejected, on the English theatre and its critics – O'Casey's revenge on the editors who had turned down his long, vituperative articles or replies to criticism.

Macmillan questioned whether the articles would still be fresh enough to warrant publication in book form; O'Casey rounded on him fiercely, saying everything he wrote had perforce to be combative, for "the sword I have swung so long is now stuck to my hand and I can't let go". His plays were, he said, important, therefore his defence of them was equally so – a questionable argument. Macmillan had also asked if the book wasn't a bit too much like "brawling in church"; O'Casey replied that Jesus Christ had done exactly that "before me, and I occasionally follow in His steps". Macmillan raised no further objection and sent him a contract, so that O'Casey could then boast to Nathan that his publishers had jibbed at the book at first, but "then fell silent when I told them that the first to create a brawl in church was Jesus Christ".

But Macmillan went on trying to persuade O'Casey to modify the contents of the collection. He visited the Overstrand Mansions flat, asked politely if O'Casey would consider changing "Coward Codology" and "The Cutting of an Agate", the main attacks on his *bêtes noires*. No, said O'Casey; Macmillan gave way. "It could have been a dangerous half hour," said Eileen, "but thanks to Harold's tact and graciousness, it was just a sensible talk."

Without doubt *The Flying Wasp* – its title taken from a remark by Agate that there was "a nest of wasps that must be smoked out, because it is doing the theatre infinite harm" – damaged O'Casey's reputation, not only because it insulted the English literary and theatrical establishment, but also because his habit of verbal intemperance had become tiresome. Even O'Casey's American friend and champion, Brooks Atkinson, called *The Flying Wasp*, in the *New York Times*, "a scrappy and truculent volume with some bright retorts tucked away in its pages but no strong line of argument or reasoning. It is petty in attitude."

––––––◆◆◆◆––––––

"Beware of entering into a sham," O'Casey wrote, "lest you become part of the sham yourself." But he wielded his own sword with a wilful disregard for truth when he rode into battle with Malcolm Muggeridge, who had attacked the Soviet system in a *Daily Telegraph* article on the Moscow treason trials of 1938. O'Casey wrote two letters to the *Telegraph*, both of which were refused publication; he then expanded the letters into an article called "The Sword of the

Soviet", which the *Daily Worker* published, and in which he taunted
Muggeridge for being "a cock that won't fight". Muggeridge rose
quickly to the taunt, saying he was ready to debate publicly with
O'Casey their respective attitudes towards the Soviet regime. However, "The Dean of Canterbury, Professor Laski, the Duchess of
Atholl, Sir Bernard Pares, the Webbs – these I can understand; but
the author of *Juno and the Paycock* – I admit I was surprised."

O'Casey, bested in the actual content of the quarrel, side-stepped
Muggeridge's arguments, ignored his challenge, and simply complained of press censorship exercised by the *Daily Telegraph* over his
two original letters. But Muggeridge would not let him get away
with it:

> O'Casey, you know perfectly well that you have behaved badly.
> You know perfectly well that no newspaper can be expected to
> publish every letter which may be submitted criticising articles
> which have appeared in its columns . . . If you have decided
> to plump for Stalin and throw in your lot with his Comintern
> sycophants inside and outside the U.S.S.R., then cut out talk about
> free play and the freedom of the press.

O'Casey replied by impishly distorting Muggeridge's words to "He
says, O'Casey knows perfectly well that no newspaper can be
expected to publish letters critical of articles appearing in its
columns". The omission of "every" can only, at best, be described
as wilful. O'Casey went on to crow about misbehaving. He knew
what he was doing; he warmed to the image of himself as a carrion
crow: to see himself as pecking at the decaying carcass of a dead
imperial system suited the by now larger-than-life O'Casey character.
Its worst trait was perverse ignorance. He refused to go and see the
Soviet Union for himself.

Soviet emissaries, such as Timofei Rokotov, the editor of
International Literature, wooed him or were wooed by him. In 1939,
for Rokotov, he wrote an article on "Literature in Ireland", in which
he said of Yeats, who had died earlier in the year, that he was the
greatest poet who wrote in the English language. In his earlier period,
building his poetry on the legends and romances of the Gaelic past,
Yeats had, O'Casey claimed, "fled too far away from the common
people, turning the poet into a cold aristocrat who turned his head
up to the heavens, looking at no-one below the altitude of a star".
However, in the last years of his life, "Yeats became much more human, drew nearer to the world's needs, and, *as he told me himself* [my

italics], became intensely interested in the new voice of the resurgent working-class speaking in its own way, and demanding the earth and the fullness thereof." Fortunately for O'Casey Yeats was not around to refute this. Even in O'Casey's account, in his autobiography, of their last meeting, Yeats was as defiantly anti-communist as ever. In fact, O'Casey had mocked Yeats's later poetry with its realistic, ordinary images: "Wedding" the sublime to the ridiculous, he had commented, polishing bone "till he thinks it ivory".

But in those hectic and arid years before the Second World War, O'Casey's claims as to what was "communist" became not only out of proportion to reality but strangely, almost insanely – if one fails to admit the coherence of his system of selective likes and dislikes – personal. "Hail to the Coming of Communism", he wrote to a Cambridge undergraduate, Peter Newmark, whom he befriended during a visit to Cambridge in 1936 to address the Shirley Society of St Catharine's College on "The Holy Ghost Leaves England".

St Francis, as well as Shaw, he told his old buttie Gaby Fallon, was "more of a Communist than he was a Bourgeois or a Conservative or a Fascist"; while his friend Nathan – no doubt to Nathan's own extreme surprise and mystification – was dubbed "the great proletarian critic" and "a red revolutionary in the theatre". Imperious Nathan had the reputation of a great snob and socialite, but for O'Casey, "You want the best that can be given to the art of the theatre, and that is the creed of the communist. It's not for nothing that your profile on the cover of your last book stands out against a background of Red." Nathan later tried to tell him that communism was bad for a playwright.

The members of the aristocracy whom O'Casey knew and liked were not exempt from this comradely hug: he tried to insinuate to Lady Astor that because of her good heart – and because of his – she must be on his side, i.e. that of communism. But he acceded at the same time to Lady Astor's charge that Russia was killing all her intelligent people, that communism hadn't come yet to Russia. The revolution, however, was definitely coming to England: to Harold Macmillan he wrote: "When I talk to you, I am in the Revolution: & when you talk to others, you are in the Revolution. How? Because we are intelligent men; & intelligent men must ever be thinking of bringing about a change."

He was even more explicit to his publisher in October 1939, when Macmillan and his family moved out of Birch Grove, which became a nursery school during the war, into a cottage in the stables: he was sure, he said, that he and Lady Dorothy would be happy in a cottage because they were "Communists in heart".

Why did O'Casey withdraw so much into a world of his own, and why did he dissipate his energies in needless but self-gratifying squabbles during the time the family lived in Battersea, from late in 1934 until late in 1938? Part of the answer lay in the nature of that twilight world of the 1930s when it was still possible in England to remain out of touch with the reality of what was happening in Central Europe, in Hitler's Germany, and to the East, in Stalin's Russia. But the main part of the answer, in O'Casey's case, lay in his relationship with Shaw.

With this last of his necessary father-figures O'Casey no longer had the thrust of cynicism – perhaps because he was now in his middle fifties – with which to penetrate the weaknesses of a man whom he worshipped with a passion bordering on idolatry. He did not perceive the appalling extent to which Shaw had suffered from shyness and vanity. He did not understand that his early setbacks had made Shaw develop a watertight but completely artificial self-esteem, or how he could, through wit, mockery and flattery, keep the whole world at a distance. O'Casey was quite needlessly in awe of Shaw: while not his equal as a rumorist, he had an emotional range and power so much greater than the older man's; greater humility and naturalness; above all, genuine passion. And, as Macmillan noted, O'Casey was always so much more attractive a character.

But he felt himself an intellectual inferior. Would Shaw disillusion him? Never; because O'Casey was for Shaw a reflection of the problems he had himself suffered as a young man: and he elicited admiration from this mirror-image of himself, whose glass had a rougher density. "Your husband was luckier than all of us," Shaw told Eileen; "my family was very middle of the road, respectable – and restricted about what the neighbours would say. But you – you got the meat."

Sometimes O'Casey would go out of his way to show subservience to him, tailoring his judgments and making quite untrue assertions, such as that when he read of Shaw's shyness, he realised "that this very shyness & pride is deeply set in my own nature." He preferred it to the hypocrisy and complacency of the English: "No wonder Swift went mad." Pride certainly was set deeply in O'Casey's nature, but not shyness.

It may be the fact that Shaw never tried to wield direct authority over O'Casey that made O'Casey blind to his shortcomings, the most significant of which Shaw was only too much aware of himself. His bid to be a sage and propagandist first, and an artist and entertainer only incidentally and second, had failed lamentably: only in the second role was he universally admired. He was the twentieth century's first and most famous victim of what later became known in some circles as "repressive tolerance": his witty castigation of morals amused those at whom it was directed, acting as a safety valve for their repressed finer feelings, enabling them to compete with each other and to exploit the poor (or the rich) even more vigorously than before.

Both Shaw and O'Casey held the belief that the mass of the people was incapable of forming its own judgments, and that, therefore, the fact that it rejected communism meant it had been seduced, bribed, or brainwashed by the capitalist authorities. Indeed, Shaw's disenchantment with the British liberal democratic process had become final: in his view Ramsay MacDonald, by reaching an accommodation with the privileged and the powerful, had put an end to socialism working. When it came to Stalin, Shaw's attitude might be summed up as, "What does a bit more slaughter matter – as long as true socialism is the result. After all, Stalin was not unique in history . . ." He didn't, perhaps, see that the slaughter would not be negligible, nor that it was unlikely to cease, in his own lifetime at least. Shaw's imagination – and by extension O'Casey's – was too gentlemanly, too much a product of the essentially decent moral atmosphere of the late-nineteenth-century British Empire, to envisage the totalitarian system of George Orwell in *Animal Farm* and *1984*.

With the new play he was writing between 1935 and 1939 in Overstrand Mansions, O'Casey remained wholly under the sway of Shaw, making a deliberately outspoken statement in favour of communism, unrelieved by even a trace of self-mockery or ordinary humour. *The Star Turns Red* was a disastrous marriage of the two least successful sides of his rich and broad talent – the tendency to crude, rhetorical propaganda, and the desire to turn the nihilism of expressionism into a poetry of optimism. Dedicated to those who "fought through the great Dublin lock-out" of 1913, the time is set as "Tomorrow, or the next day", but really smacks of the present. Red Jim, the hero, might have been based on Larkin, but he bears a greater affinity to some of the worst stereotypes of Auden and Brecht. O'Casey gives the pretty girl, Julia, who supplies some sexy touches, the most memorable line: "It's the bitter heart that flaunts the bitter word!" The play was unrepentantly expressionistic in style and overtly propagandist: the cast of characters, which includes a Purple Priest, Four Saffron Shirt Troopers, a Woman with Withered Child, a Young Man with Cough – as well as the hero, Red Jim – gives the work's flavour exactly.

O'Casey had begun *The Star Turns Red* as far back as 1925, when he was still living in Dublin's North Circular Road. At that time he called it *The Red Star*. It figured in his correspondence with a Soviet woman living in Berlin who had written to O'Casey to ask what he was working on. As he was busy attending rehearsals of *The Plough and the Stars* O'Casey made little progress, although he did tell Lady Gregory that he had hopes of writing what he called a "Labour play". The idea came from the visit of Jim Larkin to the Soviet Union in 1924, when he had gone to represent Ireland at the Fifth Communist International: O'Casey was conscious that he still hadn't paid full tribute to his old friend and hero, nor had he brought to a successful conclusion his attempt, in *The Harvest Festival*, to write a play about the great Dublin lock-out of 1913, in which he had been so active. However, before he ceased contact with his Russian admirer, Raisa Lomonosova, he sent her a telegram late in 1925: STAR STILL A NEBULA.

So it remained for over ten years. So indeed, for some, it remains today. But the metaphorical leap that O'Casey's mind accomplished in changing the title before the play was finally published, in February 1940 (causing, as he had hoped in 1937, "another bloody big row" – it was published during the period of the Nazi-Soviet pact, and therefore, at least technically, achieved the feat of serving as "enemy propaganda"), was over the gap between the Red Star of Lenin and the original Star of Bethlehem. He saw his Red Jim, based on Larkin, as John the Baptist heralding the rise of communism. By late 1938, having rejected another idea, of substituting Jack Cade as hero (and offering him to Shaw as a communist St Joan), he felt he was making progress, and he finished the script in early 1939.

Upon its completion the familiar interior self-justifying process took over. He no longer had any severe or challenging critics, although he could joke a little with Nathan when dispatching the completed *Star Turns Red*: "As well as being something of a confession of faith, it is, I think, a play; &, possibly, the best of its kind which has been written – which isn't saying a lot. There are, anyhow, some good lines in it. It is, I think, much more compact than *Within the Gates*, though I don't yet know just how much of the verse form ought to go to a play dealing with present-day life." He sent another copy to Richard Madden, one to Harold Macmillan, and a fourth, by registered post, to Timofei Rokotov in Moscow, adding "with deep regards to All who are working to add to the power and greatness of the Great Soviet Nation".

The so-called non-aggression pact which Stalin signed with Hitler in August 1939, prior to the bipartition of Poland, was cemented at the end of September by a Soviet-German treaty of friendship. Stalin then occupied Latvia, Estonia and Lithuania, and made war on Finland; while Sweden provided Germany with vital iron ore, and enabled it to overfly its country (later helping to secure the conquest of Norway), the Soviets supplied Hitler with enormous quantities of raw materials, including a million tons of grain and 900,000 tons of oil, in return for arms and ammunition. Mussolini, Hitler's long-term ally, gave it as his opinion that Stalin, no longer a Bolshevik, now practised "a kind of Slavonic fascism".

Rokotov soon wrote back to O'Casey, offering to publish *The Star Turns Red* in Moscow, which delighted the playwright; he had, however, to refuse: Macmillans declined to allow more than an extract to appear. How publication in Moscow could affect British sales – the excuse O'Casey gave Rokotov – was not explained. When, following Hitler's invasion of Poland, Britain declared war on Germany in September 1939, O'Casey realised that *The Star Turns Red* did not stand much chance of a production in England; any aspersions cast on its quality could be safely put down to the political climate.

O'Casey thought that the Russo-German pact had come about because Stalin was a "realist":

> The fact of an understanding between Nazi Germany and Communist Russia is a long story; but it was inevitable, and anyone who watched things for the past couple of years could see it coming. I myself shocked some Liberals here nearly a year ago by saying that an understanding between Germany and Russia was not only possible but certain, if England and France refused to take their chance of forming a peace front. Had Russia undertaken to fight Germany, she would have been left in the lurch as Poland was left; but Stalin is no fool, whatever else he may be. People make the mistake of thinking that communists are idealists. On the contrary, we are realists.

Harold Macmillan wrote to O'Casey in October saying he intended to delay publication of *The Star Turns Red* till the spring of 1940; but George P. Brett, president of Macmillan, New York, turned it down, saying:

> Not only do I feel that the publication of this play in America at this time would do you immeasurable damage, but by the same

token it would damage us too. America is rabid against Communism . . . it would be a sure way of alienating your friends among the readers in this country.

Turning to matters closer to hand, but not wholly forgetting Hitler, O'Casey was now also expressing his view that the partition of Ireland should be ended: "Double partition", he called it. "It divides Ireland from Ireland, and separates Ulster from herself . . . A clique isn't going to keep Dal Riada, Oriel, Tirowen, and Iveagh from the rest of Ireland. Ulster is as Irish as they make them. [In Ulster is Cave Hill, beside Belfast, where the Founders of the United Irishmen took the oath to drive the English out of Ireland. These men were Protestants, by the way.]"* He compared the English in Ireland to the Nazis, re-espousing his long-abandoned nationalism, which in the early months of the war turned to fierce support for Irish neutrality:

We understand the English far better than they understand us. There is no use mentioning "Nazi tyranny" to an Irishman. English Government in Ireland, setting aside the Black and Tans, has often been soft-brained, but never soft-handed.

In March 1940 Peter Newmark, O'Casey's left-wing correspondent at Trinity College, Cambridge, one of whose tutors was Anthony Blunt, another F. R. Leavis, helped to set up a London production of *The Star Turns Red* at the communist-inspired Unity Theatre. The management at first refused the play on the grounds that it was too critical of trade union leaders, but Newmark persuaded them it was not. Tess Mayor, another left-wing student who later married Lord Rothschild, played Julia. James Agate, intimidated or overgenerous, called the play a "masterpiece": "I find the piece to be a *magnum opus* of compassion *and* a revolutionary work," he wrote in the *Sunday Times*. "I see in it a flame of propaganda tempered to the condition of dramatic art, as an Elizabethan understood that art." Other critics were less kind, reflecting more faithfully perhaps the degree to which the allegorical clash between communism and fascism had grown out of touch with the present-day reality. Even the great American "proletarian critic" and "revolutionary red" Nathan turned on O'Casey: "Incontrovertibly poor . . . the feeblest play

* The passage in square brackets was omitted by *Picture Post* when this letter was published on 24 February 1940.

O'Casey has written. Communism, one fears, has now adversely affected Sean O'Casey as a dramatic artist."

Shaw, however, remained true to his devotee – or was at least still master of the side-stepping compliment. "I should have gone," he wrote O'Casey on a card, "to the *Red Star*, black-out or no black-out, if I hadn't read it. It shewed up the illiteracy of the critics who didn't know that like a good Protestant you had brought the language of the Authorized Version back to life. Splendid." Just what did that mean? Shaw presumably had in mind language like Red Jim's:

> Prating priest, peradventure my comrades are deaf and did not hear you. And, outside, there are many thousands as deaf as these. We have turned aside from you. The life we have lived is coming to an end: life rotten in the ear that it could not hear; life rotten in the eye that it could not see . . . Now we stand up, we turn, and go our own way, the bent back changing to the massed majesty of the Clenched Fist!

And this was hardly a tribute to Larkin, all his life a faithful practising Catholic.

Fortunately, *The Star Turns Red* marked the end of O'Casey's attempt to infuse a positive message into the experimental expressionism born of post-First-World-War nihilism. In it, as in *Within the Gates*, he showed bravery in daring to be experimental, but as with the earlier play, the experiment turned out to be primarily with his own talent. He had no gift for successful experiment, while the poetical or emotional rhetoric with which he flooded both these plays was as dead as its most successful nineteenth-century practitioners, and appears simply over-sincere, quaint, even artful. Experiment had become for him by 1940 a narrowing-down mode of expression; only in the autobiography he was writing did the urban prose dialogue – parodic, earthy, more knowing and infinitely more suggestive, with its heightened realism – still appear, if only in snatches. *Within the Gates* did, however, have one saving grace which explains why so many writers of the day – Nathan and Charles Morgan, in particular; but also T. E. Lawrence and Eugene O'Neill – liked it. O'Casey, with his instinct for disorder and chaos, had taken the deliberate, austere, harsh and generalised methods of expressionism and reversed them. The dark theatrical machinery of Toller's despair and nihilism (and O'Casey's own in *The Silver Tassie*) had been transformed into an epiphany of love: with beautiful irony, it became a celebration of life.

No such thing happened in *The Star Turns Red*: it concerned itself purely with changing the world. No play more completely ignored Lady Gregory's sound advice to concentrate on character. Like many writers of the time who scoffed at the fate of the individual, O'Casey could not see the dangers of social collectivism, nor that his zeal to reform the world reflected an indifference, or callousness, towards facing himself – possibly even an escape from it. Scrapping with others relieved loneliness, belief in communism conquered an even greater fear, that of coming to grips with what Ibsen once called the devils that infest the head and heart: to be "objective", in communist jargon, was to put as much distance as possible between yourself and your real problem. O'Casey had, alas, fallen into a lamentable self-deceit.

The harsh and hollow voice amplified in the inner coldness and emptiness of *The Star Turns Red* was that of the defeated and now aged Shaw who had turned to the brutal Stalin and his methods to bring about change in an England that would not listen. For did not he and O'Casey have in common the lack of a strong and helpful father whose influence could fruitfully have interacted with their own developing personalities? Had not both, in turn, sought father-figures elsewhere, Shaw in his imagination and in himself (creating both himself and a host of wonderful fatherly seers and wits), O'Casey in a succession of existing heroes? Had not both, stopping short of final disillusionment, now turned to a God the Father whose manifestations of crude power they worshipped as gullibly and superstitiously as the most fundamental and slavish of Christians?

Stalin was their answer. The true Protestantism both men believed they embodied – ever rebellious, ever protesting – had still to be satisfied in its need for unquestioning zeal and uncritical faith. Both men kept a photograph of Uncle Joe on the mantelpiece of his inner sanctum – like devout Irish peasants with their postcards of the Virgin Mary.

Neither man was quite capable of honesty in facing himself – facing the gap, that is, between his ideals and the reality of life. Jonathan Swift, as another Irish Protestant, had been among the first to try to do that, and he could not bridge the gap between his ideal, sanitized notion of the rational being (the Houyhnhnms) and the reality of man. His high Tory politics were somewhat different from O'Casey's and Shaw's, and where they found Stalin he found madness. None of the trio, even the Anglican Dean it seemed, could truly find the God his soul hungered for, unblocked or uncontaminated by the social and personal problems life heaped on him.

Fortunately for O'Casey, he had a greater hold on life than Shaw and a stronger hold on his sanity than Swift. Life caught him up in its humanising process, to which he always gave his first response. He describes a child as the "greatest, the loveliest, and the most delicate equipment we have for the development of life's future", and Eileen bore him another, a daughter they named Shivaun. He, Eileen, and their two boys had fled London a second time, settling in the small Devon town of Totnes. Shaw, whose suggestion that they send their two boys to the private, fee-paying school of Darting-ton Hall, outside the town, had generated the move, gave them £50 for Shivaun, telling Eileen that it was important her boys have a sister: "Sisterless men are always afraid of women".

Harold Macmillan, who had by then faithfully published *The Star Turns Red*, wrote to Eileen in 1940:

I was so glad to get your letter and its very exciting news. I do congratulate you. If your daughter is born into a temporarily unhappy time, I am confident that she will grow up into a better age, which I believe will succeed these follies and horrors which now seem so terrible.

He and Dorothy had, he told Eileen, handed over Birch Grove to the infant children; their son Maurice had joined the Field Artillery and was stationed in Brighton: "quite nice for us, for he can get home alternate Sundays". He himself was longing to get back into the Grenadier Guards.

Macmillan later commented that although O'Casey "claimed to be a Communist and, I think, an atheist, his was a truly Christian nature: one of the kindest and most genuine men I have known". It was the same transference of meaning as O'Casey, in his letter of 1938, had used to claim Macmillan as being "in the Revolution".

17

A DETRIMENTAL TEMPER

"Stalin is becoming a household name in Totnes," O'Casey remarked cheerfully in 1941. By now the Russians had changed sides. "Stalin is right," he told his renewed and faithful correspondent Fallon, in a different context. To *Time and Tide* he had written, "In Russia it is the Russians who execute Russians, and (as Shaw said in another case) who has a better right to cut a Russian's throat than another Russian?"

In moving to the small South Devon town of Totnes, O'Casey shed complexity and discomfort: he had hated the Battersea flat with its large rooms and the weary climb up the stairs to the third floor. He often complained of his loneliness there to Eileen; he could not bear roaming around in the silences of Eileen's room and of the nursery when she took the children away. In Totnes, they rented a detached Victorian house from a humourless dentist who would not accept Charlotte Shaw as a financial guarantor – only GBS was good enough for him. Totnes allowed the ageing playwright full scope for his lovable and cantankerous image to grow without threat of bombs, theatres, or other writers.

But how would the town itself have fared under Stalin in the 1930s? There could not have been a more Tory borough, with its hilltop castle ruins, dating from pre-Norman times and still under the ownership of the Duke of Somerset, and its sturdy Devon "kulaks" – "folk in the fine fair English sense of the word", as O'Casey wrote. With a brand-new police station over the road, the Conservative Club only a few hundred yards away, O'Casey found peace and tranquillity here. Totnes, with its freshwater moorings on the River Dart, where foreign vessels once added an exotic flavour, had for centuries maintained its quality as a gentle and lovely town, "like a grey-haired lady, with a young face, sitting calm, hands in lap, unmindful of time". Totnes even numbered a delightful Dublin priest among its dwellers, a Father Ned Russell after whom O'Casey named a later play, *The Drums of Father Ned*. He became a valued friend.

The move to "Tingrith", a fine white stuccoed and spacious villa, endowed with a delightful conservatory, walled garden and sizeable outbuildings, was the beginning of a truer exile than that from Ireland. For the remaining twenty-five years of his life, O'Casey left Devon scarcely half a dozen times. With *The Star Turns Red* he set a precedent of not attending a production of a new play of his, which he stuck to, saving much heartache. In his last volume of autobiography he remarked bitterly that all his plays had been betrayed by bad productions – except for those by Fagan's Irish Players, and *The Silver Tassie*.

Harold Macmillan, before joining Churchill's Government as Secretary to the Ministry of Supply and before leaving to become resident Minister in North Africa, had successfully launched O'Casey on a new course of writing which absorbed him from the late 1930s until the early '50s, namely his six volumes of autobiography. It was a huge literary undertaking, running in the end to over half a million words, but it did not cost O'Casey the effort and soul-searching he put into his plays; neither did it achieve their concentration. In strong contrast, even the least successful of his plays was highly wrought, chipped into shapes which may have shown misapplied judgment but not niggardliness of effort. Nothing he wrote for the theatre was careless.

Macmillan was justly proud of the first volume of autobiography, for not only was it, for all its faults, a striking memoir, but it had other and more wide-reaching effects on O'Casey's work: it led him out of the wilderness of experiment and political commitment in which he had been lost for most of the '30s. The mood and feeling of *I Knock at the Door*, which Macmillans published in early 1939, was centred on O'Casey's mother; it is her figure and character which give the book its thrust, its shape, and its quality of celebration at his overcoming the rigours of his early life. He succeeds in bringing Susan Casey to life again, not this time through the defiant and vivid mother images of the Dublin plays, but more directly, and at the same time more expansively, through his memories of her. Susan Casey apart, the volume contains powerful description, and some moving intimate revelations, such as those concerning his eyes. Its publication was an achievement: *I Knock at the Door* was sold to a book club, serialised in a paper, reprinted several times, while O'Casey experienced a new lease of fame.

Macmillan never had a closer relationship with an author than he had with O'Casey, and that relationship was at its closest when he wrote *I Knock at the Door*. O'Casey sent him the first batch of sketches in 1938 and the two men met and discussed them, Macmillan encouraging O'Casey to add further material until the book found its true length. Sometimes, weekending at Birch Grove, O'Casey would read the work in progress to his hosts.

An incident at breakfast one of these weekends provided an insight into the family life of his publisher and the communication he had with his own children. Sean, Eileen and Maurice were alone in the dining room. Maurice, then in his teens, was dressed very smartly for riding. O'Casey, like all Dubliners whatever their class, loved horses, and he said, "You must be enjoying going out – what a delightful thing to be doing."

"Oh no," Maurice told him, "I hate it. I can't stand it." O'Casey then enquired why on earth he did it. "I have to," Maurice told him. "It's expected of me: not worth making the fuss not to." "Well, why not say it to your father that you don't like it?" "Oh no, I couldn't do that." "Well, I'll tell him if you like," said O'Casey: Maurice said, "Oh no, no, let's leave the whole thing alone." O'Casey could not understand the lack of communication between father and son.

At one point in the discussions about *I Knock at the Door* Macmillan expressed anxiety over O'Casey's intention to do away with inverted commas for direct speech: at another he worried about O'Casey's frugal use of commas. Finally O'Casey allayed his fears by supplying more commas, and instead of quotation marks using dashes, as in Joyce's *A Portrait of the Artist* and *Ulysses*. Macmillan discussed illustrations with O'Casey, but they decided to have none. To ensure that the typography was satisfactory Macmillan sent four specimen pages for him and Eileen to choose from. O'Casey responded that he knew more about politics than about specimen pages.

I Knock at the Door covered the first twelve years of Sean's life – we have this on O'Casey's word to "Mr Harold", as he still deferentially addressed his publisher. But was it accurate autobiography? Hardly. Because O'Casey believed in "objectivity", not "truth" or "fact" in the generally accepted sense of those words, he presented his whole life faithfully in accordance with his communist ideals. In other words, it was the "gospel" of young Sean Casside's life as told in accordance with the faith and the attitudes he wished to instil in his reader. Others felt its truth differently, that it was "true" because O'Casey projected in it his own deep feelings about the characters he knew and loved: here the truth was emotional. One small by-product of writing this first volume was that he started sending his sole remaining brother, Mick, a quid at Christmas time to buy tobacco.

After some experiments O'Casey had eschewed writing in the first person, and called his hero "Johnny", then "Sean Casside" or "Cassidy". Had he worked more at the first-person technique, he might have ended by removing many of the rhetorical flights of the omniscient narrator – as well as the latter's often unnecessary and over-lengthy comments. It would have been nearer to the rigour of writing for the theatre, while he would have found it difficult – and therefore beneficial – to incorporate material outside the conscious grasp of the "I" figure: he could only have used what he had directly experienced.

Yet he wanted the chance to make an appeal on behalf of other characters when they spoke up, he wanted to show their independence. In fact the writing is often at its best when, in dialogue, he shows another character wrong-footing the two-dimensional Sean Casside. In the absence of anything other than the stereotyped reflections of Casside – he, like O'Casey himself, has a wholly extrovert and non-self-questioning personality – this is the main form of complexity or psychological resonance *I Knock at the Door* possesses by virtue of its third person narrator. Otherwise, while being an uncompromising tract against authority, the book tenderly and movingly proclaims the virtue of motherly protection, and pays off the huge debt O'Casey still owed his mother.

Dartington Hall, the leading progressive school of its time, and the favourite of such figures as Bertrand Russell and Shaw, was owned by Leonard and Dorothy Elmhirst. Elmhirst was a collector of people and it was not long before he added the O'Caseys to his collection – in particular Eileen, now dubbed by Shaw "one of the beauties of Devon". The school itself had a good or bad reputation, according to which ideology one embraced. It was co-educational, there were no formal lessons, no corporal punishment, no religious instruction. It encouraged the arts, which meant that, as well as acting and making pots, the children played poker at night, and bathed in the nude in the River Dart. Many of the avant-garde principles on which the school operated were expounded by Russell in his book on education. ("No Russell ever went to school," commented Macmillan later. "They were always slightly odd. They never met other people.") William Curry, the headmaster, was described by one pupil, Claire Tomalin, as a hydrocephalic, gnome-like creature in a dirty mackintosh. She remembered his first words to her, on her being accepted as a sixth-form pupil, were, "Promise me one thing. Don't go to bed with the boys."

He and O'Casey got on well; Curry, too, was an idealist. O'Casey recommended an Irish friend, Leslie Daiken, to apply for a job there. He also told Curry that, as a communist, he was in favour of "preferential treatment to all in all schools – that is the adopting of educational methods to each child according to its needs". The fees were eighty pounds per child per term, but as Shaw, the convinced egalitarian and socialist, told Eileen, "The higher the standard for the young, the better, so long as it is good and simple. They will try all their lives to fight for better living for themselves and others."

Yet at Dartington Hall, although recommended by Shaw, the children were expected to set their own standards – nothing was demanded or exacted from them. Neither O'Casey nor Curry seemed to know what to do if the children's standards or needs got out of hand, became violent or self-gratifying. Curry, a conscientious man whose manner inspired loyalty among the children, with time became increasingly disillusioned, suffered a nervous breakdown, and finally concluded that children, in this imperfect world, were better off under some sort of benevolent dictatorship. Dartington Hall's reformative zeal depended, in its heyday, on a strong if oppressive sense of order in society as a whole. It was, like O'Casey himself, Protestant in its inspiration. When, many years later, its principles became widely accepted in society, the school collapsed – but so, by then, had most formal values in society itself. Of course the reformers would never admit that their Protestantism was at the centre of any moral decline. Sex was the Achilles heel of Dartington Hall, although, fortunately for them, none of the O'Casey children suffered as a result of the freedom: they, perhaps more than most, were suited to attend such an establishment because early on they found agreeable pursuits they could follow. Breon became a painter and jeweller, returning after an art school course in London, to live in the South West; the daughter, Shivaun, attended the Central School of Drama, Swiss Cottage, later moving to the Drama Centre, before taking up an acting and directing career.

O'Casey had first visited Dartington Hall as a possible participant in the Elmhirsts' experiment. They proposed that he become a colleague of Michael Chekhov, nephew of the Russian playwright, who ran the school's drama department. This could have provided a secure source of funds for the children's education, but Eileen told Mrs Elmhirst, who offered the post to O'Casey, that it would be a catastrophe, and a sheer waste of anyone of his quality. Dorothy

Elmhirst, a queenly American, overwhelmed Eileen and made her feel she was returning, unconsciously, to her younger days when she had been patronised by the rich. But Leonard Elmhirst, who, according to David Astor, was a "slightly scatty agricultural reformer", gave Eileen no such feelings, and they became friends.

Although Lady Astor visited the O'Caseys in Totnes – and they saw her once in her constituency town of Plymouth – she told them playfully that it was "dreadful" of Shaw to proclaim the virtues of such a school, an opinion O'Casey hotly disputed. They had now dropped out of wartime London society, and the capital city, for O'Casey, soon became only a memory – not a very pleasant one, as he recorded; its life was "too sloven, too outspread, and too voluminous to weave any conforming pattern a human mind could frame; the world-weaving activities here created but a bewildering tangle in London's life". He even thought the poets and prelates buried in Westminster Abbey were smothered in the city's impenetrable tapestry.

Not only had London never inspired him – he had only *Within the Gates* to thank it for – it left behind its own "chassis": their lease on the Overstrand Mansions flat, in the "most snobbish, bourgeois, locality in London", still had time to run. The O'Caseys had secured, as they thought, verbal agreement to their not paying the rest of the rent, but the landlord sued for a year's rent in default of written notice. Sean and Eileen travelled to London to attend the hearing, staying at the Strand Palace Hotel. They found their plea made by an inexperienced young "junior" instead of the distinguished advocate they thought they had engaged, and lost both the case and the money.

Although still living in rented accommodation – they could at that time, when property was cheap, probably have taken out a mortgage or even bought a house outright – Devon suited them domestically. They were comfortable. O'Casey had slipped back into that familiar tenant-landlord structure which, deep inside, answered a need in him. At any time the grumpy dentist owner, having given the agreed term of notice, could have repossessed the house, but for sixteen years he did not. There were advantages to being a tenant, even if by now a tenant of a very superior and famous kind. It made O'Casey a permanent victim, kept him in touch with the poor, the underdog, his spiritual brethren to whom he returned increasingly in his autobiographical expansiveness. It kept the old wounds open while providing the fuel for class animus. The move to Devon may not have been a considered one, but it answered the needs of O'Casey's negative capability; it provided, as well as comfort and security, pain and uncertainty.

In Devon, the O'Caseys hit upon the real world again, a world they could enjoy as a family and one which re-awakened and fed O'Casey's imagination. He began chopping wood, digging the garden and working about the house; he shared positively in his children's interests – Breon had become attracted to "the Drama", as O'Casey told Nathan: "He likes American comics, films, & their broadcasts. Anyway they're better than ours." Later on the town, local park and area became flooded with American soldiers of every hue and description: O'Casey chatted at length to a homesick GI from Kansas City.

The war disrupted them at the beginning, when they had three poor East End evacuees staying in the house, but Eileen had plenty of help, a nanny for the children as well as a regular daily, and the evacuee children did not stay long. She threw herself into mastering first-aid and learnt how to deal with incendiary bombs by "creeping, done out in dungarees, on her belly into a hut filled with old furniture, set ablaze with magnesium". Later they had a refugee boarder from Dartington Hall, a boy called Peter who needed, as Eileen put it, "a different billet". The O'Casey children, however, not being boarders at Dartington Hall, coped happily with the double life of home and school, although they did not mix the two. Breon never invited other boys home to his house: Niall, more sociable, with a lively sense of humour, did not bring friends home either; later he played the trombone, and had an excellent ear for imitating accents. O'Casey, never resting from his work, happily tolerated their noise, careless as they were of "the tumult of mind afflicting the old codger".

Shivaun, with whom O'Casey developed an especially close relationship, remembered him playing games with her: Grandmother's Footsteps, Kick the Can, or Tink Tonk Tinker's Man. He would impersonate a little boy for her or turn the table upside-down to make it into a boat. He was always accessible, and not at all authoritarian. Only once did he raise a hand and threaten to smack her – she was arguing with Eileen, who seeing the expression of shock on her daughter's face, immediately took her to one side, exclaiming, "What have you done to Shivaun?" "Damn the pair of you," said O'Casey.

War had its hazards. To observe the black-out they had to cover more than twenty windows in the rambling house. Once in the night a bomb exploded locally, and O'Casey, leaping out of bed in the dark, tripped over something and "fell recklessly, dinting my back into the coal-scuttle". At another time, during an incendiary and high-explosive bomb attack, a window blew in, and the ceiling fell in the garage. Niall, aged seven, cried and "his little body shook" while he clung to his father who cuddled and kissed him "into quietness and peace". Tingrith had a comfortable warm cellar, reached by a trap door in the kitchen floor, where they could take refuge. They had also bought a steel-topped Morrison shelter which they stationed just inside the front door and under which they could also sit out the raids while the house shook from bombs falling nearby. One day when a leopard had escaped from a local zoo, O'Casey tried to stop Niall from going to school.

He kept up a stream of eccentric, uninformed comment in his letters to friends. The army needed a few slum products in it as leaders, he told Jack Daly, a former O'Tooler, now living in Oxford – like "the guttersnipe, Rommel". He began writing regularly for a Moscow magazine, while in the summer of 1942 he sent an impassioned plea to Winston Churchill to lift the government's ban on the publication of the Communist *Daily Worker*. Although some of its staff resigned, the paper had remained loyal to Russia during the Hitler-Stalin pact. "Add another horse to your chariot of war," he told the Prime Minister in Churchillian tones, reminding him that the two of them were once members of Lady Londonderry's Wednesday "Ark": Churchill had been the Warlock, wearing a "Bronze Ark in the centre of a Stuart tartan ribbon bow". He himself, he didn't remind Churchill, had been the spider. But the ban was lifted.

The Totnes Catholic priest, "Father Ned", visited O'Casey four or five times a week for a meal and a chat, so that, as O'Casey said, "we practically went through the war years arm in arm". They had much in common and would swap Dublin City lore and tales of odd encounters. Both loved this animated conversation and their shared sense of humour: "We heard the german bombs fall at midnight, and saw Plymouth a flame of fire".

O'Casey's productivity showed a steep rise during the early part of the war. The conditions of fear, physical deprivation, and hope in the England of the early 1940s were uncannily similar to those in Dublin between 1919 and 1923 – although, of course, England lacked the deep religious divisions. These conditions, and the courage he saw everywhere displayed by ordinary people, stirred O'Casey's gifts nearly as powerfully as they had been stirred twenty years earlier. Between his arrival in Totnes and the point at which the tide of war began turning, in mid-1944, he wrote two further volumes of autobiography which, though uneven, contained some of his finest prose, as well as two further plays, *Purple Dust* and *Red Roses for Me*.

Purple Dust, which he had begun in London, shows a marked improvement on *The Star Turns Red*. An elaborate burlesque, it abandons propagandist abstractions for character, albeit character on the stagey side. The Shaw of *John Bull's Other Island* was again a strong influence, as if O'Casey had set out, in a roundabout way, to update it: peasant stage Irishmen given such names as Jack O'Killigain and Philip O'Demsey, comically displace two stage Englishmen called Stoke and Poges (the village of Stoke Poges, where Gray wrote his *Elegy*, was adjacent to the unhappy Chalfont St Giles). The younger man, Poges, was based on O'Casey's old Mephistopheles, Billy McElroy, the Belfaster of Scottish extraction whom O'Casey had for a time trusted, when "just a gaum"; now he dismissed him as "the most egoistic & selfish mortal that ever crossed my path", as he told the Scots poet Hugh MacDiarmid in 1949. MacDiarmid's first wife, Peggy Skinner, had left him in 1930 to live with McElroy.

The two middle-aged Saxons in the play have settled, with their Irish mistresses, in a dilapidated mansion in a remote part of Ireland. Apart from the genial pastoral confusion – a kind of "state of chassis" *en plein air* – of conflicting cultures from which the Celts emerge as demonstrably superior to the English gulls, *Purple Dust* celebrates pagan licence and primitive joy, or the "lower inclinations of the people", as Canon Creechewel, the local priest, calls them. As the two crafty Irishmen detach the mistresses from their corrupt landlords, they echo earlier calls to freedom from Ibsen and Synge:

> An' you, young girl, sweet bud of an out-spreading three, graft yourself on to the living, and don't stay hidden any longer here. Come where the rain is heavy, where the frost frets, and where the sun is warm. Avril, pulse of me heart, listen to me, an' let longin' flood into your heart for the call of life . . .

The call of life? It may have seemed a little remote in 1940. The sound, secure, and fundamentally middle-class world which was a prerequisite for such dreams was in the process of passing, as the more brutal "freedoms" of the modern world – the imaginative self-expression of German fascism, the class "freedom" of Russian communism, the permissive, consumer "freedoms" of liberal American democracy – began their own struggle for supremacy. As an industrial power England had already fallen behind in the race, and it turned, in mid-war, to the pipe-dream of the Welfare State, in spite of each English person being said to owe "as much as it would take him to earn throughout a lifetime". Ireland was no longer the twentieth century's cockpit for revolutionary change, but a remote and idyllic backwater: left behind, who knows, perhaps for its own good. Anyway, in *Purple Dust*, O'Casey indulged its backwardness.

Devon, too, was an idyllic backwater, perfect for the cultivation of visions. Remembering his early youth in his second instalment of autobiography, *Pictures in the Hallway*, which in O'Casey's inexact chronology covered roughly the years between 1891 and 1902 (but taking a huge step out of sequence to describe his brother Tom's death in 1914), he recreated his theatrical apprenticeship as Father Dolan in *The Shaughraun*. *I Knock at the Door* had been too much a random collection of impressionistic sketches, as if the past were a religious procession of characters great and small. But, apart from re-awakening his long-neglected Boucicault instincts in playwriting (the best elements in *Purple Dust* stem from these), O'Casey gave *Pictures in the Hallway* much more dramatic timing and development. If the first book's successes – Susan Casey (or Casside) hurrying home with the dead child in her arms; the wake and funeral of Michael Casey; Bella's departure for her wedding without a word from her mother; the old vagrant Jew conned into replacing the broken window – if these are Boucicault set-pieces, in its sequel O'Casey achieves greater continuity and growth.

His mother's purchase from a kind Jew of a new suit for Sean (or Johnny, as he was still called in this instalment); the presentation of the clock to the Hampton and Leedon boss; the attempted seduction of "Alice" in the stockroom; the shenanigans over the buying and selling of damaged crockery to Biddy by the tight-fisted Mr Anthony: all these episodes are eminently actable. Other qualities in the book also reflect the renewed influence of Boucicault, now adapted to prose narrative: the awareness of vivid backgrounds (the painting of backcloths is one of the autobiography's most consistent achievements); the reduction of individual characters to stock types or "humours" so clearly incompatible that the expectation of a clash – either comic or tragic – is always being set up, then either fulfilled or delayed. The sly, comic soliloquys, and the "staged" tableaux also owe much to Boucicault's influence: "Shakespeare's good in bits; but for colour and stir, give me Boucicault."

Purple Dust had to wait to be staged; its publication, in November 1941, did little to enhance O'Casey's popularity. James Agate was re-alienated by it. When the actor-manager Alec Clunes announced in early 1942 that he had plans to present the play at his Arts Theatre

Club, in London's West End, Agate wrote disapprovingly, and telegraphed Clunes, "PURPLE DUST ALL DUST AND NO PURPLE STOP LEAVE ALONE STOP." When O'Casey with characteristic vehemence but unusual brevity told the *Sunday Times* that he had refused Clunes the play, presumably hoping by this avowal to salvage some pride, Agate turned on him savagely:

> Is he like that *diva* before whom Berlioz imagines some critic bowing low and stammering: "Your voice has the sublimity of the Heavenly Choir. Your trill is more amazing than the sun. Saturn's ring is unworthy to crown your head. Before you humanity can but prostrate itself; deign at least that it embraces your feet." In reply to which poverty-stricken meed the singer shrugs her beautiful shoulders and says, "Qu'est-ce qu'il me chante, cet imbécile?" . . .

Was he like Wordsworth, who required admirers *en masse* to service every page, every word, every comma? "Must every word about Mr O'Casey be jam scooped out of a silver tassie with a golden spoon?" Turning to the play, Agate judged that it was "not the moment to produce a witless lampoon at the expense of the English, too busy fighting for freedom to answer back". *Purple Dust* had to wait until 1943 for its first performance, by an amateur company in Newcastle upon Tyne.

A much better play, however, was under way, and for once O'Casey did not pause to take up the cudgels for it – and endure further humiliation by having his letters rejected. At first he called the new piece *At Sea in a Gold Canoe*, but later changed the title to *Red Roses for Me*. The darkening of social mood in England, as the country stood alone against Hitler, found a truer reflection of defiance, perhaps, in the way O'Casey interwove various strands of his prodigious talent in this newer play than in his "skit" on the English, which he had not intended to have taken at all seriously or symbolically – or so he said, anyway. The plot of *Red Roses for Me* was lifted almost wholly from *The Harvest Festival*, but the intensity and seriousness of the earlier, rejected play was toned down and broken up as O'Casey wove into it more autobiographical experiences from his Dublin years (he was at the same time writing *Pictures in the Hallway*), from the, by now, failed communist idealism of more recent years, and his expressionist experiments, from *The Silver Tassie* to *The Star Turns Red*.

Although he sentimentalised rather than deepened the central characters of Ayamonn and his mother, Mrs Breydon, a direct authenticity, long absent from his dramatic work, made its moving return, as when Ayamonn praises his mother for her care of him after his father's death. Maire Keating, O'Casey's long-standing early passion, reappears in the character of Ayamonn's girlfriend, Sheila, a fine figure of a girl, who carries herself with a graceful sturdiness, but whose large, sympathetic brown eyes grow dim, now and again, with "*a cloud of timidity*". Ayamonn sacrifices his love for her to his youthful idealism and his love of death.

In one way it was an indication of O'Casey's lack of development, that age and experience gave him no deeper perspective on the situation he presented in *Red Roses for Me* than the one he had known as a young man, and had written up as happening to Jack Rocliffe in *The Harvest Festival*. Yet if he never again progressed beyond re-living vivid memories of his youth, O'Casey found, in *Red Roses for Me*, a magical means of transcending those events theatrically – raising them to a level of symbolic importance – which gives that play a new dimension.

He planted this visionary element in the first act, but gradually, while skilfully employing realistic dialogue, lifted the veil of grubby Dublin away to epiphanise it in Ayamonn's imagination as the eternal city: "Oh, look! Look there! Th' sky has thrown a gleaming green mantle over her bare shoulders, bordhered with crimson, an' with a hood of gentle magenta over her handsome head – look! . . . Our city's in th' grip o' God!" By the end, when Ayamonn dies, this unreality, while remaining convincing, dominates the play. It is as if, at last, and unconsciously, O'Casey has solved all the problems he set himself in *The Silver Tassie*. Characters are symbols at the same time as being characters.

If *Red Roses for Me* significantly reversed the downward trend of O'Casey's talent, it is still not without fault, because he had now hardened into a playwright without a theatre.

Under this window, on a roughly made bench, stand three biscuit-tins. In the first grows a geranium, in the second, musk, and in the third, a fuchsia. The disks of the geranium are large and glowing; the tubular blooms of the golden musk, broad, gay, and rich; and the purple bells of the fuchsia, surrounded by their long, white, waxy sepals, seem to be as big as arum lilies. These crimson, gold, and purple flowers give a regal tint to the poor room.

As Sean O'Faolain noted of this elaborate stage direction, it was useless to anyone in the theatre: "That is not playwriting. It is a man fondling his material subjectively inside himself, as the literary novelist so often does – and safely can: as a dramatist *never* can." He might have added that O'Casey was repeating almost literally a description of his mother's flowers in the autobiography.

Each major piece of work O'Casey wrote shook up and sifted his admirers, purging some and promoting others: there were always casualties – to this extent he and Shaw, perhaps, aped the autocracy of their hero Stalin, although more gently. *Red Roses for Me* was no exception. Its main victim was Gabriel Fallon, O'Casey's Dublin buttie who – according to O'Casey's later and very one-sided version (when he fell out with friends he ruthlessly cancelled all affection) – had become increasingly pious over the years. With the enlargement of his family and with a wife, Rose, who resented his free-thinking, Fallon had taken, like a lay monk, or like Chesterton, to kneeling in his bedroom at a prie-dieu before a crucifix.

The final split between the two old friends was delayed until just after the war. Fallon had first voiced his criticisms of *Red Roses for Me* when it was given its world première in Dublin, directed by Shelah Richards, at the Olympia Theatre in March 1943. As critic of an "ultra-montane" Catholic weekly, the *Standard*, and still faithful to the O'Casey of the trilogy, Fallon had written: "My own quarrel with the work lay in its excess of sentimentality and in the inclusion of one particular scene which attempted to brand Dublin's Catholic poor as ignorant idolators, a scene in which the author is being as false to himself as he was to his characters."

O'Casey had ignored or not known of the criticism. Later, this time after a revival of *Red Roses for Me* at the Gaiety, directed by Ria Mooney, Fallon made his criticism more explicit. His main point was that, being both autobiographical and didactic, it was a play O'Casey "*insisted on writing*, rather than the play which Sean O'Casey could have written": Yeats's old criticism of *The Silver Tassie* in another form. Fallon went on in rather more detail about the hocus-pocus which O'Casey mocked concerning his "Our Lady of Eblana": "Faced with it, I find myself forced to recall the kindliness and the understanding of the personality I once knew in order to assure myself that this is not a piece of coldly-calculated bigotry."

Fallon defended himself against O'Casey's expected onslaught by saying that O'Casey had always told him to be frank and truthful. Worried lest he should lose O'Casey's friendship, he then carefully expanded his criticism in a further article in the *Standard*:

In the action of the play the statue [of the Virgin] is removed from its niche in the hallway by the Protestant Mr Brennan Moore . . . Mr Moore has the statue re-painted and returned to its niche in the hallway. Then suddenly . . . we are informed by the Protestant Hero of the play, Ayamonn Breydon, that "*th' Blessed Virgin has come back again*" . . . Men and women now appear at the door singing a hymn softly, "staring at the Image shining bright and gorgeous as Brennan made it for them." After the singing of the hymn . . . EEADA tells us "*She came back; of Her own accord.*" DYMPNA declares that "*From her window little Ursula looked, and saw Her come; in the moonlight, along the street. She came, stately*" . . . This is followed by the FIRST MAN's speech: "*My eyes caught a glimpse of Her too, glidin' back to where She came from. Regal and proud She was, an' wondrous.*"

The nub of Fallon's criticism was that although O'Casey had dealt far from tenderly with Orange ignorance and bigotry in the persons of the Dowzard and Foster, taking care to provide a carefully dramatised corrective in the dignified Protestant rector, and in Ayamonn and Mrs Breydon, "What corrective," he asked, "did you provide for the lying and the hypocrisy and the folly of your representatives of working-class Catholics?"

O'Casey said no more from this time on but cut his friend dead: later he told the editor of his letters about "the poor pious and gutless Gaby . . . in his sanctimonious glory": "All my life I've been attacked and vilified, but never for want of integrity. And I've been called a lot of nasty names, but never a coldly calculated bigot. One thing I am cold and calculated about is bigotry; and perjury, and cowardice."

Yet another old Dublin friend, his eye specialist Cummins, wrote to O'Casey in a vein similar to Fallon's, but escaped the accusation of calumny. Cummins said:

I confess I do not like the incident of the missing statue and the attendant behaviour of the simple poor Catholics of the house. Is it possible to present fairly the religious aspects of contemporary Ireland? For centuries the Catholics were oppressed by a system that aimed at destroying their self-respect as well as their material prosperity; while, under the system, indeed as an essential part of it, the Protestants, a small minority, were protected and favoured and made the lawful receivers of the looted Catholic property.

"*Et tu Brute*," O'Casey at first wrote back to him, with a long and deeply emotional defence. He saw it happen, he told Cummins, below Drumcondra Bridge, with the statue of Our Lady of the Tolka in white gown and blue mantle, behind the poor cottages on a mud bank flooded in winter.

I tell you the devotion to that statue was, in my opinion, nearer than next door to worship – and what the hell harm anyhow? She represented to them the colour and loveliness they craved for . . . their devotion was always a beautiful manifestation to me: they adored something above themselves. So do they in the play, and it is not to be condemned, or deprecated, by a fairly comfortable, safely-placed professional man. It strikes me, dear Joe, that it is you rather than I who are unjust to the simple Catholic poor.

Cummins, like Fallon a devout Roman Catholic, graciously climbed down: O'Casey had successfully stirred his middle-class guilt. "Forgive me for imputing to you a lack of sympathy with those simple people. I am shocked at having done so. I have never known a man so free from bias, so white-hot in the face of injustice as you." Yet is the compassion so powerfully expressed in O'Casey's letter there in the play? Clearly not.

There were still traces of saving humour around the edges of O'Casey's anti-Catholicism. Before he fell out with Fallon, he declared, "why in the name o' God should the Catholics care a damn of what I may say about them?" They were "a bit like", he went on, "a man going about afraid that a touch of a butterfly's wing would bring him concussion of the brain".

------◆◆◆◆------

But O'Casey carried his anti-Jesuit railings to gargantuan excess in the strange relationship he formed near the end of the war with a young Irish girl who later refused to be identified except as "Miss Sheila". Sheila Edwards was the daughter of an Irish major killed on the North-West Frontier in India; living in London, she worked in a factory, but had connections with a well-placed Catholic family and – most important of all, from the angle of O'Casey's vituperation – the Jesuits of Farm Street. She appealed to him at once – "too wild to be educated", he later called her – because when he attacked the Vatican in the *Daily Worker* in an article called "Clericalism Gone Looney" she lashed out at him in what he called "a violently abusive" personal letter, writing that it was "sad to think that the English public should be given such foul trash to read. If people administer poison causing death they are hanged, and when a person like *you* administers poison that kills the soul of the workers, nothing is said or done. The abuse in your letter shows you are a very low type." She ended her letter: "I will not call you comrade; I think of you as my brother in Christ Jesus, and will pray for you. The talents God has given you are being abused."

O'Casey found the attack not just appealing – with more than a *frisson* of sexuality, it was highly provocative. The sixty-five-year-old snatched up his battle lance, at first delicately pricked about with it – as usual not answering directly the points his correspondent made, then in a ramble of anecdotal detail and attractive self-defence (such as that he had been an unskilled labourer "for forty years") tempting Miss Sheila to launch into a second attack. Sure enough she did, with dozens of questions, flattered in spite of her hostility that so famous a man should take her seriously.

Agreeably combative to both of them, the correspondence expanded and soon, clearly to O'Casey's pleasure, it diverged from the more arid meadows of communism and Catholicism to richer fields of Mars (or Venus) where they could continue their now friendly joust on the subject of sex and chastity. Words like "vigour", "virility", "lusty", "sex", "immorality" entered the lists like eager young heroes. In one long letter, well in excess of 5,000 words (surely a record even by O'Casey's standards), he attacked Sheila's religious adviser, a Jesuit, who had categorically claimed that it was impossible to be a Catholic and a communist – the perennial favourite. But Sheila confessed that the priest was attempting to get her to take a vow of chastity; what a "dastardly thing to coax, or seduce, a good-looking girl to pledge herself by a vow to life-long chastity", O'Casey protested, then continuing, "And not only to herself does this mean torture, but it means the same thing to young men attracted towards her in a lovely and very human way. Don't forget the beautiful story of Romeo and Juliet."

He had intended when beginning this correspondence to make use of it in a collection of essays about the Irish called *The Green Searchlight*. But now it was his turn, on receiving her photograph from Sheila, to grow more personal. "A very lovely young girl," he called her, but why wasn't she married? The aura of Jesuit power which surrounded her and the weekends she spent "with big nobs", as he chuckled to a communist friend, continued for some time to excite his imagination. He sent her a second 5,000-word letter, this time revealing that Stalin had pulled Lady Astor up short, on her visit to Russia, for beating her children. However the second outpouring must have struck even him as excessive, for he then contented himself with short, hasty replies, and the whole love affair by letter cooled rapidly.

The relationship with Sheila, with its tutorial yet self-interestedly affectionate intentions, and with its touch of spirited wickedness as he irreverently tried to overturn the girl's faith, had something of a Swiftian animation. It reflected too the physical distance and isolation, and yet mental closeness, Swift had enjoyed with "Vanessa" (Hester Van Homrigh) and then with "Stella" (Esther Johnson). Its end was terrifyingly Swiftian too, when one day, many years later, Miss Sheila set out to visit O'Casey in Totnes. Having written by now what O'Casey referred to as a suitcase full of letters, still apparently in love with this elderly man – or if not in love at least curious about him – yet in no way repenting the vow of chastity and total devotion to God she had finally taken, she arrived in the small Devon town and sought out his house, which was but two minutes' walk from the station. O'Casey was expecting her. But when he saw her coming up the drive and heard her ring the bell, he would not come to the door. Later, in tears, she telephoned the house, and Eileen had to make some excuse for him.

In 1954, when he wrote *The Bishop's Bonfire*, he based one of its main characters, Foorawn, on Miss Sheila. "*She has large blue eyes*," he wrote, "*brown hair that shows reddish gleams within it . . . A thin gold chain encircles her neck, its two ends meeting to hold up a red enamel cross on her breast . . . The men, whenever they pass her, lift their hats respectfully in tribute to her reputation for piety, and in reverence for the vow of perpetual chastity with which she has burdened herself . . .*" In Act I he wrote an exchange between Foorawn and her boyfriend in which the girl wants to hide away – a reversal, as was often true in O'Casey's plays, of the real situation.

Fortunately for him he had no such disillusioning an encounter with another object of his now increasing passion for correspondence. As he edged towards seventy, every nook and crevice of his mind filled up with this correspondence, so that he soon had a cosy Dublin of the head full of the same endless chatter, gossip, chance encounters, vain boastings and endless disputatiousness, mingled with inexhaustible memory, to make up for the absence of the real place. The new correspondent's name was Ingrid Burke, a nineteen-year-old aspiring actress who wrote him a fan letter in 1948; when he met her two years later, he found her, unlike Miss Sheila, a lot prettier than her letter. This time he warned that good looks were often a handicap because many men were so selfish!

Ingrid appeared to like Virginia Woolf, provoking a typical O'Casey swipe: "a fine writer, but vague, & unacquainted with life; frightened by it, I'm afraid" – possibly one of his better literary judgments, and the stronger for being short. Stephen Spender, too, came in for some stick: "His own is the 'skeleton walking in the wilderness of tinsel stars.' I may be prejudiced, for I have an uncontrollable loathing for Cissies." "Another of the Cissie philosophers, isn't he?" he called W. H. Auden. "Afraid of life, as almost all of them are." He was also forthcoming to Ingrid on the nature of marriage (she came from an unhappy family) in a paradoxically Catholic way:

> I am sorry to hear about your unhappy connection with divorce & the quarrels of your people. The worst of poverty isn't as evil as that sort of thing. I have seen numerous children made so unhappy by the unselfishness of parents desiring a change for the better which is, as often as not, a change for the worse. Divorce should be made more difficult, as it is in the USSR, where every effort is made to keep couples together for the sake of the children.

When Ingrid told him she was thinking of becoming a Catholic, with amazing restraint he praised English Catholics, whom he found tolerant and amiable in a "Protestant or pagan, if you like, country". But he could not, even so, leave the subject without a thrust at "horrible" François Mauriac or Graham Greene. And then, of course, Hitler was a Catholic, while Cardinal Griffin, primate of England, was "a trite fellow with a trite mind".

The same kind of intimacy developed with Ingrid as had with Sheila. Ingrid had a married man friend (Sheila had revealed no great rivals to the Church for her affections), who propositioned her with notions of free love. Contrary as ever, O'Casey adopted the reactionary position, defending what he had once deemed absurd – marriage – mindful, perhaps, that he and Eileen had been married for twenty-one years. Cold, heartless, and dangerous to his wife, he called the man. It could mean permanent injury: "If she has children already, it will mean she cannot give them the attention they need; &, if her psychological nature be injured, theirs will be hurt too . . ." He did not at all refrain from being personal.

> Your friend, knowing so much, seems to know nothing at all. "If a woman *knows* he loves her, she will not mind him having affairs with other women." And how does she *know*, how does she get

to *know* he loves her? Will he answer you that? Is a woman ever assured of a man's love for her?

He definitely did not believe in the free love which a number of writers in the USSR had preached long ago, until the people got sick of it and a healthy outlook "banished" it. The land, he claimed once again, where divorce was hardest to come by was Russia – and "where the desire for it was least". No, the pleasures of free love were illusory, and people who indulged themselves generally did so because, having money, they didn't know what to do with themselves.

There are, of course, instances of grand passion . . . of men loving women belonging (as the saying goes) to other men – Parnell, for instance – but these are rare, & often lovely; but the normal, healthy life is the man, the woman, & the child – three in one, & one in three. The millions live this way, & are useful, generally happy, & often great.

The man, the woman and the three children: the O'Caseys, too, were generally happy, although there was still a suggestion of the Parnell syndrome in their lives, with Eileen slipping away to London from time to time.

❖

Harold Macmillan had wanted to re-enlist in the Grenadier Guards at the beginning of the war, but, now in his mid-forties, held a government post instead, as resident Minister in North Africa. In early 1943, at Algiers airport, he escaped a fire in the plane he had boarded, but was badly burned; on recovering consciousness in hospital his first words were, "Tell my mother I'm alive and well." She had been dead for more than five years. O'Casey had told Macmillan's brother Daniel that he wished "Mr Harold" "wasn't quite so diffident in the midst of his talents. Both of you, if I may say so as a friend, seem to pull back your intelligent desires. It's hard for an intelligent mind to plunge forward. The duffers do allright."

Later in the war Macmillan established a virtual overlordship of the Mediterranean theatre of war: "viceroy by stealth", John Wyndham called him, and he had, among other unpleasant duties, to sort out the forced repatriation of White Russians who had fought alongside the Germans and the handing over of Yugoslavs to Tito's vengeful Partisans, in the certain knowledge, as he recorded in his diary, of what would befall them. "He might have been happier among the books," O'Casey had commented to Daniel Macmillan, unaware of Harold's problems: yet he would certainly have done as Macmillan had done. He always claimed Russia had no territorial ambitions.

As well as occasionally seeing Harold, Eileen went out to dinner in London with old friends such as the impresarios Sidney Bernstein and Lee Ephraim, who could supply seats for the theatre and give her a taste of her old life. Sometimes she would take two of the children, leaving one behind with Sean and their daily. She needed these breaks, which in no way detracted from her love and esteem for Sean.

Life in Totnes did not altogether suit her, but she put up with it bravely. At one particularly bad juncture her face swelled up, her neck disappeared and her hands became grotesquely fat: O'Casey said, "It's a terrible thing to have happened. But it's a strangely interesting face, rather like some of those in Aesop's fables." Breon drove her for treatment to Torquay; the doctor there told her later that she had had a nervous breakdown, and needed more gaiety. She took up old-time dancing for a while.

O'Casey would never accompany her when she went out, or up to London. She accepted that he lived in his own world, and did not blame him for it. He was visited often by American GIs who, in civilian life, had been connected with the theatre – one such was Nathan's friend Thomas Quinn Curtiss, who later became the drama critic of the *International Herald Tribune* – or who had taken courses in Irish literature. Elderly literary figures were soon to be in demand, as subjects for postwar American doctoral theses; and American university libraries would provide a welcome source of supplementary income as they began their exhaustive trawling for memorabilia. Some friends from O'Casey's Dublin visited: Jim Larkin, in August 1943, and Jack Carney, who helped Larkin edit the *Irish Worker*, and with whom O'Casey corresponded voluminously on socialist issues. But he missed other friends; the only contact he had with Shaw for many years was a packet of signed postcards for Breon to sell at Dartington Hall to make pocket money. O'Casey still kept his life-long pleasure in smoking, cigarettes now having given way for the most part to the pipe, in which he smoked a blend of thick twist, torn into shreds and left marinating in a jar under a moist cabbage leaf.

Prior to the war he had taken out Irish nationality for his children, presumably as a precaution if the Germans invaded England. Don't, Shaw told him midway through the war, bring up Breon "as that most despicable of all shams, a stage Irishman". Breon was born an Englishman, breathed English air and knew English people, "having Raleigh for his local hero. To him his dad must always be a funny sort of fellow, let us hope beloved and admired, but still a curiosity." O'Casey let the children's Irish nationality lapse.

Although Shaw and O'Casey did not meet again, their occasional correspondence was affectionate, especially in October 1943 when Charlotte Shaw died from *osteitis deformans*. A long and ingratiating letter written in 1945 to Shaw, asking if he could borrow two books to help Breon pass an exam, received no reply. Early in 1950 the Irish High Commissioner, John Dulanty, took Eileen along to see the ninety-three-year-old Shaw, who was ailing: Dulanty told O'Casey, "Herself and myself had a pleasant hour with Bernard Shaw, who greeted her with 'Well, Eileen, you've still got your good looks.' He was obviously glad to see her. (I wandered out of the room to give them the opportunity of a mild flirtation!) Amongst other things he talked to us, God help us, about his super super tax income poverty, and how but for an annuity which he bought years ago – 'the first time I came into money' – he would now be in Queer Street."

With her eye for the great historical moment, and her great fondness for and loyalty to Shaw, Eileen went back alone to see him several times in the last year of his life. He joked with her and gave her advice about the children. He enjoyed the visits and in May wrote to O'Casey:

My dear Sean,
Eileen, still lovely as ever, gave me a photograph of the lot of you which pleased me so much that I have had it framed and look at it quite often. Your marriage has been a eugenic success: the Heir Apparent is a stalwart who must count me as a Struldbrug which is what I actually look like. I keep my wits about me much better than my legs; that is the best I can say for myself.

Eileen was one of the last to see Shaw before he died in November 1950, aged ninety-four. She found him looking "woefully thin, but his humour hadn't abated, & his eyes gleamed as brightly as ever". In his stark room, relieved only by photographs of Gandhi, Stalin and himself, Shaw told her that O'Casey was "the luckiest of us all" because he had had freedom to play in the streets as a child and had experienced the warmth, as well as the deprivation, of working-class life: "I had a skivvy and a maid who used to leave me outside pubs: poor boys of my age humiliated me when I would have liked them to accept me." He told her that "if there's an Almighty, I'll have a helluva lot of questions to ask Him". Eileen said the two of them would get on very well. He made her stroke his forehead. She thought that he was back in imagination with his mother, wanting her comfort. It was wonderful, he murmured, to feel "the touch of a soft Irish h nd & hear the soft sound of an Irish voice". Perhaps his last words were "his love to the O'Caseys".

Shaw did not remember the O'Caseys in his will, although they were perhaps the only family towards whom he had consistently felt family-minded: he left the bulk of his money and royalties to an alphabetical reform which would have made him immortal, and to institutions which had helped him and would reflect glory upon him. Yet, as O'Casey wrote in his autobiography, "His epiphany was the showing forth of man to man. Man must be his own saviour; man must be his own god. Man must learn, not by prayer, but by experience. Advice from God was within ourselves, and nowhere else."

Shaw's relationship with O'Casey had been an uncomplicated one: linear, unbroken by quarrels, serviced by common targets and mutual admiration. O'Casey once challenged him, at a lunch at Lady Lavery's, about having to keep talking – brilliantly – all the time; he also decried Shaw's taste in painting: this was about the sum of his criticism. "It's up to Sean now," Shaw had told Eileen, "to carry on the fight," no longer recalling that O'Casey was himself now an old man of seventy. "Then it's up to one or both of the boys if their lives aren't wasted in another war." And the girl? One may question how deep an instinct feminism was, even in this most famous male champion of women's rights.

O'Casey was greatly offended later when Shaw's Ulster champion, St John Ervine, left out of his biography any mention of their friendship. He wrote a long, indignant letter emphasising their similarities and the bonds between them.

Eileen, too, received much praise from O'Casey. "I'm too used to you now to feel safe & comfortable without you," he wrote during one of her absences. "I feel rotten – a full-up feeling in my belly & a stronger sense of being by myself."

Eileen's mother, still addressed as "Mrs Reynolds" by O'Casey, was settled near by in a room in Paignton. Eileen would slip out of Tingrith, not telling Sean if he had fallen fast asleep, and drive over to see her.

Kathleen Reynolds complained peevishly about every aspect of her daughter's life, not least about Sean, and she continued her emotional blackmail over her real, or imagined ill-health. She also bombarded Eileen with letters, until one day O'Casey could stand it no more, and wrote to Sister Catherine, Eileen's cousin, a teaching nun at Maynooth College, who had become something of an arbiter in these family quarrels:

> You must have heard a lot about our imperfections, it's time you heard about those of Mrs Reynolds "Something from the inner side of the world" . . . I have often wondered how an intelligent woman like you failed to see through her pietistic pretences . . . Her life, according to herself, has been but a never-ending litany of woe . . . there hasn't a year passed that she isn't dying: that a few more weeks will see the end of her in that she is riddled with disease – cancer, arthritis, valvular disease of the heart, asthma, emphysema! . . . I never met before a woman who could manufacture complaint as readily and as glibly as Mrs Reynolds . . . Ever since I came across her, eighteen years ago, she has been dying at regular intervals.

He then quoted "at random" from some of her letters to her "Dearest Eily":

> [1942:]. . . My knees are so bad I cannot walk much. Would to God I was dead and out of it all. [1932:]. . . If you had seen the sister of the ward she would have told you how very ill I was, and am, and not fit to be worried. [1942:] Since Saturday my nose running and legs aching all over. I am not fit to be moving . . . [1935:] I am quite crippled with my arthritis. It is my neck arms and legs now . . . Things have gone to the devil in this house, no maids, and Mrs Burke is drunk at all hours. [1935:]. . . My throat is bad. Between that and my heart I feel very ill. Please send me some money as unless I have nourishment I will never get well. I wish I had a chicken as I cannot eat the dinners here. ["See, however bad her throat was she was ready to down a chicken," O'Casey interjected here.] [1933:] My heart is very bad again. I don't know how I am going to get through the moving job. It's no use people with bad hearts trying to do things . . . Have you any idea where the net curtains are. ["The 'awful pain' doesn't stop her from thinking of the net curtains," noted her son-in-law.]

O'Casey concluded his *tour de force* on Mrs Reynolds's comi-tragic condition by telling the good Sister that her prayers were needed far more for this idle and selfish woman than for the conscientious, hard-working Eileen. The beautiful examples he quoted of the processes of life never, alas, found their way into a play.

Indeed, as he wrote this letter he was finishing his next piece, *Oak Leaves and Lavender*, from which it appeared that he had his priorities wrong. O'Casey tried not only to do the impossible – namely, to render the average Englishman's speech – but also to deliver a tribute to his adopted land's behaviour during the Blitz. At its most propagandist the play shares both the method and the sentiment of Coward's film *In Which We Serve* and his *Cavalcade*: yet O'Casey lambasted the British High Command for its lack of imagination after the D-Day landings, and was also at work on the third book of his autobiography, *Drums Under the Windows*, in which the abuse of his adopted land reached its peak.

J. B. Priestley, reviewing the published version of *Oak Leaves and Lavender*, found that O'Casey

> has enlarged his method, heightened his manner, done more and more telescoping and symbolising, and piled on the rhetoric, to make up for the loss of all that Dublin flung into his lap, to show us what a Communist Celt of genius can do even with English life and character. Much of the drama has gone, and we are left with opera without the orchestra.

O'Casey got back at Priestley by calling him a "minor moper acting the part of a prophet in the wilderness". He sent Nathan's comment, "a fine play – far & away above any play on war he has encountered for years", to half a dozen of his correspondents. Much later G. Wilson Knight applauded the play's "eighteenth-century spirits and its extraordinarily skilful realisation of a society on the brink of death".

Bronson Albery elected to produce *Oak Leaves and Lavender*, but as a possible director O'Casey spurned Michael Redgrave: "Pity [he] was so conceited – it is a baneful thing in any man; worse in one with talent." He declined the outstanding abilities of Hugh Hunt, calling him "not an Irish producer, anyway". He scattered misjudgments like random machine-gun fire, over friend and foe alike.

Finally Ronald Kerr was found to direct *Oak Leaves and Lavender*: he visited O'Casey in Devon, where the playwright spotted at once, he said, that Kerr wasn't the right man to do the play, but hadn't the courage to tell him so. An odd fellow, O'Casey found him, "one who could keep talking for hours without saying a single thing". O'Casey ventured out of Devon to see the play at Eastbourne before its London première at the Lyric Theatre, Hammersmith, in May 1947; he found it "a frightened thing, apologising for its appearance on the stage". Later, when he recalled it, "his heart's blood pressed into his head, and all the world became red". Yet Bronson Albery had clapped Kerr "on the back continually". Later Kerr committed suicide: O'Casey's parting shot was more in the vein of Marston than of Boucicault: "The fellow's gone now, making his exit by way of a gas-oven, giving in a kitchen a better production than he ever gave on a stage."

O'Casey afterwards owned to Breon that the play was a failure: "Even today, I leave behind me the failure of *Oak Leaves and Lavender*, having learned a lot from it, which I hope may serve me in the future." The defeat created medical problems: an X-ray of his chest showed, he told Daniel Macmillan, "the lungs scarred from silicosis", which in turn had caused the occasional pneumonic trouble. "This (they say) has wrenched the heart a little from its right place." Yet royalties from a growing number of overseas productions were on the increase, and they had changed the Morris for a Ford. "I don't get into it often."

18

DIVORCE, IRISH-STYLE

"It's hard enough to write, or try to write, one's own life, but to do justice, or injustice, to another's, is harder still," O'Casey told Lennox Robinson, who had served him faithfully as friend and enemy, when Robinson attempted to write Lady Gregory's life, an idea he abandoned later in favour of editing her journals. O'Casey in his own autobiography showed fewer and fewer qualms about the deliberate injustice done to the lives of others as he waded deeper into controversial times and areas, with the third volume, *Drums Under the Windows*, published in October 1945.

When informed that a book club wanted to distribute an edition of *I Knock at the Door* O'Casey had taken a swipe at Gollancz's Left Book Club: "I hated his vulgar, cheap-looking editions, without the least semblance of taste on cover or contents." He was frankly amazed at the good sale of *Drums* – Macmillans had 8,300 copies in print – especially as he had felt less confident in it than in the previous volumes, but happy at the money. He was now better off than he had been for ten years, despite turning down the whopping offer, of as much as $100,000, to write a screenplay of Thomas Wolfe's *Look Homeward, Angel* for David O. Selznick in Hollywood.

But if the public responded warmly to *Drums Under the Windows*, so that it quickly sold out, the critics, on both sides of the Irish Sea, treated O'Casey with the usual roughness and affection. Both the previous volumes had been banned in Ireland by the Censorship of Publications Board, for their atheism and gross immorality; *Drums* was passed, however, which led to a memorable review of all three by Padraic Colum, in *Irish Writing*:

These memoirs show Sean O'Casey as a great writer who is prone to a great fault: the fault is wilfulness; it is shown not only in the unconventional incidents and expressions which he makes use of, but in an abandonment to his own issues and his own idiom. Take the first chapter in *Pictures in the Hallway*, the description of the death of Parnell as it affects Johnny's family: it begins magnificently, goes on memorably, and then we come to lose patience because we think the writer isn't going to hold back from saying anything that comes into his head.

The main damaging influence was that of James Joyce: Colum could not bear O'Casey when he "plays Jeff to Joyce's Mutt".

Sean O'Faolain endorsed this view in his own publication, *The Bell*: whenever O'Casey "deals with the intimate, private material he can be moving, terrifying and sensible," he said; "but whenever he comes up against anything that is superficially exciting or violent, such as one of those big public things,"

he races off into pages of rhodomontade, noisy rhetoric, embarrassing jocularities, heavy-handed satire, the most naïve kind of Joyceisms ("Dominus woebuscums", "the Rebubblicans", "all bankum", "crowds of queerternions", "Mutt Talbot", "quiet as a none breathless with mad oration", "their dustiny") and into bad English.

O'Faolain accused O'Casey of carelessness and of not working over his copy enough: "arrogant and presumptuous", he called his attitude. Because, O'Faolain continued, a man had literary talent, it did not follow he had political judgment: Shaw had both, but Voltaire only the latter. O'Casey should have stuck more to literature.

Certainly it was true that neither Macmillan brother dared exercise editorial control over O'Casey (beyond Harold's advice to him to employ more commas), although they took pains over avoiding any possibility of libel in the books. O'Casey assured them that many of the passages queried had no likelihood of being read by those they concerned: that the persons mentioned were dead, that such-and-such a story was common knowledge, or, in one case, that "the 'doctor' here described never existed. He is purely a phantom of my imagination, as is most of the chapter." Clearly the publishers were not all that deeply bothered about O'Casey's methods or intentions. They certainly never challenged him in the way Yeats and Lady Gregory did with his early plays.

O'Casey, "creative and careless alike to the point of wantonness", O'Faolain summed up, left an impression of those troubled years of Irish history "as if one entered a smoky cabin and, dimly, by the flicker of a smothered fire, caught glimpses of history from the half-seen figure and mumbled speech of some old angry prophet by the hearth". Yet he conceded that the description in *Drums Under the Windows* of the first appearance of the flag of the Plough and the Stars should be in every Irish schoolbook and prose anthology.

Reviews of the first three books published in England produced significant casualties among erstwhile friends and champions. Gogarty, for example, wrote a deeply appreciative and perceptive review for *The Observer*, calling *I Knock at the Door* "powerful and unsparing", "capable and terrible", "strange and original writing", but because he expressed some unease at the whole autobiographical procedure, and stated that it seemed O'Casey "has, after all the unsurpassable hilarity of his plays, a grudge against life", O'Casey took umbrage – in the usual form of a letter, which *The Observer* refused to print.

St John Ervine, in *The Spectator*, called *Drums Under the Windows* manifestly fiction. "As a bitter invention, the book is entertaining. As an account of events, it is nonsense." As for its hero, during the troubled times of revolution and its aftermath, "we are left with the impression of very few good men on this earth, Mr O'Casey being about the best of the lot." For the style, however, Ervine reserved his most damning stricture, calling it "a mixture of Jimmy O'Dea and Tommy Handley". Far from professing himself flattered, as P. G. Wodehouse had once done when O'Casey tried to insult him by calling him "English Literature's performing flea" ("all the performing fleas I have met have impressed me with their sterling artistry and that indefinable something which makes the good trouper"), O'Casey defended at length, in a letter that was for once published, the factual content of *Drums*. This provoked Ervine's retort: "One of Mr O'Casey's most dangerous delusions is that he thinks. He does not think, he never has thought, cannot think: he can only splash about in his emotions." O'Casey's last word was calculated to make an Ulsterman twitch with rage: "The fact is, I think, that Mr Ervine hates the Irish."

All this was good knockabout stuff in the now hallowed tradition of a new O'Casey *œuvre*. But George Orwell's celebrated review of *Drums Under the Windows* in *The Observer* hit a good deal harder and hurt much deeper. Orwell had little humour (least of all about himself); he had no taste for the emotional volatility of Irishmen; he could not see that O'Casey's nationalism as expressed in the book was very much a two-edged sword – often not even cutting, just sending itself up. He addressed it with deadly seriousness. Pointing out that *Drums* contained "no reference to England which is not hostile or contemptuous", he proceeded to say that O'Casey sank to the "worst extremes of jingoism and racialism" when he wrote "Cathleen, the daughter of Houlihan, walks firm now, a flush on her haughty cheek." This passage, of course, was meant to be ironical.

Orwell expressed extreme dislike of O'Casey's writing in the third person, "which gives an unbearable effect of narcissism". Why are there, he asked – and he might have been putting the question as much to O'Casey's publishers as to the public which in its postwar, anti-Empire frame of mind applauded the book – "Irishmen whose life-work is abusing England", who are "able to look to the English public for support"? They even, "like Mr O'Casey himself, prefer to live in the country which is the object of their hatred", where they remain "almost immune from criticism".

O'Casey's letter to *The Observer* in reply was once again refused publication. In it he heaped scorn on Orwell's charge that Irish writers in England enjoyed special status; he paid his taxes, he said; moreover his Irish nationalism was completely misunderstood by Orwell. "Orwell's freedom of thought!" he commented sourly upon hearing that his letter was not to appear.

Later, in the last volume of autobiography, published in 1954, four years after Orwell's death, he took his revenge by putting the blame for the bad review on his own refusal to provide a puff for the jacket of Orwell's novel *The Clergyman's Daughter* in 1935. Orwell's publishers, Gollancz, had then, according to O'Casey, compared one scene in the novel, set in Trafalgar Square, to Joyce: O'Casey retaliated at the time (or so he said) that Orwell "had as much chance of reaching the stature of Joyce as a tit has of reaching that of an eagle". He also condemned Orwell's "Doomsday Book", *1984*, as "the decay in himself . . . transmuted into the life of the whole world . . . self-pity, wrapped sourly up in yearned revenge".

Perhaps he resented in Orwell that capacity for honest disillusionment with causes which he had once possessed himself, but upon leaving Ireland had lost. Anyway, there was no reason to believe that Orwell even knew about O'Casey's refusal to write a puff. O'Casey, and many critics and followers sharing his cast of mind, sometimes seemed unable to believe there was such a thing as a valid, honest judgment not tied to some ulterior purpose – unless, of course, that judgment was whole-hearted praise.

But paranoia, a symptom perhaps of something unfinished in the human personality trying to work itself out, never came to dominate O'Casey: as Eileen admonished R. M. Fox, who asked her, in 1955, out of his early knowledge of O'Casey in Dublin, "Is Sean as bitter as ever?" – "How can a man with a soft voice like that, be bitter?" "Indeed," O'Casey admitted to his Harvard friend, Horace Reynolds, in 1949, "it is the reviews that 'go for me' that I linger over, and love."

------◆◆◆------

Paranoia was but one weapon in a large armoury at O'Casey's disposal: he kept it in place, but always made sure that it did not grow rusty out of disuse, building up danger for himself and his family, as so often happened in the case of other writers, especially Irish. If Orwell thought his denunciation of England from the privileged position of a Macmillan author was unfair, this was nothing to the *saeva indignatio* towards Ireland expressed in the fourth volume of autobiography which he wrote during 1945 and 1946 and which was published in early 1948.

Innishfallen Fare Thee Well did not sell nearly as well as *Drums*; there was, O'Casey told his friends, a slump in the book business. But it also suffers, to an increased degree, from the faults of the three previous books. There are still magnificent set-pieces, coloured with the melodramatic tricks he had learned from Boucicault, such as his account of the raid on 35 Mountjoy Square. He chillingly depicts some of the more sinister episodes after the end of the civil war – re-using the material of the early Dublin plays, but vividly handled and with dialogue that has lost none of its earthiness or bite. The travelogue of his visit to Coole, with its affectionate character sketch of Lady Gregory, is also a highlight of this volume. But the most celebrated chapter, and justly so, is "Mrs Casside Takes a Holiday" (a play on the title *Death Takes a Holiday*, by Walter Ferris), an account of his mother's last days when she was dying from Spanish flu towards the end of the First World War. That a man in his late sixties could write so simply and movingly of his mother, who had died nearly thirty years before, showed not only how the power of the love she gave him had lasted, but how central a force of literary inspiration it still was. This was a gift that few men or women in this world, for all their privilege and success, had ever received. But O'Casey alone, in his family, had received it; he did not acknowledge Susan Casey's possible shortcomings where his brothers and sister were concerned. Had they been successful, would he have praised the system? More likely his mother.

Mick Casey died in Dublin in January 1947, at the age of eighty-one. The brothers had communicated once or twice before his death, and O'Casey still sent him the odd quid, but not the clothes he asked for: "Strange and all as it may sound," he told him in 1945, "I am wearing the eldest boy's coat and trousers which became too small for him – he's just six feet two. Both the missus and I have to give all the clothing coupons to the children – three of them, and even then these aren't enough."

In his last years Mick had become a well-known Dublin character, strutting around the cattleyards with a walking stick which he carried like a field marshal's baton, or frequenting the North Wall pubs where he made sketches of customers and gave them the finished works. He had read the first three books of his brother's autobiography: "The other fella," he commented, "you have to hand it to him."

When Harold Macmillan (having now returned to publishing during the postwar period when the Conservatives were in opposition) wrote to ask O'Casey if Mick would object to the passage in *Innishfallen Fare Thee Well* which showed him as a violent drunkard, O'Casey informed Macmillan of his death. Mick would not, anyway, have taken legal action, he said, because he would never have read the book. "He never read a line I wrote." But not only did Mick read his brother's work, O'Casey's other relatives subsequently and vehemently denied the truth of O'Casey's portrait of him.

"To be fair to myself" (O'Casey went on to Macmillan), "I may say we were friendly after separation. When he was down and I was up (in a job), I helped him to many a bit of tobacco and many a drink; and when I came to Eng., I sent him many a quid, finally paying the funeral expenses." The truth about the funeral is that O'Casey's niece, Isabella Murphy, with whom Mick had lived in Beaumont during his last eight years, paid the expenses out of her own pocket. O'Casey as next of kin received the insurance Michael had taken out and reimbursed his niece.

The Irish, left behind to live their lives in Ireland, quite naturally did not approve of O'Casey's valedictory volume: it is surprising that he should have expected them to. While one English critic, at least, approved – Desmond MacCarthy wrote that "Personally I love the superb but today despised Art of Rhetoric; and I can figure O'Casey even when he continues intoxicated with his own . . . I wait patiently for the phrase which will be final and quick as a blow – and I am seldom disappointed" – Dublin responded much less kindly. Sean O'Faolain (in fact reviewing the published version of *Red Roses for Me*) caught exactly what departure from Dublin had meant to him:

It was not the beauty of Dublin but the filth of Dublin that nourished O'Casey. He had flourished on its poverty. His passion flamed in its damp and chill . . . He had got a lift, in some mysterious way, out of the dull exasperation of his native city. His gall-sac had fattened on its fungus . . . Gauguin, who went into exile among the yellow Polynesians in Tahiti, never got more excitation than O'Casey got out of the yellow tuberculars of North Dublin. Whatever disillusion came over us this did not cease. The more we rotted the more incense there was to our foetor. Mollser is always with us.

More specifically with regard to *Innishfallen Fare Thee Well*, P. S. O'Hegarty wrote:

The four volumes have shown a progressive decline in interest . . . He can have Big Ben, and the lights of London, and the Red Flag – he is curiously irritated about the Red Flag and the refusal of Irishmen to adopt it as their flag – and we will keep the three plays. And we shall always have a corner in our hearts, not for the man he thinks he is, nor for the man he would like to be, but the man he was.

Like the marooned city of Berlin which figured so largely in the news in the post Second World War period, O'Casey's soul was now neatly divided between East and West. America held his undying allegiance, for, at a tolerable distance – and during the rest of his life – it made an increasing fuss of him. It was always the new land, the land of golden opportunity: of material opportunity as enshrined in its huge buildings of commerce and trade which dwarfed the stifling spiritual temples that suffocated his native Ireland.

At the same time Russia was the land of the future, because inevitably, as he constantly told his friends in Moscow, communism – in his own very loose and all-embracing definition of it – would win. O'Hegarty was right: he did recommend that Ireland should join the Soviet bloc. This optimism about the future, joined to a past full of privation and struggle – and he made sure that was never forgotten – endowed his rebelliousness with a saintly quality, and caused him to become an object of pilgrimage in his later years. It was yet another irony, or paradox, of his longevity that he should assume the miraculous attributes of the religious effigies he so knocked and despised in his plays.

But he did. The stream of visitors to the O'Casey house in Totnes thickened as postwar affluence grew. Ria Mooney, the Irish actress and director, noticed the "intangible middle-class atmosphere" as they sat down to high tea. It was hardly surprising that visitors from the States, which had forty million citizens of Irish descent and from which ninety per cent of O'Casey's expanding income came in his old age, should outnumber the Russians. One could view them as a religious procession, to adopt the metaphor employed so frequently in the autobiography, with a saint-like Johnny Cassidy encountering persecutors and redeemers, oppressors and victims. These dignitaries from both East and West who journeyed to Totnes all reflected the new, non-spiritual culture that came increasingly to dominate the late 1950s and the 1960s. Joined as they were in the bond of utilitarian materialism, was there anything to choose between a CBS programme director and the Soviet cultural attaché?

Honours and accolades caught up with O'Casey, although he continued to spurn them as much as he could: offered an honorary doctorate by Trinity College, Dublin, he mused, "Sean O'Casey, Litt.D.! No, Sir, this would never do. I am a wandering minstrel singing his share of songs at the corners of occasional streets: such I was, such I am, and such I shall die!" He refused a CBE from Harold Macmillan in November 1962 on the grounds that "such an honour would not be suitable for my nature or feeling".

Boris Izakov, the editor of *Sovietskaya Kultura*, on his visit to Devon, voiced the objection that the principal characters of O'Casey's plays were depicted with too great a realism and were "unattractive and unheroic". "The Soviet theatre could not reconcile itself to something so contradictory." O'Casey fixed him: "I like them just as they are." But it did not occur to him that he might not have liked the Russian workers and soldiers of the Red Army whom he so often upheld as paragons just as they were. Later he told another visitor, the Indian Saros Cowasjee, "Russia is not Communist. It will take another 60 years before it goes Communist. Your India may take as much as 150 years." At another time he told the *Life* magazine photographer, Gjon Mili, that he had no illusions about his fate had he lived in Russia: "I should be put against the wall and shot." At still another time he boasted he was a "hero over in Russia, because they never stop tellin' me, but I don't go out of my way to say particularly nice things about them."

He embarrassed correspondents everywhere by stamping on the back of his envelopes "Friends of the Soviet Union". Yet he exclaimed elsewhere, "I wish our Communists would write better than they do, or stop writing altogether." Like a great actor adept at playing himself, the largest character he ever created, he could now give many different performances of "Sean O'Casey". He stuck to main themes, but within these there were rich variations – including complete contradictions.

In the last two volumes of his autobiography, *Rose and Crown*, published in 1952, and *Sunset and Evening Star*, 1954, he sank to his nadir of literary infighting. *Sunset and Evening Star* even included chunks of his correspondence refused publication in *The Observer*, in reply to a review by Louis MacNeice of *Rose and Crown*. Both volumes are marred by his increasing need to pay off old scores, and both lack the brilliant sketches that gave the earlier instalments their distinction. As he told Ria Mooney, "When I take a pen into my hand something comes over me and I can't help being bitter, even when I write letters."

Letters, typed copies of which he now kept, were also the basis of the last two volumes, and much of the heavily condemned Joycean fantasy had vanished. "When afterwards I read his letters I felt that he was very unhappy and that he seemed to have changed," commented Dr John Larchet ("Larky"), who remembered O'Casey sitting in the Abbey stalls with Lady Gregory listening to the orchestral selections in order to choose the right ones to go with his plays. "Summing up I would say that he was unfair to those three, Yeats, Lady Gregory, and Robinson, to have forgotten what the Abbey did for him." A major chapter of *Rose and Crown* covered what the Abbey, by rejecting *The Silver Tassie*, didn't do for him.

The freshest observation and the most entertaining chapters are those covering his trip to America in 1934. In "Wild Life in New Amsterdam", he describes a dinner party at which guests are shown a photograph of the spurious hunting exploit of a rich man's son, who had, in the most expensively cosseted circumstances, killed a tiger. O'Casey reveals in this scene the sham at the centre of the American dream: an emotion of glory so much in excess of any real achievement: "Sick with ecstasy at others getting to know of his astonishing achievement. Hardly able to eat, so full of himself."

O'Casey finds for this deception a rare and perfect image – true both for the boy's mother and for the process which had resulted in the best of his own writing: "The mother seeing the sham in her heart, silvering it over, as the oyster iridescently nacres an irritation, with a sham of her own, accepting the myth, and decorating it with gravity and praise." In this chapter, and in those which precede and follow it, O'Casey is back doing what he is best at, showing the processes of life. He then concedes that "Wealth often takes away chances from men as well as poverty."

In *Sunset and Evening Star* the immediacy, even that of a new trip, has cooled. A visit to Cambridge, undertaken to deliver a talk to undergraduates, is swamped in pontification about the shortcomings of a university education, highlighted by the starkness of living conditions at St John's College. It seemed that O'Casey was appreciating more and more that the rich, and their children, were on the whole as much deprived as, if not more than, the poor, who had at least the compensation of family warmth and emotion.

Writing now more from memory than from observation and from the heart, O'Casey had become too much the victim of his own image, the "blaster and blighter", the crow, "more intelligent than most birds" but raucous, and now, as he said, "old and hoarse". Easily stirred as a controversialist who trades on his own all too palpable scars to score points in a debate, yet will hit out mercilessly at deficiencies in his enemies, O'Casey in these last volumes shows little of the compassion that marks his plays. The rhetoric of politics settles in a highly coloured mist over everything he praises or blames.

And, not unnaturally, given his own practice, he views the literary world – in particular the Irish literary world – as a nasty place: "In a society firmly based on the principle that 'what goes up must come down', everyone waits maliciously with beady eyes cocked for the collapse of the next victim."

19

TH' GENTLE RIPPLE OF A ROSE

When the last volume of autobiography was being printed in 1954 O'Casey moved, for the last time, to hilltop St Marychurch, a blowy, upper-middle-class suburb of Torquay which faced directly down to Babbacombe beach.

At first Eileen hoped that the landlord's notice to quit, after sixteen years in Totnes, would mean they would move nearer to London, where Niall was to become a student at the LSE and Breon was already a pupil at the St Martin's School of Art, having just finished his military service as a lance-bombardier in Germany. The winter before had been particularly hard; the cold-water tank on the roof burst and flooded the house, and Eileen had then broken her wrist. O'Casey confronted the disruption cheerfully, as an old man of seventy-four who had "no financial reserves, & so must try to keep going for there's five and half of us – five of ourselves & Eileen's mother".

But Shivaun was still at Dartington Hall, and refused to become a full-time boarder, so they were forced to remain in the vicinity. They chose a second-floor – or first-floor, depending from which side one viewed the house – flat in the imposing Villa Rosa, in Trumlands Road, which meant, he said, "half our present space & three times the rent". He must anyway have fancied Torquay, writing in 1946 that she was hidden to the east of Totnes, "stretching herself languorously to be fondled by a soothing sea"; prophetically he continued, "A place where many are old, some sick and resentful, trying to hear the stirring sound of the Reveille in the mournful notes of the Last Post". He did not seem much perturbed by his continued exploitation by landlords. "Remember," he told a friend when informing him of his change of address, "all the Bourgeoise [sic] aren't villains; often a damn sight more charming & interesting than those who are no more than peripathetic Communist pamphlets." Two huge adjacent churches built in local stone dominated the skyline outside the walls and cedars of the Villa Rosa garden: the Protestant church of St

Mary Virgin – like St Barnabas – and, slightly lower down, the O'Toole-like mass of the Catholic church of Our Lady of Help. Two sombre Dublin images side by side.

Eileen has given a comprehensive picture of O'Casey's routine at Torquay. He rose at nine a.m. and he and Eileen read their letters, settling together what to reply. He still received all the Dublin papers by post. During the morning he relaxed, maybe went for a walk; sometimes he might type – or, if working on a play, he would sing. After lunch he rested, mostly for the sake of his deteriorating eyesight – the threat of total blindness increased with old age, his right eye under added strain as his left eye lost virtually all its vision – then around five p.m. he would seriously start work at his typewriter and continue working all evening. Sometimes, however, he would watch TV – he liked sport most, or nature programmes – or listen to music (his preferences were Mozart, Mendelssohn and Haydn). He drank, according to Shivaun, enormous amounts of tea, sweetened with six or seven spoonfuls of sugar per cup.

His way of working, as always, was slow. He still wrote in school exercise books in minute handwriting, and would then copy on the typewriter, then revise – writing out drafts in longhand over and over again – finally making a fair copy on a typewriter. He might still, if the mood and inspiration held, work on well into the night. As in his youth in Abercorn Road, he was marvellously self-sufficient: to meet someone, "You'd never get him as far as the garden gate," commented Eileen. He had one holiday during his last years, when he and Eileen went to Salisbury and put up at the Red Lion Hotel for a fortnight, although he no longer, according to his diary, found the cathedral awe-inspiring. Hugh MacDiarmid persuaded him to visit Scotland in 1953 for Sam Wanamaker's touring production of *Purple Dust*, which opened in Glasgow but disappointingly never came to London. During a rehearsal at the Princes Theatre, Edinburgh, O'Casey met Charles Chaplin and they discussed a possible film based on *Purple Dust*. The play had to wait until 1966 to have full justice done to its "joyous blarney" – by the Berliner Ensemble in East Berlin. A trip to Stratford was the only other recorded absence from Devon, and there he was most adamant about not visiting the Shakespeare Memorial Theatre. Breon said, "He didn't really like the theatre or theatre people; he hated rehearsals of plays." He boasted in one letter of not having been in a theatre for twenty-six years. He was good at tying up parcels, but used to embarrass his family when they went out together for a meal by insisting on leaving a small, out-of-date tip like sixpence.

During his reflective hours, sitting on the shallow concrete balcony outside his front door, he would watch the poplars, white and glistening, the dark cypresses, or the pod-laden laburnums at the end of the garden – a small one, "19 paces long, 10 wide". Next door were chestnut trees, while tall firs stood not far distant; to the north lay hills covered with thick woods, to the east a glimpse of the sea. Sometimes one of his children would join him, and if it was spring they would discuss the three or four purple crocuses flowering in the grass of the tiny lawn, or the clumps of saffron ones along the flower bed running to the gate. In summer he would sit among the flowers wearing one of his coloured caps from a collection begun by Shivaun, perhaps the fez from Persia, or "a gay sparkling one from India, a brilliant crimson cap with a big peak worn by the American lorry-driver", or "a blue-black cap, red button on top, red peak, and a big red K to its front" sent him by the Chancellor of the University of Kansas.

His wonder at the flowers was kept so alive that with the sunflowers particularly in mind he thought of writing a play about Van Gogh. Twenty years earlier he had heard Irving Stone, at the New York Women's Club, "fashioning Van Gogh into life again; that odd, strange man who gave an old chair an honoured place in the universe . . . gave to roses the whiteness of priestly hands breaking the sacred bread". Van Gogh had always been one of his preferred painters, he had argued his qualities, together with those of Goya, many years before in Dublin with Joe Cummins, who was more keen on Fragonard and Boucher. Then someone sent him a play called *Vincent*, and he abandoned the idea.

But O'Casey wasn't a countryman so much as a small-town man with a penchant for municipal gardens. Battersea and Totnes supplied this need, but St Marychurch not. Here, as in Chalfont St Giles, he had to make do with the churchyard – of St Mary Virgin – where he would think about those lying buried beneath their fading headstones, with no room for more; "the yard was fat with graves that had shut up the days" of their occupants.

Although, as he said, a slight sadness came over him in the graveyard, "but no chill", he had a great deal of suffering to endure in 1956, when he had just turned seventy-five. The first New York production of *Red Roses for Me*, for which he had made revisions and added new scenes in the second half of the play, flopped at Broadway's Booth Theatre after a month. Then he had to have two major operations, one for prostate and the other for a kidney stone, with only a month between them, followed by a post-operative infection, then pneumonia. A girl in Dublin sent him a "Miraculous Medal", but the "dangling charm", as she called it, was hardly his brand of cure.

Just after their wedding anniversary, towards the end of September, when Eileen had left him to go to London to settle Niall in for a new term at LSE, O'Casey wrote to her, "I thought a lot of sending you a few flowers on the 23rd but was too shy to do anything about it, but you know how I love you." He added that Mrs Reynolds was telling Breon that "one of her heart valves is leaking".

Niall, who had turned twenty-one that January, had been a year at LSE. He had been demobbed from his national service in October 1955, after serving, like Breon, in the Royal Artillery in Germany. His subject was biology, but like his father he was passionately interested in politics. He was also a keen jazz trombonist, but his playing was frowned on by the neighbours. Though he had been popular at school, Dartington Hall had not prepared him for life in the way it had Breon; and compared to his brother he was highly strung: "When in a cricket match or taking part in a play," said his mother, "he'd get into a state of nerves and he also had migraines which the excitement made worse." "A brilliant mind, a sardonic if somewhat sarcastic sense of humour . . . a great talker," commented his father. He had his father's intellectual gifts, his mother's insta-bility.

The tensions of 1956 put a strain on Niall. First there was his father's serious illness, which forced him to travel back at weekends from London in his little emerald-green Ford van. In June came the Anglo-French invasion of Suez, a move to forestall the nationalisation of the canal by Nasser and in support of Israel, which aroused political passions everywhere – not least among students at LSE, who staged a demonstration which looked, at one stage, as if it might become violent.

Hard on the heels of that débâcle, over which father and son were united in opinion, there followed the Soviet invasion of Hungary. This caused deep divisions in the British Communist Party but also strife between father and son. Niall, as a committed left-winger, was miserably upset by the new, or imperialist, face of Russia suddenly revealed by this action. They argued hotly, O'Casey becoming "strangely stubborn and hard", insisting that anyone who was against Soviet authority should be shot. Meals at the Villa Rosa were eaten in stony silence. No one knew quite what went on in Niall's heart, but there must have been a deep conflict between his love for his father, the man of gentle nature who had told him so many colourful stories when he was young, read him the whole of *Moby Dick*, acting out the parts in different voices, or drawn for him daily strip cartoons, and the authoritarian who defended what all but a handful of Soviet sympathisers saw as a deeply inhuman and murderous response.

In cooler tones, when he was back in London, Niall wrote his father (16 November) about the "Old Guard" in the party who favoured the invasion:

> Dear Daddy
> I hope you find the enclosed press cuttings of interest from today's *Daily Worker*. The Old Guard is having quite a tough time at present. Resignations on the staff [of the *Worker*] include Malcolm MacEwan, "Gabriel", Philip Bolsover; on the verge are many others, including Sheila Lynd. The attitude of the executive over Hungary on many matters has been quite untenable. One can imagine the mistakes that have been made in Eastern Europe as being the same here, as if the Soviet Union had liberated us from Hitler, and had set up J. R. Campbell & his gang as Government. This isn't Communism at all. The "double-think" reminds me of Captain Waterhouse.
>
> Love,
> NIALL

His father did not bend an inch towards him, no doubt noting with disfavour the use of his enemy Orwell's coinage "double-think", inconceivable in his view of communism. Even though – according to Breon – Niall was his "favourite", O'Casey did not see that what distressed his son more than the invasion itself was his own support of it.

"He hides the distress under the careless scorn of his letter-writing," O'Casey wrote later in a comment at the foot of the letter. He consoled himself that the boy had little experience of war, at first hand or even second hand, while he

over a long life had known the Boer War, the First World War, the Easter Rising in Ireland, the Black and Tan terror, the Irish Civil War, and then the terrible strife let loose by Hitler, not forgetting the Western refusal to open its eyes to what Hitler did in Spain, leading to the first growth of his gigantic egomania that finally slew five million Jews, and sent to the grave many millions of old and young in almost every country in Europe, in a vast and deep attempt to make himself the Lord of Creation and stamp out the power of Socialism, fully grown in the USSR and bud-ripening in many other countries.

He [Niall] did not, and could not, see the implications of having such proud and ignorant and narrow-minded "gets" as Mindszenty, head of Hungary, Prince Primate; and Niall had never read what the Prince Primate had been in Hungary or what he could be as dictator of the country. But his hot and honest opinions, put out without hesitation, were at any rate a tribute to his home where, at all times, in every circumstance, free thought was the genre of our family life.

Clearly O'Casey suffered no guilt about the next argument they had when, two weeks later, the drawn and worried Niall came down from London to discuss it further. They ended, though disagreeing, said O'Casey, "by my putting my arms around him and looking at his face which was full of eagerness and honesty and sorrow". Neither his father nor mother – who was on Niall's side – noticed that this face was full, too, of illness. But he returned a second time to London.

Two weeks later Niall came home again for the Christmas holidays. He seemed unusually tired, and his mother thought he had, in addition to motoring home to Devon, been staying up too late playing in his band. Eileen called a doctor, and that doctor summoned a specialist, while Niall stayed in his room playing records. The specialist's confirmation of the diagnosis was swift. Niall had leukaemia. The same night he was taken to Exeter Hospital. Christmas Day, 1956, was the last time O'Casey saw Niall:

When I went to where he lay in bed, and kissed him with a kiss of love, I heard him murmur "It's hellish" in answer to my cry of my dearest, my beloved boy; no more; never again did he murmur a simple complaint; no cry of resentment; but suffered all patiently: the blood transfusions; the choking up of the voice passage, the terrible periods of icy coldness and burning heats; talking calmly and rapidly when drugs released his voice; of Hungary; of friends; and the coming Youth Festival in Moscow, for he had planned to go there.

Eileen and Breon accompanied Niall on his last journey to St Bartholomew's Hospital in London for specialised treatment. Once a bitter word escaped him, when he tried to get out of bed and Breon told him not to: "It's all very well for you. It is I who have to die and not you." Shivaun stayed behind with her father to do the cooking, while O'Casey prepared the breakfast and did the washing up. "It is hardest on you," he wrote to Eileen, staying at the Strand Palace Hotel. She did not leave her son's side until, a few days later, it was all over. He was cremated at Golders Green Cemetery in North London, where both the Shaws had been cremated.

"And the political bastards still go on with their atom-bomb tests, assuring the spread of this curse into every home, if their murderous madness isn't stopped." Childhood deaths from leukaemia had gone up by eighty-six per cent since 1938, while 2,224 had died of it in 1955, O'Casey found in a *Times* report. But this was little consolation. There was no consolation.

O'Casey continued for years to mourn his son's death. Daily he poured out his grief in words: religion was no help; a costume sewn with miraculous medals couldn't keep his beloved boy alive another hour, he railed. He wished he could swap his young son's vigorous life for his own stooped shoulders, bald head, dimming eyes and "gnarling" face. Where do the dead go? he asked at another time. "Does Mozart compose great melodies? Does Bernard Shaw write plays? Does Lady Gregory watch over her dear Willy Yeats?" He watched each spring pass into summer and wondered why his own son had not had the chance to make the same passage. He noted the date Niall would have become a full-fledged biologist – "and a handsome one, too". He dreamed of him.

He was lying in a sloping way in a bed, so that as one sat on the bed's side, my face was close to his, without need of bending. Shivaun looking the age of 6 or 7, sat on the opposite side, eating an apple.

Niall's face was not the bright and eager face I knew so well; it was paler, and the eagerness had given way to a shadow of quietness.

I clasped a hand of his in mine, and he enclosed it tightly and lovingly, I think, in both of his. He held his hands around mine so, and was silent.

– Darling, your hand is cold, I said.

– I am cold, he said, clasping my enclosed hand more closely, and said no more.

O'Casey compared himself to the Soviet Ambassador Jakob Malik whose twenty-four-hour-old infant son died in London in July 1958 and whom he took back to Mother Russia in a tiny coffin. He looked for Niall to be over his shoulder and give him advice when the *Komsomolskaya Pravda* asked for an article addressing the youth of the Soviet Union on the anniversary of the October Revolution. His grief hardly weakened for years, with every week surrounded by "a black border", passing uninterrupted through Christmases when "a shoal of gay cards came floating in . . . most from friends in the U.S.A.", through to his eightieth birthday celebrations when he was sent a beautiful bunch of eighty red roses ("Niall you went wearing a tiny nosegay of but 21"). He called out many a time, "Oh, God to think of it; I buried a Father when I was a little boy, and a Son when I was an old, old man."

He battled for a quiet eightieth, refusing to give interviews to *The Observer*, the *New York Times*, a lunch offer by Macmillans. In America Ed Sullivan had been going to include in his TV show on St Patrick's Day night a portion of a filmed conversation between Barry Fitzgerald and O'Casey. It had originally been part of the film *Cradle of Genius*, directed by Paul Rotha, called by O'Casey "a very dull tribute to the Abbey Theatre which those who paid for it find it hard to get shown". Eminent Irish-Americans, however, objected to O'Casey, so Sullivan ostentatiously announced that the conversation would be omitted, explaining that he had been told O'Casey "had been used by English communists". O'Casey was happy to have been spared: "Thank God I escaped from appearing in the midst of such horrible bog of Irish sentimentality and inanity."

Samuel Beckett sent birthday greetings to the *Irish Times*. "To my great compatriot, Sean O'Casey, from France where he is honoured, I send my enduring gratitude and homage", although O'Casey had never overcome his antagonism to what he considered the younger writer's dark view of humanity ("I have nothing to do with Beckett. He isn't in me; nor am I in him"). Beckett's honouring of him was the greater by virtue of Beckett having declined to do something similar four years earlier for the centenary of Shaw's birth:

> This is too tall an order for me . . .
> I wouldn't suggest that G.B.S. is not a great playwright,
> Whatever that is when it's at home.
> What I would do is give the whole unupsettable, apple-cart for a
> sup of the Hawk's Well, or the Saints', or a whiff of Juno, to go
> no further.

In 1960 O'Casey was one of three likely candidates for the Nobel Prize, but it was awarded to the French poet Saint-John Perse.

Somewhere inside O'Casey his creative powers were rising again during the last decade of his life. It was like the beginning of his marriage and the start of his family in reverse. At the moment of Breon's birth his playwriting fortunes, with the rejection of *The Silver Tassie*, had declined. While Niall lay dying in Bart's, he received from the New York publisher, George Braziller, $1,500 and a bunch of glowing reviews from the first American production of *Purple Dust* at the off-Broadway Cherry Lane Theatre. It ran there for over a year, the longest for any O'Casey play. Dramatised versions of the first two volumes of his autobiography, by Paul Shyre, were also performed on Broadway in 1956-7; O'Casey listened several times to tapes of them sent from New York. *Cock-a-Doodle Dandy*, the play he liked most of his later years, although written earlier, was at last staged professionally both in New York and London.

In his last three full-length plays, *Cock-a-Doodle Dandy*, *The Bishop's Bonfire* and *The Drums of Father Ned*, and the three satires he published in his eighty-first year, in 1961, *Behind the Green Curtains*, *Figuro in the Night* and *The Moon Shines on Kylenamoe*, O'Casey returned to his chastisement of Ireland for refusing to join the modern world. Yet was he now of it himself? In these fantasies of mythical places like Ballybeedhust, Ballyoonagh, Doonavale, Kylenamoe and Nyadnanave, bizarre and miraculous events unfold – a human-size cock crows with sexual urgency, and challenges the Catholic barrenness, women sprout horns, a plaster saint blows blasts on a "buckineeno", a Brussels "petit Pizzeur" sprays irreverence on a Dublin suburb. There is a huge discrepancy between these places and events and the actual reality of Ireland, a new and young country searching painfully, in tight circumstances, for a moral and material identity of her own. While critics found that this vision reduced her to a "narrow-minded", "priest-ridden", acquisitively materialistic society with bourgeois pretensions, and falsely and hollowly nationalistic, who was to say that the permissive virtues O'Casey and others preached would not have turned her, twenty years later, into the drug- and disease-ridden spiritually empty arcadias other more "liberated" countries have become?

O'Casey, however, assuming the moral right to attack his native land, had for a long time been like the ex-husband laying down rules of behaviour to the wife he has deserted, yet whose interests he still claims to know better than anyone else, including herself. He justified this because his feelings towards Ireland were still strong: he had tried to form attachments elsewhere and failed. Was it any wonder, then, that Ireland continued to reject him? But wonder he did, and again the reality lacking in the plays was compensated for by the mud slung between O'Casey and those who proscribed them.

But he had a lot of fun, both in the plays themselves, which are full of skittish humour – like the early one-act plays which punctuated the masterpieces at the Abbey – and on the hardly wider stage of Dublin life. The knockabout comedy of censorship culminated in 1958 with the Council of the Dublin Tóstal Festival, which had accepted *The Drums of Father Ned* for production, rejecting both it and a dramatisation of Joyce's *Ulysses*.

As in previous bannings it was not just the work, but the Flutherian figure of O'Casey himself, waving his fists and asking for a fight, that the authorities rejected. But O'Casey was challenging the paternal guardians, as it were, of his first wife: he provoked them to exercise their authority, and they responded by doing so. He retaliated by putting an embargo on all productions of his plays in Ireland until 1984: though different in detail, these exchanges were in essence replays of earlier quarrels. "Not quite tears," as he said of the effects of all this, "for within me the laugh comes and goes and always comes back."

Cock-a-Doodle Dandy was the best of the final pieces and the best piece of self-dramatisation since *The Shadow of a Gunman*. O'Casey refines the realistically portrayed Davoren into the beautiful and effective symbol of the cock who says nothing, only crows: the Lord of Misrule, the pagan Oisin, the jester, the dark prophet of the life force, all are suggested in this expressionistic device. The other characters take sides over real-life incidents – a dying girl's futile departure for Lourdes; the apocalyptic blow of Father Domineer which strikes dead a workman "living in sin" with a woman of the parish – in an extravagantly theatrical mixture of dance-like action and wild humour. O'Casey thought of *Cock-a-Doodle Dandy* as a morality play, with battle lines different from the usual ones drawn between good and evil, and considered it "my best".

Certainly it was the work of a happy man, for as Breon and Eileen attested, no piece he wrote caused more laughter and song in him during its labour: Breon contrasted his mood while writing it with the depression he suffered when he had to write newspaper articles. But it had little success in the US: Macmillans there refused to publish an American edition, importing instead a mere 891 copies from London. O'Casey wanted to approach another publisher, but Daniel Macmillan dissuaded him.

The play failed in New York when presented at the Carnegie Hall Playhouse at the end of 1958; O'Casey remarked poignantly to Brooks Atkinson, who had sent on the reviews, "somehow, some-day, somewhere the characters will leap & laugh a way into life. Meanwhile they are safe in limbo."

Since then, like many others of O'Casey's plays, it has been widely translated (*Cock-a-Doodle Dandy* itself into French, German, Italian, Spanish, Dutch, Polish, Romanian, Slovak, Japanese). A 1959 production, directed by George Devine, which came down from the Edinburgh Festival to play at the Royal Court, established O'Casey's link (as "Angry Old Man", a label which O'Casey resented) with John Osborne, whose plays contained a small element of the O'Casey revolt, but did not advance beyond the rhetorical self-pity and the repetitive music-hall routines used by O'Casey to command attention. Nor have later "angry" dramatists managed to achieve that special O'Casey quality of self-mockery: piling on vituperative ill-feeling and upping the stakes they have substituted obscenity for mockery, hatred for love, and have ignored the lovingly detailed processes of life or the volatile contradictions of character seen in the best of O'Casey's work. Discontent is a hard act to follow, making us seek, as Goethe wrote, "the root of all evil outside ourselves instead of finding it in our own contrariness".

The Bishop's Bonfire and *The Drums of Father Ned* lack vitality, by comparison with *Cock-a-Doodle Dandy*, although in the second O'Casey was, or so G. Wilson Knight claimed, "tidying up" his private theology. There is something too composed, too pictorial about the writing: many scenes have a painterly quality, like a Stanley Spencer, full of colour and of a distinctive character – but too finished for actors to spring inside them and mould them to their own intentions. The plays perform themselves on the printed page, and the playwright orchestrates them completely.

O'Casey described the subject of *The Bishop's Bonfire* as "the ferocious chastity of the Irish" – making it sound quite attractive – and "a lament for the condition of Ireland which is an apathetic country now, losing all her energy, enthusiasm and resolution". The expected counterblast is by no means wholly ferocious, often the reverse. In fact O'Casey told the director, Tyrone Guthrie, that one character in the play, Rankin, was based on a stone mason of the same name and that he tried to reassure this guilt-obsessed Catholic that it wasn't so hard to go through life giving little offence to God. Rankin had wheeled to face him, brought his face close and hissed out, "There's always concupiscence!" But sympathy for the enemy was something O'Casey shared with few of his doctrinaire colleagues.

The Bishop's Bonfire, when it opened in Guthrie's production at the Gaiety, Dublin, in 1955, provoked denunciations from the pulpit, in the well-hallowed tradition of O'Casey first nights, although the Vatican's ecumenical changes of the early 1960s were soon to alter Catholic thinking, even in Ireland. He and Guthrie enthusiastically fed each other with ideas and O'Casey even made a few suggestions for new dialogue, but he never attended a performance. Sidney Bernstein, who had remained friends with the O'Caseys since Eileen's Cochran days and who had sent gifts to Tingrith of tobacco and clothing during and just after the war, wanted to take him and Eileen to the first night. Eileen accepted and went, accompanied by Shivaun. O'Casey never slipped over to Dublin "quietly and unnoticed", as he intended doing if the play was a success.

The prologue of *The Drums of Father Ned*, dubbed "Prerumble", is a marvellous brief flashback to the "Troubles" of the early 1920s: a party of Black and Tans capture two Republicans, whose enmity for each other – one supports the Irish Free State, the other is a Sinn Fein Diehard – far outstrips their hatred of the English. This so mystifies their captors that the officer in charge tries to intimidate them into shaking hands; having no success he leaves them to prolong their feud. But the rest of the play, unfolding in the same town some thirty-four years later, when the "two rats" are now Mayor and Deputy Mayor, but unchanged in what they feel towards each other, dissipates the explosive comi-tragic mood of the "Prerumble". Father Ned, the revolutionary priest, never appears: he represents progress and we hear his drumming. O'Casey no doubt meant it as allegory but it slid into mere romp.

"Figuro is an abounding joy everywhere at last," says the Birdlike Lad in *Figuro in the Night*, "the instrument he was handling shows up and down in stretched dimensions." This, and *The Moon Shines on Kylenamoe*, which with its railway station setting revives ghosts of the GNR, display O'Casey's last priapic defiance of Ireland's hypocritical piety.

In *Behind the Green Curtains*, a savage, three-scene satire on Dublin's *literati* and their faint-heartedness before clerics, Michael Robartes, a famous Protestant playwright (based on Lennox Robinson, who died in 1951), causes with his death a moral dilemma: should his literary friends risk the Catholic bishop excommunicating them for attending his funeral? In the end those who are humiliated or refuse oppression leave for England – historically Ireland's oppressor, now the haven for its oppressed. Having arrived on a short visit to publicise a first night O'Casey had now resided there for over thirty-three years: "Stay in England," one of his voices had told him, "where, if there isn't wisdom, there is sense, and some decency of manner."

Eileen, in her fifties, was a strikingly handsome woman, "of auburn beauty and fine proportions, an open-faced woman with a gentle manner and a quick smile," wrote David Krause. She was now O'Casey's ambassador extraordinary to the world at large. In 1958 she visited New York to attend the first night of *Cock-a-Doodle Dandy*. She had her own little flat in London, in the Cromwell Road, a two-roomed place at a controlled rent where she could be independent. "Ideal for me," she said. O'Casey saw it only once, on his last visit to London to attend the performance of *Cock-a-Doodle Dandy* at the Royal Court.

Their relationship had mellowed now, they had few arguments, and as his eyes worsened she read aloud to him and helped him with correspondence. "My arms aren't long enough to stretch so far to hug you," he wrote to her in 1958; "& your sweet mouth has to travel a long way before I can give it a long kiss; & I miss greatly that hug and that kiss." Filled with great love, theirs was now, of course, a celibate marriage. Eileen, on her own candid admission, had strong sexual needs which she fulfilled outside. "It's a pity I'm so old," O'Casey told her once; while of their sex life she said: "After a certain point there wasn't much in that line. It all went into his writing."

O'Casey was conscious, even to the very end of his life, not only how precious Eileen had been to him personally, but how he had stolen her from her natural habitat among the rich and privileged. Her love, he wrote in the 1929 version of "Eileen most Fair", he had "claimed and laid hold of in the Frowning Face of others". There was always in him a *frisson* of pleasure at the excitement she awoke in others: "I struck away the hands that were unloosening her girdle, and tightened it again, that I myself with my own hands might loosen it."

In the summer of 1962 he had to say farewell to the joy of reading: "My eyes have slumped as low as the low market price on Wall Street." With Eileen reading the replies out to him he still remained as prolific a letter-writer as before. To Brooks Atkinson, now retired from the *New York Times*, who was writing a book on birds, he gave an impression from his window, of the "fainter beauties within my vision of life". He recalled seeing his first swallow when he was twenty-six or twenty-seven years of age, working in a gang sinking big and small sewer pipes and building a septic tank in the country outside Dublin. With his reputation as a "scholar", every Saturday he was sent to fetch the weekly wages from the cashier and carry the bag of thirty to forty pounds in sovereigns and glistening silver pieces to pay the men. Arriving at the works hut, he said, "I used to hold up the bag of money, & say, first in Irish, then in English, 'May the blessing of God be on the way this money is spent for the good of those who earned it'." The men would answer "Amen".

Leaving work one Saturday with a companion he looked into the sky at this "swarm of scimitar-winged birds", and asked what they were; his companion couldn't believe he didn't know.

> – Swallas, Jack; just common swallas.
> – An' what are they doin', dartin' about up there?
> – Eatin' insects; swarms of them in the air; gorgin' themselves while the goin's good . . . Well, so long, Jack – I'll leave you with your swallas.

Barry Fitzgerald died in 1961, leaving O'Casey a small legacy to attest to their long association and friendship. In his own will, written in late 1962, O'Casey bequeathed to Eileen "all my goods, estate valuation, and all else, to her in gratitude for many, many years of happy and fruitful companionship; and with all I bequeath to her my deep love, as deep now, deeper indeed, than the love I felt for her in our earlier years." He was now growing more blind by the month, with the plague, as he called it, "that enfolded the germ of a divine gift". After President Kennedy's death, in 1963, he wrote to one correspondent that he and his wife felt the same way after Niall's death:

> We were physically sick as well as emotionally upset; the belly heavy as lead caused by the distension of the bowels. No wonder in ancient times, these were thought to be the centre of the emotions; Gaelic mothers used to say to their babies "M'inne estigh thu", "You are my bowels within"; and remember that passage of scripture which says "If a man seeth his brother in want, and shutteth up his bowels of compassion against him, how dwelleth the love of God in that man?"

One of the witnesses to O'Casey's will was Geoffrey Dobbie, a nurseryman from Babbacombe. Dobbie, married and with an ailing wife, had been enlisted by Eileen and helped her in the garden and around the home – he sometimes, Eileen said, "remained overnight". Dobbie moved into the Villa Rosa during the late summer of 1964 when O'Casey went down with acute bronchitis and on returning home from hospital showed increasing fatigue. Now eighty-four, he was not expected to live long.

When Eileen's mother died at this time, O'Casey sent Dobbie along to the funeral. She had been fatally injured in a fall, and in a few moments of consciousness before the end Eileen gave her some brandy. Mrs Reynolds called for a priest, and Eileen told her she'd soon be with Edward, her husband. "Oh my God," exploded Mrs Reynolds, "I don't want to meet him again!"

Eileen declared, with a huge chuckle, "I upset her deathbed!"

※

When he was in the clinic at Torbay, anticipating his end, O'Casey began to write a long last letter in which he summarised, in a most eloquent and moving way, his and Eileen's life together: "Here I am like a cooped-up cock, ragged in feather, drooping in comb, the crow gone off into a cough." He described her early loveliness, her laughter, how he had "failed as 'a man of the world'" because he could not stop talking of serious things; then their marriage, their first son, little money, and all the subsequent tests and hardships they had to endure: the barrage of incoming bills without the money to meet them. "They were the necklace always twisting round your lovely neck." He had no gift for finding a ready market for his plays while the English ignored him because of his "lamentable political judgments". How she stood up to it was a mystery to him, especially when "at meal times, a silent and sullen da sat like a frozen image at the table". She might have tried to break the tension, but "Many a time a gentle remark . . . was ignored, or a tender overture of affection was banished into a deeper silence."

Here he broke off, but finished the letter on his return to the flat in Torquay: "Wherever you are, Eileen darling, is home to me." Without her the "great playwright" was "but a whimpering figure in a darkened doorway. The stalwart of the O'Casey home is not Sean, but Eileen."

A few weeks after completing this, on the morning of 17 September 1964, his nose began to bleed profusely. Eileen rushed about gathering towels and wiping up the mess. She drove him at once to the doctor's surgery where the bleeding was plugged. Later, when he was resting at home, he expressed regret at having won her away from Ephraim:

"I was selfish to take you away from him; you should have stayed with him for the security." She made him an omelette – he liked omelettes – but as soon as he began to eat, the bleeding came on again. He told her what to do with the children, pointing out dangers, telling her to sell this and that. Eileen felt that he was suffering a premonition of death.

At two a.m. on 18 September he had a thrombosis and suffered agony from a pain in his side. They drove him a little later to hospital, but on arrival found that he had died peacefully on the way. "I don't believe I can settle anywhere," he had told a friend some years earlier: "Probably I won't even be able to settle serenely in Heaven if I get there."

Eileen accepted his death with calm resignation, grateful that he had been spared both incapacity and pain. After a ten-minute Anglican service at Torquay crematorium his body, in a light oak coffin decked in family tokens of red roses, was committed to the fire. His ashes would go, as he wished, to be scattered on the same ground as those of Niall, between the Shelley and Tennyson rose beds at Golders Green.

EPILOGUE – SAINT OR GUNMAN?

*I have found life an enjoyable, enchanting, active and sometimes
a terrifying experience. A lament in one ear, maybe, but always a song
in the other.*

O'Casey believed in life before literature and gave politics more
importance than aesthetics. He was a devoted father and husband,
and had had the good fortune to marry a woman who possessed, in
her way, gifts as strong as his own: "The best thing that ever
happened to Sean O'Casey," Brooks Atkinson wrote, "was to meet
Eileen O'Casey."

With equal generosity, given the way he and O'Casey had quarrelled, Lennox Robinson told Frank O'Connor one day when they
were arguing over the value of the early O'Casey plays versus the
late – a popular pastime of the Irish literati: "I don't *mind* how many
bad plays Sean writes for the rest of his life. What*ever* they may be
like they will be the plays of a happy man." This sudden outburst
remained in O'Connor's memory, he said, not only because of its
profound relevance to O'Casey, but because it was a remark made
by a man who would never himself be happy again.

For all his waywardness O'Casey was a genuine seeker after goodness. He had overcome his personal inclinations towards activism,
and some of his best work owes everything to the disillusionment he
suffered, the depth of which revealed the enormity of his hopes for
mankind and for himself. He never saw life in terms of Yeats's
"Perfection of the life, or of the work". His pursuit was of the ordinary:
the humble life, well-lived, without exploiting others, with decent
civilised pleasures, nineteenth-century pastoral joys – and a dash of
twentieth-century television sport and nature programmes thrown
in. He was an Arcadian who liked doing the washing up:

I know what a housewife has to face & has to do . . . I did chores
before I became ill, to help my wife; & am beginning again –
washing up, peeling spuds, carrying down the garbage, etc. It is
partly good for us, for it is routine, & this checks the excitement
of the mind, & gives us rest. We cannot always suffer ecstasy.

Daily life for him was as sacramental as for the poorest of housewives or seminarists, and he often compared himself to the modest early nineteenth-century poet and country clergyman, George Crabbe.

"To me one thing alone is certain," he had written to Harold Macmillan in 1951; "we are all one in the tremendous and glorious bond of humanity. Jew, Gentile, bond and free, Tory and Communist can never break away from this grand bond." O'Casey last saw his publisher when he visited Birch Grove in 1939, but kept in touch for the rest of his life, mostly through Eileen. Harold Macmillan, who held that publishers "exist to satisfy their authors", had been an ideal choice: Edith Londonderry had introduced the two men socially just after Macmillans had published *The Plough and the Stars*. Harold had spoken to O'Casey, as he said in a letter, in two voices: "first as your friend and secondly as a publisher". It could be argued that the older man had a strong influence on the younger, giving him a relationship with that early Irish period which he much valued, and certainly Macmillan tried, unsuccessfully, to influence O'Casey to drop, in his writing, "criticism in reply to criticisms of your own work".

Macmillan's relationship with Eileen, too, had been a close one. Eileen made no bones about the fact that she "took a shine to Harold" the first time she saw him. His loyalty to his wife, Lady Dorothy, was absolute, but in 1929 she became involved with a close colleague of his, Robert Boothby – they too met at a Londonderry reception in Park Lane – by whom it was thought she had a child, Sarah, born in 1930. This caused great pain to Macmillan: as Edith Londonderry said at the time, "Harold is most upset. He spends most of his time in church. I don't think that's a good idea, do you?" Many years later, at dinner after a remembrance service at an Oxford college, he commented, rather unexpectedly, to those present on how good it had been at the service to hear the Ten Commandments read out in full: "Especially the seventh, because of course we've all had experience of it."

He did not, however, run to other women for consolation. But as time went on one of his consistent consolations was Eileen. Their relationship, a fragile and precious one, grew in strength so that over the years an understanding and affection built up between the pair which both reckoned to be unique.

Daniel Macmillan, who was chairman of Macmillan Holdings, and dealt with the financial side of the firm's relations with O'Casey, behaved with enormous generosity towards the family, guaranteeing Eileen's bank loans and suggesting solutions to their money problems until O'Casey's royalties made them more than comfortable. "Dan," said Eileen, "stood by me all the time." At one time Daniel wanted to propose O'Casey for a Civil List pension, but Eileen refused, knowing Sean would have none of it.

After the death of both their spouses – Lady Dorothy died in 1966 – Harold Macmillan and Eileen saw much of one another, and there were rumours that the two might marry. Eileen was the first woman whom Macmillan asked to sit in Lady Dorothy's place at table in Birch Grove; he also took her out frequently to dine at Buck's Club. When her memoir of O'Casey, *Sean*, was published in 1971, Macmillan gave a big party for her at the home of his grandson Alexander. When Macmillan was offered a peerage in 1984, and was in a quandary over whether to accept, Eileen was present at dinner at Birch Grove when Lord Home tried to persuade him to take it. Harold said to her, "What do you think?" and she told him, to the dismay of the others present, "I think it's better just to remain Mr Macmillan because peers are ten a penny." O'Casey would have been even more scathing: "Now it's Lord Willis," he had commented on Ted Willis's elevation in 1964, "wearing his ermine robes so that he can look like the rest of 'em. How can any self-respecting Socialist dress himself like that to parade about in a monkey-house?"

Eileen, without benefit of, as she herself admitted, "any political brain", satisfied a different side of Macmillan's nature. Both lonely, they were able to sit together for hours and be at ease: "melt into one another", in Eileen's words. Harold was not a demonstrative man, a perfunctory kiss was all he showed of his feelings, but there was great warmth in his personality. He once outlined to her his dream of living in a village in Scotland he knew well and of joining the old boys who stood together against the sea wall, quoting their own bards and swapping humorous stories till the local pub opened. "I think that would be the perfect life," he told her.

But when Eileen, by her own account, came to think seriously of becoming mistress of Birch Grove she knew she could never do it, and evaded the offer as gently and as indirectly as it had been broached. She noted, on Macmillan's part, a slight, if only temporary, cooling. But their affection continued as before, as "the best kind of love, an unfulfilled one".

As Macmillan grew into his late eighties Eileen was struck by his many affinities with O'Casey. He visited her at her ground-floor flat in Portland Place ("Don't go back to Ireland, go to Paris or London", was one of the last things Sean had told Eileen), delighted to find it so comfortable. They talked of the past, and she would hum or sing to him the old music-hall songs: he regretted never having got to see *Me and My Girl*. He told her that once when at Eton he had time off to visit his dentist but afterwards had gone with some friends to see Marie Lloyd, staying out late, for which he had been reprimanded on his return to college. The punishment was worth it.

Once when he was very ill he called her to his bedside in the nursing home and explained how bits of shot from his First World War wounds had remained in his system, causing trouble from time to time. Later, at home again, with his sight badly failing, he remarked that he couldn't really see the furniture but still had a vague idea of where everything was. Like O'Casey he would pick up a book, turn it lovingly from side to side, open it and bring it very close to his face to peer into its contents.

She saw him last a fortnight before he died, at lunch at the Carlton Club; he was very frail, and had to be brought to the table in a wheelchair. He was worried because he had just fallen out of his chair and feared, not that he would break a limb, but that he might have done something to his head. He told her how weary his day was and that he missed not being able to read: "It's amazing how much I sleep," he said. But there was still the customary wit and fire. "What do you think about Reagan?" he asked Eileen, who replied, "I think he's gaga." "Yes," he rejoined, "but gaga in a very elaborate manner." Eileen told him she was writing about Shaw. "Why are you writing about *him*?" he said with palpable displeasure. His man arrived to wheel him off and they said goodbye for the last time.

During the last year of O'Casey's life and at the prompting of two American friends, Robert Graff of NBC and Robert Emmett Ginna, a *Life* Magazine executive, Metro-Goldwyn-Mayer bought the screen rights to the first three volumes of the autobiographies for the film *Young Cassidy*. O'Casey earned £4,000 from the sale. Graff and Ginna were to co-produce and John Ford to direct. The English playwright John Whiting was commissioned to find, as Graff put it, "25 episodes of a true-to-life picture of Sean O'Casey". Whiting was considered a terse and literate writer with an eye for tight scene construction. O'Casey did not like his script and said so, but was ignored; Whiting died before shooting began.

Sean Connery, attracted by the photograph of O'Casey aged thirty and with his moustache, had almost said yes to playing "Johnny", but withdrew. Rod Taylor was cast finally as the playwright. O'Casey would have preferred Donal Donnelly, advice which was also rejected.

The million-dollar film was shot in Dublin in 1964-5 and released in 1965. John Ford, who had directed the disappointing Hollywood version of *The Plough and the Stars* in 1935, spent thousands of dollars dismantling aerials from the rooftops of old Dublin. The sixty-nine-year-old Ford, who had always wanted to make the O'Casey story, wept with nostalgia at being back in Dublin. He set up camp in the Shelbourne Hotel, started drinking heavily, stayed up all night, held levees, and finally collapsed, after shooting only a few scenes of the film, with viral pneumonia. His doctor was flown in from Los Angeles, and Ford was taken by private plane to London, and from there back to the USA. Jack Cardiff directed in his place.

As "Johnny", Rod Taylor, like some wild backwoodsman, fought all and sundry, kissed the girls and made them cry; but nowhere visible in his performance was the ascetic, self-mocking O'Casey. Michael Mullen was much upgraded from his actual importance in O'Casey's life by being made into his best friend, as well as chorus figure. Taylor apart, there were superb performances in minor roles, among them Jack MacGowran as Archie (Isaac), Maggie Smith as a bookshop assistant (an episode not even in the autobiographies) and Sian Phillips as an extraordinary, red-headed version of Bella. Flora Robson played Susan Casey. Far from being cramped in Abercorn Road the Caseys looked as if they were living in a decayed palazzo.

Michael Redgrave as the monocled Yeats, and Edith Evans impersonating a Lady Gregory as seen in the great Jack Yeats portrait, gave wonderful performances in these minor roles. As O'Casey's one-night stand from the anti-Boer War demonstration, Julie Christie supplied a revealing foretaste of roles she would play in future, more permissive films. At two a.m. one morning during shooting, writhing in pain, she was rushed to St Michael's Hospital, Dun Laoghaire, and hurriedly operated on for appendicitis: "Clean your hands and make an invisible incision," her companion told the staff.

O'Casey wrote thousands of letters, and towards the end the writing of these had become his most pressing daily task. The American scholar, David Krause, of Brown University, who visited him in Devon in the last years of his life, subsequently collected more than 3,000 letters which he sorted, in some cases selected from, dated, annotated, and assembled in three volumes of 1,000 pages each. Volumes I and II were published in 1975 and 1980 respectively; Volume III is as yet unpublished.

O'Casey and Krause discussed many aspects of his life and literary output, about which Krause asked him detailed questions. His moods, said the American, were "often mixed, and he could be an outraged comedian, a gentle genius, an insecure rebel". Sometimes, said Krause, there was a "craggy grandeur in his aquiline profile which . . . invested him with the magisterial dignity of a Renaissance Cardinal painted by El Greco, especially when he complemented his perennial red beanie by wearing his blood-red robe on chilly days". When Krause taxed him with the extremes of his nature he replied: "Tact? Polite submission, that's what tact really is, and it's something I've never learned . . . The first thing a fella has to do if he wants to accomplish anything of value is to be tactless." And then, later in their talk, "Christ was a tactless communist, God help him." O'Casey's epistolary output increased rather than diminished towards the end: a "bloody big cargo" he called it on the telephone to Krause.

"They're very dull," said Eileen about the first two volumes: "I'm afraid I've never read them through. I said to Breon once, come on, we'd better read Sean's letters . . . but we couldn't manage them, Breon no more than me!"

O'Casey's last testament as a playwright is an article entitled "The Bald Primaqueera", which he had completed about three weeks before his death. This turbulent outburst lashes the Freudians of the theatre, from Antonin Artaud through Eugène Ionesco to Joe Orton, the "dare-devil Horrorhawks of the theatre of murder, rape, and cruelty . . . arm in arm with the theatre of the Absurd". What he hates about these playwrights is their inability to love and cherish mankind: "The present literary group . . . seem to revel in the rending of all men, mentally and physically. They get sport out of it all." He attacks David Rudkin's *Afore Night Comes* for showing farm workers as "ignorant, stupid, and given to ferocity"; Harold Pinter is contemptuous of life, of "a larger part of the loveliness around him"; as for Orton's "basilisk pot of sexual distortions", it is the latest example of the theatre's sour and venomous condition of mind, the "loutish lust of Primaqueera".

Until his final days O'Casey the gunman – or what George Russell had called the annihilator, Beckett the dynamiter – kept Ireland firmly in his line of sight. Lorraine Beaver, his grand-niece, had started writing to him in 1962 when she was eighteen, telling him that he should lift the embargo on the performance of his plays at the Abbey. "What a bold and impudent letter to send to a world-famous writer!" he addressed her, going on, "There is no Abbey Theatre, young lady. That theatre died when the poet Yeats and the poet Fred Higgins died . . ." In one of his last letters to Bella's grand-daughter he told her that he was never homesick and did not miss Ireland, but added, in the ex-husband's tone: "She will have to make herself more attractive if she wishes to keep her people attached to her. If she is content to remain slovenly and shy, her people will continue to flee from her."

But after his death, when that flood of recrimination suddenly ceased, the writer and folklorist Catherine Rynne described the silence: "Nobody is scanning the papers now. No aged prophet in Devon is bothering about us any more. Loving us more than hating us through a lifetime of neglect and derision. There's no one to look out for us now. Forgive us, O'Casey."

Notes
&
Acknowledgments

The STRANGER in the HOUSE

A drawing from *An Poblacht*, 1906, by George Morrow

NOTES

List of Abbreviations

PRINCIPAL SOURCES CITED

By Sean O'Casey: *cited as*

Autobiographies, 2 vols. [I: *I Knock at the Door, Pictures in the Hallway, Drums under the Windows*; II: *Inishfallen Fare Thee Well, Rose and Crown, Sunset and Evening Star*] (London: Macmillan, repr. 1963) — **A**

Letters, ed. David Krause, 2 vols. [I: 1910–41 (London: Cassell, 1975); II: 1942–1954 (New York: Macmillan, 1980)] Vol. III: 1955–1964, in preparation — **L**

Five Irish Plays [*The Shadow of a Gunman, Juno and the Paycock, The Plough and the Stars, The End of the Beginning, A Pound on Demand*] (London: Macmillan, 1935) — **FIP**

The Complete Plays, 5 vols. [I: *Five Irish Plays* (see above); II: *The Silver Tassie, Within the Gates, The Star Turns Red*; III: *Purple Dust, Red Roses for Me, Hall of Healing*; IV: *Oak Leaves and Lavender, Cock-a-Doodle Dandy, Bedtime Story, Time to Go*; V: *The Bishop's Bonfire, The Drums of Father Ned, Behind the Green Curtains, Figuro in the Night, The Moon Shines on Kylenamoe, The Harvest Festival, Kathleen Listens In, Nannie's Night Out*] (London: Macmillan, 1984) — **CP**

The Story of the Irish Citizen Army (London: Journeyman Press, repr. 1980) — **ICA**

Under a Colored Cap: Articles, Merry and Mournful (London: Macmillan, 1963) — **Colored Cap**

Feathers from the Green Crow, ed. Robert Hogan (London: Macmillan, 1963) — **Feathers**

Windfalls: Stories, Poems and Plays (London: Macmillan, 1939) — **Windfalls**

Blasts and Benedictions: Articles and Stories (London: Macmillan, 1967) — **Blasts**

Other sources:

Eileen O'Casey: *Sean*, ed. J. C. Trewin (London: Macmillan, 1971) — **Sean**

Eileen, ed. J. C. Trewin (London: Macmillan, 1976) — **Eileen**

Mary Colum, *Life and the Dream* (London: Macmillan, 1947) — **Colum**

Gabriel Fallon, *Sean O'Casey the Man I Knew* (London: Routledge, 1965) — **Fallon**

	cited as
Joseph Holloway's Abbey Theatre, ed. Robert Hogan and Michael J. O'Neill (London: Southern Illinois Press, 1967)	Holloway
Irish Worker (Dublin, 1911–14)	*IW*
Lady Gregory's Journals, ed. Daniel J. Murphy [vol. I: 1916–1925] (Gerards Cross: Colin Smythe, 1978)	*Lady G Journals*
The World of Sean O'Casey, ed. Sean McCann (London: Four Square, 1966)	McCann
Martin B. Margulies, *The Early Life of Sean O'Casey* (Dublin: Dolmen Press, 1971); information from interview notes referred to as "MM unpub. notes"	MM

For all other sources, cited in full in the notes which follow, the place of publication is London unless otherwise indicated.

Other abbreviations (individuals and institutions):

Sean O'Casey	SO'C
Eileen O'Casey	EO'C
Gabriel Fallon	GF
Lady Gregory	Lady G
Maire Keating	MK
George Jean Nathan	GJN
Lennox Robinson	LR
George Bernard Shaw	GBS
W. B. Yeats	WBY
Berg Collection, New York Public Library	Berg
National Library of Ireland	NLI

NOTES ON SOURCES

Prologue [pp. 3–6]

3	born one of thirteen	*A* II. 14
4	"Irish fact"	Hugh Kenner, *A Colder Eye* (1983), 3
	early infant mortality	Mary E. Daly, *Dublin the Deposed Capital* (Cork, 1984), 246
	Rotunda Hospital . . . rate of mortality	Frank G. Slaughter, *Immortal Magyar* (New York, 1950), 37
	"It had often been recorded . . ."	*A* II. 231

Act One   SWORDS OF LIGHT   1880–1921

Ch. 1   *Two Eternities* [pp. 11–24]

11	"That's curious about . . ."/ "of the Limerick branch . . ."	SO'C★ to Nan Archer, 25 Aug 1945 (*L* II. 283)
	"– Is it a roman . . ."	*A* I. 198
12	"vaguely menacing us . . ."	C. S Andrews, *Dublin Made Me* (Dublin, 1979), 9–10
13	It was for one of these bodies . . ./Only Isaac, though his schooling . . .	MM, 14–15, 84–8; unpub. notes
14	the birth of a sister . . ./"dug her knees home . . ."	*A* I. 5, 2
	His mother sold the caul	to Frank MacManus, 21 Oct 1946 (*L* II. 406)
	the award of a . . . sewer contract	Daly, *Dublin the Deposed Capital,* 58
15	with a parlour kept swept	*A* I. 39
	Tenement ownership . . . was by no means	Daly, *Dublin the Deposed Capital,* 283
	"to beat the landlords . . ."	*Irish Times,* 28 May 1892

★ All letters cited hereafter are from SO'C unless otherwise indicated.

15	nearly three million pawn tickets	Sir Charles Alexander Cameron, *Reminiscences* (London and Dublin, 1913), 166
16	"below St Ignatius Road . . ."	to Frank McCarthy, 8 Feb 1949 (*L* II. 585)
	"in the spring it thrust . . ."	*A* I. 592
	Tom remained . . . immune	to Robert Ginna, 17 Aug 1953 (*L* II. 986)
	"small, hard, shiny . . ."/ "they pushed him further down . . ."/"most of it in the letter . . ."	*A* I. 12, 13, 10
17	d'Aubigné's *History* . . ./ "big enough to understand . . ."/ "sometime gentle, sometime fierce . . ."	*A* I. 27, 28
18	having visited Stonybatter	to Jack Daly, 10 May 1948 (*L* II. 522)
	"They weren't as poverty-stricken . . ."	McCann, 164
19	confidential reports from inspectors	MM, 84–8; unpub. notes
	Even he, in an unguarded moment	to Robert Ginna, 17 Aug 1953 (*L* II. 986)
	"in a bible Sean had . . ."	*A* II. 514
20	"Casey told me he is a labourer . . ."	*Lady G Journals*, 446
	"an' I'm here waitin' . . ."	*A* I. 66–7
21	"she brought from the little yard . . ."	*A* I. 67
	the sea "glide in over . . ."	unpub. notebook E 4 (Berg)
22	ship's officers, bottle-blowers and artisans	MM, 27
23	"There is to be no putting-off . . ."	*A* I. 171
24	Deverell engaged him	*A* I. 237

Ch. 2   *The First Sword* [pp. 25-38]

25	"the exalted name"	James Joyce, *Dubliners* (1914), 151
	"Parnell came down the road . . ."	W. B. Yeats, *Collected Poems* (1952), 359
26	"bringing Charlie Stewart Parnell . . ."	*A* I. 9

	"This lovely land . . ."	James Joyce, "Gas from a Burner", *The Essential James Joyce*, ed. H. Levin (1963), 349
	efforts "to serve the Irish peasant"	to Liam Shine, 5 Jan 1947 (*L* II. 433)
27	"A cloudy sneer . . ."	*A* I. 267
28	"He was clawing . . ."	*A* I. 283
29	"It was a wonderful revelation . . ."	to Eric Gorman, 30 Aug 1951 (*L* II. 822)
	"Shakespeare's good in bits . . ."	*A* I. 195; to Frank McCarthy, 24 Jan 1954 (*L* II. 1021)
31	"FATHER DOLAN: I'd rather see her . . ."	*A* I. 195, 197
	"hero–heat that surged . . ."	*A* I. 346
32	he was later to claim . . . beri-beri	to GJN, [?] Dec 1948 (*L* II. 569)
	John to Sean, "his right name"	*A* I. 325
33	the Sheelds children . . .	*A* I. 310
	sang "*Veni Creator Spiritus*" . . ./"she closed her eyes . . ."/"From the big east window . . ."	*A* I. 326
34	Fletcher . . . had to contemplate leaving	*A* I. 353
	Josie's brother . . . also owned	MM, 34; unpub. notes
35	"Now, boys and girls . . ."/ He drank not only evenings . . .	MM, 34, 35
	petticoat . . . "creased an' twisted . . ."	*A* I. 370
37	"theoretically an anarchist . . ."	G. B. Shaw, Preface to *John Bull's Other Island* (1907), xiv
	"A holy city's our city . . ."/ "Rotten Dublin; lousy Dublin . . ."	*A* I. 383, 378
38	"The Sword of Light! . . ."	*A* I. 360

Ch. 3   *Fiery Blossoms* [pp. 39–60]

39–40	letting his mother "drudge for his living . . ."	G. B. Shaw, *Man and Superman, Collected Plays*, vol. II (1971), 557
40	his body . . . fell into alignment	to Brooks Atkinson, 17 Oct 1946 (*L* II. 405)
	"slippy, hot and pungent . . ."/"Not one of these brawny boys . . ."	*A* I. 408, 421
41	St Barnabas' . . . covered with flags	MM, unpub. notes
	"Tom and Mick would drift over . . ."/"We heard his voice . . ."	MM, 39; unpub. notes
42	driven from Carlingford Road	to Leo Keogh, 12 Oct 1953 (*L* II. 1000)
	"the Civil Servants . . ."	to Francis Kelly, 15 Aug 1954 (*L* II. 1080)
	These would not attend	to D. M. Doyle, 15 May 1950 (*L* II. 711); to John Hutchinson, 10 Sept 1953 (*L* II. 990)
	"Height five feet four . . ."	unpub. ltr., J. B. Yeats to WBY, ? 22 May 1902
	He flung himself into the sport	to John Hutchinson, 10 Sept 1953 (*L* II. 990)
43	wearing a muffler	to Francis Kelly, 15 Aug 1954 (*L* II. 1080)
44	"Dotted here and there . . ."/"She had married . . ."	*A* I. 450, 446–7
45	"When Life's bright dawn . . ."/"After all, what is Irish Education . . ."	*Feathers*, 79, 7
47	"A group of them . . ."/"It wasn't a pleasant job for him . . ."	*A* I. 462, 474
48	"We thought it was time . . ."/"love of wicked politics . . ."/ "Here's a play . . ."	Gerard Fay, *The Abbey Theatre* (1958), 35, 15, 110
49	"Some blasted little theatre . . ."	*A* I. 511

"In it the comical side . . ."   Maxim Gorky in *English Review*,
                                   1924 (Fay, *Abbey Theatre*,
                                   120)

50 "Between Abbey
      Street . . ."   Colum, 95
    "The man who wrote that
      article . . ."   Preface, *Windfalls*, v
51 his sister used to solicit a few
      pence   *A* I. 480
    the struggle "between the
      artist man . . ."   Shaw, *Man and Superman*, *Collected
                                   Plays*, II. 558

    ". . . on weekends, he and
      O'Casey . . ."   MM, 49-50
52 adding parapet coping   to Frank McCarthy, 27 Mar 1949
                                   (*L* II. 603)
    he saw fields of corn   to Alec Donaldson, 13 May 1946
                                   (*L* II. 369)

    "when all
      telegraph-poles . . ."   to George Gilmore, 7 Nov 1951 (*L*
                                   II. 836)

    "Pomps and Charities"/
      withering scorn upon one
      Turkington/"Birming-
      ham and Yorkshire . . .
      importations"   *IW*, 1913: 8 Feb, 21 Jan, 8 Feb
    "new-fangled" train   unpub. notebook E 15 (Berg)
53 "a dour and fiery figure . . ." Desmond Ryan, *Remembering Sion*
                                   (1934), 82-3

54 "Dostoevsky, Chekhov,
      Ibsen . . ."   MM, 45
    "partly because he was . . ." Bulmer Hobson to MM, 8 Mar
                                   1968
    "Bulmer Hobson . . . editor
      of *Irish Freedom* . . ."   *A* I. 548
55 "giving her only a curt
      nod . . ."   MM, 51
    "fire flashing from his . . .
      eyes"   *A* I. 548
    "strictly non-sectarian . . ." Two other exhortatory letters of
                                   1910 survive, both written to
                                   Sinn Fein, the Irish nationalist
                                   weekly owned and edited by
                                   Arthur Griffith: *L* I. 5, 919.
56 "as big a slum hovel . . ."   to John Hutchinson, 10 Sept 1953
                                   (*L* II. 990)

    "Tommy Lynch and his
      brother . . ."   to Sean O'Rourke, 24 Dec 1947 (*L*
                                   II. 494)

57	"the cleverest Irishman . . ."	*A* I. 557–8
	"On the whole, they weren't . . ."	to Jim Kavanagh, 29 Apr 1951 (*L* II. 789)
	"We were then, apparently . . ."	to John Hutchinson, 20 Oct 1953 (*L* II. 990)
	"That's a feather . . ."	MM, 48
	heard "Uncle Jack's footsteps . . ."	Kit Casey in McCann, 165–6
58	"Through the streets he strode . . ."	*A* I. 572
	successfully called strikes	Deirdre Henchy, "Dublin in the Age of O'Casey", in *Essays on Sean O'Casey's Autobiographies*, ed. R. Lowery (1981), 55
59	"In the department in which . . ."	to *IW*, 5 Mar 1912 (*L* I. 12)

Ch. 4   *The Third Eye* [pp. 61–85]

62	a square-faced bottle of gin	R. M. Fox, *Jim Larkin: The Rise of the Underman* (1957), 16–17
	"Hell has no terrors . . ."/ "Once drawn into the abyss . . ."	Andrew Boyd, *The Rise of the Irish Trade Unions* (1972, repr. 1985), 80
63	"workless fathers, mourning mothers . . ."	*Dublin 1913, a Divided City* (Dublin, 1982) 70
	"The figure of St Laurence . . ."/"Then the musical voice . . ."	*A* I. 559
64	"– A man without a soul . . ."	*A* I. 559–60
	"You leave on the doorstep . . ."/ "Although we cannot agree . . ."	*IW*, 14 Dec 1912
65	"So, Euchan, you sneer . . ."	to *IW*, 8 Feb 1913 (*L* I. 13)
	"aimless futility, tinged . . ."	to *IW*, 1 Mar 1913
66	"– We can't afford to have . . ."/"me Lord Archbishop . . ."	*A* I. 525, 529
	"a great humanist . . ."	to *Irish Freedom*, May 1942 (*L* II. 46)

Pearse took the side of the
employers

67 "The Boy Corps of
Ulster . . ."

68 "SCENE: A TRAM
STOP . . ."

69 "This is not a strike . . ."
"Here it came, the *Dead
March* . . ."

70 "Sitting there, listening . . ."
According to Miss
Moloney . . .

71 resolved "not to employ any
persons . . ."

"frightened cattle in a
cattle-boat . . ."

72 "Control yourself!" . . ./
"Along a wide lane . . ."
"Looks like rain,
Mick . . ."

73 "the Irish Proletariat . . ."

"You may succeed . . ."
"O'Casey – another rebel"

74 "What life would
remain . . ."

75 "Labour in its own
defence . . ."/"surging
with a passion . . ./"not
ripe enough to be
shaken . . ."

76 "union between the
separatist . . ."
"The audience was
unanimous . . ."

77 Drills of the Citizen Army
"We are beaten . . ."/"And
so we Irish workers . . ."

78 "She had got Tom . . ."/
"Tom's yellow-skinned
wife . . ."/"I don't want
his home to be . . ."/"He
gripped her angrily . . ."

to *IW*, 21 Feb 1919 (*L* I. 27)

to *IW*, 7 June 1913

James Plunkett, *Big Jim* (Dublin,
1955), 34-5

Dublin 1913, 78

A I. 606

Dublin 1913, 70

MM, unpub. notes

Boyd, *Rise of the Irish Trade Unions*,
92

A I. 583

A I. 589

Jim Phelan, *The Name's Phelan*
(1948), 153

V. I. Lenin, *Lenin on Ireland* (1920),
7-9

Irish Times, 6 Oct 1913
to Frank McCarthy, 12 July 1949
(*L* II. 623)

IW, 27 Sept 1913

ICA, 4-5, 1, 7-8

Irish Freedom, Mar 1913

Bulmer Hobson, *A Short History of
the Irish Volunteers* (Dublin, 1918),
in *Feathers*, 179

ICA, 10-11

Dublin 1913, 99-104

A I. 423, 429, 440, 442

79   "Kerrigan in the North
     Strand . . ."/twenty
     sovereigns   MM, 60-1; Kit Casey in McCann,
                                   165; MM, unpub. notes

     "Out of Ireland have we
     come . . ."   Yeats, *Collected Poems*, 288

80   "the whole tone of his
     letters . . ."   *IW*, 1914: 25 Jan, 7, 21, 28 Feb, 7,
                                   14 Mar

     redressing "rivalled some
     of . . . Dante's *Inferno*"   *ICA*, 18
     "Captain White was indeed..." *Irish Writing*, Feb 1949 (*L* II. 580)

81   relates how he . . .
     journeyed to Lucan   *ICA*, 20-1
     "Then the flag came . . ."   *A* I. 613

82   "the attitude of the
     witches . . ."/"the ambig-
     uous principles . . ."   *ICA*, 31, 26

     "Larkin's people for some
     time . . ."   ltr. to John Devoy, 14 May 1914,
                                   in MM, unpub. notes

83   "to what a small com-
     pass . . ."/"around the
     funeral cortèges . . ."   *ICA*, 39, 43

     "spluttering Catherine-
     wheel . . ."   *A* I. 596

     At another time she held a
     rehearsal   C. Desmond Greaves, *Sean
                                   O'Casey* (1979), 81

     "Nyah – all that type ever
     wants . . ."   MM, unpub. notes

84   "for bourgeois
     tendencies . . ."/"I fear
     no man . . ."   MM, unpub. notes

Ch. 5   *They Dreamed and Are Dead* [pp. 86-103]

86   "He could relax now . . ."/
     painted them with iodine   *A* I. 641, 627

87   "the broad and crowded
     highway . . ."   *ICA*, 52

     "We all regarded Jim
     Connolly as . . ."   Tim Pat Coogan in McCann, 111

     derisive title of "the Steps
     Committee"   MM, 60

     "Where did you get your
     blighty . . ."/"You
     wouldn't get a
     mother . . ."   *A* I. 633

"There's a storm of
anger . . ."   *FIP*, 259–60

88 "romantic cult of
Nationalism . . ."   *Colored Cap*, 263

90 "too much of an Irish
heaven . . ."   to Robert Monteith, 31 Dec 1954
                                      (*L* II. 1135–6)

"Why could the Irish get
nothing . . ."   Iris Murdoch, *The Red and the
                                      Green* (repr. 1978), 212

"In a room, back of the
shop . . ."   to Jack Carney, 22 Apr 1943
                                      (*L* II. 129–30)

91 "The Irish National
Volunteer Movement had
no . . ."   J. R. White, *Misfit* (1930), 307
"a little loose on his
legs . . ."   *A* I. 647

92 "Will we have to come
back . . ."   *A* II. 56–60; MM, 68–9
"What remains to sing
about . . ."   Yeats, *Collected Poems*, 355

93 "Sometimes my heart hath
shaken . . ."   Seamus Scully, "Ghosts of Moore
                                      Street" in *Dublin Historical Record*
                                      (Dublin, 1971), 55–63

"Some say it was
burned . . ."   to Gerald O'Reilly, 26 Apr 1945
                                      (*L* II. 234)

"His great head, made
hideous . . ."   *Spectator*, 2 Nov 1945

94 the "mutiny of the British
officers . . ."   *Dublin 1916*, ed. R. McHugh
                                      (1976), 361

"like all really sincere
pacifists . . ."   White, *Misfit*, 350

95 "living antithesis of the
Easter Insurrection . . ."   *ICA*, 64
"Sean watched their
wonderful activity . . ."   *A* I. 654
"The bonfires of Sinn Fein
began . . ."   *ICA*, 63

96 "Frank kicks two
birds . . ."/"I try to
laugh at the world . . ."   to James Shiels, 14 June and 17 July
                                      1916 (*L* I. 58–9, 60)

"When I danced, & I danced
often . . ."   to Francis MacManus, 12 Apr 1942
                                      (*L* I. 42)

96   "a puzzling figure . . ."/
       "O'Casey staggered
       home alone . . ."   MM, 64–7
97   "How quickly 'Maire' may
       be written . . ."/"a love
       so ardent and so
       deep . . ."/"Forgive me for
       my execrable
       attempts . . ."   unpub. ltrs. to MK,
                                             7 May 1917 and undated (NLI)
98   "Like vultures from dark
       clouded skies . . ."   Sean McCann in McCann, 36
       "Unhappy Sean! . . ."/
       "Waited in East Road
       again . . ."   unpub. ltrs. to MK, 6 Oct and
                                             Oct 1917 (NLI)
99   "The gentle flowers . . ."   unpub. ltr. to MK, undated (NLI)
       "the bedrooms were so
       small . . ."   *A* II. 187
100   "Let me crave your
       forgiveness . . ."   unpub. ltr. to MK, 16 Aug 1917
                                             (NLI)
       "sowing the seed of Human
       Liberty . . ."   "Homage to Thomas Ashe",
                                             Feathers, 160
101   "It never made him less
       Irish . . ."   to Dublin *Saturday Post*, 6 Oct 1917
                                             (*L* I. 65)
       "It was a curious choice to
       Sean . . ."   *A* II. 4
       "Thomas Ashe, Thomas
       Ashe . . ."   *Feathers*, 163
102   *The Nabocklish*/"at the back
       of the houses . . ."   Paddy McDonnell in McCann, 171
       "You know, Sean, you could
       write . . ."   Tom Buggy, "Sean O'Casey's
                                             Dublin", *O'Casey Annual
                                             No. 1*, ed. R. Lowery (1982),
                                             94

Ch. 6   *Lethe's Wharf* [pp. 104–120]
104   "Your suggestion that I
       should . . ."   to John Gassner, 25 Sept 1954
                                             (*L* II. 1094)
105   "My mother was so
       angry . . ."   MM, 75–6
       "scraggy mare bare of a
       plume . . ."   *A* II. 490

106	"I know that wasn't true . . ."	Sean McCann in McCann, 33
	"only to make him recite . . ."	MM, 80
	"continued feebleness . . ."/ "I could call up now and again . . ."/"I cannot humiliate myself . . ."	to Fergus O'Connor, 13 and 17 Feb, 15 Apr 1918 (*L* I. 70, 71, 84)
108	"His beginning of bravery . . ."/"Life . . . had wasted all . . ."/they "were all four failures . . ."	*A* II. 21,15
109	"draped a red cloth . . ."	MM, 77
	"my mother took her part . . ."	to Robert Ginna, 17 Aug 1953 (*L* II. 986)
	Isaac (Joseph) failed to arrive	Isaac Casey was prevented by wartime restrictions from attending his mother's funeral, and SO'C never spoke to him again.
110	Maire called this the "sour pride . . ."	Sean McCann in McCann, 32-3
	"reported to be the original site . . ."	unpub. ltr. to MK, 23 July 1919 (NLI)
111	"Be kind to them . . ."	unpub. ltr. to MK, 23 July 1919 (NLI)
	"R. There is nothing solid . . ."	unpub. notebook, 1918 (Berg)
	"create things out of his own life"	*A* I. 402
	"What are they fighting for Ireland for"	MM, 81
112	onslaught on his "indecision and failure . . ."	MM, 82
	"full of confidence on . . ."	*A* II. 96
	"We wouldn't touch it . . ."	Paddy McDonnell in McCann, 171
	"splashing his thoughts over . . ."	*A* II. 95-6
113	"I wish to God this strike . . ."/"Oh, John, you wrong us . . ."	*CP* V. 435, 443
114	"I cannot turn a man away . . ."	*CP* V. 460

114	Later O'Casey recognised . . .	
	"TOM: And this is the glorious . . ."	to GJN, 21 Feb 1942 (*L* II. 2)
116	"I hope you did not forget . . ."/"My mother did speak . . ."	*CP* V. 419
		to MK, May 1919 (Sean McCann in McCann, 41)
117	"She listened – how well . . ."	*A* II. 190
	"The summer sun is tightly . . ."	
		to MK, undated (Sean McCann in McCann, 41)
118	He liked "the forword and afterword . . .	
	"He cursed us all . . ."	GBS to SO'C, 3 Dec 1919 (*L* I. 87)
	"My Dearly treasured . . ."	Paddy McDonnell in McCann, 171
		unpub. ltr. to MK, 22 Dec 1919 (NLI)
119	"I thought the world vanished . . ."	to John Gassner, 25 Sept 1954 (*L* II. 1095)
120	"We are sorry to have to return . . ."	Abbey Theatre Reader's Opinion, 28 Jan 1920 (*L* I. 92)

Act Two   ON THE RUN   1921–1927

Ch. 7   *The Shaft Which Flies in Darkness* [pp. 123-142]

123	"set too much in the one key . . ."/"This play is interestingly . . ."	Abbey Theatre Reader's Opinion, 28 Jan 1920 (*L* I. 91-2)
124	"His glittering gate . . ."/ "– Writin', be God, again! . . ."	*A* II. 194, 30
125	"– Who d'ye think y'are . . ."	*A* II. 33
	"was responsible for all the wit . . ."	Kit Casey in McCann, 165
	Mullen had been born . . ./ "odd slouching appearance . . ."	*A* I. 611; unpub. ltr. to Ronald Ayling, 26 Jan 1960 [*L* III]
126	"wriggling together like worms . . ."	to *IW*, 21 Feb 1914
	"smirched with the age-long . . ."	*A* II. 38
	"desperately superstitious and . . ."	*Feasta*, May 1955

128	between "the devil of the Auxiliary's pistol . . ."	*Irish Statesman*, 7 June 1924
	"terror in the shape of a man . . ."	*Feasta*, May 1955
129	"A shoulder-band of the overall . . ."	*A* II. 46
	"for Jim Larkin when he returned"	unpub. ltr. to Saros Cowasjee, 23 Oct 1958, quoted in S. Cowasjee, *Sean O'Casey: The Man Behind the Plays* (1965), 90
130	"a 'play of ideas' moulded . . ."	to Jack Carney, 28 Mar 1942 (*L* II. 33)
	"big sharp shit . . ."	to Jack Carney, 10 Jan 1947 (*L* II. 435)
131	"'The Crimson in the Tricolour' . . ."	LR to SO'C, 5 Nov 1921; for original version see *Lady G Journals*, 651-2
133	"I find this discursive play . . ."	play critique by WBY, 19 June 1922 (*L* I. 101-2)
	"I have re-read the work . . ."	to LR, 9 Oct 1922 (*L* I. 104)
134	"I've been among children . . ."	to Joseph Jay Deiss, 12 Dec 1950 (*L* II. 761)
135	"a man in his thirties . . ."/ "orange confetti"/"as it swirled round . . ."	R. M. Fox in McCann, 43, 45, 44-6
	"*A Return Room in a tenement* . . ."	*FIP*, 117
136	"There's a fellow that thinks . . ."/"But this is the way . . ."	*FIP*, 125-6, 167
137	"Surely a man that has read . . ."/"A Helen of Troy come to live . . ."	*FIP*, 164, 165
138	"Oh, Donal Og O'Davoren . . ."/"The poet ever strives . . ."	*FIP*, 132, 161-2
139	"The play is typed . . ."	to LR, 17 Nov 1922 (*L* I. 105)
	tried . . . "to write plays in which . . ."	*The Observer*, 10 Feb 1924
140	"What it lacked in dramatic construction . . ."	Holloway, 215-16
	"A man should always be drunk . . ."/"I'm a Nationalist meself . . ."	*FIP*, 134, 168

141 "MINNIE: I know what you
          are . . ."   *FIP*, 138
     "The characters seemed
          strangers . . ."   Holloway, 216
     "Less than four
          pounds! . . ."   *A* II. 143
142 "I forget how I came . . ."   *Lady G Journals*, 446

Ch. 8   *Hearts of Flesh and Stone* [pp. 143-162]
143 Fallon recalled seeing
          "F. J." . . .   Fallon, 3-7
144 "You're after making a
          hames . . ."   Harry Brogan in McCann, 173
     full . . . "of wild discussions
          and rows . . ."/"a
          jovial sardonic
          sketch . . ."   *A* II. 103, 144
     "Mac made one fatal
          mistake . . ."   Holloway, 218
145 "Nobody in Ireland did
          anything . . ."   *Leaders and Workers*, ed. J. W. Boyle
                                                (Dublin, 1966), 84
     Labour would "probably
          have to . . ."   *ICA*, 67
     "Of course, Jim was
          always . . ."   to Jack Carney, 10 Jan 1946
                                                (*L* II. 339)
     "Instead of counting their
          beads . . ."   *FIP*, 166-7
     "brawny and vulgar" façade   *A* II. 140
146 'Act I – Annie on strike . . ."   unpub. notebook *Juno*
147 "Somehow or other,
          despite . . ."   Holloway, 221
     his talent "would have to
          perish . . ."   *A* II. 144
     "Once inside he swore . . ."   Fallon, 17
148 taken . . . "in the middle of
          the night . . ."   Holloway, 220-1
     "more than just dead . . ."   *A* II. 8
     "JOHNNY (*passionately*): I
          won't . . ."   *FIP*, 77
149 "the kindly soul of the old
          woman . . ."   *A* II. 81
     "otherwise I fear that . . ."   James O'Connor (Seamus
                                                O'Concubhair) to SO'C,
                                                27 June 1921 (*L* I. 93)
     "B. I often of a . . .
          cold . . ."   unpub. notebook *Juno*

150	"I forgot, Mary . . ."/"MRS. I gather . . ."
	unpub. notebook *Juno*
153	Pritchett once called "the ambition . . ."
	quoted in John P. Frayne, *Sean O'Casey* (New York, 1976), 16
	"My poor little child . . ."
	FIP, 110
154	As Paul Claudel wrote . . . "Do you believe . . ."
	Fallon, 26
	"BOYLE: Won't it be a climbin' . . ."/"What did th' likes of her . . ."
	FIP, 21, 95
155	envied him "every word of . . ."
	to LR, 29 Dec 1923 (*L* I. 108)
155-6	Chekhov who "seems to let . . ."/"Lady G. enjoying her own . . ."
	Holloway, 224, 151
	"a stately-looking man . . ."/ "Away in the dim distance . . ."
	A I. 519, II. 105
157	"It seemed to be a strange . . ."
	Fallon, 19
158	"Would they . . . come to the back pit . . ."
	Lennox Robinson, *Curtain Up* (1942), 139–40
	Cummins was "a strange man . . ."
	to Robert Ginna, 17 Aug 1953 (*L* II. 987)
	"Gradually the players . . ."
	Fallon, 21
159	"A strange, odd fish,"
	Holloway, 226
160	"is at once an iconoclast . . ."
	Irish Statesman, 15 Mar 1924
	Boucicault and old melodramas
	to David Greene, 1 Jan 1953 (*L* II. 929)
	"Casey was bad in writing . . ."/"This is one of the evenings . . ."
	Lady G Journals, 511–12
161	"I asked him to come to tea . . ."
	Lady G Journals, 512
	used . . . to "buy cooked pork in . . ."
	to Frank McCarthy, 7 Mar 1949 (*L* II. 594)
	"Paddy Callan & his brother Phil . . ."
	to Jim Kavanagh, 9 Feb 1947 (*L* II. 448)
	"I wasn't working when Lady Gregory . . ."
	unpub. ltr to Saros Cowasjee, 23 Oct 1958, quoted in Cowasjee, *Sean O'Casey*

161   saying (as she recalled): " 'I
          owe . . .' "   *Lady G Journals*, 512

162   "Now I can kick
          anyone . . ."   Cowasjee, *Sean O'Casey*,
                                                    44-6

        "When the mother whose
          son . . ."   *Lady G Journals*, 513

Ch. 9   *Green, White Orange – or Yellow* [pp. 163–186]

163   "I am proud . . ."   *Seanad Eireann Parliamentary
                                                    Debates*, V (11 June 1925), 443

164   "Religion is the denial . . ."   *Further Letters of J. B. Yeats*, ed. L.
                                                    Robinson (Dundrum, 1920),
                                                    23

        "I believe that literature . . ."   *Freeman's Journal*, 13 Nov 1901
        plays should manifest "in one
          way or other . . ."/"My
          own theory of poetical or
          legendary drama . . ."   Richard Ellmann, *Yeats: The Man
                                                    and the Masks* (repr. 1979), 128

        "when I had mocked in a
          comedy . . ."   David Krause, *The Profane Book of
                                                    Irish Comedy* (1982), 45

165   "an art for the few . . ."   Ernest Fenellosa and Ezra Pound,
                                                    Noh (1916), 5–6

        "Will you come in on
          Monday . . ."   WBY to SO'C, 26 Mar 1924
                                                    (*L* I. 108)

        "immaculate in shiny sober
          black . . ."/"Yeats
          suddenly caught
          sight . . ."   *A* II. 232–3
        recommended . . . to T. S.
          Eliot   Ellmann, *Yeats*, 215
        "he wondered how they
          would feel . . ."   *A* II. 234–5

166   "happened to mention
          something . . ."   Holloway, MS Apr–June 1924,
                                                    938–9

167   "Living her own life . . ."   *The Bell*, vol. XIII (1946–7), 7
        "a mouth that was inflexible"   Colum, 120
        "Isn't it a pity . . ."   to Lady G, 2 June 1924 (*L* I. 109)
        gong, "that gave a soft,
          pensive . . ."   *A* II. 115

168   "be polite to the Spirit . . ."   *A* II. 115
        "I have long pondered . . ."   to Lady G, 12 July 1924 (*L* I. 112)

169   "the design for which . . ."   Fallon in *Modern Drama IV* (1961),
                                                    231

"I am glad that de
Valera . . ."

to Lady G, 22 July 1924
(*L* I. 113)

"all she does now,
seemingly . . ."

to Shaemas O'Sheel, 27 July 1951
(*L* II. 814–15)

170 "the greatest dramatic
find . . ."

Daniel Macmillan to James
Stephens, 27 Aug 1924
(*L* I. 115)

"He had been there
lately . . ."

Holloway (22 Aug 1924), 237

171 "He thinks Robinson
has . . ."

Holloway, MS Apr–Jun 1924, 940

"*a long, gaunt, five-story . . .*"

FIP, 278

"Its most remarkable
feature . . ."

Fallon, 2
Beatrice Coogan in McCann, 74

172 "But no sign of life came . . ."

"a discordant symphony in
greén"

A II. 125

173 the "cruiskeen lawn"
rejected . . ./"blue-prints
to see how far . . ."/
"a theocracy, fashioned
by . . ."

A II. 128–9, 135

174 unholy "Oisin spirit" as
opposed to the "St Patrick
purity . . ."

David Krause's distinctions, in his
Profane Book of Irish Comedy

175 Mark Twain . . . a "worthy
supplement" to Shaw/
"Honestly, I don't think
much . . ."

to Lady G, 22 July 1924, Sept 1924
(*L* I. 113, 118)

"*glare in the sky seen . . .*"

FIP, 340

176-7 "a sacrament to the Citizen
Army . . ."

New York Times, 4 Dec 1960

"What d'ye take
Fluther . . ."/"A man in th'
pink . . ."/"You can't
sneeze . . ."

FIP, 267, 216, 217

177 "Fight fair! . . ."/"call
themselves Catholics . . ."/
"Bloodshed is a
cleansing . . ."/"You
louse, you . . ."

FIP, 332, 259, 249, 271
Sean McCann in McCann, 35

"One evening he left off . . ."

178 the seed of Rosie in "Honour
Bright"

The Observer, 14 Feb 1926

178 all during Easter Week . . .   MM, 68
     "I . . . heard one
       workman . . ."   Holloway, 242
179 "You see, Gaby . . ."   Fallon in *Modern Drama IV*, 231–2
     "I am very busy laying
       down . . ."   to Lady G, Oct 1924 (*L* I. 119)
     "I'm afraid you'll have
       to . . ."   to R. M. Fox, 27 Oct 1924
                                         (*L* I. 120)

     "To the lovely and
       loveable . . ."   Sean McCann in McCann, 31
180 Yeats's plays had . . .
     "thinned down the
       stalls . . ."   Anthony Butler in McCann, 92
     thought "of putting actors
       into . . ."   to Sam Wanamaker, 3 Apr 1953
                                         (*L* II. 958)

     "We were to find
       ourselves . . ."   *The Story of the Abbey Theatre*, ed.
                                         S. McCann (1967), 119

181 "But actors lacking
       music . . ."/passing "from
       juvenile leads . . ."/"As he
       stepped back . . ."   *Story of the Abbey Theatre*, 119, 116,
                                         117

182 "The Allgood sisters not
       on . . ."   Cyril Cusack in *The O'Casey
                                         Enigma*, ed. Micheál Óh Aodha
                                         (Dublin, 1980), 37

183 "the Church of the Three
       Patrons . . ."   Beatrice Coogan in McCann, 77
184 another girl . . . who "had
       found . . ."   B. Coogan in McCann, 82
     "Had Joyce Chancellor . . ."   to GF, [?] May 1925 (*L* I. 135)
     "type the Caste"   to Lady G, 12 Aug 1925 (*L* I. 138)
185 "I hear you've been
       criticising . . ."   *A* II. 156
     first impressions were
       "confirmed and
       intensified"/"I have
       written . . ."   to M. J. Dolan, 13 Aug 1925
                                         (*L* I. 138–40)

186 stopped O'Casey on his
       way . . .   *A* II. 156–7

     Ch. 10 *Divine Afflatus* [pp. 187–204]

187 "It was rather
       embarrassing . . ."   to GF, 26 Aug 1925 (*L* I. 142)

"I would think twice before . . ."	*Lady Gregory's Journals 1916–1930*, ed. L. Robinson (1946), 88
188 "The lady's professional . . ."/ "O'Casey is contrasting . . ."/"I feel however that there are . . ."	George O'Brien to WBY, 5 Sept 1925; WBY and LR to O'Brien, 10 Sept 1925; O'Brien to WBY and LR, 13 Sept 1925 (*L* I. 144–7)
189 "Speaking to me across . . ."/"Jim Larkin had a great . . ."	to Lady G, 11 Sept 1925 (*L* I. 147–8)
"O'Casey," Yeats boomed . . .	*A* II. 159–63
190 "It is a great story . . ."	to Lady G, 1 Nov 1925 (*L* I. 155)
"THE COVEY (*loudly*): There's no use . . ."	*FIP*, 220
191 "FLUTHER (*scornfully*): Then Fluther . . ."/"PETER: . . . isn't it a poor thing . . ."	*FIP*, 258, 223–4
192 "as much a tragedy . . ."	*Sunday Times*, 22 Nov 1925
"A dramatic success . . ."	to Sara Allgood, 7 Dec 1925 (*L* I. 157)
193 "consciously or unconsciously . . ."	Fallon, 88
"I see where Robbie . . ."	to Sara Allgood, 7 Dec 1925 (*L* I. 161)
"any kid, livin' or dead . . ."	*FIP*, 265
"Were corrections . . ."	to LR, 10 Jan 1926 (*L* I. 166)
"more nervous than ever . . ."/ "Oh, shut up . . ."	*A* II. 147
194 eyelashes "pricked like . . ."	*A* II. 148
"You are hard . . ."/"The last act will save . . ."	Holloway, 231 (an echo of a phrase Holloway used of SO'C; cf. p. 213), 200–1
"I write it out in a verse . . ."	Yeats, *Collected Poems*, 205
195 "There was electricity . . ."	Holloway, 251
196 "carries realism to extremes . . ."	Holloway, 252
"Afterwards I met him . . ."	Ria Mooney in McCann, 167
"I'd like you to know . . ."	*A* II. 150
197 "He never fails to expose . . ."	*Irish Statesman*, 20 Feb 1926
"He's usually out for . . ."/"I only do so for young . . ."	Holloway, 253

197	"the ripest ear of corn . . ."	*ICA*, 64
198	"I suppose that some . . ."	Dr John Larchet in McCann, 176–7
	"I can still hear the Joxer-Daly-like accents . . ."	Fallon, 92
	"a genuine Fluther Good"	*A* II. 149
	"I want to make money"	Holloway, 255
199	"Mr Yeats struck an attitude . . ."	*An Poblacht*, 19 Feb 1926
	"We are now leaving the hall . . ."	Donal Dorcey in McCann, 65
	"You have disgraced yourselves . . ."	*Irish Times, Irish Independent*, 12 Feb 1926
	opportunity . . . to "throw dirt . . ."	*Catholic Bulletin*, vol. XVI (1926), 213–19
200	"Someone came knocking . . ."/"We had to go . . ."	Ria Mooney in McCann, 168
	"It is the realism that would . . ."/ "Shakespeare pandered . . ."	*Irish Independent*, 15 Feb 1926, 23 Feb 1926
201	"If squalidness, coarseness . . ."/"The safety of her brood . . ."	Holloway, 260, 257
	"Nora Clitheroe is no more 'typical . . .'"	*Irish Independent*, 23 Feb 1926
	"The Staff of Stonewall Jackson . . ."/"We know as well as Mrs Sheehy-Skeffington . . ." /"They objected to the display of . . ."	to *Irish Independent*, 20 and 26 Feb 1926 (*L* I. 169, 174)
202	"something of a whirlwind . . ."	to Sara Allgood, 23 Feb 1926 (*L* I. 174)
	"With regard to Mr O'Casey . . ."	*Irish Independent*, 2 Mar 1926
	"airless room"/"the colonel's daughter still"	*A* II. 152, 153
203	"he was clearly unwell . . ."	*The Standard*, 4 Mar 1955
	"I am anxious . . . to bring everyone . . ."	*Irish Independent*, 2 Mar 1926
	"in the little car of . . ."/"He saw now that the one . . ."	*A* II. 153, 150

he exempted Mrs
Sheehy-Skeffington

unpub. ltr. to Dr Owen
Sheehy-Skeffington, 22 July 1961
[*L* III]

204   "I was never an enemy of
his"

to F. R. Higgins, 5 June 1939
(*L* I. 803)

Ch. 11   *Free Wheeling* [pp. 205–219]

205   "tramped the quarter-
deck . . ."
"pulled here, pulled
there . . ."
"I live in the slums . . ."/
"There is material for
a . . . film . . ."

to GF, 5 Mar 1926 (*L* I. 181)

A II. 254

Daily Sketch, 24 Mar 1926; *Daily
Graphic*, 8 Mar 1926

206   " 'Didn't you think it' "

Beverley Nichols, *Are They the
Same at Home?* (1927), 275

206-7   "Never saw a hobnailed
boot . . ."
207   "cleverly placed a
mantle . . ."

A II. 254

ltr. (1934) to Lady Londonderry,
in H. Montgomery Hyde,
The Londonderrys (1979),
247

He found the bright young
things . . .
208   "Mr O'Casey's
extraordinary knowledge
. . ."
"Certainly. It is a
compliment . . ."

responded to Asquith
with . . .
". . . he was *under forty years
of age*"

A II. 251–2

Sunday Times, 22 Nov 1925

Lady Gregory's Journals 1916–1930,
256

Irish Times, 24 Mar 1926

David Krause argues in *L* I. 183
that SO'C was ignorant of his
age; but cf. pp. 205, 300

209   "great buttie now . . ."/
"This is a lonely City after
all . . ."

"Dear Maire: There is
none . . ."
"She went too far
altogether . . ."

to GF, 27 Mar and 12 Apr 1926
(*L* I. 185–6, 189)

Sean McCann in McCann, 31

Windfalls, 58–9

210	from his "angry hurt, his need . . ."
	Beatrice Coogan in McCann, 85
211	"dazed notion . . ."/"The doctor said we must . . ."/ "instead of seeing . . ."
	Eileen, 27, 41, 46
213	"Sean . . . then aged forty-six, was . . ."
	Sean, 23
	"He's a splendid fellow . . ."
	to GF, 13 May 1926 (*L* I. 194)
214	"uncanny, powerful . . ."
	to GF, 16 May 1926 (*L* I. 196)
	"It was terrible stuff . . ."
	to Frank O'Donnell, 23 Jan 1953 (*L* II. 938)
215	"There was nothing to drink but . . ."
	Augustus John, *Autobiography: Chiaroscuro* (repr. 1975), 340
	"Be brave and be confident . . ."
	to EO'C, [?] May 1926 (*L* I. 195)
216	"Receiving his royalties . . ."
	Sean, 26
	"Remember the advice of Saint Teresa . . ."
	unpub. ltr. to EO'C, 1926 (extract quoted in *Sean*, 28)
	"rarely seen a lovelier face or . . ."
	A II. 291-2
	"That sharp, sinister, cynical laugh . . ."
	unpub. ltr. to EO'C, 9 July 1929 (EO'C)
217	"quietly, patiently, and persistently . . ."/ "Ephraim & his cool-blooded . . ."
	unpub. ltr. to EO'C, 13 Sept 1929 (EO'C)
	"I must say I feel at home . . ."
	to GF, 20 June 1926 (*L* I. 201)
218	"many have I tried to love . . ."
	Sean McCann in McCann, 42
	"FORSAKING IRELAND . . ."
	Daily Sketch, 7 July 1926
	"British Drama knows its own . . ."
	Catholic Bulletin, vol. V, 803-4
219	"Now that Ireland is getting . . ."/"Monty thought this rather . . ."/ "as a depicter of the Irish . . ."
	Holloway, 270-1

Ch. 12   *A Part in Life* [pp. 220-238]

220	"When the soul of a man . . ."
	James Joyce, *A Portrait of the Artist as a Young Man* (repr. 1952), 231

221	"People just don't seem to . . ."	*Irish Independent,* 7 July 1926
	'His plays are phases of . . ."	A II. 154
222	"I turn for shelter and rest . . ."	A II. 166
	"AE liked to have every sort . . ."	Colum, 170–1
	"There's a genuine humility in . . ."	A II. 167
223	When Talbot died they found . . .	Mary Purcell, *Matt Talbot* (Dublin, 1954), 244–8
	"*Ecce hobo sapiens . . .*"	A II. 140
224	"to wrest industrial supremacy . . ."/ "I cannot see that the concept . . ."	Walter McDonald: *The Manliness of St Paul* (1958), 132; *Ethical Aspect of the Social Question* (Dublin, 1920), 217
	"A debating society or journal . . ."	to *Daily Worker,* 31 May 1948 (*L* II. 535)
225	"There are many of us who . . ."	*Irish Writing,* nos. 7–15 (1945–6)
	"You mustn't tell him, for . . ."	Lennox Robinson, interviewed by S. Cowasjee, 3 Sept 1958 (Cowasjee, *Sean O'Casey,* 87)
226	"We can't give sight to . . ."	*CP* II. 103
227	"rather shabby red-plush . . ."	Peter Quennell to the author
	telling her that "it was my name . . ."/her "big, soft . . . eyes"	unpub. ltrs. to EO'C: 13 Sept 1928, 9 July 1929 (EO'C)
	"Isn't it strange that . . ."	to GF, 1 Oct 1926 (*L* I. 206)
	"My dear child . . . you look . . ."	*Sean,* 29
	"I hope you had a good time . . ."	unpub. ltr. to EO'C, 10 Jan 1927 (EO'C)
	"Gae fetch to me a pint . . ."	A II. 270
228	"He sat in a wheeled chair . . ."	Wilfred Owen, *Poems* (1920), 32–3
229	"I suppose you think . . ."	to Lady G, 24 Dec 1926 (*L* I. 210–16)

230 "Certain plays of Ernst
     Toller . . ."/"This sort of
     destructive drama . . ."   Huntly Carter, *The New Spirit in
                                     the European Theatre, 1914–1924*
                                     (1925), 214, 217

231 "virulent Red
     pamphlet . . ."   *A* II. 295
     "within me darling as
     it is said . . ."   unpub. ltr. to EO'C, 7 July 1929
                                     (EO'C)

     frail, "but almost ready . . ." *Sean*, 31
232 "knee and thighs looking
     out . . ."/"Take care of
     yourself . . ."   unpub. ltrs.: to EO'C, 7 July, 1929;
                                     EO'C to SO'C, undated (EO'C)

     "I have no home . . ."   to GF, 25 Apr 1927 (*L* I. 215)
     "*jagged and lacerated ruin . . .*" *CP* II. 35
233 "that backboneless &
     ribless . . ."   to GJN, 28 Nov 1939 (*L* I. 8)
     escaping from
     "burlesque . . ."/"the
     worst book on . . ."   *A* II. 271, 264
     a "little manager – born
     within . . ."   to GF, 5 Jan 1927 (*L* I. 211)
     "the excitement of his
     lady's . . ."   *A* II. 295
     "one of the most truly moral
     men . . ."   EO'C to the author
234 "Bright, fascinating
     things . . ."   to EO'C, 1927 (*L* I. 216–17)
     "I have spent the passing
     hours . . ."   unpub. ltr. to EO'C, 4 Aug 1927,
                                     partly quoted in *Sean*, 33–4

235 "then getting up with that
     quick . . ."/"because of
     the possibility . . ."/
     "Very good . . ."   unpub. ltrs.: EO'C to SO'C,
                                     undated (1927); to EO'C, 10
                                     Sept 1927 (EO'C)

238 "of my own wife . . ."   to *Daily Worker* (not pub.) 31 May
                                     1948 (*L* II. 532)

Act Three   THE SHAPE OF A NEW WORLD   1927–1964

Ch. 13 *Slouching Towards Bethlehem* [pp. 241–259]
241 "humorous, watchful . . ."   *Sean*, 41
242 "I knew that I had been . . ."/
     "wonderfully
     soothing . . ."   *Eileen*, 99; *Sean*, 42

"beeches, Larches
   Willows . . ."/"solve an
   Einstein problem . . ."   to GF, 9 Sept and 13 Sept 1927
                                                (*L* I. 220, 221)

"I hope all goes well . . ."   Lady G to SO'C, 27 Nov 1927,
                                                in *Modern Drama*, May 1965,
                                                97

243 one visitor noticed   George Bishop, in *The Observer*, 6
                                                Oct 1929

"Jasus, it wasn't half . . ."   *A* II. 298
"Wherever it was, it would
   be . . ."   *Sean*, 55
244 "Lady Londonderry had to
   live . . ."   unpub. ltr. to David Krause, 1963
                                                [*L* III]

"You will find there a
   Queen . . ."   Lady Londonderry, *Retrospect*
                                                (1928), 247

"content with her
   friendship . . ."   unpub. ltr. to D Krause, 1963
                                                [*L* III]

"They are of a different
   race . . ."   Londonderry, *Retrospect*, 189
245 "I know some of these . . ."   *A* II. 295
"a close tyrannical
   bureaucracy . . ."   Ronald Clark, *Life of Bertrand
                                                Russell* (1975), 380

"a level of physique
   and . . ."   Paul Johnson, *A History of the
                                                Modern World* (1983), 275–6

246 "so that I may be able . . ."/
   "I don't believe you'll
   ever . . ."   to Lady G, 28 Feb 1928 (*L* I. 230,
                                                233)

247 "I absolutely agree with . . ."   Lady G to SO'C, 27 Apr 1928, in
                                                Modern Drama, May 1965, 100

"You were interested
   in . . ."   WBY to SO'C, 20 Apr 1928
                                                (*L* I. 268)

249 "the blood–dimmed tide
   is . . ."   Yeats, *Collected Poems*, 211
250 "When 'A.E.'
   experimented . . ."   St. John Ervine to SO'C, 6 June
                                                1928 (*L* I. 263)

251 "I think I ought to . . ."   Lady G to SO'C, 27 Apr 1928, in
                                                Modern Drama, May 1965, 100

252 "What the hell are you . . ."   *Sean*, 59
"the doctor taking fifty
   pounds . . ."   *A* II. 301

252–4   He had anticipated . . .
         two months later

rough draft of a ltr. to GBS, 5 July
1928 (*L* I. 297); it is not known if
the letter was sent.

253, 254 spirited caricatures

two cartoons, 9 June 1928,
apparently unsent (EO'C)

255   "I have no intention . . ."

to Daniel Macmillan, 12 May 1928
(*L* I. 244–5)

       "Could anything equal . . ."

on WBY to Lady G, 25 Apr 1928
(*L* I. 238)

       "I am too big for . . ."

to LR, 2 May 1928 (*L* I. 240)

256   "You seem Mr Yeats, to
       be . . ."

to WBY, 11 May 1928 (*L* I. 273)

       "Does he take me to be . . ."

to Lady G, undated (*L* I. 270)

       "You can take it from
       me . . ."

to George Russell, 2 June 1928
(*L* I. 257)

257   "In *The Silver Tassie* . . ."

Walter Starkie to WBY, *Irish
Statesman*, 9 June 1928

       "hopping about like a gold
       finch . . ."

unpub. notebook E 6 (Berg)

       "tossed the names of Yeats
       and O'Casey . . ."

A II. 277

       "Mr S. O'Casey, dramatic
       writer . . ."

Catholic Bulletin, vol. XVIII (1928),
676

258   "So far as Dublin is
       concerned . . ."

unpub. ltr. WBY to Lady G, 4 June
1928

       "that he might see there was
       nothing . . ."

Lady Gregory's Journals 1916–1930,
110

       Starkie became "a toff"

to *Nineteenth Century*, Sept 1928
(*L* I. 306)

       "Born into the
       proletariat . . ."

A II. 284

       "I am convinced . . ."

Sir Barry Jackson to SO'C, 28 June
1928 (*Sean*, 62)

       "justifiable anger . . ."

St. John Ervine to SO'C, 6 June
1928 (*L* I. 263–4)

Ch. 14   *A New Character* [pp. 260–278]

260   "You really are a ruthless . . ."

GBS to SO'C, 19 June 1928 (*Sean*,
63)

       "Give him a job . . ."

GBS to Lady G, in *Lady Gregory's
Journals 1916–1930*, 110–11

261   Cecil L'Estrange Malone

quoted in Andrew Boyle, *The
Climate of Treason* (1980), 31

"You are suspected of . . ."
GBS to SO'C, 19 June 1928 (*Sean*, 63)

262 "And there I'll leave you . . ."
to *Irish News* (not pub.), 4 July 1928 (*L* I. 295)

263 "the same gesture . . ."/ "eight years later . . ."
Sean, 64

"towards the silencing of Sean . . ."
A II. 279

264 "Through the delicate fume . . ."
A II. 279–80

"Say that he is the rottenest . . ."
GBS to SO'C, 3 July 1928 (*Sean*, 65)

tried "to prevent the publication . . ."/"the one criticism that was . . ."
to GBS, [5] July 1928 (*L* I. 297)

265 "a silly little temple . . ."
to GBS, [5] July 1928 (*L* I. 297)

"I do feel 'Sean' wants . . ."
Charlotte Shaw to EO'C, 8 July 1928 (*Sean*, 66)

"He had refused the counsel . . ."/"Mrs Shaw, in her heart, resented . . ."
A II. 280

"Try to be a little good natured . . ."/"DEAR SEAN—You are creating . . ."
Irish Statesman, 4 Aug 1928

266 "He would fight alone . . ."
A II. 280

"clasping in my arms once again . . ."
unpub. ltr. to EO'C, 24 Aug 1928 (EO'C)

wanting to "get as far away from . . ."
to GF, 28 July 1928 (*L* I. 302)

267 "Isn't Jude a tragic tale . . ."/ "Even if nothing should happen . . ."
unpub. ltrs.: EO'C to SO'C, undated; to EO'C, 20 Sept 1928 (EO'C)

omissions or modifications in the text
Lord Chamberlain to C. B. Cochran, July 1928 (*L* I. 299)

268 our "classical war play . . ."
J. L. Hodson, *No Phantoms Here* (1932), 144

pictures by "Cezanne, Renoir, V. Gogh . . ."/ "We have six originals now . . ."
to Lady G, 7 Nov 1928 (*L* I. 320, 319)

268 "so you see my boy . . ."/
   "Did you see see pee see's
   praise . . ."   to GF, 29 Nov 1928 (*L* I. 323)
   "I've read Yeats's 'The
   Tower' . . ."   to Oliver Gogarty, 5 Feb 1929
                                      (*L* I. 334)

269 "There is no greater
   artificiality . . ."   O. Gogarty to SO'C, 8 Feb 1929
                                      (*L* I. 336)

   "I don't know . . . whether
   to condemn . . ."   to GF, 28 Feb 1929 (*L* I. 341)
   "on every house you can
   see . . ."/"her good &
   impetuous nature . . ."   to Augustus John: 20 Feb 1929
                                      (*L* I. 340); unpub. ltr.,
                                      15 Jan 1929

270 "I was very young . . ."   David Astor to author
   "peevishly proclaiming his
   hunger"   *Sean*, 48

271 "Breon must only take you
   away . . ."/"Gold and
   Silver . . ."   unpub. ltrs. to EO'C, 9 July 1929
                                      (EO'C), 14 July 1930 (*Windfalls*,
                                      35–42)

   "deep, burning
   longing . . ."/"Would it
   really be wrong . . ."   unpub. ltrs., EO'C to SO'C,
                                      undated and 6 July 1929 (EO'C)

   "believe me
   affectionately . . ."   Lady G to SO'C, 15 July 1929, in
                                      Modern Drama, May 1965, 105

   things that had "entrenched
   themselves . . ."   to Lady G, 18 July 1929
                                      (*L* I. 350–1)

272 "not only an open mind
   but . . ."/"It was,
   however, the first . . ."   Raymond Massey, *A Hundred
                                      Different Lives* (1979), 86–7

273 "It was all out and no
   holds . . ."   Massey, *Hundred Different Lives*, 87
   "with amazing strength . . ."   to GF, 18 Sept 1929 (*L* I. 366)
   "every day after
   rehearsal . . ."/"*Christ
   these Irish parts . . .*"   Emlyn Williams, *An Early Autobio-
                                      graphy, 1927–1935* (1973), 114

274 "The journalist claimed . . ."   unpub. ltr., WBY to Lady G, 30
                                      Oct 1929

   "The story of Mr Sean
   O'Casey . . ."   *The Observer*, 6 Oct 1929

"The production has made my mind . . ."

to Lady G, 15 Oct 1929 (*L* I. 369)

275 "of whom he had so often . . ."

A II. 336

"In the harsh work lights . . ."

Massey, *Hundred Different Lives*, 90–1

"the greatest thing of our time"

Augustus John to SO'C, 21 Oct 1929 (*Sean*, 87)

276 "Cochran the infallible . . ."

Williams, *Early Autobiography*, 117

"I hear only of people who . . ."/"I had tea with Gerald Heard . . ."

unpub. ltrs.: WBY to Lady G, 10 Nov 1929; to LR, 16 Nov 1929

"fine houses"

to GF, 3 Dec 1929 (*L* I. 384)

"I fancy that Dublin . . ."

Catholic Mind, Sept 1930

"Vox AEius non vox Dei . . ."

Irish Statesman, 30 Nov 1929

277 "I advise you to say . . ."

Irish Statesman, 14 Dec 1929

"Any more strokes . . ."

to *Irish Statesman*, 7 Jan 1930 (*L* I. 392)

"AE has been unhorsed too . . ."

to Oliver Gogarty, 14 Apr 1930 (*L* I. 404)

"like a little cuckoo clock . . ."

Irish Statesman, 30 Nov 1929

Ch. 15   *The Phantoms of Hyde Park* [pp. 279–302]

280 "I never saw it"

unpub. ltr. to Charles Rosenberg and Martin Kesselman, 23 Mar 1955 [*L* III]

"From the little cockey'd sparrow . . ."

to Lady Londonderry, 14 July 1930 (*L* I. 413)

"Had he found the gathering . . ."

Bonar Thompson, *Hyde Park Orator* (1934), Preface, xii

281 "Sooner or later an Archdeaconship . . ."

to GF, 4 Nov 1930 (*L* I. 423)

"he was all . . . for quoting . . ."

Leslie Rees in *Meanjin Quarterly*, vol. XXIV, no. 4, 416

starting to dread . . . "its powers . . ."/"imposing prisons for . . ."/"that I may talk in secret . . ."

unpub. ltrs. to EO'C, 15 Feb 1932 and undated (EO'C)

282 "I'll see to it . . ."/"Do you miss . . ."/a "pity these things . . ."

unpub. ltrs. to EO'C, 11 July 1929 and undated (EO'C)

283 | "without prim and purposeful . . ." | *A* II. 423

"I'm going to have . . ."/"an operation at midnight . . ." | *Sean*, 90–1; *Eileen*, 121–2

284 "glorious irresponsibility" | to GJN, 12 Feb 1953 (*L* II. 940–1)

285 "A mass of wriggling . . ." | *A* II. 363

"I rejoice to think of you . . ." | Charlotte Shaw to EO'C, 15 Nov 1931 (*Sean*, 94)

"God be my judge . . ." | to Charlotte Shaw, [?] Nov 1931 (*L* I. 443)

"*after a year*, they moved . . ." | *A* II. 366

"I have, at last, got a chance . . ." | to GF, 21 Oct 1931 (*L* I. 438)

286 to "get back to the play . . ." | to Charlotte Shaw, [?] Nov 1931 (*L* I. 441)

"that the next may be a great play . . ." | Hodson, *No Phantoms Here*, 147–56

"My thoughts, Eileen . . ." | unpub. ltr. to EO'C, 15 Feb 1932 (EO'C)

287 "Eileen, dear, I don't think . . ." | *Eileen*, 127

"dear and lovely" body | unpub. ltr. to EO'C, 10 Mar 1932 (EO'C)

"You crept into a father's place . . ."/"The other night I had . . ."/"How often have I told you . . ." | *CP* II. 141, 140, 145

288 "Five pounds to keep the wolf . . ." | to J. R. Storey, [?] July 1932 (*L* I. 445)

289 "That's the last penny . . ." | *FIP*, 409

"triumph of the principle . . ." | Samuel Beckett, *Disjecta*, in *Bookman*, Christmas 1934, 82–3

she died at Coole . . . | Elizabeth Coxhead, *Lady Gregory* (1961), 192

290 "absurdly bad bargain . . ." | GBS to SO'C, 23 July 1932 (*Sean*, 107)

"Once Sean had turned against . . ." | *Sean*, 105

"It can't be worse there than . . ." | unpub. ltr. to EO'C, 27 Dec 1932 (EO'C)

291 "Anyhow what more can they teach . . ." | unpub. ltr. to EO'C, 18 Jan 1933 (EO'C)

"hardest job that I have
ever . . ."
"I wish it were a hundred . . ."

to GJN, 30 May 1933 (*L* I. 457)
unpub. ltr. to EO'C, 20 May 1933
(EO'C)

"You have written some
grand stuff . . ."

C. B. Cochran to SO'C, 1 Aug
1933 (*L* I. 460)

292   attempt to "release drama
from . . ."
"It's not 'ims afryde . . ."
"Your advice to go
back . . ."

Blasts, 111–17
CP II. 208

to C. B. Cochran, 7 Aug 1933
(*L* I. 462)

"Instead of being a
drunkard . . ."
293   "We were thinking of the
main . . ."
"Sean O'Casey is all right
now . . ."

EO'C to author

EO'C to author

Hesketh Pearson, *Bernard Shaw*
(1987), 413

"It is a splendid piece of
work . . ."

Eugene O'Neill to SO'C, 15 Dec
1933 (*L* I. 482)

"How far he has gone
since . . ."

T. E. Lawrence to Lady Astor,
15 Feb 1934, *The Letters of T.E.
Lawrence*, ed. D. Garnett (1938),
510

294   "which is really pretty
subtle . . ."

unpub. ltr. Augustus John to
SO'C, 11 Jan 1934

"or wish to be saeculo
saeculorum . . ."

to Lady Astor, 6 Jan 1934
(*L* I. 486)

"with a twisted smile,
listening . . ."
295   "Mr O'Casey's fierce
play . . ."
"My mission in life is not to
give . . ."
"Mr O'Casey is
essentially . . ."
"A big sneer and a little
snarl . . ."
296   "Curious they can't see . . ."

"It is a proud thing . . ."/"It
will be good . . ."

Daily Express, 8 Feb 1934

The Times, 8 Feb 1934

Daily Express, 12 Feb 1934

Sunday Times, 11 Feb 1934

Sunday Times, 18 Feb 1934
to Macmillan & Co., 5 July 1934
(*L* I. 511)

to GJN, 1 Nov 1933, 21 July 1934
(*L* I. 477, 516)

297   "Don't look on the dull
      side . . ."
                                            unpub. ltr., EO'C to SO'C,
                                              undated (EO'C)

298   "The Commies are
      comin' . . ."   *A* II. 387
      "Brigid and Columcille . . ."   Hyde, *The Londonderrys*, 248
      the *Britannic*   *A* II. 393
299   "a melancholy sight . . ."   unpub. ltr. to EO'C, 16 Sept 1934
                                              (EO'C)

      overblown praise of the
      American   *A* II. 403
      "I've rarely seen such a
      man . . ."   unpub. ltr. to EO'C, undated
                                              (EO'C)

      "Come unto me all you . . ."   *A* II. 407
      "bit too gorgeous . . ."   unpub. ltr. to EO'C, undated
                                              (EO'C)

300   "good though she is . . ."/
      "Don't say anything . . ."   unpub. ltrs. to EO'C, 21 Oct and
                                              26 Nov 1934 (EO'C)

      "He was born in 1880 . . ."   *New York Times*, 14 Oct 1934
      "like a monkey on a stick . . ."   unpub. ltr. to EO'C, 31 Oct 1934
301   "and not a pretty girl . . ."/
      "tattered, worn . . ."/
      "After we have nursed . . ."   unpub. ltrs. to EO'C, 14 Nov, 2
                                              Oct, between 4 and 20 Oct 1934
                                              (EO'C)

      "Nationality was something
      even . . ."   *A* II. 440

Ch. 16   *Pink Wilderness* [pp. 303–323]

304   "wobbling walk of the
      housemaids . . ."/
      a "celibate cleric stay
      with . . ."   *A* II. 472, 479
      "the missus protesting & half
      afraid . . ."   to GJN, 30 Nov 1935 (*L* I. 536)
      substantial royalties   unpub. notebook E 8 (Berg)

305   "either dead before it was
      taken . . ."   *New Statesman and Nation*, 9 Feb
                                              1935

      "He has attacked . . ."/"He
      is very emotional . . ."   WBY to Ethel Mannin, 4 Mar
                                              1935, *The Letters of W. B. Yeats*,
                                              ed. A. Wade (1954), 831–3

306   "to say silently so that . . ."/
      a "truer rebel than
      truest . . ."   *A* II. 342, 343

307   "What is its divinity?"
       "He used to come in
          unannounced . . ."

       "rather lightweight . . ."
308   The reason . . . "was the
          reason all . . ."
       "Harold Macmillan is one
          of . . ."
       "The dynamic of social
          change . . ."

       "fine character, who
          wore . . ."/"something of
          the greatness of Hardy . . ."
309   "My dear Sean . . . I have
          almost had . . ."

310   "the best feelings"

       "there is no force on
          earth . . ."

       "ridiculous BA hood . . ."

       "stepping back from a kind
          of . . ."

311   a "born Communist . . ."

       "I would like to take
          you . . ."

       "lovely Eileen Carey . . ."
       "He is, as you say, a fine
          fellow . . ."

       "O'Casey lived very
          much . . ."
312   "Capitalism is the
          regimentation . . ."/
       "soldiers of rotten
          cardboard . . ."

       "I am praying to God . . ."

       "He wasn't much of a
          thinker . . ."/"bits of his
          autobiography"

A II. 345

Nigel Fisher, *Harold Macmillan*
   (1982), 20
H. Macmillan to author

H. Macmillan to author

to GJN, 1 Dec 1935 (*L* I. 597-8)

Harold Macmillan, *The Middle Way*
   (1938), 373

H. Macmillan to author

J. Ramsay MacDonald to SO'C,
   10 Jan 1934 (*L* I. 487)
Michael Holroyd, *Lytton Strachey*
   (1971), 212

John Strachey, *The Menace of
   Fascism* (1932)
Malcolm Muggeridge, *Chronicles of
   Wasted Time*, vol. I (1978), 205

Harold Macmillan, *Winds of Change*
   (1966), 359
G. B. Shaw, *Immaturity* (1931),
   Preface

Lady Astor to SO'C, 8 Nov 1935
   (*L* I. 593)
A II. 600

unpub. ltr. to EO'C, 13 Oct 1934
   (EO'C)

H. Macmillan to author

to *Time and Tide*, 23 May and
   6 June 1936 (*L* I. 628, 632)
to Harold Macmillan, 13 Nov 1936
   (*L* I. 642)

H. Macmillan to author

313 "the sword I have swung so
       long . . ."   to Harold Macmillan, 25 Sept 1936
                                             (*L* I. 637–9)

     "then fell silent when I . . ."   to GJN, 28 Oct 1936 (*L* I. 639)
     "It could have been a
       dangerous . . ."   *Sean*, 138
     "a scrappy and truculent
       volume . . ."   *New York Times*, 6 June 1937
     "Beware of entering
       into . . ."   to Lady Rhondda, [?] Dec 1937
                                             (*L* I. 688)

314 "a cock that won't . . ."/
     "The Dean of
       Canterbury, Professor
       Laski . . ."   *Forward*, 6 Apr and 30 Apr 1938
     "O'Casey, you know
       perfectly . . ."/"He says,
       O'Casey knows
       perfectly . . ."   *Time and Tide*, 4 June and 11 June
                                             1938

     Yeats had . . . "fled too far
       away . . ."/"Yeats became   *International Literature* (Moscow),
       much more human . . ."   Dec 1939 (*Blasts*, 176)

315 "Hail to the Coming of . . ."   to Peter Newmark, 7 June 1937 (*L*
                                             I. 673)

     St Francis . . . was "more
       of a Communist . . ."   to GF, 29 Oct 1936 (*L* I. 641)
     "You want the best that can
       be . . ."   to GJN, 28 Oct 1936 (*L* I. 639)
     "When I talk to you, I am
       in . . ."   to Harold Macmillan, 9 Sept 1938
                                             (*L* I. 736)
316 "Communists in heart"   to Harold Macmillan, 22 Oct 1938
                                             (*L* I. 820)

     "Your husband was
       luckier . . ."   EO'C to author
     "that this very shyness . . ."   to GBS, 24 Nov 1937 (*L* I. 685)
317 "It's the bitter heart
       that . . ."   *CP* II. 252
318 "STAR STILL A NEBULA"   unpub. telegram to Raisa
                                             Lomonosova, 17 Nov 1925
                                             [*L* III]

     "another bloody big row"/
     "As well as being
       something of a . . ."   to GJN, 8 Mar 1937 and 8 Feb 1939
                                             (*L* I. 655, 775)
319 "a kind of Slavonic fascism"   quoted in Johnson, *History of the
                                             Modern World*, 361

"The fact of an
  understanding . . ."

                to Richard Madden, 19 Oct 1939
"Not only do I feel . . ."   (*L* I. 817)
                George P. Brett to SO'C, 16 Feb

320 "Double partition . . ."   1940 (*L* I. 845)
                to *Picture Post*, 24 Feb 1940

"I find the piece to be a   (*L* I. 846)
   magnum opus . . ."
"Incontrovertibly poor . . ." *Sunday Times*, 13 Mar 1940
321 "I should have gone to the *Newsweek*, 29 Jan 1940
   Red Star . . ."
                GBS to SO'C, postcard, 22 Apr
                1940 (*Sean*, 162)
"Prating priest,
   peradventure . . ."   *CP* II. 325–6
323 "greatest, the loveliest . . ." *A* II. 512
"Sisterless men are
   always . . ."
                GBS to EO'C, 4 Oct 1939 (*Sean*,
"I was so glad to get your 156)
   letter . . ."
                Harold Macmillan to EO'C, 5 Oct
O'Casey "claimed to be a 1939 (*Sean*, 156–7)
   Communist . . ."
                Macmillan, *Winds of Change*, 187

Ch. 17 *A Detrimental Temper* [pp. 324–348]

324 "Stalin is becoming a
   household name . . ."   to Lovat Dickson, 20 Dec 1941
                (*L* I. 917)
"In Russia it is the
   Russians . . ."   to *Time and Tide*, 5 Mar 1938
                (*L* I. 705)
"folk in the fine fair English
   sense . . ."   *West Country Magazine*, Winter
                1946
"like a grey-haired lady . . ." *A* II. 523
325 In his last volume of
   autobiography   *A* II. 655
326 "Oh no," Maurice told
   him . . .   EO'C to author
327 "No Russell ever went . . ." H. Macmillan to author
328 "preferential treatment to
   all . . ."   to William Curry, 22 Apr 1944
                (*L* II. 166)
"The higher the
   standard . . ."   *Sean*, 143
329 "too sloven, too
   outspread . . ."   *A* II. 406

329	"Most snobbish, bourgeois . . ."	to GF, 3 Apr 1945 (*L* II. 224)
330	"He likes American comics . . ."	to GJN, 11 May 1943 (*L* II. 13?)
	flooded with American soldiers/She threw herself into mastering . . ./"the tumult of mind afflicting . . ."	*A* II. 577, 576, 661
	"fell recklessly, dinting . . ."	to Jack Carney, 23 Feb 1943 (*L* II. 125)
	"his little body shook"	unpub. diary, 6 Dec 1958 (EO'C)
331	"the guttersnipe, Rommel"	to Jack Daley, 26 June 1942 (*L* II. 62)
	"Add another horse to your . . ."	to Winston Churchill, 4 July 1942 (*L* II. 67)
	"we practically went through . . ."/"We heard the german bombs fall . . ."	unpub. ltr. to Brooks Atkinson, 1943/1944 [*LIII*]
332	"the most egoistic & selfish . . ."	unpub. ltr. to Hugh MacDiarmid, 9 Oct 1949
	"An' you, young girl . . ."	*CP* III. 106
	"as much as it would take . . ."	*A* II. 658
334	"Is he like that *diva* . . ."	*Sunday Times*, 3 May 1942
335	"*a cloud of timidity*"/"*Under this window* . . ."	*CP* III. 138
336	"That is not playwriting . . ."	*The Bell*, 1943, 119
	"Faced with it, I find myself . . ."	*The Standard*, 28 June 1946
337	"In the action of the play . . ."	*The Standard*, 9 Aug 1946
	"All my life I've been attacked . . ."	SO'C to David Krause, 1963 (*L* II. 386)
338	"I tell you the devotion . . ."/"Forgive me for imputing . . ."	to Joseph Cummins, 26 Nov 1942; Cummins to SO'C, 4 Dec 1942 (*L* II. 97)
	"why in the name o' God . . ."	to GF, 20 Feb 1943 (*L* II. 226–7)
	"sad to think that the English . . ."	Sheila Edwards to SO'C, 9 Apr 1945 (*L* II. 226–7)

339 a "dastardly thing to
       coax . . ."

to Sheila Edwards, [?] June 1945
(*L* II. 258)

340 "*She had large blue
       eyes . . .*"

CP V. 38–9

341 "a fine writer, but
       vague . . ."/"a trite fellow
       with . . ."

unpub. ltr. to Ingrid Burke, 6 July
1948 [*L* III]

342 wished . . . "wasn't quite so
       diffident . . ."

to Daniel Macmillan, 18 Feb 1942
(*L* II. 17)

343 "It's a terrible thing to
       have . . ."

Sean, 191

344 "that most despicable of all
       shams . . ."

unpub. ltr. GBS to SO'C, 14 Nov
1942

       "Herself and myself had a
       pleasant . . ."

John Dulanty to SO'C, 13 Jan 1950
(*Sean*, 194)

       "My dear Sean, Eileen,
       still . . ."

GBS to SO'C, 5 May 1950
(*Sean*, 195)

       "the luckiest of us all"
345 "if there's an
       Almighty . . ."/"the
       touch of a soft Irish
       hand . . ."

EO'C to author

to GJN, 3 Nov 1950 (*L* II. 749–50)

       "His epiphany was the
       showing . . ."

A II. 623

346 "You must have heard a
       lot . . ."

unpub. ltr. to "Sister Catherine",
14 Feb 1945 (EO'C)

347 "has enlarged his
       method . . ."
       "eighteenth-century
       spirits . . ."

Our Time, June 1946

G. Wilson Knight, *The Christian
Renaissance* (1962), 342

       "Pity [he] was so
       conceited . . ."

to Beatrix Lehmann, 5 Nov 1945
(*L* II. 302)

348 "one who could keep
       talking . . ."/"a frightened
       thing, apologising . . ."

to Jill Howard, 5 June 1947
(*L* II. 466)

       "his heart's blood
       pressed . . ."/"The
       fellow's gone now,
       making his exit . . ."

A II. 655

348 "Even today, I leave behind
        me . . ."   to Breon O'Casey, 28 May 1947,
                                              in Ronald Ayling and Michael J.
                                              Durkan, *Sean O'Casey: A
                                              Bibliography* (1978), 76
       the lungs scarred from . . ."   to Daniel Macmillan, 29 Aug 1947
                                              (*L* II. 474)

Ch. 18 *Divorce, Irish-Style* [pp. 349–358]

349 "It's hard enough to
        write . . ."   to LR, 25 Oct 1943 (*L* II. 149)
       "I hated his vulgar . . ."   to Daniel Macmillan, 21 Dec 1942
                                              (*L* II. 109)
       "These memoirs show . . ."   *Irish Writing*, vol. I (1946–8), 68
350 "whenever he comes up
        against . . ."/"the 'doctor'
        here described . . ."/   *The Bell*, vol. II (1945–6), 815
        creative and careless   to Lovat Dickson, 8 July 1945
        alike . . ."   (*L* II. 276)
351 "powerful and unsparing
        . . ."/"As a bitter
        invention . . ."   *The Observer*, 12 Mar 1939;
                                              Spectator, 2 Nov 1945

       "all the performing fleas I
        have met . . ."   P. G. Wodehouse, *Performing Flea*
                                              (repr. 1961), 254

       "One of Mr O'Casey's
        most . . ."/"The fact is, I
        think . . ."   *Spectator*, 3 Nov and 7 Dec 1945
       "no reference to England
        which is not . . ."   *The Observer*, 28 Oct 1945
352 Orwell "had as much
        chance . . ."/"the decay in
        himself . . ."   *A* II. 547, 542
       "Is Sean as bitter . . ."   R. M. Fox in McCann, 49
353 "Indeed, it is the reviews . . ."   to Horace Reynolds, 17 Feb 1949
                                              (*L* II. 588)
354 "Strange and all as it
        may . . ."   to Michael Casey, [?] Jan 1945
                                              (*L* II. 201)
       "The other fella . . ."   MM, 86–7
       "He never read a line . . ."   to Harold Macmillan, 15 Oct 1948
                                              (*L* II. 558)
       "Personally I love the
        superb . . ."   *Sunday Times*, 30 Jan 1949
355 "It was not the beauty
        of . . ."   *The Bell*, vol. V (Oct–Mar 1942–3),
                                              115

"The four volumes have shown . . ."

Irish Book Lover, vol. XXXI (1949–51), 44

356 "Sean O'Casey, Litt.D.! . . ."

unpub. ltr. to J. P. Mitchell, 4 Feb 1961; see *Eileen*, 189–90

"such an honour would not be . . ."

unpub. ltr. to I. J. Bligh, 28 Nov 1962 (EO'C)

"unattractive and unheroic . . ."

Sovietskaya Kultura, 15 Dec 1955

"Russia is not Communist . . ."

Irish Times, 25 July 1959

"I should be put against . . ."
was a "hero over in Russia . . ."

Life Magazine, 9 Oct 1964

interview in *The Sting and the Twinkle*, ed. E. H. Mikhail and John O'Riordan (1974), 108

"I wish our Communists would . . ."

to Frank McCarthy, 24 Mar 1951 (*L* II. 782)

357 "When I take a pen . . ."/
"When afterwards I read his letters . . ."

Ria Mooney, Dr John Larchet in McCann, 170

"Sick with ecstasy . . ."/
"The mother seeing the sham . . ."

A II. 433

358 "Wealth often takes away . . ."

A II. 429

"blaster and blighter . . ."

Fallon, 159; *New York Herald Tribune*, 16 Nov 1958

"In a society firmly based . . ."

A II. 640

Ch. 19 *Th' Gentle Ripple of a Rose* [pp. 359–374]

359 "no financial reserves, & so . . ."

to Gordon Rogoff, 9 May 1954 (*L* II. 1048)

"half our present space . . ."

to Frank Morell, 6 Apr 1954 (*L* II. 1040)

"A place where many are old . . ."

West Country Magazine, Winter 1946

"all the Bourgeoise . . ."

to Frank Morell, 6 Apr 1954 (*L* II. 1040)

360 a comprehensive picture

EO'C to author

360   Salisbury . . . Red Lion
         Hotel   unpub. diary, 7 Sept 1950 (Berg)
      "joyous blarney"   *New York Times*, 18 May 1966
      He boasted in one letter   to Frank McCarthy, 4 Nov 1954
                                                    (*L* II. 1106)

361   "19 paces long, 10 wide"   unpub. diary, 6 Aug 1960, 26 July
                                                    1958 (EO'C)
      "a gay sparkling one . . ."   unpub. ltr. to Brooks Atkinson, 16
                                                    Apr 1958 [*L*III]

      "fashioning Van Gogh into
         life . . ."   *A* II. 444
      "the yard was fat . . ."   unpub. diary, 16 Nov 1957
                                                    (EO'C)

362   "I thought a lot of
         sending . . ."   unpub. ltr. to EO'C, 28 Sept 1956
                                                    (EO'C)

      "When in a cricket
         match . . ."   EO'C to author
      "strangely stubborn and
         hard . . ."   *Sean*, 239

363   "Dear Daddy, I hope you
         find . . ."   Niall O'Casey to SO'C, 16 Nov
                                                    1957 (*Sean*, 238)

      "over a long life had
         known . . ."   *Sean*, 238–9

364   "by my putting my
         arms . . ."   *Sean*, 239
      "When I went to where . . ."   unpub. diary, 5 Oct 1957 (EO'C)

365   "And the political
         bastards . . ."/"Does
         Mozart compose . . ."/
      "He was lying in a sloping
         way . . ."   unpub. diary, 6 Dec 1958, 27 Feb
                                                    1960, 4 July 1958 (EO'C)

366   "a black border . . ."/"Niall
         you went wearing . . ."/
      "Oh, God to think of
         it . . ."   unpub. diary, 12 Dec 1959, 2 Apr
                                                    1960, 13 Apr 1957 (EO'C)

      "had been used by English
         Communists . . ."/
      "Thank God I
         escaped . . ."   unpub. ltrs. to Brooks Atkinson,
                                                    19 Mar and 30 Mar 1960 [*L* III]

      "I have nothing to do with
         Beckett . . ."   unpub. ltr. Dec 1955 [*L* III]

367   O'Casey listened several
         times   unpub. ltr. to Tyrone Guthrie, 9
                                                    Mar 1958

368   "Not quite tears . . ."

Introduction to *Selected Plays* (New York, 1954)

369   "somehow, someday, somewhere . . ."

unpub. ltr. to Brooks Atkinson, 1958 [*L* III]

"the root of all evil . . ."

J. W. von Goethe, *Wisdom and Experience* (New York, 1949), 218

O'Casey told . . . Tyrone Guthrie

unpub. ltr. to Tyrone Guthrie, 12 Feb 1955

370   "quietly and unnoticed . . ."

EO'C to Sidney Bernstein, 10 Feb 1955

"Figuro is an abounding joy . . ."

CP V. 361

371   "Stay in England . . ."

A II. 641

"of auburn beauty and . . ."

David Krause in McCann, 140

"My arms aren't long enough . . ."

unpub. ltr. to EO'C, 16 Nov 1958 (EO'C)

"claimed and laid hold . . ."

undated TS (EO'C)

"fainter beauties within . . ."

unpub. ltr. to Brooks Atkinson, 30 June 1962 [*L* III]

372   "–Swallas, Jack; just common . . ."

unpub. ltr. to Brooks Atkinson, 30 June 1962 [*L* III]

"We were physically sick . . ."

unpub. ltr. Jan 1964 [*L* III]

373   "Oh my God . . ."

EO'C to author

"Here I am like a cooped-up cock . . ."

to EO'C, 12 Aug 1964 (*Sean*, 281–3)

374   "I don't believe . . ."

TS National Broadcasting Company interview with Robert Ginna, 22 Jan 1956

Epilogue [pp. 375–381]

375   I have found life . . .

"The best thing that ever happened . . ."

TS NBC interview, 22 Jan 1956

The Sean O'Casey Reader, ed. Brooks Atkinson (New York, 1968), Introduction, xxii

"I don't *mind* how many . . ."

Frank O'Connor, *My Father's Son* (1971), 140

"I know what a housewife . . ."

unpub. ltr. 3 June 1956 [*L* III]

376   "To me one thing alone is . . ."

to Harold Macmillan, 29 Sept 1951 (*L* II. 828)

377 "Now it's Lord Willis . . ."   *Daily Worker*, 30 Mar 1964

380 "often mixed, and he could
     be . . ."   David Krause in McCann, 143-4

     "dare-devil
     Horrorhawks . . ."   "The Bald Primaqueera", in *Blasts*,
                                            63-76

     "What a bold and impudent
     letter . . ."   unpub. ltrs. to Lorraine Beaver,
                                            1962-3, in MM, unpub. notes

381 "Nobody is scanning the
     papers now. . ."   Catherine Rynne in McCann, 251

FURTHER SOURCES

James Agate, *Ego* (9 vols., 1935–48)
Ronald Ayling (ed.), *O'Casey: The Dublin Trilogy* (1985)
Deirdre Bair, *Samuel Beckett* (1978)
J. C. Beckett, *The Making of Modern Ireland* (1966)
Barrett H. Clark, *European Theories of the Drama* (New York, 1965)
The Life of George Crabbe by his Son (1947)
R. M. Fox, *Rebel Irishwomen* (Dublin, 1935)
——"*The History of the Irish Citizen Army*" (Dublin, 1943)
Lillian Gish, with Ann Pinchot, *The Movies, Mr Griffith and Me* (1969)
Tyrone Guthrie, *A Life in the Theatre* (1960)
Robert Hogan, *The Experiments of Sean O'Casey* (New York, 1960)
——"*Since O'Casey*" *and Other Essays on Irish Drama* (1983)
Michael Holroyd, *Augustus John: The Years of Experience* (1975)
Hugh Hunt, *Sean O'Casey* (Dublin, 1980)
Denis Johnston, *Collected Plays* (2 vols., 1960)
P. W. Joyce, *English as we speak it in Ireland* (1910)
Robert Kee, *The Green Flag* (1972)
G. Wilson Knight, *The Golden Labyrinth* (1962)
David Krause, *Sean O'Casey: The Man and his Work* (1960)
——*A Self-portrait of the Artist as a Man: Sean O'Casey's Letters* (Dublin, 1968)
——(ed.), *The Dolmen Boucicault* (Dublin, 1964)
Mary Lou Kohfeldt, *Lady Gregory: The Woman behind the Irish Renaissance* (1985)
E. Larkin, *James Larkin* (1965)
Sybil Le Brocquy, *Cadenus* (Dublin, 1962)
F. S. L. Lyons, *Ireland Since the Famine* (1971)
Hugh MacDiarmid, *The Company I've Kept* (1966)
Walter McDonald, *Reminiscences of a Maynooth Professor* (1925)
M. J. MacManus, *Eamon de Valera* (New York, 1946)
E. H. Mikhail (ed.), *Lady Gregory: Interviews and Recollections* (1977)
Charles Morgan, *The House of Macmillan* (1943)
David Nokes, *Jonathan Swift: A Hypocrite Reversed* (1985)
Diana Norman, *Terrible Beauty: A Life of Constance Markievicz* (1987)
Simon Nowell-Smith (ed.), *Letters to Macmillan* (1987)
Eoin O'Brien, *The Beckett Country* (1986)
Sean O'Faolain, *Constance Markiewicz* (1934)
Padraic O'Farrell, *Who's Who in the Irish War of Independence, 1916–1921* (Dublin, 1980)
P. S. O'Hegarty, *Sinn Fein: An Illumination* (Dublin, 1919)
John O'Riordan, *A Guide to O'Casey's Plays* (1984)

Sir William Orpen, *Stories of Old Ireland* (1924)
George Orwell, *Collected Essays* (vol. 4, 1968)
Peter Quennell, *Customs and Characters: Contemporary Portraits* (1982)
Desmond Ryan, *The Rising* (Dublin, 1949)
Ann Saddlemyer (ed.), *Theatre Business* (1982)
Anthony Sampson, *Macmillan: A Study in Ambiguity* (1967)
Kenneth Tynan, *Curtains* (1961)
Oscar Wilde, *De Profundis and other writings* (1973)
John Willett, *The Theatre of Bertolt Brecht* (1959)

ACKNOWLEDGMENTS

I would like to thank Eileen O'Casey for her many kindnesses to me during the writing of this book, not least for responding patiently to the questions I asked. While I must emphasise that the interpretation I place upon personalities and events is my own, and is not to be attributed to her, I am deeply grateful to her for permission to quote from Sean O'Casey's private correspondence, her own correspondence, and his literary works both published and unpublished.

My warmest thanks to Ion Trewin, who has given generous support at all stages, as well as valuable comments on successive drafts. My thanks likewise to Thomas A. Stewart and Susan Leon of Atheneum; to John Trewin, for introducing me to the *dramatis personae* of O'Casey's life who are still alive, and for reading and commenting on the finished book; to David Krause for the advice he gave me in Dublin (including a copy of the indispensable *Sean O'Casey: A Bibliography* by Ronald Ayling and Michael J. Durkan) and for his patient answering of many queries and unstinting supply of unpublished letters and other material; to John Kelly for allowing me to consult the unpublished letters of W. B. Yeats, and for reading the book in draft; to Michael Holroyd for his advice vis-à-vis George Bernard Shaw and Augustus John and for reading the book at proof stage (and with the unfortunate omission of the bottom line of each page, not the easiest of tasks). To Roy Foster, for help with the historical accuracy of some passages; to Deborah Rogers, for her help in a variety of ways.

I must thank the following for consenting to be interviewed, for sending or collecting letters or information, and for help in one or more of innumerable other ways: Rosemary Aimetti, Clare Astor, The Hon David Astor, Adrian Barr-Smith, Lord Bernstein, James Bosley, John Bright-Holmes. A. J. Cockshut, Julian Curry, Thomas Quinn Curtiss, Frank Delaney, Margaret Drabble, Lady Caroline Faber, T. M. Farmiloe, Edward Fowler, Angela Fox, Robert Emmett Ginna, Lillian Gish, Robert Graff, Derek Granger, Rose Fallon, Sir Peter Hall, David Horan, H. Montgomery Hyde, Rory Johnston, Christine Kelly, Linda Kelly, Robert G. Lowery, Brian Martin, the late Siobhan McKenna, Barbara McKenna, Peter Newmark, Trevor Nunn, Kate O'Callaghan, Breon O'Casey, Shivaun O'Casey, Andy O'Mahony, Anna von Planta, Peter Quennell, Maureen Roche (*née* Fallon), Teresa Sacco, Brian Silcock, the late Lord Stockton, Wolf Suschitzky, Claire Tomalin, John Tydeman, Sam Wanamaker, Carole Welch, Terence de Vere White, Roma Woodnutt.

My particular gratitude is due to Seamus Scully for introducing me to O'Casey's Dublin; by enabling me to see Dublin through his eyes, Mr Scully brought me many insights into my subject. I must thank Bernard

O'Donoghue for his translations of Gaelic, for reading the typescript and checking the spelling of proper names. My thanks, too, to Martin Lubikowski for the map of Dublin. In attempting to recreate the atmosphere and processes of O'Casey's early life I have been helped not only by Martin B. Margulies's book, *The Early Life of Sean O'Casey*, but by his generous loan of notes on his interviews in 1963–4 with the following (their relationship with O'Casey is identified by the key: F = family; N = neighbourhood; M = friends of Mick Casey; IRB = Irish Republican Brotherhood; ICA = Irish Citizen Army; GNR = Great Northern Railway; L = Laurence O'Tooles):

Alicia Beaver – F (Bella's daughter-in-law); Ernest Blythe – IRB; Mrs Rose Brady (maiden name Fitzpatrick) – N; John "Fooker" Brown – M; Paddy Buttner – ICA; Jim Caffrey – N; Christopher Casey – F (Tom Casey's son); John Joseph Casey – F (Tom's son); Joseph Casey – F (Isaac's son); Mrs Tom Clarke – IRB; Mr and Mrs P. Cullen – F; Mrs Jim Cunningham – N; Mr and Mrs Liam Daly – L; Mrs Kate Doherty (maiden name Shields) – N; Susan Elliott (maiden name Beaver) – F (Bella's daughter); P. A. Foley – GNR; R. M. Fox – ICA; Mrs J. Hanratty – ICA; Mr and Mrs William and Margaret Hart – N (landlords, 8 Church Place); Brendan Herlihy – M; Bulmer Hobson – IRB; Kit Kearney – M; Mrs Chris Keeley (maiden name Caffrey) – N; Katie Kenna – N (Abercorn Road); Nan Kenna – N; "Rabbit" Kelly – M; George Kilbride – N; Kathryn Langan – N; Jack McCabe – ICA; John McDonald – L (Patrick's brother, despite different spelling); Mr and Mrs Patrick McDonnell – L; Ellen McGraham (maiden name Fairtlough) – F (niece of Isaac's wife); Joseph McGrath – ICA; William Middleton – N (son of George Middleton); Miss Helena Moloney – ICA; Bridget Mulhall (maiden name Casey) – F; Mick Mulvihill – M (owned North Wall bar where Mick Casey drank and sketched); Anne Murphy – F and N; Mrs Frances Murphy – N (neighbour of Isaac's); Isabella Murphy (maiden name Beaver) – F (Bella's daughter); Mrs P. Murphy – N (Abercorn Road – father kept shop where Caseys purchased groceries); Prof. Liam O'Briain – N; Christina O'Rourke – N (Seville Place); Frank Robbins – ICA; George Rocliffe – N (O'Casey schoolmate at St. Barnabas'); Mr and Mrs James Shiels – L; Michael Smith – L; Mr and Mrs Stephen Synott – L (also owned bookstore where SO'C shopped); George Wisdom – GNR.

I thank the following for kind permission to use copyright material:

Macmillan and Co. Ltd, London (from the published plays and prose of Sean O'Casey)

The Society of Authors, London, as the literary representative of Bernard Shaw

John Kelly and Oxford University Press (from the letters of W. B. Yeats)

I am grateful to the editors of and contributors to the following newspapers and magazines in which articles, reviews, etc. I have consulted appear:

American Spectator
An Poblacht (The Republic), Dublin
Catholic Bulletin, Dublin
Catholic Mind, Dublin
Daily Express, London

Daily Sketch, London
Daily Telegraph, London
Daily Worker, London
Dublin Evening Telegraph
Dublin Saturday Post
Forward, Glasgow
Guardian, London
International Herald Tribune, Paris
International Literature, Moscow
Irish Freedom, London
Irish Independent, Dublin
Irish Press, Dublin
Irish Statesman, Dublin
Irish Times, Dublin
Irish Worker, Dublin
John O'London's Weekly, London
The Leader, Dublin
Modern Drama, Lawrence, Kansas
Nation and Athenaeum, London
New Statesman, London
Newsweek, New York
New York Times
Nineteenth Century, London
Observer, London
Peasant and Irish Ireland, Dublin
Picture Post, London
Sinn Fein, Dublin
The Star, Dublin
The Standard, Dublin
The Standard, London
Sunday Times, London
Time and Tide, London
The Times, London
Totnes Times, Devon

Much kindness has been shown me by the staff of the following libraries and institutions where I have obtained material: BBC (Sound and Written) Archives; British Film Institute; the British Library; Imperial War Museum; British Library Newspaper Library, Colindale; Public Record Office, Kew; Bodleian Library, Oxford; Central Library, Westgate, Oxford; National Library of Ireland, Dublin; Trinity College Library, Dublin; Bibliothèque Nationale, Paris; New York Public Library; Society of Authors, London.

Finally my warmest gratitude to Catharine Carver for her editing. My thanks to Hazel Bell for making the index; to Maria Rejt, Stephanie Darnill, Evan Oppenheimer, for invaluable editorial help; to Linda Rowley and Maureen Grant for typing the manuscript.

G.O.C.

Oxford
December 1987

INDEX

Note: page references to line illustrations are in italics; photographs are between pages 214 and 215, and are indicated by *il.*; SO'C refers to Sean O'Casey.

Abbey Theatre, *132*; opening, 48; productions, 152, 164; Shaw's plays, 48, 141, 147, 172, 184–5, 225; *The Playboy of the Western World* performed, 49–50; SO'C first visits, 102; *The Frost in the Flower* submitted to, 112, 120, 123; *Harvest Festival* submitted, 116, 120, 123–4; *The Crimson in the Tricolour* submitted, 131–4, 139, 141; *The Seamless Coat* submitted, 132; *On the Run* submitted, 138–9; *Shadow of a Gunman* performed, 139–41, 143–4; company, 143, 181–2; finances, 143, 180, 187; *Juno and the Paycock* performed, 155, 157–62; SO'C's relationship with, 138, 142, 143–4, 155–6, 170–1, (deterioration) 179–86, 225, 250–1; payments to SO'C, 152; and Yeats's plays, 180–1; *The Plough and the Stars* (submitted) 185, 187–91, (production) 191–202, 218, (programme) *195*, (controversy following) 197–204, 218, 221; and *The Silver Tassie*, 234, 243, 246–59, 357, (production) 274; production of *King Lear*, 268; tours, 207, 242; players in New York, 300; film on, 366; SO'C's final view of, 380

Adams, Joe, 108, 110

Agate, James, criticism by, 182: of *Juno and the Paycock*, 192, 207–8; of *Within the Gates*, 295–6; of *The Star Turns Red*, 320; of *Purple Dust*, 333–4; SO'C attacks, 313

Albery, Bronson, 347–8

Allgood, Sara: in *Juno and the Paycock*, 157, 158, 159, *159*, 192, 207, *il.*, (film version) 279; in London, 182, 192, 202, 205, 213, 233, 276; SO'C's letter to, 192

America, *see* United States of America

American Spectator, 290

Amersham, 266–7, 284

Anglicanism, *see* Protestant faith

Anglo-Irish war, *1918–20*, 127–32, 135–6, 139

Angmering-on-Sea, Sussex, 267

'Angry Old Man' label, 369

anti-semitism, 280

Archer, Abraham (grandfather of SO'C), 11

Archer, Nan, 11

Archer, Susan, *see* Casey, Susan

Archer, William, *The Old Drama and the New*, 233

Archer family, of Galway, 11

Arnott, Sir John, 33

Artaud, Antonin, 380

Ashe, Thomas, 56, 100–1

Asquith, H. H., Earl of Oxford and Asquith, 208, 218

Assembly of Ireland (Dáil Éireann), 127

Astor, David, 270, 329

Astor, Nancy, Viscountess, 294, 298, 303, 311, 315, 329, 339

Atkinson, Brooks, 296, 300, 301–2, 313, 369, 371, 375

Aud (German ship), 90

Auden, W. H., 341

Auxiliaries, 128

Ballynoy (arsenalist), 129

Ballynoy, Mrs, 129

Barlow, Seàghan, 186, 225

Barnes, Binnie, 273

Bartlett, Sir Basil, 294

Baylis, Lilian, 48

Beaver, Bella (*née* Isabella Casey; sister of SO'C), birth, 13; career, 19; marriage, 20–1; and SO'C, 21, 23–4, 44–5, 46–7, 50–1, 104, 105; children, 41; after madness of husband, 43–5, 46–7, 50–1; death, 104–5, 106; *il.*

Beaver, John (nephew of SO'C), 104–5, 116

Beaver, Lorraine, 380–1

Beaver, Nicholas (brother-in-law of SO'C), 20, 23, 41; madness, 43–4; death, 46; *il.*

Beaver, Nicholas (nephew of SO'C), 41

Beaver, 'Sonny' (nephew of SO'C), 104

Beaver, Susan (niece of SO'C), 18, 33, 45, 104; *il.*

Beaver, Valentine (nephew of SO'C), 104

Beckett, Samuel, 29, 116, 289, 302, 366, 380

Beckles, Gordon, 294–5

Belfast, 61, 75, 135, 320

Bennett, of O'Toole Club, 161

Berkeley, George, Bishop, 17, 25

Berlin, 360

Bernstein, Sidney, Lord Bernstein, 343, 370

Berry, Tom, 214

Birch Grove, Sussex, 312, 315, 323, 326, 376, 377

Birmingham Repertory Company, 242

Birrell, Augustus, 45

Bishop, George, 274

Black, Revd John, 13

Black and Tans, 126, 127–9, 197; in *The Drums of Father Ned*, 370

"Bloody Sunday" (31 August *1913*), 70–2

Blythe, Ernest, 43

Boer War, 35, 75, 210; demonstration against, *1899*, 35–6, (filmed) 379

Bognor Regis, 235

Bolshevik Revolution, 85, 99

Boothby, Sir Robert, Baron, 376

Boston, 301, 303

Boucicault, Dion (Dionysus Lardner Boursiquot), 29–31, 160, 353; *Arrah-na-Pogue*, 30; *The Colleen Bawn*, 30;

The Shaughraun, 28, 29, 30, 31, 49

Boughton, Rutland, 243; *The Immortal Hour*, 286

Bowen-Colthurst, Captain, 94–5

Boyle, of Dublin, 151, 161–2

Boys of London and New York, The, 24

Brady, Canon, 106, 145, 281

Brady, Mrs (wife of publican), 109

Bray, visit to, 21

Braziller, George, 367

Brecht, Bertolt, 70

Breen, Father, 90

Breen, Dan, 200

Brentwood, Ursuline Convent, 211

Brett, George P., 319–20

Britannic (liner), 297, 298–9, 301

British, in Ireland, 18, 30, 91, 136, 320

British Army, 20, 48, 87

British Communist Party, 362

British Government, 57, 127, 320

British International Pictures, 270, 288

Brittain, Vera, 301

Brugère, Raymond, 184

Burke, Ingrid, 340–2

Burke, John, 219

Burns, Robert, poems by, 126, 228

Byrne, Alfred, Lord Mayor of Dublin, 241

Byrne, James, death of, 69

Byron, Lord George Gordon, 137

Cahill, Frank, 51–2, 95–6, 97, 102, 111–12; portrayed in *The Frost in the Flower*, 138

Cahill, Josie, 81, 96

Callan, Paddy, 42, 161

Callan, Phil, 161

Cambridge, 315, 320, 358

Cardiff, Jack, 379

Carey, Eileen, *see* Casey, Eileen

Carney, Jack, 343

Carpenter, Walter, 53

Carroll, Matt, 99

Carson, Lord Edward, 75

Carter, Huntly, 230

Casement, Sir Roger, 76, 90

Casey, Christopher (Kit; nephew of SO'C), 18, 56, 57, 77, 79, 125, 176

Casey, Eileen (niece of SO'C), 41

Casey, Isaac ("Joseph"; brother of SO'C), 43, 109; childhood, 13; career, 13, 20–1, 35; as actor, 28–9, 30–1; marriage, 34, 35; and Volunteer Army, 83

Casey, Isabella Charlotte (Bella; sister of SO'C), *see* Beaver

Casey, Johanna ("Josie"; sister-in-law of SO'C), 34–5, 41

Casey, John, *see* O'Casey, Sean

Casey, John (two infant brothers of SO'C), 13–14, 26

Casey, John Joseph (nephew of SO'C), 18

Casey, Mary (*née* Kelly; wife of Tom), 37, 77–9

Casey, Michael (father of SO'C), 14–15; family, 11; career, 11, 12–13; character, 16–17, 20; reading, 17, 29, 32; marriage, 11; as father, 13, 16, 20; death, 16, 17, 20

Casey, Michael (Mick; brother of SO'C), 19, 35, 56, 57, 70, 154; childhood and education, 13, 26; career, 13, 39; army service, 20, 28, 35, 86; discharged, 107; drinking, 57, 116, 124–5, 152; relations with SO'C, 43, 112, 116, 124–5, 327, 353–4; death, 353–4; portrayed in *The Plough and the Stars*, 176–7; portrayed in SO'C's autobiography, 354; *il.*

Casey, Susan (*née* Archer; mother of SO'C), 39–40, 44–5; appearance, 18; family, 11; marriage, 11, 13; bringing up children, 3–4, 14, 16, 17, 18, 23; on children's marriages, 23, 34–5, 37; SO'C living with, 36, 37, 39–40, 44, 57, 86; last illness and death, 106, 107–9, 124, 353; SO'C's relationship with, 23, 31–2, 36, 59–60, 88, 115–16, 119, 152, 153, 353; portrayed in SO'C's plays, 112–13, 115, 149, 174; portrayed in SO'C's autobiography, 325, 333, 353; *il.*

Casey, Thomas (brother of SO'C), 28, 32; childhood, 13, 16; career, 13, 20, 37, 41; army service, 20, 35, 37; marriage, 37, 41; death, 77–9; *il.*

Castletown of Upper Ossory, Lord, 55

Catherine, Sister (cousin of Eileen Carey), 346–7

Catholic Bulletin, 218, 257

Catholic Church: in Belfast, 135; and Casey family, 11–12, 34–5; SO'C's attitude, 34, 51, 65–6, 78, 79, 106, 145, 173, 183, 223–4; and socialism, 223–4; in *Red Roses for Me*, 337–8; in Irish Free State, 173; Eileen and, 242; in America, view of SO'C's plays, 300, 303

Catholic Mind, 276

celibacy, 153

censorship, 107, 164, 267, 303, 349, 368

Chalfont St Giles, 284–6, 288, 290, 292, 361; *il.*

Chamberlain, W. H., 312

Chancellor, Joyce, 184

Chaplin, Charles, 360

Chapman, Edward, 280

Chekhov, Anton, 152, 156

Chekhov, Michael, 328

Christie, Julie, 379

Churchill, Sir Winston, 244, 245, 331

CID, 148

Clarke, Austin, 200, 221

Clarke, Tom, 55, 75–6, 82, 89, 92; death, 93, 102

Clarke, Mrs Tom, 55, 86, 102, 197

Claudel, Paul, 154

Clery, Arthur, 202

Clitheroe, Jenny, 33

Clondalkin, 81

Clunes, Alec, 333–4

Cochran, C. B.: and Eileen, 270, 271, 290; PRODUCTIONS: revue in New York, 268; *Bitter Sweet*, 270, 271, 272; *The Silver Tassie*, 262, 266–8, 269, 275–6; *Mother of Pearl*, 290; rejects *Within the Gates*, 291–2

Collins, Michael, 147

Collins, publishers, 296

Colum, Mary, 50, 222

Colum, Padraic, 349–50

communism, 85, 87; SO'C and, 223, 231, 298, 311, 312, 313–16, 323, 355; Niall's attitude to, 362–3; *The Star Turns Red*, 317–21; *see also* Russia

Connery, Sean, 378

Connolly, James, 26–7, 35, 77, 84, 95; in Easter Rising, 67, 89, 91–3

Connolly, Sean, 176

Coogan, Beatrice, 172, 183–4, 209–10

Coole Park, Co. Galway, 158, 167, 168, 187, 189

Cooperative Society, 73

Corby, Captain, 238

Corkery, Daniel, *The Labour Leader*, 131–2, 152

Cosgrave, W. T., 147, 172

Coward, Sir Noël, 231, 271, 347; SO'C attacks, 313; *Bitter Sweet*, 268, 270, 271, 272, 283; *Conversation Piece*, 300; *The Vortex*, 206

Cowasjee, Saros, 356

Crabbe, George, 376
Cradle of Genius (film), 366
Craig, May, 178, 192, 193, 194
Crowe, Eileen (Mrs McCormick), 185,
    191–2, 193
Cumann na mBan (Society of Women),
    83, 197
Cummins, Dr Joe, 158, 192, 194, 241,
    242, 337–8, 361
Cunningham, Mrs Jim, 124
Curry, William, 327–8
Curtis Brown agency, 289–90
Curtiss, Thomas Quinn, 343
Cusack, Cyril, 182

Daiken, Leslie, 328
Dáil Éireann, 127
Daily Express, 294–5
Daily Express (Dublin), 21
Daily Sketch, 205–6
Daily Telegraph, 275, 313–14
Daily Worker: SO'C writes to, 224–5,
    314, 338–9; banned, *1942*, 331; on
    invasion of Hungary, 362
D'Alton, Charles, 29, 31
Daly, Jack, 151, 161–2, 331
Daly, P. T., 81, 87
Dartington Hall, 323, 327–9, 330, 359
de Valera, Eamon, 93, 127, 132, 147–8,
    172–3; *1924* release, 169; SO'C's
    opinion of, 101, 172–3
de Valera, Sinéad (*née* Ni Fhlannagáin),
    42, 169
Deakin, Seamus, 42, 54, 75–6, 82, 90
Delaney, Maureen, 192
Deverell, Anthony, 24, 27
Devine, George, 369
Diehards (Irregulars), 132, 135, 139,
    158; in *1923*, 147–8
divorce, 341–2
Dobbie, Geoffrey, 372–3
Dolan, Michael J., 144, 146, 155, 157,
    160, 165, 180, 191, 219; director of
    Man and Superman, 185–6; opinion of
    The Plough and the Stars, 187–8
Donaghy, Lyle, 203
Donnelly, Donal, 378
Dostoevsky, Fyodor, 189; *The Idiot*,
    189–90
Douglas-Home, Sir Alexander, 377
drama revival, Irish, 47–50; *see also*
    Abbey Theatre
Dublin: map, 8–9; late 19th–cent.
    conditions, 4, 12–13, 15, 27;

portrayed by Joyce, 27; Casey family
    homes in, 11–24, 27–38, 39–47,
    50–1, 57, 86, 104–9, *il.*; drama
    revival, 47–50; *1912–14* labour
    troubles, 14, 62–74, 77, 111–15, 318;
    Citizen Army in, 74–7, 79–84; Easter
    Rising, *1916*, 89–96; SO'C's view of,
    37, 354–5, 360; SO'C visits, *1926*,
    218; SO'C rejected by, 218–19;
    honeymoon in, 241; *Young Cassidy*
    filmed in, 378–9; Abbey Theatre, *see
    separate entry*; Abercorn Road, 32–3,
    35, 37, 46–7, 50, 57, 105, 124–5, 281,
    il.; Brady's Lane (Seery's), 42, 50, 56;
    Burgh Quay, 177–8; Central Model
    Schools, 13, 45; Chamber of
    Commerce, 62–3; Charlemont
    House, 241; Church Place, 50;
    Clontarf parish, 33; docks, 69;
    Drumcondra Gaelic League, 41–3, 53;
    Empire Theatre, 102; Forester's Hall,
    129–30; Four Courts, 51, 135; Fowler
    Hall, 135; Gaiety Theatre, 370;
    Hawthorne Terrace, 21–2, 23, 28;
    Hotel Russell, 241; Imperial Hotel,
    69, 70, 71; Innisfallen Parade, 15–16,
    134; Jacob's Biscuit Factory, 91, 178;
    Kenilworth Square, 183–4; Labour
    Exchange, 170; Liberty Hall, 64, 67,
    69, 73–4, 74, 83, 87, ("Steps
    Committee") 87; (in Easter Rising)
    91, 138; Liberty Hall Players, 30–1;
    Mechanics' Theatre, 31, 48; Merrion
    Square, 165–6, 189, 202; Mills Hall,
    202; Mount Jerome Graveyard, 11,
    14, 105; Mountjoy Gaol, 69, 100, 197;
    Mountjoy Square, 125, 126, 127,
    129–30, 134, (raided) 128–9, (in *On
    the Run*), 135–6; North Circular
    Road, 130, 134, 148, 171, 188,
    189–90, 209, 241, *il.*; O'Connell
    Street, 69, 70–1, 92; Olympia
    Theatre, 336; Post Office, 20, 41, (in
    Easter Rising) 92; Queen's Theatre,
    29; Richmond District Lunatic
    Asylum, 43–4; Rotunda Hospital, 4;
    St Barnabas' church and parish, 22,
    32, 41, 50, 91, *il.*; St Barnabas'
    National School, 21, 22–3; St Enda's
    College, 67; St Mark's Ophthalmic
    Hospital, 18; St Mary's church, 56; St
    Mary's Infants' School, 19, 20–1; St
    Laurence O'Toole church, 32, 51,
    223, 281, *il.*; (Christian Brothers'

School) 51, 97, (SO'C turns against) 145, (*see also* Laurence O'Toole Club); St Vincent de Paul Hospital, 87, 236; Seery's Lane, 42, 50, 56; Stonybatter, 18; Trinity College, 241, 356; Upper Dorset St, 14–15; Webb's Bookstore, 54

Dublin Drama League, 175
Dublin Tóstal Festival, 368
Dublin United Tramways Company, 67–8
Duffy, Bernard, *Special Pleading*, 130
Dulanty, John, 311, 344

Earle, Mrs (dresser), 243, 281, 282, 284
Eason and Son (newsagents): SO'C works for, 31, 32; strike, 67
Easter Rising, *1916*, 27, 34, 89–96; in *The Plough and the Stars*, 88, 91, 94, 95, 172, 173–4; Yeats writes of, 194–5
Edinburgh, 360, 369
Edward VII, King, coronation, 40–1
Edwards, Sheila, 338–40, 341
Elliott, Helen, 235–6, 238
Elmhirst, Dorothy, 327, 328–9
Elmhirst, Leonard, 327, 329
Emmet, Robert, 11, 26, 110
English–Speaking Union, 218
Ephraim, Lee: before Eileen's marriage, 212, 213, 216, 226–7, 231, 232, 238, 373–4; after, 282–3, 343
Ephraim, Mrs Lee, 227
Epstein, Sir Jacob, bust of Lady Gregory, 241
Ervine, St John, 93–4, 250, 258–9, 345, 351
Evans, Dame Edith, 379
expressionism, in drama, 230

Fagan, J. B., 192, 203, 205, 207, 213, 233; *And So To Bed*, 233
Fairtlough, Johanna ("Josie") *see* Casey
Fairtlough, William, 34
Fallon, Gabriel: as actor, 143–4, 191; in *The Plough and the Stars*, 192, 193; correspondence with SO'C, 232, 268, 276, 281, 304; SO'C's letters to, 209, 213, 217–18, 227, 242, 267, 268, 269, 273, 276, 285, 315, 324, 338; records cited, 157–8, 158–9, 168–9, 171, 179, 181, 184, 187, 198; on *Red Roses for Me*, 336–7; final estrangement from SO'C, 336–7; *il.*
Fallon, Rose, 336

Fay, Frank, 48, 180
Fay, Mrs Frank, 219
Fay, W. G., 48, 180
Federation of Employers, 59, 67, 71, 77
Fenians, 30, 43
films, 360; SO'C asked to write screenplays, 270, 349, 358; of *Juno and the Paycock*, 270, 279–80, 281, 288; of *The Plough and the Stars*, 304, 312; of SO'C's autobiography, 378–9
Finglas, 100, 148, 149
Fitzgerald, Barry (William Shields), 184, 185; as actor, 143, 181–2; in *Juno and the Paycock*, 143, 157, 159, 181, (film) 280; in *The Plough and the Stars*, 191, 193, 194, 198, 200; death, 372
Flannagan, Patrick Joseph, 178
Fletcher, Revd Harry Arthur, 22, 32, 34, 36–7, 114
Fletcher, Revd J. S. ("Hunter"), 22–3, 32
Flood, Father, 116–17
Ford, John, 270, 312, 379
Fox, R. M., 134–5, 179, 200, 221, 352–3
French, Samuel, publisher, 289–90
Friml, Rudolf: *The Desert Song*, 231; *Rose Marie*, 212

Gael, The, 135
Gaelic Athletic Association, 56, 76
Gaelic League, 26, 37–8, 41–3, 46, 49, 51, 53–4, 55, 64–6, 76; Drumcondra branch, 42, 53–4; Mulcahy branch, 41–2
Gaffney, Father Michael, 276
Garrick Club, 209, 233
Gassner, John, 104
General Strike, *1926*, 214
Gifford, Grace, 93
Ginna, Robert Emmett, 378
Gish, Lillian, 300
Glasnevin village, 109, 110
Gogarty, Oliver St John, 214, 222, 268–9; and Harold Macmillan, 307; reviews *I Knock at the Door*, 351; *Blight*, 102
Gollancz, Victor, 349, 352
Gonne, Maud, (Mrs MacBride), 26, 35, 47–8, 194, 202, 203
Good, John ("Fluther"), 176
Gordon, C. L. (censor), 267
Gore-Booth, Constance *see* Markiewicz
Gore-Booth, Sir Henry, 70
Gorki, Maxim, 49

Gow, Ronald, and Walter Greenwood, *Love on the Dole*, SO'C reviews, 305, 312

Graff, Robert, 378

Great Northern Railway, 23, 43; SO'C works for, 39–41, 47, 52–3, 58–9; SO'C writes of, 52–3, 59

Greene, Graham, 341

Greenwood, Walter, *Love on the Dole*, *see* Gow, Ronald

Gregory, Augusta, Lady, 3, 19–20; character, 166–7; SO'C caricatures, *253*; family, 167–8; at Coole, 167–8, 187; reading, 189, 222; and Abbey Theatre, 49, 141, 156, 157, 158, 160, 162, 166, 180, 187, 242; critique of *The Crimson in the Tricolour*, 131–2, 138–9; plays by, 26, 48, 164, 166; relations with SO'C, 142, 160–1, 162, 166–8, 175, 179, 184, 189, 190, 207, 208, 229, 246, 271–2, 274–5, 289, 305, 306; and *The Plough and the Stars*, 187; and *The Silver Tassie*, 247, 250–2, 260–1, 262, 275–6; death, 289; *il.*

Gregory, Robert, 167

Grey, Mary, 207, 213

Griffin, Cardinal Bernard, 341

Griffin, Revd Edward Morgan, 37, 41, 50, 78, 109, 112, 127; portrayed in *The Harvest Festival*, 113–14

Griffith, Arthur, 35, 43, 63, 89, 147, 201

Guthrie, Sir Tyrone, 369–70

Hampton and Leedon (chandlers), 24, 27–8, 31

Hardy, Thomas, 308–9; *The Dynasts*, 168, 175; *Jude the Obscure*, 267

Harvard, 301, 303

Hawthornden Literary Prize, 208, 218

Helga (British gunboat), 91

Herald Tribune, 300

Higgins, Fred, 380

Hitchcock, Alfred, 279–80, 281

Hitler, Adolf, 319, 320, 363–4

Hobson, Bulmer, 54–5, 75, 76, 82; and Easter Rising, 89–91

Hodson, J. L., 208, 286

Hogan, Captain, death of, 148, 149, 229

Hogan, John (school teacher), 22

Holloway, Joseph, 183, 200, 250; diary cited, 131–2, 140, 141, 155–6, 157, 158, 159, 170–1, 178–9, 225; on *The*

Plough and the Stars, 194, 195–6, 197, 198, 203; antagonism to SO'C, 219

Hollywood, 312, 349, 358, 379

Home Rule policy, 25, 45, 66

Horniman, Annie M., 48

House of Commons, 25, 127

Howell, Father Perceval, 238

Howth, 52, 83, 241

Hughes, Herbert, 299

Hungary, Soviet invasion, 362–4

Hunt, Hugh, 347

hurling, 38, 42–3, 56

Hutchinson, Harry, *il.*

Huxley, Sir Julian, 245–6

Huxley, Juliette, 245

Hyde, Douglas, 26, 42, 51, 64, 65, 66, 96; translations, 99

Ibsen, Henrik, 59, 114

Inghínídhe na hÉireann (Daughters of Erin), 47–8

International Literature, 314

Ionesco, Eugène, 380

Ireland: partition, 320; SO'C rejects, 220–6, 380–1

Irish Citizen Army (ICA), 75, 76–7, 80–3; in Easter Rising, 89–96; becomes Irish Republican Army, 127; flag, 81–2, 91, 93, 168–9, 201–2

"Irish fact", 3–5

Irish Free State, 132, 144, 145; and Abbey theatre, 139, 180, 187, 188; Army of, 139, 147–8; SO'C's attitude to, 172–3

Irish Freedom, 54–5

Irish Home Rule Party, 25

Irish Independent, 200, 218, 221; in labour dispute, 67, 69; reviews SO'C's plays, 140, 160, 196

Irish language, 173; SO'C learns, 34, 39, 54; proposed as compulsory at University, 65–6; *see also* Gaelic League

Irish News, The, 262

Irish Opinion, 100

Irish Parliamentary Party, 63, 102, 127

Irish Republican Army (IRA; formerly Irish Volunteers *and* Irish Citizen Army), 127–8

Irish Republican Brotherhood (IRB), 43, 54, 55, 66; and labour unions, 58; Teeling Circle, 43, 55, 67; SO'C leaves, 75–6; and Volunteer Army, 76–7; *1919*, 118; *see also* Diehards

Irish revival, dramatic, 47–50, *see also* Abbey Theatre
Irish Statesman, 160, 196–7, 255, 256, 257, 258, 265, 276–8
Irish Times, 140, 196, 198, 199, 208, 258, 267, 366
Irish Trades Union Congress, 95
Irish Transport and General Workers' Union (ITGWU), 34, 130; under Larkin, 58–9, 62, 64; 1913–14 lock–out, 67–74, 77; Employers' Federation bans, 59, 67, 71, 77; under Connolly, 87; rejects Larkin, 130, 145
Irish Volunteers, 76–7, 79–80, 82, 83–4, 101; in Easter Rising, 89–96; *see also* Irish Republican Army
Irish War Pipes, 55–6, 96
Irish Worker, 39, 52, 58, 59, 63, 64–5, 69, 79, 86, 125
Irish Workers' Union, 58
Irish Writing, 349–50
Irregulars, *see* Diehards
Irving, Ernest, 286–7
Izakov, Boris, 356

Jackson, Sir Barry, 233, 242, 246, 258, 286
Jews, 280, 301
John, Augustus, 207, 213–15, 298; set painter for *The Silver Tassie*, 269–70, 272, 275; opinion of *Within the Gates*, 293–4; works by owned by SO'C, 243
Johnston, Denis, 225
Joyce, James, 15, 352; on Parnell, 25, 26; and Ireland, 220; influence on SO'C, 350; *Dubliners*, 27, 28; *A Portrait of the Artist as a Young Man*, 28; *Ulysses*, 368
Judge, Peter *see* McCormick, F. J.

Kavanagh, Jim, 134, 209, 229
Keating, "Birdie", 98–9
Keating, Mary (Maire), 97–100, 101, 102–3, 106, 109–11, 116–17, 118–19, 177–8, 179, 183, 190, 209, 218; parents, 98, 99–100; portrayed in SO'C's plays, 137, 154–5, 335
Kelly, John, 36
Kelly, Mary, *see* Casey
Kelly, Tom, 11
Kelly, William, 99, 102, 105; shop, 92
Kenner, Hugh, 3
Kerr, Ronald, 347–8
Kettle, L. J., 76

Kilkenny, 26
Knight, G. Wilson, 347, 369
Komsomolskaya Pravda, 366
Krause, David, 371, 379–80

Labour Exchange, 172
Lane, Sir Hugh, 167; picture collection, 167–8, 246
Larchet, Dr John, 143, 198, 357
Lardner, Dionysius, 29
Larkin, Delia, 84, 127, 129, 134
Larkin, Jim, 87; early career, 58, 61–4; edits *Irish Worker*, 58, 59, 63, 64; organizes ITGWU, 62–3, 64, 67–74, 77; "Bloody Sunday" appearance, 69–71; and Citizen Army, 74–5, 82, 84, 86; in America, 61–2, 84–5, 126–7, 129–30, 145; return to Ireland, 145; visits Soviet Union, 318; in *1925*, 189; marriage, 127, 145; portrayed in *The Star Turns Red*, 85, 134, 317, 318, 321; SO'C's attitude to, 57, 58, 64, 84–5, 113, 156
Laughton, Charles, 273–4
Laurence O'Toole Club, 51, 86, 96, 97, 111, 112; pipers' band, 55–6, 96; mock attack by SO'C, 118; in *1924*, 161
Lawrence, T. E., 275, 293, 321
Lawrence, W. J., 160
Lehmann, Beatrix, 273
Lenin, V. I., 73, 99, 261
leukaemia, 364–5
Life, 356
Liverpool, 58, 61; University, 192
Lloyd, Marie, 378
Lloyd George, David, 127, 132
Lomonosova, Raisa, 318
London: SO'C's first visit, 205–10, 220–3; SO'C rejects, 329; Apollo Theatre, 275; Arts Theatre Club, 333–4; Battersea, 297, 305, 316, 324, 329; Bethlehem Royal Hospital, 210–11; Bloomsbury, 245; Chelsea, 215, 218, 238, 269; Cromwell Road, 371; Drury Lane Theatre, 212, 231; Fortune Theatre, 205, 207, 210, 231; Golders Green Cemetery, 365, 374; Hampstead, 269; Hyde Park, 215, 279, 280–1, 292; *Juno and the Paycock* productions in, 179, 192, 203, 205, 207–8, 210; Kensington, 218, 234; Lancaster Gate, 223, 306; New Theatre, 217; Old Vic Theatre, 48;

London – cont.
Park Lane, 243–3; *The Plough and the Stars* in, 182, 213, 216, 217, 233; Queen's restaurant, 214, 227, 235; Royal Court, 233, 234, 242, 369, 371, *il.*; Royalty Theatre, 192, 293, 294; St James's Square, 294; St John's Wood (Woronzow Rd), 242–3, 252, 266, 269, 281–2, 284, *il.*; *The Shadow of a Gunman* production in, 233, *il.*; *The Silver Tassie* production in, 267–8, 269–70, 272–6, 325; Unity Theatre, 320; *Within the Gates* production, 293–6
London School of Economics, 362
Londonderry, Edith, Lady, 231, 292, 298, 308; London hostess, 207, 243–4; in Ireland, 297, 298; SO'C's letters to, 231, 280
Lonsdale, Frederick, 231; *The Street Singer*, 216, 226
Lord Chamberlain's office, 267
Lucan, 81
Lynch, Liam, death of, 139
Lynch, Tommy, 56

MacBride, Major John, 194
MacBride, Maud, *see* Gonne, Maud
MacCarthy, Desmond, 354
McCormick, Eileen, *see* Crowe
McCormick, F. J. (Peter Judge): as actor, 143, 181, 182, 268; in *Shadow of a Gunman*, 139, 144; in *Juno and the Paycock*, 157, 159, *il.*; in *The Plough and the Stars*, 191, 197, 198, 225; in *Man and Superman*, 185; and SO'C, 144, 157, 183, 219
MacDermott, Norman, 293, 294
MacDermott, Sean, 92
MacDiarmid, Hugh, 332, 360
MacDonald, Ramsay, 243, 245, 261, 317; correspondence with SO'C, 288, 309
McDonald, Dr Walter, 66, 173, 224
McDonnell, Johnny, 91, 95–6
McDonnell, Paddy, 53, 91, 96, 102, 118
McElroy, Evelyn, 284
McElroy, William (Billy), 214, 227–8, 233, 234, 238, 283, 284; portrayed in *Purple Dust*, 332
MacGowan, James, 80, 138
MacGowran, Jack, 379
McKenna, Siobhan, 182
MacLean, Joan, 212
Macmillan, Alexander, 377

Macmillan, Daniel, 342, 343, 348; as SO'C's publisher, 169–70, 255, 307, 350, 368; after SO'C's death, 376–7
Macmillan, Lady Dorothy, 316, 323, 376, 377
Macmillan, Maurice (father of Earl of Stockton), 209
Macmillan, Maurice (son of Earl of Stockton), 323, 326
Macmillan, Maurice Harold, 1st Earl of Stockton: character, 307–8; family, 308, 326; marriage, 376; career, 307, 308, 310, 325, 342–3; political views, 309–10, 312; in World War II, 342–3; relations with SO'C, 307–9, 312–13, 323, 342, 356, 376; as SO'C's publisher, 307, 312–13, 319, 323, 325–6, 350, 354, 376; and Eileen, 311–12, 323, 376–8; books by, 308, 309
Macmillans (publishers): authors handled by, 307; publish SO'C's works, 169, 179, 246, 255, 262, 297, 307, 312, 319, 349, 376; New York, 301, 319–20, 368
MacNamara, Brinsley, 218–19
MacNeice, Louis, 357
MacNeill, Eoin, 65, 76, 82, 89–90
MacSwiney, Terence, *The Revolutionist*, 144
Madden, Richard (agent), 296, 318
Maguire, Nurse, 199
Mahaffy, J. P., 214
Malik, Jakob, 365
Malone, Andrew E., 221
Malone, Cecil L'Estrange, 261
Manchester, 48, 270, 271, 290
Manchester Guardian, The, 258, 310
Mannin, Ethel, 305–6
Manning, Eve, 291
Mansfield, Frederick W., Mayor of Boston, 303
Margate, 282
Margulies, Martin, 41, 51–2
Markiewicz, Count Casimir, 70
Markiewicz, Constance, Countess (*née* Gore-Booth): in 1913 lock-out, 70, 73; and Citizen Army, 81, 83–4; in Easter Rising, 93, 94; elected MP, 127; SO'C's opinion of, 83–4
Markle, George, 296, 298, 299, 300
Mars, Marjorie, 294
Martin, Kingsley, 312
Marx, Karl, 70, 311

Massey, Raymond, 272–3, 275
Maunsel & Co. (publishers), 106, 107
Mauriac, François, 341
Maxwell, General Sir John, 93
Mayor, Tess, 320
Metro-Goldwyn-Mayer, 378
Middleton, George, 39, 50
Mili, Gjon, 356
Milton, John, 284
miners' strike, *1926*, 214, 227–8
Mitchel, John, 79
Moloney, Helena, 70, 83
Montgomery, James (censor), 219
Mooney, Ria, 185, 336, 356, 357; in *The Plough and the Stars*, 192, 193, 194, 196, 200
Moore, George, 42, 164; *Principia Ethica*, 310
Moore, John, 130, 134, 149, 151
Moore, Mrs John, 148, 149
Moore, Mary, 148
Morgan, Charles, 295, 297, 321
Morgan, Sidney, 279–80
Morrell, Lady Ottoline, 245, 276
Morrow, George, drawing by, *384*
Mount Pleasant, County Down, 298
Moylan, Thomas K., *The Nabocklish*, 101–2
Muggeridge, Malcolm, 310–11, 313–14
Mullen, Michael, 135, 141; shares room with SO'C, 125–6, 128–9, 130; portrayed in *On the Run*, 136; portrayed in *Young Cassidy*, 379
Murdoch, Dame Iris, *The Red and the Green*, 90
Murphy, Gertrude, 139
Murphy, Isabella, 354
Murphy, William Martin, 67, 69, 71
Murray, T. C., *Sovereign Love*, 139

Nathan, George Jean: as critic, 293, 309, 320–1, 347; relations with SO'C, 296, 299, 301, 304, 315; correspondence with SO'C, 313, 318
National Dramatic Company, 48
National University, 65
nationalism: American, 301; Irish, 26–7, 30, 51, 261; drama revival, 47–50; SO'C's, 36, 37, 65–7, 88, 320, 351–2
Nelsons, publishers, 307
New Statesman, SO'C reviews for, 305
New York: Larkin in, 61–2; Eileen Carey in, 212–13; SO'C's plays published in, 179, 368; PRODUCTIONS IN: *Juno and the Paycock*, 179, 207, 212–13; *The Plough and the Stars*, 242; *Within the Gates*, 296–7, 299–301; *Red Roses for Me*, 361; *Purple Dust*, 367; *Cock-a-Doodle-Dandy*, 369; Cochran revue in, 268; SO'C in, 296, 297, 299–301
New York Times, 296, 300, 366
Newmark, Peter, 315, 320
Nichols, Beverley, 206–7, 279
Nineteenth Century, 265
Nissé, Dr Bertram, 293
Nobel Prize, 367
Nolan, James, death of, 69

O'Brien, George, Professor, 187–8
O'Brien, Susie, 109
O'Brien, William, 130
Observer, The: interviews SO'C, 208, 274, 366; publishes SO'C's letters, 255, 256; reviews in, 351–2, 357
O'Casey, Breon (son of SO'C), 348, 362, 363, 364, 368, 380; birth, 252; childhood, 266–7, 269, 270–1, 282, 290–1, 330, 343–4; education, 328, 359, *il.*
O'Casey, Eileen (*née* Reynolds; stage name Carey; wife of SO'C): early career, 210–13; appearance and character, 281, 282, 371; meets SO'C, 210, 213; theatrical career, 213, 216, 226, 231, 233, 270–1, 281, 286, 290–1; developing relationship with SO'C, 213, 215–17, 226–7, 231–2, 233–5, 237; engagement, 234–5; wedding, 237–8, *il.*; honeymoon, 241–2; first pregnancy, 234, 242; first childbirth, 252; abortion, 283; third pregnancy, 296–7, 303–4; as SO'C's wife, in London, 242–3, 245, 252, 263–5, 269–72, 281–3, 297, 303–4, 371; in Chalfont St Giles, 284–7, 290–1, 292–3, 296–7; in Devon, 324–5, 327–31, 340, 342–3, 354, 359–60, 364, 368; SO'C's ambassador, 370, 371; at son's death, 364–5; at SO'C's death, 373–4; portrayed in SO'C's plays, 236–7, 266, 287–8; *il.*
RELATIONSHIPS: with Lee Ephraim, 212, 213, 216, 226–7, 231, 232, 282–3, 373–4; with SO'C, as wife, 266–7, 270–1, 281–2, 288, 298, 345–7, 352–3, 362, 371, 372, 373, 375; with her mother, 211–12, 345–7, 373;

O'Casey, Eileen – *cont.*
with other men, 269–70, 286–7, 311, 343, 371; with Shaw, 311, 327, 344–5, 378; with Harold Macmillan, 311–13, 323, 376–8: *Sean*, 377

O'Casey, Niall (son of SO'C), 330–1; birth, 304; education, 359, 362; character, beliefs and relations with SO'C, 362–4; death, 364–6, 372; *il.*

O'Casey, Sean (*né* John Casey): family, 3–4, 11–12; birth, 3–4, 14; name, 3, 32; character, 3, 5–6, 23, 40, 170, 206, 352–3; childhood, 14–24, 25–7; first trip to seaside, 21; education, 19–20, 21, 22–3; reading, 19, 54, 82, 126, 142, 168, 175, 189–90, 221–2, 281, 302; works of art liked by, 192, 243, 268, 281, 361; appearance and clothes, 19, 281, 380; eye problems, 16, 18, 54, 158, 194, 234, 360, 371; health, 32, 86–7, 269, 292–3, 348, 361–2; finances, 105–6, 107, 288–90, 291, 303, 304; early jobs, 23–4, 27–8, 31–2, 39–41, 47, 52–3, 57, 58–9; early sexual relationships, 28, 36, 81, 129; celibacy, 153; political development, 25–7, 43, 45–6; first theatrical experiences, 28–31; turns to writing, 38, 88, 102, 105; taste for drama develops, 82; first visits Abbey Theatre, 102; Protestantism, 33–4, 36–7, 45–6, 50–1, 108, 142; and Gaelic League, 41–3, 46, 51, 53–4, 55, 64–6; and labour unions, 58–9, 61, 63–74, 87, 88–9; and Citizen Army, 74–86; and Easter Rising, 90–6, 173–4; first published works, 105–6, 107; after mother's death, 107–9, 123–4, 353; leaves home, 124–5; at Mountjoy Square, 125–36, (raided), 128–9; in North Circular Road, 130, 134, 148–9, 155, 171, 179; first play performed, 139–41; involvement with Abbey Theatre, 120, 123–4, 131–4, 138–42, 143–4, 146–7, 155–62, 163–8, 170–2, 179–86, 187–201, 234, 242, 246–59, 262–6, 268–9, 274–7, 289–90; at Coole, 167–8, 187; in public debate, 202–4; departure from Ireland, 216–19, 220–6; first comes to London, 205–10, 220–3, 279; wins Hawthornden Prize, 208; international reputation, 230;

Communism, 223, 231, 298, 311, 312, 313–16, 317–21, 323, 355, 362–4; wedding, 237–8, *il.*; honeymoon, 241; life in London, 242–6, 252, 263–8, 269–75, 279–84, 289, 297, 304–6, 308, 329; in Chalfont St Giles, 284–8, 290–2; visits Ireland, *1934*, 297–8; visits America, 296, 297–302, 303; in Totnes, 323, 324–5, 327–31, 333, 340, 342, 343, 347–8, 355–6, 359; in Torquay, 359–67, 371–4; honours, 356, 377; eightieth birthday, 366; death, 373–4; will, 372; assessment of, 375–6; *il.*:

ATTITUDES: to mothers, 87, 115–16, 149, 162; to his family, 108; to love, 283; to men, 153:

RELATIONSHIPS: with Larkin, 57–9, 64, 84, 85, 113, 129–30, 134, 145, 156, 189; with Maire Keating, 97–100, 106, 109–11, 116–17, 118–19, 177–8, 179, 183, 190, 209, 218 (in plays) 137, 154–5; with mother, 23, 31–2, 36, 59–60, 88, 115–16, 119, 152, 153, 353; with brother Mick, 43, 112, 116, 124–5, 327, 353–4; with sister Bella, 21, 23–4, 44–5, 46–7, 50–1, 104, 105; with Tom's wife, 77–9; with Yeats, 156–7, 161, 163, 165, 268–9, 305–7; with Lady Gregory, 142, 160–1, 162, 166–8, (at Coole Park), 167–8, 187; with Beatrice Coogan, 183–4, 209–10; with Shaw, 5, 111, 190–1, 209, 223, 263–5, 316–17, 321, 322–3, 343–5; with wife, Eileen, 266–7, 270–1, 281–2, 288, 298, 345–7, 352–3, 362, 371, 372, 373, 375; with George Russell, 222–3, 276–8; with Harold Macmillan, 307–9, 312–13, 323, 347, 356, 376; with Sheila Edwards, 338–40; with Ingrid Burke, 340–2; with Kathleen Reynolds, 346–7; with son Niall, 330–1, 362–6:

WORKS: caricatures, 96, 115, 254–5, 257, 7, 88, 239, 253, 254, *il.*; songs, 101, 105–6, 110, 116; poems, 117; letters, published, 379, 380; collections published, 312–13; *Autobiographies*, 4–5, 270, 312, 321, 349–55, 357–8, (dramatised) 367, (filmed) 378–9, (*see also* titles); "The Bald Primaqueera", 380; *Behind the Green Curtains*, 367, 370; *The Bishop's Bonfire*, 340, 367, 369–70; *The Call of* the Tribe, 97–8; *Cathleen Listens In*, 144, 147, 172; *Cock-a-Doodle-Dandy*, 367, 368–9, 371; *The Cooing of Doves*, 144; *The Crimson Cornkrakes*, 111; *The Crimson in the Tricolour*, 130, 131, 132–4, 139, 146, 160; *The Drums of Father Ned*, 123, 325, 367, 368, 370; *Drums Under the Windows*, 347, 349, 351–2; *The End of the Beginning*, 288–9; *Figuro in the Night*, 367, 370; *The Flying Wasp*, 313; *The Frost in the Flower*, 102, 111, 112, 119, 123, 138; "Gold and Silver Will Not Do", 271; "The Grand Oul' Dame Britannia", 98; *The Green Searchlight*, 339; *The Harvest Festival*, 111, 112–16, 123–4, 231, 318, 334; *I Knock at the Door*, 325–7, 333, 349, 351; "I Wanna Woman", 290; *Inishfallen Fare Thee Well*, 125, 353, 354, 355; *Juno and the Paycock*, 236, (writing of) 131, 146–7, 148–55, 172, (Abbey Theatre production) 155, 157–62, *il.*; (London productions) 179, 192, 203, 205, 207–8, 210, (New York productions) 179, 207, 212–13, (tours) 207, 242, (publication) 169, 179, 296, (film) 270, 279–80, 281, 288; *The Moon Shines on Kylenamoe*, 367; *Nannie's Night Out*, 169, 172, 175; *Oak Leaves and Lavender*, 347–8; *Pictures in the Hallway*, 333, 350; *The Plough and the Stars*, 91, 94, 95 (writing of) 88, 166, 168–9, 172, 173–9, 184, (expressionism) 230, (submitted to Abbey Theatre) 185–6, 187–91, (Abbey Theatre production) 191–202, 218, (programme) 195, (controversy following) 197–204, 218, 221, (London production) 183, 213, 216, 217, 233, (New York production) 242, (filmed) 304, 312, 379, (publication) 312; *A Pound on Demand*, 288–9; *Purple Dust*, 331–4, 360, 367; *Red Roses for Me*, 331, 334–8, 361; *Rose and Crown*, 357; *The Seamless Coat of Kathleen*, 132, 134; *The Shadow of a Gunman* (formerly *On the Run*), 128, 129, (writing of) 135–9, (first performance) 139–41, 143, (publication) 169, 179, (London production) 233, *il.*; *The Silver Tassie* (writing of) 17, 226, 227–33, 234, 236–7, 242, 246, 262–3, 268,

(submitted to Abbey Theatre), 246–56, (Starkie's opinion of) 256–7, 258, (publication) 255, 262, 289–90, (Shaw's opinion of) 260–3, (London production) 267–8, 269–70, 272–6, 325, (denounced in Ireland) 276, 278, (Abbey Theatre Production) 274; "The Soul of Man", 45; *The Star Turns Red*, 85, 304, 309, 317–23; *The Story of the Irish Citizen Army*, 83, 95, 106–7, 110, 197, 204; *The Story of Thomas Ashe*, 101; *Sunset and Evening Star*, 357–8; *Three Shouts on a Hill*, 117–18, 262, 263; *Windfalls*, 270, 289, (banned) 303; *Within the Gates* (writing) 279–80, 283, 285–6, 287–8, 290, 291, 321, (submitted) 291–2, (London production) 293–6, (New York production) 296–7, 299–301, (refused in Boston) 303, (publication) 307, 309

O'Casey, Shivaun (daughter of SO'C), 323, 328, 330, 359, 361, 365, *il.*
O'Cathasaigh, Sean, *see* O'Casey, Sean
O'Concubhair, Seamus (James O'Connor), 130, 149
O'Connor, Fergus, 101, 102, 103, 105–6
O'Connor, Frank, 375
O'Connor, Joseph, *Blight*, 102
O'Donnell, Frank Hugh, 203
O'Faolain, Sean, 5, 336, 350–1, 354–5
O'Farrel, Ayamonn, 34, 49
O'Flaherty, Liam, 200, 221; *The Informer*, 270
O'Flanagan, Sinéad, *see* de Valera
O'Growney, Frank, 76, 99
O'Hegarty, P. S., 128, 355
O'Hickey, Revd Michael P., 65–6, 224
O'Higgins, Fred, 200, 221
O'Higgins, Kevin, 147
O'Lochlain, Kevin, 56–7, 63, 76, 99
O'Murchadhu, Michael, 161
O'Neill, Eugene, 293, 299–300, 321; plays by, 175
O'Nuallain, Peadar, 41–2, 43
O'Rahilly, "The", death of, 92
Orange Order, 34, 61, 135
O'Regan, Kathleen, 213, 216
O'Rorke, actor, 182
Orpen, Sir William, drawing by, 74
Orton, Joe, 380
Orwell, George, 317, 351–3, 363
Osborne, John, 369
O'Shea, Kitty, 25

O'Shea, Captain William, 25
Owen, Wilfred, "Disabled", 228–9, 236
Oxford, 376

paintings, 192, 243, 268, 281, 361
Parnell, Charles Stewart, 25–6, 57, 342, 350
Pearse, Padraic, 56, 75, 76, 80, 156; in *1913* lock-out, 66–7; in Easter Rising, 89, 92, 93; portrayed in *The Plough and the Stars*, 175, 177, 179; death, 93–4; SO'C's opinion of, 66–7; *The Cattle Raid of Cooley*, 67
Pearse, Mrs Padraic, 197
Peasant and Irish Ireland, 45–6
Perse, Saint-John, 367
Phillips, Sian, 379
Picture Post, 320
Pinero, Arthur Wing, 233
Pinter, Harold, 380
Plato, works of, 139, 142
Plunkett, Grace, drawing by, *159*
Plunkett, Joseph, 92, 93
Poblacht na h'Éireann, An, 36, 132, 199, *384*
political idealism, in 1930s, 309–11
Pound, Ezra, 164–5
Priestley, J. B., 347
prostitutes: in *The Plough and the Stars*, 188, 194, 196; in *Within the Gates*, 295
Protestant faith: and Casey family, 11–12, 32, 33–4, 108; SO'C's, 36–7, 45–6, 50–1, 108; SO'C confirmed in, 33–4; renounces, 50–1, 142; Yeats declares, 163; *see also* Irish Citizen Army

Quennell, Peter, 227

Rankin (stone mason), 369
Reagan, Ronald, 378
Redgrave, Sir Michael, 347, 379
Redmond, John, 76, 192
Rees, Leslie, 281
Reid (GNR foreman), 52, 58–9
Reinhardt, Max, *The Miracle*, 290
Reynolds, Edward, 210–11, 373
Reynolds, Eileen Carey, *see* O'Casey, Eileen
Reynolds, Horace, 353
Reynolds, Kathleen (*née* Carey; mother-in-law of SO'C), 210–12, 231–2, 234–5; at wedding, 237–8; at childbirth, 252; and SO'C, 345–6, 362; death, 373

Richards, Shelagh, 191, 194, 196, 200, 210, 336
RKO, 312
Robinson, Lennox, 167, 370; as director of Abbey Theatre, 147, 152, 182, 225; rejects SO'C's early plays, 132; and *The Crimson in the Tricolour*, 131, 133–4, 250; and *Shadow of a Gunman*, 139; and *Juno and the Paycock*, 155, 157–8; and *The Plough and the Stars*, 187, 188, 191, 193, 194; and *The Silver Tassie*, 246–7, 250–1, 253–6, 264, 267, 276; at US University, 268; relations with SO'C, 156–7, 183, 349, 375; plays by, 171, 183, 276, 309; *The Whiteheaded Boy*, 146, 155
Robson, Dame Flora, 379
Rocliffe, George, 22, 23, 50
Rokotov, Timofei, 314, 318, 319
Rose Marie, London production, 212
Rotha, Paul, 366
Royal Dublin Fusiliers, 20, 32, 37
Royal Engineers, 86
Royal Irish Constabulary, 127
Rudkin, David, 380
Rush, Leo, 88
Russell, Bertrand, 3rd Earl Russell, 245, 327
Russell, Charlie, 99
Russell, George ("AE"), 169; in *1913* lock-out, 73; editor of *Irish Statesman*, 256, 258, 264, 265, 276–8, 380; SO'C's opinion of, 222–3, 276–8; plays by, 250, 309
Russell, Father Ned, 324–5, 331
Russia and Soviet Union: in *1913*, and Ireland, 73; Revolution, *1917*, 77, 85, 99, 261; Larkin visits, 318; in 1930s, 310–11, 312, 313–14; in *1938*, 313–14; in World War II, 319, 324, 331, 343; invasion of Hungary, 362–4; SO'C's attitude to, 230, 231, 342, 355–6, 366; in *The Star Turns Red*, 317–21; *see also* communism
Ryan, Frank, 200, 204
Rynne, Catherine, 381

Salisbury, 360
Saturday Post, 100, 101, 102
Shakespeare, William, 29, 281
Yeats' view of, 247–8; *Henry IV*, 200; *Henry V*, 29, 172; *Henry VI Part 3*, 28–9; *Julius Caesar*, 106; *King Lear*, Abbey Theatre production, 268

Shakespeare Memorial Theatre, 360
Shaw, Charlotte, 263–5, 284, 285, 324, 344
Shaw, George Bernard, 57, 324; SO'C requests preface from, 117–18; relations with SO'C, 5, 209, 223, 263–5, 316–17, 321, 322–3, 343–5; influence on SO'C, 190–1, 317; SO'C writes on, 111; SO'C's opinion of, 366; opinion of *The Silver Tassie*, 259, 260–3, 275; opinion of *Within the Gates*, 293; opinion of *The Star Turns Red*, 321; and Eileen, 311, 327, 344–5, 378; and Breon, 343–4; attitude to Ireland, 57, 220; attitude to Russia, 311, 322; views on education, 328, 329; death, 344–5; quoted, 5, 37, 51, 93–4; plays published, 307; plays and Abbey Theatre, 48, 141, 147, 172, 184–5, 225; *Back to Methuselah*, 169, 252; *John Bull's Other Island*, 57, 64, 88, 136, 332, (rejected by Abbey) 48, 261; *Man and Superman*, Abbey production, 184–5, 225; *St Joan*, 175, 262
Sheehy-Skeffington, Francis, 94–5, 197, 204
Sheehy-Skeffington, Hanna, 197–8, 199, 200–1, 202–4
Sheehy-Skeffington, Owen, 203, 241
Sheelds family, 32–3
Shelley, Percy Bysshe, 137
Sheridan, Peter, 67
Sheridan, Richard Brinsley, 15
Sherriff, R. C., *Journey's End*, 233
Shields, Arthur, 139, 197
Shields, William, *see* Fitzgerald, Barry
Shiels, Jimmy, 91, 95–6
Shyre, Paul, 367
Sinclair, Arthur, 207, 233
Sinclair, Upton, *The Singing Jailbirds*, 175
Sinn Fein, 76, 95, 101, 105, 126, 130, 145; and Irish language, 65–6; *1918–19*, MPs, 127
Skinner, Peggy, 332
Smith, Maggie, 379
Smith, Mick, 91, 178
socialism, British, 245, 261
Society for Church Missions, 13
Soviet Union, *see* Russia
Spanish Civil War, 312
Sparrow, Mrs (landlady), 215
Spectator, The, 351

Spender, Sir Stephen, 341
Stalin, Joseph, 311, 317, 319, 322, 324
Standard, 336–7
Starkie, Dr Walter, 196–7; opinion of *The Silver Tassie*, 256–7, 258, 260, 264, 265
Stephens, James, 162, 170, 243; *The Wooing of Julia Elizabeth*, 132
Stephenson, John, 191
Stitt, Nicholas, 33
Stone, Irving, 302, 361
Strachey, John, 310
Stratford, 360
Suez, Anglo-French invasion of, 362
Sullivan, Charlie, 31
Sullivan, Ed, 366
Sunday Times, 207–8, 295–6, 334
Swaffer, Hannen, 274
Swift, Jonathan, 100, 284, 316, 322–3, 340
Synge, J. M., 164; *In the Shadow of the Glen*, 48; *The Playboy of the Western World*, 114, 137, (Abbey Theatre production) 49–50
Synott, Stephen, 54

Talbot, Matt, 223
Taylor, Rod, 378–9
television, American, 366
Temple, William, Archbishop, 245
Tessa, employed help, 284, 290
Thompson, Bonar, 280
Thorndike, Dame Sybil, 209
Time and Tide, 290, 312, 324
Times, The, 233, 275, 295
Tobin, Mr (surgeon), 87
Toller, Ernst, plays by, 175, 230, 236
Tomalin, Claire, 327–8
Tone, Wolfe, 26
Torquay (St Marychurch), 359–61, 373, 374, *il.*
Totnes, Devon, 323, 324–5, 327–31, 333, 340, 342, 343, 347–8, 355–6, 359, *il.*
Townsend Dramatic Society, 30
Trim, Nanny, 284
Tuerk, John, 296, 298, 299
Twain, Mark, 175

Ulster, 147
United States of America: Larkin in, 61–2, 84–5, 126–7, 129–30, 145; Robinson in, 268; SO'C's trip to, 296–302 (in autobiography), 357–8;

United States of America – *cont.*
and funds for IRB, 127; universities, 343; visitors from, 343, 356; *see also* New York
University of Michigan, 268

Van Gogh, Vincent, 302, 361
Vane, Major Sir Francis, 94–5

Waller, Harold, 272
Walters, Evan, 255
Wells, H. G., 307
West, Robert, 21
Whilden (GNR engineer), 59
White, Captain Jack, 74, 77, 80–1, 83–4, 91, 94, 173
Whiting, John, 378
Wilde, Oscar, 5
Williams, Emlyn, 273–4, 275–6
Willis, Ted, Lord Willis, 377
Wilson, A. P. ("Euchan"), 65; *The Slough*, 152
Wisdom, George, 58
Wodehouse, P. G., 351
Wolfe, Thomas, *Look Homeward, Angel*, 349
Wolfe Tone Memorial Committee, 65
Women's and Children's Relief Fund, *1913*, 73, *74*
women's clubs, American, 301–2, 361
Woolf, Virginia, 341

World War I, 84, 86–7; in *The Silver Tassie*, 247
World War II, 319, 324, 330–1, 342–4, 347
Wren Boys, 105
Wyndham, John, 342

Yeats, Jack Butler, 162, 187; *The Tops of the Mountains*, 192
Yeats, John Butler, 163–4
Yeats, Mary, 187, 306
Yeats, William Butler, 79, 168, 202; character and beliefs, 163–4, 307; reading tastes, 189–90, 222, 302; dramatic theory, 164–5, 180–1; politics, 25, 26, 47; and Abbey Theatre, 48, 49, 141, 160, 180–1, 234; relations with SO'C, 161, 163, 165, 305–7; criticism of *The Crimson in the Tricolour*, 132–3, 160; and *The Plough and the Stars*, 187–9, 194–5, 198–9, 200; and *The Silver Tassie*, 247–51, 252–8, 261–3, 274, 275–6; compared with Shaw, 260–1, 263; SO'C's opinion of, 156–7, 222, 268–9, 314–15, 380; SO'C caricatures, *253*, *254*, 257; late poetry of, 249, 315; *At the Hawk's Well*, 165; *Cathleen Ni Houlihan*, 48; *The Countess Cathleen*, 164; *On Baile's Strand*, 48; *The Player Queen*, 164; *The Tower*, 268–9; il.
Young Cassidy (film), 378–9

Biography in Paladin Books

Aneurin Bevan (Vols 1 & 2)　　　　　　　　£3.95 ☐
Michael Foot　　　　　　　　　　　　　　　　each
The classic political biography of post-war politics.

The Unknown Orwell　　　　　　　　　　　£2.95 ☐
Peter Stansky and William Abrahams
Introduces Eric Blair, of Eton and the Indian Imperial Police. In analysing his background, the authors have given us a uniquely valuable key to one of our most important literary figures.

Orwell: The Transformation　　　　　　　　£2.95 ☐
Peter Stansky and William Abrahams
This covers the period of four crucial years, in which Eric Blair, minor novelist with little or no interest in politics, emerged as George Orwell, an important writer with a view, a mission and a message.

Oscar Wilde　　　　　　　　　　　　　　£2.95 ☐
Philippe Jullian
Still the best biography of Oscar Wilde, This book presents his astonishing life, work, wit and trials.

Welsh Dylan　　　　　　　　　　　　　　£1.95 ☐
John Ackerman
This penetrating biography throws new light on Dylan Thomas's identity as a Welshman, showing the close relationship between his work and his Welsh background.

Virginia Woolf (Vols 1 & 2)　　　　　　　£1.95 ☐
Quentin Bell　　　　　　　　　　　　　　　each
Acclaimed as one of the outstanding literary biographies of the century, these books trace the troubled development of Virginia Woolf as a writer and as a woman.

Solzhenitsyn　　　　　　　　　　　　　　£9.95 ☐
Michael Scammell
'A comprehensive picture of the man . . . This superb biography will certainly be the standard account of the most remarkable literary life story of our time.' *Times Literary Supplement*. Illustrated.

To order direct from the publisher just tick the titles you want and fill in the order form.

Biography in Paladin Books

Mussolini £3.50 ☐
Denis Mack Smith
'Will be remembered . . . for the exceptional clarity and brilliance of
the writing. His portrait of Mussolini the man is the best we have.'
Times Literary Supplement.

Karl Marx: His Life and Thought £3.95 ☐
David McLellan
A major biography by Britain's leading Marxist historian. Marx is
shown in his private and family life as well as in his political
contexts.

Miles Davis £3.95 ☐
Ian Carr
'For more than a quarter-century Miles Davis has personified the
modern jazz artist. Mr Carr's biography is in a class by itself. He
knows his music and his Miles.' *New York Times Book Review*.

Freud: The Man and the Cause £3.95 ☐
Ronald W. Clark
With great objectivity, Ronald Clark provides a new, human and
revealing portrait of the physician who changed man's image of
himself. He also gives a clear and balances account of the medical
world of Freud's early professional years; the conception of psycho-
analysis; Freud's struggle for recognition; and how his achievement
can be viewed in the light of contemporary knowledge. Illustrated.

Chaplin: His Life and Art £8.95 ☐
David Robinson
In this definitive biography, the only one to be written with full
access to the Chaplin archives, David Robinson provides a uniquely
documented record of the working methods and extraordinary life of
the mercurial genius of early cinema. Illustrated.

To order direct from the publisher just tick the titles you want
and fill in the order form.

Anthropology in Paladin Books

Humankind £2.95 ☐
Peter Farb
A history of the development of man. It provides a comprehensive picture of how we evolved to reach our present state, and analyses the remarkable diversity of human beings.

Shabono £2.95 ☐
Florinda Donner
'A masterpiece ... It is superb social science because in describing her experiences among the Indians of the Venezuelan jungle Florinda Donner plummets the reader into an unknown but very real world.'
Carlos Casteneda.

The Mountain People £2.50 ☐
Colin Turnbull
A remarkable and gripping account of two separate periods in which Turnbull lived with a declining African tribe, the Ik, in a mountain area on the borders of Uganda and Kenya.

The Forest People £2.50 ☐
Colin Turnbull
A fascinating study of the Pygmies of the Ituri Forest – a vast expanse of dense, damp and inhospitable forest in the heart of Stanley's 'Dark Continent'.

The Human Cycle £2.95 ☐
Colin Turnbull
An illuminating comparison of Western industrial society and smaller-scale societies elsewhere in the world. Far from believing in the superiority of 'advanced' societies, Turnbull shows how we could refashion our own ways by learning from them.

Lucy: The Beginnings of Humankind £2.95 ☐
Donald C. Johanson and Maitland A. Edey
'A riveting book that is at once a carefully documented report, an exciting adventure story, and a candid memoir of a brash young palaeoanthropologist ... What Lucy suggests about our forebears will keep palaeanthropologists arguing for years.' *Publishers Weekly*.
Illustrated.

To order direct from the publisher just tick the titles you want and fill in the order form.

Politics in Paladin Books

Aneurin Bevan (Vols 1 & 2)   £3.95 ☐
Michael Foot   each
The classic political biography of post-war politics.

Karl Marx: His Life and Thought   £3.95 ☐
David McLellan
A major biography by Britain's leading Marxist historian. Marx is
shown in his private and family life as well as in his political
contexts.

The Strange Death of Liberal England   £2.95 ☐
George Dangerfield
This brilliant and persuasive book examines the forces responsible
for the breakdown of Liberal Society in England. At once an expo-
sition of the causes for the dissolution of a great period in English
history and a reluctant threnody for the age of purpose and order. 'A
brilliant analysis.' *The Times*.

War Plan UK   £2.95 ☐
Duncan Campbell
The secret truth about Britain's civil defence. The result of more than
five years' research, the book reveals the incredible history of how
one government after another has planned to protect itself and
survive. 'An unprecedented break in the secrecy surrounding civil
defence planning.' *The Observer*, Fully illustrated.

The Plutonium Business   £2.95 ☐
Walter C. Patterson
Concerned by the rarity of uranium at the dawn of the nuclear age,
physicists came up with a compelling concept – the fast breeder
reactor. But uranium is no longer scarce and a great vision has gone
sour. In this searching analysis, Patterson argues that the plutonium
people must be stopped – for the sake of all humanity.

Going Critical   £2.95 ☐
Walter C. Patterson
An unofficial history of British nuclear power. 'No other industry has
been so obsessively coddled by its official mentors, backed without
stint or hesitation for so long through such a chronicle of arrogant
ineptitude.'

To order direct from the publisher just tick the titles you want
and fill in the order form.

All these books are available at your local bookshop or newsagent, or can be ordered direct from the publisher.

To order direct from the publishers just tick the titles you want and fill in the form below.

Name _____

Address _____

_____

Send to:
Paladin Cash Sales
PO Box 11, Falmouth, Cornwall TR10 9EN.

Please enclose remittance to the value of the cover price plus:

UK 60p for the first book, 25p for the second book plus 15p per copy for each additional book ordered to a maximum charge of £1.90.

BFPO 60p for the first book, 25p for the second book plus 15p per copy for the next 7 books, thereafter 9p per book.

Overseas including Eire £1.25 for the first book, 75p for second book and 28p for each additional book.

Paladin Books reserve the right to show new retail prices on covers, which may differ from those previously advertised in the text or elsewhere.